The
COUNSELING
SOURCEBOOK

The Counseling Sourcebook

The
COUNSELING
SOURCEBOOK

*A Practical Reference
on Contemporary Issues*

JUDAH L. RONCH, Ph.D.

WILLIAM VAN ORNUM, Ph.D.

NICHOLAS C. STILWELL, Ph.D.

Editors

CROSSROAD / NEW YORK

This printing: 2000

The Crossroad Publishing Company
370 Lexington Avenue, New York, NY 10017

Printed in the United States of America

Library of Congress Cataloging-in-Publication Data

The Counseling sourcebook : a practical reference on contemporary
    issues / Judah L. Ronch, William Van Ornum, Nicholas C. Stilwell,
    editors.
        p. cm.
    Includes bibliographical references.
    ISBN 0-8245-1241-3 (pbk.)
        1. Counseling. 2. Psychoanalysis. 3. Psychotherapy. I. Ronch,
    Judah L. II. Van Ornum, William. III. Stilwell, Nicholas C.
    BF637.C6C654   1994
    361.3'23—dc20   93–45447
                                                            CIP

*This book is dedicated to
our teachers, mentors, clients,
colleagues and families—
past, present and future*

Contents

PART 3

Counseling Approaches Throughout the Life Span

Introduction

This book is for everyone interested in counseling, whether practitioners, students, "consumers," or general readers. We have attempted to bring to the professional and lay reader alike a compilation of practical counseling approaches written specifically for *The Counseling Sourcebook* by experienced counselors and recognized experts about topics that are both contemporary and timeless. Above all, we hope these contributions will be useful to a wide range of counselors, psychologists, nurses, clergy, teachers, social workers, school counselors, doctors, and others in the helping professions.

Anyone who helps others has undoubtedly discovered a growing abundance of information about an ever-diversifying array of diagnostic issues and problems for which clients request counseling intervention. Whether counseling is the primary focus of professional activity or an adjunct to other services, we hope that helpers who read this volume will find that the chapters offer practical suggestions to help them with problems of immediate concern in their work. We also believe that this comprehensive array of chapters by counseling experts will give undergraduate and graduate students alike a down-to-earth look at the nature of counseling and a sense of the wide variety of issues counselors are daily asked to help with in the 1990s. Practitioners and students will also find discussions of theory that provide helpful answers to essential, practical questions about why a particular counseling approach is as it is, how it developed, or what it can accomplish. At the same time, we hope that students and others will achieve increased understanding and empathy for persons with difficulties that they perhaps have not encountered before or thought much about but that are discussed in this volume.

We have tried to achieve a synergy between technical, theoretical, and practical concerns. While some articles present theoretical issues, they provide the practical implications of the ideas involved. Likewise, practical articles are based on relevant theory or on their established presentation. Our major goal has been to present useful information soundly based on research and theory so that practitioners, students, and general readers might appreciate the empirical and theoretical evidence for the successful approaches described by the authors.

This book will not make the reader an instant counseling virtuoso. We hope that reading the contributions will give the reader a sound orientation to practical counseling approaches in a wide variety of areas, sensitivity to the special issues that counselors face every day, and encouragement to do further, in-depth reading if their interests or their clients stimulate that need.

This book is the product of and a tribute to the expertise of many people. It is our pleasure to express our gratitude to them for their generosity, interest, and wisdom, all of which were in abundant supply and of invaluable assistance as we developed this volume.

Michael Leach and Werner Mark Linz at Crossroad Publishing Company were the original wellspring of the idea from which the sourcebook evolved. Mike's consummate editorial skills and personal commitment to this project minimized any difficulties we encountered and made them opportunities to learn and grow.

We owe a debt of gratitude to the contributors, who not only took time from busy schedules to write these chapters, but also enthusiastically endorsed the idea of such a sourcebook and believed in its importance as we did. Their desire to share their skills with a broad range of colleagues and nonprofessional readers attests to their excellence as teachers and to their professional leadership.

Our editorial assistants, Susan DiUglio and Lynn Tocci, made vital contributions to the book's structure and format. As experienced counselors, they also provided valuable input about the content. We thank them for their many hours of diligence, good humor, and attention to the details of a project like this. We are pleased that they are both continuing to demonstrate the professional skills that we found so helpful.

The editorial advisory board responded to our invitation to participate, as well as to our requests for assistance, with grace and an outpouring of invaluable assistance. Their recommendations were pivotal in the development of the sourcebook. Our sincere thanks to all of them.

The clerical/coordinating components of a volume such as this can be daunting. We were fortunate to have the able assistance of Kim Trama, Sheila Bogart, Donna Molinaro, and Judy Barba, who were able to attend to the many details necessary to make the book possible.

Finally, we thank our teachers, mentors, supervisors, and clients, who gave us the perspectives from which to develop *The Counseling Sourcebook.*

Judah L. Ronch, Ph.D.
William Van Ornum, Ph.D.
Nicholas C. Stilwell, Ph.D.

1

FOUNDATIONS: A CENTURY OF APPROACHES

The seven chapters in this section of *The Counseling Sourcebook* highlight key concepts from some of the major schools and approaches to counseling. Knowledge of these basic principles is helpful to all practicing counselors.

A knowledge of psychoanalytic principles provides the counselor with tools to help understand the complete personality, as this approach reminds us that current behaviors are often rooted in the past developmental history. Gestalt therapy provides the counselor with a helpful outlook toward recognizing the presence and depth of emotions. Two chapters emphasizing behavior therapy and cognitive therapy demonstrate the power and effectiveness of cognitive and behavioral approaches in treating a range of conditions. Brief therapy provides approaches for a focused and concentrated look at problematic life issues. In the climate of managed mental health care, brief therapy is being considered more and more the treatment of choice. Finally, a review of medication therapies gives the counselor knowledge of these options, which often need to be considered, and can provide significant help and relief when prescribed for the appropriate condition. This information is also helpful when counselors need to refer to and interact with medical professionals.

Taken together, these seven chapters offer a practical grounding in the principles of counseling. They offer significant information regarding major ways of looking at human problems and providing assistance.

1

Psychoanalysis

RICHARD FRIEDMAN, Ph.D.

Psychoanalysis refers to a theory of normal and abnormal development of the mind, a system of therapy developed to apply treatment based on the theory, a profession that administers the therapy, and a method of research. All four of these developments will be discussed in this article.

Although there were precursors to psychoanalysis and independent developments, the towering figure of Sigmund Freud (1856–1939) gave psychoanalysis its shape, vocabulary, and dominating metaphors. Freud was so important to psychoanalysis that some people speak of "Freudian psychoanalysis" or refer to themselves as "Freudians." Many practitioners who have left strict Freudian theory still acknowledge their debt to Freud, and many still consider themselves psychoanalysts. However, even among those who adhere closely to Freud, there are differences of opinion about psychoanalytic theory. Because a thorough discussion of the current status of psychoanalytic theory would easily fill an entire volume the size of this one, the following is a brief overview to familiarize readers with terms and ideas they might encounter in further readings.

NORMAL DEVELOPMENT OF THE MIND

Freud discovered the unconscious by listening to his patients talk about their innermost feelings and report their dreams. For Freud the unconscious—among psychoanalysts, this is never called the "subconscious"—includes not just the passive part of the mind containing memories, but also a dynamic system in which wishes and feelings, prohibitions and fears all interact with one another in a constantly active process. While most of the unconscious mind is unknown to the conscious self, Freud discovered that we have indirect access to a patient's unconscious through *free associations,* that is, through following the instruction to speak freely without the patient censoring what he says during therapy.

Psychoanalytic theory rests on an assumption of symbolic and metaphoric communication. What might have been dismissed before Freud as nonsensical or criticized as immoral or savage became raw material that could be understood much the way poetry or myth can be understood once the interpreter knows the hidden keys. Freud noticed patterns in communication from many of his patients. When he began to look for similiar patterns in other patients, he discovered they were there as well, although hidden behind multiple layers of symbolism. Freud discovered that dreams are coded messages from the unconscious consisting of *manifest content,* which is the narrative of the dream as reported by the dreamer, and *latent content,* which is the meaning (or meanings) expressed symbolically in the latent content. The latent content expresses a wish (disguised through processes of condensation, displacement, symbolization, denial of time and space, and tolerance of contradictions) that is unacceptable to the dreamer's conscious mind (or waking ego). Once a therapist understands these mechanisms and knows the thoughts and feelings associated with the various manifest parts of a dream, an interpretation of the underlying wish is possible.

To Freud's (and the world's) surprise, people were commonly found to have different kinds of sexual wishes beginning with infancy. These unacceptable wishes are repressed in the unconscious, but they are never destroyed. We all spend our lives working out the tension between wishes and prohibitions. Freud then discovered similar indirect messages from the unconscious in the study of slips of the tongue and other "mistakes," jokes, enactments, or repetitions of past traumas or injuries in the present, and in the patient's own symptoms. In some ways, of course, Freud's discoveries were not altogether new; what Freud added was a systemic understanding and explanation for aspects of human behavior that had long been known to poets and philosophers.

Freud based his theory of the mind on the developmental model revealed through dream interpretation. In his view people go through normal stages of emotional growth, experienced in the unconscious mind, with the most important stages occurring during the first six years of life. Sexual energy (called *libido*) is present from birth. The child's main focus of pleasure is in that zone of the body where the most libido is temporarily concentrated or *cathected.* If the child is fortunate in his or her experience during each phase of cathexis, he or she can move with full energy on to the next stage of development. If the specific phase is somehow unsuccessful, the child will forever be stuck or *fixated* at least partially at that stage and have diminished energy for the subsequent stages. Most psychoanalysts today generally recognize four main phases of early sexual development: the *oral,* the *anal,* the *phallic* (the three considered together to be the pre-oedipal period), and the *oedipal.*

The oral phase of development is marked by the very young infant's first need: to take pleasure in sucking to gain nurture in order to survive. The oral stage begins at birth, and psychoanalysts now identify several substages. What starts out as a biological need for food also involves a relationship with the food giver, usually the mother. Starting around age 1 the child begins to develop sphincter control and the anus becomes the major center of sexual pleasure. For the first time, the child discovers a part of his or her body that is completely under the child's own control and independent of his or her parents. Now the child can learn to give (originally feces, but this is soon generalized to other things). As toilet training is one of the first conspicuous acts of socialization, the child enjoys improved reality testing. This is the age of discovering ambivalence. In the phallic phase, starting around age 2, for the first time the primary focus of sexual pleasure is in the genitals themselves. This is the age when boys' and girls' development becomes clearly distinct and the age when infantile masturbation focuses on the genitals for the first time. The issues of the pre-oedipal stages are mastery of actual and symbolic tasks associated with these body zones. The oedipal phase overlaps the last part of phallic development and ends around age 6 or 7. At this stage the child wants to marry his or her opposite-sex parent and displace his same-sex parent.

With the end of the oedipal period, the child's libido is quiescent or sublimated into social and intellectual activity until the onset of puberty five to seven years later, a period psychoanalysts call the *latency stage*. This hiatus in sexual development is a time of intellectual growth. With the onset of puberty the child's sexuality is reawakened and the latency period is over. Many modern psychoanalysts also invest adolescence with considerable importance for adult emotional well-being; and increasingly, theorists tend to see each stage of life, from birth to senescence, as a growing out of dynamic processes that continues throughout life. While the healthy adult has gone through these stages in sequence, he or she will maintain erotic pleasure in each throughout life. For example, kissing and sucking, pleasures from the earliest days of life, continue as normal components of adult foreplay.

Some analysts postulate a second drive or instinct of aggression to balance the sex drive. Those theorists who believe in primary aggression describe the role of both instincts, sex and aggression, in normal and abnormal development. Another way of saying this is that children, from birth, have drives toward pleasure and aggression concentrated in various parts of the body. The pleasure is energized by the same source that energizes mature sexuality. However, most psychoanalytic theorists tend to emphasize the primacy of sexual energy over aggressive energy, if in no other way than in the absence of any systematic nomenclature of aggressive development paralleling the widely accepted names of the stages of sexual development.

While there have been some controversial modifications of Freud's proposed stages of development, all psychoanalysts agree that early development, no matter how it is understood, is crucially important to enhancing or undercutting emotional health. By understanding the symptoms of his adult patients as residues of unfinished childhood growth, Freud was able to postulate normal infantile development. In the process he made some startling discoveries, the most important of which were the interrelated notions of an active unconscious filled with wishes, desires, and fears, and the parallel discovery that people have sexual feelings from the beginning of life. When he first published his findings, Freud's discovery of infantile sexuality was perhaps his most controversial idea; and to this day virtually every important revision of Freudian thought, while acknowledging his contributions to our understanding of the mind, explicitly rejects this one feature.

Eventually Freud's model of the mind included complicated unconscious structures, differentiating between the part of the unconscious from which all drives and impulses stem (the *id*), the part that gives us a moral sense of right and wrong (the *superego*), and the mediator between these and between the individual and the outside world (both the conscious and unconscious parts of the *ego*). He felt that babies are born all id and have only rudimentary egos, and that one of the outcomes of good parenting is the development of a healthy ego and superego.

PATHOLOGICAL DEVELOPMENT OF THE MIND

Freud suggested that pathology is a maladaptive compromise worked out in the unconscious part of the ego between the demands of the id for gratification and those of the superego for restraint in order to protect the ego from being overwhelmed by either desire or guilt. Typically, the compromise symbolically portrays the stage of development that represents the time of greatest conflict. By understanding the patient's conflict through understanding his symbolic communication, a psychoanalyst can arrive at a psychoanalytic diagnosis, that is, an understanding of her[1] patient's problems based on his age at the origin of the problems in early childhood.

Emotional symptoms are marked by a tendency toward extremes. One widely held assumption about symptoms is that if a person demonstrates a tendency toward one extreme, he is defending against impulses toward the opposite extreme. Reacting against opposing tendencies

---

1. As a matter of practice, no meaningful generalizations can be made about same-sex or mixed-sex combinations of psychoanalyst and patient; however, for the sake of clarity and succinctness, all subsequent references in this article to psychoanalysts in general will be with a female pronoun and all references to patients will be with a male pronoun.

causes wishes and fears to become fused: The symptom is both an expression of a desire and the fear of realizing that desire. The compulsively neat person is unconsciously afraid to make messes while simultaneously yearning to make messes. These symptoms can be understood as representing another kind of conflict as well. Impulses and desires that emanate from the id come into conflict with prohibitions from the superego. The ego mediates between the two, often with compromises that produce and shape symptoms depending on the person's unconscious fantasies and the amount of aggression unneutralized by love.

In going through normal developmental stages, the individual can experience difficulties. While the difficulties are not remembered consciously, there are symbolic signals in the form of symptoms that something went wrong. Pathologies of the oral period, stemming from the earliest part of life, a time when the infant was without speech, are the most difficult to treat by psychoanalysis—"the talking cure," as the first psychoanalytic patient called it. Oral problems include the various addictions and eating disorders. Orally fixated personalities are either passive, needy people or aggressive in a consuming or biting way. Those around people with oral fixations will sometimes complain of being sucked dry.

People who have been toilet trained at a very early age and in an aggressive manner might have symptoms directly related to anal-intestinal disorders (either a tendency toward diarrhea or a tendency toward constipation) or symbolically related problems such as extreme sloppiness, compulsive neatness, or an obsessive concern with detail and control. The complaint that people make about anally fixated individuals is that they are controlled, controlling, obsessive, or (at the other extreme) slobs or rebellious.

Pathologies from the phallic stage tend to blend into the Oedipus complex. These people typically have difficulty with competition, either suffering from the inability to compete and be successful or being obsessed with winning at all costs. Boys, fearing retaliation from their fathers in their rivalry for their mothers, begin to fear castration. People fixated at the oedipal stage are either mother- or father-fixated and will choose sexual partners who remind them of their parent or are an exaggerated opposite version of their opposite-sex parent. Many marital difficulties stem from the compulsion to choose a spouse based on unresolved oedipal issues.

What has been presented so far is a very brief synopsis of one aspect—the developmental—of traditional Freudian psychological theory. However, it is not necessary to view theory exclusively within any one model. It is possible to understand development from many different perspectives while still remaining within a psychoanalytic framework. One school of psychoanalysis, for example, feels that libidinal drives, rather than simply seek parts of one's own body, seek other people, starting with the mother's breast and eventually encompassing an awareness of, empathy with, and love for significant others. Following Cartesian precedent in philosophy, other people are called *objects* (as opposed to the self who is the subject), and such practitioners consider themselves *object relations analysts*. For these analysts, pathology is the inability to see other people as wholly separate from themselves; the confusion of self and others is a condition known as *narcissism*. Object relations theory is implicit in some of Freud's writings. Freud, in fact, wrote the seminal acticle on narcissism.

Other psychoanalytic perspectives on psychology include Freud's *dual drive theory*—sex and aggression—and what Freud called *metapsychology*, or his most general theories about the structure of the mind. These approaches were, for the most part, first suggested by Freud. Some psychoanalysts choose to emphasize one view over another because they feel that it has greater explanatory power or is more useful for reaching therapeutic conclusions. A small number of psychoanalysts feel that all traditional theories are too limiting and propose more or less sweeping overhauls of the entire theoretical underpinnings of psychoanalysis. The difference between more classical psychoanalytic theorists and other theorists, such as the object relations thinkers, is first one of emphasis, and second one of explaining metaphor. Of course, different theoretical emphases can lead to differences in therapy, and the controversies among psychoanalysts are sometimes sharply debated.

THERAPY

What we might today call psychotherapy existed in many forms prior to the discovery of psychoanalysis: shamanism, religious confession, or heart-to-heart talks. However, prior to Freud's pioneering work, psychotherapy tended to be unsystematic and inefficient. Some particularly charismatic healer might achieve dramatic results, only to find that he or she was unable to teach the technique to any disciples no matter how dedicated and enthusiastic they were. By approaching psychotherapy with a consistent view both of the healthy mind and of pathology, Freud began to work out techniques that could be taught and were predictable. Today, virtually all psychotherapies that rely primarily on talk have learned from psychoanalysis or were derived directly from it.

Everyone experiences feelings without language; indeed, we begin to experience feelings before we have language. Psychoanalysis was discovered by listening to the patient's free associations, and psychoanalysis as practiced today continues to use listening as the most important tool. When the patient talks about feelings, he translates his nonverbal experiences into words. The words are always inadequate because they are necessarily metaphors. We have no direct language of feelings and never will have. Good therapists help their patients develop an expanded language that facilitates saying more and more about feelings.

If psychoanalytic theory can be understood as developmental, the therapy based on psychoanalysis can be seen as regressive. As the patient talks and the analyst listens without trying to guide or shape what the patient is saying, the patient tends to begin experiencing (during sessions) a regression to early childhood emotional states. This is possible because of the human tendency to repeat emotional experiences when frustrated and because most patients find the relative silence of the analyst to be frustrating. It is usually necessary for the patient to reexperience, in the treatment, the original emotional process that has produced the symptom in order to achieve a state of emotional receptivity to change. At the same time that the patient is regressing, he is also expanding (with the analyst's help) the range of emotions that he experiences consciously and can talk about.

The story of the patient's life is told in ways that distort what really occurred: he omits some details and exaggerates others. What the patient does not alter consciously he alters unconsciously. A patient might feel that he has nothing more to say, that his mind is blank, or that he cannot remember years of experience or last night's dream. A patient will, in all conscious innocence, report what might be seen objectively as a triumph to have been a failure—or a failure as a triumph. These obstacles to free association are normal in the course of psychoanalysis and are expected by the analyst. Psychoanalysts call the inevitable inability to free associate *resistance*. Paradoxically, patients tell the story of their lives through their unique patterns of resistance—which can also be called their character—as well is in what they articulate clearly and directly.

Reexperiencing early feelings with and for the psychoanalyst is called *transference*. Psychoanalysts are carefully trained to control their patient's regression and to convert the patient's emotional experience in therapy into an instrument of useful change through interpretation. Symptoms appear in the therapy in the relationship between patient and analyst. Psychoanalysts analyze resistance and transference.

Just as patients have feelings about their psychoanalysts and tend to form transferences, analysts have feelings toward their patients. Psychoanalysts call these feelings *countertransference*. In the early days of psychoanalysis strong countertransference feelings were considered problematic. Gradually analysts have come to recognize the inevitability and usefulness of feelings about patients. Most analysts today are concerned about countertransference only if their feelings interfere with their work. Sometimes these feelings are difficult for the analyst to acknowledge to herself. If the analyst is not aware of these feelings in her work with a patient, that area of the patient's mental life will be left unanalyzed, or worse, she might be able to rationalize taking unethical action with a patient. Therefore, to protect both patients and analysts, all training institutes require student psychoanalysts to undergo their own psychoanalysis. In her own psychoanalysis the analyst in training learns that she has unconscious wishes and fears that are little different from those of her patients. Armed with a good personal analysis, the practitioner has a basis in personal experience for empathy with her patients and the self-knowledge needed for disciplined work.

To illustrate how a psychoanalyst might apply these ideas of symbolic communication from the unconscious, stages of development, transference, and resistance, let us look at two case vignettes. An anally fixated patient might have entered treatment complaining of difficulty with his wife's excessive neatness and unwillingness to compromise. The analyst will note the complaint and listen for it to come up in the transference. Eventually the patient might find himself getting into a struggle with his analyst over payment of fees. He might insist on paying weekly when she had requested monthly payments; he might forget his checkbook; he could bounce checks repeatedly; or the check could be made out to the wrong person, or for the wrong amount, or left unsigned. The unconscious is endlessly inventive when it comes to symbolic representation. At first the patient will see his "mistakes" as inconsequential, meaningless, or even the analyst's fault. He might experience her as rigid, demanding excessive orderliness in his bookkeeping. Gradually his analyst will help him understand that his complaints about his wife and about the analyst express part of his own early struggle with his parents' demand for fecal production. What had been experienced first as a baby later becomes an adult symptom and is finally reenacted symbolically with his analyst.

Similarly we can see trauma and fixation from the oedipal period in transference and resistance phenomena. The patient might present a dream in which a policeman chases him for looking through an office window. As the patient talks about the dream, he thinks perhaps the window was to his analyst's consulting room. The analyst could understand this symbolically: the patient wishes to know the analyst's secrets and fears punishment. Transferentially, the patient wishes to know his mother's secrets and fears his father's retaliation for seeing his mother undress or for seeing (or hearing) his parents engaging in sex. The analyst uses this material to help the patient understand his unconscious wishes and fears.

In therapy the psychoanalyst assumes that if the patient can bring unconscious conflicts into consciousness, the patient can be helped to understand the origins of his conflicts and will feel better and have increased energy available for current life. This is an emotional process, not an intellectual one. It is seldom helpful for an analyst to offer an interpretation to a patient of his unconscious conflict early in the treatment. Many analysts have experimented with very early interpretations in an effort to find ways of speeding the therapeutic process. What they have learned is that a patient can sometimes be trained to accept an interpretation intellectually but that little or no change follows. Therapeutic change comes about slowly and only as part of an emotional process. Only when the patient actually feels what has informed the symptom is he able to begin the struggle for change. In the example of fee payments, the analyst might begin by pointing out to the patient that there seems to be some difficulty with money and ask the patient what he thinks it is about. Gradually the patient might begin to remember other struggles and contests of will. He might assume that his analyst is controlling and demanding. Eventually, when the patient is caught up in the feelings he experienced as a child going through toilet training, his analyst can interpret the symbolism of the struggle over fee payment. The patient then begins to assimilate the interpretation through further associations and by further awareness of other instances of similar struggles. The patient becomes more self-observing and can give up the compulsive need for conflict in this area.

Most psychoanalysts consider the setting of the therapy extremely important to achieve good results. As is true for most psychotherapies, confidentiality is a sine qua non of psychoanalysis. While there are a few major exceptions, most analysts feel that a full analysis can only be carried out three to five times a week in sessions lasting 45 or 50 minutes and extending over many years. The patient should be lying down and the analyst should be behind the patient so that he is not influenced by her facial expressions or body language. These conditions all help the patient develop transference and foster free association.

Freud felt that only a few categories of patients could form transference relationships with their analyst and that psychoanalytic therapy was appropriate only to those few types of patients. Much analytic work since has been devoted to developing techniques to help an ever broader range of patients form transferences and thereby become eligible for psychoanalysis. As is true for virtually every aspect of psychoanalysis, these expanded techniques are cause for lively debates. Many analysts today use modified psychoanalytic technique in conducting what they call *psychoanalytic psychotherapy* with a very wide spectrum of patients. Some of these modifications include scheduling fewer sessions per week, keeping the patient in a sitting posture, and limiting the depth of the interpretations. There are also analysts who make no distinction between psychoanalysis and psychoanalytic psychotherapy and will psychoanalyze virtually any patient.

While psychoanalysis demands a greater commitment from both patient and practitioner than most other therapies, virtually all psychoanalysts are convinced that psychoanalysis provides the deepest and most thorough therapeutic changes for many people suffering from many types of pathology.

PROFESSION

In most large urban areas of the country, psychoanalysts have developed networks of membership societies and training institutes. The main function of the analytic groups is to provide training. Psychoanalytic training has three parts: formal academic course work, usually in small seminars; supervision by experienced psychoanalysts of clinical work; and the future psychoanalyst's personal analysis conducted by someone who has been approved by the training society. While most training institutes require only 3 or 4 years of course work, the required hours of supervised clinical work and personal analysis can result in many years of training. After graduation psychoanalysts are expected by their societies to continue learning. Because supervisors and training analysts must be paid, psychoanalytic education is very expensive.

Subgroups of institutes, usually centered around a particular variant of psychoanalysis, have banded together in several organizations that offer mutual recognition. However, psychoanalysis is unique among the learned professions in the United States in its nonrecognition by state regulating and licensing boards and in its requirements of prior professional training. Until the 1940s, psychoanalysis in this country was dominated by psychiatrists, and all institutes required a medical degree (and usually psychiatric residency) as an admission prerequisite. This was not true in most other countries, and the situation changed in the United States in part because large numbers of well-trained nonphysician analysts fled here from Europe just before World War II. Today only a minority of students at psychoanalytic institutes are physicians; the majority come from psychology and social work, and smaller numbers from school counseling, nursing, the clergy, and various academic disciplines. Although psychoanalysis has no legal status as a profession, the various institutes and societies train future psychoanalysts, set standards for practice, and function much like other professional associations.

RESEARCH

Psychoanalysts talk about something real—the mind—that has no material existence. Therefore, research on the mind is impossible to quantify, and psychoanalytic theory and therapy is virtually ignored in American university departments of psychology and psychiatry. Because behavior, the brain, and neurological responses can all be quantified, they have become the stuff of most academic research. Freud was a physician with a specialty in neurological research. He wrote pioneering papers on polio and the medical uses of cocaine before turning to his study of hysteria that lead to the development of psychoanalysis in the late 1880s and 1890s. He retained strong roots in medicine and biology. While he always insisted that nonphysicians be allowed to practice psychoanalysis, and in fact wanted psychoanalysis to be established as a completely independent profession, he approached his new science with medical models in mind. This has been a mixed legacy. On the one hand, psychoanalysis holds itself to the highest standards of truth and engages in rigorous self-purging of tendencies toward the irrational, mysticism, or spiritualism. On the other hand, psychoanalysis has been saddled with a misleading set of medical metaphors and a frustrating inability to submit itself to laboratory proof.

Perhaps the most pernicious medical legacy is the idea of cure. Unfortunately, we have no generally accepted alternative metaphor for emotional change through therapy. Held to conventional medical standards, it is difficult to discuss the "cure rate" of psychoanalysis in any meaningful terms. It is necessary, therefore, to note that when psychoanalysts speak of cure, they speak of a never fully completed process akin to the learning of a foreign language rather than of a closed-end system such as a course of antibiotics to kill a bacterial infection. While some psychoanalysts conduct sophisticated research *on* psychoanalysis, their work in this area more nearly resembles the work of historians or literary critics than that of, say, microbiologists. One partial exception is the work of scientists investigating the validity of psychoanalytic concepts of infant and child development. Other research involving psychoanalysis *uses* psychoanalytic concepts as research tools in such nonquantified areas as history, religion, education, and literary criticism. Scholars in these fields find psychoanalysis to be a powerful conceptual tool that has provided rich insights. An intellectual history of Western culture since World War I that ignored the impact of psychoanalytic thinking on virtually all of the arts, social sciences, and humanistic studies would be woefully inadequate.

FOR FURTHER READING

Bettleheim, B. (1983). *Freud and man's soul.* New York: Knopf.

Fenichel, O. (1945). *The psychoanalytic theory of neurosis.* New York: Norton.

Fine, B. E., & Fine, B. D. (Eds.). (1990). *Psychoanalytic terms and concepts.* New Haven and London: American Psychoanalytic Association and Yale University Press.

Freud, A. (1946). *The ego and the mechanisms of defense* (C. Baines, Trans.). (1966). New York: International Universities Press.

Freud, S. (1966). *The standard edition of the complete psychological works of Sigmund Freud*

(Vols. 4, 5, 7, 9, 15–16, and 18–20) (J. Strachey, Ed. and Trans.). London: Hogarth Press.

Greenson, R. (1967). *The technique and practice of psychoanalysis* (Vol. 1). New York: International Universities Press.

Laplanche, J., and Pontalis, J.-B. (1973). *The language of psychoanalysis* (D. Nicholson-Smith, Trans.). New York: Norton.

Menninger, K. (1958). *Theory of psychoanalytic technique*. New York: Basic Books.

Rycroft, C. (1972). *A critical dictionary of psychoanalysis*. New York: Viking Penguin.

Schafer, R. (1982). *The analytic attitude*. New York: Basic Books.

Strean, H. (1990). *Resolving resistances in psychotherapy*. New York: Brunner/Mazel.

2

Gestalt Therapy

DOUGLAS M. DAVIDOVE, Ph.D.

1. In *Gestalt therapy* the diagnosis and treatment of "neuroses" means attention is paid to a loss of ego-functioning that also assumes a certain degree of unawareness in a person's characteristic ways of coping. Normally, in the deliberate exercise of his (or her) best powers, a person may not achieve what he sets out to do; and may find frustration as the outcome of his trials. Still he may not be unaware of how he might have gotten in his own way, or of how the environment, for its part, is obdurate. And it is not unlikely in this case that he will again attempt to get his needs met using his "same" resources, tempered now with knowledge gained through (tough) experience, a new estimation of things. In this not abnormal situation then, the person has *not* interfered with his own growth (and is not likely a candidate for psychotherapy.)[1]

The person coming for the help of a therapist is not merely frustrated however; generally he is fearful as well, and usually unable to shake free of the annoying thought that he is, in some way, to blame for his predicament, that is, for its disappointment. Further, he may be confused about how and why this is happening (though he's usually quite sure he's suffering). Then in therapy, it is a question of clarifying the functional relations, for instance, between the pains of failure and some unawareness of how the failure is made; and all of this in relation to how one keeps going (or becomes paralyzed) in moments of anxiety.

2. Anxiety is problematic, or can become so, depending, of course, on the extent to which a person maintains inflexible attitudes, rigid behav-

---

1. Many clinically oriented individuals are too eager to see almost "everything"—each mistake or miscalculation—as a "neurotic symptom." On the other hand, depending upon the therapist's abilities to tolerate his (her) own anxiety, he may, unaware, be abetting neurotic elements that are best faced with skepticism (e.g., much of the treatment of so-called self-esteem problems relieves some of the present suffering while promoting a conceit of one's self-importance—and deepening isolation).

iors, and so on. To those who find anxiety threatening, or who fear the threat of anxiety, and who are disabled (by unawareness) from coping with what seems to want to shake them to pieces, anxiety is felt as menacing. In Gestalt therapy, an encouraging hypothesis of theory is that the toleration of anxiety is rewarded: It can be made a functional advantage, a motivational force in furthering aggressive action on the way toward one's goal (as anxiety, in general, is also an organismic excitation).

In locating and treating problems of the loss of ego-functioning, the presence of anxiety is almost always a symptom of inhibition, unawareness, fixation, and so on. Therefore, the "art" of intervening is found in the abilities of the therapist neither to alleviate anxiety (and its latent excitement) to a point of extinction, nor to heighten it beyond the patient's endurance (e.g., to a level of panic).

3. An intervention is a deliberate action taken by a therapist, in the presence of anxiety, that intends to make a lasting difference in the awareness, and to the experience, of the patient. Any technique of intervention is an artifice of practice, even when it consists in holding one's tongue; and what often matters most is the delivery, for example, the timeliness, or appropriateness of what is said (or withheld in silence). How and when a Gestalt therapist will intervene is based on the level at which a patient's tolerance of anxiety is functional or can become so: as part of integrating one's felt concern for one's situation, including oneself in it, with other possibilities (e.g., in learning something about oneself and this becoming part of one's cumulative self-awareness).

Now there is a vast array of contexts, including one's presence in therapy, that may elicit anxiety. And in every case it is detectable since, in essence, it presents sensible manifestations: When anxious, a person holds his breath. This indicator is, to an observant therapist trained to perceive it, something to note. It is always the case that when a patient is holding his breath, there is an accompanying disturbance in the ongoing functioning (in the creative excitement), though we may not yet know what is "lost," being unaware, alienated (e.g., the patient could be trying to avoid a particular, unacceptable thought—about himself or the therapist).[2]

4. The findings and insights of Gestalt psychology, incorporated into

---

2. Some *psycho*therapists who teach their patients "breath-mechanics" and call it (or actually, confuse it with) Gestalt therapy seem to think the symptom of anxiety is the same as asphyxia, and that people cannot spontaneously exhale and inhale unless tutored. This method, far from being an aid to psychotherapy, can be a positive interference. One may, in the deliberate instruction, drive out opportunities for learning the more relevant facts about the underlying, psychological, basis of the anxiety. Holding one's breath in anxious moments and situations is a way anxiety is manifested; it is not its "cause."

the theory of Gestalt therapy, have to do with "whole" functioning and thus provide a substantial basis for a theory of the Self. The Self (its ego-functioning, personality- and id-functioning, etc.) is not a "thing"; it is realized in terms of the structure of a figure *(gestalt)* in awareness that refers to the *field* (of the organism and environment). For in the end, no matter how great the temptation to discuss, for instance, the "privacy" of thought, elements of the environment are included in every figure-formation. And if this may not always appear to be the case, it is the case. Figure-formation is energized by both poles of the field: the experiencing organism and the environment that is contacted.

In terms of practice, therefore, when a patient is speaking of what he may be presently aware of—whether a memory, a wish, some anxiety, a dream, and so on—it is necessary to discern the environmental aspects in the report that are neglected (or minimized) or included (and exaggerated). This simple test of awareness is always available and verifiable in practice, as in every present moment there is always an environment. Indeed, *no* figure appearing in a person's awareness in a contact situation can be sufficiently explained when aspects of the environment are left out, disregarded, or trivialized. So any patient will, through manifest expressions, reveal something of his reality and of his ability to make contact.

This is not to say that Gestalt therapy professes to have found the "one and only" reality toward which the health of any patient must attain. In fact, in a sense, in experience, the contrary is also true: it is the function of good therapy to enable the patient to "find and make," as it were, his own "reality," his own *increasing* reality.[3]

5. In theory, the Self is essentially known as a spontaneous power or process of figure/ground formation. In principle, the process is a natural one in which a dominant (though transient) *figure,* dynamically related to its *ground,* is given and experienced in awareness. Along with figure-formation (and included in it) is an aspect of this same "Self" that, theoretically and practically, is discussed as a separate and interrelated function. This part (identifying with, or alienating the figure), called *Ego,* is most present wherever and whenever deliberate choice, acceptance or rejection, are present. So in a psychotherapy session, while the

---

3. There may be difficulty in the discussion at this point because of inherent questions about the meaning of *reality*. Obviously, what is not being said is that everyone lives in his (or her) own little world; if this were the case, it might be wondered how any significant, meaningful, directed, need-fulfilling contact (including psychotherapy) would be possible at all. But we're also not saying that there is an exclusive, purely "objective" reality that exists, has always existed, and will go on existing, unchanged, and that the problem of therapy is to get the patient to see it (and, of course, to live in it). What we are trying to show is that, in a way, "reality" is both "objective" and "subjective" and that it is what is given in moments of contact.

patient is selecting what is safe, useful, frightening, interesting, urgent, and so on, it is the same as saying that he is alienating and identifying with the possibilities; that is, this is the "Ego" at work.

6. It is always interesting and clinically relevant to notice the variety of ways in which patients order their priorities, from the moment the hour begins through the ending of the session. It is in what is brought in (and in what is avoided), and importantly, in *how* it is conveyed, that the therapist gets the intimate view of the kind of self-regulation the patient has taken on (e.g., how the patient is burdened by his ordering).[4]

Self-regulation of some kind occurs, of course, regardless of how aware a patient is of any hierarchy to which his values conform (e.g., in his belief that what he wants is more important than what he can have). So Gestalt therapy is supported by a basic theory of human nature (giving meaning to what is spoken of as a "person") that presumes an arrangement of structures and functions in the field that relate to the well-being of the human (social, animal, physical) organism. And this framework, like others in the theory, is an orientation for the therapist and is most profitably used as an exploratory device. After all, it is the patient's own awareness of what is important and what isn't that is ultimately the factor that will decide how this particular, aggregate individual will cope. (One of Brecht's choices, for instance, tells of what ends he pursued when flattened by desperate circumstances: "Grub first, then ethics.")

7. A person sustains himself, completes his situations, only by getting from the environment what is assimilable, useful for growth and preservation. From any patient's perspective, the context of psychotherapy is such an environment (with the therapist playing a critical role in it). If treatment is to succeed the patient must be offered and he must find what is likely to increase self-awareness (a gain that, in turn, can be transferred to his ordinary life). Therefore, it is intrinsic to the practice of Gestalt therapy that the therapist be aware of how the patient makes contact (or fails to do so) *in the on-going present* of any and every therapy hour.

To repeat: A person seeks therapy because in his misery he sees himself as failing; and psychologically, failure always involves some amount of made interruption or disturbance in contacting the environment. Therefore, the way in which a disturbance is made (e.g., where there is neurotic inattentiveness or rigidity) must be brought to the patient so he can *experience* it (and therefore identify with it as his own). Then it is on the basis of the various inhibitions to contact-making, as evidenced

---

4. One may find oneself wanting to say, gently, as Kafka said of himself, "You've harnessed yourself ridiculously for this world."

in the therapy session and observable by the practitioner, that the Gestalt therapist intervenes.

8. A central orientation in Gestalt therapy is respectful of the philosophical judgment that whatever happens (including acts of anticipation and remembering), happens in an *on-going present*. This temporal aspect, considered simply, means that events unfold and develop (in therapy as elsewhere) and can be viewed as occurring in a sequence. A sequence begins with an awareness of an *appetite* (what one needs, desires, wants, etc.) and passes into the next development in which the environment is purposefully contacted and manipulated until the need is gratified and the situation finished.

It is also the case that, due to anxiety and a consequent loss of ego-functioning that may occur at any point in the interaction, gratification may be thwarted. Then it is likely that each patient will present, to the eye of the therapist, a number of ways in which he may be *unaware* that he is disturbing his efforts at contact-making.

Every patient reveals, in a sense, two kinds of evidence regarding when, how, and where efforts of contact-making fail or are inadequate to resolve some problem. Normally, as in any therapy, there's the "complaint" of the typical dissatisfactions with one's day-to-day existence that are verbalized to the therapist. Additionally, the manner, style, attitude, and so on of the patient's presentation is very much the raw material to be worked over. In treatment, *how* a person addresses his problems *in the presence of a therapist* will display adequate samples of essential background traits—of ego functioning, personality, and so on—that this individual typically employs. So it is in their inevitable combination—the patient's details of his dissatisfactions and in the delivery—that the Gestalt therapist gains insights into areas of the patient's unawareness, the structure in which anxiety is likely to be present.

9. Within its temporal context any event can be divided into phases (e.g., beginning, middle, end). In the language of Gestalt therapy, wherever "Ego" is, psychological events are described as consisting of "Fore-Contact," "Contacting," and "Final Contact" phases. It is understood then and accepted that in any phase, at any point, something other than what may be "intended" can occur. Further, that the occurrence of the "unwanted" may lead to a fixation rather than to successful organic completion.

At any place in the matrix of contacting, the Gestalt therapist would diagnose and treat a particular loss of ego-functioning observable in terms of specific psychological functions. The neurotic case is where a particular "mechanism" appears and is used instead of, rather than along with, the efforts to press on in the engagement.

10. It would be useful before going into the descriptions of diagnosis and treatment of neurotic structures to illustrate a bit more expansively how events "normally" occur in the on-going, felt experience of the individual. We may begin by assuming that the person is "at rest" and that a more energized status is aroused when a *deficit* (e.g., the need for food, an interest) occurs, or if there is stimulation from the environment (e.g., tempting a vaguely perceived need or interest). Normally, in this stage an appetite, desire, and so on appears as figure and, by becoming part of the ground support, contributes to activating means for contact-making in the environment. One of these means is a building sense of felt excitation useful in every outgoing action (that when unsupportable is also a source of anxiety).

Now aware of a need (desire, etc.), one next confronts an environment in which *objects* are available. It is not extraordinary then, given the complexity of sociocultural life, that obstacles will appear that may be overcome only with some degree of conflict. Assuming one proves adequate to the difficulties and can overcome the obstacles and obtain what is gratifying, the urge would appear of giving oneself over (psychologically) to the experience. Then with the organism/environment concern resolved, what follows would occur with diminished awareness as one is "returned" to the quiescence of rest.[5]

In all of this it is not difficult to imagine how a person may interfere with the developing sequence: He may shrink from aggressive contact with the environment, or even before that he may blot out awareness of what he needs or wants. And it is just this, just what is done or avoided, that guides the therapist in the intervention paradigm of Gestalt therapy. The vital question concerns whether or not the situation is still alive with possibilities *(on-goingness)* or has been negated (by *fixation*).

11. "On-goingness," it must be emphasized, is of especial importance to the life of *any* situation. It means that a problem can at least be *worked at* without a neurotic outcome (given that such an outcome is "defined," essentially, as a loss or fixation of one's *boundaries*); that occasion for novelty (e.g., unpredictable favorable or unfavorable occurrences) are inherent everywhere and at any time (as this moment, indeed, has never before occurred). To the Gestalt therapist, one's sense of vitality applied to what would resolve a human problem is given the available capacity, to use a mundane phrase, to continue to "do one's best."

To reiterate: It is in the occasion of intolerable anxiety that the same *mechanism*, which when functioning normally assists one in contact-making, now becomes "neurotic" because of the fixation. Or looked at from

---

5. The last phase known, "Post-Contact," in situations that are successfully completed is *out* of awareness and does not involve ego-functioning.

a situation of tolerable excitement, the mechanisms do not permanently disable the ego-functioning; they participate, even if mistakenly, as belonging to an increasing awareness of what is there and what can be done.

INTERVENTIONS OF A GESTALT THERAPIST

12. We can begin arbitrarily with a scene of the patient having *falsely* "completed" doing something (e.g., "explaining" his latest romantic débacle) where essentially "nothing" occurred that he could gain from in terms of increased self-awareness. Though other interpretations of this evident failure are likely quite important,[6] in this somewhat idealized example we'll take up with the patient showing, more or less, to the therapist and himself that the therapy is going nowhere. What we have here is a *fixation*—of the conditions of "failure"—in which the patient, now frustrated and angry, falls silent, betraying an attitude of positive determination to move no further (e.g., by "cooperating" with the therapist).

This position (as a "mechanism") is a demand for *confluence* containing evidence that nothing novel is relevant, or relevant enough; a strong figure of concern (desire, need, appetite, stimulation from the environment, etc.) is kept from developing. If there is interest at all, it is in the direction of having the therapist ply more of his skills and "wisdom" to bring about an unblocking of the now-stagnant conditions.

For the Gestalt therapist, the "choice" of interventions here would include what may appear to the patient as (antagonizing) passivity. The option taken could be a refusal in a sense to "help," based on an assessment that additional dependency now would interfere with, rather than increase, the self-awareness. The intervention may be, e.g., not to become bored, provoked, distracted, excessively "kind," to lose patience. That is, the therapist would be "all there" (and available), but the aggression, the experimental initiatives, belong mainly to the potentialities of the patient.

It is not inconceivable here that the situation can become even more fixed, more "deadened"; and also in this case the patient may cleverly find a manipulation that succeeds in drawing the therapist into going out to rescue him.[7] But let's assume the patient is able to mobilize some of the energies dammed up in confluence: He may consider that perhaps he is expecting too much from the therapist and other people. In

---

6. The "secondary gains of illness" and so on are important also, but will be disregarded in this illustration.
7. Here, as throughout, the therapist's own capacity to tolerate anxiety comes to the foreground.

this case, he may attempt to "compensate," for example, by asserting that "a man should be strong and not have to rely on anybody" as he gloomily struggles to do something for himself (striking a "macho" pose).

To the Gestalt therapist, however, the interpretive understanding of such a clichéd remark is direct evidence of the patient's identifying (unaware) with an *introject;* and it is the introjection of the masculine role that is now assumed to be interfering with the spontaneity of the stronger figure relevant to the underlying motivation. In this case the therapist may intervene, this time by questioning and challenging the patient's remarks, for example, "What do you find wrong (dangerous, disgusting, etc.) with needing another person?"

13. If we return again to the idea of the unfolding of the contact-sequence, what we have to this point is the transition from (a) a situation of no-contact (with appetite, environment, etc.) to (b) a figure-formation hampered by the inclusion of a social ideology (i.e., of male prowess), that is, an introject that draws away from the excitement (or anxiety) latent in the more accurate evaluation of one's present context. Since in Gestalt therapy it is understood that unassimilated introjections are mostly useless to creativity, an intervention would have to be made on the basis of the patient's incapacitating identification with it.

It is certainly not the case that introjection is useless as an adjustive function, as "going along with the crowd" has considerable meaning in terms of the social feeling that one "fits in." But if in the therapy situation one cannot experimentally invent as yet untried solutions to problems, the possibilities—in terms of discovery—of increasing self-awareness and growth are reduced. Considered as part of the series of fixation, the therapist's questioning of the identification with the introject would again rouse anxiety in the patient. And consequently, the next fixation would be made in terms of the meaning to the patient of the therapist's question.

14. It is not uncommon to find in the anxiety aroused when one's cherished beliefs are questioned that this lends to *projecting.* In this illustration one can conceive that the patient, confronted by a testing of the authenticity of what he thinks he believes, may find "proof" for accusing the therapist of trying to encourage him to become "feminine," weak, and so on. Then in the attempt to ward off the threat of anxiety that would occur here (e.g., in identifying with aspects of his personality that do *not* fit his male stereotype) the patient again fixates his present achievement, that is, the conviction given in the projection that the therapist is interested in emasculating him.

15. A fixation now is indicative of the patient's difficulties in confronting the environment; and again an intervention would be made in terms of establishing a *boundary of contact*. As before, a noncoercive questioning, this time aimed at what the patient finds as the evidence for his assertion, may be the best technique. If the question succeeds, if the patient comes to realize that what he is attributing to the therapist may in fact be emotionally his "own," the next anxiety, brought on by the turning of the aggression against the self instead of toward the environment, will also be fixated, now by "retroflecting."

16. *Retroflection* is a dynamic "mechanism" in which the person (his body, personality) becomes the target for the conflict now stirred up. Instead of perhaps "having it out" with the therapist or some other "enemy," the patient safely engages in combat with "inner" forces (e.g., the mother who forced him to learn what it means to be a "man"). Of course, in front of the therapist, the patient may give voice to the battle by belittling the responsible parties, criticizing himself for his limitations, and so on. Nevertheless, however honest or well intended the "confession," the fact that hostile aggression is turned against the Self is evidence to the therapist of lost ego-functioning, and calls for an intervention meant to bring the organism/environment context back into awareness.

As a way of attending to a patient's retroflecting, the therapist may inquire as to what present threat (e.g., from Mama, from the therapist) exists, is perceived, now and here. And indeed, unless it is the therapist who is effectively preventing the ongoing contact (as it possibly may be), it is always interesting when some kind of pertinent knowledge is attained that the difficulty is not released or in some small way integrated.

So the patient "agrees" that Mother is not here and as a present obstacle is out of the way. Still, this is unsatisfactory to one who demands assurances (that he is, for instance, "irrefutable") and who will not risk himself until he is convinced that possibilities of being "caught" off guard have been eliminated. This condition, known in Gestalt therapy as "Egotism," is the last fixation, preventing "Final Contact."

17. In a certain sense, Egotism can be regarded as an "informed" confluence: The main difference between them is that in the former, given its degree of awareness, there is too much for the patient to talk about (which is used to interfere with his letting go). But however impressive and vast a patient's "awareness" about things, the therapist can avoid being duped. Even if the patient is shrewd enough and verbal enough to articulate all that he has learned in his experiences in therapy (demonstrating, for example, how well he knows himself or the therapist), it is not adequate as proof that final contact has been achieved.

Final contact, by definition, involves a degree of *not* knowing, an element of risking oneself, for growth occurs just where the functioning of the ego, the sense of "I" in the situation, is no longer a fixed concern. And though it may be extremely difficult to pull off, if in the face of the potentially surprising and unpredictable factors that are *always* there, regardless of how fine-tuned the "Ego" is, a patient manages to cope and "give in" to the created figure, the possibilities for completing his unfinished situations and growing from the novelties of the present environment are now strengthened.

As for the therapist's contribution to the likelihood of a patient's ever exercising the "faith" involved in risk, he (or she) can, as in the earlier stages, make an intervention in terms of ego-functioning only in the areas of unawareness. Nevertheless, this is the most complicated and difficult of all the contexts in any session of psychotherapy: One cannot "teach" faith or risktaking, but one can to the extent possible prepare the grounds (in therapy but not, for better or worse, in the "real" world) for what Gestalt therapy refers to as an *experimental safe emergency*. That is, if the patient can discover, in the presence of the therapist, that he will not collapse if he risks himself, it is more likely he can take over on his own.

18. For any psychological experience to be truly completed, assimilation and growth ("Post-Contact") must have occurred. But in psychological experience, assimilation and growth essentially pass into the physiological and take place in the organism (but "outside" its awareness). The limits of practice in Gestalt therapy are reached when it is clear that grounds for Final Contact in the release of the aware functioning of the "Ego" have been prepared.

No person can, without being coercive, demand of another that he grow. And it is likely that in modern society the emphasis is in the contrary direction: not on growth per se, but in the direction of acquiring status (e.g., becoming rich, beautiful, successful, etc.). As Goethe observed: "Everybody wants to *be* somebody: nobody wants to grow." However, whether or not this or similar aspects of human life are worthwhile is not a question for Gestalt psychotherapy.

CONCLUSION

19. Because of space constraints the discussion in this work was limited to a more or less "typical" clinical situation, to concentrating on some common events within the context of psychotherapy (e.g., on what basis as a practitioner of Gestalt therapy one can expect to intervene). Many of the concepts and terms could not be fully explicated, and much of the intellectual texture of theory was sacrificed to the presentation of the closer connections between method and application.

The theory of Gestalt therapy is complex and extensive, and most completely articulated in volume 2 of *Gestalt Therapy* (Perls, Hefferline, & Goodman, 1951). As what was presented here is drawn from that source, it is recommended that that work be read for an elaboration and clarification of the vocabulary, specialist items, and overarching theoretical assumptions and insights.

REFERENCES

Perls, F. S., Hefferline, R. F., & Goodman, P. (1951). *Gestalt therapy: Excitement and growth in the human personality.* New York: Dell.

3

Behavior Therapy

CYRIL M. FRANKS, Ph.D.

Most systems of psychotherapy stem from a mixture of clinical experience and the fertile mind of the originator. Psychoanalytic and Gestalt therapies are cases in point. Few attempts are made to engage in independent investigation, and validation remains largely a matter of clinical impression. Behavior therapy, a term used here synonymously with behavior modification, is unique in that clinical insight and creativity serve primarily as important starting-off points in the development of a therapy model that rests upon principles derived experimentally prior to direct clinical application. In this respect, behavior therapy is an approach rather than, as many non-behavior therapists erroneously believe, a set of techniques. One hallmark of this approach is an allegiance to independent data and the methodology of the behavioral sciences coupled with some form of stimulus-response learning theory.

Developed largely by experimental psychologists dissatisfied with the prevailing psychotherapy scene, it is only within the past 3 or 4 decades that behavior therapy has become a viable alternative. One chapter cannot do justice to these events, and those who wish to delve further should consult the relevant literature. Kazdin (1978a) has written an informative history of behavior therapy and, in 1973, Franks and Wilson inaugurated a still ongoing, annual chronicle of theoretical, practical, and professional developments in behavior therapy. While the latter is not recommended since it runs strongly counter to the raison-d'être of behavior therapy, readers interested primarily in techniques could consult one or more of the readily available practice-oriented manuals or, better yet, attend a clinical workshop geared toward their specific needs. My purpose here is to provide an overview of origins, concepts, basic techniques, current issues and future directions. In so doing, I have no wish to engage in polemics or blanket endorsement of behavior therapy. The key word is *different* rather than *better* or *worse*.

Myths about behavior therapy abound, some of them arising from the

misguided enthusiasm and naive pronouncements of early practitioners. These include the notion that even contemporary behavior
therapy rests exclusively upon some form of simple conditioning and
that it is effective primarily for the treatment of specific problems such
as public speaking anxiety or fear of riding in elevators. It is also erroneously believed that behavior therapy is dictatorial and that warmth, empathy, and the development of trusting relationships are still of little
clinical concern. Other incorrect beliefs are that behavior therapists
treat something called "the symptom" and ignore hidden problems and
that thought processes and affect are ignored. I can think of no qualified
behavior therapist who functions in this way today. Other incorrect
charges leveled against behavior therapy are that biological and constitutional differences are discounted and that behavior therapists deal
exclusively with the here and now. Not all the myths are negative. Many
are seemingly positive but equally inaccurate. For example, it is commonly believed that most bad habits can be successfully eradicated by
behavior therapy in a small number of sessions and that virtually anybody can become a behavior therapist after a few sessions of training.
Both beliefs are quite false.

THE FOUNDATIONS OF BEHAVIOR THERAPY

Behavior therapy has a long past but a short history. While reinforcement has been used intuitively for thousands of years, it was not until
psychology abandoned philosophical speculation in favor of data that
the ground became ready for behavior therapy to germinate. The
burgeoning impact of Pavlovian classical conditioning, Watson's neobe-
haviorism, Thorndike's laws of learning, and Skinner's operant conditioning—names and principles that can be found in most psychology
texts—facilitated this process. Dissatisfaction with the prevailing psychotherapeutic status quo led to the search for new systems and new ways
of thinking about old problems. Then as now, no one country or school
of thought could lay exclusive claim to behavior therapy and no one
leader or technique stood out.

Behavior therapy is now entering its fourth decade. The 1960s, the
first decade, was a pioneering era of ideology and polemics in which
behavior therapists tried to present a united front against the common
psychodynamic "foe." It was during these turbulent times that, despite
resistance from the mental health establishment, behavior therapy began to receive acceptance from both lay persons and an increasing number of professionals. As behavior therapy became more secure, behavior
therapists gradually abandoned missionary zeal in favor of a search
for new horizons within their own domain. This was the era of biofeedback, behavioral psychopharmacology, ecological psychology, behavioral

medicine, and more—now all firmly established facets of behavior therapy. Sophisticated methods of treatment, improved methodology, and better outcome procedures were developed. Perhaps the most significant event that occurred in this era, to be discussed shortly, was that behavior therapy, along with much of psychology, "went cognitive."

In the second and third decades this trend continued. Forward-looking behavior therapists identified themselves as social learning theorists, and therapeutic change became dependent upon cognitive processing activated through behavioral procedures. Conditioning responses were seen as self-activated, situation-sensitive reactions based on learning expectations rather than as invariant, automatic processes. Private events, cognition, affect, empathy, and verbal interchange between patient and therapist became fair game for this new breed of behavior therapists. Whereas the focus of traditional behavior therapy was overt behavior and that of cognitive therapy was the putative causal roles of maladaptive thought patterns, cognitive/social learning therapists sought to integrate both sets of variables into one common process. To cognitive behavior therapists, focusing exclusively on either behavior or cognition is too restrictive; both sets of variables have to be taken into consideration. Thus, in the fourth and present decades, the emphasis has been on even greater conceptual and clinical sophistication together with a healthy recognition of limitations and, possibly less positive, a diversity that could contain the potential for disintegration—but more on this shortly.

With the growing acceptance of behavior therapy, non-behavioral clinicians began to acknowledge that viewing behavioral techniques as a device for the correction of specific malfunctions interfered with the real order of business: psychodynamically oriented psychotherapy. Behavior therapists tried to draw attention to the fact that behavior therapy is a conceptual approach that has led to the development of various procedures rather than a collection of techniques per se. While virtually anybody, it was pointed out, could learn how to carry out most of these procedures in a mechanical fashion, in no way would this entitle these individuals to call themselves behavior therapists. From this perspective, it is quite inappropriate for psychodynamic clinicians to regard themselves as psychodynamic therapists who occasionally use adjunct behavioral procedures to facilitate depth therapy. Unfortunately, psychodynamically oriented clinicians choose either to ignore or to dismiss this note of caution.

The term *behavior therapy* was introduced independently by three groups of researchers: In the United States, Lindsley, Skinner, and Solomon (1953) referred to their use of operant conditioning with hospitalized psychotic patients as behavior therapy. In the United Kingdom, Eysenck (1959) used the term to refer to his new learning theory approach to therapy. In South Africa, Lazarus (1958) used the term to refer to the addition of objective laboratory procedures to traditional psychotherapy. As of 1993, some 40 regularly published behavior therapy journals, mostly in English, are available. Large national and international groups form part of a still evolving network. Themes covered range from children to geriatrics, from practical case management to esoteric theoretical interests, from working with the individual to the resolution of large-scale problems in business and government, from specific stimulus-response units within a school or hospital setting to field-oriented programs involving complex interactions, and more.

CHARACTERISTICS OF CONTEMPORARY BEHAVIOR THERAPY

Since behavior therapy is an approach rather than a set of techniques, it is applicable, at least in principle, to virtually all disorders. (This should not be taken to imply that behavior therapy is ideal for all disorders or that it is always going to be readily effective.) The competent behavior therapist takes into account relevant past events and their possible impact upon the present, listens carefully to what the patient has to say, and then embarks upon a fact-finding assessment process to shed light upon what the patient perceives as problems and what the therapist feels are more relevant issues. Patient and therapist then engage in mutual discussion of salient issues and a very provisional contractual agreement is negotiated.

Early behavior therapy was understandably simplistic. The technology for more complex application had not as yet emerged, and the emphasis has been upon specific, one-to-one stimuli. In addition, largely as an overreaction to prevailing psychodynamic influences, early behavior therapy was anticognitive and antimentalistic. As behavior therapy became more secure and more cognitively oriented, this defensive stance was no longer necessary. Whereas it used to be that the opponents of behavior therapy were its strongest critics, informed criticism now came from within. Failures were viewed as theoretical and clinical challenges.

Contemporary behavior therapy reflects a combination of doing and talking, multidimensional methods, and a problem-solving approach in which assessment and intervention are intermingled to generate periodic reevaluation. When appropriate, psychoactive medication may be combined with behavior therapy (Van Hasselt & Hersen, 1993). In principle, if not always in practice, clinical activity arises out of data-based formulations and tested predictions rather than intuition and clinical impression alone. By these criteria, rational-emotive therapy (RET) is not behavior therapy, no matter how effective it may be, because the procedures stemmed originally largely from clinical observation and the gifted mind of Ellis rather than from any independent data base

(Ellis, 1979). To his credit, it must be placed on record that Ellis and his associates are now developing a research program and a data base for RET.

Modern behavior therapy is able to accommodate considerable diversity. There are those who accept personality dimensions and enduring personality traits as highly consistent with a behavioral position and there are those who take a diametrically opposite point of view. Some individuals believe that self-control cannot possibly exist since there is no such thing as the "self"; for others self-control is a primary goal. There are those who lean heavily on physiological and genetic factors and there are those who believe that such determinants are either non-existent or, at best, irrelevant. Then there are those for whom the guiding framework is radical behaviorism, with its complete denial of any intervening variable between the stimulus and the response, and there are those whose only allegiance is to the methodology of behavioral science. For some, the principles of classical and operant conditioning, with the possible addition of modeling, are sufficient, and for others conditioning is but one part of the story. Finally, some behavior therapists believe that theory is essential and others insist that data are sufficient in themselves. (More on these matters shortly.) Contemporary behavior therapy is able to accommodate all of these perspectives and more. Whether behavior therapy will assume a possibly retrogressive corrective rigidity or whether it will fragment into disparate and potentially antithetical entities is for the future to decide. In 1981 I wrote an article titled "2081: Will We Be Many or One—Or None?" This issue is as much a concern in 1993 as it was over a decade ago (Franks, 1981).

THE COGNITIVE REVOLUTION

Without doubt, one of the most exciting developments in behavior therapy is the rise of cognitive behavior therapy and cognitive social-learning theory. According to its more enthusiastic proponents, cognitive behavior therapy is a paradigm shift, a new era in behavior therapy. Others disagree (see Mahoney and Kazdin, 1979, among many others, for more extensive dialogue). Reactions against the "stigma" of mentalism had led early behavior therapists to focus on overt responses and to ignore completely all cognitive processes. It was also much easier to work with specific reinforcers than with more nebulous procedures. Furthermore, at that time the technology for working with group processes and systems did not exist. And so it is understandable that early behavior therapists stressed specific procedures geared toward specific problems. Then came the "cognitive revolution," a development of still uncertain significance despite its popularity among behavior therapists. What is needed, if light rather than heat is to be generated, is for the argument to be moved from the theater of debate to the arena of empirical investigation. Necessary prerequisites include consensus about a definition of behavior therapy, specification of investigational methods, and compliance with these methods by behavior therapists. It should also be recognized that several different therapy models have emerged, of which cognitive behavior therapy is but one. These include *applied behavioral analysis,* based on Skinnerian operant conditioning; *Pavlovian-based learning or conditioning therapies,* as filtered through the visions of such neobehaviorists as Hull, Spence, Eysenck, Rachman, and Wolpe; and *social-learning therapy,* for which Bandura (1982) is its foremost spokesmen. From my perspective, it is difficult to envisage any form of therapy without some cognition, and it is the relative emphasis on the extent of the cognition that determines whether a particular strategy is to be regarded as primarily cognitive. In some procedures, such as aversion conditioning, cognitive input is relatively minimal and in others, such as cognitive restructuring, cognitive variables predominate.

DEFINING BEHAVIOR THERAPY

In 1978, Kazdin listed the more salient characteristics of behavior therapy: a focus on current rather than historical determinants; an emphasis on overt behavior change as the main criterion by which treatment is to be evaluated; specification of treatment in objective terms so as to make replication possible; a reliance upon basic research to generate testable hypotheses about both treatment strategies and specific intervention techniques; and finally, specificity in definition, accountability, treatment, and measurement (Kazdin, 1978b). Over the last 15 years, while these criteria are still relevant, certain conditions need to be taken into account. These include but are not limited to an emphasis on patient-clinician interactions, exploration of perceived and possibly unrecognized patient needs and goals, consumer satisfaction, greater recognition of cognitive and affective elements, and enhanced awareness of the therapist's responsibilities toward society.

Early definitions strove to link behavior therapy to specific doctrines, theories, laws, or principles of learning. For example, Eysenck (1959) was satisfied with a vague definition predicated upon so-called modern learning theory and, somewhat idiosyncratically, Yates (1970) thought systematic investigation of the single case was the essence of behavior therapy. The definition of behavior therapy that follows, originally endorsed in 1975 by the Association for the Advancement of Behavior Therapy (AABT) and still in effect with minor modifications, reads as follows:

> Behavior therapy involves primarily the application of principles derived from research in experimental and social psychology for the

alleviation of human suffering and the advancement of human functioning. Behavior therapy emphasizes a systematic evaluation of the effectiveness of these applications. Behavior therapy involves environmental change and social interaction rather than the direct alteration of bodily processes by biological procedures. The aim is primarily educational. The techniques facilitate improved self-control. In the conduct of behavior therapy, a contractual agreement is usually negotiated in which mutually agreeable goals and procedures are specified. Responsible practitioners using behavioral approaches are guided by generally accepted ethical principles. (Franks & Wilson, 1973–1975, vol. 3, p. 1)

This definition attempts to cover all fronts. Most definitions tend to fall into one of two classes: doctrinal or epistemological. Doctrinal definitions attempt to link behavior therapy to various theories, laws, or principles of learning. Epistemological definitions are more inclined to characterize behavior therapy in terms of the various ways of studying clinical phenomena. By and large, doctrinal definitions tend to be narrow and thereby fail to accommodate all of behavior therapy, whereas epistemological definitions, as above, tend to be excessively accommodating and hence applicable to almost all therapies. It may be that a definition of behavior therapy that is acceptable to the majority of behavior therapists is not possible at this time. Perhaps with this in mind, Erwin (1978) rests content to characterize behavior therapy as "a nonbiological form of therapy that developed largely out of learning theory research and that is normally applied directly, incrementally, and experimentally in the treatment of specific maladaptive patterns" (p. 146).

Given what has been written so far, it is not surprising that lively controversy occurs within and outside behavior therapy. In the next section, I highlight a few of these areas.

SOME CURRENT ISSUES

The role of stimulus-response learning theory and conditioning in behavior therapy. Behavior therapy is supposed to be based on conditioning. Is cognition likewise governed by conditioning mechanisms? Are the principles of conditioning as applicable to covert and inner-directed processes as they are to external situations? Other than Bandura's social learning and modeling, no new behavior therapy principle seems to have been developed for decades. Is it now necessary to broaden the foundations of behavior therapy to include knowledge drawn from social psychology, physiology, and sociology? If behavior therapy is broadened in this fashion does it take on a new identity or even no identity? In the long run, does this matter?

The nature of behaviorism and its relationship to behavior therapy. Contrary to the belief of many professionals, both those outside behavior therapy and those within who should know better, behaviorism is not a monolithic concept. At the very least, two major kinds of behaviorism can be identified: *methodological behaviorism* and *metaphysical or radical behaviorism.* In methodological behaviorism, mental states and mediational variables are accepted. Methodological behavior therapists tend to refer to themselves as *behavioral* rather than *behaviorist,* a distinction that frequently goes unrecognized. Nowadays, most behavior therapists are behavioral rather than behaviorist, and notions such as free will, self-control, cognition, and awareness are given full recognition. By contrast, the metaphysical or radical behaviorist denies the existence of mental states as useful postulates. Radical behaviorists tend to be nonmediational, antimentalistic, and never inferential. Individuals such as Watson were metaphysical behaviorists, whereas Hull, Spence, Eysenck, and the majority of contemporary behavior therapists are more appropriately viewed as methodological behavior therapists. It is indeed difficult to see how any behavior therapist can work with a patient in a meaningful relationship that is totally devoid of cognition. It is equally difficult to see how a patient can respond to even a circumscribed procedure, such as a token reinforcement or aversive stimulus, without some cognition or awareness. Be this as it may, the debate about the nature, role, and significance of behaviorism in behavior therapy remains lively and is likely to continue in the foreseeable future. It is far from an academic matter because the intellectual stance adopted determines the therapist's approach to his or her patients.

Social-learning theory and reciprocal determinism. In its most advanced form (e.g., Bandura, 1982), social-learning theory is interactional, interdisciplinary, and multimodal. While radical behaviorists tend to ignore or de-emphasize the role of cognition and cognitive therapists are inclined to minimize the importance of performance, social-learning theorists stress both cognition and performance. And while classical conditioning focuses on external events and operant conditioning is a matter of reinforcement contingencies, social-learning theory takes into account both sets of determinants, using concepts derived from self-efficacy theory and modeling to bring about the necessary bridging mechanisms. According to Bandura, self-efficacy influences thought patterns, actions, and emotional arousal across a broad range of human experience, extending from the individual to the collective efforts of the group. There is continuous and reciprocal interaction among behavioral, cognitive, and environmental performance patterns. For those who resent the popular equating of behavior therapy with coercive manipulation and the curtailing of free choice, reciprocal determinism is an enticing notion. For others, reciprocal determinism creates more of an illusion of human freedom than freedom itself—but this is ultimately a philosophical issue that is hard to resolve by experiment.

The importance of theory, the growing gap between theory and practice, and the problem of technical eclecticism. Unfortunately, relatively few behavior therapists consistently practice what they preach. It is difficult to focus on data and external corroboration when confronted by the pressing demands of a patient with an immediate problem. Similarly, despite the best of intentions, there is a gap between clinical research and clinical practice. Given the different priorities, contexts, and demands of practice and research, this is understandable if not acceptable. In clinical practice, the primary goal is treatment. In contrast, clinical research has as its primary goal the testing of specific hypotheses. Integrating the divergent demands of practice and research is likely to tax the ingenuity of the clinician to the utmost (see Kazdin, 1993).

In his spirited defense of what he calls *technical eclecticism,* Lazarus (1981) takes the position that, if a scientist cannot afford to be eclectic, the clinician cannot afford *not* to be eclectic. By this he means that, while theoretical eclecticism is logically impossible (to adopt one conceptual orientation one day and another the next is tantamount to intellectual schizophrenia), technical eclecticism, the use of any validated technique regardless of origin, is essential when the main concern is the welfare of the patient. Unfortunately, this is easier said than done because the only way to know what works is through good validating studies and these are rare. Too often, the clinician takes refuge in the argument that it is preferable to rely on intuitive trial and error—a latching on to anything that might help. This is a far cry from the principles of empiricism and rational investigation based on hypothesis testing that triggered off much of behavior therapy in the first instance. The debate continues unabated as proponents on both sides develop elaborate arguments in defense of their positions. Meanwhile, the gaps between theory and research and between what behavior therapists write and what they do grows wider.

Behavior therapy, psychoanalysis, and integration. In its formative years, behavior therapists engaged in antagonistic, self-defeating, and potentially destructive feuding with psychoanalysts. Within recent years, both camps became more tolerant, and there is now a limited but growing call for conceptual as well as practical rapprochement. Whether this heralds ecumenical progress or a specter of regressive futility is a matter of opinion. My position is clear: Behavior therapy and psychoanalysis are fundamentally irreconcilable at both theoretical and clinical levels (Franks, 1984). It is not a matter of better or worse so much as difference. Behavior therapists and psychoanalysts deal with different paradigms, under-stand and formulate psychological problems differently, rely on very different methods of verification, and accept different "facts" as legiti-mate data. For example, clinical impression is often sufficient validation for the psychoanalyst but less than satisfactory, in itself, for the behavior therapist. Proponents of either position who are logically consistent within their respective models thereby arrive at conclusions that are in-compatible with those of the other faction. To my way of thinking, at least for the foreseeable future, it would be better for each camp to do its own thing and go it alone. Many competent behavior therapists take diametrically opposing positions and argue that some form of integra-tion, perhaps leading to a new conceptual model, is feasible (e.g., Gold-fried, 1978; Wachtel, 1977). In my opinion, if such a synthesis is eventually to come about, it is more likely to arise as a by-product of calculated, goal-directed program research within each camp. But this is a point of view not shared by all behavior therapists, and the debate continues.

Behavior therapy and the rise of professionalism. The AABT began as an interest group rather than a guild. But, as with the American Psycho-logical Association, professional concerns now take increasing prece-dence. Perhaps as a consequence, while clinical know-how advances significantly, conceptual innovations remain lacking. In an attempt to reverse this trend, a small but growing number of behavior therapists are striving to return to the founding principles of the AABT. Whether this is a positive step forward or an ostrichlike retreat from reality re-mains to be seen.

The image of behavior therapy. There is a regrettable tendency for the public to view behavior therapy as a collection of powerful, potentially harmful techniques for the promotion of conformity and the control of human behavior with little regard for the rights and feelings of others. Behavior therapy is sometimes equated by the uninformed with psycho-surgery, the use of drugs, sensory deprivation, and even torture. This view continues to be promulgated by less than well informed writers in popular books and in the media. These negative images are inadvert-ently reinforced by unfortunate behavioral terminology such as *control,* *punishment,* and *aversive conditioning,* all of which impact negatively on the willingness of the public to consider behavior therapy as a viable treatment option (Mays & Franks, 1985). Somewhat tangentially related is the vexing matter of terminology and the medical model. We still think, speak, and write about *patient, treatment, therapy,* and the like. One advantage of this association with medicine is that behavior therapy is less likely to be construed as something malevolent. On the other hand, behavior therapy began as a radical departure from the medical model, a departure that is not advanced by the perhaps now unavoidable continuation of this terminology.

These are some of the issues for behavior therapists to ponder as they go about their daily clinical business. There are many others. For example, when modifying client behavior, which behavior should be changed and in what sequence, and what are the determinants? What ethical and legal justifications are to be invoked in attempting to answer such questions? Are the answers to be found through the application of behavioral principles or through subjective preferences? While there are few legal decisions that apply exclusively to behavior therapy, there are some rulings that are particularly relevant. For example, in planning a token economy for a psychiatric setting, court rulings affirming the rights of all patients to basic amenities have to be met. It is then up to the ingenuity of the behavior therapist to develop acceptable and meaningful reinforcers that do not interfere with the rights of the individual patient. Part of the problem is that behavior therapists and lawyers employ different language systems. Law is steeped in mentalistic language in which terms like *free will, duress,* and *coercion* are commonplace. If these words are anathema to many behavior therapists, behavioral terms such as *control* and *behavioral modification* are equally offensive to many lawyers.

Although guidelines have been tentatively established by professional organizations for the protection of both patient and research subjects, consensus is less than total. This is equally true of attempts by behavior therapists to develop appropriate procedures for working with specific populations such as prison groups or families of autistic children. Fortunately, most professionals share similar concerns when it comes to the welfare of their clients, and probably the best that behavior therapists can do at this time is to be guided by the policies that prevail in their parent professions.

BEHAVIORAL INTERVENTION: SOME STRATEGIES AND TECHNIQUES

There are literally hundreds of behavioral assessment and intervention procedures in current use. Most have adequate empirical validation, some few are theory generated, and virtually all are reevaluated periodically. With the possible exception of standardized intelligence and attainment tests, certain personality questionnaires, and measures of sensorimotor/memory functioning, the traditional test battery is not used.

In behavior therapy, assessment and intervention are continuous, closely related processes. A fully trained behavior therapist has at his or her command numerous assessment procedures geared toward cognitive, affective, or behavioral areas or relevance. These range from sophisticated physiological indices through self-report and behavioral observation to information gleaned from meaningful others. An important first step is to identify and prioritize treatment goals (Kazdin, 1993).

Reinforcement in some form is probably the procedure most readily associated with behavior therapy. The notion of reinforcement is not unique to behavior therapy. What behavior therapists have contributed is the specification of principles and the development of systematic application strategies. Reinforcement refers to the strengthening of the behavior to increase the probability of performance of a desired response. The individual is reinforced to engage in the desired activity. The reinforcement, which has become contingent upon performance, always involves an increase in frequency of the desired behavior. Presentation of the consequence whenever the behavior is performed is known as positive reinforcement, and the consequence is termed a *positive reinforcer.* In negative reinforcement, an unpleasant consequence can be avoided by performance of the desired behavior. Both positive and negative reinforcement are very different from punishment, a procedure that, for obvious reasons, is rarely used nowadays. In punishment, the frequency of occurrence of an undesired response is decreased by the presentation of an aversive stimulus whenever the undesired behavior occurs. These three procedures, positive and negative reinforcement and punishment, are sometimes confused by individuals not well versed in behavior therapy.

Reinforcement can take many forms, ranging from material rewards through praise, social interaction, or other intangibles. Tokens can be exchanged for some mutually agreed reward at a later date. Within a well-constructed token economy, the reinforcers become part of a program for modifying the daily life of entire groups, such as the residents of psychiatric wards, prison inmates, or school children. Token economies are most effective when combined with a program of individualized behavior therapy.

Reinforcement can be delivered in a real-life, in vivo situation or through the imagination with a procedure known as *covert conditioning.* Studies show that appropriately paired and monitored stimuli, pleasant or unpleasant, can serve as effective behavioral change agents even when they occur only in the imagination. With certain physiological exceptions, all behaviors are maintained by reinforcement. If the reinforcement is no longer available, sooner or later the individual stops engaging in the behavior. This is known as *extinction.*

Systematic desensitization (Wolpe, 1958) is a laborious process that has proven its value in countless situations. Here, too, it is important to begin with adequate assessment because the presenting problem may not be the one that is most relevant or most urgent. Beginning usually in the imagination and then extending into the real-life situation, systematic desensitization generally involves three steps. First, the patient is trained to respond in a manner that is incompatible with both subjective and manifest anxiety. It is difficult to feel anxious and relaxed at the same time, and muscular relaxation can be used to counter anxiety. Many training procedures have been developed to this end, most of which involve the graduated relaxation of various muscle groups. Once relaxation training and mapping out an individualized hierarchy of anxiety-provoking situations are completed, desensitization to events associated with specific anxiety can begin. Mildly anxiety-provoking images are switched to increasingly threatening situations in small, successive steps, and the patient is trained through the relaxation process to feel at ease in circumstances that used to cause anxiety. Many variations have been developed. Sometimes the process is facilitated by associating the anxiety-provoking stimulus with an imagined pleasant scene. If feasible, the patient is exposed to gradually augmented real-life encounters with anxiety-provoking situations. This procedure, known as *in vivo desensitization*, is particularly helpful with problems such as fear of public speaking or performance anxieties related to a negative self-image.

Literally hundreds of behavioral techniques have been validated for incorporation into planned behavior therapy programs. In *flooding*, the patient is exposed in the imagination to a highly aversive situation for a period long enough for discomfort to reach a maximum and then decline. This is a drastic treatment and should be used with caution only after consideration of all relevant parameters. In *modeling*, the observer watches either a live model or a video reenactment. Modeling is useful in teaching new behavior, in motivating more effective performance in existing behavior, in reducing associated anxiety, or in discouraging unwanted behavior. Ample evidence shows that people can benefit from the experiences of others, and modeling uses a variety of strategies to maximize these benefits. Performance difficulties are sometimes related to interpersonal skill deficits, and a variety of skill-deficit training programs is now available. In *social skills training*, the individual is taught to function assertively but not aggressively.

Behavioral contracting is a procedure that is sometimes employed as a precursor to formal behavior therapy. Client and therapist work out a mutually acceptable contractual agreement that specifies positive or negative consequences for compliance or noncompliance with the agreement. Therapists working with adolescents and children often find this arrangement to be helpful.

In *cognitively oriented behavior therapy* the emphasis is on strategies for modifying the faulty cognitions that are assumed to maintain the disorder. In *cognitive restructuring therapies,* patients learn how to modify the distorted or otherwise incorrect thinking that maintains the problem behaviors and to replace these thoughts with more adaptive cognitions. Cognitive restructuring therapies are of particular value when the problems are reinforced by excessive maladaptive thoughts. *Thought stopping,* in which the patient is trained to distract the disturbing thought whenever it becomes too intrusive by some procedure, such as a loudly shouted "Stop!" or a painful flick of a rubber band attached to the wrist, is sometimes effective as an adjunctive behavioral strategy, especially if a pleasant thought is substituted immediately for the unpleasant one.

Ideally, a new behavioral technique emerges out of some theoretical framework. It then gets investigated under controlled conditions and, finally, it is tried out by clinicians in their everyday practices. This is an important stage because acceptability to patient and client and appropriateness for the population on whom it has been validated are essential prerequisites for good behavior therapy. If there is no theoretical rationale, empirical validation will suffice. After all, many effective, commonly used procedures in medicine rest on empirical validation devoid of theory in the first instance.

PRESENT STATUS, FUTURE DIRECTIONS

Technologically, much has happened since Kazdin wrote his comprehensive *History of Behavioral Modification* in 1978; conceptually, little has occurred. But on the positive side, behavior therapists are now accepted members of the mental health community and able to take time out to think about present and future concerns.

Behavior therapists can justifiably feel pleased with their accomplishments. This does not mean, however, that behavior therapists are living in the best of all possible worlds. Clinicians do not always practice what they preach, and the gap between research and clinical practice remains great. Other problem areas, such as the rise of professionalism and its impact on the practice of behavior therapy, the de-emphasis of theory, and the many conceptual and theoretical issues that await resolution, have been outlined briefly in this chapter. Among the more important concerns that will need to be examined more closely are the feasibility of integration with a psychodynamic model and the scientific integrity of cognitive behavior therapy. There is a regrettable tendency for many, but not all, cognitive therapists to think in terms of clinical impression rather than objective data. Fortunately, even though the reinforcements for professional success are more compelling than the advancement of knowledge, there is a small but growing movement within the ranks of behavior therapy to return to a theoretical and conceptual frame of reference. The shift a from stimulus-response model to a nonlinear, more sophisticated, multicausal perspective is still in an early stage. As part of this process, many behavior therapists are now beginning to think in terms of systems rather than specific stimuli and responses, a trend that augers well for the future of behavior therapy.

To the extent that behavior therapy is a flexible approach, it lacks unity and cohesiveness. Variations flourish and are even encouraged. There is no generally accepted definition of behavior therapy, no one leader and no technique that is regarded as more "pure" than any other. While these are healthy developments, they also carry with them the seeds for fragmentation. Whether behavior therapy will be able to resolve these problems and integrate itself into an organized whole, or whether, like the Soviet Union, it will dissolve into a series of localized fragments remains for the future to decide.

Behavior therapists, who are still mostly psychologists, are searching for ways to take into account other disciplines, other professions, and thinking derived from new sources. How this is to be accomplished, whether this will limit the present uniqueness of behavior therapy, and how this is going to change the already extensive training requirements for behavior therapists are further issues that await resolution. If behavior therapy is to become interdisciplinary, it will have to feature much more prominently in the training of psychiatrists and social workers. Can behavior therapists incorporate innovative developments from other disciplines into an overall model that still retains that spirit of scientific integrity which brought behavior therapy into existence in the first place?

Finally, a note of caution: Behavior therapy is an emerging new science, evolutionarily akin to the relatively primitive status of physics and medicine in the 16th and 17th centuries. It is too early to expect most problems to be resolved, and it is premature to think in terms of large-scale integration either within behavior therapy or between behavior therapy and other conceptual systems. What can be said with more certainty is that behavior therapy, now a far cry from its unsophisticated beginnings, is a flourishing and accepted part of the mental health scene and that it is likely to continue in this fashion in some form in the years that lie ahead. On the other hand, we have to remind ourselves that, in the unlikely event that behavior therapy as we know it today should vanish from the face of the earth, this does not have to be a total disaster if the goals and aspirations toward which we all strive are brought about. After all, our primary concern as theoreticians is with the advancement of knowledge, and our primary concern as mental health professionals is with the alleviation of suffering. It is my hope that this brief overview will place behavior therapy in perspective, pointing out accomplishments and limitations, issues that await resolution, and the potential as well as the hazards for the future. Behavior therapy may or may not be more effective than other forms of treatment. Perhaps the best that can be said at this time is that it is conceptually unique among psychotherapies, that it is continually evolving, and that it lends itself to objective evaluation and the recognition of deficiencies.

REFERENCES

Bandura, A. (1982). A self-efficacy measure in human agency. *American Psychologist, 37*, 122–147.

Ellis, A. (1979). *The essence of rational psychotherapy: A comprehensive approach to treatment.* New York: Institute for Rational Living.

Erwin, E. (1978). *Behavior therapy: Scientific, philosophical, and moral foundations.* Cambridge, England: Cambridge University Press.

Eysenck, H. J. (1959). Learning theory and behaviour therapy. *Journal of Mental Science, 105*, 1–75.

Franks, C. M. (1981). 2081: Will we be many or one—or none? *Behavioural Psychotherapy, 9*, 287–290.

Franks, C. M. (1984). On conceptual and technical integrity in psychoanalysis and behavior therapy: Two fundamentally incompatible systems. In H. Arkowitz & S. B. Messer (Eds.), *Psychological therapy and behavior therapy* (pp. 223–244). New York: Plenum Publishing.

Franks, C. M., & Wilson, G. T. (1973–1975). *Annual review of behavior therapy: Theory and practice* (Vols. 1 and 3). New York: Brunner/Mazel.

Goldfried, M. R. (1978). On the search for effective intervention strategies. *The Counseling Psychologist, 7*, 28–30.

Kazdin, A. E. (1978a). *History of behavior modification: Experimental foundations of contemporary research.* Baltimore: University Park Press.

Kazdin, A. E. (1978b). Behavior therapy: Evolution and expansion. *The Counseling Psychologist, 7*, 34–37.

Kazdin, A. E. (1993). Evaluation in clinical practice: Clinically sensitive and systemic methods of treatment delivery. *Behavior Therapy, 2L*, 11–45.

Lindsley, O. R., Skinner, B. F., & Solomon, H. D. (1953). *Studies in behavior therapy. Status report 1.* Waltham, MA: Metropolitan State Hospital.

Lazarus, A. A. (1958). New methods of psychotherapy: A case study. *South African Medical Journal, 32*, 660–663.

Lazarus, A. A. (1981). *The practice of multimodal therapy.* New York: McGraw-Hill.

Mahoney, M. J., & Kazdin, A. E. (1979). Cognitive behavior modification: Misconceptions and premature evaluation. *Psychological Bulletin, 80*, 1044–1049.

Mays, D. T., & Franks, C. M. (Eds.). (1985). *Negative outcome in psychotherapy and what to do about it.* New York: Springer.

Van Hasselt, V. B. & Hersen, M. (Eds.). (1993). *Handbook of behavior therapy and pharmacotherapy for children: A comparative analysis.* Boston: Allyn & Bacon.

Wachtel, P. L. (1977). *Psychoanalysis and behavior therapy.* New York: Basic Books.

Wolpe, J. (1958). *Psychotherapy by reciprocal inhibition.* Stanford, CA: Stanford University Press.

Yates, A. J. (1970). *Behavior therapy.* New York: Wiley.

4

Group Counseling and Therapy

RICHARD PANMAN, Ph.D.
SANDRA PANMAN, M.P.S.

WHAT IS GROUP THERAPY?

Group counseling and psychotherapy involves the treatment of several clients at the same time under the guidance of a therapist or leader. While there may be considerable differences in the theoretical orientation and skills of group counselors and therapists, certain similarities exist in all forms of group therapy. Groups are usually composed of 5 to 10 persons who meet with a leader at least once a week, anywhere from 1 to 4 hours. A common arrangement is to have everyone in the group sit in a circle. This arrangement encourages both visual and verbal communication among members. Groups can be organized around a type of problem such as alcoholism or a type of client such as single parents. The therapist's role is that of a guide or facilitator who keeps the group focused on interaction and self-exploration.

HOW DOES GROUP THERAPY WORK?

Fundamental to the practice of group therapy is the principle that a small group can act as the agent of change and strongly influence those who choose to be members. This is in contrast to *individual therapy,* in which the therapist is the sole agent of change. In a group, under the guidance of an effective leader, members learn to explore their problems in the presence of others. As they share experiences and react to one another's feelings and behavior, group members begin to find emotional release and a sense of well-being.

The advantages that group therapy offers clients, when compared with individual therapy, are substantial. Working in a group is a more natural situtaion than the one-to-one relationship of therapist and patient. As patients listen to each other, they realize that many people struggle with problems similar to their own. Therapy group members are often relieved to discover that they are not alone in fearing death or worrying about going crazy. This awareness strengthens each person's belief that he or she will improve, an important contributing factor to actual improvement in all forms of treatment.

The increased acceptance, trust, and support that members experience in group therapy leads to group cohesiveness, a sense of togetherness. The self-esteem of each client is enhanced by the unconditional acceptance that he or she receives from other group members. In this atmosphere of mutual respect, clients learn from one another by giving each other feedback and sharing ideas for solving problems. Patients, especially those with low self-esteem, benefit from their experience of being helpful to another person (Yalom, 1985).

If you are a helping professional working with people in groups, an educator or student interested in group therapy, or someone who would like to join a therapy group, then knowing about both historical and current trends in group therapy will be important to you.

EARLY GROUP THERAPY

In the late 19th and early 20th centuries, millions of immigrants moved to America from Europe. These people, some of whom were our grandparents and great grandparents, became slum dwellers in larger cities. Organizations such as Hull House in Chicago were founded to help the poor immigrant population. Known as *settlement houses,* these social agencies organized self-help groups to lobby for better housing, recreation, and working conditions. These social work groups emphasized the value of social participation, the democratic process, and personal growth. Although the idea of treating people in groups had not yet evolved, the social work group set the stage for the emergence of group psychotherapy.

In 1905, Joseph Pratt, a Boston physician, formed groups composed of patients who all had the same illness, tuberculosis, and came from similarly impoverished environments. Pratt recognized the therapeutic value of mutual support that patients with similar problems gave to each other. While Pratt's background was medicine, not social work, he utilized social work concepts that stressed the positive influence that one patient could have on the others. Credited with being the first practitioner of group therapy, Pratt emphasized a psychological approach that was encouraging and supportive (Kaplan & Sadock, 1971).

Alfred Adler, a Viennese psychiatrist and student of Sigmund Freud, emphasized social and interpersonal factors in the formation of personality. Society's problems, he argued, played an important role in the development of emotional disorders. To counter this, he had patients meet in peer groups because he strongly believed that the sharing of problems would be therapeutic. Adler was especially interested in the upbringing and education of children and established many child guidance clinics in the 1920s and 1930s. His emphasis on family environment led to child therapy sessions that included parents, teachers, and doctors. He was a pioneer in both group and family therapy (Ansbacher & Ansbacher, 1956).

Working parallel to Adler's approach was the *social work group*, which, by the 1930s, had become more concerned with the immediate personal needs of members and focused on the use of groups for treatment purposes. Group therapy or counseling was offered in mental hospitals, child guidance clinics, prisons, and public assistance agencies. A modern day descendent of the social work group is the *support group*, which helps people come to terms with a common problem or goal. Support groups, like the earlier settlement house self-help groups, reflect the concerns of the larger community. People that face similar difficulties can provide mutual support and inspiration when they meet in groups such as Alcoholics Anonymous, Overeaters Anonymous, and Survivors of Incest. Any of the approaches to psychotherapy discussed in this paper might be used in conducting a support group, depending on the purpose of the group and the orientation of the leader.

THREE APPROACHES TO GROUP PSYCHOTHERAPY

Social group workers, psychologists, and psychiatrists have long shared a common body of knowledge about group treatment. During the 20th century three major theoretical orientations and treatment approaches to both individual and group psychotherapy have emerged: *psychodynamic, phenomenological,* and *behavioral.* Psychoanalysis, the prototypical psychodynamic therapy, has been widely accepted because it has offered the most comprehensive theory of mental illness and a clearly specified set of techniques for treatment.

Phenomenological therapies, which emphasize each person's experience of reality and the personal meaning the individual gives to those experiences, stress the uniqueness of the individual. Behavior therapy assumes that all behavior, normal and abnormal, is learned, and has developed effective treatment methods for changing unwanted behavior. Because there is a good amount of interchange between these three approaches to therapy, each has influenced the others. This chapter traces the major historical and theoretical aspects of each approach to group counseling and psychotherapy.

1. PSYCHODYNAMIC THERAPIES

Psychotherapy began with the work of Sigmund Freud, who established the psychodynamic approach to the study of personality. This theory proposes that unconscious psychological processes determine thoughts, feelings, and behavior. Each person must figure out how to meet his or her needs in a world that often frustrates these efforts. Personality, according to Freud, develops out of each person's struggle with this task.

Freud described personality as having three major components: the *id*, the *ego*, and the *superego*. The id, a reservoir of unconscious energy, includes basic instincts, desires, and impulses with which we are all born. The id functions according to the pleasure principle, wherein the immediate gratification of needs is primary, regardless of the rights or feelings of others. The ego, or self, develops as parents, teachers, and other authority figures place restrictions on the expression of id impulses. The ego operates on the reality principle, making compromises between the unreasoning demands of the id and the constraints of the real world. The third component of the personality, the superego, consists of internalized parental and societal values, the "shoulds" and "should nots" of the social world. The superego functions according to the morality principle that distinguishes between right and wrong and causes feelings of guilt when the rules are violated. These three components of personality, along with other concepts developed by Freud, provide a basis for *psychoanalysis, group analysis,* and *transactional* analysis, the approaches to therapy discussed below (Greenson, 1967).

Psychoanalysis

Psychoanalysis, founded by Sigmund Freud, while typically one-to-one therapy between therapist and patient, did not ignore interpersonal relations. Psychoanalytic concepts such as *free association, resistance, interpretation,* and *transference* used in individual therapy were later applied by others in group settings. By the 1930s group therapy fit more and more within the framework of psychoanalysis. Trignant Burrow, a psychoanalyst, first used the term *group analysis*. Burrow treated patients in groups because he felt that a patient was less resistant to the treatment process in a group than in individual therapy. Within the group setting, Burrow helped patients become aware that they share many things with one another: they are not alone, their problems are not unique, and they welcome the support of the group (Greenson, 1967).

In the 1940s and 1950s, group therapy developed into the psychoanalytic model as practiced by Samuel Slavson and Alexander Wolf. Slavson's approach to analytic group psychotherapy focused on the individual rather than the group process. Serving as a substitute family, the group, with Slavson acting as a permissive parent, helped each member understand his or her emotional conflicts. Slavson believed that by awakening long buried memories people would gain greater awareness of themselves (Slavson, 1964).

Wolf's model of a group, like Slavson's, was that of the primary family. In a simulated family setting, he encouraged patients to work through their unresolved conflicts. Wolf believed that group support helped each member better tolerate anxiety. Group members were encouraged to free associate about one another and to report their dreams. Resistances and transference feelings that developed toward group members, including the analyst, were analyzed, often by other group members. Interpretations by the analyst were kept to a minimum (Wolf, 1975).

Wolf is credited with having introduced the use of free association to groups. Free association, a method first developed by Freud, assumes that the constant stream of thoughts, feelings, memories, and images that we all experience serve as clues to what lies in the unconscious mind. Wolf adapted free association to a group context by asking a patient to go around to each person and say the first thing that comes to mind about him or her. Whenever these associations were acknkowledged as correct by a group member, the patient was reinforced for being intuitive and spontaneous, leading to higher self-esteem and lower anxiety.

In a psychoanalytic group, the analyst acts as a catalyst by listening to the free associations of the patients, making inferences about the unconscious conflicts in their dreams, and helping interpret their transference reactions. The analyst offers interpretations that enable patients to gain insight into their unconscious conflicts and to learn how to resolve them. During this process, patients will show resistance to awareness and change, a way of protecting themselves against the analyst who is about to expose their hidden fears. When this happens in a group, patients can be a great source of support for one another.

Transference, a core concept in psychoanalysis, occurs when patients experience feelings toward the therapist that reflect unconscious conflicts about their childhood experiences with parents and other significant people. Transference may take different forms: falling in love with, becoming dependent on, or being hostile toward the therapist. Patients reenact their family drama with the therapist, transferring to him or her their feelings from earlier relationships. Psychoanalysts believe the interpretation of transference allows clients to see how old conflicts affect their relationships in the present. The key to treatment is for the therapist and patient to examine and work through these transferences.

Although Freud never practiced group therapy, his analysis of groups was based on the same principles he had developed to explain individual behavior: unconscious processes such as resistance and transference. His group psychology was based on understanding members' unconscious relationships to the group leader and to one another. The great lesson that Freud taught us is to examine what lies beneath the surface in order to gain a fuller understanding of and appreciation for the complexities of human behavior.

Group Analytic Therapy

The group analytic or group dynamic approach to psychotherapy emphasizes many psychoanalytic concepts, such as unconscious conflicts, resistance, and transference. In contrast to psychoanalysis, which emphasizes individual psychology, the group dynamic approach views the group as a coherent entity with its own inherent laws. Borrowing a "here and now" focus from phenomenological therapies, the goal of this type of group is to give its members an opportunity to learn about the interpersonal life of the group as it happens. The group analytic approach is used not only for therapy, but also to nurture personal growth and development.

Two models that focus on group dynamics are the *Tavistock* and *T-groups*. The Tavistock group, developed in the 1940s by Wilfred Bion, originated in Great Britain in a hospital setting and was psychoanalytically oriented, while the T-group, also called a training or sensitivity training group, developed at the same time in the United States as a growth experience within the scope of behavioral science theory. Both were directed toward helping people to become more knowledgeable about group dynamics, both saw the learning group's task as that of studying its own behavior, and both attempted to keep this learning group as unstructured as possible. The Tavistock group is discussed here because of its psychodynamic tradition, while the T-group will receive further attention in the section on phenomenological therapies (Bion, 1961).

The leader/consultant in a Tavistock group makes interventions directed toward what the group as a whole is doing rather than focus on individual group members. Initially, the group tries to get the consultant to be directive: to tell the group what to do. The leader frustrates this behavior and explains it as an infantile attempt by the group to avoid working at its task. There is a tendency in this setting to expect magic from the leader, to blame the leader for failure as a defense against feelings of helplessness, and to see the consultant as the source of all good feelings experienced in the group.

In group dynamic therapy models, the therapist attends to group interaction in order to understand the overall theme or group tension common to all patients. The members' concern with the distribution of authority (their relationship to the leader) and with the distribution of affection (their relationships with one another) are two sources of tension. The group, like a patient in analysis, is encouraged to examine feelings and behavior during the session to better understand group resistance and transferences. The leader's interpretations are always about the group as a whole, rather than about any of its individual members.

Another variation on the group analytic approach is *family therapy*, a model that is based on the theory that psychological disorders are rooted in family conflicts (Haley, 1971). Family therapy involves treatment of two or more members of the same family, where the problems of one person make him or her the identified client. From an initial focus on the most troubled person, attention shifts to the entire family as a "system." In the systems approach, the client's disorder reflects conflicts, communication problems, and other difficulties in the family as a whole. Based on the idea that the family is the client, all members must take part in resolving family conflicts. The goal of family therapy is to create harmony within the family by helping each member better understand the family's interactions.

Transactional Analysis

Eric Berne, a rogue psychoanalyst, developed an interpersonal therapy in the 1950s that reduced the complex language of psychoanalysis to layman's terms. Transactional analysis (TA), focuses on the patient gaining insight and awareness of his or her ego states, psychological games, and scripts or life plans. According to Berne, our personalities consist of three *ego states*—child, adult, and parent—which approximate Freud's id, ego, and superego (Berne, 1964). An ego state is a phenomenological reality that can be directly observed, rather than a theoretical construct such as id, ego, or superego. An ego state is a pattern of feelings and experiences that correspond to a pattern of behavior. The child ego state is a carryover of behavior patterns from childhood. When people are in the child ego state, they sit, stand, speak, think, perceive, and feel as they did in childhood. The adult ego state, like a computer, gathers and processes data for making predictions and decisions. The adult acts logically and is the best evaluator of reality because it is not clouded by emotion. The parent ego state incorporates behavior from our own parents and other parental models. The Parent is controlling and limit-setting, nurturing and comforting. The Parent also passes on traditions and values that are vital for the survival of culture.

In the TA group, the therapist analyzes the transactions between and among group members, especially the games people play. Games are common rituals of everyday life that help us to avoid intimacy with others. The prototype game in TA is called Why Don't You—Yes But, and involves what is referred to as "one-upmanship." Susan asks Mary for advice about her relationship with Jim. Mary suggests a solution to Susan, which she, in turn, discounts by saying, "Yes, that's good advice, but I can't do that because I'm not ready." At this point Mary offers an alternative solution, still believing that Susan is seriously looking for a way out of her problem. This game may continue for several rounds until Mary admits defeat, the satisfaction that Susan sought in the first place. Susan is now one up on Mary. When TA is conducted in groups, a substantial amount of time is spent analyzing the games played by the various group members.

Early in life, each person makes decisions about how to survive in the world. These decisions become part of a life plan, or script, which the person relies on to meet his or her needs. TA identifies four life positions that are the basis of a person's script: *I'm OK, You're OK* reflects self-acceptance and the acceptance of others. *I'm OK, You're Not OK* is the position of angry, paranoid, and other highly suspicious persons. *I'm Not OK, You're OK* is the point of view of people who are sad and depressed. *I'm Not OK, You're Not OK*, which involves rejection of self and others, is the frightening position of schizophrenics and other seriously disturbed people. The transactional analyst uses techniques such as questioning, confronting, and interpreting to help patients make adult choices that result in more satisfying, game-free behavior. The goal is for group members to understand their games and change self-defeating aspects of their scripts.

2. PHENOMENOLOGICAL THERAPY

Until the 1940s, almost every psychotherapist used some form of psychoanalysis. Alternatives were developed by therapists who had been trained in the psychodynamic tradition but adopted the phenomenological approach. These newer therapies promote insight into current feelings and perceptions, unlike psychoanalysis, which delves into unconscious childhood conflicts. Phenomenological therapies focus on the subjective interpretations people place on events, and view humans as capable of consciously controlling their actions and taking responsibility for their decisions. Among the phenomenological group therapy approaches are *psychodrama, person-centered psychotherapy, Gestalt therapy, T-groups,* and *encounter groups.*

Psychodrama

Psychodrama, developed by Jacob Moreno, an Austrian psychiatrist, is the oldest model of group psychotherapy. In 1921, Moreno opened his Theatre of Spontaneity in Vienna and presented a formal model for psychodrama. *Role-playing,* a technique Moreno developed for use in psychodrama, has been used widely in other forms of group psychotherapy. By combining psychoanalytic and phenomenological approaches to therapy, Moreno was the first to produce a true form of group therapy. In fact, Moreno is credited with having coined the term *group psychotherapy* (Moreno, 1978).

Moreno used the method of *dramatic action* as a way of helping patients present their problems in a "here and now" drama, so that both patient and audience could experience it in an immediate way. In psychodrama, as in other forms of group therapy, each patient serves as a therapeutic agent for the other patients. Central to the action method is the notion of *catharsis*, the therapeutic release of the patient's deepest feelings and conflicts. Moreno's action approach contrasted with analytic models that encouraged patients to talk about their problems in "there-and-then" ways, just as one might recount the plot of a play rather than enact it.

Psychodrama encourages patients to work through old situations and learn to express themselves spontaneously and creatively in new situations. Moreno's techniques are particularly useful with patients who find it difficult to get in touch with their feelings or express them in words. Psychodrama's emphasis on both verbal and nonverbal techniques and on the acting out of feelings has been influential in the development of phenomenological group therapies such as Gestalt and encounter groups.

Person-Centered Therapy

Although Carl Rogers was trained in psychodynamic methods, he soon began to question their value. Rather than consider the therapist as all-knowing expert, Rogers's therapy relied more on the client's own drive toward growth and self-actualization. To stimulate this process, he developed a nondirective treatment technique that created a permissive, nonjudgmental atmosphere in which clients were free to explore their feelings and fulfill their potential. The therapist's role was to clarify the client's feelings and perceptions in the immediate situation and to help the client gain insight and plan positive action. In this approach, the therapist used his or her empathy skills to reflect the client's affect rather than the content of his or her statements.

Rogers believed that constructive personality change can occur if the attitudes of the therapist foster it in the following ways. The therapist is *congruent,* genuine, and authentic in the relationship, experiencing his or her own feelings and communicating them. The therapist experiences *unconditional positive regard* for the client, accepting the person in a warm, positive way without placing conditions on the client. The therapist has *empathy* for the client, an emotional understanding of what he or she might be thinking and feeling. An empathic therapist makes clients feel valued and, as a result, more confident and motivated to solve their own problems (Rogers, 1961).

Rogers's group model for therapy developed into what he called the *intensive group experience* or *basic encounter*. Rogers made no distinctions between therapy goals and growth and development goals; that is, the group experience could benefit anyone, not just clients in therapy. The leader's goal was to bring into the open participants' here and now feelings about one another and, through the group experience, to effect permanent changes within the individual. Rogers emphasized the value of honest feedback and the awareness, expression, and acceptance of feelings. He also believed that a trusting and cohesive group climate was one of the most therapeutic elements of the basic encounter group. Rogers minimized his own interventions so that each participant could become, at different times, a facilitator or therapist for other participants in the group (Rogers, 1970).

Gestalt Therapy

Fritz Perls, trained in medicine and psychoanalysis, challenged orthodox psychoanalytic theory and practice with the introduction of his Gestalt therapy technique in the 1940s. The focus of Gestalt therapy is always on what *is*, on awareness of the present moment, and not on what might have been (regrets about the past) or on what should be (worry about the future). Gestalt therapists try to keep clients' attention focused on what they think and feel in the here and now. Gestalt therapy seeks to create conditions in which clients can become more self-aware and self-accepting (Perls, Hefferline, & Goodman, 1951).

The therapist's role in Gestalt therapy, more than just telling clients why they behave the way they do, is to help them see how they prevent themselves from getting what they want. Gestalt therapists prod clients to become aware of feelings and impulses that they have denied or disowned. In the process, the therapist must remain alert to the use of interpersonal "games," ways in which patients manipulate others as a way of avoiding emotionally painful issues. The focus throughout is on the moment, the here and now.

In group Gestalt therapy, the leader works with one group member at a time by putting him or her in the "hot seat." Across from the patient is an empty chair that may represent people with whom the client has unfinished business, or parts of himself or herself that are in conflict. Perls found the group format to be very effective because the presence of other people gave the therapist an opportunity to see the patient's self-defeating behaviors and fantasy projections as revealed in their interactions with others. Additionally, group members reinforced the patient for developing self-awareness and practicing new behaviors.

The T-Group

While the settlement house provided a setting for the application of social group work, and the psychiatric hospital an environment for group therapy, business and industry was the context for the development of T-groups. In 1946, Kurt Lewin and his colleague Ronald Lippitt helped to organize a conference of business and community leaders (Shaffer & Galinsky, 1974). The purpose of this meeting was to discuss the improvement of relations between groups and the ways groups can be used to foster better relations within and among communities.

Conference members were there to participate in a group and at the same time examine their own behavior. The expectation was that group members would be better able to understand both group processes and their own individual styles of relating to others in groups. Like the Tavistock group, the T-group was also concerned with group processes and with encouraging members to become aware of the dynamics of a group. Unlike the Tavistock model, the T-group attended to individual differences and the roles participants played within the group structure. Some members emerged as leaders while others were followers, and this was regarded as important information to be discussed by the group.

The task of the T-group is to understand its own behavior. The group leader or trainer does not lead in the traditional sense but asks questions and makes comments that help the group learn from its experience. The covert dynamics in real-world groups are usually hidden by the daily pressures of ongoing business activity. In the T-group environment, where they are free of the usual pressures and structures, members are better able to see and understand interpersonal interaction as it happens. When participants return to their home organization, they are more aware of the group dynamics that help or hinder a group's task and of their own role in these processes.

Encounter Groups

T-groups with their group relations and organizational emphasis evolved into encounter groups that had a personal-interpersonal focus. In contrast to the unstructured T-group, encounter groups used verbal and nonverbal exercises to create intensive interpersonal experiences in a shorter time period. The evolution of the encounter group was strongly influenced by Carl Rogers's interest in what he called the *intensive group experience*. This basic encounter group helped people find authenticity in the way they related to others and themselves (Rogers, 1970). It was not designed to develop interpersonal skill or increase understanding of group dynamics.

The open encounter model developed by William Schutz (1973) extended Rogers's approach by adding an emphasis on body work. Schutz saw body tensions as blocks against feeling and created group exercises that emphasized physical relaxation in the individual and bodily contact with other members. These exercises led to a reduction of body tension and consequent emotional release. For example, if an individual felt immobilized and constricted, Schutz used an exercise in which the participant attempted to break out of a tight circle formed by the other group members. He encouraged the mistrustful participant to fall back into the arms of the other members, trusting them to catch him or her. Schutz, who emphasized trust, openess, and self-disclosure of his own experiences in the group, led group members to a high level of intimacy and a strong feeling of unity.

A further development of the encounter group technique is the *marathon,* an extended group session first used by Fred Stoller and George Bach (Stoller, 1972). Marathons usually take place on weekends, lasting anywhere from 1 to 2 days. Participants remain together for the entire session, eating and sleeping as necessary. While the marathon is similar to Rogers's basic encounter group in method, the extended-time format creates a pressure-cooker atmosphere in which fatigue lowers defenses. This results in more open, honest, and intense communication among participants, especially those individuals who tend to be resistant to change.

Bindrim (1968) first described the use of *clothing-optional or nude marathons.* These groups follow the same format as other marathons but use nudity to hasten emotional exposure. Nakedness makes it more difficult to maintain the usual social and economic façades. Once past the initial embarrassment of being nude, participants begin to shed their inhibitions and decrease their sense of personal isolation. The nude marathon was helpful to people with sexual problems and led to greater self-acceptance.

3. BEHAVIOR THERAPY

Psychodynamic and phenomenological therapists believe that when clients gain insight into their underlying problems, the symptoms created by those problems disappear. The contrasting view of behavior therapists was that clients' problems are learned behaviors that can be changed without searching for hidden meanings or unconscious causes. If previous learning experiences can produce problems in the way people think and behave, new learning experiences might help solve these problems. The emergence of behavior modification as an alternative approach to psychotherapy was a very significant development within the field of clinical psychology during the late 1950s and early 1960s. While there are many behavioral techniques, this section outlines two ways in which behavior therapy is practiced in groups: *systematic desensitization* and *behavioral rehearsal.*

Systematic Desensitization

Systematic desensitization, developed by Joseph Wolpe (1987), is a behavioral treatment that helps clients cope with phobias and other irrational fears. Most behaviorally oriented groups are characterized by a high degree of structure provided by the leader. Clients first go through training to achieve a state of deep relaxation. While in a relaxed state, the client imagines one of a graduated series of anxiety-producing stimuli. A client who fears flying, for example, might be asked to visualize reading an ad for an airline, traveling in a taxi on the way to the airport, boarding the aircraft, and looking out the window as the plane leaves the ground. The client gradually works through this anxiety hierarchy, imagining a more difficult scene only after being able to tolerate the previous one without feeling any stress. Once clients can calmly imagine being in feared situations, they are better able to deal with those situations when they actually occur.

Behavioral Rehearsal

Behavioral Rehearsal, or practice groups, first developed by Arnold Lazarus (1987), use role-playing to help clients overcome such inadequacies as the inability to assert oneself effectively or to express feelings openly. *Assertiveness training,* a form of behavioral rehearsal, revolves around the issues of asking for what one wants and being able to say no, while *expressive training* groups are concerned with helping people to get past inhibitions about expressing warmth, tenderness, and love to others. Leaders help group members to identify the nature of ineffective behaviors and the kinds of situations in which they occur and to specify new responses that would be more effective. One at a time, group members role-play new responses to their problems, discuss the strengths and weaknesses of the role-playing with other group members, and evaluate their problems with the help of the group. Then the role-player has the opportunity to rehearse the situation a number of times, continuing to get feedback about where his or her performance needs improvement. As members progress, they are instructed to try out the new behaviors in actual life situations outside the group, which are, in turn, discussed in subsequent group meetings.

Early behavior therapists focused on observable behavior and not on the inner thoughts of their clients. In the late 1960s and early 1970s, many behavior therapists came to recognize the important effects that thoughts, perceptions, and feelings have on behavior. *Cognitive behavior therapy* helps clients change the way they think as well as the way they behave. Instead of practicing new behaviors in assertiveness training, clients need to identify habitual thoughts that get in the way of self-expression. The therapist encourages the client to try new ways of thinking that will make it easier to behave more assertively. Two examples of this type of therapy, *rational-emotive therapy* (RET) and *cognitive therapy*, are discussed below.

Rational-Emotive Therapy (RET)

Developed by Albert Ellis (1987), rational-emotive therapy (RET) is based on the principle that anxiety, guilt, depression, and other psychological problems are not caused by frightening or upsetting events but by how people think about those events. Ellis says that you get upset not because you fail a test, but because you believe failure to be a disaster that indicates you are no good. RET aims first at identifying self-defeating, problem-causing thoughts. Among the most common of these thoughts are the beliefs that we must be loved by everyone, that we must be achieving at all times to be considered worthwhile, and that unhappiness is caused by outside forces over which we have no control. Once the client recognizes these thoughts and sees how they cause problems, the therapist helps the client to replace them with more realistic and beneficial ones.

Cognitive Therapy

Aaron Beck (1987) developed cognitive therapy for the treatment of depression. Depressed clients tend to exaggerate the importance and frequency of negative events ("This always happens to me!") and minimize the value of personal accomplishments ("It was nothing!"). The cognitive therapist helps clients identify logical inconsistencies and other errors in thinking that lead to depressive feelings. Homework assignments help clients keep track of positive events and personal skills, enabling them to develop more optimistic ways of thinking and reduce self-blame for negative outcomes. Clients are encouraged to gather information about themselves that will disconfirm their false beliefs. The client's assumptions, beliefs, and expectations are formulated into hypotheses to be tested. Therapist and client then design ways for the person to test these hypotheses in the real world.

RESOURCES FOR MORE INFORMATION

American Association for Marriage and Family Therapy
1100 Seventeenth Street, NW
Washington, DC 20036
(202) 452-0109

American Group Psychotherapy Association
25 East 21st Street
New York, NY 10010
(212) 477-2677

American Psychoanalytic Association
309 East 49th Street
New York, NY 10022
(212) 752-0450

American Society of Group Psychotherapy and Psychodrama
6728 Old McLean Village Drive
McLean, VA 22101
(703) 556-9222

Association for the Advancement of Behavior Therapy
15 West 36th Street
New York, NY
(212) 279-7970

Association for Group Psychoanalysis and Process
501 East 79th Street
New York, NY 10021
(212) 288-2297

Association for Humanistic Psychology
1772 Vallejo Street
San Francisco, CA 94123
(415) 346-7929
Person-centered therapy, Gestalt therapy, encounter groups

Esalen Institute
Big Sur, CA 93920
(408) 667-3000
Gestalt therapy, encounter groups

Gestalt Institute of Cleveland
1588 Hazel Drive
Cleveland, OH 44106
(216) 421-1700

Institute for Rational-Emotive Therapy
45 East 65th Street
New York, NY 10021
(212) 535-0822

International Transactional Analysis Association
1772 Vallejo Street
San Francisco, CA 94123
(415) 885-5992

National Institute for Applied Behavioral Sciences
(Formerly the National Training Laboratories)
1240 North Pitt Street
Alexandria, VA 22314
(703) 548-1500

A. K. Rice Institute
1610 New Hampshire Avenue
Washington, DC 20009
(202) 363-5443
Tavistock groups

REFERENCES

Ansbacher, H. L., & Ansbacher, R. (1956). *The individual psychology of Alfred Adler*. New York: Basic Books.

Beck, A. T. (1987). Cognitive therapy. In J. K. Zeig (Ed.), *The evolution of psychotherapy* (pp. 149–163). New York: Brunner/Mazel.

Berne, E. (1964). *Games people play*. New York: Grove Press.

Bindrim, P. (1968). A report on a nude marathon. *Psychotherapy: Theory, Research, and Practice, 5*. 180–188.

Bion, W. R. (1961). *Experiences in groups*. New York: Basic Books.

Ellis, A. (1987). The evolution of rational-emotive therapy (RET) and cognitive behavior therapy (CBT). In J. K. Zeig (Ed.), *The evolution of psychotherapy* (pp. 107–125). New York: Brunner/Mazel.

Greenson, R. R. (1967). *The technique and practice of psychoanalysis*. New York: International Universities Press.

Haley, J. (1971). Family therapy: A radical change. In J. Haley (Ed.), *Changing families: A family therapy reader* (pp. 272–284). New York: Grune & Stratton.

Kaplan, H. I., & Sadock, B. J. (1971). *Comprehensive group psychotherapy.* Baltimore: Williams & Wilkins.

Lazarus, A. A. The need for technical eclecticism: Science, breadth, depth, and specificity. In J. K. Zeig (Ed.), *The evolution of psychotherapy* (pp. 164–175). New York: Brunner/ Mazel.

Moreno, Z. T. (1978). Psychodrama. In H. Mullan & M. Rosenbaum (Eds.), *Group psychotherapy: Theory and practice* (2nd ed., pp. 352–376). New York: Free Press.

Perls, F. S., Hefferline, R. F., & Goodman, P. (1951). *Gestalt therapy.* New York: Julian Press.

Rogers, C. R. (1961). *On becoming a person.* Boston: Houghton Mifflin.

Rogers, C. R. (1970). *On encounter groups.* New York: Harper & Row.

Schutz, W. C. (1973). Encounter. In R. J. Corsini (Ed.), *Current psychotherapies* (pp. 401–443). Itasca, IL: Peacock.

Shaffer, J. B., & Galinsky, M.D. (1974). *Models of group therapy and sensitivity training.* Englewood Cliffs, NJ: Prentice-Hall.

Slavson, S. R. (1964). *A textbook in analytic group psychotherapy.* New York: International Universities Press.

Stoller, F. H. (1972). Marathon groups: Toward a conceptual model. In L. N. Solomon & B. Berzon (Eds.), *New perspectives on encounter groups* (pp. 171–187). San Francisco: Jossey-Bass.

Wolf, A. (1975). Psychoanalysis in groups. In G. M. Gazda (Ed.), *Basic approaches to group psychotherapy and group counseling* (2nd ed., pp. 101–119). Springfield, IL.: Thomas.

Wolpe, J. (1987). The promotion of scientific therapy: A long voyage. In J. K. Zeig (Ed.), *The evolution of psychotherapy* (pp. 133–143). New York: Brunner/Mazel.

Yalom, I. D. (1985). *The theory and practice of group psychotherapy* (3rd ed.). New York: Basic Books.

5

Cognitive Therapy

ARTHUR FREEMAN, Ph.D.

FRANK M. DATTILIO, Ph.D.

The purpose of this section is to provide a broad overview of cognitive therapy, theory, and techniques.

Cognitive Therapy (CT) is an active, directive, structured, collaborative, and psychoeducational model for brief psychotherapy. While originally developed by Dr. Aaron T. Beck for the treatment of depression, the model has been expanded over the last dozen years to effectively treat anxiety and panic disorders, eating disorders, substance abuse, personality disorders, and schizophrenia. CT has been successfully used in individual, couples, group, and family formats.

Rooted in both the behavioral and the psychodynamic traditions, CT can be readily adapted and included into the therapeutic armamentarium of all mental health professionals, regardless of their previous training. A short-term therapy model is a requirement in today's complex system of mental health service delivery. CT has been demonstrated to meet that need for a broad range of mental health professionals including counselors, psychologists, pastoral counselors, social workers, and nurse practitioners.

The theoretical underpinnings of cognitive therapy have been developed and shaped by a variety of approaches which include the phenomenological approach, structural theory, and cognitive psychology. Albert Ellis, the grandfather of cognitive behavior therapy, developed his *Rational-Emotive Therapy* (RET) 30 years ago (1962). Beck's work in developing cognitive therapy began in the early 1960s as a result of his research on depression (Beck, 1963, 1964, 1967). His first writings grew out of his earlier attempts to validate Freud's theory of depression as the result of anger turned toward the self. In trying to substantiate this theory, Beck made clinical observations of depressed clients and investigated their treatment under traditional psychoanalysis. Rather than finding retroflected anger in their thoughts and dreams, he observed a negative bias in the cognitive processing of depressed individuals. As a result of clinical observation and experimental testing, he developed the cognitive theory of emotional disorders and, in particular, the cognitive model of depression (Beck, 1976).

According to Ellis (1973, 1980), RET therapists would work to persuade the individuals that the beliefs they have are irrational, offering to teach them a more adaptive philosophy of living. Beck, on the other hand, attempts to collaborate with the clients in testing the validity of their cognitions (Beck, Kovacs, & Weisman, 1979).

The theories of rational-emotive therapy and cognitive therapy both contend that individuals adopt reasoning patterns and either possess control over their thoughts and actions or can be taught to take control through the adoption of a different style of response. Both approaches view the individuals' underlying assumptions generating these thoughts as targets of the interventions in therapy, not merely as symptoms of some vague unconscious conflict.

Research has provided empirical support for the model and its effectiveness in cases of unipolar depression (Beck & Rush, 1978). Studies comparing cognitive therapy and antidepressant medications have also been conducted (Beck, 1986; Hollon et al., 1985; Murphy, Simmons, Wetzel, & Lustman, 1984). In several outcome comparisons, cognitive therapy was shown to be equal in effectiveness to antidepressant medication in treating depression. Still more impressively, the double-blind study of Rush, Beck, Kovacs, and Hollon (1977) demonstrated that cognitive psychotherapy was more effective than medication in the alleviation of depression. The research of Kovacs, Rush, Beck, and Hollon (1981) suggested that cognitive therapy tends to produce longer-lasting effects, and other studies have supported this finding (Blackburn, Bishop, Glen, Whalley, & Christie, 1981; Murphy, Simmons, Wetzel, & Lustman, 1984).

As an offshoot of the work on depression, the development of theoretical concepts of treatment for suicidal clients has gained attention (Beck, Weisman, Lester, & Trexler, 1974). A major finding of that work was that hopelessness was a key component of suicidal intent and outcome. As a result of his work, Beck generated a number of assessment scales for depression and suicidality, such as the Beck Depression Inventory (Beck, Ward, Mendelsohn, Mock, & Erbaugh, 1961), the Scale for Suicide Ideation (Beck, Kovacs, & Weisman, 1979), the Suicide Intent Scale (Beck, Schuyler, & Herman, 1974), the Hopelessness Scale (Beck, Weisman, Lester, & Trexler, 1974), and the Beck Anxiety Inventory (Beck, Epstein, Brown, & Steer, 1985).

Cognitive therapy has also devoted research to the study of anxiety disorders (Alford, Beck, Freeman, & Wright, 1990; Beck & Emery,

1979; Beck, Emery, & Greenberg, 1985; Beck, Laude, & Bohnert, 1974; Dattilio, 1986, 1987, 1988, 1990; Ottaviani & Beck, 1987; Sokol, Beck, Greenberg, Wright, & Berchick, 1989), as well as marital discord, (Beck, 1988; Dattilio, 1989, 1990; Dattilio & Padesky, 1990; Epstein, 1986; Schlesinger & Epstein, 1986), and personality disorders (Beck, Freeman et al., 1990; Pretzer, 1983).

THEORY OF PERSONALITY

Cognitive therapy views personality as being shaped by *schemas* or *rules of life* which develop early in life as a result of several factors. These schemas constitute the basis for coding, categorizing, and evaluating experiences. Psychological problems are perceived as stemming from commonplace processes such as faulty learning, making incorrect inferences on the basis of inadequate or incorrect information, and not distinguishing adequately between imagination and reality (Kovacs & Beck, 1979). Individuals often formulate rules or standards that are excessively rigid and absolutist, based on erroneous assumptions. Such standards are derived from what Beck et al. (1979), Beck, Freeman et al. (1990), and Freeman and Leaf (1989) term *schemas* or *complex patterns of thoughts,* which determine how experiences will be perceived and conceptualized. These schemas or thought patterns are usually employed even in the absence of environmental data and may serve as a type of *procrustean mold,* which shapes the incoming data so as to fit and reinforce preconceived notions (Beck & Emery, 1979). This distortion of experience is maintained through the operation of characteristic errors in information processing. It has also been proposed that several types of fallacious thinking contribute to the feedback loops that support psychological disorders: for example, systematic errors in reasoning, which are termed *cognitive distortions,* are present during psychological distress and include arbitrary inferences, selective abstraction, overgeneralization, magnification and minimization, personalization, labeling and mislabeling, dichotomous thinking.

The cognitive therapist works to obtain both the *specific content* of the clients' cognitions and/or beliefs, and the *style* of thinking. Clients are taught to obtain and report, in detail, their dysfunctional cognitions, including when they occur and their impact on the clients' feelings.

COGNITIVE MODELS FOR DEPRESSION AND ANXIETY

In the cognitive model of depression, Beck (1967) emphasized the *cognitive triad* to characterize depression. Depressed individuals maintain a negative view of self, the world and experiences, and the future. They perceive themselves as inadequate, deserted and worthless. The negative view of the world is apparent in the beliefs that they have been burdened with enormous demands and impenetrable barriers which exist between the individual and their goals. The world appears devoid of pleasure or gratification and the future is viewed pessimistically, reflecting the belief that the current problems will only become worse.

As a reality-based intervention, cognitive therapy accepts the life situations of individuals and focuses on altering only the biased views of themselves, situations, and the impoverished resources which limit their response repertoires and prevent them from generating solutions. Cognitive therapy is therefore an active, structured, and usually time-limited approach to the treatment of depression. It teaches clients to take a number of steps in combating depression, including monitoring negative automatic thoughts; recognizing connections between cognition, affect and behavior; critically examining these underlying thoughts; substituting more objective interpretations for these negative cognitions; and learning to identify and alter the "higher order" dysfunctional beliefs that predispose individuals to distortions in interpreting experience (Beck & Rush, 1978).

The collaborative empiricism that occurs between client and therapist is what ties these strategies together in a system which consists of identification of the problem, design and execution of tests of specific hypotheses, and evaluation of certain beliefs. With mild to moderate depression (scores of 15–22 on the Beck Depression Inventory), it is possible to begin immediately with the clients' misinterpretations and negative beliefs about themselves, their personal world, and the future.

In the most severe cases of depression (scores of 22 and higher on the BDI), it is often important to start out with behavioral tasks, such as designing a daily activity schedule with the client to monitor day-to-day tasks; getting out of bed when not sleeping, tending to essential hygiene details, and attempting to be more active overall. Specific tasks may be agreed upon and worked into the graded task assignment, the rationale of which is to start with easily mastered tasks and then work up to the more difficult ones. Frequently, specific cognitions can be set up as hypotheses which the client can then test as part of the graded task assignments.

Once the client is more active, more of the cognitive procedures may then be used, and the client can track his or her automatic thoughts, particularly when they precede or accompany a negative feeling. Clients are asked to fill out the Daily Record of Dysfunctional Thoughts and are trained to give reasonable or rational responses to their negative automatic thoughts. As the client progresses through treatment, more attention is focused on the client's underlying assumptions. These assumptions are examined in the same manner as automatic thoughts—

that is, by scrutinizing the evidence or the logic which upholds them and testing them empirically.

THE PRACTICE OF COGNITIVE THERAPY

As with most other modalities of therapy, one of the initial goals of treatment is to develop rapport with the client. This is particularly important in light of the fact that cognitive therapy involves a collaboration between client and therapist that is essential in the change process.

Providing a rational and effective structure is also a key issue in therapy for both the course of treatment and the individual therapy session itself. This assures continuity and focus on the issues at hand and also makes the best use of time and effort. Once a structure has been established, the collaborative process is employed to aid the therapist and client in developing a list of specific problems to address in therapy.

Once the problem list has been established, the therapist may begin to narrow the focus in therapy and, in collaboration with the client, develop an agenda for the succeeding sessions. Often this involves a review of the past week's events. In addition, homework assignments are discussed, along with any difficulty which was experienced while completing them. It is understood that some flexibility be maintained with the structure of the sessions should the client wish to focus on a more immediate or urgent problem. The specific interventions or strategies will be contingent on the skill level of the client, as well as the nature of the presenting problem.

The last stage of the session is devoted to collaborative assessment and evaluation of homework from the previous session. Any homework assignment for the subsequent session are discussed at this time as well. This period is also set aside for receiving feedback from the client in evaluation of what they have learned from the current session. As a result of this format, a gradual yet structured termination occurs which also sets the stage for the succeeding session.

TREATMENT STRATEGIES

There are a number of strategies within the armamentarium of cognitive therapy which were designed specifically to aid clients in testing the reality of their cognitions.

These strategies can be classified as either cognitive or behavioral in approach, but some overlap may occur. The following approaches are adapted from Freeman and Greenwood (1987).

Cognitive Strategies

Downward arrow. This term first coined by Beck et al. (1979) is phrased because of its actual use of downward pointing arrows to aid clients in understanding the logic and sequencing of their reasoning. The therapist follows a client's statement by asking, "Then what?" This elicits the sequence of thoughts and beliefs which aids in uncovering the client's underlying assumptions.

Idiosyncratic meaning. This is the process of clarifying a term or statement made by the client so that the therapist may have a high level of understanding of the client's "reality."

Labeling of distortions. By labeling distortions, clients are able to automatically identify any dysfunctional thoughts and monitor their cognitive patterns. Through this type of monitoring a more accurate route towards change occurs. For a more detailed description, see Burns (1980).

Questioning the evidence. Once the client learns to question the actual evidence, the process of substantiation is initiated and becomes an automatic procedure following any irrational thought statement. This allows clients to decide whether or not their statements are based on erroneous information.

Examining options and alternatives. This entails going back over all of the possible options and alternatives which exist in attempts to avoid the trap of seeing "no way out" of a circumstance or situation. The specific task is to work until the individual is generating new options.

Reattribution. Placing all of the blame on oneself is a common occurrence seen with clients, particularly in the guilt-ridden or depressed cases. Reattribution involves the individual appropriately distributing responsibility to the rightful parties and dispelling the notion that any single individual is responsible for all problems and difficulties.

Decatastrophizing. Those who engage in catastrophic thinking are individuals who choose to focus on the most extreme negative outcome of any given situation. Decatastrophizing involves aiding them in balancing out their focus on the worst anticipated state by evaluating the situation and asking oneself "What is the worst thing that might occur?" This can be followed by "If the worst occurred, would it be so horrible or unbearable?"

Advantages and disadvantages. In attempts to have the client sway away from dichotomous thought patterns, instructing them to list advantages and disadvantages of a situation allows them to change their perspective and balance out the alternatives.

Paradox or exaggeration. A technique which may be viewed as the inverse of decatastrophizing. This involves the therapist taking an issue or idea to the extreme, allowing the client to view the absurdity of an exaggerated viewpoint. This often aids the client in developing a more balanced perspective on the issue.

Turning adversity to advantage. Taking an unfortunate situation and using it as an advantage can be very helpful, for example, being rejected by the school of your choice may be an indirect route toward a more promising alternative.

Replacement imagery. We all image to a greater or lesser degree. Negative dreams and images can often have powerful emotional sequelae indicating the strength of the imagery. Clients can be helped to change the direction of the negative and depressogenic/anxiogenic dreams and images to more positive, successful coping scenes with a consequent change in affect.

Cognitive rehearsal. Many of the target behaviors for change rely on the strength of visualizing in the mind the desired outcome. The use of cognitive rehearsal may aid individuals in practicing assertiveness, the awkwardness in confronting others, and so on.

Behavioral Techniques
While the mechanics involved with cognitive therapy involve the primary use of cognitive techniques stated previously, behavioral techniques are also used as supportive measures, in addition to a means for collecting information in facilitating change.

The following behavioral techniques are the more frequently used techniques in cognitive therapy.

Assertiveness training. A large component of assertiveness training involves both cognitive processes as well as behavioral rehearsal. This, in essence, consists of the therapist's teaching or modeling for the client those desired behaviors in social situations. This is particularly so for the anxiety disorders such as social phobias or agoraphobia. The term *in vivo* is used to indicate that the behaviors are acted out in real life.

Behavioral rehearsal. This is the behavioral counterpart to cognitive rehearsal. The difference lies with the actual behaviors themselves being the subjects rehearsed: asserting oneself in public, getting up and going to work, and so on. Feedback from the therapist to the client is then given as a means of guidance and development of effective responses and styles. This also involves the reinforcing of existing skills.

Graded task assignments. This is the process of establishing a hierarchy of events which involves the target behaviors, whether they are approaching a parent or overcoming a fear of meeting new people. The specific tasks are arranged in steps from least anxiety-producing or threatening to most anxiety-producing. This allows for a gradual approach to facing the threatening object/event.

Bibliotherapy. The prescription of reading assignments has always been a strong characteristic of cognitive therapy. There are many readings that can be assigned to clients as homework. Most are those books which were designed for the general public, such as *Love is Never Enough* (Beck, 1988), *Feeling Good* (Burns, 1980), *Cognitive Therapy and the Emotional Disorders* (Beck, 1976), *Own Your Own Life* (Emery, 1984), *Talk Sense to Yourself* (McMullin & Casey, 1975), *New Guide to Rational Living* (Ellis & Harper, 1976), *Woulda, Coulda, Shoulda* (Freeman & DeWolf, 1990), *The Ten Dumbest Mistakes That Smart People Make* (Freeman & DeWolf, 1992). A visit to a large bookstore's self-help section will net the counselor a number of excellent readings. For a smaller group of clients, certain of the available texts might be helpful as bibliotherapeutic reading. Many of these books have assessment forms, homework forms, exercises to be done, and summary forms to be used as templates for various activity recording. These are not meant to replace the therapy, but are assigned as an adjunct to therapy and are primarily to serve as a supportive and educational tool to the actual therapeutic process.

Relaxation and meditation. The use of programs, including relaxation, meditation and focused breathing, have proven to be helpful with anxiety clients in learning to distract themselves and gain control over their anxiety.

Overbreathing. Teaching the client how to overbreathe and to then encourage the client to hyperventilate in the office is an effective technique for helping clients learn that they can attain breathing control and reduce many of their symptoms.

Social skills training. This involves reviewing and instructing the client in behaviors which are necessary to social interaction: maintaining conversations with others, posture, eye contact, and assertiveness skills, in addition to developing techniques for self-expression and conveying individual thoughts and opinions.

Shame-attacking exercises. An exercise promoted most by RET therapists involves having the client engage in activities that emphasize their concern for what others may think of them. A typical example might be to have the client announce out loud each stop that a public bus makes while en route and carrying a full load of passengers. The point is to aid the client in seeing how people really react and that their thoughts really do not matter.

HOMEWORK

One of the most important features of cognitive therapy is the use of homework assignments. Because the actual therapy sessions are limited to only one or two hours per week in the office, it is imperative that activities which support the treatment continue outside of the sessions. The emphasis is placed on self-help assignments which serve as a continuation of what was addressed in the preceding session. This is also an integral part of the collaborative process between the client and the therapist. Assignments typically include those techniques listed above. The assignments are tailored according to the specific problem and are a result of the collaborative process which occurs during treatment.

SUMMARY

The cognitive therapy approach has been empirically demonstrated to be an effective method for the treatment of a broad range of clinical problems and clinical populations (Freeman & Dattilio, 1992). Cognitive therapy is an active, directive, structured, problem oriented, collaborative, dynamic, and psychoeducational approach. Utilizing both cognitive and behavioral interventions, the client's problems are elucidated, clarified and become a direct focus of the therapy. Clients are taught to identify cognitive distortions and to learn self-help techniques for adaptive responding. Homework is used to add to the in-office treatment and to help the client test out new ideas and behaviors.

FOR FURTHER READING

Beck, A. T. (1976). *Cognitive therapy and the emotional disorders.* New York: International Universities Press.

Beck, A. T., & Emery, G., with Greenberg, R. (1985). *Anxiety and phobias: A cognitive approach.* New York: Basic Books.

Beck, A. T., Freeman, A. & Associates. (1990). *Cognitive therapy of personality disorders.* New York: Guilford.

Beck, A. T. & Weishaar, M. E. (1986). *Cognitive therapy.* (Available from the Center for Cognitive Therapy, 133 South 36th Street, Philadelphia, PA 19104.)

Dattilio, F. M. (1989). A guide to cognitive marital therapy. In P. A. Keller, & S. R. Heyman (Eds.), *Innovations in clinical practice: A source book.* Sarasota, FL.: Professional Resource Exchange, Vol. 8, 27–42.

Dattilio, F. M. & Padesky, C. A. (1990). *Cognitive therapy with couples.* Sarasota, FL: Professional Resource Exchange, Inc.

Epstein, N., Schlesinger, S. E., & Dryden, W. (1988). *Cognitive-behavior therapy with families.* New York: Brunner/Mazel, 380.

Freeman, A., & Greenwood, V. (Eds.). (1987). *Cognitive therapy: Applications in psychiatric and medical settings.* New York: Human Sciences Press, Inc.

Freeman, A. & Dattilio, F. M. (Eds.). (1992). *Comprehensive Casebook of Cognitive Therapy.* New York: Plenum Press.

Freeman, A., Simon, K. A., Beutler, L. E., & Arkowitz, H. (Eds.). (1989). *Comprehensive handbook of cognitive therapy.* New York: Plenum Press.

Meichenbaum, D. (1977). *Cognitive-behavior modification: An integrative approach.* New York: Plenum Press.

Ritter, K. Y. (1985). The cognitive therapies: An overview for counselors. *Journal of Counseling and Development, 64,* 42–46.

REFERENCES

Adler, A. (1936). The neurotic's picture of the world. *International Journal of Individual Psychology, 2,* 3–10.

Alford, B. A., Beck, A. T., Freeman, A., & Wright, F. (1990). Brief focused cognitive therapy of panic disorder. *Psychotherapy 27(2),* 230–234.

Beck, A. T. (1963). Thinking and depression: 1. Idiosyncratic content and cognitive distortions. *Archives of General Psychiatry, 9,* 324–333.

Beck, A. T. (1964). Thinking and depression: 2. Theory and therapy. *Archives of General Psychiatry, 10,* 561–571.

Beck, A. T. (1967). *Depression: Clinical, experimental, and theoretical aspects.* New York: Hoeber. (Republished as *Depression: Causes and treatment.* Philadelphia: University of Pennsylvania Press, 1972.)

Beck, A. T. (1976). *Cognitive therapy and the emotional disorders.* New York: International Universities Press.

Beck, A. T. (1986, June 28). Treating depression: Can we talk? [Letter to the editor.] *Science News, 129(6),* 12.

Beck, A. T. (1988). *Love is never enough.* New York: Harper and Row.

Beck, A. T., & Emery, G. (1979). *Cognitive therapy of anxiety and phobic disorders.* Philadelphia: Center for Cognitive Therapy.

Beck, A. T., & Emery, G., with Greenberg, R. (1985). *Anxiety and phobias: A cognitive approach.* New York: Basic Books.

Beck, A. T., Epstein, N., Brown, G., & Steer, R. A. (1985, November). *An inventory for measuring clinical anxiety.* Paper presented at the annual meeting of the Association for Advancement of Behavior Therapy, Houston, TX.

Beck, A. T., & Freeman, A., & Associates. (1990). *Cognitive therapy of personality disorders.* New York: Guilford.

Beck, A. T., Kovacs, M., & Weisman, A. (1979). Assessment of suicidal intention: The scale for suicidal ideation. *Journal of Consulting and Clinical Psychology, 47,* 343–352.

Beck, A. T., Laude, R., & Bohnert, M. (1974). Ideational components of anxiety neurosis. *Archives of General Psychiatry, 31,* 319–325.

Beck, A. T. & Rush, A. J. (1978). Cognitive approaches to depression and suicide. In G. Serban (Ed.), *Cognitive defects in the development of mental illness* (pp. 235–257) (published under the auspices of the Kittay Scientific Foundation). New York: Brunner/Mazel.

Beck, A. T., Schuyler, D. & Herman, I. (1974). Development of the suicidal intent scales. In A. T. Beck, H. L. P. Resnik & D. J. Lettieri (Eds.), *The prediction of suicide* (pp. 45–56). Bowie, MD: Charles Press.

Beck, A. T., Ward, C. H., Mendelsohn, M., Mock, J. E. & Erbaugh, J. K. (1961). An inventory for measuring depression. *Archives of General Psychiatry, 4*, 561–571.

Beck, A. T., Weisman, A., Lester, D., & Trexler, L. (1974). The measurement of pessimism: The hopelessness scale. *Journal of Consulting and Clinical Psychology, 42*, 861–865.

Blackburn, I. M., Bishop, S., Glen, A. M., Whalley, L. J. & Christie, J. E. (1981). The efficacy of cognitive therapy in depression: A treatment trial using cognitive therapy and psychotherapy, each alone and in combination. *British Journal of Psychiatry, 139*, 181–189.

Burns, D. (1980). *Feeling good: The new mood therapy*. New York: Signet Books.

Dattilio, F. M. (1986). Differences in cognitive responses to fear among individuals diagnosed as panic disorder, generalized anxiety disorder, agoraphobia with panic attacks, and simple phobia. *University Microfilms International*, Pub. No. 8711320, p. 216.

Dattilio, F. M. (1987). The use of paradoxical intention in the treatment of panic attacks. *Journal of Counseling and Development, 66*, 102–103.

Dattilio, F. M. (1988). Relation of experiences in sex and panic: A preliminary note. *The Cognitive-Behaviorist, 10*(3), 3–4.

Dattilio, F. M. (1989). A guide to cognitive marital therapy. In P. A. Keller, & S. R. Heyman (Eds.) *Innovations in Clinical Practice: A Source Book.* Sarasota, FL: Professional Resource Exchange, Vol. 8, 27–42.

Dattilio, F. M. (1990). Symptom induction and de-escalation in the treatment of panic attacks. *Journal of Mental Health Counseling, 12*(4), 515–519.

Dattilio, F. M., & Padesky, C. A. (1990). *Cognitive Therapy with Couples.* Sarasota, FL: Professional Resource Exchange, Inc.

Ellis, A. (1973). Are cognitive behavior and rational therapy synonymous? *Rational Living, 8*, 8–11.

Ellis, A. (1980). Rational-emotive therapy and cognitive-behavior therapy: Similarities and differences. *Cognitive Therapy and Research, 4*, 325–340.

Ellis, A., & Harper, R. (1976). *New guide to rational living.* New York: Lyle Stuart.

Epstein, N. (1986, Spring/Summer). Cognitive marital therapy. *Journal of Rational-Emotive Therapy, 4*(1), 68–81.

Freeman, A., & Dattilio, F. M. (Eds.) (1992). *Comprehensive casebook of cognitive therapy.* New York: Plenum.

Freeman, A., & DeWolf, R. (1990). *Wouda, coulda, shoulda: Overcoming mistakes, regrets and missed opportunities.* (New York: HarperCollins)

Freeman, A., & DeWolf, R. (1992). *The ten dumbest mistakes that smart people make and how to avoid them.* (New York: HarperCollins)

Freeman, A., & Greenwood, V. (Eds.) (1987). *Cognitive therapy: Applications in psychiatric and medical settings.* New York: Human Sciences Press, Inc.

Freeman, A., & Leaf, R. C. (1989). Cognitive therapy applied to personality disorders. In A. Freeman, K. Simon, L. E. Beutler, & H. Arkowitz (Eds.), *Comprehensive casebook of cognitive therapy* (pp. 403–433). New York: Plenum.

Hollon, S. D., DeRubeis, R. J., Evans, M.D., Tauson, V. B., Weimer, M. J., & Garvey, M. J. (1985). *Combined cognitive-pharmacotherapy versus cognitive therapy alone in the treatment of depressed outpatients: Differential treatment outcomes in the CPT project.* Unpublished manuscript, University of Minnesota and St. Paul–Ramsey Medical Center, Minneapolis–St. Paul, MN.

Kovacs, M., & Beck, A. T. (1979). Cognitive-affective processes in depression. In C. E. Izard (Ed.), *Emotions in personality and psychopathology* (pp. 417–442). New York: Plenum.

Kovacs, M., Rush, A. J., Beck, A. T., & Hollon, S. D. (1981). Depressed outpatients treated with cognitive therapy or pharmacotherapy: A one-year followup. *Archives of General Psychiatry, 38,* 33–39.

Murphy, G. E., Simmons, A. D., Wetzel, R. D., & Lustman, P. J. (1984). Cognitive therapy versus tricyclic anti-depressants in major depression. *Archives of General Psychiatry, 41,* 33–41.

Ottaviani, R., & Beck, A. T. (1987). Cognitive aspects of panic disorder. *Journal of Anxiety Disorders, 1*(1), 15–28.

Pretzer, J. L. (1983, August). *Borderline personality disorder: Too complex for cognitive therapy?* Paper presented at the annual meeting of the American Psychological Association, Anaheim, CA.

Schlesinger, S. E., & Epstein, N. B. (1986). Cognitive-behavioral techniques in marital therapy. In P. A. Keller and L. G. Ritt (Eds.), *Innovations in clinical practice: A source book* (Vol. 5, pp. 137–156). Sarasota, FL: Professional Resource Exchange, Inc.

Solkol, L., Beck, A. T., Greenberg, R. L., Wright, F. D., & Berchick, R. J. (1989). Cognitive therapy of panic disorder: A non-pharmacological alternative. *Journal of Nervous and Mental Disease, 177,* 711–716.

6

Brief Therapy:
The 20-Minute Hour

CHARLES H. HUBER, Ph.D.

Training in counseling and psychotherapy has traditionally emphasized long-term efforts. Counseling has been described as a process continuing for a specific number of sessions or for a number of years, sessions themselves minimally accorded the proverbial "50-minute hour." But the counseling process can successfully occur in the course of a few moments, with only a few words being exchanged. Assuming they are the right words, spoken at the right time and in the right way, clients are quite likely to profit (Sperry, 1989). Embedded in the hallowed tradition of counseling and psychotherapy, however, has been the belief that there is a direct relationship between the length of treatment and client improvement: the longer the course counseling, the greater the improvement (Fiester & Rudestan, 1975).

Neither clinical experience nor research has supported the assumption that more is better. By contrast, experience indicates that when counselors respond to almost any encounters with clients—even unscheduled ones such as telephone calls or curbside consultations—as potential therapeutic transactions, the outcome is likely to be therapeutic (Sperry, 1989). Research has consistently shown that briefer modes of counseling are at least as effective and sometimes even more effective than longer-term approaches (Perry, 1987).

Making the transition from a traditional, long-term approach to a brief therapy mode such as a 20-minute hour orientation requires letting go of the idea that counseling is about exploring problems. Instead of tuning into what is wrong with clients, counselors assist clients in finding the resources they already possess in order to move toward more effective solutions. This focus on solutions defines the ambiguous concerns clients bring to counseling in more manageable ways that elicit their own natural competence. If done with skill and sensitivity, 20-minute hour counseling sessions can become the norm. The following discussion is offered to convey the context of counseling within a 20-minute hour.

COMPLAINTS AS GOALS

Much of the information traditional counselors typically look for may be unnecessary. Background information is useful, but following a rigid pattern of elaborate history taking before initiating intervention can discourage client cooperation (Walen, DiGiuseppe, & Wessler, 1980). Some clients feel threatened by so much self-disclosure; others believe that much of the material is irrelevant and that the counselor is wasting valuable time that could be used to help them. If clients are apprehensive about exposing their "real" problems, they are just as likely to hide them during an extensive assessment as during a very short, concise one.

The counselor who employs a 20-minute hour orientation assumes that clients will be best served by working efficiently on issues they themselves are willing to discuss. Competence in addressing these presenting issues is more than enough motivation for clients to divulge their "secrets" at some later time. Further, such divulgence frequently becomes unnecessary given what clients learn in more successfully dealing with their presenting concerns. Thus, there is little need to wait for the "real" problems to emerge or to seek a list of all of the client's problems before proceeding to identify ineffective and effective solutions relating to the client's complaint.

To optimize time and effort, clients' presenting concerns are immediately tied to therapeutic goals. Following the initial inquiry, "What are the concerns that bring us together today?" with a statement such as "In answering that question, you might want to focus on how you would like to see things differently" sets a goal-oriented tone. Ideally, this goal setting will be a cooperative endeavor between client and counselor. This typically calls for the counselor to be an active participant, not simply a recorder of what clients want to do.

Small change leads to additional changes. Therefore, the counselor should logically start small. When asked about goals, many clients express unrealistic or utopian objectives, that is, what they tend to see as ultimate, end goals. For example:

CLIENT: I'd like to get better grades.
COUNSELOR: What are your grades now and what would you see as a goal for yourself?
CLIENT: I'm getting D's and F's now. I'd love it if I could get all A's.
COUNSELOR: A's are fine as a longer-term goal, but perhaps we might want to consider moving one step at a time. Keeping in mind all

A's as un ultimate objective, what might be one or more shorter-range objectives?

CLIENT: I see what you mean. Perhaps moving to C's this coming semester, then B's and A's the following semester.

COUNSELOR: That sounds like a fine focus for you to pursue.

Setting goals in increments of small changes allows clients to experience success relatively quickly. Thus encouraged, clients become empowered to make increasingly greater changes in their circumstances.

Another important aspect of goal setting is that goals should be as concise and concrete as possible. Goals such as "more self-confidence" and "feeling better" are only starting points in coming to some negotiated understanding. When vague goals such as "I want to feel better" are offered, the counselor responds, "What will you be doing differently to indicate to you that you are feeling better enough?" to illustrate:

CLIENT: I think that if I felt better, I'd be able to get out more.

COUNSELOR: For example?

CLIENT: Well, for one thing, I'd begin exercising more regularly. I belong to a health club and used to go there fairly regularly.

COUNSELOR: How many days per week are you getting in an exercise session at the health club now, and what would be an indication that you are feeling better?

CLIENT: I may get there once a week now if I'm lucky. I think that three visits per week would be good. That's how often I typically used to go.

COUNSELOR: So if you were to return to visiting the health club at least three days per week, you'd know you'd be "feeling better enough."

Upon negotiating a realistic and concrete goal, it is then important to get a description of the unsuccessful solution(s) clients have employed in pursuit of their goal (the goal being a more positive reframing of their complaint). Continuing with the above illustration, the counselor might respond, "I can't imagine that you haven't already tried several ways to get yourself out more often, in particular to get yourself to the health club on a more regular basis. What might be some of the solutions you've tried that just haven't been effective enough?"

Since complaints are seen as persisting because of clients' unsuccessful efforts to resolve them, a clear understanding of these unsuccessful efforts is critical. Emphasis is placed on what is currently being done by clients to attain their goal (resolve the complaint). A detailed description of the thoughts, feelings, and actions experienced is sought. When the description is too vague to provide an almost cinematic picture of the circumstances surrounding the unsuccessful solution, more focused questioning is used. For example:

COUNSELOR: When your son begins to act out, openly disobeying your requests, what do you do to try to change things?

CLIENT: I usually try to explain to him the reasons for my request.

COUNSELOR: What exactly do you say? Can you think of an example of the most recent time this occurred?

CLIENT: Just this morning, actually. I asked him to clean up his room before school and he just balked at me and continued playing with his Nintendo.

COUNSELOR: You said what exactly and did what next?

CLIENT: I told him that we all have jobs and cleaning his room was his job. When he didn't respond, I began to get more upset and yelled at him, "Get the room cleaned up now!" Then I pulled the Nintendo control from him.

COUNSELOR: And then he said and did what?

CLIENT: He yelled at me to get off his back and just sort of sat there staring at me.

COUNSELOR: And then you said and did what, and how were you feeling at that point?

Formulating goals from clients' complaints and then getting descriptions of the unsuccessful solutions being employed to attain the goals (resolve the complaints) should never be framed as all-or-nothing propositions. The emphasis is on the relative as opposed to the absolute. The counselor never suggests to clients that their complaints will be totally resolved or that their ideal goals will be completely attained. Circumstances can be "significantly improved," and "meaningful progress toward a goal attainment" can be achieved. Likewise, the counselor does not suggest to clients that their attempted solutions have been totally unsuccessful; rather, he or she suggests that these solutions have not been successful enough, which is the reason the clients are seeking assistance.

EXCEPTIONS

The counselor working from a 20-minute hour orientation next seeks to determine what happens when the complaint is not occurring or has only minimal impact on the client's daily life. What happens when the goal the client has identified is being achieved in some manner? Further, what is the client doing to make this happen? The counselor maintains the basic assumption that regardless of the magnitude or chronicity of the difficulties clients experience, there are always times when, for some reason, these difficulties are seemingly resolved or only minimally influence clients' lives. Depressed persons feel okay, combative couples have peaceful days, and children comply without question to their parents' requests. Most persons, many counselors included, consider these seeming problem-free times to be unconnected or unrelated to the problematic times and so do little to understand them better or to amplify them (O'Hanlon and Weiner-Davis, 1989). In fact, such exception times frequently go entirely unnoticed, their significance unappreciated until recalled in counseling.

Exceptions to times when difficulties are present in their full furor offer a tremendous amount of information about potentially successful solutions. More successful solutions that clients have already proven effective can readily evolve from examination of times when the complaint is not actively occurring. Clients frequently need to do little more than amplify what is already working for them to resolve even the most persistent of difficulties. They don't necessarily need to learn new solutions, a process that takes up the majority of time spent in traditional counselling approaches.

Clients typically respond in curious ways when questioned about expectations. They are often quiet momentarily and then appear lost in thought. This happens because most people generally cast their life circumstances in black-and-white, either-or terms: "That child never obeys me" or "I walk around angry all the time." Although it is highly unlikely that a child would be able "never" to obey any rule or request, or that a person could be angry 24 hours a day every day, many persons nonetheless perceive things this way. So when clients are asked, "What is different about those times when you're not angry or only minimally upset?" the counselor is requesting that clients report on experiences to which they have paid almost no attention. Up to this point all they have been noticing is their child's disobedience, the feelings of anger. They have simply not attended to or viewed with any real significance the occasional time when their child goes out of the way to be cooperative, or when they feel relatively calm and satisfied. As a consequence, they also have given little or no credence to the more successful manner in which they were resolving what at other times they experience as a persistent difficulty.

O'Hanlon and Weiner-Davis (1989) offered comment on clients' frequent surprise at being asked to attend to exceptions to those times when their complaint is not present:

> Another reason clients sometimes seem a bit unprepared ... pertaining to exceptions is that they do not expect therapy to be a place where one discusses what is going right. Therapy is a place to talk

about problems. After all, no TV or movie therapist ever asks about what is going right. In asking about exceptions, we are not only attempting to redirect people's attention to what is already working but also orienting people as to what we think is important to know and talk about in therapy. (p. 83)

O'Hanlon and Weiner-Davis (1989, p. 85) went on to note their observation that exceptions relative to clients' complaints are "there for the asking." They offered a number of areas of invaluable inquiry for eliciting information about exceptions, and with them more successful solutions that clients can employ for the better resolution of their recurring difficulties. (It is important to note here the idea that exceptions are not being sought to identify exceptions per se, but rather to identify situations that illustrate more successful solutions. The counselor's objective is to unearth these more successful solutions.)

The primary area of inquiry for the counselor involves one major question: "What is different about the times when . . . (your child obeys or you're feeling okay)?" Any difference that can be seen from those times when the complaint circumstances are actively occurring normally provides an illustration of an exception. Initially, some clients find it difficult to pinpoint an exception, but with persistence and an attitude of "You can do it with some extra thought" on the part of the counselor, most clients eventually describe situations during which they are not experiencing their complaint (they are progressing in the direction of their stated goal). To encourage this, the counselor assumes a stance that suggests he or she would be very surprised if there were no exceptions. This is done by asking, "What is different about the times when . . . ?" as opposed to "Have there been times when . . . ?" The first question implies a certainty on the part of the counselor that a difference has occurred. Further, the question is asked in terms of clients' expressed goals ("when you're feeling okay" instead of "when you're not feeling angry"). "Not feeling angry" only conjures up occasions related to anger, whereas "feeling okay" focuses on more satisfying circumstances. Occasionally, a client will insist that there have been no times that the complaint has not been present. When this occurs, the counselor looks instead to identify exceptions when the complaint was not as bad or only minimally experienced, the "best of the bad times."

Upon describing a difference, the focus shifts to highlighting what the client did to make this difference occur. "What did you do to contribute to that happening?" "How did you get yourself/him/her/them to . . . ?" "How did you handle that differently from the way you normally do?" On the simplest level, this subsequent focus on clients' different thoughts, feelings, and actions provides information about what clients have done to better deal with their difficulty—a more successful solution.

CONTRASTS AND A COMMON DENOMINATOR

The concept is a simple one: If clients want to experience less stress and greater life satisfaction, they need only be able to assess better what is different about the times when they are already experiencing greater life satisfaction and less stress and what they themselves are doing to make this occur. Therein lies the more successful solution: clients increasing their awareness of these differences that have a track record of achieving (even for short periods of time) their desired goal and clients recognizing their personal contribution to the occurrence of these differences (O'Hanlon and Weiner-Davis, 1989).

At this point in the process, the counselor and the client have (a) addressed the client's presenting complaint and reframed it as a goal, (b) assessed those solutions the client is repetitively although unsuccessfully using to seek goal attainment, and (c) identified at least one exception time when the goal is seemingly attained (the complaint is not present or is minimally present), along with the client's contribution to that goal attainment. The next task is to determine the logic, rule, or basic emphasis of the solutions, both successful and unsuccessful. By studying the various individual solutions described, the counselor looks for their common denominator and then seeks to answer the question "What is the basic rule underlying this client's successful and unsuccessful problem-solving efforts?

For example: two parents' presenting complaint was their teenage son's noncompliance. Their goal was to have him obey them more readily. They had several specific house rules to which the son's attendance at least two-thirds of the time would offer evidence that their goal had been attained. In relaying their present efforts at attaining this goal, they reported several unsuccessful solutions: "We've done just about everything imaginable. We've warned him. We've taken away his allowance and other money privileges. We've grounded him for weeks at a time. We've sat him down and explained that this is our house and he has to abide by our rules. Several times, we've even hit him. We've tried to keep him away from those lowlife friends of his who are constantly in trouble by sending him to a private school. He was expelled after a month and a half. We've tried just about everything we can."

"Everything" consisted of variations of the same basic belief accompanying all these unsuccessful solutions: "He must obey us" (expressed as an irrational, absolute demand.) Regarding identification of exceptions, when queried concerning times when circumstances were different, the parents after some reluctance related two seeming fluke situations. One concerned a recent weekend vacation the family had taken to the mountains. The parents related wanting to have some "together time" as a couple, and so they selected a resort where specific attractive activities were planned for children and teens to allow parents time to themselves. They further reported deciding to let their son "take responsibility for his own enjoyment," not feeling obligated to see to it that he had a good time.

The second exception occurred only the day before, when both were unexpectedly called at the last minute to work at a church dinner in place of a couple who were ill. They described rushing from their home to the church and telling their son he would have to fend for himself for dinner. Upon returning home they discovered he had not only made his own dinner, but also cleaned the kitchen "spotlessly" afterward.

Both situations were attributed to the fact that "he was just in a good mood." In response to specific questions ("What did you two do differently to contribute to that 'good mood'?"), the parents were able to see that they had "backed off" both times. While they still expected their son to attend to the house rules, they didn't press him about doing so.

Assessing clients' basic rule relative to their unsuccessful solutions indicates what might be done to resolve their complaints by suggesting what to stay away from: the "mine field," those comments and recommendations that are simply a variation of their unsuccessful rule (Fisch, Weakland & Segal, 1982). The easiest way to avoid the mine field and to arrive at truly different and potentially more successful solutions is to determine an alternative solution 180° toward the opposite direction of the basic rule leading to the unsuccessful solutions. The 20-minute counselor emphasizes the *toward* in looking for a rule that is rational and relative in nature, not absolute, and thus the complete opposite of a client's unsuccessful rule. In the case example above, the counselor contrasted "not pressing" their son (although still reasonably desiring that he obey) and "demanding that he obey" (unreasonably and absolutely) by highlighting the successful and unsuccessful solutions reported and the parents' emotional experience during both types of solution situations. Demanding that the boy absolutely obey the house rules was tied to unsuccessful solutions and intense, angry, hurtful emotions. Not pressing the boy, but rather wanting him to obey the house rules, was tied to more successful solutions and satisfactory emotional experiences, for example, offering structured situations that allow their son to assume greater responsibility, expecting him to be able to take that responsibility, and feeling relief and pride when he did just that.

While the specifics of clients' basic unsuccessful and successful rules differ from client to client, unsuccessful rules generally have a strong element of absolutism and demandingness attached to them. More successful rules are 180 degrees toward the opposite direction and have a strong element of relativism and desirability of flexibility attached to them. The specifics of the unsuccessful solution attempts, more successful exception times, as framed by the goals identified by the client, provide the evidence bearing out this assumption with clients.

AMPLIFYING SUCCESSFUL SOLUTIONS

Most clients tend to categorize their unsuccessful solutions dichotomously, that is, in black-and-white, either-or terms. They believe that the only way their difficulty can be addressed is the way it is now being addressed. For example, a husband might blame all his difficulties on his wife. Although this may seem foolish to the objective observer, it is a premise the husband maintains, even though it presently contributes to significant marital discord (it may, however, relieve him of having to take responsibility for his contribution to the discord). As long as this premise is the basis of the husband's view, and therefore of the way he feels and behaves, then amplification of his more successful solutions is unlikely. But once the husband begins to doubt this premise, he becomes open to alternative solutions.

This greater openness is generated through a process of debate. *Webster's* (1976) defines *debate* as "a process wherein a question is discussed by considering opposing arguments." The counselor employing a 20-minute hour orientation challenges clients to consider the opposing arguments presented by their unsuccessful solutions and accompanying rule and their more successful solutions and accompanying rule. Once clients' successful and unsuccessful solutions and respective rules have been assessed, the counselor's focus for amplifying the successful solutions comprises three main tasks. The first task is to facilitate doubt about the sanctity of clients' unsuccessful solutions/rule by coupling their unsuccessful solutions/rule with their successful solutions/rule and then compiling disconfirming data relative to the unsuccessful solutions/rule. The second task is to encourage clients' exploration of the more successful solution/rule in a way that affirms the greater helpfulness and sensibleness of this solution/rule by highlighting the future benefits. The third task is to review and confirm the step-by-step manner in which the successful solution/rule will be carried out in the coming days. This process offers enhanced opportunity for greater emotional satisfaction (or less dissatisfaction) as well as goal attainment (complaint resolution).

Debate begins by highlighting the contrasts between the client's successful solutions and unsuccessful solutions, emphasizing the relevant rule accompanying each. For example:

COUNSELOR: You noted that you do all you can to avoid disagreements with your boss. You mentioned several solutions that have not worked satisfactorily in that you continuously come away dissatisfied. We identified a basic rule that appears to inform all your relatively unsuccessful attempts: "I must not argue with the boss." You also noted that the two times you can recall that you were more assertive with the boss, you made your point and came away satisfied and proud of yourself. The rule that accompanied those two occasions, what you saw as exception times, we agreed was something like "I'd rather not argue with the boss, but there are times I will gain by taking a stand." Which of these times are the ones you benefited most from?

CLIENT: When I was more assertive, but the boss was also in a better mood those days.

COUNSELOR: True, the boss was in a better mood, but perhaps your assertiveness significantly contributed to the better mood. The point we need to stress now, though, is would you rather experience the good feelings that accompanied your thinking "I must not argue no matter what"?

CLIENT: The times I was thinking "I'd rather not argue, but it's better to sometimes."

The client's confirmation, even though minimal, signals the counselor to move the debate forward and begin to highlight the successful solution and accompanying rule in a way that affirms the greater helpfulness and sensibleness of this direction. The counselor promotes this by facilitating the client in consequential thinking (Spivack, Platt, & Shure, 1976). This refers to the ability to predict the probable consequences of a possible solution. Although having seen the successful solution as an exception time ("but the boss was in a better mood those days"), the client has already experienced success and it is on this success that consequential thinking is focused. To continue with the above case illustration:

COUNSELOR: Based on those times you were successful with your boss when thinking, "I'd rather not argue, but . . . ," would it not be likely that your success will continue if you acted similarly, but just more often?

CLIENT: Possibly. However, I do think much of it had to do with the boss's being in a better mood.

COUNSELOR: Well, that may be second part of your success in dealing with the boss. Perhaps you can look for times when the boss is in a better mood and think, "I'd rather not argue, but . . . ," and then act in an assertive manner as you did on the two occasions you reported feeling very good about the stand you took. Given your past success, how likely is it that this method has a better chance of succeeding than avoiding all disagreement whatsoever?

CLIENT: I'd probably feel better knowing I did something instead of backing off.

COUNSELOR: And how would that affect your job performance?

CLIENT: Definitely better. I wouldn't feel so helpless and put upon. I'm sure I'd get a lot more work done.

Once the client has evaluated the more satisfying consequences likely to occur as a result of increasing the frequency of thinking based on the more successful rule and enacting previous "exception time" successful solutions more often, the debate concludes with means-ends thinking (Spivack, Platt, & Shure, 1976). Client and counselor review the sequence of events that have been successful in a step-by-step manner. They then rehearse exactly how the client will increase the frequency of the more successful solution and its accompanying rule in the coming days and how the boss will likely react, how the client will react to the boss's reactions, and so on. Typically, role-playing or use of imagery is employed to facilitate the rehearsal. For example:

COUNSELOR: We've confirmed that a more helpful thought is "I'd rather not argue, but at times I will gain by taking a stand." I'd like you to keep the thought firmly in your mind.

CLIENT: Okay.

COUNSELOR: Now close your eyes and picture yourself approaching your boss about that memo you recently received on working extra hours over the weekend. Picture yourself saying to the boss, "My work is up-to-date and I don't need the weekend hours to catch up like some of my co-workers." You've already ascertained that the boss is in a fairly good mood. You're speaking slowly and clearly. Tell me when you get that picture clear in your mind. *(Pauses and waits for the client's response.)*

CLIENT: I've got it clear.

COUNSELOR: Now what are you saying to the boss and how are you feeling about it?

CLIENT: I'm feeling a bit anxious. I'm saying, "I have something I'd like to speak with you about. I realize the reason for your memo about extra hours on the weekend is for the work to become caught up. I've worked extremely hard during the week, skipping my lunch and breaks occasionally to keep up-to-date, and I am ahead on my work as a result. Thus, I don't feel it's necessary for me to be here on the weekend."

COUNSELOR: How are you feeling as you state your case assertively?
CLIENT: I'm definitely feeling better, more empowered.

MAINTAINING AND CONTINUING
SUCCESSFUL SOLUTIONS

Maintaining and continuing successful solutions amplified during the session can be accomplished by *follow-up* and *feedback*. The term *homework* is frequently used as synonymous with follow-up. Counselors working from a 20-minute hour orientation do not merely engage in "talk therapy"; rather, they stress that a significant portion of "session time" is best spent outside of session. Clients are encouraged to take what was addressed in the session and regularly use it in their daily lives. "Action" follow-up assignments are therefore the major emphasis of counseling.

Follow-up assignments that are action oriented share four important characteristics:

1. **Consistency**. The assignment is consistent with the work done during the session. Assignments should follow naturally from the main theme of the session. Typically, this will be amplification of successful solutions addressed during the session.
2. **Specificity**. The assignment is delineated in sufficient detail and clear steps to take are provided. This should flow from amplifying successful solutions via means-ends thinking; summary/review, however, is frequently helpful.
3. **Small Steps**. Like the goals for counseling, the probability of success is increased if steps are reasonably small and attainable. Small, attainable steps lead to initiation of beneficial cycles of a larger nature.
4. **Seriousness**. When addressing follow-up assignments, it is important to do so in a serious manner. Assignments that the counselor presents off-the-cuff or in a reluctant, apologetic manner will decrease client compliance. In is important that the counselor review the assignment carefully with the client, including the rationale for it, as understanding increases client compliance.

Feedback is a process whereby clients verify the effects of their successful solutions. The more successful solution is implemented outside of the session. Its effects are evaluated. How well did it work? If more satisfactory than previous unsuccessful solutions, self-affirmation is in order. If not satisfactory, what was different from previous times when the solution was successful? Feedback basically involves encouraging clients to be scientific in their examination of results and the conclusions they draw from them (Wallen, DiGiuseppe, & Wessler, 1980).

Good scientists gather information as impartially as possible, attempting to observe and report their observations objectively and accurately. Two primary habits that interfere with scientific information gathering are *selective abstraction* and *magnification/minimization*. (Beck, Rush, Shaw, & Emery, 1978). Selective abstraction "consists of focusing on a detail taken out of context, ignoring other more salient features of the situation, and conceptualizing the whole experience on the basis of this element" (Beck et al., 1978, p. 7). Magnification/minimization "is reflected in errors of evaluation that are so gross as to constitute a distortion" (p. 8). In both types of interferences, clients ignore certain features of their circumstances and thus gather biased information. In selective abstraction, clients focus on one category of information only and ignore others; in magnification/minimization, they ignore information within a category. With feedback, the counselor facilitates clients in agreeing on what information is most relevant, thus avoiding selective abstraction. Second, keeping a written account or log of where, when, and how often helps clients avoid the problem of magnification/minimization.

EPILOGUE

The counselor employing a 20-minute hour orientation seeks consistently to do brief, efficient, and effective counseling; he or she works to promote positive change sooner than later. This is not to say, however, that all counseling efforts can occur in 20-minute sessions. Although most can, it is important not to rigidly repeat a solution that is unsuccessful. Movement in a different direction—longer and/or more sessions—is called for when briefness is not working well enough.

It is hard, however, to think of a moral or ethical justification for spending a long time counseling a client when a shorter time will suffice. There is no reason to believe that anything will be lost when counseling is begun with briefness as its focus and then extended in length of sessions and/or number of sessions as necessary. If a client's counseling experience does by necessity extend past that time identified as "brief," it should still continue only for the most minimal time possible to attain the agreed-to counseling goals.

REFERENCES

Beck, A. T., Rush, A. J., Shaw, B. F., & Emery, G. (1978). *Cognitive therapy of depression: A treatment manual.* Unpublished manuscript.

Fiester, A., & Rudestan, K. (1975). A multivariate analysis of early treatment dropout process. *Journal of Consulting and Clinical Psychology, 48,* 528–535.

Fisch, R., Weakland, J., & Segal, L. (1982). *The tactics of change: Doing therapy briefly.* San Francisco: Jossey-Bass.

O'Hanlon, W. H., & Weiner-Davis, M. (1989). *In search of solutions.* New York: Norton.
Perry, S. (1987). The choice of duration and frequency for out-patient psychotherapy. In R. Hales and A. Frances (Eds.), *Psychiatric update: The American Psychiatric Association annual review.* Washington, DC: American Psychiatric Press.
Sperry, L. (1989). Contemporary approaches to brief psychotherapy. *Individual Psychology: The Journal of Adlerian Theory, Research, and Practice, 45,* 3–23.
Spivack, G., Platt, J., & Shure, M. (1976).*The problem-solving approach to adjustment.* San Francisco: Jossey-Bass.
Walen, S., DiGiuseppe, R., & Wessler, R. (1980). *A practitioner's guide to rational-emotive therapy.* New York: Oxford University Press.
Webster's new collegiate dictionary. (1976). Springfield, MA: G. & C. Merriam.

7

Medication Therapy

RANDY IAN PARDELL, M.D.

DONNA D. STEIN, R.N., M.A.

Over the past 30 years the advancement of medication therapy in treating emotional disorders has had a profound effect on people suffering from mental illness by reducing disabling psychiatric symptoms and enhancing improved functioning in society. This chapter presents an overview of current psychopharmacological and other somatic treatments of mental disorders. In this section medication treatment regimes for depression, anxiety, and schizophrenia are presented.

MOOD DISORDERS AND DEPRESSION

A *mood disorder* is characterized by a disturbance in emotional affect that is pervasive and is not due to any physical or other mental illness. The emotional disturbance may include abnormal feelings of depression or elation. There are two major categories of mood disorders: *bipolar disorders* and *depressive disorders.*

Sadness, sorrow, and discouragement are normal reactions to disappointments or losses. When these moods become prolonged and intense and are associated with a number of physical and psychological symptoms, a diagnosis of a depressive episode can be made (see DSM-III-R, American Psychiatric Association, 1987). *Depression* is a common illness that affects 7% of the population. Women are affected twice as often as men. Age at onset is most commonly in the late 20s, but a major depressive episode may begin at any age, including during childhood. Major depression is often unrecognized by family physicians, and accepted methods of treatment are often underprescribed (Katon, Von Korff,

The authors wish to acknowledge the invaluable assistance of Phyllis R. Freeman, Ph. D., in the preparation of this chapter.

Lin, Bush, & Ormel, 1992). Left untreated 60% of patients have suicidal ideation and 15% commit suicide (Kaplan & Sadock, 1990).

ANTIDEPRESSIVE AGENTS

The tricyclic antidepressants (TCAs) have been used for more than 30 years. In 1957 Kuhn found that imipramine had mood-elevating and behavior-activating properties. Structurally related tricyclic agents have been synthesized and in controlled comparisons with placebos are found to be effective in the treatment of depression (Quitkin et al., 1991). These medications inhibit the reuptake of the neurochemicals norepinephrine and serotonin into nerve cells and hence increase the amount of these chemicals in the brain. It is hypothesized that this effect of TCAs is associated with the mood-elevating effect of these antidepressants. The major TCAs used are imipramine, desipramine, amitriptyline, and maprotiline. These medications do not have an immediate action and require 1–2 weeks before the antidepressant effects are obtained. Initial symptoms such as insomnia and anorexia are the first to improve prior to mood elevation (Lickey & Gordon, 1991). In three antidepressants, imipramine, desipramine, and nortryptiline, studies have shown that particular blood levels are associated with the antidepressant response (Risch, Janowsky, & Huey, 1981). Some common side effects of the tricyclic antidepressants include blurred vision, dry mouth, urinary retention, headache, weight gain (a common cause of noncompliance), constipation, drowsiness, dizziness, orthostatic hypotension, heart palpitations, and an absence of bowel motility (paralytic ileus).

The tricyclic antidepressants are contraindicated in patients with cardiac electrical conduction abnormalities or pregnancy and in use with alcohol. These medications may be lethal in overdosage and may cause agranulocytosis and leukopenia (low white blood count) (Kaplan & Sadock, 1990). TCAs in the elderly population should be used cautiously due to their effects on the cardiovascular system. When prescribed, close monitoring of cardiac status and plasma levels is indicated.

The newer antidepressants have fewer troublesome or intolerable side effects. Reduced side effects may lead to an increase in patient tolerance and compliance and ultimately to a reduction in the symptoms of depression. Although the newer antidepressants have not been proven more effective than standard TCAs, some previously unresponsive patients respond to these novel agents (Baldessarini, 1989). Among these atypical antidepressants are fluoxetine (Prozac), sertraline (Zoloft), trazodone (Desyrel), and bupropion (Wellbutrin).

Fluoxetine is a potent serotonin reuptake inhibitor with antidepressant properties as favorable as those of the TCAs but with little or none of the usual side effects common among the TCAs. The possible side effects from fluoxetine are rash, weight loss, nausea, nervousness, anorgasmia or delayed orgasm, and insomnia, all of which usually subside after the first week of therapy. One of the benefits of this agent is its relative safety in overdosage due to the lack of adverse cardiovascular effects. Fluoxetine has been useful in treating seasonal affective disorder as well as other atypical depressive syndromes, and in the treatment of eating disorders (Kaplan & Sadock, 1991). The effect of fluoxetine in treating obsessive-compulsive disorders has been encouraging (Kaplan & Sadock, 1989).

Though there has been recent controversy in the media about fluoxetine inducing suicidal and homicidal behaviors, the Food and Drug Administration (FDA) found no convincing evidence of this. In fact, there is no statistical difference between standard TCAs and fluoxetine in treatment of emergent suicidal ideation. The highest incidence of suicidality is in *untreated* depressed patients (Fava & Rosenbaum, 1991).

Clomipramine (Anafranil), a recently released TCA, is effective in the treatment of obsessive-compulsive disorder (OCD), depression, and anxiety disorders. It is the only TCA that has been shown effective for the treatment of OCD due to its potent serotonin reuptake blockade. Clomipramine has been shown to possess specific antiobessive effects that are independent of its antidepressant effects (Mavissakalian, Turner, Michelson, & Jacob, 1985). Clomipramine shares a similar side effect profile with other TCAs.

Bupropion (Wellbutrin) has properties that differ from other antidepressants in their effect on dopamine reuptake, as opposed to their action on the serotonin and norepinephrine systems. The advantages of bupropion include no clinically significant effects on cardiac conduction or pulse rate. It also produces little or no weight gain or daytime drowsiness. The occurrence of generalized seizures is slightly higher than with other antidepressants. Bupropion should be avoided in patients with histories of seizures or supporting diagnosis of anoxexia or bulimia nervosa because they have a higher incidence of bupropion-induced seizures than the general population (Kaplan & Sadock, 1990).

Trazodone (Desyrel) is a highly specific serotonin reuptake blocker, and its efficacy resembles the TCAs although it is safer in overdosage. The most common side effect of trazodone is sedation. A troublesome but infrequent side effect in men is priapism (prolonged erection), which if sustained may require surgical intervention. Some physicians use trazodone as a hypnotic agent, and it is useful in treating depression with severe insomnia (Baldessarini, 1985).

Sertraline (Zoloft), a recently released antidepressant, is a potent and specific serotonin reuptake inhibitor that has a similar side effect profile to fluoxetine. There is clinical evidence that sertraline may improve psychomotor performance and may be effective in treating OCD. Minimal side effects, lessened propensity to interact with other medications, and short half-life make sertraline a welcome novel antidepressant (Aya, 1992).

In the late 1940s a treatment used for tuberculosis, isoniazid (INH), was found to have mood-elevating properties. In the late 1950s chemically related compounds were synthesized from INH and used in the treatment of depression. Although INH is not used as an antidepressive agent, its composition allowed scientists to create compounds that are chemically related. These compounds are the monoamine oxidase inhibitors (MAOI) used in the treatment of depression. The action of an MAOI is to inhibit monoamine oxidases, the enzymes that breakdown the neurotransmitters, norepinephrine and serotonin (5-HT), thus allowing more neurotransmitter to cross the synapse to reach the receptor sites.

MAOIs are useful in the treatment of both classical and atypical depression. Although atypical depression is not a DSM-III-R category, it is used by research psychiatrists. Symptoms of atypical depression include mood reactivity (the patient feels better when something good happens), overeating, oversleeping, extreme fatigue, and chronic oversensitivity to rejection (Lickey & Gordon, 1991). MAOIs have recently been used in the treatment of panic disorder (Kaplan & Sadock, 1990). Some other indications for the use of MAOIs are posttraumatic stress disorder, bulimia, and obsessive-compulsive disorder (Baldessarini, 1985).

The MAOIs in current use are phenelzine (Nardil), tranylcypromine (Marplan), and isocarboxazid (Parnate). The main reason MAOIs are not prescribed as often as TCAs is the potentially dangerous side effect of a hypertensive crisis when MAOIs are combined with tyramine-containing foods such as aged cheeses, chocolate, fermented meats, chianti wines, and soy sauce (Baldessarini, 1985). Strict adherence to the diet is essential to avoid complications.

Other adverse effects of the MAOIs include hypertensive crisis, interaction with other drugs (e.g., narcotics such as Demerol) which can be life threatening, orthostatic hypotension, severe weight gain, sexual dysfunction, lower extremity edema, dizziness, blurred vision, weakness, dry mouth, headache, insomnia, excessive sweating, and constipation (Poling, Gadow, & Cleary, 1991). MAOIs are generally prescribed when TCAs have failed to produce the desired effect. The patient must be aware of and compliant with the dietary restrictions.

ELECTROCONVULSIVE THERAPY AND SLEEP DEPRIVATION

Electroconvulsive therapy (ECT) is most useful when there is an urgent need for intervention, such as in cases of high-risk suicide or depression with psychotic features. Some patients simply do not respond or cannot tolerate medication therapy. ECT is also appropriate in pregnancy and for patients who have a severe medical illness and cannot take antidepressant medication. Though ECT is an extremely effective treatment for depression, there is a high relapse rate, and indications are that maintenance treatment is needed every 2 weeks to a month for 6 months to provide continued antidepressant effect (Lickey & Gordon, 1991).

The mode of therapeutic action of ECT is unknown, but may be secondary to elevation of brain serotonin and norepinephrine levels. The major side effects of ECT are reversible short-term memory impairment and mild confusion after the actual treatment. There are extremely rare (1 in 10,000) severe complications from ECT, such as stroke or sustained seizures. Though there is much fear and controversy about ECT by the general public, ECT is an effective, safe, and rapid treatment for severe depression or agitated behaviors that are unresponsive to medication therapy (Baldessarini, 1985).

ECT has been used successfully for the treatment of depression for more than 50 years. Before the discovery of antidepressant agents, it was the only efficacious treatment for depression and to this date remains the most rapid and effective treatment for acute severe depression.

A recent review of the literature on the clinical aspects of sleep deprivation in the treatment of depression (Leibenluft & Wehr, 1992) showed that noninvasive sleep deprivation can potentiate the response to antidepressant medication or lithium. The studies reviewed have used sleep deprivation as both a treatment of depression and a diagnostic and prognostic instrument in assessing the disorder. The noninvasive nature of sleep deprivation provides an optimistic alternative for the treatment of depression. However, it has little clinical value since depression recurs rapidly after sleep deprivation therapy is discontinued.

BIPOLAR DISORDER

Bipolar disorder is a cyclical syndrome that manifests itself by alternating periods of depression and mania. A bipolar disorder can manifest itself in a depressive phase with symptoms of a major depressive episode, a manic phase, or both, each occurring at different times (see DSM-III-R, American Psychiatric Association, 1987). Bipolar disorder is found in the general population at a rate of 0.4–1.2% and affects men and women equally. The onset of the disorder is usually during adolescence or early adulthood (Poling, Gadow, & Cleary, 1991).

Lithium

Lithium is the drug of choice in the treatment of bipolar disorder. It was discovered in 1949 by John Cade when he noted its calming effect on animals. Today there are several preparations of lithium carbonate available in the United States that are used primarily to treat mood disorders.

The initial treatment of lithium is usually during the manic phase when the patient may be hospitalized. In the first 5–10 days of treatment, a sedative or antipsychotic may be given while waiting for the therapeutic blood levels of lithium (0.6–1.2 MEq per liter) and the antimanic effects to begin, usually in 5–10 days. Due to the low therapeutic index of the lithium ion, blood levels can become toxic; therefore, careful monitoring of blood concentrations is crucial. In rare cases, lithium can negatively affect thyroid gland or kidney function, effects that are reversible when the medication is discontinued (Baldessarini, 1985).

Once the proper dose of lithium is reached, the most common side effects are nausea, vomiting, diarrhea, mild confusion, light-headedness, and slight motor tremor, but typically patients rarely complain of feeling medicated or mentally dull (Baldessarini, 1985). Serious lithium intoxication warrants the immediate withdrawal of the medication and evaluation of blood levels. The early signs of a toxic reaction are increasing tremor, weakness, ataxia, giddiness, drowsiness, blurred vision, and slurred speech. In severe intoxication, lethargy and stupor may lead to coma.

Lithium is an effective treatment for acute mania. In addition, lithium can reduce the frequency and intensity of future episodes of mania or depression. Hence, many patients diagnosed with bipolar disorder will be prescribed lithium on a maintenance basis for a year or longer to prevent future recurrence of mania or depression. Bipolar disorder is also treated with carbamazepine (Tegretol), valproate (Depakene), and calcium channel inhibitors for patients who do not respond to lithium.

In the treatment of bipolar disorder, carbamazepine (CBZ) has been found to be an effective maintenance treatment for bipolar disorder by preventing recurrence of mania and depression. It is also useful in the treatment of acute mania and depression in patients with bipolar disorder (Post, Uhde, & Ballenger, 1983). There may be a synergistic response to adding CBZ to lithium in both acute and maintenance treatments. Initial and treatment emergent blood levels of CBZ, liver chemistries, and a complete blood count should be performed because a rare complication of CBZ therapy is bone marrow suppression, (leading to severe infection and blood disorders) and hepatitis. CBZ can also affect and lower blood levels of other drugs metabolized by the liver by inducing the cytochrome P-450 enzyme pathway system (Roose & Glassman, 1990).

Valproate has also been shown to be effective in acute and maintenance treatment of bipolar disorder (McElroy, Keck, & Pope, 1988). It is usually well tolerated. The major side effects are weight gain, hair loss, tremor, and sedation. A rare occurrence of liver failure has been a significant concern, but occurs almost exclusively in children, many of whom have inborn errors of metabolism and or are taking other anticonvulsant medications (Roose & Glassman, 1990).

ANXIETY DISORDERS

Anxiety becomes a mental disorder when it is more intense than is justified by the actual threat. Kaplan and Sadock (1991) define anxiety as "a pathologic state characterized by a feeling of dread accompanied by somatic signs indicative of a hyperactive autonomic nervous system. Anxiety is differentiated from fear, which is a response to a known cause" (p. 310). There are five types of anxiety disorders: *panic disorder, generalized anxiety disorder, phobic disorder, obsessive-compulsive disorder,* and *posttraumatic stress disorder.* Thirteen percent of Americans have suffered from an anxiety disorder. Symptoms of anxiety and avoidance behavior are common among this group of disorders.

In this section each type of anxiety disorder will be discussed briefly and followed by the medical treatment regime currently used.

Panic Disorder With or Without Agoraphobia
A panic attack is characterized by a sudden onset of intense fear or terror (see DSM-III-R). The average age of onset is in the late 20s. Panic disorder without agoraphobia is seen equally in both males and females. Panic disorder with agoraphobia is diagnosed twice as often in women than in men. According to the NIMH Epidemiologic Catchment Area survey, approximately 1.4% of the population has suffered from panic disorder during their lifetime (Myers et al., 1984). There is a 30% concordance rate among monozygotic twins and a 15% chance among first-degree relatives who have had a panic disorder to experience the disorder (Tomb 1988). Panic disorder with agoraphobia includes symptoms of the fear of being in places or situations from which escape might be difficult or embarrassing or in which help might not be available in the event of a panic attack (American Psychiatric Association, 1987).

The current pharmacologic agents used to treat panic disorder include benzodiazepines, such as alprazolam and clonazepam; tricyclic antidepressants, such as imipramine and desipramine; and monoamine oxidase inhibitors (McGlynn & Metcalf, 1989). Treatment lengths vary according to patient response. In a long-term treatment model, Ballenger (1991) describes the changes in medication during different phases of panic disorder with different goals for each intervention and the gradual tapering of the medication. Although medication treatment is effective in controlling the actual panic attacks, it does not relieve the anticipatory anxiety experienced by some patients (DuPont, 1990).

Patient support and education are most useful to ensure patient understanding, cooperation, and compliance. Groups for patients with panic disorder with agoraphobia are available in many communities. These groups serve to provide education, support, encouragement, and an opportunity to see how others have overcome their affliction (McGlynn & Metcalf, 1989).

Social Phobia

Social phobia is the persistent fear and avoidance of social situations where the person may be judged or scrutinized by others. The individual fears performing an embarrassing act in which he or she will be humiliated (McGlynn & Metcalf, 1989). Slight social anxiety is common to most people during certain social interactions, but when it becomes excessive or debilitating, a social phobia may exist. The social fear may be specific, such as the fear of being unable to speak in public, choking on food while eating in front of others, or experiencing hand tremors when writing in front of others; or the phobia may be generalized to social situations.

According to DSM-III-R: "A diagnosis of Social Phobia of is made only if the avoidant behavior interferes with the occupational functioning or with usual social activities or relationships with others, or if there is marked distress about having the fear" (American Psychiatric Association, 1987).

Physiological symptoms include blushing, increased heart rate, palpitations, and difficulty breathing in anticipation of the phobic reaction. According to the NIMH Epidemiologic Catchment Area survey (Myers et al., 1984), social phobia is a common disorder with a 6-month prevalence rate of 0.9–1.7% in men and 1.5–2.6% in women.

Treatment of social phobia includes medication and/or cognitive-behavioral approaches. MAOIs have been shown to be the most effective in treating social phobias, but as previously discussed, these have many adverse reactions. The benzodiazepines, such as alprazolam, may be beneficial in some patients. However, these agents are prescribed with caution due to the high rate of substance abuse among this population, though this concern may be overrated (Schneier, 1991). The beta blockers such as propranolol benefit patients with specific fears in predictable situations when taken 45 to 60 minutes before the feared activity. Patients with more generalized symptoms may respond to a daily beta blocker such as atenolol. The side effects generally are limited to fatigue (McGlynn & Metcalf, 1989).

Simple Phobia

A simple phobia is a persistent fear of a certain object or situation. Avoidance of the specified anxiety-provoking stimulus perpetuates the phobia. The more common phobias include the fear of snakes, mice, dogs, insects, airline travel, closed spaces, and heights. Many people with phobias do not seek care. The lifetime prevalence rates of simple phobia were approximately 4% for men and 9% for women (Robins et al., 1984). Treatment for simple phobias includes cognitive and behavioral psychotherapies. Fear of flying is treated with therapy, hypnosis, and medication.

Obsessive-Compulsive Disorder

Obsessive-compulsive disorder (OCD) is characterized by obsessive thoughts and compulsions that are distressing and that significantly interfere with the person's daily life. Obsessions are intrusive, unwanted, and involuntary ideas, thoughts, or images that seem senseless to the person. The most common obsessions are thoughts of violence, contamination, and doubt (American Psychiatric Association, 1987). Compulsions are repetitive, purposeful behaviors that serve to prevent discomfort. The acts are ritualistic in nature and, when not performed, the person encounters much anxiety and tension. The more common compulsions include counting, washing, and checking.

Ninety percent of patients with OCD experience both obsessions and compulsions. The other 10% describe only obsessional thoughts (McGlynn & Metcalf, 1989). People so affected recognize that their ritualistic behaviors are excessive; they would like to stop but feel powerless and cannot. The NIMH Epidemiologic Catchment Area survey found that 1.5% of the American population met the criteria for OCD within a 6-month period and that the disorder occurs equally among men and women (Myers et al., 1984). The treatments for OCD include cognitive-behavioral therapy (exposure and response prevention) and medication therapy. (See "Antidepressive Agents" for medication therapy for OCD.)

Posttraumatic Stress Disorder

Posttraumatic stress disorder (PTSD) is characterized by extreme anxiety produced by a traumatic life event. This extraordinary event is relived through nightmares, flashbacks, and conscious thoughts (see DSM-III-R for complete symptom list). PTSD is common, with the lifetime prevalence between 1% and 15% of the general population. Some individuals may experience symptoms of PTSD after severe trauma, such as physical attack or combat (Helzer, Robins, & McEvoy, 1987). Associated with PTSD are symptoms of anxiety and depression that sometimes are severe enough to be classified as an anxiety or depressive disorder.

The pharmacologic approach to PTSD is aimed at reducing the symptoms of anxiety and depression in conjunction with supportive psychotherapy. The standard medication regimes for anxiety and depression have been shown to be effective in the treatment of PTSD (Kaplan & Sadock, 1991). (For specific information, see "Antidepressive Agents" and "Anxiety Disorders" for medication therapies for PTSD.)

Generalized Anxiety Disorder
In a recent article Rapee (1991) concluded that generalized anxiety disorder (GAD) can be considered the "basic" anxiety disorder with worry as its characteristic feature (see DSM-III-R). Patients with GAD usually complain of somatic distress in the form of headaches or abdominal discomfort. Substance abuse tendencies may be present, especially in men (McGlynn & Metcalf, 1989, p. 54).

MEDICATION TREATMENT FOR ANXIETY DISORDERS

Since the 1970s, the benzodiazepines have been the most widely prescribed medication for the treatment of anxiety, insomnia, and seizure disorders. Currently, there are 14 benzodiazepines available for clinical use in the United States. At least 10% of the population uses one of these drugs each year. The benzodiazepines have a mechanism of action with diffuse inhibitory effects in the central nervous system (CNS) and anticonvulsant activity. They also function as a muscle relaxant by inhibiting reflex activity (Baldessarini, 1985).

The pharmacological effects of the benzodiazepines include sedative effects (in the treatment of insomnia), conscious sedation (e.g., as a pre-anesthetic), and as a treatment for alcohol withdrawal. Benzodiazepines are used to treat anxiety disorders such as panic attacks and generalized anxiety disorder; they are also used as anticonvulsants. Clonazepam (Klonopin) has been shown to be effective in infantile myoclonic seizures. Midazolam (Versed) is used as an adjunct to anesthesia. It has potent sedative and relaxant effects and also causes an amnestic response during invasive procedures such as endoscopies. Versed is used only in settings where the patient can be continuously monitored (Physician's desk reference, 1992). Benzodiazepines are also used as an anti-stress medication to treat irritable bowel syndrome and angina pectoris during the acute treatment of myocardial infarction.

In comparison to antipsychotic and antidepressant medications, the benzodiazepines produce few systemic side effects and are relatively safe. Benzodiazepines are safe when taken alone or even in overdosage. However, if they are combined with alcohol or other CNS depressants, an overdosage can be lethal (Lickey & Gordon, 1991).

Most side effects are mild, but some can produce significant impairment. The most common side effect is CNS sedation. This may cause daytime sleepiness and impaired concentration. Other side effects include amnesia with mild forgetfulness and some memory impairment for new learning. Sometimes there is psychomotor impairment related to difficulty in coordination and accidental falls. There can be behavioral side effects with disinhibition and increased agitation in some patients (Baldessarini, 1985).

Benzodiazepines can cause physiological dependence. Discontinuation of benzodiazepines can cause symptom recurrence, or rebound, which is a worsening of the pretreatment symptoms or withdrawal symptoms. A withdrawal syndrome is an emergence of new symptoms related to physiological dependence. Although the danger of physiological dependence should lead to caution in prescribing benzodiazepines, it should not cause avoidance of using these medications when indicated. Some patients who take benzodiazepines for years do not develop withdrawal symptoms, where others do exhibit these symptoms shortly after treatment is initiated. Rickles, Schweizer, Case, and Greenblatt (1990) found that the type of benzodiazepine used, the dosage of the medication, and nondrug factors such as dependent personality and baseline psychopathology contributed to the withdrawal severity.

To minimize the dependence and withdrawal effects, benzodiazepines should be used intermittently or on an as needed basis (prn). In most cases they should be prescribed for short periods of time, no longer than a few weeks. The half-life of the medication plays a major role in both the treatment effects and the withdrawal symptoms. The elimination half-life is the relative rate of medication excretion from the body. There are several factors that contribute to the development of benzodiazepine withdrawal syndromes. High-potency, short half-life compounds such as alprazolam, (Xanax) triazolam (Halcion), and lorazepam (Ativan) are most often implicated in withdrawal symptoms. Longer duration of treatment, higher doses, and abrupt withdrawal are all implicated in the development of withdrawal symptoms. The symptoms of benzodiazepine withdrawal include anxiety, insomnia, sensitivity to light and sound, tachycardia, mild systolic hypertension, abdominal distress, headaches, tremor, craving, and in the worst cases, seizures. The longer the elimination half-life, the greater the chance for build up of high levels of these medications. In the elderly, this may cause excessive daytime sedation, confusion, and amnesia (American Psychiatric Association, 1990).

The long half-life benzodiazepines appear to be helpful in patients with generalized anxiety disorder (GAD) in which a once-a-day dosing with a long half-life medication may have a beneficial effect that lasts throughout the day. Shorter half-life benzodiazepines have the advantage of producing less cognitive impairment with regular use. However, they appear to produce more severe withdrawal symptoms as well as more symptoms of anxiety between doses. Typical long half-life benzodiazepines include diazepam (Valium), chlordiazepoxide hydrochloride (Librium), and clorazepate (Tranxene). The shorter half-life benzodiazepines include lorazepam (Ativan), oxazepam (Serax) and alprazolam (Xanax).

Benzodiazepines also differ in potency, which is the number of milligrams needed to achieve the comparable clinical effect. The high-potency benzodiazepines have their clinical effect in dosages of 1–4 mg per day, and the lower potency benzodiazepines require 10–30 mg per day. The high-potency benzodiazepines appear to be more effective in suppressing panic attacks than the lower potency medications of this class (Baldessarini, 1985). The benzodiazepines are absorbed rapidly and completely through the gastrointestinal tract, although some presence of food may delay the process. Medications such as diazepam (Valium), or triazolam (Halcion) have a rapid onset, whereas chlordiazepoxide hydrochloride (Librium) and oxazepam (Serax) work more slowly. Most intramuscular injections of the benzodiazepines are absorbed poorly except for lorazepam (Ativan) (American Psychiatric Association, 1990).

There has been recent concern over triazolam (Halcion) and its behavioral manifestations. In a newsletter, Upjohn (1991) reported that memory impairment, "traveler's amnesia," confusion, agitation, and behavioral changes have been seen in patients taking triazolam. It is not evident whether these symptoms are due to the triazolam or to other confounding variables, such as other medications or the underlying illness. More controlled research is needed in this area.

Buspirone (BuSpar) is an azapirone derivative and a partial serotonin agonist that is unrelated to the benzodiazepine class. It appears in early clinical trials to be as effective as the benzodiazepines in the treatment of generalized anxiety disorder (see "Anxiety Disorders"). The recommended dosage of buspirone is 20–60 mg per day.

Buspirone appears to be safe in combination with other medications except monoamine oxidase inhibitors, which can cause elevated blood pressure. It is also contraindicated in combination with haloperidol, as it can increase the blood levels of haloperidol.

In contrast to the rapid onset of the benzodiazepines, buspirone has a gradual onset of 3–4 weeks before a significant clinical effect is obtained. In a clinical study, Rickles (1990) found that clorazepate (Tranxene) produced significantly better relief from anxiety in the early stages of treatment than did buspirone. However, after 4 weeks of treatment the two medications showed equal results. Patients should be aware of buspirone's delayed onset of action to maintain compliance with the medication treatment.

Buspirone produces relatively little sedation or interaction with central nervous system depressants and no enhancement effect with alcohol. Therefore, in patients with histories of alcohol of substance abuse, benzodiazepines may be contraindicated because of abuse potential. Buspirone, however, does not cause physiological dependence or withdrawal symptoms and can be used in the chemically dependent population. Buspirone produces unpleasant reactions in doses above therapeutic levels, which dissuades patients from abusing the medication (Kaplan & Sadock, 1990). The major side effects of buspirone include dizziness, headache, nausea, light-headedness, and excitement (Rickles, 1990).

The treatment of anxiety disorders is not as well defined as in other disorders due to the overlap of symptomatology and subjective etiology. Antidepressants such as the tricyclic antidepressants, the monamine oxidase inhibitors, and the newer-generation antidepressants such as fluextine (Prozac) in some cases appear to be as effective as the benzodiazepines in treating anxiety disorders. (See "Antidepressive Agents" for more information.)

SCHIZOPHRENIA

Schizophrenia is a serious debilitating mental illness with disturbances in many psychological processes. Since the development of the first antipsychotic agent, chlorpromazine in 1952, there has been much progress in the development of medications to treat schizophrenia. In this section the discrete characteristics of schizophrenia will be briefly discussed, followed by the current medication treatments.

Schizophrenia is a thought disorder in which a cluster of psychotic symptoms significantly impairs daily functioning. The diagnosis is made when the symptoms are not due to a mood disorder, organic syndrome, psychoactive substance abuse, or schizoaffective disorder. The disorder is chronic with a prodromal, an active, and a residual phase. The prodromal phase is characterized by a steady decrease in functioning with marked impairment in social isolation and personal hygiene. During the active phase hallucinations and or delusions are present along with characteristic disturbances in affect or thought. The residual phase follows the active phase of the disturbance with persistence of marked social isolation, markedly peculiar behavior, for example, hoarding food, collecting garbage, talking to self in public, disturbances in speech, blunted or inappropriate affect, and odd beliefs (Kaplan & Sadock, 1990). The duration of the time spent in each of the phases must total 6 months. This is to help ensure that schizophrenia can be differentiated from brief psychotic episodes. For the complete description of the criterion, the DSM-III-R must be consulted.

The similarities between amphetamine-induced psychoses, Parkinson's disease, and schizophrenia have lead scientists to construct the dopamine hypothesis, a theory that implicates the role of dopamine in causing schizophrenia. The theory postulates that an abundance of dopamine postsynaptic receptor sites or an overproduction of dopamine at the presynaptic terminal causes the symptoms of schizophrenia (Pincus & Tucker, 1985).

Schizophrenia is not caused by a single factor. The differentiation between Type I and Type II schizophrenia is seen in the different spectrum of symptoms. This system classifies schizophrenic patients into either Type I, productive or positive symptoms, and Type II, deficit or negative symptoms. The positive symptoms refer to additions to the patient's behavioral repetiore such as delusions, hallucinations, loosening of thought associations, bizarre behavior, and increased speech. Negative symptoms include flattened affect, social withdrawal, anhedonia, poverty of speech or content, and cognitive and attention deficits.

The symptoms are a reflection of the underlying defect. Negative symptoms usually reflect structural changes in the brain. The patients with Type II symptoms respond poorly to medication and have a grave prognosis (Rosenhan & Seligman, 1989). Positive symptoms have been associated with an excess of catecholamines (Volkow et al., 1988). The patients with Type I symptoms respond well to antipsychotic medications and have a much more favorable prognosis.

The antipsychotic agents include a large number of compounds that are useful in the treatment of not only schizophrenia but also mania, organic psychosis, and Guilles de la Tourette's disorder (Mason & Granacher, 1980). The term *neuroleptic* is often used synonymously with *antipsychotic agent* due to the neurological effects of these medications (Baldessarini, 1985). There are six classes of antipsychotic agents, of which the phenothiazines are the more commonly used.

The basic property that all the antipsychotic medications share is the inhibition of dopamine in the brain. The areas of the brain that are abundant with dopamine cells are the nigrostriatal pathway, the mesolimbic pathway, and the tuberoinfundibular pathway. Antipsychotic medication binds to the dopamine receptor and blocks the dopamine from binding to the cell receptor. Antipsychotic medications differ in potency, that is, the ability of the size of the dose to alleviate the symptoms of schizophrenia.

The phenothiazine chlorpromazine (Thorazine) was initially introduced in France in the early 1950s as a preanesthetic agent. Because of its calming effect, it was tried on psychotic hospital populations and was found to be the first effective treatment for psychosis and behavioral agitation. This was a true milestone in the development of psychopharmacology as a discipline and introduced a more humane treatment of schizophrenia (Baldessarini, 1985).

The phenothiazines are divided into three classes of medications, each varying in potency and side effect profile. High-potency medications are linked to extrapyramidal side effects, whereas the low-potency compounds produce more sedation, orthostatic hypotension, and anticholinergic side effects, including weight gain, dry mouth, blurred vision, constipation, and urinary retention. Extrapyramidal side effects are movement disorders associated with tremors, muscular rigidity, and loss of movement.

Chlorpromazine (Thorazine) is a widely used aliphatic phenothiazine with low potency. The piperazine group of the phenothiazines has a higher potency than the aliphatics that create less sedation but also cause a high degree of extrapyramidal side effects. The medications in this group include perphenazine (Trilafon), trifluoperazine (Stelazine), fluphenazine (Prolixin), and acetophenazine (Tindal). Perphenazine seems to produce slightly more sedation and cardiovascular effects than the other medications in this group. Trifluoperazine is generally well tolerated and the neurological side effects are treated with other medications, such as benztropine (Cogentin). Fluphenazine is available in an injectable form with long-acting properties that allow the patient to receive an injection once every 2 weeks.

The last subgroup of the phenothiazines is the piperidines, which include thioridazine (Mellaril), and mesoridazine (Serentil). Thioridazine is used more often and produces a lower incidence of extrapyramidal symptoms. The other side effects are similar to chlorpromazine's.

Haloperidol (Haldol) is one of two in the class of the butyrophenones that are widely used. The antipsychotic effects of this compound were discovered accidentally by Paul Janssen in Belgium while he was experimenting with derivatives of Demerol to find a new analgesic. Haloperidol is highly potent due to its blocking action on the D2 receptors. Although haloperidol has high potency and produces less hypotension, it also increases the risk of extrapyramidal side effects. This medication is widely used by physicians; it has few cardiovascular and anticholinergic side effects. Haloperidol also produces less sedation than the phenothiazines. The side effects of haloperidol are treated as they emerge in each patient.

The patients who are treatment resistant or do not respond to the typical antipsychotic medication have always posed a challenge to physicians. Clozapine (Clozaril) is a newer antipsychotic medication that is classified as a dibenzodiazepine. It is atypical due to its unique way of binding to the dopamine receptors. It does not appear to cause extrapyramidal side effects due to the location of the dopamine receptors to which clozapine binds. It is more active at the limbic than at the striatal dopamine receptors. It has been proposed that the blocking action in the limbic system is associated with antipsychotic effects, whereas the blockade of dopamine receptors in the striatal system is associated with extrapyramidal side effects. This medication shows promise with patients who experience more negative symptomatology and who previously would have had a chronic prognosis.

The most adverse reaction to clozapine is the development of agranulocytosis, a dangerously low white blood cell count due to bone marrow suppression. Although the drug is controversial, in the United States strict monitoring and control of clozapine use has been instituted to assure compliance with blood screening to avoid lethal reactions. Other side effects of clozapine include low blood pressure, fever, increased heartbeat, and sedation (Lieberman, Kane, & Johns, 1989).

Antipsychotic medications produce a wide range of side effects as a result of the number and type of neurotransmitter systems affected. Many patients become discouraged and abandon treatment due to the side effects. The more disturbing neurological side effects, such as *acute dystonias, akathisia, tardive dyskinesia, neuroleptic malignant syndrome,* and *Parkinsonism,* are unique to the antipsychotics. This is indicative of central nervous system toxicity because symptoms are manifested through these motor syndromes. It is vital for the clinician to recognize these symptoms as side effects of the medication and not as an exacerbation of the disease.

Acute dystonias usually occur rapidly and are associated with the more potent neuroleptics. Symptoms are involuntary muscle contractions that cause uncontrolled movements of the face, neck, tongue, and back. Oculogyric crisis is a dystonic reaction where the eyes roll uncontrollably. These symptoms respond well to antiparkinsonian medication.

Akathisia is an inner sense of restlessness sometimes accompanied by motor restlessness. The patient may report this subjectively or it may be observed objectively. These symptoms may be confused with schizophrenic agitation. Akathisia responds to the antiparkinsonian medications as well as beta blockers (propanolol), although a decrease in the neuroleptic is also warranted.

Tardive dyskinesia is a late onset disorder which occurs months to years after beginning neuroleptic treatment. This condition may be irreversible even after withdrawal of the antipsychotic medication. The syndrome consists of involuntary movements of a rapid, ticlike (choreiform) nature. It begins as jerky movements of the tongue and face and can progress to writhing movements of the entire body. Patients diagnosed as having mainly negative symptoms, or those with mood disorders, have been shown to be at higher risk for developing tardive dyskinesia. The younger the patient, the better the prognosis for reversal of the syndrome. There is also a higher risk of developing tardive dyskinesia in people who are older and in women (Lickey & Gordon, 1991).

Neuroleptic malignant syndrome, or "hypothalmic crisis," usually occurs early in treatment and is a severe reaction that manifests itself in high fever, catatonia, and extreme muscular rigidity. Neuroleptic treatment is immediately discontinued and hospitalization is required to monitor vital signs and for intravenous medications. There has been a reported 20% mortality rate associated with this syndrome; however, early diagnosis has significantly reduced this rate. The antiparkinsonian medications are not routinely beneficial and may worsen the syndrome. The dopamine agonist bromocriptine mesylate (Parlodel) seems to be helpful and the symptoms usually abate gradually within a week or two (Baldessarini, 1985).

These symptoms seem logical due to the depletion of dopamine that occurs in both Parkinson's disease and in the presence of the neuroleptics. Both can produce similar manifestations: an expressionless face, shuffling gait, and severe tremor. These symptoms are treated effectively with the antiparkinsonian medications that partially block acetycholine synapses or that indirectly increase dopamine. Conversely, some abnormal movements that resemble parkinsonian symptoms are actually schizophrenic symptoms not controlled by medication. The physician is able to distinguish between the two by administering an antiparkinsonian medication such as benztropine (Cogentin) or trihexylphenidyl (Artane).

CONCLUSION

Medication and other somatic therapies can alleviate, and in some cases even eradicate, the symptoms and illnesses that are prevalent throughout society. These somatic treatments have afforded relief and freedom to many people who otherwise would have been institutionalized for life. There is a promising future for further advances and refinement in somatic therapies that will provide clinicians with potent treatments with minimal side effects in the years to come.

The advantage of medication advancement to non-physician counselors is the ability of the therapist to work more effectively with the patient. Severe psychiatric symptoms can interfere with progress in psychotherapy. The medication, if properly monitored, can actually provide patients with relief from the symptoms that impair their functioning in daily life and in the therapeutic process of psychotherapy thus allowing the benefits of psychotherapy to be utilized. The use of pharmacotherapy in conjunction with psychotherapy has been shown to be more effective in some patients than either medication or psychotherapy alone (Klerman, 1991).

Over the past decade more non-physician counselors have been primarily responsible for providing mental health care services to the population. The integration of pharmacotherapy and psychotherapy has become an important issue for discussion and understanding. Although attitudes and ideologies regarding medication therapy differ among clinicians, it is important for counselors to examine the cost and benefit to the patient when selecting a mode of therapy.

FOR FURTHER READING

Gitlin, M. J. (1990). *The psychotherapist's guide to psychopharmacology.* New York: Free Press.

Schatzberg, A. F. & Alan, J. O. (1991). *Manual of clinical psychopharmacology* (2nd ed.). Washington, DC: American Psychiatric Press.

Kaplan, H. I., & Sadock, B. J. (1990). *Pocket handbook of clinical psychiatry.* Baltimore: Williams & Wilkins.

REFERENCES

American Psychiatric Association. (1987). *Diagnostic and statistical manual of mental disorders* (3rd ed. rev., DSM-III-R). Washington, DC: Author.

American Psychiatric Association. (1990). *Benzodiazepine dependence, toxicity, and abuse.* Washington, DC: Author.

Aya, F. J. (Ed). (1992). Sertraline: The latest FDA approved serotonin uptake inhibitor antidepressant. *International Drug Therapy Newsletter.* Baltimore: Aya Medical Communications.

Baldessarini, R. J. (1985). *Chemotherapy in psychiatry.* Cambridge: Harvard University Press.

Baldessarini, R. J. (1989). Current status of antidepressants: Clinical pharmacology and therapy. *Journal of Clinical Psychiatry, 52,* 18–23.

Ballenger, J. C. (1991). Long-term pharmacologic treatment of panic disorder. *Journal of Clinical Psychiatry, 52,* pp. 18–23.

DuPont, R. L. (1990). Thinking about stopping treatment for panic disorder. *Journal of Clinical Psychiatry, 51.* 38–45.

Fava, M., & Rosenbaum, J. F. (1991). Suicidality and fluoxetine: Is there a relationship? *Journal of Clinical Psychiatry, 52,* 108–111.

Helzer, J. F., Robins, L. N., & McEvoy, L. (1987). Post-traumatic stress disorder in the general population: Findings of the Epidemiologic Catchment Area survey. *New England Journal of Medicine, 317,* 1630–1634.

Kaplan, H. I., & Sadock, B. I. (1989). *Comprehensive textbook of psychiatry,* (5th ed.). Baltimore: Williams & Wilkins.

Kaplan, H. I., & Sadock, B. I. (1990). *Handbook of clinical psychiatry.* Baltimore: Williams & Wilkins.

Katon, W., Von Korff, M., Lin, E., Bush, T., & Ormel, J. (1992). Adequacy and duration of antidepressant treatment in primary care. *Medical Care, 8,* 67–118.

Leibenluft, E., & Wehr, T. (1992). Is sleep deprivation useful in the treatment of depression? *The American Journal of Psychiatry, 149,* 2.

Lieberman, J. A., Kane, J. M., & Johns, C. J. (1989). Clozapine: Guidelines for clinical management. *Journal of Clinical Psychiatry.* 50, 319–338.

Lickey, M. E., & Gordon, B. (1991). *Medicine and mental illness.* New York: Freeman.

Mason, A. S., & Granacher, R. P. (1980). *Clinical handbook of antipsychotic drug therapy.* New York: Brunner/Mazel.

Mavissakalian, M., Turner, S. M., Michelson, L., & Jacob, R. (1985). Tricyclic antidepressants in obsessive-compulsive disorder: Antiobsessional or antidepressant agents? *The American Journal of Psychiatry, 142*, 572–576.

McElroy, S. L., Keck, P. E., & Pope, H. G. (1988). Valproate in the treatment of rapid-cycling bipolar disorder. *Journal of Clinical Psychopharmacology, 8*, 275–279.

McGlynn, T. J., & Metcalf, H. L. (Eds.). (1989). *Diagnosis and treatment of anxiety disorders: A physician's handbook.* Washington, DC: American Psychiatric Press.

Myers, J. K., Weissman, M. M., Tischler, G. L., Holzer, C. M. III, Leaf, P. J., Orvaschel, H., Anthony, J. C., Boyd, J. H., Burke, J. D., Kramer, M., & Stoltzman, R. (1984). Six-month prevalence of psychiatric disorders in three communities: 1980–1982. *Archives of General Psychiatry, 41*, 959–967.

Physicians' desk reference. (1992). Montvale, NJ: Medical Economics Data.

Pincus, J. H., & Tucker, G. J. (1985). *Behavioral neurology.* New York: Oxford University Press.

Poling, A., Gadow, K. D., & Cleary, J. (1991). *Drug therapy for behavior disorders.* New York: Pergamon Press.

Post, R. M., Uhde, T. W., & Ballenger, J. C. (1983). Prophylactic efficacy of carbamazepine in manic-depressive illness. *American Journal of Psychiatry, 140*, 1602–04.

Quitkin, F. M., McGrath, P. J., Rabkin, J. G., Stewart, J. W., Harrison, W., Ross, D. C., Triamo, E., Fleiss, J., Markowitz, J., & Klein, D. F. (1991). Different types of placebo response in patients receiving antidepressants. *American Journal of Psychiatry, 148*, 197–203.

Rapee, R. M. (1991). Generalized anxiety disorder: A review of clinical features and theoretical concepts. *Clinical Psychology Review, 11*, 419–440.

Rickles, K. (1990). Buspirone in clinical practice. *Journal of Clinical Psychiatry, 51* (Suppl. 9), 51–54.

Rickles, K., Schweizer, E., Case, G., & Greenblatt, D. J. (1990a). Long-term therapeutic use of benzodiazepines: 1. Effects of abrupt discontinuation. *Archives of General Psychiatry, 47*, 899–907.

Risch, S. C., Janowsky, D. S., & Huey, L. Y. (1981). Plasma levels of tricyclic antidepressants and clinical efficacy. In S. J. Enna, J. B. Malick, and E. Richardson (Eds.), *Antidepressants: Neurochemical, behavioral, and clinical perspectives* (pp. 183–217). New York: Raven Press.

Robins, L. N., Helzer, J. E., Weissman, M. M., Orvaschel, H., Gruenberg, E., Burke, J. D., & Regier, D. A. (1984). Lifetime prevalence of specific psychiatric disorders in three sites. *Archives of General Psychiatry, 41*. 949–958.

Roose, S. P., & Glassman, A. H. (Eds.). (1990). *Treatment strategies for refractory depression.* Washington, DC: American Psychiatric Press.

Rosenhan, D. L., & Seligman, M. E. P. (1989). *Abnormal psychology.* New York: Norton.

Schneier, F. R. (1991). Social phobia. *Psychiatric Annals, 21*, 349–353.

Tomb, D. A. (1988). *Psychiatry for the house officer.* Baltimore: Williams & Wilkins.

Upjohn. (1991). *Important information about Halcion tablets.* Michigan: The Upjohn Company.

Volknow, N. D., Wolf, A. P., Van Gelder, P., Brodie, J. D., Overall, J. E., Cancro, R., & Gomez-Mont, F. (1987). Phenomenological correlates of metabolic activity in 18 patients with chronic schizophrenia. *The American Journal of Psychiatry, 144*, 151–158.

2

SENSITIVITY:
ISSUES FOR
CONTEMPORARY
COUNSELORS

This section of *The Counseling Sourcebook* looks at issues that affect the counseling relationship. When two people meet for the first time, there are many conscious and unconscious factors—assumptions, appraisals, feeling, and so on—at work that fill the gaps where information about each other ultimately will go.

Contemporary approaches to counseling increasingly recognize and assertively articulate that counselors should be aware of how culture, religion, ethnicity, gender, socioeconomics, and other counselor-client differences affect counseling. When counselors are unaware of these variables, they may inappropriately use their personal biases and value systems as internal, absolute standards of normalcy or "good adjustment."

Freud long ago spoke of *countertransference*, the therapist's irrational attitudes toward the patient, and thereby cautioned us about "blind spots" that interfere with accurate perception or optimal therapeutic relationship with the client. All counselors have values and make judgments, but if they have genuine regard for clients, they will be watchful that their biases will not become the focus of counseling. In evaluating the impact of culturally based assumptions or their ability to help persons with diverse lifestyles and cultural backgrounds, practitioners from the various counseling professions should undertake a self-appraisal to determine where value judgments might lead to insensitivity and harm to the client.

Counseling is an activity that is designed neither to validate another's lifestyle nor to approve of a client's cultural, gender, racial, or ethnic identity. Counselors must therefore be alert to the feelings they bring into the counseling session that can be communicated as messages of criticism, devaluation, or hostility. It is probably accurate to state that no counselor is entirely free of bias and value judgments. Counselors can serve clients better when they monitor and understand their own countertransference and biased conscious appraisals.

In the same vein, counselors must be sensitive to the burden of trust they bear when a client comes to them and to their many responsibilities to practice ethically and within the law. Ethical standards are becoming more clearly developed, and counselors must increasingly be made aware of the interpersonal and legal consequences of their failure to know and comply with these ethical standards. Awareness and monitoring of such issues often supply another level of stress to an already stressful occupation, but vigilance and knowledge are vital.

Contemporary counselors need to be as up-to-date about legal and ethical factors as they are about the latest treatment methods. Unethical or extralegal behavior by counselors may introduce iatrogenic or doctor-caused difficulties for the client—an unneeded source of difficulty in an already complex but potentially rewarding relationship.

8

Counseling People with Communication Disorders

GERARD B. BROOKS, M.A., C.C.C.

I communicate, therefore I am. The messages I communicate are temporary, abstract, yet they are my sole means of externalizing my otherwise hidden "inner self." Communication is the primary means by which we experience each other. It is a means of experiencing myself through interaction with others, and therefore communication contributes to the creation of my "identity."

Communication helps me succeed in the world. I use it to gain recognition and approval for my ideas. I learn, inform, persuade, request, beg indulgence, gain compliance, and win cooperation from others through the communication that takes place via my words and actions.

Communication is a bridge to intimacy and self-exploration. It is a means of showing my concern and affection for others. It allows the wonder, doubt, hurt, joy, and all the other emotions I feel inside to be expressed and shared. Skillful communication can transform inevitable interpersonal conflicts into ever more fulfilling relationships. My life's purpose can become clearer by communicating my experiences with others. No less than how instinct serves our less brainy fellow creatures, communication is how I—how we humans—survive.

Whether or not we acknowledge it, communication is challenging for all of us. But for 1 in 10 children and adults who experience a speech, language, or hearing disorder, reliable communication is simply out of reach.

Most people with these disorders struggle daily and mightily with the process, grasping for a hold in our hyperverbal society, attempting to escape agonizing isolation. Because of the high incidence and emotional consequences of communication disorders, a counselor is very likely to come into contact with a number of communicatively disordered individuals or their family members. It is hoped the information in this chapter will provide a background and some specific recommendations that the professional counselor will find valuable.

In an attempt to organize the information in this chapter for ready reference, first decide which of these two designations best fits the individual in question:

1. **Acquired Disability.** This term applies to individuals who communicated normally until the onset of some illness or injury.
2. **Developmental Disability.** This term applies to individuals who did not develop effective communication skills as a result of some defect present at birth, or whose problem occurred early enough in life to prevent normal development from taking place. It also includes individuals who may have achieved functional communication skills, but only as a result of some specialized treatment or device.

TERMINOLOGY

Many terms are used to describe communication and its defects. The lay person might use such terms as *speech, articulation, voice,* and *language* more or less interchangeably. Speech-language pathologists use these terms with more precision, but there is still considerable terminological inconsistency. For the purposes of this chapter, the following definitions apply:

1. **Communication.** A total interpersonal event involving the intentions, verbal messages, physical actions, and outcomes of human interactions.
2. **Speech disorder.** A difficulty producing any of the sounds of speech used to convey language orally.
3. **Language disorder.** Any difficulty comprehending or expressing oneself by oral or written means not primarily attributable to perceptual, motor, general intellectual, emotional, or speech disorders. When language disorder is acquired as a result of some illness or injury affecting the brain, it is referred to as *aphasia.*

Speech disorders can be caused by defects in either the structure or function of the speech system, a system that includes the respiratory system, the voice box or larynx, and certain other key physical structures involved in the reinforcement of the voice and the articulation of speech sounds within the throat and mouth.

Speech disorders can be further subdivided into *voice disorders* and *articulation disorders.* In general, problems with audibility, pitch, or the underlying tonal quality of speech are considered voice disorders (section 1). Problems with the intelligibility or pronunciation of specific words are considered articulation disorders (section 2 and 3). Note: Some problems create both voice and articulation disorders, for example, cleft palate speech.

A language disorder may manifest itself primarily in oral communication. However, individuals who have difficulties in oral communication frequently have difficulties in reading and writing as well.

1. VOICE DISORDERS

In general, any speech problem involving audibility, pitch, or the quality of the underlying voice tone is considered a voice disorder if it interferes with effective message production or otherwise detracts from communication. This is as contrasted with problems that affect the quality of particular speech sounds, or words, which are referred to as *articulation disorders* (see sections 2 and 3).

Physical Causes
The human voice depends on respiration, vocal cord vibration, and reinforcement of vocal cord vibration by various other resonating structures. Therefore, difficulties with breathing, problems affecting the vocal cords, or significant variations in key resonators—especially those immediately adjacent to the airway—can produce a voice disorder.

Some examples of physical causes of voice disorders are improper development of the larynx or pharynx, neurological disease, paralysis of one or both vocal cords, growths on the vocal cords, surgical removal of the voice box, and emphysema.

Functional Causes
Many individuals experience temporary voice problems as a result of a cold, allergies, laryngitis, excessive vocal use, or stress. The vocalist may unconsciously adopt a new way of producing voice under such conditions in an understandable attempt to maintain his or her voice. However, these compensations are often based on improper techniques that create strain, and if they are habituated, a chronic functional voice disorder may result.

Many people produce voices in ways that are adequate under conditions of modest vocal demand. However, such voices may not be equal to the demands of frequent public speaking, teaching, lengthy sales presentations, and other such vocal challenges. Individuals who have been promoted, changed jobs, recently reentered the work force, or changed careers are at risk for voice problems if their new circumstances involve vocal demands that are significantly greater than the previous circumstances.

Some people unintentionally abuse the voice mechanism with excessive throat clearing, smoking, yelling, and other behaviors that undermine the ability of the voice mechanism to function naturally. Chronic vocal irritants can cause chronic voice problems.

Puberphonia or "mutational falsetto" is a condition of inappropriately maintaining a preadolescent voice after physical maturation has occurred. This may not be a "functional" disorder, however. Among the possible causes of this condition listed by Aronson (1985) are psychologic immaturity, delayed maturation due to an endocrine disorder, severe hearing loss, neurologic disease during puberty, and general debilitating illness during puberty.

Psychological Causes

There may be some psychological involvement contributing to many cases of voice disorder. In some cases, voice disorder may reflect frank underlying psychopathology. A landmark work that associates specific voice characteristics with various psychological states is Moses's *The Voice of Neurosis* (1954).

Conversion muteness is a condition where an emotional conflict is somatized in the form of complete inability to generate voice, except perhaps in a whisper. But many less dramatic conditions often have some basis in the underlying emotional state of the individual. A psychogenic basis for a voice disorder can only be considered after a medical basis has been ruled out.

Once a medical evaluation has ruled out physical problems, a speech-language pathologist's assessment is appropriate because despite the initial cause of a voice disorder, vocal habits form quickly. As a result, psychotherapy alone may not resolve even a "purely psychogenic" voice symptom unless the maladaptive vocal habits are reversed by voice therapy.

Removal of the voice symptom through voice therapy has been shown to be highly effective with a brief course of treatment. Symptomatic voice therapy is not generally associated with psychological side effects, and, in the case of a conversion reaction, typically does not result in *symptom replacement* (the emergence of a new psychosomatic symptom to take the place of the one removed).

Finally, people can of course have psychological problems complicated by, yet largely unrelated to, functional dysphonias. This is one more reason why collaboration between the mental health professional and a speech-language pathologist can be fortuitous.

The interested reader is referred to Aronson (1985) for an excellent discussion of evaluation and treatment techniques for voice disorders, including an in-depth discussion of the complex interrelationship of psychological, organic, and functional factors that both precipitate and maintain these disorders.

Voice disorders should never be ignored. Several serious adult diseases show themselves first in a subtle change in voice quality or in a frank tremulousness of the voice. Growths on the vocal cords can be produced by chronic abuse of the voice. Such growths may continue to worsen and further degrade the voice without some form of intervention.

Treatment Considerations and Making Referrals

In all cases individuals with suspected voice disorders should have a thorough medical evaluation. Such an evaluation should include a laryngoscopic examination.

Treatment may involve simple voice rest, medication, surgery, voice therapy, or some combination, depending on the cause and severity of the voice disorder. When medical problems are ruled out, or as they are being treated, treatment of the voice itself by a speech-language pathologist is often appropriate. Even in cases where there appears to be a clear psychogenic basis, psychotherapy alone may not alleviate the voice symptom, as discussed above. Symptomatic voice treatment is usually quick, effective, and safe.

2. DEVELOPMENTAL ARTICULATION DISORDERS

Articulation is the act of producing—and sequencing into words—the individual sounds of speech that roughly correspond to the letters of the alphabet. Speech begins with air being first pushed up from the lungs and then vibrated by the vocal cords. This vibrated column of air is then "valved" from second to second as a result of being forced through various narrowings or past obstructions in the throat and mouth. Each individual speech sound is a result of one or more of these valving actions. A congenital problem that affects any of the structures along this pathway may cause a developmental articulation problem.

A child may also fail to produce standard speech sounds because he or she has developed a habit of mispronunciation. Such a habit may relate to underlying developmental problems. For example, a habit of mispronunciation can begin when a child must simplify, omit, or distort certain sounds or sound combinations in order to accommodate an immature perceptual, motor, and linguistic system. Finally, a child may fail to produce standard speech sounds due to a hearing loss.

Not every misarticulation is a "disorder." It takes a while for a child to distinguish all of the English speech sounds and then to produce each of them perfectly and in the proper sequence within each word. Many interrelated yet separate skills are developing at slightly different rates during childhood. Basic perceptual and motor skills are developing. Vocabulary, reasoning, and grammatical skills are growing. Even the mouth and throat themselves are changing.

Think of communication as a football game in which the "ball" is a message and the "goal" is a listener's mind. The child is like the quarterback of a team of rookies. Eventually the team comes together, but fumbles and misarticulations are a normal part of development.

However, we know that some children who misarticulate will not develop adult-sounding speech without professional help. In some cases, distinguishing who will from who will not is quite clear. Children born with cerebral palsy or cleft palate will usually require some degree of professional intervention. But there are many less straightforward cases.

When to Refer for an Evaluation
Because a child who needs help is much better off getting it early before speech and socialization patterns are entrenched, a referral should be considered whenever there is doubt. The longer misarticulation remains unresolved, the greater the potential for serious developmental consequences, especially if the misarticulations are significant enough to attract attention to themselves or to interfere with intelligibility.

Either of the following is a specific criterion for referring a child for an evaluation:

1. if the child is unintelligible to significant others, especially members of the immediate family and peers
2. if the child shows signs of embarrassment over his or her speech, or reluctance to speak at all

Note: Some children appear to react to not being understood by becoming domineering rather than by becoming communicatively passive. This may be because incessant talking serves to keep others at a safe distance.

Don't "wait and see." If a child meets the criteria described above, delaying professional attention threatens social and emotional development and academic achievement. Sometimes parents just need the reassurance that can only occur after they feel that their child has had a thorough "going over" and after they have specific information concerning their child's development, for example, test scores pertaining to the components of communicative development. This may be reason enough to justify referring for an evaluation.

In cases where your concern is *not* shared by a parent, an evaluation is a method by which to present the facts in a highly objective manner that will hopefully serve to motivate the parent to take the next step (treatment).

How to Refer
Speech-language pathologists are the professionals trained to evaluate and to treat communication and swallowing disorders. Most states license speech-language pathologists and the American Speech-Language-Hearing Association (ASHA) certifies speech-language pathologists. The initials *C.C.C.* after a professional's name indicate possession of ASHA's board certification.

The professional should be experienced with children. The setting may be the private office of an independant practitioner, a school, a hospital, or a free-standing rehabilitation center.

The interpretation of testing and of clinical observations of the child must be made within the context of a larger picture created from input from other professionals. You can expedite the referral by having the child's parent arrange for the following to be available to the speech-language pathologist:

- medical history
- developmental history
- academic history (if applicable)
- psychoeducational summary (if available)
- social history
- a complete hearing test

Counseling Parents
Here are some important points to make in speaking with parents about speech difficulties:

Reinforce the idea that misarticulations are common in childhood. Try and put them at ease, whether or not you intend to refer them for an evaluation. Most children outgrow their misarticulations. The majority of children who do require treatment fully resolve their difficulties.

In particularly severe cases, normal or intelligible speech may be a long-range goal or an unattainable one. In this case speech-language pathologists have at their disposal a wide array of what are referred to as "augmentative" communication devices. With such devices, individuals without speaking ability can communicate quite extensively. The more sophisticated devices rely upon assistance of a microcomputer.

Offer reassurance that they did nothing to cause the problem. Virtually all speech disorders are organically based and not caused by "bad parenting."

Instruct parents that speech errors are not due to the child's "laziness." With very rare exceptions, children want to be understood and they are making the very best of what they have.

A child who is in therapy needs a lot of praise and encouragement. As normal speakers, we take for granted the freedom to focus on our thoughts, words, and our listener's reactions. We expect our words to come off of our tongues automatically. When they don't—when we occasionally get tongue-tied—we get embarrassed and may lose our train of thought. Paying attention to one's speech is very unnatural and very difficult, yet this is precisely what therapy requires of a child. Adults in general must understand that the tongue of a child with an articulation disorder is "tied up" all the time.

Some parents may need to be sensitized to the need to provide support for their child. Others may need to be shown *how* to support their child emotionally during a course of speech therapy that may last a year or more.

Teach parents how to adjust their communication behavior. (See suggestions given under "Counseling Children.")

Counseling Children

Assume the child is aware of the problem. In most cases it's safe to assume that the child has some awareness of their speech problem ranging from vague to acute. A child with an articulation problem severe enough to degrade intelligibility is frequently asked to repeat by adults. Some well-meaning adults may interrupt virtually every statement the child makes to correct one or more words. Very young children may get a variety of puzzling responses from peers. Older children are often the brunt of jokes and teasing.

It may be helpful to gently probe a child's level of awareness of their problem with questions such as "Is it hard to talk sometimes?" or "Do people say 'I don't understand you' a lot?" You may receive reactions ranging from a shy nodding of the head to abrupt tearfulness. Speech-impaired children are relieved to know someone understands.

It may also be helpful to provide them with the language for labeling their problem. Some children are never told they have a "speech problem" until they are seen by a speech-language pathologist. Identifying the entity responsible for puzzling reactions and negative or previously inchoate feelings can be quite a relief. This is especially true if a child had learned to identify his or her problem as "stupidity," "laziness," or in other less perjorative but equally inaccurate terms.

Adjust your communication behavior. You must compensate for a child who has difficulty speaking clearly.

1. Look relaxed and slow your pace of speaking. If you hurry, or appear to be in a hurry, the child may experience anxiety and feel the need to speak quickly, which adds to their problem in most cases.
2. Be very clear that you are aware of their difficulty speaking. Establish an attitude of working together to gain understanding. Explain that sometimes *you will need to help* if you get "stuck" trying to understand.
3. When you do "get stuck," remark calmly and casually, "Okay, now I'm stuck. I need your help. Will you try and help me?" Wait for a response. Assuming it is positive, proceed. "Maybe if you say it again I'll be able to understand you." Other strategies for getting "unstuck" include asking the child to use different words, asking the child to "say more and maybe I'll get unstuck," and asking the older child to repeat the most important word.
4. When you can't get unstuck, then remain calm and say something like the following in a positive tone of voice. "Well you're trying very hard to help me get unstuck. That's real good effort. I'm still stuck though, aren't I?" Wait for a response. "Let's talk about something else for now."

Over time this type of an approach will be acceptable to most children even if you get stuck quite often. Perhaps this is because you are demonstrating a willingness to *try* and understand, you are sharing the burden of communication with them, and you are demonstrating that relationships don't have to break down even though communication often does.

3. ACQUIRED ARTICULATION DISORDERS

Any injury, disease process, or surgery that affects any of the structures along the pathway between the lungs and mouth (see section 2) may cause an acquired articulation problem. Many acquired articulation disorders arise from disease or injury affecting the central nervous system, such as stroke, Parkinson's disease, multiple sclerosis, or head injury. Cancer of the head and/or neck can also result in articulation disorder as a consequence of changing essential oral structures, for example, cancer of the tongue.

Many times articulation, voice, and swallowing problems are acquired simultaneously. Because virtually the identical musculature is employed for speech and swallowing, some individuals with acquired articulation disorders also have difficulties with voice (see section 1) and/or swallowing. Swallowing difficulty is referred to as *dysphagia,* and speech-language pathologists play an integral role in the treatment of dysphagia caused by oral or pharyngeal dysfunction.

Treatment Considerations

There are many treatment options. As with developmental articulation disorders, acquired articulation disorders occur in varying severities, from mild to profound. Most are treatable to some extent, and the individual's speech can often be returned to a highly functional state if not to complete normalcy. Some individuals can recover functional speaking ability through a combination of restorative therapy in addition to the use of a prosthetic of some kind.

The most severe cases may not significantly respond to treatment. In such cases the speech-language pathologist has a wide array of nonoral assistive devices that can allow the person to communicate—sometimes quite extensively—without speech. Many of the newer devices employ microcomputer technology.

Treatment can be complicated by concurrent disabilities or by the concurrent treatments necessitated by the same disability. For example, it is not uncommon for stroke patients to have co-occurring difficulties with swallowing and voice (see section 3) and with articulation and language (see section 4). Cancer patients must often undergo radiation treatments that produce side effects that may serve to limit, at least temporarily, the individual's response to treatment. Medications or multiphase surgical treatments are other examples of influences that may interfere with treatment.

Counseling Families

Assume the family is in virtual disarray. One of the primary difficulties in a family's attempt to cope with a member with an acquired communication disorder is the extraordinary suddenness with which it occurs. Strokes and head injuries happen "out of the blue," and families often suffer disorganization caused by the abrupt role shifts that can result.

Furthermore, acquired communication disorders most often occur within a context of complex and severe medical disability. The family's physical, emotional, and economic resources are severely challenged and may be quickly depleted.

The health care system adds its own unique stresses. With the current emphasis on reducing lengths of stay in hospitals, patients may return home totally incapacitated within weeks or even within days of the accident or illness. They may be accompanied by intimidating medical paraphernalia required to maintain their health, with complex treatment regimens such as those required for wounds or bedsores, and they may be quickly followed by an army of nurses and therapists for many months afterward. All of this serves to transform the patient's home into something that more closely resembles a MASH unit.

Obviously, some families deal with the sequelae of such a catastrophy more readily than others. But it would be hard to argue that any family is prepared for such an event, and many must deal with the emotional aftermath entirely on their own. Mental health services are often not considered until long after a family has become severely dysfunctional—if they are ever considered at all. Families themselves may not realize the need for such support as long as they continue to operate in a "survival mode." Therefore, assume the family is in need of a hand with practical "damage control" before attempting to engage them in emotional issues.

Some of the best support for the family is information. A number of specialized support and consumer groups exist that can be helpful. Some possible resources for support and/or information are listed at the end of this chapter.

Additionally, it is essential to have open lines of communication with the professionals who are engaged with the family or patient. Most speech-language pathologists would welcome such dialogue and could provide valuable insight into a particular patient's immediate situation, in terms of both rehabilitation potential and observations over the family's reactions to the patient.

Meet the patient yourself if at all possible. The emotional impact of a person's communication disability is not something that is well conveyed in a report. Therefore, it may be very instructive for you to experience communicating with the patient firsthand before attempting to counsel the family in this regard. What appears from accounts provided in professional reports to be a relatively superficial alteration in communication may represent something far more profound to a parent, child, or spouse.

It is sometimes more difficult for a family to accept communicative limitations as compared with limitations upon mobility or self-care. A change in the communication pattern of an individual may be perceived as a fundamental change in his or her personality, one that is difficult and sometimes impossible for the family or spouse to accept. For example, individuals who sustain even mild and moderate articulation problems may also exhibit problems with facial and vocal muscles that make them appear to have little or no affect because facial and vocal expressiveness is lacking. Of course, articulation problems may co-occur with actual changes in the person's thought process, mood, social behavior, and ability to use language.

Sometimes when families see someone else enjoying an interaction with a communicatively impaired loved one, they realize that relationship is still possible, that their loved one is still a person, still socially viable. Providing such a model for the family is another reason to meet the patient. While it is true that the speech-language pathologist already provides one communication role model, families may fail to identify with the speech professional in this regard. That is, they may continue to feel inadequate in relating to the patient because they believe that only the speech-language pathologist—by virtue of his or her special training—can do so. Receiving a "demonstration" from a second individual without the speech professional's degree of technical familiarity may be most helpful. Even witnessing you struggling good-naturedly to interact may be a powerful therapeutic.

A word of caution: Don't underestimate the patient's disability. It may be necessary to set aside several sessions before you can relate fairly comfortably with the patient and thus be in a position to model a "viable" exchange for the family. Consultation with the speech-language pathologist before meeting the patient may be helpful here, especially if the patient is using some assistive device to communicate. The speech-language pathologist may be able to offer tips on improving the naturalness of conversation within the patient's limitations that can then be modeled for the family.

Counseling Patients

Relax and slow your internal tempo. Individuals with acquired articulation disorders are usually adults, have most often had a catastrophic medical event, have many understandably conflicted emotions over themselves and their circumstance, may be physically disfigured, are probably struggling to communicate, and may be angry or depressed. For all of these reasons you should expect that your first and any subsequent interviews as well are not going to go smoothly.

It is possible that the patient will have (at least superficially) a good deal more tolerance for his or her circumstance than you will have with yourself in trying to communicate with him or her. So try to physically relax yourself and slow your own "internal metronome" as much as possible in order to accommodate what is likely to be a very slow-moving interaction.

I have trained myself to stop outside a patient's room before entering, take a breath, and then walk slowly into the room. This serves to relax the patient and allay anxieties that I am going to overwhelm him or her with the sheer swiftness of my entry.

Help the patient practice the skill of tolerance. If you have knowledge of the patient's disability from consultation with the speech-language pathologist, demonstrate that you are a person with whom he or she can practice a more leisurely pace of interaction. Suggest to the patient that this can be one purpose of your time together.

Whether the patient has a mild or severe problem, it is likely that more time is going to be required to convey messages. The patient must come to learn that because he or she cannot count on others to slow down, he or she must slow down. This takes practice, not only to acquire the skill to communicate with whatever technique or device is required, but also to acquire an adequate tolerance for a slowed interaction pace. Highstrung individuals are of course more challenged in this regard.

Be open about the difficulty you experience in communicating with the patient, while demonstrating a positive tone that indicates you're going to be satisfied with whatever you can accomplish, by whatever means of message exchange.

Help the patient understand that communication is something you do, not something you are. While this is obviously a complicated issue, many patients feel that their value as individuals and perhaps their meaning for living is as degraded as their ability to communicate. It is typical of reactions to catastrophic illness in general to engage in an "all-or-nothing-at-all" type of thinking. This type of thinking might be characterized by the statement "Before this illness I was whole, intact, happy, productive, needed, valued . . . Now, I am nothing."

The pre-morbid life is idealized and the current situation is just as distorted, but in a negative way. Therefore, it may be helpful if the changes in their role within their family and community, changes in their career aspirations, and their rehabilitation potential were closely scrutinized in objective terms.

It is also important to help the patient note those areas of his or her life that have survived relatively untouched. Many patients lead lives before their illness or injury that were less than ideal, challenged by uncertainty, worry, and and doubts about their personal worth. It may be possible for them to see that the "before and after" in their life are not as dissimilar as they first felt, and that their feelings now are a part of the catastrophe that will diminish over time along with the other, more physical sequelae.

Encourage the patient to participate in a support group or to accept a visitation by another individual who survived a similar catastrophe. Despite your best efforts, it's not likely you'll be entirely successful in "selling" the perspective outlined above to the victim of a catastrophic illness or injury. However, a peer just might, and peer group counseling is widely acknowledged as a most potent form of emotional rehabilitation in such circumstances. Once again, the support groups and professional organizations listed at the end of this chapter may be helpful in this regard. If no support group exists, consider starting one.

4. DEVELOPMENTAL LANGUAGE DISORDER

Language competence involves the ability to both process and produce words, sentences, and longer verbal units, both orally and in written form, in order to effectively communicate around a variety of ideas with a variety of people. A language-disordered individual may have difficulty with one or several of the skills underlying language competence, as defined above. A particular profile of strengths and weaknesses distinguishes developmental conditions such as deafness, mental retardation, autism, dyslexia, nonverbal learning disability, and others.

Some indications include age-inappropriate difficulties with any of the following:

1. Comprehension difficulties
   - poor understanding of or generally unpredictable response to speech
   - failure to note inconsistency, illogic, absurdity, or other manifestations of inadequate listening behaviors
   - failure to infer meanings of statements based on the context (e.g., physical surrounding, overall purpose of meeting, role relationship with communication partner, etc.)
   - failure to appreciate nonliteral language, meanings, humor, irony, indirect requests, etc.
   - inability to follow stories or lengthier descriptions, narratives, lectures, and so on, and to make appropriate inferences/conclusions regarding same
2. Expressive difficulties
   - inappropriate word choices
   - agrammatical speech
   - vague or confusing speech, especially in longer explanations/descriptions, and so on
   - difficulty pronouncing words
   - social style that is either overly passive or overly dominating
   - tendency to provide either excessive or inadequate detail and background information
   - tendency to initiate inappropriate topics or to develop a topic either inadequately or in too much detail
   - inappropriate manner in initiating interactions (e.g., initiating conversation before greeting or otherwise preparing an intended listener)

- irrelevant, off-topic, or tangential speech
- failure to note or react appropriately to feedback (e.g., no reaction to listener's obvious confusion)
- failure to develop reading and writing skills

The above list makes it clear that competent language use requires cognitive and social skills in addition to "pure" linguistic proficiency. Language is always used in a context that requires adaptations. Therefore, true mastery of a language necessarily involves learning to speak, listen, read and write differently depending on who is involved, what is being communicated, why it is being communicated, and in what social/cultural circumstance.

Counseling Parents
Encourage early evaluation and early intervention. There is virtually no disagreement among professionals who deal with developmental disabilities: It is far better to catch any disability early, language disorder included.

More specifically, the following actions are recommended:

1. If there is any doubt about a child's speech or language development, take advantage of screening services offered by hospitals, clinics, and private practitioners. Such services are often made available free of charge during May, "Better Speech and Hearing Month." A failed screening should be followed by a complete speech and language evaluation and a complete audiological examination.
2. If the speech and language evaluation indicates a delay, follow up with assessments by an educational psychologist. Integrating the data from the speech-language pathologist, audiologist, psycholgist, and pediatrician should suggest the child's level of risk for future difficulties and guide intervention planning.
3. Closely monitor progress relative to language development of any child with identified risk factors who does not appear to require immediate intervention, at least through the primary grades where problems are most likely to show up.

Expect grief reactions in parents of seriously language-impaired children, and support the grieving process. Moses (1986) explains that "Dreams are the way we attach . . . disability, in children, shatters parental dreams," and therefore the natural emotional attachment between parent and child. Moses views grieving as a natural process through which parents can separate from lost dreams, develop new ones, and "re-attach" with their child.

The seriously language-disordered child often has other developmental disabilities as well, so it is reasonable to assume that parents are engaging in some manner of grieving. Because parental involvement is crucial in habilitating any developmental disability, helping parents to work through grief reactions can be the single-most important function of a counselor.

Grieving may be demonstrated subtly at times. Some parents appear to be "handling things well" and to be actively involved in the habilitation process. However, a closer look may reveal that they reject particular intervention methods, modalities, or professionals because they provoke feelings that the parent cannot bear.

For example, a parent of a severely disabled, nonverbal child may be willing to come to the school, to meet with therapists, and to be generally involved. But this same parent may resist a recommendation to learn sign language even though it is explained that the sign language may eventually help the child to learn to speak and will help the parent and child to communicate in the meantime.

One explanation for such a reaction is what Moses calls "denial of implication." A parent who exhibits such a reaction may accept the immediate disability but denies the implication that speech is at best a long-term goal, possibly an unattainable one.

Counseling Children

Acknowledge difficulty and slow the turn-taking pace. Be prepared to openly acknowledge the difficulty a child is having in expressing himself or herself, but cast your comments as "I" statements rather than "you" statements, that is, "I'm trying to understand you but I'm stuck" vs. "You're having a hard time expressing yourself." Speak slowly, in a casual and relaxed manner, as if to say, "We don't have to rush here." Over time, this approach may help a verbally disorganized child to slow down too and to speak a bit better because of it.

It's not what you say. . . . Language-disordered children often have difficulty understanding speech, and some naturally attend more to facial expression and tone of voice than to speech. Therefore, it's important that your tone of voice and other nonverbal communication match what you are saying. Avoid monotone and "deadpan" deliveries in general, and speak simply in short, connected sentences rather than in long run-on sentences.

Encourage and praise good communication skills, especially:

- initiative and persistence in trying to explain something difficult or understand something you are saying (e.g., "You're trying hard to make me understand [to understand me] aren't you? Thank you for that");

- eye contact (e.g., "It's easier for me to talk to you when you look at me like that. Thank you!"); and
- requests for clarification ("Thank you for asking me to explain").

Counseling the Mentally Retarded Adult or Young Adult with Language Disorder

Mentally retarded individuals are not simply "slower" versions of intellectually normal individuals. A variety of specific types of communication and other cognitive disorders can interefere with relationships just as in the normal population, such as attention deficits, memory problems, mood disturbances, auditory disorders, neurolinguistic deficits, speech disorders, and many more. A complete evaluation is essential to uncover the inidividual's potential and determine the best strategies for improving and compensating for communication deficiencies.

It is also true that many mentally retarded individuals—especially adults and young adults—have learned certain maladapative communication skills that make them appear more intellectually impaired than they actually are. Some of these learned behaviors are the result of having been treated like children well into their adult lives.

Despite their obvious handicap, a mentally retarded adult is an adult, first and foremost. With this as a starting point, here are some things you can do to help overcome some of the most common "bad habits" of communication.

Speak less. Assume that your verbal facility is intimidating. In general, say it simply and briefly. We who are fluent speakers of a language fail to realize how much we dominate interactions with those who are not. Too much talk can create overload and trigger mental withdrawal from the conversation.

Promote thoughtful responses vs. passive compliance or glib superficial responses. Be willing to give the individual time to think and to talk. If the individual feels you are an impatient listener, he or she may begin to rely on automatic, reflexive responses rather than thinking along with you.

In general, mentally retarded individuals are more comfortable with silences than we are and so your silence will facilitate active thought process. Beware of trying to "draw out" the individual by continually asking leading questions. Such a strategy may succeed in allaying your anxiety in having to wait for a thoughtful response yet actually prevent one from occurring! If you are generally a fast-paced individual, you will need to develop extraordinary discipline in this area.

Don't reinforce inappropriate responses. Mentally retarded individuals living in a fast-paced society learn certain communication survival skills.

One of these is to develop a repertoire of more or less automatic responses that are used indiscriminately and that give the often mistaken impression of poor comprehension.

Such automatic responses may be inappropriate or inadequate in terms of content, but at the same time they are a way coping with any perceived pressure to "get on with it." Out of politeness most of us will humor inappropriate responses, and this is exactly how they are reinforced.

It is important to try and establish rapport before making demands of any kind, but once established, challenge the individual to respond thoughtfully and then give him or her enough time to do so.

Encourage and praise good communication skills. (See suggestions given under "Counseling Children" in section 2.)

Team up with a speech-language pathologist if you are engaged in a long-term counseling relationship. Emotional, cognitive, and speech/language factors interact in complex ways that defy traditional therapeutic methods. Therefore, the mentally retarded often require a true team approach that allows for a long-term, dynamic strategy addressing these interacting areas through counseling, specific speech/language and cognitive therapies, group interaction training, and sometimes involving alternative therapies (e.g., movement/music therapy or art therapy).

Autism and Language Disorder

Beware generalizations. There are probably subtypes of autism. Autism is a diagnostic category that probably includes several different developmental disorders that future research will come to clearly distinguish. Therefore, it is particularly dangerous to try to apply current generalizations about this disorder to specific individuals for the purpose of creating treatment approaches and making predictions about future development.

Because autistic individuals can be different from each other in important ways, what helps one might not help another. However, there are a variety of medical and nonmedical intervention methods, and most autistic individuals benefit from treatment.

The degree of improvement that can be expected from treatment depends largely on the severity of the autism. while severely involved individuals will likely always require some degree of assistance throughout their lives, more mildly impaired individuals may grow up to live virtually normal lives.

"Don't judge a book by its cover." I believe this old proverb is instructive about autistic individuals. My experience tells me that many autistic individuals possess surprising capabilities. Assume that the individual be-

fore you is capable of understanding you both emotionally and intellectually. Make no hasty prejudgments regardless of what you see and hear during initial contacts. Autistic individuals may produce a variety of unusual behaviors that suggest a much greater level of intellectual and emotional impairment than may actually exist. Many individuals who work with autistic people believe that establishing trust and respect is the key to disclosing and building upon hidden talents.

About echolalia. Echolalia is the repetition, or "echoing," of something the individual producing it has heard. It may be the repeating of something immediately preceeding the echoed utterance or it may be an echo of an utterance from another time and place that is stimulated by some internal impulse, circumstance, person, or statement. Sometimes the source statement is echoed verbatim, sometimes with some modification by the echoer.

There are different notions about what causes echolalia and about what should be done about it. Some consider the behavior communicative and therefore purposeful and deserving of careful consideration. Others consider it reflexive, extraneous to communication, and a behavior to be "extinguished."

I believe that echolalia is a social-communicative reflex. The impulse to respond promptly when someone speaks to us reflects a social rule we all feel compelled to obey. The rule is formally referred to as the *adjacency rule.* I believe the echoer is appropriately compelled by this social rule, but due to an underlying language defect, he or she is unable to produce an original, appropriate utterance. The echolalic response, therefore, represents a partially adaptive trade-off.

I feel the reason an echo is produced rather than some other form of deviant utterance is that the echoer is trapped in some sort of cognitive, motor, or cognitive-motor "closed loop." I presume that the individual would say more if they could.

In some cases echolalia seems to be stimulated by mental or emotional overload. In others—especially when the echo is not of an immediately preceding source statement—it appears that the echoer is selecting from a limited set of boilerplate utterances in order to convey a notion that they cannot convey more originally. In still other cases I have felt that the echoer echoed out of sheer habit and a lack of appropriate training. With training, many echolalics can develop the ability to produce utterances with some degree of originality and appropriateness.

Depending on which theory you entertain, different approaches are appropriate. But regardless, it is my practice to involve the individual in my hypotheses about his or her echolalia. I attempt to solicit input from the individual about why he or she echoes and what should be done about it. Whatever I decide can be done to help, I take pains to make sure the individual understands what I am going to do and why I am doing it.

In any case, if one accepts that echolalia is an attempt to respond to a basic social expectation, it represents intelligence and prosocial motivation that should be developed. I doubt whether such motivation is nurtured by approaches that attempt to simply eliminate the echolalia without trying to replace it with more functional behavior.

Pragmatic Communication Disorders and Nonverbal Learning Disability

Pragmatic communication disorder represents a range of behaviors that violate interaction rules implicit in all verbal encounters. Interaction rules govern such things as when to listen and when to speak, eye contact, how to start a conversation, how to interrupt, whether to provide a lot or just a little detail, when to employ a formal vs. a familiar style of speech, how to recognize nonliteral or indirect messages (e.g., "Can you open the window?" is an indirect way of requesting that the listener do it). These are skills most of us learn through experience. They govern the way language is to be used, but they are distinct from language itself.

There may be a variety of neurologically based cognitive deficits underlying these and other pragmatic deficits, and therefore the term *pragmatic disorder* describes a symptom rather than a cause. It should be clear, however, that the counselor who observes such deviant communicative behaviors should pause to consider other than psychogenic causes. The presence of a neurologically based cognitive disability may contraindicate the use of therapies used for psychogenic difficulties.

Nonverbal learning disability (NLD) is a developmental syndrome that has major implications for socioemotional development. It is asserted that NLD represents a developmental disability distinguishable from autism, while others argue NLD is a "shading" of autism. One of the clearer distinctions is in the degree to which both populations exhibit language vs. pragmatic deficits.

There is a pragmatic deficit apparent in the communication of virtually all individuals with both developmental and acquired language disorders. But it is also possible to have fairly strong test scores in such areas as vocabulary, grammar, formulation, comprehension, decoding, and spelling and still have pragmatic difficulties. This is often true of those with nonverbal learning disability and unlike those with autism.

The following adaptation from Rourke (1989) is offered to further assist the clinician in identifying this developmental disability:

- poor adaptation to novel situations with overreliance on prosaic, rote behaviors in such situations
- poor social perception, social judgement, and interaction with

marked tendency toward social withdrawal and social isolation with advancing years
- emotional disturbance, acting out, or conduct disorder in early childhood; excessive anxiety, depression, and associated internalized forms of socioemotional disturbance that tend to increase with advancing years
- hyperactivity in childhood that gradually changes to hypoactivity with advancing years

Dyslexia and Oral Language Disorder

Dyslexia is more than being a "slow reader." Dyslexia is a term that is often misused to refer to any type of difficulty learning to read. Correctly applied, it refers to a failure to benefit from systematically administered traditional methods of reading instruction due to an underlying perceptual and/or linguistic disorder, the cause of which is associated with differences in the structure and function of the dyslexic's brain. Dyslexia can be developmental, and it can be acquired through damage to the brain such as that caused by stroke.

Be alert to co-occuring oral language disorder. There are differences between dyslexics. Most, however, have difficulties with language that include oral language as well as written language. Sometimes the co-occuring oral language problem is subtle, sometimes not. Sometimes the oral language difficulty is outgrown, sometimes it persists.

5. ACQUIRED LANGUAGE DISORDER

Acquired language disorder is referred to as *aphasia*. Aphasia is not a speech disorder (see sections 1 and 2) but a language disorder that affects one's ability to use language to perform in the four language domains of oral comprehension, oral expression, reading comprehension, and written expression. It is not primarily a disorder of thought process or memory (i.e., dementia), nor is it an emotional (i.e., mood) disorder. This having been said, the underlying causes of aphasia (e.g., stroke or head injury) can also cause co-occuring generalized dementia, various specific cognitive disorders (e.g., attention and concentration problems), and mood disorders.

Aphasia can be specific to one of the four language domains mentioned above, but more often it affects all domains to some extent, involvement that is readily revealed if performance in the respective domain is sufficiently challenged.

Aphasia can be so mild that the individual can function adequately in most situations, perhaps only exhibiting problems of word finding *(anomia)* on occasion or difficulty with the most complex language tasks (e.g., giving a lengthy, complicated explanation). In its most severe form there can be essentially no residual ability to comprehend others or to express oneself verbally, a condition referred to as *global aphasia.*

Treatment Considerations

While the brain damage is irreversible, aphasia therapy can help the undamaged brain manage language better. Speech-language pathologists provide treatment of aphasia, ideally beginning as soon as the patient can tolerate and actively cooperate with a therapist. A variety of techniques are used in both individual and group contexts aimed at maximizing residual ability within each of the language domains and compensation for deficits by developing auxiliary or replacement forms of communication (e.g., gesture, pantomime, or drawing).

Progress is most swift during the so-called period of spontaneous recovery, a period of some three to twelve months following onset. But significant improvement can continue to be made years after onset. This is especially true if therapy extends beyond the aphasic individual to include family members and friends.

Including significant others is particularly essential in more severe cases where auxiliary or replacement forms of communication are being developed that require practice on the part of both the aphasic individual and any prospective communication partners, be they family members or friends. Some speech-language pathologists have formalized the use of communication partners to begin to reestablish functional relationships from very nearly the beginning of treatment (Lyon 1988).

The counseling emphasis must be on restoring familial and social relationships. Deprived of the ability to communicate verbally, family members and friends are often deprived of a strong sense of familiarity with the aphasic individual. Near total social isolation can occur quickly after onset as the patient, family, and friends lose hope of regaining their former relationship.

Counseling can provide invaluable support to family members, either collectively or individually, as each one attempts to sort through feelings and maintain his or her respective relationship with the patient.

Early consultation between a mental health practitioner and the speech-language pathologist should be undertaken whenever possible. Teamed intervention should be the goal where the mental health practitioner works with the family to prevent disaffection and hopefully nurtures a willingness to explore new ways of communicating in order to maintain vital relationships. The speech-language pathologist works with the patient to accept, develop, and use alternative communication methods within primary relationships.

Counseling Family Members

Reinforce frequently that the patient's ability to think, remember, and feel are far less impaired than his or her ability to handle language.

The patient's need to understand what has happened to him or her, to communicate, and to feel a part of the family is as great or greater than before, whether or not this need is currently masked by depression.

Family members must meet the aphasic individual halfway. They must demonstrate their willingness to work through the frequent interferences in communication if the patient is to maintain or regain his or her motivation to relate. Family members need not protect the aphasic individual from their feelings, whatever they may be. They must simply be willing to learn how to express those feelings and still own them. Sharing feelings of loss, frustration, hope, and so on in most cases will probably serve to increase closeness and help everyone through the grief process.

Try to raise awareness of feelings related to factors specifically attributable to the aphasia rather than to the catastropic event as a whole, and problem solve. For example, a hallmark of aphasia is anomia, or word finding problems. Proper names are particularly difficult. The aphasic patient may be unable to recall the name of a spouse, child, or friend. Many times we can feel hurt when someone cannot remember our name. Especially amidst the smoke and ruin of catastrophic illness, a relatively minor thing like a husband's not remembering his wife's name can be particularly damaging to their relationship.

Once such issues have been raised, you may be able to devise solutions. In the above example, if the patient were equipped with a folder in which all family members' pictures and names were pasted or simply stored, the patient could point to or otherwise display the picture/name corresponding to the person he wanted to communicate about or with. Such a strategy may significantly reduce the depersonalization that family members feel and that aphasic patients feel guilty about.

Pragmatic Communication Disorders
Pragmatic communication disorder represents a range of behaviors that violate interaction rules governing turn-taking, eye contact, what style of speech to use, and more. The term refers to behavioral mainfestations that may be developmentally based: the sequelae of a stroke, neurological illness, or head injury (even a very mild one); or indications of emotional disturbance. For a more complete description of pragmatic communication disorders, please refer to the discussion in section 4.

It is beyond the scope of this chapter to provide a detailed description of what is a complex and highly interdisciplinary field. However, suffice it to say that distinguishing the cause of pragmatic communication disorders is vital to the counselor. The treatments used for psychogenic behaviors are often contraindicated in the treatment of neurological, cognitively based social-communication disorders. The latter often require a team treatment approach, cognitive retraining, behaviorally oriented intervention methods, and vocational counseling. Consultation with a specialist is indicated in cases of head injury.

6. STUTTERING

Contrary to one of the longest running myths about human behavior, stuttering is not a symptom of emotional disturbance. For years research has conclusively demonstrated that stuttering is not associated in any causal fashion with emotional disturbance. On the contrary, a formidable body of research supports a physical basis for stuttering, and hopefully scientists will converge upon the specific physical factor or factors responsible for stuttering. Some other interesting facts about stuttering include that most people who stutter are male, left-handed, and of average or above average intelligence. Most speak fluently when alone and do not stutter when singing.

The biomechanical failure seen and heard as stuttering appears to be centered on the workings of the larynx. Stuttering may seem to be a breakdown in the workings of the mouth during the attempt to speak. In fact, most recent research has focused upon the air valving function of the larynx (see section 1) as the precipitating event in a series of mechanical events that together comprise the phenomenon of stuttering.

Dysfluency in childhood is quite common and most often resolves spontaneously. A careful speech evaluation can disclose factors that will help predict children at risk for developing a chronic stuttering pattern. More importantly, early intervention in the form of parent education can help parents avoid exacerbating developmental dysfluency and perhaps learn ways to more quickly resolve this normal occurence in order to minimize anxiety and embarrassment.

There is currently no scientifically validated nor generally accepted method of curing chronic stuttering. However, there are treatments that can significantly improve fluency provided by speech-language pathologists who often specialize in such tratment. There are also peer support groups for people who stutter. See the resources listed at the end of this chapter.

Counseling Parents and Communicating with Dysfluent Children

Anxious parents should always be referred to a speech-language pathologist for consultation. A child with a suspected chronic stuttering problem should have an evaluation by a speech-language pathologist experienced with fluency disorders. This professional is best suited to provide training for parents to help reduce the dysfluency and negative social impact of this disorder.

However, as mentioned above, most children will outgrow dysfluent speech. Despite such assurances, some parents remain anxious about their child's speech. It is prudent in such cases to refer the parents for a consultation with a speech-language pathologist who may or may not wish to see the child on the first visit. Excessive parental anxiety alone can exacerbate dysfluency, and referral can constitute an aggressive "reassurance progam" that may be all that is needed.

In communicating with dysfluent children, don't tell children to "talk slowly," "take a deep breath," "relax," or "say it again." Try not to bring attention to the dysfluency in any way at all. Focus on what the child is saying rather than on how he or she speaks. Give extra evidence that you are listening by paraphrasing what he or she is saying to you in your own words, for example, "You mean you wish you didn't have to go to bed so early." After paraphrasing, you can go ahead and respond with your own thought or reaction.

If you don't have time to listen, then tell your child when you will be ready to listen. But be flexible enough to postpone what you are doing if your child really needs your ear at that moment. None of us tolerates being put off routinely. Don't try to do two things at once. Many of us experience increased anxiety if we feel we have to compete for someone's attention at a particular moment.

When you are listening, look like you are listening. Stop what you're doing, move closer, look at your child in the eyes. Don't interrupt. Children experiencing dysfluency need us to be better listeners than we perhaps are for others. When you speak, model slow, relaxed speech patterns. Don't allow your child to interrupt you either. Practice deliberate, considerate turn-taking where each of you gets to talk and both listen. Try and build in some unhurried time each day for talking, reading stories, or just playing together.

RESOURCES FOR MORE INFORMATION

American Speech-Language-Hearing Association
10801 Rockville Pike
Rockville, MD 20852

Speech Foundation of America
P.O. Box 11749
Memphis, TN 38111

National Stuttering Project
1269 7th Avenue
San Francisco, CA 94122
Provides support and publishes a
newsletter.

FOR FURTHER READING

Ainsworth, S. & Fraser, J. (1988). *If your child stutters: A guide for parents.* (Publication No. 11). (Available from the Speech Foundation of America, P.O. Box 11749, Memphis, TN 38111)

REFERENCES

Aronson, A. E. (1985). *Clinical voice disorders: An interdisciplinary approach* (2nd ed.). New York: Thieme.

Lyon, Jon G., & Prescott, T. E. (Eds.). (1988). *Clinical Aphasiology* (Vol. 18, pp. 11–18). Boston: College-Hill Press.

Moses, K. (1986, February). *Counseling: A critical part of our practice.* Paper presented at the American Speech-Language-Hearing Association Teleconference.

Moses, P. J. (1954). *The voice of neurosis.* New York: Grune & Stratton.

Rourke, B. P. (1989). *Nonverbal learning disabilities: The syndrome and the model.* New York: Guilford Press.

9

Counseling Persons with Vision Impairment

BARBARA SILVERSTONE, D.S.W.

BETTY BIRD, Ed.D.

MARY ANN LANG, Ph.D.

In the past, blind people or those with significant loss of sight were educated and counseled in specialized settings. The climate of opinion was that vision impairment is so disabling and its effects so unique that only specialists in vision rehabilitation could understand the problems presented by visually impaired people. Additionally, individual counselors outside the field of vision rehabilitation were reluctant to work with these blind clients, who they felt were beyond their capability to help.

Blind and partially sighted people, however, comprise a heterogeneous population, differing from sighted people only in their visual functioning and related issues. Similarly, they seek counseling for a wide variety of problems including those related to parent/child and marital relations and to personal and career adjustment. Sometimes, these problems are intertwined with issues related to vision impairment. In numerous situations, vision impairment is irrelevant to the problem at hand.

Whatever the case, counselors outside the field of vision rehabilitation can certainly work with visually impaired persons. Those with expertise in other fields have much to offer persons who happen to be blind or partially sighted. It is to the counselor's advantage to be alert to the ramifications of vision impairment and sufficiently knowledgeable about resources to refer the client to specialized vision rehabilitation services if appropriate. This chapter will give a brief overview of vision impairment and rehabilitation, as well as the common features of vision impairment in persons at different life stages and in persons with AIDS.

OVERVIEW OF VISION IMPAIRMENT AND REHABILITATION

Vision impairment encompasses *blindness,* a condition where there is no usable vision, and *partial sight* or *low vision,* where there is some degree of residual vision that can be enhanced through special aids. *Legal blindness* defines acuity and vision field requirements for government entitlements. Not all visually impaired persons meet the standards for legal blindness.

Vision impairment can be caused by disease, accident, or genetic disorders. In infants a leading cause is retinopathy of prematurity. In adults, retinal diseases predominate, such as diabetic retinopathy and macular degeneration. Today the most accurate predictor of vision impairment is advanced age. While vision impairment can occur at any age, it is most frequently found in the older age brackets, particularly the over 75 population.

A national network of private and public vision rehabilitation services has the mission of training and counseling visually impaired persons to enhance their independence and quality of life. The Rehabilitation Act of 1973 as amended mandates that every state provide these services, many of which are contracted out to private agencies. Legally blind persons are entitled to the services, equipment, and technology required for rehabilitation. Advances in computer-assisted technology enable vision-impaired people to carry out a variety of work-related tasks at a speed and accuracy commensurate with that of their sighted counterparts. Given appropriate equipment and training, blind and partially sighted persons can participate fully in the workplace.

CHILDREN, ADOLESCENTS, AND THEIR FAMILIES

Early intervention for infants and children who are blind or visually impaired is highly recommended. Specialized programs for infants and preschool children are available. Although, historically, visually impaired children attended schools for the blind, now for the most part they go to integrated schools with special provisions for their training. Intervention begins, however, between counselor and family.

A family with a visually impaired child may or may not come into counseling because of concerns related to the child's impairment, but either way, the impairment is always significant and emotionally charged. Following discovery of a child's visual impairment, relationships among family members may be strained, the parents' marriage may end, or family members may experience career difficulties. Behind such responses is the fact that, in anticipating the birth of a child, family members create an image of who that child will be. They imagine how the baby will look, the things they will do with him or her, what he or she will become, and how the family's life will evolve with the child as a part of it. If he or she is born blind or with partial sight, the image created during pregnancy is shattered. Under these circumstances, parents often experience the emotional states associated with mourning. The mourning for the loss of the imagined child takes place while the family is facing the complex needs of a neonate, whose presence activates all the family stresses associated with a new baby as well as those related to his or her specific vision problems. The intensity and complexity of the situation is expanded by reactions of grandparents, aunts, uncles, and siblings. Friends and strangers add their unique contributions through looks, comments, and questions.

The counselor who becomes part of this highly charged system must help the family recognize the imagined child, deal with that loss, and develop a realistic picture of the new baby. In doing so, the counselor must inform the family about the process and stages of child development and the ways visual impairment impacts on it. The counselor needs to convey an array of strategies for facilitating the development essential to the child's well-being. Usually these techniques are outside the experience of counselors who lack training and experience working with visually impaired children. In that event, counseling involves case management or resource coordination.

As the counselor works with the family on these issues, he or she may observe a tendency for the family to withdraw from contact with relatives and friends and to include the child in this protective reaction. Although the family's need for time to mourn must be respected, the child has a concurrent need to become aware of and interact with the physical and social world. Unlike the adult who loses vision and is faced with adapting a previously existing repertoire of cognitive, physical, and social skills, the child and family are faced with the enormous task of creating concepts and skills without visual input. Lack of vision can exert a powerful indirect influence on physical growth and development by depriving the infant of visual motivation to reach out to the environment. Additionally, when parents are overly concerned about the child's safety, they may further circumscribe his or her interactions.

The counselor's role is to help the family recognize and respond appropriately to the child's need for cognitive and affective growth while addressing the family's own emotional and informational needs. Where conflicts exist between the family's needs and those of the child, the counselor's role becomes one of helping the family to recognize these competing needs and to develop ways to address their own emotional and informational needs. At the same time, the counselor needs to help the family to provide the immediate assistance that their child requires to achieve developmental milestones and avoid the secondary handicaps associated with limited interaction with the physical and social world.

ADOLESCENTS

When an adolescent or his or her family comes into the counseling situation for reasons not directly related to the adolescent's vision problem, the counselor should be as alert to the impact of the disability and to his or her related needs as when a young child is visually impaired.

The adolescent with a visual impairment presents issues related to the transition from childhood to adulthood. He or she will usually need help acquiring social skills, making career preparations, and gaining employment. Unfortunately, social maturation often lags behind that of peers; likewise, age-appropriate vocational experiences are not routine in the lives of young visually impaired persons.

One important function of the counselor working with visually impaired adolescents is to provide honest reality checks. People this age need feedback about themselves and the impression they make on others because a great deal about behavior, gestures, posture, movement, and dress is learned through visual observation. Achieving adult competencies requires self-esteem. Counselors can provide valuable assistance in this realm by working directly with the young person as well as with his or her family.

Strained relationships between the adolescent and parents are often part of the process through which the young person defines his or her own adult identity. The tension generated by an adolescent's need and desire to be independent and by his or her concomitant anxiety about assuming responsibility are part of the problem. The parent's desire for the young person to assume responsibility, as well as his or her concern for the young person's well-being, provides another element. When the adolescent has a visual impairment, the situation is compounded by the young person's uncertainty about having appropriate skills to participate in the adult world and the parent's concern for safety because of lack of vision. These added elements may cause the young person to precipitate a more intense conflict or to withdraw from the confrontation that may be necessary to establish his or her own adult identity.

Visually impaired adolescents and their parents can benefit greatly during this period from contact with adult role models who have visual impairments. Both parents and young people can expand their concepts of what is possible and acquire information about strategies for coping effectively with realistic problems related to being an adult with a visual impairment. The counselor can help the family realize the importance of developing a clear picture of adult possibilities and skills for accomplishing goals. Although there is little published material incorporating adult role models with disabilities, this resource is growing. Counselors can help families locate these materials by contacting libraries, bookstores, and publishers, many of which are now establishing collections on this theme. Local organizations of visually impaired persons and agencies that work with visually impaired individuals can put families in contact with visually impaired adults who might provide assistance as role models.

WORKING-AGE ADULTS

To function well and happily, adults need strategies and techniques to meet their needs in three primary areas: personal daily living tasks, family and social gratification, and employment. Loss of vision will affect all three areas regardless of the individual's age. The point at which vision loss occurs will influence the relative difficulty of adjusting in these areas. The individual who loses vision in adulthood is likely to have well-developed social skills as well as job experience, but will need help in applying his or her existing knowledge using new techniques for doing things.

In the ideal world, visually impaired teenagers get summer jobs where their parents work, baby-sit for younger family members and neighbors, work as camp counselor aides, or volunteer to stuff envelopes or answer the phone at their community center, church, or scout troop. If young visually impaired adults missed these early work experiences, they will need extra career counseling and support group assistance to deal with their fears about job demands, as well as internships with job coaches or trial work experiences to make the transition into employment. The support groups will spend an equal amount of time on issues pertaining to both work skills and interpersonal skills.

Talking through ways to handle the discomfort of sighted colleagues and set them at ease about one's own blindness is a skill any visually impaired person will need throughout life. Support group members will share their frank approaches, their humorous approaches, and sometimes their frustrated approaches. Social workers and other professional counselors should not be afraid to deal with the dynamics of self-esteem, interpersonal relations, or coping with blindness. Much of the adjustment to visual impairment, however, depends on the individual's acquiring a new body of knowledge and practicing new techniques. Early in the adjustment, the enriched counseling skills and knowledge of rehabilitation counselors and career specialists for the visually impaired are imperative.

By contrast, people who lose their vision in adulthood bring their lifetime of skills and experiences with them. Learning new methods for accomplishing objectives is their major challenge. Shaving or putting on makeup without a mirror seems impossible at first. Inability to perform personal care tasks becomes debilitating when family and friends step in and help too much. The danger lies in their taking over and reinforcing the fears and dependence of the visually impaired person. Connecting the person and his or her family and supporters to rehabilitation specialists is a key service that any counselor should provide immediately.

The tendency is to view adjustment as a series that follows a chronological sequence: first, psychological adjustment to loss; then, personal skill acquisition; and later, worry about social gratification and working. Actually, adults need to progress along these avenues in a balanced way. Naturally, individuals will work on the aspects of their lives that are the most important to them and for which they are ready. Progress usually occurs as small advances in first one area and then another. Learning to shave or apply makeup builds confidence and encourages one to try other things, and these positive experiences build emotional strength and reduce fear, thus furthering psychological adaptation. If the tendency to take these issues in sequence is rigidly followed, it is likely that the job and sometimes friends will be lost. Then the person will have to work at recovering them, which is far more difficult than retaining them. Losing a job is a massive blow to the ego, while retaining it can avoid loss of self-esteem.

Families and supporters invest a great deal in promoting adjustment during the transition period. Most cope well and are still there after transition, close and helpful. At times, however, marriages break up and friendships dissolve, leaving the visually impaired person faced with building new relationships. These matters can be alleviated by any trained counselor or therapist.

On the other hand, dealing with employment issues takes a specialist. Most adults draw a great deal of their identity and positive self-image from work. Two-thirds of all Americans participate in the labor force and about 7% are unemployed at this time. By contrast, one-third of all visually impaired people participate in the labor force. Where is the other third? Unfortunately, they have been discouraged from seeking employment, have left their jobs on disability when they lost their vision, or are unaware that they can work. The challenge for the medical professional or counselor is to refer the visually impaired person to a vision rehabilitation specialist early after vision loss. Again, knowing that you can learn methods that will enable you to keep your job may be the best "medicine" a person can receive. If the family, employers, and the visually impaired person can be helped to avoid panic and to get rehabilitation training and counseling, much of the loss can be avoided and the adaptation process will be smoother.

In summary, the young blind person is still maturing, acquiring social skills and job training in order to assume adult responsibilities. Conversely, the mature adult has knowledge and life experience so that the major task is to learn new methods of accomplishing objectives. Counseling can be provided by any trained professional for psychological adpatation, marital problems, and self-esteem enhancement. However, learning adaptive techniques for personal needs and job retention or acquisition requires the training of rehabilitation specialists.

PERSONS IN LATE LIFE

Vision impairment in late life is most often a phenomenon associated with aging experienced by individuals who were fully sighted earlier in their lives. It affects almost 13% of noninstitutionalized older adults with proportionally higher frequencies in the very old age groups. Vision impairment ranks third (after heart disease and arthritis) among the physical disabilities restricting the daily activities of older persons, and blindness is one of the most feared human conditions. Not infrequently for older persons, the negative effects of vision impairment are compounded by other physical conditions including poor hearing and severe arthritis. Increased social isolation has been observed, particularly among very old single persons, and reactive depressions commonly accompany severe impairment.

Age-related vision impairment rarely results in total blindness. Partial sight is far more common among older persons. The residual vision remaining to an older person can often be enhanced by the use of special optical devices, adaptive technology, and proper lighting. These low vision interventions also include training in a variety of skills that enable vision-impaired older persons to travel and function independently in their homes.

Paradoxically, the attitudes of some older persons toward these rehabilitation opportunities is often passive, in spite of the anticipated and real consequences of vision loss. Often, vision impairment is either trivialized as a normal consequence of aging or is succumbed to as being totally incapacitating. If it has occurred over a period of time, accommodations may have been made that suffice even though the social world or independence of the older person has been constricted. These passive attitudes are often reinforced by eye care professionals who indicate that nothing more can be done surgically or medically for them, as well as their own fear of being considered "blind." Older persons, however, vary in their adaptation to vision impairment, and include those who realistically accept the condition and have an optimistic attitude toward the importance and potential for learning new skills.

Professionals counseling older persons and their families should be alert to the possibility of vision impairment, its emotional consequences, and the varying adaptations made to it by older people. The total context of the older person's situation must be assessed, including the presence of other health and functional problems; financial, social, and psychological conditions; and family attitudes and behaviors associated with adaptation to vision loss. By the same token, the recognition and measure of the impact of vision impairment will clarify the assessment of other problems for which the older person is being counseled.

The effects of vision loss are often compounded by other losses that can occur simultaneously. In counseling, vision-impaired older persons will often share losses of family members and friends who gave them support and even pets for whom they can no longer care. Attention must be given in the counseling situation to the impact of those losses and ways to develop and/or sustain the older person's motivation and confidence to remain in the community and develop a realistic plan of care at home. Insecure, isolated, older visually impaired people with an inadequate support system at home may not respond positively to rehabilitation training if they feel unsafe or insecure in their own environment.

In situations where the long-term care needs of older persons (usually those over 80) are paramount, vision rehabilitation should still be encouraged. The enhancement of quality of life and even minimal functional improvements can make a significant difference. Older workers, usually those under 70, who have left employment because of their vision problems, should be encouraged to use vocational rehabilitation services.

Resistance by older persons to seeking rehabilitative help is often evident in individual counseling situations. Referral to a peer support group for visually impaired older persons is a useful intervening step to rehabilitation services and can be enormously therapeutic as the visually impaired older person discovers that his or her problems are not unique.

The number of family members and friends and the frequency of contacts with them are not in and of themselves predictors of successful adaptation. The quality of these relationships is critical to psychological adaptation, including the older person's perception of emotional bonding with a close relative and realization that the family truly understands the nature of the vision disability. Now, as visual impairment occurs at earlier life stages, overprotectiveness by family members that could prove counterproductive to rehabilitation requires family counseling and education. Visually impaired older persons should be encouraged to involve close family members in discussions related to the emotional and practical impact of vision loss and planning for rehabilitation.

PERSONS WITH AIDS

Opportunistic diseases associated with AIDS have resulted in severe vision loss for thousands of persons within the last decade. The person with AIDS (PWA) with a vision loss requires the assistance of a counselor. Emotional problems must be dealt with, skills must be learned, and resources must be identified and coordinated. Although PWAs with vision loss do not conform to any single profile, they do come into the counseling situation with a number of common elements. PWAs are often in the prime of life, yet the health problems, rehabilitation issues, and necessary decisions are usually ones that normally affect much older people. Their fluctuating health also complicates planning and intervention and may require many sudden changes of goals and strategies. In addition, the counselor will find that the possibility of death impinges on the work to a greater extent than with most other groups.

The client's awareness of his or her own mortality often translates into a high motivation to make the most of time. This high motivation will often bring the PWA into the rehabilitation or counseling process at an earlier state of adjustment than is the case with many other people with vision impairments. Because of the highly emotional context of AIDS, many counselors may need to be reminded that the essential process of working with PWAs remains the same as when working with anyone else. There are, however, unique practical and emotional challenges because of the radical, fast-paced changes that are often a part of living with AIDS. For example, the high motivation related to the acute awareness of limited time poses a dilemma for the professional: how to encourage it and still minimize disappointment. In addition, AIDS tends to impact on every aspect of the individual's life, causing the PWA to feel that he or she has lost control of his or her life. In many cases, the loss of vision can take on great intensity because it is a pervasive impediment to control and independence.

The professional can support the PWA's control of daily life by helping him or her to define realistic goals; assisting in developing plans that actualize goals in small, achievable steps; and preparing the PWA for the inevitable frustration intrinsic to constantly changing health. It may be helpful to introduce the paradigm "Doing alone, doing with, and having others do for you." It can be stressed that having someone do something with or for you does not mean that you have surrendered control. You are still in charge, still the one making the decisions.

CONCLUSIONS

Whatever the age of onset, vision impairment is commonly viewed as a catastrophic loss with unfortunate implications for an individual's quality of life and autonomous functioning. While these implications and their remediation take on varying meanings at different life stages, several commonalities can be found.

Most striking is the emotional intensity accompanying vision loss both for the individual and family. The tendency to withdraw or deny the condition is common, as are depressive reactions. If withdrawal, denial, or depression are not addressed, the potential for secondary handicaps increases in the forms of retarded learning for children and unecessary dependence for adults.

Interventions to deal with the emotional concomitants of vision impairment may be required before essential training in development, vocational, or daily living skills is initiated. Timing patterns, however, vary. With infants and persons with AIDS, the person and family generally come into the education or rehabilitation situation while still in an intense emotional crisis. With older persons, the situation has generally evolved and is less intense and volatile.

Interventions to address the psychosocial problems accompanying vision impairment can range from individual and family counseling to mutual support groups. In any situation involving vision impairment, however, a systems approach is essential. The family, workplace, home environment, school, or nursing home must be assessed and included in the counseling plan where appropriate.

FOR FURTHER READING

Corn, A. L., Muscella, D. B., Cannon, G. S., & Shepler, R. C. (1985). Perceived barriers to employment for visually impaired women: A preliminary study. *Journal of Visual Impairment and Blindness, 79*, 458–461.

Dickson, M. B., & Macdonell, P. K. (1982). Career club for blind job seekers. *Journal of Visual Impairment and Blindness, 76*, 290–292.

Dixon, J. M. (1983). Attitudinal barriers and strategies for overcoming them. *Journal of Visual Impairment and Blindness, 77*, 290–292.

Horowitz, A., & Reinhardt, J. P. (1992, July). *Assessing adaptation to age-related vision loss.* Paper presented at the annual meeting of the Association for Education and Rehabilitation of Blind and Visually Impaired Persons, Los Angeles.

Kirchner, C., & Petersen, R. (1988). Employment: Selected characteristics. In C. Kirchner (Ed.), *Data on blindness and visual impairment in the U.S.* (pp. 169–177). New York: American Foundation for the Blind.

Lang, M. A., Sussman-Skalka, C., & Galligan, M. (1992). *AIDS, blindness, and low vision: A guide for service providers* (2nd ed.). New York: Lighthouse.

Nicholson, J. R., & Tobayen-Wyssmann, S. (1984). Client centered rehabilitation: a method for setting realistic goals to meet client needs. *Journal of Rehabilitation, 50*, 39–41.

Perlman, L. G., & Hansen, C. E. (1990). *Employment and disability: Trends and issues for the 1990s.* A report on the 14th Mary E. Switzer Memorial Seminar, National Rehabilitation Association, Alexandria, VA.

Scholl, G. T. (Ed.). (1986). *Foundations of education for blind and visually handicapped children and youth.* New York: American Foundation for the Blind.

Tuttle, D. W. (1984). *Self-esteem and adjusting with blindness.* Springfield, IL: Thomas.

Warren, D. H. (1984). *Blindness and early childhood development* (2nd ed.). New York: American Foundation for the Blind.

Weber, N. (Ed.). (1991). *Vision and aging: Issues in social work practice.* New York: Harworth Press.

Wolffe, K. E., Roesler, R. T., & Shriner, K.F. (1992). Employment concerns of people with blindness or visual impairments. *Journal of Visual Impairment and Blindness, 86,* 185–187.

10

Counseling Gay Men and Lesbians and Their Families

HELEN B. McDONALD, C.S.W.

AUDREY I. STEINHORN, C.S.W.

Homosexuality is assuredly no advantage, but it is nothing to be ashamed of, no vice, no degradation. It cannot be classified as an illness. . . . Many highly respected individuals of ancient and modern times have been homosexuals, several of the greatest men among them (Plato, Michelangelo, Leonardo da Vinci, etc.). It is a great injustice to persecute homosexuality as a crime, and a cruelty, too.

—Sigmund Freud
"Letter to an American Mother"

Of all the people in minority groups in our country, perhaps the members of sexual minorities such as lesbians, gay men, and bisexuals are the least visible, least understood, and most feared. Issues about human sexuality and sexual orientation are often not talked about openly or spoken of negatively within the general population. Knowledge about human sexuality and sexual orientation is not always taught and discussed freely among those who are in the professions that deal with helping others. Therefore, it can be very confusing to counsel people about their sexual orientation. It is crucial for counselors to learn as much as possible about lesbians, gay men, and bisexuals so they can be in touch with their own biases and those of others.

A gay person is one who is attracted socially, physically, and emotionally to others of the same sex. Although *gay* is often used to refer to both men and women, most typically it applies to men. *Lesbians* are women who are attracted socially, sexually, and emotionally to women. *Bisexuals* are people who can establish emotional and physical relationships with people of both genders. Most lesbians and gay men prefer not to use the word *homosexual,* another word used to refer to a person who is attracted to someone of the same sex.

Many people believe lesbians and gay men are easily identifiable. Gay men are thought of as effeminate and swishy. Lesbians are thought to be tough and masculine. While it is true that some lesbians and gay men do fit these stereotypes, there are many heterosexual people who do also. Stereotypes or prejudgments do exist for all groups and say nothing about who these people really are. Today's lesbians, gay men, and bisexuals are as varied a group of people as you will find anywhere in our society. There are senior citizens, adolescents, people from all racial and religious groups, those who are or have been married, those with and without children, those who are in a couple, and those who are single. They come from all socioeconomic strata. Many are happy, well adjusted, and well functioning. Some have mental and/or physical disabilities. Some struggle with addictions. Some are open about their sexual orientation to others and some hide it by "being in the closet" because of their great fear of the effects of being stigmatized emotionally, socially, or economically and their fear of losing jobs, friends, the love of family members, and so on. Whether they are young or old, some have known they were lesbian, gay, or bisexual for a long time, and some are just finding out. Some are your relatives, your neighbors, or your friends.

Many people have heard the phrase "coming out" or "coming out of the closet" and wondered what it means. Most typically, *coming out* refers to the process that lesbians and gay men go through when they discover that they are attracted to and prefer to have intimate relationships with people of the same sex. It is the process that bisexuals go through when they discover that they are attracted to and capable of having intimate relationships with people of either sex. Coming out is a time when a person focuses on the ways in which he or she differs from the mainstream of the population.

As defined by the authors, coming out is a lifelong process that all people experience when they allow themselves and/or others to discover who they really are. The term refers in particular to those aspects that are the most difficult for the individual and others to accept. The process can begin at any time.

Cass (1979) has described the following six stages in the process of coming out:

1. *Confusion:* An adolescent may begin to suspect that something is "wrong" with him or her and realizes with much bewilderment that he or she is attracted to people of the same sex.
2. *Comparison:* The adolescent feels very different from others and very alone. He or she tries to deny his or her feelings and becomes very flirtatious with a member of the opposite sex in school; the adolescent dates as often as possible.
3. *Tolerance:* When the adolescent goes to college, he or she meets lesbians and gay men and is relieved to find out that they are no more weird than most of the heterosexual people he or she knows. Although the now young adult does not identify as lesbian/gay, he or she does socialize with groups of lesbians and/or gay men in various activities in an effort to make friends and see what they are like.
4. *Acceptance:* As the young adult makes new lesbian and/or gay male friends, he or she becomes more aware of how comfortable it is to be in their company. He or she even becomes attracted to a particular member of the same sex and begins having fantasies about getting involved with that person. The young adult stops dating members of the opposite sex and sees old friends less frequently. He or she may begin to have a same-sex relationship.
5. *Pride:* The young adult now prefers to be in the company of lesbians and/or gay men and consciously seeks out conferences, literature, and social events that focus on lesbian and gay issues. He or she becomes more aware of the various ways in which *homophobia,* the irrational fear and/or hatred of anyone or anything connected with lesbians and gay men, presents itself in everyday life situations. He or she may only feel comfortable to "come out" to a few carefully selected people.
6. *Synthesis:* As the young adult becomes more comfortable with life as a lesbian or gay man, he or she may slowly start to renew contacts with some old heterosexual friends, being very selective about with whom to share this very special information.

Coming out is a painful process for most lesbians, gay men, and bisexuals. The fear of anticipated rejection is an extremely distressing experience. One of the most confusing aspects of the coming out process is that of not knowing in advance when one is going to meet with negative responses. The many fears involved in coming out have to do with such things as the person's own homophobia, age, gender, religious upbringing, racial and cultural background, and so on.

There are many theories about what "causes" homosexuality, but no one knows what causes either homosexuality or bisexuality just as no one knows what causes heterosexuality. Our society has conditioned people to be negatively biased toward anyone who is not heterosexual. In our work as counselors, we need to examine our own beliefs about the origins of homosexuality and bisexuality so that our own biases will not interfere in our work. The question for all of us is to find out how open we can be, especially in view of the fact that society is so closed.

ISSUES FOR COUNSELING

Acceptance

In working with any clients about issues of sexual orientation, it is important to have a basic understanding of what homosexuality and bisexuality are all about. It is also of utmost importance that we be aware of our own negative feelings toward lesbians, gay men, and bisexuals. Because of the nature of the society that we live in, all of us have some homophobia, regardless of our own sexual orientation.

With this understanding and acceptance of our limitations, counselors will be better able to listen for clues and ask questions that will open up possible discussion about sexual orientation issues. This can help the counselor to be more ready to ask questions and less ready to assume that he or she knows what the client is talking about. For example, rather than assume that the client is heterosexual when he or she mentions dating, the counselor may ask whether the person dates men or women or both.

As counselors, our most important task is to help people accept who they are. This means that we need to help lesbians, gay men, and bisexuals accept the fact that they are different. It is not our job to change people but it is our job to accept where they are in their process and to help them understand as much as possible that various options and choices may be available to them.

Youths

The development of social and sexual identity begins at birth and continues until we die. In our society, the assumption is made that all children will grow up to be heterosexual. There is very little acknowledgment that some children are or may grow up to be lesbian, gay, or bisexual.

Many lesbian and gay youths have known about their feelings for members of the same sex from a very early age. Problems can arise for them if they are afraid to discuss these feelings with parents, peers, or other significant people in their lives, even though they may want to, because they know their parents expect them to be heterosexual. They may become withdrawn, secretive, hyperheterosexual, angry, hypersensitive, or disdainfully judgmental toward lesbians and gay men.

Lesbian or gay youths are often also afraid to share their feelings with people they are attracted to because they know they may be rebuffed, publicly ridiculed, scorned, or rejected. A variety of problems can arise from these and other negative interactions. Problems can range from poor self-esteem to poor school attendance or performance, substance abuse, participation in prostitution and pornography (both male and female), suicidal ideation or attempts, and running away from or leaving home.

All adolescents are limited by stereotypical sex role behavior, but lesbian and gay teenagers are even more limited. They will often be more secretive about their feelings and possible actions because of their fear of being labeled "deviant." Adolescents are also limited by their parents' assumption of the adolescents' heterosexuality and the parents' expectations of what they want them to grow up to be. Adolescent sexuality can be a difficult topic among adults, including counselors.

Adolescents need to be taken very seriously as they explore their sexual orientation. They need to be helped to understand that it can take time to find out whether they are really lesbian, gay, or bisexual or whether they are merely going through a phase in their development. Counselors may hold back from an exploration of sexual orientation because of their fear that they will be held responsible for the behavior of minors once they begin to explore questions of sexual orientation.

It is important to help the adolescent anticipate his or her parent's response to the news that he or she is not heterosexual. Some may be accepting, but more will not be. Some may even blame themselves. It is important to help the adolescent realize that his or her problems are separate from those of the parents.

Parents

Parents have their own problems. The parental question, "What did I do wrong?" has nothing to do with the adolescent. It is important for the counselor working with parents to encourage them to express and explore as much of their guilt as possible. For example, parents often feel that their child "became" lesbian or gay because of something that the parents did. Thorough exploration of what it is that they think they did will help parents understand that it is not about them, and that as a matter of fact, this is something that is completely beyond their control.

In thinking about parents, it can be helpful to realize that in all likelihood they had some image of what their child was going to grow up to be like even before conception. It will be very difficult for some, and impossible for others, to give up that image because it would have provided the parents with new socially accepted roles (e.g., grandparents) when their own parenting role was completed. Not only will they lose these hoped-for roles, but they may also feel stigmatized for having had a child who belongs to a sexual minority.

Because the parents experience their loss as a death, they will have to go through a mourning process very similar to that which Kubler-Ross (1969) has written about. These parents may very well find themselves in a closet of their own because of their own homophobia, their own fear of being rejected by their peers, and their not knowing (or thinking that they did not know) any other parents in the same situation. Referral to an organization called Parents and Friends of Lesbians and Gays (Parents FLAG) can be helpful (see the resources listed at the end of this chapter).

Adults

Not all people who explore or deal with their sexual orientation are adolescents. In fact, most people are young adults and older before they begin the questioning process.

How does the counselor differentiate between a client who is truly homosexual or bisexual and one who is simply going through a temporary phase of sexual questioning? Initially you cannot, and you do not have to differentiate, but you can be certain that the person's struggle is real and to be taken seriously.

During the course of this struggle, the counselor must be careful not to become impatient. The process of self-discovery unfolds slowly and the process can be very confusing because the final outcome may not be predictable from the various stages traveled through. Sometimes individuals can be absolutely certain that they are lesbian or gay from the very beginning of their quest. They get involved in same-sex relationships, come out to family and friends as homosexuals, and later discover that they are in fact heterosexual or bisexual.

After much confusion and exploration, some may decide that although they experience themselves as lesbian, gay, or bisexual, they will choose to live the lifestyle of a heterosexual because the alternative is too painful. Some may decide to "stay in the closet," to keep their sexual orientation a secret. Others will decide to live their lives as lesbians, gay men, or bisexuals in as open a manner as possible.

It is important for counselors to realize that any choice a client makes is valid, extremely difficult, and typically very painful for the person making the choice. The belief that homosexuality and bisexuality are very undesirable attributes continues to prevent many lesbians, gay men, and bisexuals from tuning in to themselves. It has also kept many who think of themselves as being homosexual or bisexual from sharing this insight with their friends and family. Because they do not want to be seen as insensitive or insulting, many heterosexuals may not ask questions or otherwise raise the issue of homosexuality or bisexuality with their reticent friends or clients.

Religion

All of us have been brought up with some kind of religious orientation, even if we consider ourselves atheists. It is very helpful and often enlightening to make a point of asking about a client's religious beliefs because of how they affect one's sexual orientation and behavior. For example, a person could go through a counseling experience without ever discussing his or her religious and spiritual beliefs and regard the counseling experience as having been successful. However, that person might find that he or she continues to experience a sense of guilt, shame, or discomfort whenever the topic of God or a supreme being is raised in a conversation. These feelings might not arise if the counselor had explored religion and spirituality.

Suicide

Some people will come to counseling wanting a promise that they will be lesbian, gay, or bisexual. Others will insist that they end up as a heterosexual, being convinced that their life will be ruined otherwise. They may even insist that they have no alternative but to commit suicide if they are not heterosexual. A lot of pressure is thereby placed on the counselor.

The counselor in this circumstance must ask himself many questions, some of which include:

1. Do you think that you have the power to make a person either straight or gay or bisexual with your counseling?
2. Do you agree that suicide is a valid option for homosexuals and bisexuals—or for anyone for that matter?
3. Do you think you would feel or even be responsible if the client made a suicide attempt?
4. What problem do you focus on—suicide or sexual orientation?
5. Do you think that it is possible to decide on one's sexual orientation in a single counseling session or rap session with a friend?

At this point, the counselor may find it necessary to tell the client that it is impossible to promise that the client will discover his or her sexual orientation to be heterosexual, homosexual, or bisexual. The counselor can assure the client that everything possible will be done to help the client understand what is happening. The counselor may also find it advisable at this time to have the client promise not to do anything self-destructive while going through the exploration.

Since these are cries for help, it is important to indicate concern and involvement, without becoming panicked or being judgmental. It is very helpful to pay attention to thoughts of death as an expression of fear and self-hatred because if the client later considers coming out to family, he or she may express that fear in very similar terms (e.g., "The news will kill my parents").

CIVIL RIGHTS

In counseling lesbians, gay men and bisexuals, it is important to understand the place of civil rights in their lives. This means both those civil rights that do exist and those that do not exist. At the time of this writing, according to the 1992 American Civil Liberties Union Handbook "The Rights of Lesbians and Gay Men," only California, Connecticut, the District of Columbia, Florida, Illinois, Iowa, Minnesota, Nevada, New Hampshire, New Jersey, Oregon, Vermont, and Wisconsin have "statewide hate or bias-crime legislation that explicitly includes sexual orientation." Other states or cities have assorted "civil rights acts or orders prohibiting discrimination based on sexual orientation." Still other states have sodomy laws that give a clear message that it is criminally wrong to be homosexual.

Many people may have difficulty understanding and appreciating the important need for the current civil rights movement in which lesbians and gay men are fighting. The reality is that most homosexuals do not have equal protection under the law. A "straight" person usually does not lose a job because he or she is a heterosexual, but a lesbian or a gay man can lose a job because he or she is homosexual. Gay parents can lose their children. Most lesbian and gay couples do not have the legal rights heterosexual married couples have. They are not allowed to file a joint tax return, and they usually do not qualify for family insurance coverage. Gay people are allowed but not welcome in the military. They are often faced with security clearance problems, and some who are foreign born are returned to their country of origin.

Not only are lesbian and gay men the recipients of much discrimination, but they also are the victims of a rising tide of antigay violence. Counselors need to realize that lesbians' and gay males' anxieties about their personal and physical safety are very often rooted in reality. Their insecurity is also affected by the lack of positive lesbian and gay role models. Little is written in history books or described in the media to encourage people to feel good about being lesbian, gay, or bisexual.

RESOURCES

Counselors can feel very isolated and alone in their work with lesbian, gay, and bisexual clients. Knowledge of resources within the lesbian, gay, and bisexual community can help the counselor work effectively with sexual minority clients. Counselors may find it helpful to refer someone to a house of worship where lesbians and gay men are known to be welcome, or to use as a resource an organization devoted to lesbian and gay youths. One way the counselor can begin to get more information is to talk to others, share concerns and needs, and develop a network. It is often amazing how helpful this can be: One person can know another who knows another who happens to have information and/or happens to be lesbian, gay, or bisexual.

Many major cities have lesbian or gay hotlines, newspapers, or magazines that can direct counselors to resources. Twelve-step programs such as AA and Al-Anon may have exclusively gay or lesbian meetings, particularly in large cities. The book *Gay Yellow Pages* (see the resources listed at the end of this chapter) covers various regions of the United States. This book is sold in many women's and alternative bookstores that also carry many of the numerous other books written about lesbians, gay men, and bisexuals.

In areas where the above resources are not available, try national professional groups. They usually have lesbian and gay caucuses. Counselors can network with such organizations as the National Association of Social Workers, American Psychological Association, American Psychiatric Association, and similar affiliations.

RESOURCES FOR MORE INFORMATION

Gay Yellow Pages
Renaissance House
P. O. Box 292, Village Station
New York, NY 10014

Parents and Friends of Lesbians and
  Gays
(Parents FLAG)
P. O. Box 20308
Denver, CO 80220
(303) 321-2270
Send $1 and a self-addressed stamped envelope for brochures and information on having gay or lesbian children.

Organizations for lesbian and gay youths:

The Gay and Lesbian Community Service Center
1213 North Highland Avenue
Hollywood, CA 90038
(213) 464-7400

The Hetrick-Martin Institute
401 East West Street
New York, NY 10014
(212) 633-8920

Horizons
3225 North Sheffield Avenue
Chicago, IL 60657
(312) 472-6469

Sexual Minority Youth Assistance League
1228 Seventeenth Street, NW
Washington, DC 20036
(202) 296-0221

Selected organizations providing legal services:

American Civil Liberties Union
AIDS Project and Lesbian and Gay Rights Project
132 West 43rd Street
New York, NY 10036
(212) 944-9400, ext. 545

Center for Constitutional Rights
666 Broadway, 7th Floor
New York, NY 10012
(212) 614-6464

National Center for Lesbian Rights
1663 Mission Street, 4th Floor
San Francisco, CA 94103
(415) 621-0674

Lambda Legal Defense and Education
Fund, Inc.
666 Broadway, 12th Floor
New York, NY 10012
(212) 995-8585

606 South Olive Street, Suite 580
Los Angeles, CA 90014
(213) 629-2728

FOR FURTHER READING

Allen, P. G. (1984). Beloved women: The lesbian in American Indian culture. In T. Darty & S. Porter (Eds.), *Women-identified women* (pp. 83–96). Palo Alto, CA: Mayfield.
Berger, R. M. (1982). The unseen minority: Older gays and lesbians. *Social Work, 27,* 236–242.
Berzon, B., Ph.D. (1984). *Positively gay.* Los Angeles: Mediamix Associates.
Berzon, B., Ph.D. (1988). *Permanent partners.* New York: Dutton.
Boswell, J. (1987). *Christianity, social tolerance, and homosexuality.* Chicago and London: University of Chicago Press.
Bozett, F. W. (1981). Gay fathers: Evolution of the gay-father identity. *American Journal of Orthopsychiatry, 51,* 552–559.
Brant, B. (1984). Reclamation: A lesbian Indian story. In T. Darty & S. Potter (Eds.), *Women-identified women* (pp. 97–103). Palo Alto, CA: Mayfield.
Coleman, E., Ph.D. (1985). Bisexual and gay men in heterosexual marriage: Conflicts and resolutions in therapy. In J. C. Gonsiorek (Ed.), *A guide to psychotherapy with gay and lesbian clients* (pp. 93–103). New York: Harrington Park Press.
Corwell, A. (1983). *Black lesbian in white America.* Tallahassee, FL: Naiad Press.
Cowan, T. (1988). *Gay men and women who enriched the world.* New Canaan, CT: Mulvey Books.
Duberman, M., Vicinus, M., & Chauncey, G., Jr. (Eds.). (1989). *Hidden from history: Reclaiming the gay and lesbian past.* New York: New American Library.
Finnegan, D. G., & McNally, E. B. (1987). *Dual identities: Counseling chemically dependent gay men and lesbians.* Center City, MN: Hazelden.
Hidalgo, H. (1984). The Puerto Rican lesbian in the United States. In T. Darty & S. Potter (Eds.), *Women-identified women* (pp. 83–96). Palo Alto, CA: Mayfield.
Hunter, N. D., Michaelson, S. E., & Stoddard, T. B. (1992). *The rights of lesbians and gay men: The basic ACLU guide to a gay person's rights* (3rd ed., Appendix C, D). Carbondale and Edwardsville, IL: Southern Illinois University Press.
Isay, R. A., M.D. (1989). *Being homosexual: Gay men and their development.* New York: Farrar, Straus, & Giroux.
Klein, F., M.D., & Wolf, T. J. (1985). Bisexualities: Theory and research. *Journal of Homosexuality, 11,* 1–232.
Lopez, D., Jr., & Getzel, G. S. (1984, September). Helping gay AIDS patients in crisis. *Social Casework,* pp. 387–394.
Marmor, J. (1980). Clinical aspects of male homosexuality. In J. Marmor (Ed.), *Homosexual behavior: A modern reappraisal* (pp. 267–279). New York: Basic Books.
Martin, D. A. (1982). Learning to hide: The socialization of the gay adolescent. In S. C. Feinstein, J. G. Looney, A. Z. Schwartzberg, & A. D. Sorosky (Eds.), *Adolescent psychiatry: Developmental and clinical studies* (vol. 10, pp. 51–65). Chicago: University of Chicago Press.

McDonald, H. B., & Steinhorn, A. I. (1990). *Understanding homosexuality: A guide for those who know, love, or counsel gay and lesbian individuals.* New York: Crossroad.

Miller, N. (1989). *In search of gay America.* New York: Atlantic Monthly Press.

Moses, A. E., & Hawkins, R. O., Jr. (1982). *Counseling lesbian women and gay men: A life issues approach.* St. Louis: Mosby.

Muller, A. (1987). *Parents matter: Parents' relationships with lesbian daughters and gay sons.* Tallahassee, FL: Naiad Press.

Nelson, J. B., Ph.D. (1985). Religious and moral issues in working with homosexual clients. In J. C. Gonsiorek (Ed.), *A guide to psychotherapy with gay and lesbian clients* (pp. 164–175). New York: Harrington Park Press.

Rafkin, L. (1987). *Different daughters: A book by mothers of lesbians.* Pittsburgh and San Francisco: Cleis Press.

Reiter, L. (1989). Sexual orientation, sexual identity, and the question of choice. *Clinical Social Work Journal, 17,* 138–150.

Steinhorn, A. I. (1979). Lesbian adolescents in residential treatment. *Social Casework, 60,* 494–498.

Steinhorn, A. I. (1982). Lesbian mothers—the invisible minority: Role of the mental health worker. *Women and Therapy, 1,* 35–48.

Steinhorn, A. I., & McDonald, H. (1988). Lesbian and gay parents. In M. Shernoff, & W. A. Scott, (Eds.), *The sourcebook on lesbian/gay health care* (2nd ed., pp. 246–249). Washington, DC: National Lesbian/Gay Health Foundation.

Vacha, K. (1985). *Quiet fire: Memoirs of older gay men.* Trumansburg, NY: Crossing Press.

White, E. (1983). *A boy's own story.* New York: New American Library.

REFERENCES

Cass, V. (1979). Homosexual identity formation: A theoretical model. *Journal of Homosexuality, 4,* 219–237.

Freud, S. (1987). Letter to an American mother. In R. Bayer (Ed.), *Homosexuality and American psychiatry* (p. 27). Princeton; Princeton University Press. (Letter originally written 1935.)

Kübler-Ross, E. (1969). *On death and dying.* New York: Macmillan.

11

Clinical Treatment Issues Regarding Black African-Americans

MICHAEL BARNES, Ph.D.

Considerable controversy exists in the psychiatric epidemiological literature concerning the incidence and prevalence of mental disorders for African-Americans in the United States. At best the research is contradictory and conflicting. For example, Fried (1969) concluded that the weight of the evidence suggests that serious mental disorder is common among blacks. On the other hand, Fischer (1969) emphasized that it is a myth that blacks have more mental illness than whites. Neighbors and Lumpkin (1990) have concluded that no definitive conclusions can be drawn about the mental health status of African-Americans based on treatment rate studies.

The mental health of African-Americans has been extensively researched. Jackson (1988, 1991) indicated that while the mental health problems of blacks have been repeatedly documented over an extended period of time, this work has not resulted in much needed knowledge in the areas of psychiatric epidemiology, service delivery, and treatment. Instead, this research has provided evidence suggesting both a need to clarify these problems and a direction for future research inquiry. For example, many researchers have abandoned the biological notion of race in their inquiries, deciding to utilize social definitions of race and ethnicity as mere clues in searching for environmental causes of observable group differences (Cooper, 1984). Many researchers have come to treat ethnicity as one of many sociocultural factors rather than as distinct cultural and social environmental indicators (Wolinsky, 1982). Indeed, many researchers have questioned the appropriateness and validity of socioeconomic status (SES) and other sociocultural measures (occupation, coping resources, lifestyle factors, etc.) when comparing across racial/ethnic groups (Allen & Britt, 1983; James, 1984; Myers, 1984).

The Subcommittee on the Mental Health of Black Americans of the President's Commission on Mental Health (1978) stated that the environment, which is created by institutional racism, rather than intrapsychic deficiencies in black Americans, is largely responsible for the overrepresentation of blacks among the mentally disabled. Therefore, it is especially important that the mental health of any black person be viewed in terms of his or her socioeconomic and cultural background. This socioeconomic/cultural context is shaped and influenced by a society in which racism is pervasive. Jackson (1991) called for renewed emphasis on the nature of the social environment and contextual factors, including general health and health care, and their relationships to mental health and mental health illness among African-Americans. Fried (1969) concluded that neglecting to consider psychosocial stressors before diagnosing black patients results in improper diagnoses and diagnostic bias. Several authors have pointed out that the study of social status, social mobility, and African-American reactions to economic and political circumstances are important topics in their own right, having significant mental health implications (Allen & Britt, 1983; Jackson, Neighbors, & Gurin, 1982).

Jackson (1991) stated it succinctly when he said that the "mental health problems of African Americans have to be understood within historical, political, social and economic contexts" (p. 33). Mental health is influenced by one's interaction within the social environment. Many African-Americans continue to endure poor economic circumstances and social discrimination, which affect the mental health status of this group. Failing to take these external factors into consideration when attempting to diagnose, assess, and otherwise provide mental health services to members of this group is inadequate (Snowden & Todman, 1982) and results in bias (Neighbors & Lumpkin, 1990).

Despite the fact that African-Americans are exposed to social conditions considered to be antecedents of psychiatric disorder, epidemiological studies have not conclusively demonstrated that African-Americans exhibit higher rates of specific mental disorders than whites (Allen & Britt, 1983; Fischer, 1969; Myers, Weissman, & Tischler, 1984; Neighbors, 1984; Robins, Helzer, & Weissman, 1984; Williams, 1986). Myers et al. (1984) suggested that it is crucial to understand the processes by which racial differences influence mental health status. According to the authors, such a research approach should not only consider the stressors unique to African-Americans, but also examine their coping responses.

UTILIZATION OF SERVICES

Until the late 1960s the needs of ethnic minorities for mental health services were not taken into account by mental health planners. However, beginning with the civil rights movement in the 1960s, there has been an increasing awareness of the need for responsive service delivery for minorities. Despite this increased awareness, and increases in service provision, there are still language and cultural barriers to using existing services.

A comparison by race and ethnicity of the use of mental health services in 1983 showed that there was a higher rate of utilization of services by African-Americans, especially in inpatient care and residential care, relative to their proportion in the general population. Their use of these services was 21% and 20.1%, in the areas of inpatient and residential care, respectively (Cheung, 1991). Furthermore, there was a large increase in the number of hospitalizations of minorities between 1970 and 1980, and African-Americans accounted for most of the increase. This finding is upsetting because there is no convergent evidence of a greater prevalence of mental illness associated with minority status. To explain this phenomenon, Poussaint (1990) has suggested that blacks often have fewer financial and social supports available for a return to the community, halfway houses are overcrowded, and it is difficult to find living quarters for marginally functioning mental patients. Furthermore, follow-up care for discharged patients has been poor or poorly funded. Lastly, much of the overutilization may be due to the overuse of federally funded drug abuse centers. Other explanations offered by Cheung (1991) include declining mental health resources in communities, fewer available programs for the chronically mentally ill, and misdiagnosis of symptoms due to cultural and language barriers.

There is contradictory data concerning the rate of utilization of outpatient mental health services by African-Americans. A study by Sue (1977) involving the mental health system in Seattle, Washington, indicated that African-Americans overutilized services, relative to their proportions in the population. However, a study by O'Sullivan, Peterson, Cox, and Kirkeby (1989) of the same population 10 years later failed to replicate these findings. More recently, a study of the Los Angeles County outpatient mental health system by Sue, Fujino, Hu, Takeuchi, and Zane (1991) found utilization rates consistent with Sue (1977).

Perhaps more important than the findings concerning utilization rates of outpatient services are the findings concerning dropout rates and length of service. A study by Sue and Sue (1974) found that 50% of black clients terminate therapy after the first session, while the corresponding percentage for whites is 30%. They also found that black clients attended an average of 4.68 sessions, while white clients attended an average of 8.68 sessions. The study by Sue, Fujino, Hu, Takeuchi, and Zane (1991) also found that African-Americans terminate quickly and average fewer sessions than other ethnic groups.

It has been proposed that this black/white difference is due to a negative view of mental health services held by African-Americans. However, research does not seem to support this notion; according to Sue and Sue (1990), black Americans seem to view counseling positively. To explain what seems to be a contradiction, blacks have difficulty with the process and content of "traditional" therapy; yet when therapy is consistent with their values, life experiences, and cultural ways of responding, therapy is viewed not only as positive, but also as effective.

PRACTICAL SUGGESTIONS FOR PROMOTING EFFICACIOUS TREATMENT

Before the process and content of treatment is discussed, a word of caution is in order. It is critical to recognize the great diversity that exists *among* black Americans. Variables such as socioeconomic status, educational attainment, cultural identity, and reaction to racism are only a few of the factors on which African-Americans differ. Therefore, it is difficult to say that the following will apply to all African-Americans. The discussion will include suggestions to (a) foster a sense of alliance between client and therapist, (b) foster a sense of empowerment, and (c) involve the family and resources from the broader social context of African-Americans in treatment.

Given the discussion above on premature termination and short treatment duration, it is apparent that the initial focus in treatment with an African-American client should be on getting the client to return for subsequent sessions. Establishing a therapeutic alliance, therefore, is vital. In order to do this, one must first recognize the potential barriers to this process. First of all, many African-Americans have been victims of discrimination and oppression. In order to survive in a white racist society, many blacks have developed *cultural paranoia* (Grier & Cobbs, 1968). This refers to a survival mechanism used to protect against both physical and psychological harm. Thus, many blacks enter therapy with a hesitancy to self-disclose out of a fear of being misunderstood, hurt, or taken advantage of in the event that personal information is shared (Ridley, 1984). Second, many clients do not come to therapy of their own volition; they are often referred by a variety of social agencies and may therefore be somewhat resistant to therapy. Third, black clients may be hypersensitive to the interaction process between therapist and client. The client may "size up" the therapist by remaining aloof and "test" the therapist by posing questions regarding the therapist's values or qualifications (Jenkins, 1985). If the therapist does not meet the client's expectations, presumably the client will terminate early in the process, typically after one or two sessions.

The above issues must be dealt with in the first few sessions of therapy because if an alliance is not established, progress will be hindered. Ridley (1984) believes that most black clients will demonstrate "healthy cultural paranoia," and he suggests two processes that should be used to combat this phenomenon. First, feelings of suspiciousness, anger, and frustration on the part of the client must be brought to the surface. Second, since disclosing to all persons is not adaptive, the therapist must acknowledge this fact to his or her client. The therapist must then encourage the client to discern those occasions when he or she should self-disclose, based on sitational demands. Third, to deal with the possible resistance, the therapist must deal with his or her own fears and prejudices and make an effort to prohibit these feelings and cognitions to interfere with the therapy. Fourth, open discussion regarding the therapist's relationship to the referral agency, obtaining the client's expectations about therapy, contracting with the client, and setting short-term goals aid in overcoming resistance (Sue & Sue, 1990). In response to testing behaviors, Gibbs (1989) maintains that the therapist must avoid being drawn into a power struggle with the client. In addition the therapist must draw firm limits for sessions. Several authors have stressed the need for outreach services with African-American clients to ensure the engagement process. Boyd-Franklin (1989) indicates that it is often important for the therapist to reach out to the client by means of letters, phone calls, and home visits.

A second process important to therapy with African-Americans is building a sense of client empowerment. Ziter (1987) indicates that powerlessness is pervasive in many black communities because of the extent to which blacks have received negative valuation from the larger society. Boyd-Franklin (1989) points out that many African-American families have a multigenerational history of victimization due to poverty and racism, and by virtue of their skin color, have constant visible reminders of the inequities of society. This leads to a sense of powerlessness and entrapment in which individuals feel unable to make and/or implement basic decisions regarding their own lives and the lives of their families. *Empowerment* refers to the identification of blacks to power, as well as the development of skills in individuals that help them to feel that they can effect important changes in their lives and take control of events over which they previously felt powerless.

To build this sense of empowerment, many authors have stressed the importance of taking an active approach to therapy. Involvement of the therapist in solving problems of day-to-day living is essential to this process as it allows for assessment of the sources of powerlessness and for the effecting of change (Thomas & Dansby, 1985). For example, the therapist can simply encourage a mother to call her child's teacher or the representative of an agency when the mother has been feeling as if she is at the mercy of child welfare agencies. If further support is needed, the therapist can role-play with the mother and be present when the call is made. The important point is that by assisting in the achievement of a small success, it helps the client to feel as if he or she is able to assume control (Boyd-Franklin, 1989).

Other writers have suggested assertiveness training as being beneficial for empowerment. As assertiveness techniques are learned, the client can implement them in situations where the client previously has been silent, withdrawn, or inarticulate despite feeling angry and frustrated. In this way, the client can develop a sense of mastery and empowerment (Baker, 1988).

A third consideration of treatment with African-Americans involves the consideration and inclusion of the family and the informal social network of the client. This is true for several reasons. As a group, black Americans tend to be more group-centered and oriented toward interpersonal matters. For many, there is an extended family (or otherwise informal social) network that provides emotional and economic support. Child rearing is often shared among a number of relatives, older children, and even close friends. Aside from family and friends, the church is often a central focus of social and civic activities in the black community. Lastly, black families are being referred to clinics, hospitals, and mental health centers in record numbers (Boyd-Franklin, 1989). Thus, it is significant that treatment of the black individual without consideration of the broader social context leads to an unrealistically narrow focus and may ignore important resources of the client.

Boyd-Franklin (1989) points out that although it may be essential to ultimately engage the whole family in therapy, it may be better to first see the identified client. Since therapy may be new to black families, this individual can often help to speed up the process of building credibility and trust. Also, many black families may feel that they will be viewed negatively by the therapist due to factors that make them differ from the ideal family, such as the presence of illegitimate children, absence of spouses, and various paternities of children of the same family. Therefore, it is recommended that therapists postpone extensive information gathering about the family until trust has been established. Boyd-Franklin (1989) recommends the use of the *genogram* or family tree for gathering information about family constellations. This approach may be more appropriate than the usual intake forms that ask for the mother's name, father's name, and number of children in the family.

Another important process of treatment is to focus on building strengths that already exist in many black families. Rather than "deficit" theories and practices to guide treatment, strengths such as the bond of the extended family, adaptability of family roles, strong religious orientation, belief in the value of education and the work ethic, and the ability to use effective coping skills should be capitalized upon and encouraged when dealing with African-Americans (Boyd-Franklin, 1989).

Lastly, in light of the importance of religion in the lives of African-

Americans, clinicians should identify local black ministers and view them as resources in helping clients.

FOR FURTHER READING

Boyd-Franklin, N. (1989). *Black families in therapy: A multisystems approach.* New York: Guilford Press.
Cheung, F. (1991). The use of mental health services by ethnic minorities. In H. F. Myers, P. Wohlford, L. P. Guzman, & R. J. Echemendia (Eds.), *Ethnic minority perspectives on clinical training and services in psychology* (pp. 23–31). Washington, DC: American Psychological Association.
Jackson, J. S. (1991). The mental health service and training need of African Americans. In H. F. Myers, P. Wohlford, L. P. Guzman, & R. J. Echemendia (Eds.), *Ethnic minority perspectives on clinical training and services in psychology* (pp. 33–42). Washington, DC: American Psychological Association.
President's Commission on Mental Health. (1978). *Report to the President's Commission on Mental Health* (Vol. 1). (PR 39.8:M52/R29/V1). Washington, DC: U.S. Government Printing Office.
See, J. J., & Miller, K. S. (1973) Mental Health. In K. S. Miller & R. M. Dreger (Eds.), *Comparative studies of blacks and whites in the United States* (pp. 448–464). New York: Seminar Press.
Sue, D. W., & Sue, D. (1990). *Counseling the culturally different* (2nd ed.). New York: Wiley.
Thomas, A., & Sillen, S. (1972). *Racism and psychiatry.* New York: Brunner/Mazel.

REFERENCES

Allen, L., & Britt, D. W. (1983). Black women in American society: A resource development perspective [Special issue]. *Issues in Mental Health Nursing, 5,* 41–79.
Baker, F. M. (1988). Afro-Americans. In L. Comas-Diaz & E. E. H. Griffith (Eds.), *Cross-cultural mental health* (pp. 151–181). New York: Wiley.
Boyd-Franklin, N. (1989). *Black families in therapy: A multisystems approach.* New York: Guilford Press.
Cheung, F. (1991). The use of mental health services by ethnic minorities. In H. F. Myers, P. Wohlford, L. P. Guzman, & R. J. Echemendia (Eds.), *Ethnic minority perspectives on clinical training and services in psychology* (pp. 23–31). Washington, DC: American Psychological Association.
Cooper, R. (1984). A note on the biologic concept of race and its application in epidemiological research. *American Heart Journal, 108,* 715–723.
Fischer, J. (1969). Negroes, whites, and rates of mental illness: Reconsideration of a myth. *Psychiatry, 32,* 428–446.
Fried, M. (1975). Social differences in mental health. In J. Kosa & I. Zola (Eds.), *Poverty and health: A sociological analysis* (rev. ed.) (pp. 135–192). Cambridge: Commonwealth Fund/Harvard University Press.
Gibbs, J. T. (1989). Black American adolescents. In J. T. Gibbs, L. N. Huang, & Associates (Eds.), *Children of color: Psychological interventions with minority youth* (pp. 179–223). San Francisco: Jossey-Bass.
Grier, W. H., & Cobbs, P. M. (1968). *Black rage.* New York: Basic Books.
Jackson, J. S. (1988). Mental health problems among black Americans: Research needs. *Division of Child, Youth, and Family Services Newsletter, 11*(2), 18–19.
Jackson, J. S. (1991). The mental health service and training need of African

Americans. In H. F. Myers, P. Wohlford, L. P. Guzman, & R. J. Echemendia (Eds.), *Ethnic minority perspectives on clinical training and services in psychology* (pp. 33–42). Washington, DC: American Psychological Association.

Jackson, J. S., Neighbors, H. W., & Gurin, G. (1982). The mental health status of older black Americans: A national study. *Black Scholar, 13,* 21–35.

James, S. A. (1984). Coronary heart disease in black Americans: Suggestions for research on psychosocial factors. *American Heart Journal, 108,* 833–838.

Jenkins, A. H. (1985). Attending to the self-activity in the Afro-American client. *Psychotherapy, 22,* 335–341.

Myers, H. F. (1984). Summary of workshop: 3. Working group on socioeconomic and sociocultural influences. *American Heart Journal, 108,* 706–710.

Myers, J., Weissman, M., & Tischler, G. (1984). Six-month prevalence of psychiatric disorders in three communities. *Archives of General Psychiatry, 41,* 971–978.

Neighbors, H. W. (1984). The distribution of psychiatric morbidity: A review and suggestions for research. *Community Mental Health Journal, 20,* 5–18.

Neighbors, H. W., & Lumpkin, S. (1990). The epidemiology of mental disorder in the black population. In D. S. Ruiz (Ed.), *Handbook of mental health and mental disorder among black Americans* (pp. 55–70). New York: Greenwood Press.

O'Sullivan, M. J., Peterson, P. D., Cox, G. B., & Kirkeby, J. (1989). Ethnic populations: Community mental health services 10 years later. *American Journal of Community Psychology, 17,* 17–30.

Poussaint, A. F. (1990). The mental health status of black Americans. In D. S. Ruiz (Ed.), *Handbook of mental health and mental disorder among black Americans* (pp. 17–50). New York: Greenwood Press.

President's Commission on Mental Health. (1978). *Report to the President's Commission on Mental Health* (Vol. 1). (PR 39.8:M52/R29/V1). Washington, DC: U.S. Government Printing Office.

Ridley, C. R. (1984). Clinical treatment of the nondisclosing black client. *American Psychologist, 39,* 1234–1244.

Robins, L., Helzer, J., & Weissman, M. (1984). Lifetime prevalence of specific psychiatric disorders in three sites. *Archives of General Psychiatry, 41,* 949–958.

Snowden, L., & Todman, P. A. (1982). The psychological assessment of blacks: New and needed developments. In E. E. Jones and S. J. Korchin (Eds.), *Minority mental health* (pp. 193–226). New York: Praeger.

Sue, D. W., & Sue, D. (1990). *Counseling the culturally different* (2nd ed.). New York: Wiley.

Sue, S. (1977). Community mental health services to minority groups: Some optimism, some pessimism. *American Psychologist, 32,* 616–628.

Sue, S., & Sue, D. W. (1974). MMPI comparisons between Asian- and non-Asian-American students utilizing an university psychiatric clinic. *Journal of Counseling Psychology, 21,* 423–427.

Sue, S., Fujino, D. C., Hu, L., Takeuchi, D. T., & Zane, N. W. S. (1991). Community mental health services for ethnic minority groups: A test of the cultural responsiveness hypothesis. *Journal of Counseling and Clinical Psychology, 59,* 533–540.

Thomas, M. B., & Dansby, P. G. (1985). Black clients: Family structures, therapeutic issues, and strengths. *Psychotherapy, 22,* 398–407.

Williams, D. H. (1986). The epidemiology of mental illness in Afro-Americans. *Hospital and Community Psychiatry, 37,* 42–49.

Wolinsky, F. D. (1982). Racial differences in illness behavior. *Journal of Community Health. 8,* 87–101.

Ziter, M. L. P. (1987). Culturally sensitive treatment of black alcoholic families. *Social Work, 32,* 130–135.

12

Gender Issues

ILENE C. WASSERMAN, M.A.Ed., L.C.S.W.

As a counselor, I often work with individuals, as well as with couples, who are seeking guidance with problems in their relationships, both at work and in their personal lives. Generally speaking, my approach with these clients is to help them to understand their own role in the difficulties they are experiencing and to help them to understand these difficulties in a broader social context. One way of accomplishing the latter is to stimulate clients to expand their notions of the social world by proposing a perspective that may be new to them. Particularly in the area of male/female relationships, the perspective of gender style differences is an important lens through which to view the difficulties and frustrations a client may be experiencing.

There is, of course, an inherent risk in any discussion of gender differences that one will fall into the trap of promoting stereotypes. The patterns of gender behavior discussed in this chapter are meant only to outline and describe observed tendencies in the most general terms, and not to define or label the inevitable behavior of either sex. It would be inaccurate and counterproductive to the therapeutic process to make the claim that men always respond to certain situations in a specific way or that women always view interaction in a particular light. It is, however, clear that men, as a group, tend to respond to certain situations in a specific way and that women, as a group, tend to view interaction in a particular light. It is the purpose of this chapter to show that understanding these tendencies and using them as tools with which to work with clients will greatly enhance the therapist's effectiveness.

As the therapist, your own awareness of gender issues is of critical importance. Such awareness includes both how you relate to male and female clients and how they may be relating to one another, as well as how your own biases and stereotypes may influence the way you frame therapeutic goals. Do you feel more empathy for or resonate with resistance to the typically female approach? To the male? These are important questions to ask yourself. No interaction, and therefore no intervention, is gender free.

While there are innumerable ways in which to structure a discussion of male/female style differences, I have, for the purposes of this chapter, concentrated on three themes. These are styles of relating, going about one's business, and defining oneself. In discussing each of these themes, I first describe the contrasting tendencies of men and women and then suggest some of the ways in which an awareness of these tendencies is of critical importance to the process through which a counselor frames the material a client raises.

STYLES OF RELATING

Independence versus Connectedness

Women tend to view relationships in terms of feelings of connectedness and mutual dependencies and to emphasize "likeness" in their social interactions. Men tend to view themselves as self-reliant and independent and to value those qualities in others (Gilligan, 1982). These different tendencies can be traced to early stages of gender identity development.

Gender identity begins to formulate between the ages of 2 and 3, but it is not until 5 or 6 that the notion of gender permanence is formalized. It is at this point that a child is capable of the thought "I am a girl and will always be a girl" or "I am a boy and will always be a boy." Since women in our society are still, in most instances, the primary caretakers of children at this age, this process of identifying oneself as belonging permanently to one of the two genders is a very different process for girls and boys. Young girls define themselves as being "like Mom," while boys define themselves as being "different from Mom" (Chodorow, 1978, p. 174). To be female is defined early in life as being "like" the other person in a primary relationship. To be male is defined early in life as being "different." This sets the stage early on for women to emphasize connection and similarity in relationship while men seek independence and self-reliance.

One of the most common areas in which this difference between men and women is played out is that of communication. Men and women not only have different preferences for how conversations are conducted, they also have different agendas for what a conversation should accomplish. Men tend to be primarily concerned with the *content* of what is said. They view conversation primarily as a method of conveying information and are therefore listening for the bottom line. Women are also concerned with what is being said, but are often even more concerned with how it is said, or the *process*. They view conversation primarily as a means of building relationships, in addition to viewing it as a means of conveying information. Conversation, for women, is an important factor in establishing that sense of connection they seek.

Very often, a couple or individual seeking help from a counselor for heterosexual relationship issues will have difficulties in this area. The woman desires a feeling of connectedness through conversation with her partner and does not feel satisfied with either the quality or the quantity of their contact. Her partner may be aware of her discontent, but may be confused as to how to address the problem. Additionally, it is often true that the woman experiences the more typically male approach to conversation as rejective. It may feel to her that he either is disinterested in what she has to say or fails to put enough energy into the relationship.

This incompatibility is not only evident in the words exchanged, but can also be seen in the accompanying nonverbals. Men tend only to make listening noises to indicate agreement. They participate at the point at which some concrete information is exchanged. Women are more likely to make listening noises simply to show that they are listening and understanding (Tannen, 1990). A typical exchange over this issue might run as follows:

SUSAN: You don't seem to be listening to me. You just sit there when I'm talking. How do I know you're paying attention?
TOM: Just because I don't say anything doesn't mean I'm not listening. I'm listening. I just don't want to interrupt you.

She is seeking evidence that the conversation is connecting them in some way; he is waiting to hear her point. She feels rejected; he feels unfairly accused.

There are several ways in which a counselor can use knowledge of these gender style differences to help a couple deal with such problems. As a starting point, it can be extremely helpful to educate the couple about the very problems that they are experiencing. This involves explaining to the couple that these difficulties are common and are often based in gender style differences. This explanation can have the effect of refocusing the couple away from the question of who is at fault and onto the project of working together. The problem is defined, not as something that they are doing to each other for reasons of either hostility or excessive neediness, but as a common situation with which they can learn to work together. While this work is obviously very personal in its nature and very different depending on the people involved, the issue itself has been somewhat depersonalized. The couple's frustrations shift away from one another and are directed toward dealing with a problem that they share.

It is important in all such work that a counselor be careful not to view or present the traditional man's more independent stance as a superior position to the woman's desire for connectedness. Connection is not the same thing as weakness or neediness, just as the avoidance of connection is not the same thing as strength or autonomy.

Counseling itself, by its very nature, can also accomplish a great deal in such situations, since it is intrinsically involved with process and not only with the bottom line. It resembles in this way the kind of communication for which the woman is likely to be thirsty. Counseling sessions become an arena in which some of that thirst can be quenched. In that setting she is by definition involved in conversations with her partner that are focused on connecting and finding common ground. This experience not only helps as a model for communication; it can also help to take some of the pressure off at home.

It is equally important for the counselor to help the woman to frame her partner's conversational style as just that, and not as a personal rejection. Again, some explanation of gender style differences can be very helpful with this. His seeming unresponsiveness does not mirror a lack of interest in her, but simply reflects his accustomed conversational approach. Some emphasis on the need that she allow him to continue to adopt that approach at times can help to offset the man's sense that the counseling, which structurally resembles what the woman is seeking, is prejudiced against his more typically male view.

This issue can be evident also in situations involving a female counselor and a male client. The counselor, seeking to connect both for therapeutic reasons and through typically female ways of relating, may find that the male client responds by escalating his own attempts to differentiate himself from her and pull back. The result can be a dialogue that resembles a chase. By being aware of this possibility, the counselor can seek ways of connecting to the client that are less likely to evoke a flight response. A male counselor might focus more on helping the client to establish boundaries. In either instance, the related transference is valuable to the therapeutic process.

GOING ABOUT ONE'S BUSINESS

Task versus Process

Men and women tend to go about their business with different perceptions of what it is they are doing. A situation in which a woman feels that she is involved in a process may feel to a man like one in which he must accomplish a task. As with conversation, this difference in approach to doing things can cause friction and misunderstanding between the sexes in their relations to one another, but it also has implications for individuals of each sex outside man/woman relationships.

Consider the case of a man and a woman, each of whom engages in a project that involves assembling a team. The criteria by which the man and woman choose their teams are likely to be different. He will focus on who is most likely to accomplish the task. She will focus on whom she would most enjoy working with. For him, satisfaction with the project is primarily related to the end product. For her, it is more likely to relate to the quality of the process through which the end product is achieved. Additionally, when working with someone, she is more likely than a man to see the opportunity of forming a friendship. Once again, a woman's tendency to focus on process is deeply rooted in her desire to discover common ground and connect with those around her.

The two genders' respective foci on process and relationship on the one hand and task and accomplishment on the other are often reflected in the issues that bring men and women into counseling. Women are often prompted to seek help because they feel that they are failing in their relationships. Men are often prompted by their own failure at a task. A classic example is the man who has lost his job and is contending with a resultant crisis of self-esteem. It is very important in either instance for counselors to be aware that they may not be hearing the whole story. Because a woman is predisposed to view her life and measure her self-worth in terms of personal relationships, she may fail to recognize the importance of accomplishment to her own sense of well-being. Similarly, because a man is likely to measure his worth by his accomplishments, he may not perceive how the nature of his relationships affects his self-esteem and sense of well-being. It is the counselor's role, in either case, to help the client to expand his or her view of life. Both views should be balanced by an understanding of the ways in which both personal relationships and achievements help to build and maintain a healthy self-esteem.

The fact that men and women can perceive the same situation or activity as a task on the one hand and a process on the other has strong implications for relations between them. For example, with a couple entering counseling, the woman commonly will complain that the romance and passion of their courtship period is long gone. "You never tell me you love me anymore," she says. "I don't have to," he responds, "I married you, didn't I?" His view of the courtship has been that it was a task, a goal-oriented activity. The courtship period is defined as successful by the end product: marriage. For the woman, the success of the courtship is dependent on her experience of it as a time of closeness and romance, and she needs for those aspects of the process to continue.

A similar disparity can be seen in sexual relations. For many men, lovemaking, like conversation, has a bottom line: in the case of sex, orgasm. For many women, sexual activity is not defined by the event that completes it, but by the entire experience or process of being close and intimate. Often, when couples are experiencing sexual difficulties, these difficulties parallel the sorts of conversational difficulties described earlier. She is looking for sustained contact. He is trying to achieve a goal or complete a task. As in the area of conversation, it can be helpful for a counselor to educate the couple about the role that gender style differences may play in these seeming incompatibilities. This will help the couple to forge a shared approach when they are able and to understand where the other is "coming from" when they are not.

In counseling, this style difference often emerges around understanding the experience of the therapy itself. A male client may need the framework of what task is being accomplished in order to stay with the process.

DEFINING ONESELF

Cooperation versus Competition

Men tend to be affirmed by achievements that set them apart. Women, on the other hand tend to be affirmed by events that bring them closer together. These tendencies make the issue of individual achievement and accomplishment a very different matter for the two sexes. In fact, much has been written about the observation that woman's fear of achievement is related to the threat of being disconnected from relationships (Horner, 1970). It has also been observed that these differences are apparent even in early childhood.

An often-noted classic difference in the socialization of young girls and boys is that boys are socialized to be competitive through sports while girls play more "turn-taking" games (Tannen, 1990). For boys, games result in a winner who is better and a loser who is not as good. Girls are more likely either to play (or frame) games in which there is the possibility of more than one winner or to engage in pretend play in which the concept of winning or losing is not involved. Again, the female emphasis is on shared experience and connection, the process of playing together. The male emphasis is on the bottom line, the result: who won? While there are no clear answers regarding the origins of these observed differences, it is clear that they carry implications for both sexes in the area of defining oneself through achievement, failure, and competition with others.

In my own experience as a counselor, I have observed that women tend to externalize success and internalize failure. Women don't take clear ownership for their accomplishments, or will try to spread the credit around. "We all did a great job," she might say. On the other hand, when confronted with failure, a woman's response is to take as much responsibility as she can. "I'm sorry," she might say, or "What did I do wrong?" Men, however, are more likely to take credit for what has gone right and to spread the blame for failure. "Whose fault is this?" a man might ask, not assuming as a woman is likely to do that it is his own fault. Men internalize success and externalize failure.

In the counseling relationship, these different approaches are played out in many ways. It is common for a woman seeking help to feel unhappy. At least some of her unhappiness is traceable to her avoidance of success and achievement in any realm other than that of personal relationships. Because her tendency is to define herself by her relations to others, she herself may be mystified as to the origin of her unhappiness or lack of fulfillment. It can, however, become evident that because she cannot reconcile an image of herself as successful with an image of herself as related and connected to other people, she has been denying herself the gratification of experiencing her own successes. This pattern is related to something known as the *double bind of female authority*. Young-Eisendrath and Wiedeman (1987) summarized this condition as follows: "If they claim their power directly they will be considered 'too much' (too emotional, too intellectual, too masculine or too weird); if they disclaim it they will be forced to identify with being childlike and immaturely dependent in ways that will increase their anxiety about being separate individuals" (p. 2). Either way, she cannot get it right. A counselor who is aware of these common predispositions in women can be most effective in breaking the perceived link between success and isolation.

Men, who tend to externalize failure, bring a very different set of issues into counseling. The example of the man who loses his job is pertinent. A man who habitually defines himself by his successes and distances himself from his failures has a very difficult time when so massive a disappointment as the loss of a job occurs. Part of the counselor's work in such an instance is to help the man to expand the terms by which he defines himself and to combat his impulse to define himself as a "loser" because he has failed at a task.

IMPLICATIONS FOR THE COUNSELING RELATIONSHIP

A knowledge of gender style differences can be a powerful tool for a counselor working either with a client individually or with a couple who have come together for help. As illustrated in this chapter, these tendencies are strong and have significant implications for many areas of everyone's lives, affecting how people communicate, how they work, and how they view themselves.

In the area of communication between the sexes, the counselor who encounters a couple with clear gender style differences has many ways to use that observation to foster their understanding of one another. To review, by educating the couple themselves on the subject, the counselor can help them to channel their energies away from conflict and into productive work together. By encouraging the use of the counseling time to engage in the kinds of communication that promote contact and intimacy, the counselor can help to relieve some of the woman's frustration with what may be lacking in her conversations at home. Finally, by validating both the woman's and the man's approach to communication, the counselor can play an important role in helping the couple to build respect for their differences and a caring relationship.

The key for a counselor in applying a knowledge of gender style differences to help a client who is experiencing difficulties in the area of personal accomplishment lies in broadening the client's own view of his or her life. The woman who seeks counseling because of her perception that her personal life is in some way failing may actually need guidance in learning to emphasize other, more stereotypically male, aspects of her life. She may in fact be frustrated because she has failed to account for her need to feel a sense of accomplishment outside of her personal life. Even a woman who is very involved in her career and her accomplishments may need help recognizing the degree to which she measures her success based on her personal interactions. Similarly, the man who enters counseling because of some work-related problem or frustration may need help expanding his worldview to include his social and personal needs. A man who lacks intimate personal contact in his relationships may not be aware that this lack is causing him pain, because it is not typically male to expect or emphasize such relationships. The counselor needs to bring into the counseling relationship the knowledge that personal relationships and personal accomplishment play crucial roles in helping people to feel strong and the knowledge that each gender has a tendency to overlook one or the other of these areas.

In helping clients to attain a strong sense of themselves, the counselor can again use a knowledge of gender style differences. A woman who is having difficulty allowing herself to succeed to her own potential may need to work on understanding and disentangling her concern that achievement will somehow isolate her from other people. A man who is faced with a failure, such as the loss of his job, may benefit from help in expanding his own way of defining himself and understanding the value of connecting with people around him in this situation. Having failed does not make him a "failure," but to the man who has spent a lifetime defining himself by his successes, it can certainly seem that way.

By recognizing the powerful effect that gender style differences can have both on male/female relationships and on issues of self-esteem and performance for both sexes, the counselor acquires a powerful tool for working on these areas. As noted earlier, for counselors to make the most of this tool, it is essential that they be aware of the gender biases they themselves bring into the counseling relationships. It is also important to recognize that counseling itself is a gender-biased process.

The entire enterprise of coming to talk with another person about troubling and intimate issues comes more naturally to women than to men, as does the very process-oriented nature of counseling. It is critical, in this context, that men not be made to feel that their natural tendencies are either inappropriate or "bad." Rather, both men and women should be encouraged to value their own way of doing things as well as that of the opposite sex.

Gender style differences cannot unravel the entire story behind any client's struggles or any relationship's problems. When understood, however, they do provide both counselor and client with a viable and enlightening framework around which to structure productive work.

IMPORTANT POINTS IN SUMMARY

1. Framing of gender style differences is necessarily very general and is by no means meant as a guideline for stereotyping or strictly categorizing men or women.
2. A counselor's awareness of basic gender style differences provides a useful lens through which to view the material a client brings to the counseling situation.
3. Women tend to seek connection to other people, where men seek differentiation.
4. Women tend to focus on process in contexts in which men are more likely to focus on task or result.
5. Women tend to internalize failure and externalize success, while men are more likely to internalize success and externalize failure.
6. Counseling, especially psychotherapy, by virtue of its structure is inherently more like and therefore more favorable to the traditionally female approach. A counselor should be aware of the ways in which this fact creates a potentially threatening climate for a male client and creates a reinforcing climate for a female client.
7. A counselor should be aware of his or her own gender style tendencies and biases. Does he or she reinforce or criticize aspects of the client's behavior because of these biases?
8. A gender-aware model for intervention needs to acknowledge the different developmental histories of men and women as well as the different expectations society holds for each gender.
9. The counselor's goal, whether working with an individual or a couple, is to integrate the traditionally male qualities such as autonomy and self-differentiation with the traditionally female ones such as connectedness and interdependency.
10. Gender styles, and the issues that surround them, provide one of

many contexts in which issues of transference and countertransference manifest. Others include sexual preference, marital status, presence or absence of children, and literally an endless number of other factors. Gender does not provide a complete definition of any person, but gender styles do provide one tool with which a therapist can work.

FOR FURTHER READING

Walters, M., Carter, B., Papp, P., and Silverstein, O. (1988). *The invisible web: Gender patterns in family relationships.* New York: Guilford Press.

REFERENCES

Chodorow, N. (1978). *The reproduction of mothering.* Berkeley: University of California Press.

Gilligan, C. (1982). *In a different voice.* Cambridge: Harvard University Press.

Horner, M. (1970). *Feminine Personality and Conflict.* Monterey, CA: Brooks/Cole.

Tannen, D. (1990). *You just don't understand.* New York: Morrow.

Young-Eisendrath, P. (1984). *Hags and heroes: A feminist approach to Jungian psychotherapy with couples.* Toronto: Inner City Books.

Young-Eisendrath, P. & Wiedeman, F. (1987). *Female authority: Empowering women through psychotherapy.* New York: Guilford Press.

13

Ethical Issues

CELIA B. FISHER, Ph.D.

JAMES HENNESSY, Ph.D.

Counseling, as conceptualized in this article, is a professional service provided by a competent counselor, psychologist, or other mental health specialist (hereinafter referred to as the counselor) that is intended to promote individual adaptability to changing life demands by helping clients develop or enhance a variety of personal-social, coping, and decision-making skills or by helping clients to alter dysfunctional or undesired patterns of living. In pursuing these objectives, counselors recognize that their interventions hold the potential for great benefit as well as considerable harm to their clients and, therefore, are aware of the standards for practice stipulated by the professional organization(s) to which they belong.

The major professional organizations concerned with the delivery of counseling services have codified these standards into statements generally referred to as *ethical principles.* Included among those organizations that have published their own code of ethics are the American Counseling Association (until July 1992, the American Association for Counseling and Development), whose ethical standards were first published in 1961 and most recently revised in 1992; the American Pyschological Association, whose standards were first issued in 1953 and most recently revised in 1992; American Association for Marriage and Family Therapy (1988); National Board for Certified Counselors (1987); and the National Association of Social Workers (1979). Other useful guides for ethical counseling practices have been written by Biggs and Blocher (1987), Carroll, Schneider, and Wesley (1985), Corey, Corey, and Callanan (1988), Herlihy and Golden (1990), Keith-Spiegel and Koocher (1985), Pope and Vasquez (1991), and Van Hoose and Kottler (1985). We have drawn upon these excellent resources in discussing the following four major categories of ethical concern: competence and responsibility, confidentiality, dual relations and allegiances, and respect for the person.

Ethical principles are manifestations of a profession's efforts to guide and regulate the practices of members of that profession. In many states the principles of specific professions have been incorporated into the licensing and certification regulations enacted by state governments to protect consumers and to control entry into a profession. In those states, members of a profession have both a legal and an ethical responsibility to be guided in their professional functioning by those principles. It should be clearly understood, however, that ethical standards are binding on members of a profession, even when those standards have not been incorporated into state regulations. The standards of the several organizations differ in their scope, specific emphases, and level of detailed specification. However, all of them hold that counselors have ultimate ethical responsibility for the procedures and outcomes of their services, and further hold that counselors must strive to promote the welfare and respect the rights and dignity of those with whom they work.

COMPETENCE AND RESPONSIBILITY

Counselors seek to facilitate effective functioning through the application of scientific and professional principles, methods, and techniques. On this basis, counselors have the obligation to maintain the highest standards of competence, and clients have the right to receive services of the highest quality. Competence is commonly defined in terms of formal education, professional training, and supervised experience in the knowledge and techniques necessary to effect desired change (Carroll et al., 1985). The counselor's awareness of ethical and practice guidelines for the delivery of specific counseling services is critical, as is knowledge and understanding of the local and state laws that govern one's practice. Over the course of their careers, counselors should be able to show evidence that they are maintaining and enhancing their professional competence through various forms of continuing education. Using outdated assessment or treatment techniques indicates that the counselor is behaving incompetently, and thus unethically (Pope & Vasquez, 1991).

Counseling services are used by a wide variety of clients (individuals and couples and younger and older adults), for a variety of problems (e.g., education, career choice, personal adjustment, work, and social relations) and in a variety of settings (e.g., health, educational, and rehabilitative institutions, and independent individual and group practices). Given the extensive array of settings in which professional services are provided, counselors must limit their practice to their demonstrated areas of competence as defined by verifiable training and experience.

Competent professional service also includes the counselor's sensitivity to his or her own implicit biases and to overcoming stereotypic thinking and value judgments based on gender, race, age, or sexual orientation. However, the absence of such biases is not sufficient to work competently with different populations. Knowledge and understanding of the client's social-cultural background and situational demands is equally important, as is familiarity with the proven efficacy of treatment strategies or assessment techniques for different social groups. At the same time, the counselor must guard against interpreting a client's problems in terms of group rather than individual factors and characteristics.

When extending services beyond the range of their usual practice, counselors must obtain pertinent training or appropriate supervision. In areas where there is little or no established opportunity to gain such experiences, empirical validation and discussion of treatment options with experienced colleagues is required. If therapeutically feasible, counselors should also alert clients when they are utilizing techniques that are new or of limited familiarity. Counselors do not withhold services from potential clients on the basis of race, gender, national origin, or sexual orientation. The situation may arise, however, where it is the responsibility of the counselor to withhold services, if offering such services would require going outside one's area of demonstrated competence (e.g., treating a child when one's training was in counseling adults) or providing assessments that may be needed but for which the counselor lacks expertise (e.g., where a battery of neuropsychological tests rather than standard psychological tests are more appropriate for the client's presenting problem).

Sometimes in the course of counseling, new problems arise that differ dramatically from those presented by the client at the outset of treatment. For example, a client may have requested career counseling, but later reveal that he or she is a substance abuser. In these situations the counselor must decide whether through consultation and/or supervision he or she can provide the best treatment for the client's problems or whether the client should be referred to a specialist in the particular area of concern. Referrals may not be a realistic alternative in an isolated or smaller community where other service providers are unavailable. Under such conditions, counselors must monitor their own skills, and continuously evaluate the effectiveness of the service provided.

To practice competently also means that counselors must monitor their own psychological health so that personal distress or dysfunction does not impair their ability to provide adequate services. Under most professional ethics codes, personal problems do not excuse incompetent, and thus unethical behavior. Personal problems can include major physical or mental illness, distress over current life situations and relationship difficulties, or problems related to alcohol or substance abuse. Counselors need to be alert also to signs of fatigue or burnout that may interfere with professional effectiveness and be aware that the work of counseling itself (e.g., a client suicide) may sometimes produce stress that may temporarily impair the quality of services. Counselors should refrain from undertaking professional activities when their personal problems are likely to lead to inadequate service or harm and should seek assistance for such problems at an early stage.

Competent counseling includes plans for interruptions in services. Counselors need to develop procedures in advance for emergencies, such as checking messages frequently on a daily basis, and when planning vacations or absences due to personal or health-related issues, arranging coverage by qualified colleagues. Counseling responsibilities include preparing clients for absences and informing them of procedures that will be followed as well as discussing procedures for "making up" any missed appointments. A counselor must also be prepared to handle client reactions to service interruptions, such as feelings of panic or abandonment.

Counselors are responsible for providing services that are effective, economical, and humane. Ongoing evaluation of service goals and outcomes should thus be considered an integral part of counseling activities. Part of the counselor's responsibility is to consider terminating services if the results cannot be improved. When the counselor decides to terminate services, he or she must prepare the client by providing the reasons for termination, the number and goals of sessions remaining, the nature of follow-up and counselor availability, and an appropriate referral.

When a client seeks to terminate services, the counselor should maintain a professional attitude, discuss the reasons for termination, express professional views about the advisability of termination, and provide a referral, if appropriate. Counselors must also be familiar with dependence needs that may exist as a result of the client's condition or prolonged treatment, and conduct termination in a manner sensitive to those needs. For example, posttermination communication with an overly dependent client may be a helpful transition or result in increased, maladaptive dependence behaviors.

CONFIDENTIALITY

Over the past 25 years, counseling has become generally regarded as an effective means through which individuals can be assisted in living more effectively. Concomitant with this attitude is the prevalent belief by clients that the communications between a counselor and a client are made in private between the two parties, and the belief that such communications will not, and should not, be divulged by the counselor to anyone without the permission of the client (Miller & Thelen, 1986). These beliefs touch on an area of ethical concern that likely is the most problematic for the professional counselor, namely confidentiality. The ethical standards of the various professions generally hold that the counselor has a primary obligation to respect the confidentiality of information obtained in the course of their professional work (American Psychological Association, 1992, Principle 5). The standards also hold that confidence is to be maintained unless (a) the client or the client's legal representative consents to release of the information, (b) if in maintaining confidentiality the client or someone else is in clear danger of harm, or (c) the counselor is under a positive legal obligation to inform an appropriate governmental agency of suspected child or elder abuse.

As is apparent, the ethical requirements for confidentiality are relative, not absolute, standards that are constrained by other rights and values held by society. A counselor, therefore, cannot convey to a client the impression that the client is free to divulge information of any kind without fear of having the confidence broken by the counselor. The counselor has an ethical responsibility to discuss the limits of confidentiality with clients *in advance* of full initiation of services and to inform the client prior to releasing information to any other professional, to such state authorities as the courts or social service agencies, or to third-party insurers who may be reimbursing the client for the costs of the counselor's services.

Because confidentiality is a relative concept, professional judgment often is involved in deciding on its limits. In forming these limits, Biggs and Blocher (1987) recommend conceptualizing confidentiality at three basic levels. At the first level, information is handled "in a fully professional manner that respects the dignity, privacy, and worth" (p. 77) of clients by not divulging information in careless, casual, or irresponsible ways. The most frequent breaches of confidentiality occur at this level when counselors share information with colleagues over lunch or coffee, when clerical staff are given unlimited access to records, or when information is shared with administrators in schools or agencies without first obtaining a client's permission. Clearly, failure to safeguard information at this level is unethical.

The second level of confidentiality occurs most often in clinical settings and concerns the release of information that is in the best interests of the client. Examples of this include sharing information with another professional who may have some involvement with the client, sharing information with people who are "significant others" to the client, such as parents of a child client, the spouse or family of an adult in treatment for a substance abuse problem, or a third-party insurer who is paying for the costs of services. In each of these instances the client should be advised in advance of any plans to share information and should agree to that sharing. An issue at this level (and at the third level) arises when a counselor feels compelled, or is legally required, to divulge information without the client's consent and yet is still acting in the best interests of the client. Corey (1991) described four circumstances that require counselors to report information:

1. when the client poses a clear danger to self or others (referred to as the *duty to warn principle*);
2. when the counselor suspects child abuse of any kind (a legal mandate in most states that carries severe penalties for noncompliance);
3. when the counselor determines that a client requires hospitalization; and
4. when ordered by a court to divulge the information.

In each of these instances the counselor is acting in the best interests of the client and therefore would not be acting contrary to either the ethical standards or the law. Once again, however, it must be emphasized that the ethical counselor explains these exceptions to the client before beginning counseling.

At the third level, all information divulged by a client is kept in confidence by the counselor, except in the rare instance where there is a clear and direct threat to human life. At this level the counselor understands that information cannot be shared, even when ordered to do so, and the counselor is willing, in extreme cases, to accept the consequences of noncompliance. Certainly, a counselor should not convey to a client that this level of confidentiality exists, unless the counselor fully understands the ramifications of such an agreement. As Biggs and Blocher (1987) stated: "Counselors who break such confidences will soon have no confidences to keep" (p. 80).

While confidentiality is basically an ethical concern, many states have recognized that it is a necessary component of therapeutic services and have therefore extended legal protection to clients who use those services. The right of *privileged communication,* which derives from English common law and the attorney-client relationship, was formulated to prevent lawyers from divulging information that is given by the client and that as such is his or her right and can be waived only by the client. For those professions for which the state has enacted privileged communication statutes, the counselor is bound by law not to divulge information without a client's consent unless there is imminent danger of loss of life or where other statutes delimit the right, as is the case with most child-abuse reporting laws. The protection afforded by these statutes extends only to clients of specific professions and does not extend to other professions offering comparable services. Counselors must be aware of the specific laws guiding their practice and should take care not to confuse the ethical standards with legal ones.

DUAL RELATIONSHIPS

A dual relationship can occur whenever a counselor interacts with a client in more than one capacity, for example, entering into a business relationship with a client or counseling students or employees. Having both a personal and a professional relationship with a client is also a dual relationship, as in providing professional services to a friend, relative, or colleague. Dual relationships are harmful for several reasons. First, a personal or business relationship with a client may jeopardize objectivity on the part of the professional, leading to inadequate services. Second, the dual relationship may create a situation in which the counselor's self-interest conflicts with the best interests of the client, compromising the integrity of the counseling goals and the evaluation of the services provided. Third, power inequities intrinsic to a counselor-client or counselor-supervisee relationship can result in client exploitation. For example, the personal knowledge that a counselor has about a therapy client with whom he or she has entered a business relationship can intimidate the client and have harmful effects on financial or social transactions; or graduate students who are in both therapy and supervision with a counselor may be afraid to terminate an unsuccessful therapeutic relationship for fear that it will negatively impact their professional record. Finally, counselors need to be aware that they may at any point be subpoenaed to offer testimony regarding a client's treatment, and that the integrity of such testimony may be questioned in light of the dual relationship. (For a more detailed discussion see Pope & Vasquez, 1991.)

Some dual relationships are unanticipated or unavoidable, as when a counselor finds that a client has become the coach of the sports team of the counselor's child or when the only counselor within traveling distance of a rural community is asked to provide services to a relative of an acquaintance. Under those circumstances the counselor needs to monitor the relationship closely, weigh the benefits of service against the risks of impaired professional judgment or exploitation, continually evaluate the effectiveness of the service, and provide referrals or abstain from entering a professional relationship if appropriate.

Service bartering for professional treatment is another situation in which the counselor needs to assess the potential for exploitation, for example, whether a client providing clerical services feels free to express opinions about the number of hours or amount of work required, for fear of terminating the therapy. Similarly, the counselor must consider how to communicate to the client if the counselor were unhappy with the services provided and consider the potential impact on the counseling relationship.

For all the reasons cited above, counselors do not engage in sexual relationships with clients and avoid such relationships with former clients. Sexual relationships with current students or supervisees also are unethical and exploitative. There is now sufficient evidence that sexual relationships with therapists harm clients by creating sexual confusion, guilt, impaired trust, role confusion, cognitive dysfunction, and increase suicidal risk (see Pope & Vasquez, 1991); a growing number of states now have laws against such behaviors. Research further suggests that therapists who engage in sexual intimacies with clients have personal problems, such as poor impulse control, high need for positive regard, or depression (Keith-Spiegel & Koocher, 1985). Self-awareness and self-monitoring are therefore essential procedures for avoiding sexual relationships with clients.

Nonsexual dual-relationships often precede engagement in sexual dual relationships (Pope & Vasquez, 1991). Thus counselors need to monitor role boundaries in all professional relationships. Counselors must also be sensitive to behaviors that may be misinterpreted by the patient as a sexual overture. Nonsexual touching of clients, the revealing of personal information, or socializing with a client or student outside the work setting may create the impression that the counselor is seeking a nonprofessional relationship. Counselors need to be aware that clients often develop feelings of attraction toward their therapists and that many counselors are at times attracted to clients. It is the responsibility of the counselor, not the client, however, to maintain a professional relationship and to be familiar with techniques that can deal with these issues in a productive and professional manner.

RESPECT FOR THE PERSON

The overarching standard in the ethical principles of all counseling professions is that the counselor respects the integrity, dignity, and welfare of the client, regardless of who the client is. In meeting this standard, counselors fully inform their clients as to the purpose and nature of treatment and the client's freedom of choice regarding participation (American Psychological Association, 1992, Principle 4). Counselors also inform clients of any conflicts of interest that may arise between the clients' and the counselors' employing institutions or agencies.

Professional services generally are offered only to clients who have sought those services and only after the nature of the service has been

explained by the counselor. As modifications to the agreed upon services are made during the course of treatment, the client is informed of,
and consents to, these changes. As noted above, the client retains the
right to discontinue treatment and cannot be compelled to continue.
That general standard is challenged regularly in those service settings
in which "mandated" counseling is provided. It is fairly common today
for children to be referred to mandated counseling when they exhibit
undesired or unacceptable behaviors in school. It is also common today
for convicted felons to be ordered to participate in treatment as a condition for parole, for substance abusers to be required to undergo treatment to avoid incarceration, and for a married couple filing for divorce
to be ordered into marital counseling.

In each of these instances, the client is offered little realistic choice
and enters counseling as a "reluctant" or "resistant" client who needs
"pretreatment induction" before eventually agreeing to treatment. In
these cases the counselor confronts an ethical dilemma that has no simple solution. Coercion is considered both unethical and ineffective, yet
the agencies of society insist that treatment be provided. The resolution
of this conflict must take into consideration the possibility that the referred client will not participate and thus suffer some negative sanction,
while at the same time the counselor must strive to convey to the individual the possible benefits (beyond simply avoiding sanctions) that may
come about through counseling.

The problems of dual allegiance arise from situations such as those
just described. The counselor has an obligation to his employer (e.g., the
school, prison, or court) to provide certain services that may be unwanted by the client. As stipulated in the ethical standards of the American Association for Counseling and Development (1992), counselors
should seriously consider terminating affiliation with employers when,
despite concerted efforts, the counselor and employer cannot reach
agreement as to acceptable standards of conduct. The clear intent of
that statement is that the counselor does not engage in activities that are
contrary to the ethical principles concerning the rights of clients, even
when such refusal may lead to loss of employment.

CONCLUSION

While space does not allow for a discussion of other important principles, our intention is to convey to the professional counselor the importance of knowing and being guided by the ethical standards
appropriate to his or her specific profession. Those standards are not
detailed "how-to" manuals, but rather convey the general principles that
underlie all professional practice. The standards also are not laws and
for some may even supersede laws, as in instances where coercion is used

on clients. Unless, however, all members of a profession strive to maintain the highest level of ethical practice, the time may come when government regulation will replace the standards. Were that to happen, the very basis of counseling as a profession that regulates itself would be removed with unknown effects on both the professionals and their clients.

FOR FURTHER READING

American Psychological Association. (1990). *Guidelines for providers of psychological services to ethnically and culturally diverse populations.* Washington, DC: Author.

Biggs, D., & Blocher, D. (1987). *Foundations of ethical counseling.* New York: Springer.

Carroll, M. A., Schneider, H. G., & Wesley, G. R. (1985). *Ethics in the practice of psychology.* Englewood Cliffs, NJ: Prentice-Hall.

Van Hoose, W., & Kottler, J. (1985). *Ethical and legal issues in counseling and psychotherapy* (2nd ed.). San Francisco: Jossey-Bass.

Corey, G., Corey, M., & Callanan, P. (1988). *Issues and ethics in the helping professions* (3rd ed.). Pacific Grove, CA: Brooks/Cole.

Pope, K. S., & Vasquez,. M. J. T. (1991). *Ethics in psychotherapy and counseling: A practical guide for psychologists.* San Francisco: Jossey-Bass.

REFERENCES

American Association for Counseling and Development. (1992). *Ethical standards for counselors.* Alexandria, VA: Author.

American Association for Marriage and Family Therapy. (1988). *Code of ethical principles for marriage and family therapists* (rev. ed.). Washington, DC: Author.

American Psychological Association. (1981). *Specialty guidelines for the delivery of services.* Washington, DC: Author.

American Psychological Association. (1992). Ethical principles of psychologists and code of conduct. *American Psychologist, 47,* 1597–1611.

Biggs, D., & Blocher, D. (1987). *Foundations of ethical counseling.* New York: Springer.

Carroll, M. A., Schneider, H. G., & Wesley, G. R. (1985). *Ethics in the practice of psychology.* Englewood Cliffs, NJ: Prentice-Hall.

Corey, G. (1991). *Theory and practice of counseling and psychotherapy* (4th ed.). Pacific Grove, CA: Brooks/Cole.

Corey, G., Corey, M., & Callanan, P. (1988). *Issues and ethics in the helping professions* (3rd ed.). Pacific Grove, CA: Brooks/Cole.

Herlihy, B., & Golden, L. (1990). *Ethical standards casebook* (4th ed.). Alexandria, VA: AACD Press.

Keith-Spiegel, P., & Koocher, G. P. (1985). *Ethics in psychology.* New York: Random House.

Miller, D., & Thelen, M. (1986). Knowledge and belief about confidentiality in psychotherapy. *Professional Psychology: Research and Practice, 17,* 15–19.

National Association of Social Workers. (1979). *Code of ethics.* Silver Springs, MD: Author.

National Board for Certified Counselors. (1987). *Code of ethics*. Alexandria, VA: Author.

Pope, K. S., & Vasquez, M. J. T. (1991). *Ethics in psychotherapy and counseling: A practical guide for psychologists*. San Francisco: Jossey-Bass.

Van Hoose, W., & Kottler, J. (1985). *Ethical and legal issues in counseling and psychotherapy* (2nd ed.). San Francisco: Jossey-Bass.

14

Legal Issues

THOMAS L. HAFEMEISTER, J.D., Ph.D.

OBTAINING THE CLIENT'S INFORMED CONSENT

Counseling, to be effective, generally relies on the establishment of a trusting relationship between the client and the counselor/therapist. The law has attempted to promote this bond by taking steps to encourage and protect this relationship, including affording the therapist with certain privileges. At the same time, it imposes on the therapist given responsibilities. One of these responsibilities is to obtain the client's informed consent to participate in treatment before that treatment commences. To fulfill this responsibility, first the therapist must appropriately disclose the necessary relevant information to the client so that the client can make an informed decision on whether to proceed with treatment, and second, the client must affirmatively indicate a willingness to begin treatment (i.e., consent).

Evolution of the Doctrine

The doctrine of informed consent was initially an attempt to regulate and broaden the discourse that occurs between a physician and a patient prior to treatment. It evolved from the general principle that everyone should have the right to determine what should be done with his or her own body, or in other words, that patients should have the right to make their own decisions regarding the course of their medical treatment.

Historically, this requirement was not particularly stringent. The physician had only to describe what was likely to occur in relatively broad terms, the patient was only expected to have a rather vague understanding of the course of treatment, and the patient had only to express a general permission to proceed. It was generally believed that because of the physician's superior expertise in providing medical treatment, the physician should be accorded considerable discretion in selecting the course of treatment.

However, since the 1960s the nature of the dialogue between physician and patient prior to treatment has been more closely scrutinized. A physician is expected to inform the patient about the possible risks that may accompany the proposed treatment, as well as about alternative treatments that might be available. No longer is the physician imbued with an aura of omniscience. Instead, the patient is generally regarded as the ultimate decision maker in deciding upon the course of treatment.

In addition, in recent years there has been a growing recognition that the doctrine of informed consent applies as well to nonphysicians who provide treatment for mental rather than physical disabilities. It may be argued that a therapist will only be held liable to a client for failure to obtain informed consent when a physically intrusive treatment is involved. Nevertheless, obtaining informed consent prior to treatment as part of the process of obtaining the client's active participation in and support of the treatment is widely viewed as clinically sound practice and is encouraged for its own sake.

Necessary Elements for Informed Consent

While the notion that the client's informed consent should be obtained prior to instituting treatment is relatively well established, controversies continue to exist over how that consent should be obtained and expressed. There are three elements that are widely viewed as necessary for a legally acceptable consent to participate in a treatment program.

Capacity. First, the individual must possess the requisite capacity to give consent. In other words, the individual's intelligence and mental status must be sufficient to allow the individual to understand what he or she is consenting to. For example, a client with a severe mental disability may not be capable of providing consent. However, the mere fact that an individual has been involuntarily civilly committed does not necessarily remove the individual's ability to consent to treatment, but rather must be determined on an individualized basis. Nonemancipated minors are also considered to generally lack capacity to provide consent (although exceptions are made in some jurisdictions for "mature" minors). For clients who lack capacity to consent, consent may be obtained from someone authorized to consent on their behalf, such as a parent or legal guardian. Nevertheless, it is generally considered clinically sound practice to involve these clients in the decision-making process to the fullest extent possible.

Knowledge. The second component is that the individual be fully informed of the risks and benefits of the program and available alternatives. For a therapist providing counseling to an individual with mental illness, where both the course of the illness and the treatment may be relatively uncertain, this component may appear to require a virtually impossible degree of clairvoyance by the counselor. Furthermore, there has been considerable controversy over whether every possible risk must be disclosed, or only those risks that are significant and probable.

However, in most jurisdictions the counselor is only expected to make the same disclosure as a reasonable counselor would disclose under the same or similar circumstances. This provides the counselor with considerable flexibility and discretion in determining whether the possibility of adverse consequences is so remote as not to warrant disclosure. In addition, the counselor may properly determine under this standard that disclosing certain possible risks might have such an adverse effect on the client as to jeopardize the success of the proposed therapy.

This very flexible standard is based on the rationale that the treatment provider is best suited to determine what the likely effect of the disclosure will be on the client, that there may be insufficient time for all risks to be explored and explained to the client, and that any other rule would subject treatment providers unjustly to second-guessing and the 20-20 vision that accompanies hindsight. Nevertheless, this standard generally does not warrant a counselor in not making any disclosure at all (except perhaps in the case of a genuine emergency), and generally it is considered wise to disclose as much relevant information as the counselor possesses unless the counselor has a specific reason for not disclosing certain information and has recorded that reason in the client's case record.

It should be noted, nonetheless, that in a few jurisdictions the standard for disclosure is what a reasonable patient or client would require to make an informed decision under the circumstances. This standard has generally been imposed in order to encourage the therapist to expand the scope of disclosure and to more actively include the client in decisions about the course of treatment. It is predicated on the belief that whether adequate disclosure has been provided should be judged from the perspective of the client, and not from that of the treatment provider. In conjunction with this belief, it is argued that: (a) the average client on his or her own has little understanding of treatment and is thus dependent on the treatment provider for enlightenment, (b) while the appropriate course of treatment may seem clear to the treatment provider, the client needs information to make a reasonable decision, and (c) once given this information, the client will generally make a reasonable decision.

However, regardless of the standard adopted, the counselor is not expected to make a full disclosure of every possible risk and alternative to the client, but only to provide sufficient information to enable the client to make an informed choice. This is generally measured by what a reasonable client in that situation would attach significance to. For example, a reasonable client will probably want to know all likely and significant risks associated with a given treatment and alternative treatments that might be less risky, as well as the benefits of the various treatments. Nevertheless, as a general rule, the treatment provider is not expected to be prescient, but only required to disclose that information known by a reasonable practitioner in that situation.

In addition, there are two relatively widely recognized exceptions to the duty to disclose. The first involves genuine emergencies where the well-being of the client (and perhaps others) demands an immediate response. Typically, the client will be physically or mentally incapable of providing consent, and although it may be generally advisable to secure the permission of a relative or some other individual closely associated with the client, securing consent can generally be omitted where the exigencies of the situation demand an immediate response.

The second exception occurs where the disclosure is likely to be detrimental to the client. Examples of this are where the disclosure of a certain risk is likely to foreclose a rational decision by the client, to complicate or hinder the treatment that is necessary, or to result in psychological damage to the client. However, because this exception has the potential to eviscerate the informed consent doctrine in general, it tends to be applied relatively narrowly, and failures to disclose pursuant to it will be examined closely. For example, the mere fact that the client would refuse the proposed treatment if told about the risks associated with the treatment is not a sufficient basis for not providing disclosure. If this exception is claimed as a basis for not disclosing certain treatment risks, the treatment provider should carefully document the rationale for not making the disclosure and try to discuss the risks with a relative or some other individual closely associated with the client who can appropriately consider the information and make a recommendation based upon it.

Voluntary. The third and perhaps most overlooked component is that the choice be voluntary and not coerced. Consent may be particularly suspect when given within an institutional environment where various pressures can be applied to "encourage" an individual to agree to treatment. For example, where release from a facility may be contingent on demonstrating recovery, the giving of consent may reflect a belief by the client that providing consent will be viewed favorably by supervisory personnel and hasten release. In such situations, the treatment provider may want to more closely examine a consent that is forthcoming under circumstances that would ordinarily result in hesitancy and perhaps reluctance on the part of the client.

Nature of Client's Expressed Consent
Historically, it was sufficient if the client expressed a generalized assent to the proposed treatment (e.g., "Do whatever you think is best, Doc"). However, there has been increased emphasis on obtaining and establish-

ing specific consent to the treatment under consideration. This has led to increased reliance on the use of standardized written consent forms. A difficulty with this approach is that attention may focus on obtaining the client's signature on a piece of paper (which the client may not understand), rather than fully discussing the proposed treatment with the client and ensuring that the client truly understands what is about to transpire. Alternatively, the written form may not convey all of the necessary information to the client, while a relatively brief dialogue between the treatment provider and the client might easily provide necessary clarifications. Under such circumstances, the patient's signed consent form may not fulfill the requirements for obtaining informed consent. Another possible difficulty with relying too heavily on obtaining a signed consent form is that the standardized form is unlikely to capture dialogues between the treatment provider and the client about the proposed treatment, and thereby likely to fail to record the substance of these supplemental discussions and fail to establish that informed consent was indeed provided.

As a result, it is generally recommended that treatment providers complement any signed written consent forms with discussions with their clients that explain the nature of the proposed treatment. It is also recommended that the treatment provider subsequently document in the clients' records that these discussions took place and the nature of the discussions.

Effect of Doctrine of Informed Consent
To the extent the legal doctrine of informed consent is applied to non-physically intrusive treatments, many counselors may find it disquieting that it is not a sufficient defense to establish that the counselor did everything right in the subsequent treatment (i.e., exercised reasonable skill). The legal wrong is the failure to obtain the informed consent, and that is what liability can be established upon. It should be noted, however, that to date there are few cases where a client has recovered monetary damages for a therapist's failure to obtain informed consent before proceeding with counseling. Nevertheless, it has been argued that this requirement may become routine for nonmedical treatment, particularly where the treatment is relatively intrusive in nature.

Furthermore, in a recent opinion handed down by the U.S. Supreme Court, it was ruled that the patient was entitled to pursue a federal action for a violation of his civil rights if he could show he was incompetent at the time he signed forms requesting voluntary admission to a psychiatric hospital and authorizing the treatment provided there (Zinermon v. Burch, 1990). The Court noted that the presence of mental illness may require treating staff to exercise additional caution in obtaining informed consent.[1] As a result, the Court ordered that the patient be given an opportunity to prove his or her allegations that the patient was hallucinating, confused, disoriented, and clearly psychotic at the time he or she signed the forms. Pursuant to such a claim, a plaintiff can recover from an individual acting on behalf of a state (e.g., a state employee) monetary damages for the violation of his or her civil rights. These damages are directly assessed to the individuals responsible for the civil rights violation, although typically if the individuals can establish that they were acting within the scope of their duties, they will be indemnified by the state.

CLIENT CONFIDENTIALITY AND PRIVACY

In addressing client confidentiality and privacy, the law has also attempted to foster the necessary trusting relationship between a client and counselor/therapist. For a number of professional groups, including attorneys, physicians, and clergy, the importance of maintaining confidentiality and protecting their clients' privacy has been explicitly recognized. Promoting respect for confidentiality and privacy, however, is especially important for establishing the trusting relationship that is essential to interactions between the counselor/therapist and his or her client.

Assurances of confidentiality and privacy encourage the client to speak freely, without inhibitions, to the therapist. By fully communicating all thoughts and feelings, the therapist is able to gain a clearer understanding of the client's difficulties and to better formulate an appropriate response. Typically clients are expected to explore and discuss their most private thoughts and emotions with their counselors. Public disclosure of these interactions has the potential to be extremely embarrassing to the client and could seriously damage the client's reputation in the community. The mere fact that the client is undergoing therapy could expose him or her to social stigma. Indeed, without initial assurances of confidentiality and privacy, the client may be unwilling even to undertake counseling.

At the same time, however, a number of reasons have been articulated for breaching these assurances of confidentiality and privacy or limiting their scope. They include the duty of counselors to protect the safety of the client and the community, their obligation to assist the fact finding conducted in conjunction with criminal and civil trials, and the need to

1. "The characteristics of mental illness thus create special problems regarding informed consent. Even if the State usually might be justified in taking at face value a person's request for admission to a hospital for medical treatment, it may not be justified in doing so, without further inquiry, as to a mentally ill person's request for admission and treatment at a mental hospital" (p. 987, n. 18).

advance scientific knowledge through research, debate, and teaching. In a given instance, the rationales for and against confidentiality and privacy may both come into play, potentially placing a counselor in the difficult position of weighing conflicting interests and determining which interest should be given priority.

Legal and Ethical Requirements of Confidentiality and Privacy
The therapist's obligation to maintain the confidentiality and privacy of communications with a client is both ethical and legal in nature. Virtually all professions that provide counseling have articulated within their respective codes of ethics a confidentiality requirement. For example, Ethical Standard 5.02 of the American Psychological Association's (1992) "Ethical Principles of Psychologists and Code of Conduct" reads:

> Psychologists have a primary obligation and take reasonable precautions to respect the confidentiality rights of those with whom they work or consult, recognizing that confidentiality may be established by law, institutional rules, or professional or scientific relationships. (p. 1606)

Furthermore, under Ethical Standard 5.05(a):

> Psychologists disclose confidential information without the consent of the individual only as mandated by law, or where permitted by law for a valid purpose, such as (1) to provide needed professional services to the patient or the individual or organizational client, (2) to obtain appropriate professional consultations, (3) to protect the patient or client or others from harm, or (4) to obtain payment for services, in which instance disclosure is limited to the minimum that is necessary to achieve the purpose. (p. 1606)

A counselor who violates such ethical principles can be subjected to administrative review by his or her state licensing board. In turn, this can result in sanctions and could lead ultimately to the revocation of that professional's license to practice. These licensing boards often stress the importance of assuring the public and future clients that treating professionals will respect clients' confidences. Indeed, this assurance is considered so important that the licensing board may continue its investigation even after an initiating complaint is withdrawn.

In addition, there are a number of legal remedies available to clients who feel their counselor has broken his or her responsibility to maintain the confidentiality of communications with the client. Although it has been asserted that suits successfully establishing liability for a counselor's breach of a client's right to confidentiality are extremely rare (although much discussed), there are cases where courts have ruled in favor of the client.

For example, the client may file a tort action for invasion of privacy seeking financial compensation for harm resulting from a wrongful disclosure of information obtained in the course of counseling. Although the exact nature of this legal remedy varies from state to state, almost every jurisdiction recognizes some type of legal action based on an invasion of privacy.

Alternatively, where there has been a "publication" (i.e., an unauthorized release to a third party, such as a book or a speech by a therapist describing case histories) of confidential (and false) information injuring the reputation of the client, the client may pursue a legal action based upon the tort of defamation. If the publication is oral, the tort is typically referred to as *slander*; if it is written, the tort is called *libel*.

In some states, a third possible tort has been recognized by the courts. It explicitly recognizes that because of the special nature of their interactions with their clients, counselors have a fiduciary duty to keep communications occurring during this relationship confidential. The breach of this duty will entitle the client to recover from the therapist any resulting damages caused by the disclosure. It has been argued that this tort has the potential to be particularly broad, encompassing all unauthorized disclosures made without justification or excuse (e.g., to prevent the client from harming others), regardless of whether there was an intentional invasion or reasonable expectation of privacy.

It may also be claimed that there was a contractual relationship between the client and the counselor that required the counselor to keep in confidence all disclosures made by the client or all discoveries made by the counselor in the course of their interactions. Where it is established that a contract was established and that this contract has been breached, the client is entitled to damages resulting from the breach of the contract.

Finally, a specific statute may have been enacted within a given state that directly authorizes various sanctions for wrongful disclosure of information generated during client-therapist interactions. Typically clients being provided services within state-operated or licensed institutions will be protected by such a provision. In recent years, such protections also have been extended to AIDS patients and are being discussed widely in connection with genetic counseling.

At the same time, a state statute may require a therapist to disclose certain information that would otherwise be kept confidential. The most pervasive requirement is that a counselor report evidence of child abuse, a requirement recognized in all jurisdictions. Other mandatory reporting requirements that have been recognized in some jurisdictions include the reporting of communicable diseases, gunshot injuries, and drug addiction. In addition, there may be an access to records provision that sets forth a mechanism whereby a client can gain access to his or her clinical records and in certain instances challenge or modify these records. There may also be a means established for the sealing of a client's records.

A statutory provision may also grant access to a client's clinical records to specifically delineated third parties that the legislature has determined have an appropriate need for these records. Limitations, however, may be placed on when this may occur and what the third party can do with the records. These third parties may include the client's attorney or other individuals designated by the client, a court of record, endangered individuals and relevant law enforcement agencies, third-party payors, select patient advocacy groups or agencies monitoring the care of clients, and qualified researchers.

Scope of Confidentiality

A broad range of communications occurring during client-counselor interactions are typically protected from disclosure, although perhaps even more so under governing ethical principles than under legal standards.[2] This protection has been held not to be limited to the words spoken by the client, but to extend as well to communications from the therapist to the client, clinical records, and opinions or impressions formed by the therapist that were based on communications with the client. It should also be noted that family members such as a spouse are not typically privy to the information arising in the course of a client-therapist relationship without the permission of the client.

However, in order to recover under a lawsuit for wrongful disclosure, generally the client must establish that there was a protected client-therapist relationship (i.e., that there was a reasonable expectation that therapy had been undertaken), that the communication occurred in the course of this relationship, that the invasion of privacy or breach of confidentiality was intentional, that the intrusion would be offensive to a reasonable person, and that the client incurred damages.[3]

Certain exceptions to the general rule of confidentiality have been noted. First, if disclosure is made pursuant to a court order or in the course of a judicial or quasi-judicial proceeding, even if the basis for the disclosure is subsequently reversed on appeal, the treating professional

---

2. In addition, the requirements that the intrusion would be offensive to a reasonable person and that the invasion of privacy was intentional may not apply to a licensing board's review of a complaint of wrongful disclosure where the board is applying a more restrictive ethical (as opposed to legal) standard designed to guide professional conduct in general rather than to redress individual wrongs.

3. The client also may be able to recover punitive damages if it can be shown that the wrong committed was willful and malicious.

is typically immune from sanction. Second, if there is no expectation of confidentiality by the individual receiving services, there will be no sanction for subsequent disclosures (e.g., the release of information occurred with the patient's informed consent).[4]

Third, the treating professional is not subject to sanction if there was a legal excuse or justification for the disclosure, such as attempting to protect others from danger (indeed, the therapist may be subject to sanction for failing to act under such circumstances). However, this dangerousness exception has been variously construed. In some instances it has been limited to only where "life and limb" are in danger, while other judicial rulings have expanded it to include the potential for emotional or psychological harm.

Unfortunately, there are few bright lines to guide the treating professional as to when and to whom it is appropriate to disclose information under various circumstances. This, in turn, has led to extensive discussion and concern by therapists about their potential liability should they make the wrong choice.

Judicial Proceedings and the Testimonial Privilege
Although confidentiality and privilege are related, there are distinctions between these legal concepts. A *privilege* is typically established and defined by statute, focuses on specific relationships (e.g., attorney-client, doctor-patient, psychologist-client, clergy-confessor), is relatively narrow in scope, and is generally restricted to placing limitations on the testimony an individual (e.g., a therapist) can provide at a trial. In contrast, the duty of *confidentiality* tends to be a product of common law rather than a statutory creation (although portions of it may be codified), encompasses all client-staff relationships within the clinical setting, is relatively broad in nature generally including all communications and records, and is not limited to trial testimony but includes all unauthorized disclosures.

Proponents of both privilege and confidentiality assert that the principle of nondisclosure is necessary to encourage frank and full discussions between the therapist and client, discussions that treatment would be impossible without. However, because they are typically asserted in different contexts, each has additional and somewhat different justifications. Nevertheless, the basic underlying principles for the two are relatively similar and many of the same principles govern both.

In general, an applicable testimonial privilege will preclude a thera-

---

4. However, as discussed previously in the section on informed consent, the circumstances under which this consent is generated may call into question the validity of the consent (e.g., a client who is being treated for a mental disability at the time consent was given, may lack the requisite capacity to provide that consent).

pist from testifying to communications occurring during therapy when the privilege has not been waived by the client, absent the presence of one of a number of special exceptions that are often set forth in the statute that created the privilege. For example, disclosures may not be prohibited where there was no expectation that the communications were to be confidential or private (e.g., the defendant requested and submitted to a psychiatric exam with full expectation and knowledge that it would be used to assist the court, or the client made the statements to other individuals as well or in the presence of others who were not part of the therapeutic relationship); where fairness and justice require disclosure (e.g., the defendant raised a defense based on his or her mental status and then attempted to assert a client therapist privilege to suppress available proof regarding this status); or where necessary to protect the safety of the community (e.g., the privilege may be overridden in the context of a determination on whether an individual who has been dangerous in the past ought to be released from institutional care).

TREATMENT REFUSALS

A third area where the law has considerably influenced the interactions between the counselor/therapist and his or her client involves the client's right to refuse treatment. Although it was perhaps not always the case, it is now widely recognized that a client has a right to voice an objection to treatment and have it heard. What has been the subject of considerable recent litigation is who, if anyone, is empowered to override such objections, under what circumstances, and by what procedure.

Policy Concerns

In general, this issue has the potential to sharply divide client advocates from treatment providers. Client advocates argue that within the therapeutic relationship, clients should retain decision-making authority and be able to exert considerable, if not exclusive, control over the course of treatment. It is asserted that a relatively broad right to refuse treatment will appropriately increase the client's involvement in the treatment provided. Rather than being a passive recipient, the client will become an active partner who more fully understands the goals and objectives of the treatment and what can be expected in the course of the treatment. By increasing the dialogue between the client and counselor, the latter will gain a richer understanding of the client and the client's treatment needs. Furthermore, if the client has been involved in setting the goals and parameters of the treatment, the client will be more highly motivated to comply with the treatment regime and work toward accomplishing the treatment goals.

In addition, the argument continues, the recognition of a broad right may correct some past widespread treatment abuses, such as overdosages of medication and polypharmacy. Also, it may encourage therapists to pay more attention to side effects clients experience during treatment—side effects that left unattended could be dangerous—and to consider less intrusive means of treatment.

Individuals who argue for a relatively narrow right to refuse treatment assert that at a certain point it is both necessary and appropriate for the therapist to become the primary decision maker and to assume responsibility for the course of treatment. The therapist, because of professional training and experience, is best equipped to make the necessary treatment decisions and better prepared to remain objective and cognitive of necessary long-range ramifications. In contrast, a client's objectivity may be clouded by the problems that led the client to seek treatment, and the client may be unwilling to surmount temporary discomforts that are necessary for a successful treatment outcome.

Furthermore, this argument continues, by imposing a relatively elaborate review mechanism for considering whether a client's objection to treatment should be overridden, the authority and status of the treatment provider are undercut and treatment delayed, potentially harming the client. For example, delay may prolong hospitalization, permit decompensation or deterioration, and increase the likelihood of behavioral outbursts, placing the client, therapeutic staff, and others, including the general community, at risk of harm. In addition, a treatment provider pursuing a nonaggressive treatment regime to minimize client treatment objections may also increase the likelihood of such harms occurring. Relatedly, any review process imposed may be perceived as requiring an unproductive expenditure of staff time and resources.

It also is asserted that the significance to the client of this right and any associated review mechanism is overexaggerated, as the majority of clients are both content and prefer to have the therapist make the necessary treatment decisions. In addition, the objections raised may be more a reflection of the problems that brought the client to therapy in the first place or reflect other problems unrelated to the treatment modality than a representation of genuine concerns about treatment.

Status of the Client
It should be noted that generally the contours of the right to refuse treatment differ depending on the status of the client. The relevant case law has almost exclusively focused on the right to refuse treatment of clients who are involuntarily placed within a state-operated or licensed institution or subjected to state supervision as part of an outpatient placement. In such settings, where the placement typically stems from an initial court order, the state, as the custodian of the individual receiv-

ing treatment, is able to assert an interest in requiring the client to undergo treatment.

However, a counselor who is seeing a client as part of his or her private practice generally lacks the authority to force the client to undergo treatment against the client's wishes. The therapist is typically forced to rely upon his or her powers of persuasion or encouragements forthcoming from concerned family and friends of the client. At the same time, this therapist will generally be free to discontinue the therapeutic relationship if the therapist concludes that the client's unwillingness to adhere to a given treatment regime makes the continuation of treatment futile (although the termination of the treatment relationship may not end the therapist's responsibility to the client or others if the therapist reasonably believes that the client is likely to imminently engage in dangerous behavior).

State versus Federal Law

The right of a client in the state's custody to refuse treatment is made particularly complex by the fact that the nation's federal courts have tended to take a very different position on this matter than have state courts. Since the state courts have tended to place greater restrictions on a counselor's ability to override the objection to treatment of such a client, it is imperative that the counselor determine what the applicable law is within his or her state before attempting to override a client's objection to treatment.

In general, the federal courts have expressed a reluctance to recognize a broad right to refuse treatment and have carefully circumscribed it. They have tended to conclude that under federal law the state's interests in overriding a treatment refusal can outweigh the client's interests. However, they have not precluded the state courts from reviewing the right to refuse treatment under state law. In recent years, state courts have indeed been willing to do so, and many have independently established such a right and recognized the client's interests as paramount.

Typically at issue is not whether such clients have the power to voice an objection and have it heard. This has been widely recognized and accepted. Even the federal courts tend not to give the treatment provider carte blanche in overriding a client's objection. Instead, the issue has centered on who is empowered to override the client's objection, under what circumstances, and by what procedure. The federal courts have tended to favor review systems internal to the treating facility that do not require a judge to make the final decision, with professionals associated with the treating facility included on the review panel (although the client's current treatment provider is typically excluded). In contrast, some state courts leave the ultimate decision in the hands of a judge, concluding that an internal review panel will not be sufficiently objective to protect the rights of the client.

It should be noted also, however, that judicial opinions recognizing a right to refuse treatment and to have a judge serve as the final arbiter extend only to antipsychotic medication, electroconvulsive therapy, and psychosurgery. Other forms of treatment, because they are not considered intrusive, onerous, or irreversible, have not generally had these heightened procedural requirements specifically attached to them.[5]

Emergency Treatment

Although it is sometimes overlooked, it should be kept in mind that a therapist generally retains the ability to administer treatment over objection in a true emergency. Most states assign to the treating physician responsibility for decision making in an emergency that would endanger the life or pose a serious threat to the health of an individual. Under the common law (codified in many states), a physician is not generally required to obtain the patient's consent (or a court order) to provide treatment in an emergency. Similarly, common law and statutory law authorize physicians to treat minors in emergency situations.

Treatment for Minors

When the client is a minor, the parameters for accepting and refusing treatment are somewhat altered. For purposes of making treatment decisions, minors frequently are divided into three categories. The first category includes *emancipated minors*. Generally, emancipated minors are under the age of 18 and have either (a) married, (b) enlisted in the armed services, (c) made a valid declaration of emancipation or established their independence, or (d) obtained their parents' consent to assume this status.[6] The second category includes *mature minors* who are not emancipated but who have the ability to understand the nature and consequences of a proposed treatment, deliberate about their options (including alternative outcomes), and make voluntary decisions about their treatment options, including the option of nontreatment. The third category, *non-mature minors*, includes all minors that are neither emancipated nor mature. Unless dictated otherwise by state law, emancipated minors are treated as adults for treatment decision-making purposes.

If a minor is not emancipated, a surrogate decision maker will have

---

5. Although it is not an issue likely to be faced by most counselors, it should be noted that the U.S. Supreme Court and a number of state courts have uniformly ruled that competent patients have a right to refuse life-sustaining medical treatment. Less guidance, however, has been provided on the related issue of whether an incompetent patient has the same or a similar right.
6. The exact definition of an emancipated minor is often a matter of state law.

to speak for the minor.[7] Thus, where the parent is the minor's lawful surrogate, parental consent is generally required for a minor's treatment, even if the minor is mature. Nevertheless, if the minor is a mature minor, the minor's preferences should generally be given great weight by the surrogate decision maker and, in some jurisdictions, are considered dispositive.[8] In general, it has been widely suggested that a minor's wishes regarding treatment should be respected where the minor is capable of participating in the decision-making process, and, at a minimum, the minor should be involved in the decision making as much as possible.

Generally, the decisions of parents or legal guardians regarding treatment of a non-mature minor prevail and the state refrains from unreasonably interfering with parental autonomy. Pursuant to both common law and constitutional principles, parents have the right to the care, custody, and control of their minor children. This includes parents' right to control most treatment decisions for their children. State intervention is appropriate only when "it appears that parental decisions will jeopardize the health or safety of the child" (Wisconsin v. Yoder, 1972). The treatment decision of a parent or legal guardian may be overridden if a court finds that the parent or legal guardian is unfit or the child is neglected within the meaning of those terms as set forth in that state's child abuse/neglect statute.[9] However, if a parent's objection to treatment for a minor is based on a religious conviction, the terms unfit or neglected as used in statutes or case law may have a limited meaning.

Typically, in order for the state to intervene and override a parental decision to refuse treatment, the benefits of a treatment and its potential success must be substantial and the minor's life must be threatened or the minor is threatened with a serious or permanent disability by a lack of treatment. Ordinarily, it would appear unlikely that counseling would be considered a life-saving intervention or one that would protect the minor from serious or permanent disability. However, as a minor's problems become more serious, it may be possible to successfully establish

---

7. Who this surrogate decision maker will be is typically a matter of state law. It may include (a) a parent or legal guardian, (b) a social service agency with legal custody of the minor, or (c) a court with jurisdiction over medical treatment for minors.

8. Where there is a disagreement between a mature minor and a parent over treatment, many experts dealing with pediatric ethics believe there should be considerable reluctance to act contrary to the wishes of the minor.

9. When a court overrides a parent's decision to forgo medical treatment for a child, the court generally gives custody of the child to the state for purposes of providing the treatment. Many jurisdictions recognize the right of a court to authorize state custody of a minor when the minor is in need of medical care and the parent is neglectful in providing that care.

that the parents' objection to treatment (including those of a religious nature) should be overridden.

REFERENCES

American Psychological Association. (1992). Ethical principles of psychologists and code of conduct. *American Psychologist, 47,* 1597–1611.

Brakel, S. J., Parry, J., & Weiner, B. A., The mentally disabled and the law. (1985). Chicago: American Bar Foundation.

Perlin, M. L. (1989 & 1992 Cum. Supp.). Mental disability law: Civil and criminal. Charlottesville, VA: Michie.

Reisner, R., & Slobogin, C. (1990). Law and the mental health system: Civil and criminal aspects (2nd ed.). St. Paul, MN: West.

Wisconsin v. Yoder, 406 U.S. 205, 234 (1972).

Zinermon v. Burch, 494 U.S. 113 (1990).

15

Religious Issues

ROBERT J. LOVINGER, Ph.D.

A variety of difficulties emerge when a client raises a theme with religious content or connotations. Society avoids religious or political conversations, recognizing that these topics generate intense reactions. When people are taught about religion as children, it is presented in a concrete manner, suitable to the child's understanding. Religion is often sanitized to avoid embarrassing questions. Abstract thinking flowers in adolescence, about the time that most people discontinue religious instruction and walk away feeling that religion is childish and punitive.

To avoid feelings aroused by religious themes in counseling, the counselor may suggest that religion, like politics, is personal. Counseling itself is personal, so to know if the material is relevant requires exploration. Ignoring religion or dismissing enthusiastic interest will interfere with the exploration and resolution that counseling provides.

DEFINITIONS OF RELIGION

Simply stated, *religion* is "a system of beliefs in a divine or superhuman power, and practices of worship or other rituals directed towards such a power" (Argyle & Beit-Hallahmi, 1975, p. 1). Another view (Berger, 1974) is that:

1. Religion is a structured pattern of relations (beliefs and rituals) to some divine (superhuman, otherworldly) power(s).
2. Religion is centrally concerned with ethical relations among individuals and groups in society.

These definitions include belief as a component of religion. In this regard, Judaism differs partly from Islam and significantly from Christianity. Judaism is founded on God's promise of a land (Canaan) to live in, contingent upon the people's fulfillment of their covenantal relationship between them and God. The Israelites agreed to live in accord with a moral/ritual code.

Central to Christian thought are three concepts: Creation, Redemption, and Resurrection. While not the only way to construe these concepts, Creation means that the world and humanity are God's doing. Further, the world is good even if people are unable to maintain that goodness. They needed Redemption through God's presence in the world through Jesus, whose death was an atoning vehicle for reconciliation with God. God is present to human beings through multiple facets (the Trinity). The Resurrection's central theme is that God is faithful to humanity, even in death.

Islam comes from a word meaning primarily "peace" *(salaam)* but secondarily "submission" (to God's will). It contains clearly stated beliefs, systematically set forth in the Koran as dictated by Muhammad, and practices set within a community, organized within a code called the Shari'a. There are six central beliefs (Booth, 1988):

1. one God,
2. angels who act as God's agents,
3. books, including Jewish and Christian Scripture,
4. prophets or messengers,
5. a Day of Judgment, and
6. predestination (all that occurs is God's will).

Islam is often regarded negatively because of its association with terrorism. Black Muslims were considered deviant from normative Islam but are now mainstream and form an important segment of the Islamic community in the United States.

American Black Churches
Christianity had a slow start among black slaves, partly due to opposition by owners who felt it made the slaves troublesome. Eventually, Methodist and Baptist clergymen began to license black men to preach, who ministered directly to black people. Many whites were displeased by black churches, the only institutions over which blacks exercised control. These churches fostered black leadership and ameliorative activities during and after slavery.

White efforts to control black churches were defeated in court battles. This defeat mobilized blacks to organize the African Methodist Episcopal Church in 1816. When the Montgomery bus boycott was organized in 1955, Baptist minister Martin Luther King, Jr., was asked to be spokesman. His practical and philosophical positions were not fully accepted within the African-American community, and the alternative presented by the American Muslim Mission (Black Muslims) was also attractive although a majority of African-Americans with a church affiliation were with Protestant churches.

American Indigenous Churches

The Mormons (properly, the Church of Jesus Christ of Latter-day Saints) was founded by Joseph Smith in the 1820s on a new scriptural revelation, The Book of Mormon. Much movement and turmoil led to the murder of Smith in 1844, followed by the exodus to Utah under Brigham Young in 1847. The Mormon church eventually entered the mainstream of American church life.

The Seventh-Day Adventists, activated by intense hopes for the return of Christ predicted by William Miller, endured repetitive failures of prediction to form an ongoing, congregational structure.

Christian Science was founded by Mary Baker Eddy on the idea that illness arises from incorrect thinking. She developed a theological healing system in which the only medical treatment was prayer, except for setting broken bones.

Charles Russell's religious doubts, although helped by Adventist beliefs, led to a series of radical writings to aid Bible study. The Jehovah's Witnesses, organized into groups called Kingdom Halls to promote Russell's views, rejected military service, blood transfusions, or recitation of the Pledge of Allegiance by their children. They received considerable abuse as a result of their aggressive proselytizing.

The "frontier" churches, a group of mainstream, moderately conservative churches, arose from an effort to reunify Protestant denominations. These churches (Church of Christ; Disciples of Christ, or Christian Church; and the United Church of Christ) arose mainly at the frontier and avoided divisive creedal or hierarchical structures.

Cult, Sect, and Church

Cult is a usually disparaging term applied to a religious group that is "(1) unconventional and esoteric; (2) controversial and the target of allegations of harmful acts; (3) authoritarian; (4) close-knit and communal; (5) aggressively proselytizing; (6) intense and emotional in its indoctrination practices or group ritual; and (7) charismatic in its leadership" (Robbins & Anthony, 1988, p. 741).

Sociologically, cult refers to a religious group that arises spontaneously, not from a church. The Church of Jesus Christ of Latter-day Saints (Mormons) began as a cult. A *sect* begins as a group within a church, such as the Methodists, who began within the Church of England. Christianity began as a Jewish sect. Sects tend to withdraw from their environment, while churches do not. When a sect opens to the world, it becomes a church.

PERSONALITY IMPLICATIONS OF MODERN AMERICAN RELIGIONS

Judaism

The four main Jewish subgroups are *Hasidic*, or ultraorthodox; *Orthodox*, or traditional Jewish life; *Reform*, or a modernization of tradition; and *Conservative*, or counterreaction to the Reform movement. In Judaism the family is the crucible of character formation and socialization to group norms. "Jewish mother" jokes reflect the determining influence of a powerful mother while the father's impact comes somewhat later in the child's life. The boy's ritual duties make inequities between men and women, and boys frequently are more esteemed. Only a man can give a legal divorce under Jewish law, but only a Jewish mother can make a person a Jew by birth.

Comprising less than 3% of the American population, Jews have thrived through values of industriousness, adult study, and educational accomplishment. Familial devotion, joy, ritual and ethical practices, and charity were traditional values inculcated in the child, through parental behavior, the synagogue, and the Jewish school. In the past, group cohesion usually prevented intermarriage. Even now selection of a non-Jewish partner suggests significant issues in areas related to intimacy, autonomy, and/or control. Jews are more likely to feel guilt over independence and autonomy vis-à-vis the family. Intellectual debate and criticism are esteemed. Long centuries of confinement in cramped ghettos led to strong restraints on sexual satisfaction, and emotional conflicts are frequent. Alcohol use begins very early; wine is a sacramental part of many activities, but drunkenness is strongly disapproved of.

Catholicism

The Eastern church was highly creative in early Christianity. The Eastern Orthodox church is much more federated in character and closer to its Hebraic base and its mystical roots in thought, liturgy, and ritual. Theological differences include a married priesthood, certain sacramental practices, and primacy of the Roman papacy. In the United States the 52 million Roman Catholics are the largest Christian denomination. The past prejudices and discrimination suffered by Catholics have declined greatly, and the parochial system of education still functions.

The Catholic churches saturate the lives of their adherents, affecting life and death, procreation, and celebration, but there are major national differences. Irish and Italian Catholics typically show considerable differences with regard to patterns of alcohol use, degree of emotional expressiveness, and ease of self-disclosure. Family factors also have powerful effects; guilt and shame often accompany many activities related to autonomy or violation of childhood precepts.

Skepticism toward the therapist's authority, particularly after earlier exposure to significant failings in parents, priests, monks, and nuns, is not uncommon. Significant inhibitions are found over (a) bodily pleasure (erectile or orgasmic dysfunction), (b) satisfaction over accomplishment (excess humility), or (c) bodily adornment.

Protestantism

Most of the 2,000 Protestant denominations in this country can be grouped into nine general types of churches: *Mainline, Unionist, New Scripture, Millennial, Inner Light, Fundamentalist, Holiness, Pentecostal,* and *Non-Trinitarian.*

Mainline churches. These are the Lutheran, Presbyterian, Reformed, Episcopal, and Methodist denominations. Lutheran and Episcopal churches retain more of their Roman Catholic roots in liturgy, ritual, and sacraments and are diverse in their degree of sacramental practice, emphasis on biblical literalness, and political liberality.

The Episcopal church is very disparate, ranging from "high church" or Catholic liturgy, to the "broad" or middle church, to a more austere "low" church with very little sacramental emphasis. Part of the Episcopal church is evangelical; other parts actively promote political or social improvement.

The Presbyterian and Reformed churches are characterized by presbyterian (eldership) governance, some sacraments (baptism and communion), and moderate pressure for doctrinal uniformity. These churches range from liberal to conservative, both theologically and regarding social action vs. evangelical activity.

Methodist was a derogatory name applied to John Wesley for his methodical approach to *holiness,* a state of spiritual development. Methodists are serious about their faith, but genial in practice, without an emphasis on doctrinal minutia or scholarly activity. Social action is an expression of faith.

Unionist churches. As mentioned earlier in "American Indigenous Churches," these denominations bypass creedal or hierarchical strife. They are earnest, theologically diverse, conservative churches.

New Scripture churches. The Church of Jesus Christ of Latter-day Saints (Mormons) and the Christian Science church both have scriptures on a par with the Bible. For Mormons, missionary endeavors and social welfare activities are expected, at least at some time in everyone's career, to help develop a material perfection of their lives. Relationships are very important, but there are very strong prohibitions against premarital and extramarital sex. Celibacy is strongly disapproved of, while alcohol, tobacco, and caffeine are forbidden, although some use occurs among college-age students. If alcohol or tobacco is used, there is no level of acceptable use once temperance is breached. Autonomy issues and conflicts over control are likely, especially where the person's life trajectory or wishes exceed the permissible boundaries.

Christian Science is markedly different from the Latter-day Saints. In Christian Science, evil is a false perception and illness arises from incorrect thinking. With proper thinking and prayer, a trained Christian Science healer can induce healing. Setting broken bones and assistance at birth is permissible. With its strong emphasis on thought, meditation, and imagery, there may be a propensity for withdrawal in interpersonal relations.

Millennial churches. The Seventh-Day Adventists and Jehovah's Witnesses both are deeply rooted in the apocalyptic imagery of Revelation. *Millennial* refers to the thousand-year period described in Revelation, after which a great struggle between Jesus and Satan will end with Satan's defeat and various fates for the faithful and for sinners.

Adventist practice emphasizes a good deal of social service, education, and practical achievement. The Adventists support many schools and a large number of medical facilities. Their observance of the Saturday Sabbath, avoidance of meat (if not kosher), and proclivity toward vegetarianism are not especially provocative. Experiencing temptation is not a sin, but giving in is, so sin is a choice. Success, hard work, and its attendant satisfactions are supported.

Jehovah's Witnesses attribute many of the world's ills to government, religion, and commerce and regard the papacy as having deliberately mistranslated the Bible. They also view the world as a cataclysmic struggle between evil and good. Their originally aggressive missionary activity is now more circumspect. This denomination is sometimes characterized as more pathological than others, but the evidence is anecdotal (Montague, 1977; Botting & Botting, 1984). The elders who direct each Kingdom Hall are reputedly unfavorable to psychotherapy.

Inner Light churches. Amish, Church of the Brethren, Mennonites, and Quakers are included in the Inner Light churches. The Quakers, whose humanitarian activities have earned them prominence, are composed of several groups. Some resemble other Christian churches, while others conduct the silent services for which the Quakers are known.

Inner Light refers to openness to an inner light from God. Community is very important, and the quiet and decorous behavior of people in these churches may obscure their passionate attachment to their way of life. Emotional difficulties may center around guilt or shame over not meeting community standards. Feelings of disloyalty may trouble a member who has abandoned the community because of advanced learning or not following the community's practices.

Fundamentalist, Holiness, Pentecostal, Evangelical, and Charismatic churches. Many, but not all, Baptist churches can be included. Some northern and general American Baptist churches are much more centrist in thought than Southern Baptists. Fundamentalism began about 1900 to protest changes in traditional Protestantism introduced by liberal pastors and theologians. The "fundamental" principles include a belief that the Bible is to be taken literally for it is without error, a belief in the Trinity, and a belief in the substitutionary death of Jesus. Typically, fundamentalist worship is relatively restrained, avoiding *glossolalia* (speaking in tongues).

In Holiness churches, although Wesley's concept of entire sanctification is regarded as something that could happen through a brief, intense change, glossolalia is not typical. Pentecostalism originated from the Holiness movement and went beyond the "second blessing" of holiness to the "third blessing" of baptism in the Holy Spirit. This was characterized by "gifts of the Spirit," such as glossolalia. Some Pentecostal churches may use *Holiness* in their name, but few Holiness churches will use *Pentecostal.*

Evangelical refers to the Christian impetus not only to give others the good news of the atoning death and resurrection of Jesus, but also to bring others into communion with Jesus and other Christians to receive salvation. *Charismatic* refers to expression of intense emotion in a religious service. Charismatic typically refers to Catholics. Pentecostal is the more accustomed term among Protestants.

Non-Trinitarian churches. This includes two extreme churches, "Oneness" Pentecostal churches and the Unitarian Universalist Association. The former sees Jesus as God and rejects the Trinity. Its members resent being classed with Unitarians, whom they often regard as not being Christian. Unitarians are noncreedal; goodness and improvement are seen as a human potential.

Islam
Islam rejects racism, making it an attractive faith for those African-Americans who reject religions associated with whites. The separatist movement led by Elijah Muhammad—whose work began in the mid–

1930s and continued until his death in 1975—emphasized self-improvement, economic independence, hard work, moral behavior, and self-reclamation, while rejecting white society for the injuries it inflicted. Upon Muhammad's death in 1975, his successor, Wallace Deen Muhammad, startled his followers by proclaiming that whites are not devils. He began to direct the movement toward more orthodox Islamic teachings, changed the name to American Muslim Mission, and was subsequently accepted by the World Muslim Council. In reaction, some members followed Louis Farrakhan, who reconstituted the separatist Nation of Islam.

Muhammad's efforts made the Nation of Islam effective in fostering pride and integrity, especially among imprisoned African-Americans. Other factors, individual to the person's family of origin, are also of importance and need to be understood in counseling an American-born member of the American Muslim Mission.

The Personal Meanings of Religion

Religions mobilize thought and emotion to generate cognitive and affective states in the adherent. When these fit the child's understanding and emotional maturity, then growth and altruism are promoted. When they are aversive or exceed the child's understanding, disaffection may later ensue. The young adult may feel that religion is childish if he or she stopped learning at ages 12–14, just when the capacity for abstract thought has begun. If parents or clergy suppress questions or show hypocrisy, the child may be convinced that religion is a charade. Among the worst behaviors is sexual seduction by clergy. Counselors must understand that the client's anger over unempathic or abusive approaches is a response to disappointment and hurt. One client reported family prayer sessions that prayed for another member to be able to stay on her diet, but for the client's devils to be driven out—a devastating message.

In our society the developmental thrust is for children to differentiate from their parents. Religious parents may find that their children have declared themselves nonbelievers, while nonreligious parents sometimes find that their children have been converted. When parents maintain a steady attitude, their children eventually evince values little different from those of the parents.

A client's particular interest in the Bible's violent imagery, God's punishment, or prescription to parental authority merits exploration in counseling. Some clients may ask a counselor to pray with them, or some counselors may offer this. This is a highly personal matter, and counselors should avoid this if they are uncomfortable because they risk being seen as insincere. Where the counselor is comfortable, then the client's intent deserves exploration.

What is being prayed for? A client may be making an effort to achieve closeness, to secure comfort from a ritual activity, to partake of the counselor's greater "power," to divert attention from a problem area, or to test the counselor's attitudes.

Shame and Guilt

Shame (humiliation, embarrassment, chagrin) seems to develop earlier than guilt. Shame involves an interpersonal relationship, and often the client fears, or has experienced, damage to that relationship. Shame also occurs when the client's integrity or body has been violated (e.g., rape or incest).

Guilt and shame are very important emotions to deal with in counseling. Mere reassurance is not very effective. Guilt is frequently displaced; detailed exploration frequently shows that the client feels guilty about some idea, impulse, or feeling that, if enacted, would merit guilt feelings. Shame is harder to expunge in counseling and takes prolonged work. Sometimes it seems to diminish as if by desensitization. The counselor's steady, reliable acceptance also helps. Shame also seems related to repetitively frustrated childhood needs that were perhaps followed by ridicule. Subsequently, shame has been used to deflect desires for closeness if that need became a precursor of subsequent rejection.

SELECTED RELIGIOUS CONCEPTS

Religion has special perspectives and issues, only a few of which are dealt with in this section.

Abortion

Counselors will inevitably have feelings about a client's problem pregnancy. Client requests for advice will test the counselor's professional neutrality. Neutrality is not permissiveness but the counselor's withholding personal reactions to promote client introspection to uncover personal attitudes and feelings.

The early Judeo-Christian limitation on abortion was likely part of the Jewish principle of care for the child and prohibition of either infanticide or child sacrifice. Islam allows abortion to save the life of the mother, although a minority opinion allows abortion until the end of the fourth month (Abdul-Rauf, 1977).

Helping clients to come to an understanding of their choices, consequences, and motives is probably most useful in the long run. The counselor must be clear about his or her values while recognizing that to offer or assert these values may leave the client with consequences the counselor does not have to shoulder.

Alcoholism

Islam and some Christian churches regard any use of alcohol as sinful. For these clients the disease concept may be useful if it does not foster a retreat from responsibility. The Bible accepts wine or beer in moderation, while also setting limits. Even where a client's church prohibits alcohol, pastors are usually cooperative with a parishioner who is struggling with an alcohol problem, and will generally collaborate with the counselor.

Death, Grief, and Mourning

Theologically, Judaism and Christianity regard what happens after death as known only to God, but God is faithful. Heaven, Purgatory, Limbo, and Hell were a folk addition to Christianity that has been tacitly dropped, but many people think that there is an immediate life after death. Some Christian denominations (Latter-day Saints) are quite explicit about a very concrete afterlife, while Christian Science appears to see disease, and perhaps death, as false thinking. The Koran is specific about what awaits after death.

Most people experience death as an uncontrolled loss that is often dealt with through explanations and guilt. Feelings of guilt, through conjuring up something we could/should have done, reduce feelings of helplessness and loss.

The presence of others helps the mourner remember the good (and bad, if needed) and feel the appropriate pain and sadness. Failure to grieve leaves one's emotions bound to a person who can no longer give anything back, causing long-term consequences.

Depression

The counselor needs to distinguish between a *depressed mood* and a primary *depressive problem*. It is also important to make a distinction between *depression* and *sadness*. For mild to moderate depressions, most benign psychological interventions help. Suicide is the major risk in depression (as discussed later in this section).

Depressed clients may depict their unhappiness in religious terms. They feel sinful, unforgivable, or alienated from God or Jesus. Such clients usually distort their denomination's theology. Challenging the religious basis of a client's depressive ideas and feelings has risks, but showing the client how his or her religious feelings also operate with other people may give better traction.

Devil, Satan, and Angels

Angel derives from the Greek word for "messenger." The Hebrew word *sahtan* means "adversary"; hence, *satan* was not originally a name. When the Bible was translated, the Greek for "accuser" or "slanderer" was *diabolos*, from which is derived "devil." The malignant figure of Satan can permit the client to evade responsibility for his or her behavior.

Holy Spirit

For Christians, God operates through the Holy Spirit, while Jews and Muslims tend to see God's effect on the world directly, or through angels. For many conservative churches, grace or salvation is through baptism in the Holy Spirit. Not necessarily pathological, reports of direct experiences with God are uncommon and may be more serious.

Homosexuality

Gay or lesbian clients typically seek counseling for similar reasons as straight clients: depression, relationship problems, and self-esteem difficulties. When there are conflicts in clients between sexuality and religious orientation, these conflicts need attention.

The Bible's statements on homosexuality *seem* very clear—for men. Female homosexuality is never mentioned in the Old Testament, while New Testament references are vague. Probably pagan ritual sexuality was the target of Old Testament prohibitions. Greco-Roman practices were the dominant New Testament backdrop, yet the Gospels and Acts seem unconcerned with homosexuality. In Romans 1:18–32, Saint Paul condemns homosexuality. However, careful study demonstrates that the prevailing model of homosexuality was pederasty ("love of boys"). Saint Paul was probably attacking the exploitative pederasty also condemned by many pagan writers. Saint Paul might have also been condemning the modern model of adult, caring, mutual homosexuality, but there is no way to know (Scroggs, 1983). It is important to note that the Bible does not forbid homosexuality, only homosexual acts.

Pleasure and Sex

Most people erroneously view sexuality as a drive or as an impulse the person must resist or control. Yet nearly all of sexual functioning is brain-based, determined by the mind and the social situation. True drives *require* satisfaction, for if the person is deprived beyond the organism's capacity to sustain itself, the lack of satisfaction is fatal. Not so for sexuality. Sex involves human *relationships*. Even masturbation usually involves fantasies.

Extramarital sexual activity has a diverse range of meanings. For the client who has had an affair, or affairs, and feels guilt based on having transgressed biblical commandments, it helps to examine the symbolic meaning of the affair. Judaism, Islam, and Christianity all offer ample means to expiate guilt. Confession is one attractive alternative, but this may also express hidden hostility by the confessing person. Such a disclosure needs careful consideration.

Love, Marriage, Annulment, and Divorce

The Old Testament accepts sexual love between adults, bounded between husband and wife, forbids it with children, as a religious act, in prostitution, between relatives, or between men. In Judaism, marriage provides satisfaction, mutual care, help and support, rearing of children, and a structure within which the religious life of the family can flourish. A woman cannot divorce her husband, although she may compel him to divorce her. Divorce (a *get*) requires a rabbinic court and is easily secured, but is a major failure. Jewish parents are more likely to worry about intermarriage than divorce. A Jewish couple who secure a civil divorce without a religious divorce impose on any subsequent children a very severe ban.

The early church chose between the two conflicting statements of Jesus (Matthew 19 vs. Mark 10 and Luke 16), and decided that divorce was not permissible. These texts represented progressive attempts to change the position of women from possessions to people. In the Catholic church, when the necessary conditions of marriage are absent (lack of consummation, lack of understanding, or inability to live out the ideals of marriage), annulment is available.

Islamic law views marriage as "a legal commitment sanctioned by God and acknowledged by society" (Abdul-Rauf, 1977, p. 39). Marriage is a religious and civil act that leads to children, family, companionship, and sexual satisfaction. Homosexuality and celibacy are rejected. Choosing a spouse involves the entire family, and women may have little or much to say, depending on the culture—although in theory both should consent. Divorce in Islam is theoretically easy, although strongly discouraged. In Islam a woman's right to divorce can be written into the marriage contract.

Sin

Sin, often defined as deliberate violation of God's law, arises from a common Hebrew word most simply meaning "error." Deliberate sin in either the Old or New Testament is designated by other less frequently used words.

A client's intense sense of sinfulness may arise from anger at someone else that has been turned inward to avoid self-awareness. Clients burdened by a desire to be perfect typically find reassurance or support to be of little permanent help. To initiate inquiry I may say, "Perfection is your antidote for worthlessness." An alternative I also find useful is "You seem to have a defect in your conscience." Since such people are actually scrupulous about their behavior, this gets their attention. I tell them, "A conscience should do three things: warn you against wrongdoing, make you feel bad if you do, and reward you for doing well. Your conscience does fine on the first two but fails on the third." Lamsa (1985) renders Jesus' injunction to "be perfect" as to be "all inclusive. To know all lines of a trade" (p. 51), suggesting that Matthew and Luke may have used an Aramaic word that could mean "whole" or "generous."

Some clients develop a detailed list of specific sins. Such lists are inconsistent with either Jesus or Saint Paul, who were much more concerned with attitudes than behavioral trivia, with alienation from God than empty ritual. Such clients may be communicating their alienation from God and significant people. I find that trying to open up such feelings is initially painful, but if the counselor does so in a manner that expresses interest in the client's feelings without endorsing their accuracy, then a healing process can be initiated.

Women and Men

A woman's consent to marriage is deduced from Genesis 24:55–58 and her independent business activity is extolled in Proverbs 31:10–31. The Old Testament took a more complex, humane view of women, than did Greek and Roman law. In the New Testament, Jesus associated with both men and women with remarkable openness. Sometimes Saint Paul was quite radical on equality of men and women; other times less so. The most radical position on male and female equality is in the Koran, although local customs often reign.

Many Protestant denominations ordain women as ministers; the struggle is often over whether a woman can be a bishop. The Reform and conservative movements in Judaism accept women as rabbis. In the Roman Catholic church women have long served as teaching and nursing nuns and currently serve as lectors and administrators, but this is a ceiling.

WHAT IS A CULT?

In sociology, a *church* is connected with the outside world, a *sect* has split from a church and withdrawn from its environment, and a *cult* is an innovative religious group. "Cult" has such negative meanings that I will use *new religious movement* (NRM) for more objectivity about these new religions, the people they attract, how they retain members, and what concerned parents can do when a relative has joined one.

The Unification Church of America. The Unification Church of America (UCA) arose from an organization founded by the Reverend Sun Myung Moon in 1954. Moon moved to the United States in 1971 to concentrate his efforts, arousing intense interest. Large numbers of young people were "converted," but their involvement dissipated and the UCA's estimate of 5,000–7,000 members in the mid-1970s is probably much lower now.

While Moonies acknowledge Jesus' salvific death, they reject the Trinity and hold central the failure of Adam and Eve to develop the perfect spiritual family after Eve's seduction by Lucifer. Moon expects the return of a messiah, who may perhaps be himself.

Hare Krishna. The Hare Krishnas, arising from a Hindu sect from 15th-century India, was brought to America in 1965 by a retired Indian businessman. The Hare Krishnas are monotheistic, as is Hindu theology, even though God is represented in three aspects: Brahma (creator), Siva (destroyer) and Vishnu (preserver). Krishna is an avatar of Vishnu. Their theology differs from orthodox Hindu thought. Membership is estimated to be 3,000–4,000.

The Church of Scientology. Dianetics, started by science fiction writer L. Ron Hubbard, resembles psychoanalytic concepts grafted onto a computerlike model of the mind. Purporting to bring about a state of being "clear" through a few hours of "auditing," Scientology was received with intense interest in 1950. Then Hubbard added spiritual dimensions, which coalesced in the Church of Scientology. Hubbard centralized control, and by the 1960s his organization was well structured. Reported membership is in the tens of thousands.

Why Do They Join?

The convert to an NRM receives immediate acceptance, warmth, and purpose. Competitiveness is rejected, basic needs are met, and the convert's contribution is immediate. Strong idealism and involvement in a program untainted by sordid society attracts late adolescents and young adults.

Most adults do *not* join NRMs as their ordinary emotional attachments strengthen their personality, enhance self-worth and frustration tolerance, and fortify impulse control. When conversion stabilizes a precarious sense of self, interference is a severe threat to personal integrity and emotional coherence that is strongly resisted.

Brainwashing, Deceptive Recruiting, Violence, and Fund-Raising

"Brainwashing," deception, and unethical recruitment techniques are common accusations against NRMs. Brainwashing actually requires much control of the person and is expensive and ineffective. While deceptive recruitment is sometimes used, attempts to influence attitudes, not brainwashing, are operative. NRM members are not turned into zombies, for attrition is substantial.

Although frequently charged with violence, modern NRMs are more likely to be recipients of violence than initiators. Both NRM and anti-NRM groups have engaged in violence, but for NRMs it seems more reactive to harassment. Parents have hired deprogrammers to kidnap their children from NRMs. Such kidnapping is a serious offense that sometimes leads to conviction.

Fund-raising by NRMs has been strongly criticized. Many have relatively small needs for money that are met through small businesses or member donations. Moonies and Hare Krishnas need more money, and sometimes their begging and soliciting is harassing. Scientology raises money through lesson sales and perhaps through other businesses.

Deprogramming

Because NRM members have not been brainwashed, deprogramming does not work. Deprogrammers attempt to persuade, influence, and undermine a person's beliefs. The process has no legal support, but is potentially dangerous to mental health. The similarity of stories from people after deprogramming springs from the basic ideology and justification of the deprogrammers.

Perhaps a third of the persons forcibly deprogrammed return to the NRMs, perhaps more confirmed in their faith and less able to leave when they otherwise might wish to. Those whose forcible deprogramming has "taken" are more likely to be involved in the anticult movement and to more vehemently reject their former NRM. People who have left after their own reevaluation rarely have horror stories to tell and are less involved in the anticult movement.

Joining a New Religious Movement: Between Parent and Child

The parent/child dialogue, seen on a television program whose theme was deprogramming, resembles family therapy. Parents' hopes and plans for their children are disrupted, their children are not responsive to parental influence, and hopes for grandchildren are imperiled. The primary conflict is familial, as the NRMs do not really affect the interests of government or church. Converts will likely renew their family ties if the families have not made this impossible.

NRMs may be regarded as opportunities for young adults to:

1. grow up and separate from their families,
2. repair earlier losses through new committed relationships,

3. provide meaning to their lives, or
4. get off drugs and acquire skills on which they missed out.

Satanic "Cults"

The worship of Satan is intimately tied to Christianity with satanism's inversion of symbols and rites of the mass. Many media reports of satanism either are mislabeled or deflect attention from ordinary crimes. Sensational reports of animal and human sacrifices and ritual abuse are often unfounded or the evidence is ambiguous (Lyons, 1988).

There are three types of satanic groups: "(1) solitary Satanists, (2) 'outlaw' cults, and (3) neo-Satanic churches" (Lyons, 1988, p. 9). The solitary Satanists are typically disturbed adolescents who concoct their own rituals. The outlaw cults seem similar, with larger numbers. The Church of Satan, originated by Anton LaVey in San Francisco in 1966, and the Temple of Set, founded by Michael Aquino and his wife Lillith Sinclair, are flamboyant but prohibit harm to people or animals, sacrifices, and the use of blood in rituals.

Solitary Satanists and "outlaw" cults can be harmful because their practice "has great emotional intensity and includes strong overtones of ventilation of anger against God and society. Needless to say, Satanism attracts its share of sociopathic persons" (Ellwood, 1988, p. 721).

But Shouldn't Something Be Done?

Sexual or ritual abuse of children or adults and abuse of animals are illegal and merit prosecution. Freedom of religion is not a defense. Offensive acts (group sex, excrement in a Black Mass, reading the Mass backward, or using an inverted cross or black host) while abhorrent are not illegal, and the "cure" of suppression risks the religious liberties of all.

Similarly, heavy metal music has generated intense opposition from fundamentalist Christian groups, who claim that these recordings contain subliminal messages that can only be decoded when the tape is played backward. While this music may be loud, tasteless, and simple, the hearing of healthy youngsters seems more at risk than their mental health. It may further destabilize an already disturbed adolescent, however. "Demetaling" or other "rehabilitations" are likely secular disguises for fundamentalist views. The fears of a satanic network attempting to destroy American youth has little foundation. What little danger there is comes from loners or small groups of disturbed people.

State police organizations around the country are definitely interested in satanic groups and follow up reports. There are instances of outlaw cults, but reports of wide conspiracies do not pan out. Either satanic groups are uniformly more effective in cloaking felonies from well-trained investigators, or there is less here than meets the eye. Some are dangerous, but current laws are sufficient. Prohibition increases attractiveness, a counterproductive action.

Involvement with a satanic church may indicate considerable isolation, alienation, and rejection of one's family values. In adolescents, this may be an expression of ordinary anger or a way to differentiate from the family. While an interest in satanism is cause for neither panic nor disinterest, family counseling may be desirable since the adolescent may reject being the sole problem. If the adolescent acknowledges serious personal distress, individual treatment as an adjunct is an alternative. Satanic interests may also indicate the formation of an accepted sense of oneself as evil. This is a malignant development in which distress that might motivate accepting professional help may be absent (Magid, 1988).

ILLNESS, PAIN, AGING, AND DEATH

Pain and suffering happen to some good people without apparent justification, while some evil people prosper. If God is just, how can this be understood? This is exactly the problem faced by Job. Kushner (1981) discusses this in *When Bad Things Happen to Good People*, using three true but conflicting statements:

A. God is all-powerful and wills everything that happens in the world.
B. God is just and fair, so the good prosper and the wicked are punished.
C. Job is a good person.

Logically, when Job suffers, only two of the three statements hold, and the choice is which statement to drop. Kushner opts to modify statements A and B by proposing that God tries to make the world fair and just, but cannot always do so. Kushner quotes from Job 40, in which God tells Job, *"You* tread down the wicked" (p. 43) and then God will acknowledge Job's power. Kushner concludes that while God may not be omnipotent, God offers comfort and guidance.

"Answers," "Explanations," and Responses

In counseling, clients may want, even demand, answers to make the person's world whole again. Kushner (1981) lists well-meaning but devastating "answers" meant to comfort the bereaved. These include:

1. It was a punishment for sin. (If not the deceased's, then yours).
2. God needed him more. (You did not need him enough.)

3. She is now free from pain and in a better world. (You did not make this world nice enough for her.)
4. If only. . . . (It's really someone's fault.)
5. Don't cry, he wouldn't want you to. (Don't burden *me* with your pain.)
6. God does not give you a heavier burden than you can carry. (The bereaved person's strength caused the pain.)

And there is the classic "I don't know what to say," meaning, I cannot bring the deceased back to life. While the dead cannot be revived, the living can be comforted and their pain ameliorated through support. Prolonged stifling of pain is damaging. Finally, the living may be angry at the dead, both for real hurts as well as angry grief over feeling abandoned by the person who died.

Suicide

A strong religious affiliation will reduce the risk of suicide *somewhat*. Risk factors include being older, unmarried, in poor physical health, unemployed or retired, or from a broken home, living alone, infrequent use of health agencies, severe emotional difficulties, membership in certain groups, and prior suicide attempts. Women are three times as likely as men to attempt suicide; men are three times as likely to succeed. Adolescents are at higher risk than mature adults, but preadolescent children do make suicide threats and sometimes execute them. Elderly adults are also at risk when health and finances decline and important relationships are lost.

However, employment and financial status can sometimes be improved. Relationships, and sometimes health, can be enhanced. Where a client is at risk for depression, part of the interview should evaluate suicidal potential. Even children can be asked.

The counselor's appeal to religious prohibitions is a desperate intervention. Suicide seems to be largely independent of religious affiliation in this country, although there are some differences among groups as a function of age, gender, and ethnic membership. However, some clients regard suicide as a slap at God or a great sin. The client who sees suicide as a slap at God likely is angry at God. God can tolerate the client's anger and will not strike back in anger—but someone in the client's life probably did. As for suicide being a sin, one may agree in the original meaning of the word—suicide is an error.

ASSESSMENT AND TREATMENT

Religious Differences and Similarities

When a client challenges the counselor's status on personal salvation, exploring this question's meanings is indicated. The client is asking the counselor, "Are you totally reliable or identical with me?" or "Will you judge me as does my pastor?" The question "Are you a Christian?" has multiple meanings but most extremely asks "Have you taken Jesus as your personal Savior?"

The client's need for total trust at the start of counseling suggests fragility, an abusive history, or great difficulty with ambiguity. Accepting assurances without qualm connotes considerable desperation, jeopardizing the counseling process later from the ordinary disappointments and failures inherent to counseling. The wish to be identical indicates a poorly organized self. Absent a direct question, offering such information without understanding its meaning may burden a client with unnecessary knowledge. But if a client inquires and the question has been explored, a direct answer is preferable to evasion.

Initial Appraisal of Client Difficulties

Some counselors take acceptance and understanding to mean they should not appraise the adaptiveness of the client's behaviors, feelings, or attitudes. But an appraisal can lead to different responses that affect progress in counseling.

If the client begins to recount personal religious experiences, it is important to try to set these experiences into the context of both the client's childhood and his or her current denomination.

Religious behaviors implicated with emotional problems (Pruyser, 1971, 1977; Rubins, 1955; Salzman, 1953) include:

1. *Self-oriented display:* Exhibition of one's good deeds, piety, charity, and so on.
2. *Religion as reward:* Expecting the world (or God) to treat the client well, based on good behavior or piety.
3. *Scrupulosity:* An overriding preoccupation with never doing anything wrong or sinful. The client sometimes hurts others in this pursuit; the client's underlying pride is sometimes the worst sin of all.
4. *Relinquishing responsibility:* Saying "The Devil made me do it" evades accountability for one's behavior.
5. *Ecstasy or frenzy:* Personal ecstasy may express early emotional deprivation and an intense effort to restore a sense of personal wholeness and vitality.
6. *Recurrent church-changing:* Persistent inability to connect with a congregation signals difficulties in sustaining relationships.
7. *Indiscriminate attitudes:* No religion is perfect. A client's persistently enthusiastic, indiscriminate attitude expresses a response typical of childhood.
8. *Double-sided "love":* Love can also express anger, dependence, and

immaturity. The feelings that arise after affirmations of love are a better guide than verbalizations.

9. *The Bible as a guide to everything:* The Bible is a complex text spanning some two millennia. Considering it a guide to *all* of life's daily choices and problems is an evasion of responsibility.

10. *Possession:* Where a client reports possession, and where major personality changes appear, the counselor should consider a multiple or borderline personality disorder. Consultation is definitely indicated unless the counselor is well experienced with these problems.

Not all religious expression reflects dysfunction. Some aspects show creative coping with life's problems. These include:

1. *Awareness of complexity:* Religious problems are often complex, and an awareness of their multifaceted nature suggests intellectual and emotional maturity.

2. *Willingness to try alternatives:* The religion of the client's parents may be suitable, but if the client has experimented, the final choice more likely is a mature one.

3. *"Conversion":* This is not taken in the usual meaning, but rather signifies that the client went through a period of struggle before coming to a resolution.

4. *Coherence:* While all religions have complexities, the adherent's task is to organize his or her life coherently. Clients who extol love but are brutal to their children are not coherent.

5. *Integrity:* All religions make demands, some of which are inconvenient or difficult. Integrity implies that falling short indicates the need for effort rather than an adjustment of standards.

6. *Respect for boundaries:* A religious affiliation may engender a good deal of enthusiasm. In American society, there are limits beyond which enthusiasm is intrusive.

FOR FURTHER READING

Alter, R. (1981). *The art of biblical narrative.* New York: Basic Books.

Asimov, I. (1968). *Asimov's guide to the Bible: The Old Testament.* New York: Avon Books.

Asimov, I. (1969). *Asimov's guide to the Bible: The New Testament.* New York: Avon Books.

Cole, W. G. (1959). *Sex and love in the Bible.* New York: Association Press.

Josipovici, G. (1988). *The book of God: A response to the Bible.* New Haven: Yale University Press.

Kosnik, A., Carroll, W., Cunningham, A., Modias, R., & Schulte, J. (1977). *Human sexuality: New directions in American Catholic thought.* Mahwah, NJ: Paulist Press.

Lamsa, G. M. (1985). *Idioms in the Bible explained and a key to the original Gospels.* New York: Harper & Row.

Lippy, C. H., & Williams, P. W. (1988). *Encyclopedia of the American religious experience.* New York: Scribner's.
Patai, R. (1960). *Family, love, and the Bible.* London: MacGibbon & Kee.
Pruyser, P. W. (1974). *Between belief and unbelief.* New York: Harper & Row.
Stacey, D. (1977). *Interpreting the Bible.* New York: Hawthorn Books.

REFERENCES

Abdul-Rauf, M. (1977). *The Islamic view of women and the family.* New York: Speller.
Argyle, M., & Beit-Hallahmi, B. (1975). *The social psychology of religion.* London: Routledge & Kegan Paul.
Berger, P. L. (1974). Some second thoughts on substantive versus functional definitions of religion. *Journal for the Scientific Study of Religion, 13,* 125–133.
Booth, Jr., N. S. (1988). Islam in North America. In C. H. Lippy & P. W. Williams (Eds.), *Encyclopedia of the American religious experience* (pp. 723–729). New York: Scribner's.
Botting, H., & Botting, G. (1984). *The Orwellian world of Jehovah's Witnesses.* Toronto: University of Toronto Press.
Ellwood, R. S. (1988). Occult movements in America. In C. H. Lippy & P. W. Williams (Eds.), *Encyclopedia of the American religious experience* (pp. 711–722). New York: Scribner's.
Kushner, H. S. (1981). *When bad things happen to good people.* New York: Avon Books.
Lamsa, G. M. (1985). *Idioms in the Bible explained and a key to the original Gospels.* New York: Harper & Row.
Lyons, A. (1988). *Satan wants you: The cult of devil worship in America.* New York: Mysterious Press.
Magid, B. (1988). The evil self. *Dynamic psychotherapy, 6,* 99–113.
Montague, H. (1977). The pessimistic sect's influence on the mental health of its members: The case of Jehovah's Witnesses. *Social Compass, 24,* 135–147.
Pruyser, P. (1971). Assessment of the patient's religious attitudes in the psychiatric case study. *Bulletin of the Menninger Clinic, 35,* 272–291.
Pruyser, P. (1977). The seamy side of current religious beliefs. *Bulletin of the Menninger Clinic, 41,* 329–348.
Robbins, T., & Anthony, D. (1988). Cults in the late 20th century. In C. H. Lippy & P. W. Williams (Eds.), *Encyclopedia of the American religious experience* (pp. 741–754). New York: Scribner's.
Rubins, J. L. (1955). Neurotic attitudes toward religion. *American Journal of Psychoanalysis, 15,* 71–81.
Salzman, L. (1953). The psychology of religious and ideological conversion. *Psychiatry, 16,* 177–187.
Scroggs, R. (1983). *The New Testament and homosexuality.* Philadelphia: Fortress Press.

3

COUNSELING APPROACHES THROUGHOUT THE LIFE SPAN

The chapters in this section provide information to address two tasks that face the contemporary counselor. The first is a need for the general practitioner to gain increased understanding of a life-span perspective. The second is the ability to be conversant with the wide range of contemporary issues.

The ability to understand life-span development has become an important issue as the age range for vital living increases physically, socially, and psychologically. The life-span perspective is represented clinically by articles ranging from decisions regarding testing of children, treatment of adolescents, family and marital counseling, understanding adult development and aging, and issues related to death and dying. The result is that the counselor is asked to consider the interactive impact of all age-appropriate tasks.

The scope of more specific issues is also represented by chapters from a life-span perspective. Problems such as child abuse, eating disorders and addictions, phobias, AIDS, marital problems, and organic disorders are included. Some topics included are less detailed, as they are less likely to be encountered during the course of general practice but still require a level of awareness on the part of counselors. If a need for additional information arises, we refer you to the further reading suggestions at the end of each chapter.

These issues can occur as problems in several generations of the same family at the same time. This section necessarily provides the counselor with an appreciation of both the age and clinical dimensions of counseling in order to increase awareness of the life-span challenge.

16

Treatment Planning in Counseling

JOHN B. MORDOCK, Ph.D.

While *Webster's Dictionary* (Webster's II New Riverside Dictionary, 1988) defines counseling as "to give counsel or advice," Campbell's (1989) *Psychiatric Dictionary* defines counseling as "a type of psychotherapy of the supportive or re-educative variety." Turning to Walrond-Skinner's (1986) *Dictionary of Psychotherapy,* we find that the word *psychotherapy* is difficult to define, with definitions ranging from narrow ones based on a particular school of thought to broad ones where any exchange between a help giver and a help seeker is considered psychotherapy. The word *counseling* has lost its original, specific meaning and has become a general term to denote any helping relationship where an individual is guided in understanding, gaining control over, and modifying attitudes, feelings, or behaviors that interfere with interpersonal adjustment.

Years ago it was thought that the advice of a trained, knowledgeable, and experienced counselor would help clients. In some cases, it did. But in other cases, the client did not follow the advice, actively resisted it, or could not generalize principles underlying the advice to other similar situations. As a result, counselors had to develop other techniques to help a client resolve interpersonal difficulty. Counselors holding particular philosophies of human nature evolved techniques out of their belief systems (e.g., client-centered counseling or existential counseling from humanistic theories). Therapies developed from interpersonal theory, group and family theory, learning theory, and so on. As a result, a variety of counseling approaches fall under the headings of *insight therapy*, with examples being client-centered, rational-emotive, cognitive-behavioral, and psychoanalytic therapies; or *behavior therapy*, with behavioral contracting, desensitization, and modeling as three major techniques used by practitioners. The *group therapies* include marital and family counseling, with family counseling further subdivided into structural, strategic, multigenerational, and functional counseling.

How does the counselor know which modality of counseling to employ with a particular client or when to involve the client's family in the counseling process? If the counselor is well trained in one approach, this approach may be applied to all clients or only to those clients considered likely to profit from the approach. Clients also are self-selective, with young adults preferring individual-oriented client-centered counselors, for example, and older adults preferring Jungian counselors.

Many counselors do not adhere strictly to one approach, choosing to borrow from several to meet the needs of their clients. Often their choice of an approach rests on the maturity of the client, his or her intelligence, the severity of the presenting problem, and the client's expectations about and motivation for help. In other words, the client's level of emotional and cognitive development dictates the choice of modality. While rational-emotive therapy (RET) has been utilized with children, it is better suited for adults. Psychoanalytic therapists employ play therapy with children because children's cognitive development limits the use of free association. Client-centered counselors also use play therapy because the child has limited verbal skills. Adaptations in technique are made to accommodate the immature client. It follows that if adaptations are made for children because of their immaturity, then adaptations need to be made for clients who may be emotionally immature or developmentally arrested. Forms of play therapy have been utilized with retarded clients, and parents have been helped to play so they, in turn, could play with their child. Even play therapy techniques have been modified for children at different levels of emotional development (Mordock, 1978, 1991; Thompson, 1991).

Families also have been categorized developmentally. Based on Sandor Rado's Motivational Framework (Rado, 1962), Lantz (1987) categorizes families as *magical-craving, parental-invocating, cooperative-striving, and realistically self-reliant.* The magical-craving family responds best to suggestion and charismatic permission; the parental-invocating family to empathy, ventilation acceptance, encouragement, and environmental manipulation; the cooperative-striving family to pattern clarification, social skill training, cognitive restructuring, and behavior modification; and the realistically self-reliant family to interpretation, encounter, and socratic search for meaning.

The counselor desirous of helping each of his clients needs to select a course of action from among the array of alternatives available. He or she needs to match the client's problems, capacity for problem solving, and motivation with the counseling modalities most likely to help the particular client to resolve his or her particular difficulties. Not only are particular modalities selected for use, but the sequences and timing of their use are considered in the planning process.

While a large body of literature exists to teach and guide the counselor to deliver specific modalities of counseling, very little literature exists to help the counselor in modality selection, often referred to as *treatment planning*. Steps in the process of treatment planning have not been well articulated. Treatment planning is often an intuitive process for many skilled clinicians, and it is difficult to define what actually transpires between the beginning and end of their creative acts (Looney, 1984).

TREATMENT PLANNING

Recently, Frances and his colleagues (Frances, Clarkin, & Perry, 1984; Perry, Frances, & Clarkin, 1985; Beutler & Clarkin, 1960) have articulated the concept of *differential therapeutics*. Differential therapeutics is an effort to define enabling factors and indicators for a wide range of treatments. From the indicators, counselors can define contraindicators and enabling factors for predicting a client's probable response to a particular course of action. The treatments considered extend beyond counseling to include consideration of an array of treatment settings, the selection of medication, and the assignment of treatment mode, frequency, duration, and format.

Beutler and Clarkin (1990) present four general steps for "fitting" the treatment to the client:

1. fitting the focal goals and objectives of the treatment to the complexity of the client's problems;
2. selecting the level of intervention to fit the client's methods of coping;
3. altering treatment menus to fit mediating tasks and goals that define the phases through which treatment progresses; and
4. adapting specific-in-therapy procedures to the moment-by-moment treatment states that occur between a client and a counselor.

Looking more closely at the first step, formulating treatment goals, Beutler and Clarkin discuss selecting a therapeutic focus. The counselor must answer the question "Are these problems isolated symptoms that are environment specific, or are they supported by reinforcing symptom patterns that are indicative of underlying conflict?" In well-executed treatment, the focus involves a chain of hypothesized relationships between precipitating events and final objectives of change, often referred to as a *psychodynamic formulation*.

Once the counselor has decided whether the problem is a transient response or a persistent, recurring pattern maintained by conflict, the task then becomes one of defining the specific symptoms or conflicts that require work. If the symptoms are viewed as situationally specific, then the counselor begins to develop the therapeutic focus by identifying each symptom and assigning it a priority for intervention.

The selection of goals is more complex when the symptoms are conflict based. Patient complaints cannot always be trusted to define the most beneficial objectives of treatment (Beutler & Clarkin, 1990). Symptoms can be vague and can change across situations. The counselor must observe in the symptoms common symbols and certain patterns within the recurrent events. The focus of treatment is organized around a psychodynamic formulation that explains the common elements that exist across situations and that are not readily apparent in the concrete events that occur in the client's life.

The counselor must also select the depth of intervention. Traditionally, therapeutic approaches were ordered along a continuum of depth, ranging from behavioral interventions, through supportive and crisis counseling approaches, to psychoanalysis, the "deepest" approach. More recently, Beutler and Clarkin (1990) propose that the levels of experience to which change mechanisms are addressed can be ordered as (a) unconscious motivations, wishes, and conflicts; (b) unidentified feelings and sensory experiences; (c) dysfunctional cognitive patterns; and (d) behaviors of excess and insufficiency. The counselor matches the depth of intended intervention both with the coping style of the patient and with the outcome expected. The counselor moves toward the development of a specific treatment menu.

Beutler and Clarkin (1990) review the literature on the relationship of client coping style to modality effectiveness. For example, clients who tend to externalize their problems by blaming others or blaming conditions (a less mature coping style) respond best to behaviorally oriented modalities. Those who internalize their problems (take responsibility for them) respond best to therapies that are designed to magnify and expose feelings. Clients who habitually repress feelings respond best to methods directed at uncovering the needs and wants that underlie current problems.

Less mature clients become extremely anxious when faced with loss of perceived control or freedom. They maintain their fragile self-image by efforts at exerting control over a self-limited environment. Consequently, they resist the counselor's influence. "To take advice or direction from a counselor is to admit to being a failure." Such clients respond best to nondirective counseling approaches. Somewhat more mature and less resistant clients who have established some trust in the counselor can make better use of more structured approaches where questions are asked, feelings clarified, limits set, and guidance and advice provided. With well-developed clients, interpretive activities, guided fantasy, dream analysis, and confrontation can be utilized if done carefully and slowly so as to preserve the therapeutic attachment (Beutler & Clarkin, 1990).

My own interest as a counselor of families whose children have been referred for help, most often for conduct problems, has been in selecting the correct modalities to employ with family members and in determining the sequence and length of the modalities selected. When family therapy was in its infancy, we were trained to insist that all family members attend each session and to discourage individual members from talking to us individually. As we gained increasing experience in working with families, we learned that other approaches were more effective in achieving the goals of treatment. For example, Abelsohn (1983) and McPherson, Brackermanns, and Newman (1974) present cases of drug-abusing adolescents where the adolescent was initially seen alone for several sessions, followed by several sessions with the mother alone, and then family members were brought together for family therapy. The rationales for these procedures were based on assessment of the assets and deficits of each family member and his or her particular needs at the time. Improving the adolescent's relationship with the mother involved individual counseling to help the adolescent understand the mother's problems. The mother was seen alone to develop a therapeutic alliance that would enable both the mother and the adolescent to tolerate the stress that would arise in the family sessions to follow.

Minuchin (1974) presents a case where case management/linking with the school was the first step, accompanied by seeing the referred child in companionship counseling while he or she waited for assignment to a Big Brother; the mother was seen individually to help her prepare for a mother's group or an ongoing codependence support group. Minuchin (1974) presents another case where the family was seen initially to help strengthen the boundary around the parent's relationship; the child was then seen alone, followed by sessions with siblings to help them support one another's noninvolvement in parental conflicts.

Selecting appropriate "homework" assignments outside counseling sessions is an important part of treatment planning. Plans often call for increasing one parent's involvement with a child and decreasing another parent's involvement with the child's pathological behaviors (Dalton, 1983), decreasing a parent's involvement with a grandparent (Minuchin & Fishman, 1979), increasing parental transactions (Minuchin,1974), and seeking support from collaterals by asking them to respond to the child in a particular manner. The sequence of these assignments also is important. Often parents or collaterals cannot follow advice until other modalities of counseling have been offered to prepare them to accept taking directions from others.

SETTING GOALS

Counselors must also direct their efforts at helping the client to reach reasonable goals. For example, the attention-deficit disordered child who is immature may never be able to play with same-age peers but may be able to relate to younger children.

Realistic goals for family counseling have been based on an assessment of three levels of goal attainability (Terkelson, 1980). The highest level is *full restoration.* At this level, counseling helps the family recapture its capacity to promote need attainment. The second level is *supplementation.* Here the counselor does not expect the family to attain sufficiency in and of itself. The counseling plan deliberately includes creation of some more or less permanent attachment between the family and an external helping agent (Lamb, 1980). The family becomes semiautonomous. Involvement in self-help support groups or continual support by school staff will always be required to preserve family stability. The lowest level is *replacement.* Too much is missing in the family, resulting in the family needing extensive supplementation to function adequately. One or more of its members will require periodic placement in foster homes, group homes, or other institutions. These supplemental services should be used in the context of a relationship established with a family member and with awareness of the member's needs for control. Whereas some counselors may view the use of such facilities as treatment failure, their use may create some family stability. The family members should participate in the finding, planning, and utilization of these services. Such planning helps to promote a member's growth, the ability to cope more effectively, and self-esteem. When concrete services are provided outside this context, strong regressive tendencies are encouraged and only temporary and sporadic relief occurs (Newman & Martino, 1973).

The counselor who considers each client's developmental level and developmental needs is one who goes beyond his subjective preference for a particular counseling approach and instead selects the approach or approaches best suited to the client who presents himself for help. *The Counseling Sourcebook* is designed with this in mind.

FOR FURTHER READING

Beutler, L. E., & Clarkin, J. F. (1990). *Systematic treatment selection.* New York: Brunner/Mazel.

Frances, A., Clarkin, J. F., & Perry, S. (1984). *Differential therapeutics in psychiatry.* New York: Brunner/Mazel.

Mordock, J. B. (1991). *Counseling children: Helping the troubled and defiant child.* New York: Crossroads.

REFERENCES

Abelsohn, D. (1983). Dealing with the abdication dynamic in the post-divorce family: A context for adolescent crisis. *Family Process, 22,* 359–383.

Beutler, L. E., & Clarkin, J. F. (1990). *Systematic treatment selection.* New York: Brunner/Mazel.

Campbell, R. J. (1989). *Psychiatric Dictionary* (6th ed). New York: Oxford University Press.

Dalton, P. J. (1983). Family treatment of an obsessive-compulsive child: A case report. *Family Process, 22,* 99–108.

Frances, A., Clarkin, J. F., & Perry, S. (1984). *Differential therapeutics in psychiatry.* New York: Brunner/Mazel.

Lamb, H. R. (1980). Therapist-case managers: More than brokers of services. *Hospital and Community Psychiatry, 31,* 762–764.

Lantz, J. E. (1987). Emotional motivation for family treatment. *Social Casework, 68,* 284–289.

Looney, J. G. (1984). Treatment planning in child psychiatry. *Journal of the American Academy of Child Psychiatry, 5,* 529–536.

McPherson, S. R., Brackermanns, W. E., & Newman, L. E. (1974). Stages in the family therapy of adolescents. *Family Process, 13,* 77–94.

Minuchin, S. (1974). *Families and family therapy.* Cambridge, Harvard University Press.

Minuchin, S., & Fishman, H. C. (1979). The psychosomatic family in child psychiatry. *Journal of the American Academy of Child Psychiatry, 18,* 76–90.

Mordock, J. B. (1978). The separation-individuation process and developmental disabilities. *Exceptional Children, 45,* 176–184.

Mordock, J. B. (1991). *Counseling children: Helping the troubled and defiant child.* New York: Crossroads.

Newman, M. B., & Martino, M. S. (1973). The child and the seriously disturbed parent. *Journal of the American Academy of Child Psychiatry, 12,* 162–181.

Perry, S., Frances, A., & Clarkin, J. F. (1985). *A DSM-III casebook of differential therapeutics: A clinical guide to treatment selection.* New York: Brunner/Mazel.

Rado, S. (1962). *Psychoanalysis of behavior* (Vol. 2). New York: Grune & Stratton.

Terkelson, K. G. (1980). Toward a theory of the family life cycle. In E. A. Carter & M. McGoldrick (Eds.), *The family life cycle: A framework for family therapy* (pp. 21–52). New York: Gardner Press.

Thompson, T. C. (1991). The place of ego building work in psychotherapy with children. *Child and Adolescent Social Work, 8,* 351–367.

Walrond-Skinner, S. (1986). *A dictionary of psychotherapy.* New York: Routledge & Kegal Paul.

Webster's II new Riverside dictionary. (1988). New York: Riverside Publishing.

17

Why Psychological Testing?

MILTON F. SHORE, Ph.D., B.A.P.P.

PATRICK J. BRICE, Ph.D.

BARBARA G. LOVE, Ph.D.

> This is really silly; what does it show anyway?
> —14-year-old girl halfway through
> the testing session

Why is psychological testing utilized? To answer this question clearly, it is important to understand the unique characteristics of psychological tests, the context in which testing is done, and the value, as well as limitations, of psychological testing.

WHAT IS A PSYCHOLOGICAL TEST?

The word *testing* frequently elicits a number of associations. People think of school where tests are used to find out who has done the homework assignment and learned the material. If the material was learned, students passed; if not, they failed. This success/failure model arouses much anxiety among people being tested. Indeed, "test anxiety" is an experience many people have and one that has been studied extensively in psychology.

Another meaning of *testing* is associated with medical examinations. There are a number of medical tests (e.g., blood tests) that are used to determine whether or not a disease is present in the body. Traditional medical/laboratory tests are designed to discover physiological causes underlying symptoms. The results are independent of time and place. Thus, a high white blood cell count would strongly suggest a systemic

This chapter is adapted from Shore, M. J., Brice, P., and Love, B., *When Your Child Needs Testing* (New York: Crossroad, 1992).

infection, regardless of when or where the test was conducted. Electro-encephalograms, CAT scans, and magnetic resonance imaging techniques are tests of the neurological system that will yield the same results regardless of where they are given.

Psychological testing differs markedly from medical testing. In psychology, testing is a way of collecting information that helps the counselor understand psychological processes and behavior. Since behavior is multidetermined, that is, has biological, psychological, social, and cultural influences, it is important that psychological testing be distinguished from many other kinds of testing. And, unlike traditional medical/laboratory testing, the context can have significant effects. A test administered in a group setting, such as a classroom where there are many students, may yield significantly different results than if it were administered individually in a psychologist's office. The result of a test given by someone who is liked by a child and where the child is relaxed differs from one where the child feels uncomfortable.

The very idea of measurement in psychology is abstract and complex. A physician can see or detect the physical presence of a tumor, aberrant blood cells, a virus, or bacteria with sophisticated laboratory tests and techniques. However, no one can see intelligence, memory, personality, or cognitive style. We can only deduce something about these characteristics from behavior. Therefore, measuring these psychological entities is more difficult and as a result, less accurate than well-developed medical/laboratory tests. Because of these limits in psychological tests, multiple testing procedures and techniques are used as part of a process, usually referred to as *psychological assessment*.

WHAT IS PSYCHOLOGICAL ASSESSMENT?

Psychological assessment is the procedure whereby a psychologist gathers information about a person in an attempt to answer some questions about behavior, emotions, personality, or cognitive (intellectual) abilities. An assessment typically encompasses several means or methods of collecting and distilling information. It is then up to the psychologist performing the assessment to integrate the information, develop and test hypotheses about the psychological process in question, and formulate answers to those questions.

The first source of information for a psychological assessment is gathered from existing documents, including files and records (e.g., court records, school records). For example, current testing should always be compared to previous testing to see what, if any, changes have occurred. School records are a picture of how the child is perceived by others in different situations. Records from other agencies assist in giving not only background data, but also in giving an understanding of where to begin and in indicating differences in behavior across contexts. The psychologist doing the testing will evaluate the material for accuracy and will judge its relevance. The psychologist is alert to opinions, biases, and judgments made by others and will not have these influence findings in an inappropriate manner. This extremely important information cannot be obtained without written permission from parents.

A second technique for gathering information for assessments is observation. Commonly, the psychologist observes how the child performs on the tests and observes how the child is behaving in the waiting room. Still, the psychologist may want to supplement the testing with other observations (for instance, at home or in the classroom). Observations are extremely important as a way of collecting information about specific problem behaviors. Observations permit a total picture of the natural context in which the problem behavior occurs over time. It is particularly useful when cooperation is a problem. It is possible to observe subtle changes and the impact of the situation as the behavior unfolds in interactions. The behavior is observed firsthand rather than reported. One difficulty with observations is that the behavior may not show at the time of the observation (people are often on their best behavior when being observed). The person's behavior at the time of the observation also may not be typical behavior. Observation also does not "reveal" the reason behind the particular behavior.

A third technique for gathering information for an assessment is the interview. A psychologist may use the interview to supplement testing. An interview is a communication between people to gather information. The interview may be an individual interview, a family or group interview, or a play interview with a child (play is the medium through which children communicate their thoughts and feelings). There is a common feature in each of these interview strategies: an opportunity to explore or proceed in a particular direction to gather more in-depth information. Through interviews, it is possible to gain anecdotal and observational data that help put together a picture of the child and family in interactions.

The highly individualized aspect of the interview is its greatest asset. It gives people an opportunity to communicate in ways that are characteristic for them. The greatest asset of the interview, however, is also its disadvantage. Each interview is unique. It is practically impossible to compare one interview with another—the interviewers' styles differ, the material obtained differs, and there are often areas that are not explored. This may be because the client was unaware, unable, or unwilling to share certain things. Or the interviewer may have felt that pursuing a certain area would not be helpful or would be impossible to follow up. A great deal of the material obtained in an interview depends on the skill and training of the interviewer. Gaining the cooperation of the interviewee and overcoming social graces that can cover significant areas of concern—and present the person in "the best light"—are issues that are difficult to deal with in an interview.

This brings us now to psychological testing as the last major means of collecting data. Psychological testing is a "picture" of behavior at a given point in time. It has unique advantages and contributes a great deal to the assessment process. There are five major characteristics to psychological testing, which also help define it:

1. Psychological tests present a standard situation. All individuals who take the test are given the same instructions and the same questions. This is an attempt to make the experience similar for everyone so that the responses or reactions are not a result of different questions or cues, as is often the case in interviews. This contributes to the objectivity in testing that makes it a valuable part of assessment.
2. Efforts are made to objectively score the responses given. Testers are required to be trained in administration and scoring, and often their results are checked to make sure they are scoring correctly.
3. A test is administered to a number of individuals who form a normative group. An individual child's answers (responses) are compared to the responses of that group. Thus a more objective judgment can be made as to whether the person is or is not like others in certain ways.
4. Well-designed testing can answer some questions quickly; for example, whether or not someone is developmentally functioning significantly below mates his or her age.
5. It is almost impossible to fabricate on most tests (many tests have no right or wrong answers). This allows information to be obtained that might otherwise be unavailable or inaccurate.

There are several distinct advantages that testing provides when gathering information needed for a decision. For example, Lisa's parents wonder about her development. At the age of 3 she seems to have delayed speech, trouble separating from her parents, and perhaps even motor coordination problems. However, many children grow and develop at different rates. Some children seem to have a lot to say at young ages, others develop language a little later. Yet parents may not know the difference. So how do Lisa's parents get answers to their questions about her development? By giving a standardized test that allows comparisons of Lisa's scores in language, motor, and social skills to others of her age, a psychologist can begin to evaluate how much Lisa is like or different from her peers.

In a similar way, testing can be very helpful in Tommy's situation. In the second grade, he is having problems in math. Interview and observation data can help to define his problems, see how he behaves in school and in math class, notice how his teacher responds to him and approaches him and gather impressions and opinions. However, test data would be the critical factor in determining how far behind his peers Tommy is in math, plus what other sorts of weaknesses and strengths he may have that might suggest a true deficit for learning math.

USE OF TESTS IN ASSESSMENT

Psychological tests have been used in a number of ways. Often they have been used in mechanical, routine ways to make decisions. Sometimes that is appropriate. For example, tests are given in a group setting to find out for whom further testing might be necessary or to find candidates for special programs or admission. This is called *screening*. Screening is usually completed with measures and techniques designed for group decisions. Thus screening tests cannot and should not be used for determining what is underlying a behavior or as a substitute for a complete assessment. Their purpose is to eliminate those who do not require further consideration or attention or to select children for inclusion in certain programs.

With children, one might use screening tests to see if they are ready for certain workbooks in school, to determine the need of tutoring or special help, or for some other similar purpose. Screening offers an efficient way of using resources to identify a specific group needing attention. However, screening is a first step in certain types of decision making. The tests used are often brief and designed for group administration, thus will only provide crude "pictures" of the behaviors of concern. This will necessarily lead to some errors in decision making. Whenever an error is suspected, further testing is warranted.

Routine testing is common in some agencies where all clients take the same tests irrespective of the referral problem or issue. For example, in some correctional settings everyone gets an intelligence test; in another, an MMPI (an adult personality test). This mechanical testing procedure puts psychological testing on the same level as height, weight, and temperature measurements in a doctor's office. Psychological tests should be selected to answer certain questions, not used in a ritualistic manner. When used, they should be part of an assessment process or used for a specifically stated purpose (e.g., screening). Testing children simply for the sake of testing has little merit.

In addition to screening, another reason for psychological testing is to determine if a *referral* for intervention is necessary. These tests can range from assessing for referral for a medication evaluation or review, to referrals for psychotherapy, to referrals for tutoring or a school change. Psychological tests can often provide information that will help in the assessment required to form the basis for a referral for intervention.

A frequent purpose for using tests in an assessment process is to help in making a *diagnosis*. The value of a diagnosis lies in being able to select appropriate treatment when necessary. The case of José provides an example where an accurate diagnosis of the ongoing psychological process is important. José, 10, was born in El Salvador, where his uncle was kidnapped and murdered. José shows symptoms that could be attributed to a posttraumatic stress disorder resulting from the traumas he witnessed in his home country of El Salvador. Those same symptoms, though, are also symptomatic of attention-deficit disorder, a disorder affecting many children. Psychological testing can be instrumental in diagnosing which of the two possible disorders underlies the observed behaviors. An accurate diagnosis is critical here since the intervention for posttraumatic stress disorder is quite different from the treatments normally recommended for attention-deficit disorder.

Another case where diagnosis becomes important is that of young Brad. Brad is an 8-year old child whose parents divorced when his mother was 3 months pregnant. He has been threatening other children, is described as "spaced out," and refers to himself as Michael. Some of the behaviors he has shown and others described may be suggestive of severe emotional disturbance. Calling himself another name, "spacing out" in the middle of a conversation, and fighting and threatening are characteristics seen in pervasive developmental disorder. This is a disorder where children have poor understanding of reality and often lag behind in many areas of development. Yet, the disorder may have a different underlying cause. It could be functional in nature, simply a strategy Brad has found to garner a great deal of adult attention. It could also result for a variety or combination of neurological difficulties such as an atypical seizure disorder. Psychological testing in this assessment can be helpful in discerning which of these factors is playing a major role.

Beyond screening, referral, and diagnosis, the most common use of psychological testing is in making plans for children. And the most common planning for children is educational. Psychological testing is usually seen as instrumental in placement decision making whenever any sort of special education options are being considered for children. These decisions, for example, could be whether a special school is necessary for a student, whether a self-contained classroom in a regular school will meet the needs in question, or whether resource room assistance will provide the required support.

Jeremy, 4 1/2, is the son of two university professors. His parents have raised the question of placement in a private school, believing he needs a gifted and talented program. If this is true, he may benefit from special classes or perhaps special schools to optimize his potential. Psychological testing will be a valuable aid to this process, not only in determining whether Jeremy is "gifted," but also in providing insight into Jeremy's emotional maturity and perhaps his capacity to handle the pressures often experienced by gifted children.

Psychological testing can also be helpful to those planning instructional curricula. All children have different strengths and weaknesses in their learning styles. Knowing a child's learning style (e.g., experiential, visual, observant) helps the teacher/instructor plan the curriculum.

Placement decisions in education are not the only planning processes that take place. Testing may be requested to assess whether a child needs treatment of one sort or another. Brian, 15 years old, has been in treatment for some time. Yet the recent behavior his therapist reports in therapy is worrisome and could be suggestive of suicide. While psychological testing cannot predict suicide with 100% accuracy, a full battery of testing with other data-collection methods can shed light on the kinds of despair Brian is feeling, the depths of that despair, as well as problem-solving approaches and coping strategies. In Brian's case, the testing can help in planning whether he can continue to be treated as an outpatient or needs a more restricted/residential environment.

One more important use of psychological testing in assessments is evaluating change over time. Children in special education programs are required to have periodic reevaluations by psychologists to monitor changes in abilities. Because of the features of testing described earlier in this chapter, the availability of normative information, the standardized testing situation, and the objectivity of scoring in many tests, tests provide a means by which to track change. It is certainly true that repeated testing or repeated exposure to the same test materials over a short time period biases the results. However, not all tests will be significantly influenced by practice effects. Furthermore, even tests influenced by practice can have that influence minimized by extending the time between testing.

Evaluating change in children through psychological testing is very common when children have experienced a head injury. There is often a predictable period of recovery for various kinds of injuries. It is possible, then, through observing changes in functioning on standardized psychological tests to track a child's recovery or lack of recovery. Similarly, children who have experienced significant psychological trauma, such as abuse or neglect, can be periodically reassessed to observe improvements in psychological functioning over time, as can children who receive special education services, whether in public or private schools or from a tutor.

These are some of the more common uses of psychological tests in assessments or evaluations. Obviously, children may be evaluated for some other purpose not described here. For example, judges may order children evaluated when there is a custody dispute in the courts or when consultation by a psychologist may be seen as useful. These reasons for referrals, while growing in number, are less frequent than the ones already described. Whereas psychological testing can be very helpful in many of these situations, it does have its limitations.

LIMITATIONS TO PSYCHOLOGICAL TESTING

Limited Predictability

As mentioned earlier, human behavior is multidetermined, with many factors interacting to influence behavior and functioning. Development does not occur in a vacuum. It takes place in a context that includes immediate family, community, and the larger society. A natural consequence of this is a limited ability to predict future behavior based on current psychological test data. This is especially true when a very young preschool child or infant is the subject in question. Psychological measures at young ages have little ability to predict later performance. This can be comforting to parents whose infant was assessed as having difficulties; there is hope that with help and an enriched environment the child can blossom. It should also serve as a caution to parents whose child was assessed as gifted or precocious in preschool.

Development also does not proceed in a step-by-step manner. There are peaks and valleys, periods of rapid change, and periods of consolidation. Each new period or stage in development brings new expectations, new environmental demands that hopefully match the newly emerging talents and abilities. Tests done at one point in time may not accurately predict how children will function at the next developmental level. What psychological testing can do is portray the child as he or she is at the given moment and provide insight regarding current underlying psychological processes. Based on these insights, psychologists can offer recommendations that will facilitate development, guide treatment or intervention, and address the referral question.

Overinterpretation of Scores

Some people may have a tendency to see tests as the "ultimate decision maker." No action is taken until the test results are seen, that is, until the numbers are obtained. It is almost "number worship," or the tendency to attribute "power" to the numbers. Private schools sometimes set IQ cutoffs for entrance to the school. As a result, there may be a search for that IQ score by parents who want that school for their children. Strategies may be taught that will help children to achieve certain scores ("numbers") on entrance exams or on achievement tests. Psychological tests are seen as useful only in that they may provide numbers needed as entry tickets for the most sought after programs. This is a use of psychological testing that we do not support or encourage. It places minimal emphasis on what is actually best for the child, on what the child is ready to handle, and major emphasis on competition and achievement. Often this happens at an age where children are not ready emotionally to handle that kind of competition.

Parents, not psychological tests, are the ultimate decision makers regarding children. Psychological test data can be useful and hopefully will help professionals make useful and appropriate recommendations using other information as well; thus, parents get help making difficult decisions about their children. In the end, it is the psychologist, not the test data, and the parents, not the test data, who after interpretation will use the material for the benefit of the child. When the numbers are taken out of the context of the testing and the child's life, they lose meaning. For example, Jeremy may be intellectually gifted. Yet, other facts such as social and emotional maturity may suggest that he not be enrolled in a gifted program.

Numbers do not stand by themselves. In the same way that development does not occur in a vacuum, tests do not answer questions by themselves. Only when well-trained professionals integrate the data from tests with observations, interviews, and so on, can appropriate opinions be offered and recommendations made.

Limited Comparison Groups

Some of the features of tests that make them valuable are also drawbacks. The fact that standardized tests have normative data allows comparisons of children with similar-aged peers as a way to gauge development and progress. *Normative data* refers to the scores obtained from the comparison group that will serve as the standard for judging performance. Unfortunately, normative data is sometimes limited when special populations are considered. For example, few measures of intelligence have included children who are deaf or hard-of-hearing in their normative sample. Therefore, when evaluating a deaf child, it is much harder to find a test that was developed using an appropriate comparison group. The same problem is true with other special populations, as well as ethnic or racial minorities. When the group of children upon which test norms were established does not include a cultural subgroup, that test cannot be used in the same way with children from that particular subgroup.

Inappropriate Uses

Tests are constructed to measure specific traits or characteristics (e.g., intelligence, personality, etc.). They are constructed with certain assumptions in mind. For example, since it is assumed that boys and girls are intellectually equal, IQ tests have been constructed so that those items that showed marked differences between the sexes were eliminated. A test that measures knowledge of math facts cannot be used as a measure of creativity or artistic ability. A test set up to measure personality cannot be used to assess cognitive or intellectual abilities. This is because the tests were constructed to focus on issues related to intelligence, knowledge of math facts, or personality and to minimize the focus on other characteristics. Because of this, tests cannot and should not be used to assess other characteristics not built into the design of the measure.

This limitation is included because it does happen that psychological tests developed for one purpose have been used for something very different. Such uses are inappropriate. If there is need for measurement of a particular characteristic, then a procedure for measuring that characteristic should be used or developed.

Limits in Generalization

Test data are also time limited. As a "snapshot" of behavior, they lack the dynamic qualities that define the transactions between people. Generalizing from the results of a single, brief testing session to a child's life must be done with great caution and care. A long list of factors can color test results, such as the attitude of the child toward the testing, the child's health on the day of the testing, whether he or she remembered to bring his or her glasses (and whether the examiner even knew glasses were used), and even the weather can influence this snapshot of behavior. Test interpretation, therefore, is always done from a cautious stance with a vigilant approach that seeks to encompass and explain behavior within context(s).

The thoroughness of the evaluation also has an impact on generalizability. When the evaluation is a simple screening, with one test given, there is very limited generalization. In contrast, when the test is part of a complete battery of a carefully selected group of tests and assessment procedures, psychologists can have more faith in how the results generalize to the child's life.

Psychological testing is a useful and effective way of collecting information about a child. This information, when supplemented with facts, impressions, and descriptions from other sources, leads the psychologist to form an opinion regarding the referral question. The psychologist also evaluates the confidence he or she has in the data and the results and how accurately they characterize the child.

FOR FURTHER READING

American Psychological Association. (1981). Testing: Concepts, policy, practice, and research. *American Psychologist, 36,* 10.

A volume of a professional psychological journal devoted solely to the current technical and conceptual issues and problems in psychological testing.

American Psychological Association, American Educational Research Association, and the National Council on Measurement in Education. (1985). *Standards for educational and psychological testing.* Washington, D.C.: American Psychological Association.

Ethical and professional guidelines adopted by the professional organizations to regulate the development and use of psychological testing.

Anastasi, A. (1988). *Psychological testing* (6th ed.) New York: Macmillan.

Primarily an undergraduate textbook focusing on test construction, principles of testing, and current testing practices. Includes a list of test publishers and a classified list of some 240 representative tests.

Barker, P. (1990). *Clinical interviews with children and adolescents.* New York: Norton.

A book for students that describes the variety of interviewing techniques useful with children from infancy through adolescence. The structure and stages of interviewing are discussed, along with a chapter on interviewing mentally retarded children.

Children's Defense Fund. (1978). *Your child's school records: Questions and answers about a set of rights for parents and students.* Washington, DC: Author.

A booklet put out by an advocacy organization that answers questions parents ask about school records. It also contains the names and addresses of advocacy groups for legal assistance and the addresses of state departments of education.

Children's Defense Fund. (1989). *PL 94-142 and 504: Numbers that add up to educational rights for children with disabilities.* (3rd ed.) Washington, DC: Author.

A guide for parents and advocates that answers questions about the special education and civil rights laws and lists state and local advocacy groups, national disability associations, national and regional offices of federal agencies, and state special education departments. Legal references.

The Exceptional Parent (Magazine). P. O. Box 300, Dept. EP, Denville, NJ 07834 (telephone 800-247-8080).

A journal written by professionals that is intended for parents who have disabled children to assist them in practical matters of daily life and education.

Galvin, M. (1987). *Ignatius finds help.* New York: Magination Press.

Designed for children and their parents to be read separately or together to allay anxiety about seeing a psychotherapist. Story is of a bear who has troubles getting along with others.

Joint Committee on Testing Practices. (1988). *Code of fair testing practices in education.* (Available from the American Psychological Association, 1200 Seventeenth Street, NW, Washington, DC 20036.)

Major obligations to test takers of professionals who develop and/or use educational tests. Directed primarily at professionally developed tests.

Koocher, B. P. & Keith-Spiegel, P. C. (1990). *Children, ethics and the law.* Lincoln, NE: University of Nebraska Press.

A volume intended for professionals who are concerned about the appropriate practice in the specialized psychological work with children and their families. Deals with issues such as confidentiality, informed consent, and children's rights.

Nemeroff, M. A., & Annuziata, J. (1990). *The first book of child therapy.* Washington, DC: American Psychological Association.

Intended for children aged 4–7 to introduce them to play therapy; aimed at answering common questions children and parents have regarding therapy process.

Salvia, J., & Ysseldyke, J. (1991). *Assessment.* Boston: Houghton Mifflin.

A comprehensive introductory-level textbook on assessment practices in special and remedial education.

Sattler, J. M. (1988). *Assessment of children.* (3rd ed.) San Diego; Author.

A comprehensive, widely used graduate school-level textbook on the psychological assessment of children.

Wodrich, D. L. & Kush, S. (1990). *Children's psychological testing: a guide for nonpsychologists* (2nd ed.). Baltimore: Brooks.

Intended for nonpsychological professionals, it describes various psychological tests used for children of different ages and discusses general diagnostic issues and ways of judging test findings.

18

Teaching Children
Self-Control
through Counseling

JOHN B. MORDOCK, Ph.D.

To take arms against a sea of troubles . . .
—William Shakespeare

In this chapter, I list and define the various defense mechanisms children use to manage anxiety and to maintain a sense of well-being. For heuristic purposes, the defenses are divided into two categories: *primitive* and *mature*. After defining the defenses, I present ways to encourage children to use the more mature defenses. These procedures include teaching them to play, to change their mood, and to develop mechanisms of restraint. The difference between uncovering repressed memories and structuring memory is featured as traumatized children misperceive and distort reality when under stress, particularly if traumatized before the development of speech.

When we experience something that makes us anxious, we tend to find ways to exclude the experience from conscious awareness should we experience it again. This process has been called *selective inattention, dissociation,* or *repression.* This mechanism helps us to avoid situations that could make us anxious. No one thinks clearly when anxious, and the discomfort anxiety causes is avoided whenever possible. Unfortunately, it is not possible to avoid many experiences, particularly inner experiences. We can't avoid our own unacceptable impulses. Consequently, we develop inner strategies to avoid anxiety stimulated both from within and from without. These strategies are called *defense mechanisms.*

This chapter is adapted from Mordock, J.B. *Counseling Children* (New York: Continuum, 1990). Republished as *Counseling the Defiant Child* (New York: Crossroad, 1993). Chapter 6.

Frequently, we hear one person say to another before a confrontation, "Now don't get defensive, but you hurt my feelings with that remark." When the offender simply says, "I feel bad, I really blew it making that tactless remark, I realize now that it hurt," he[1] is not being defensive. He feels bad that he hurt his friend, but what is done is done. If he says, "That's not how I intended that remark; you misinterpreted what I said," he is being defensive; that he had not intended to hurt his friend is not relevant. His friend was hurt and he is *denying* that fact. If he says, "I didn't mean to hurt you, what I meant was . . . ," he is now trying to *minimize* his friend's pain. He could combine minimizing with *blaming* by suggesting to his friend that he is too sensitive, that others would not have been hurt by the remark. Or he could claim that this is unlike anything he has ever done before. He is now using *negation* to avoid his anxious feelings. Suppose he takes every opportunity to compliment his friend during the rest of the evening. He is now trying to undo the effects of his tactless remark. The anxiety he feels is decreased by his *undoing* efforts. Or he could explain to his friend that he recently became aware of his tactless behavior and that he is taking corrective action through a planned series of readings on proper etiquette. He is now using *intellectualization* as a defense. He controls his anxious feelings by thinking about them instead of experiencing them.

But suppose he felt nauseous all evening, could not eat, felt tired, or got a headache. Now he has used *somatization* as a defense. He has converted the painful affect into bodily sensations. He could also decide that his friendship with this individual is not that important. "So who cares if I hurt his feelings!" This defense is called *rationalization*. In the future, he could *avoid* being in situations where he would run into his friend and reexperience the embarrassment of his tactless remark. He could use a combination of defenses. Initially, he could minimize his remark and avoid his friend in the future.

All of us behave like the insulter on numerous occasions. But if we never admit to ourselves any wrongdoing, because we cannot tolerate the anxiety of being imperfect, we would be viewed as being very defensive and possibly as maladjusted. But if we had no defenses, and each time we got anxious we also became overwhelmed and could not function, we would also be maladjusted.

The well-adjusted person uses defenses sparingly when faced with low levels of anxiety. When faced with high anxiety, he will use them initially and then gradually drop their use as the anxiety state becomes more manageable. When a child dies, a parent's first reaction is denial.

---

[1] The use of the pronoun *he* in this chapter is intended for purposes of succinctness and is not meant to exclude persons of feminine gender, who also experience anxiety and use defense mechanisms.

Only with time does the parent accept the finality of the child's death, and even then the child's room may remain unchanged for a long period.

Most of us are defensive when our anxiety is high, but after the passage of time we reevaluate our behavior and give up our defensive posture. Later we admit our mistake to ourselves and resolve not to repeat it. *This fact is very important.* Rarely will an individual whose defenses are made clear to him during a counseling session give up his defenses at that time. Each time the counselor points out how the client has used a defense to avoid experiencing a feeling, the client will resist accepting this fact. He most likely will increase the use of the defense for a time because his anxiety has increased following the interpretation.

Only with time and repeated revelations will the client begin to accept that he makes use of certain defenses to contain his anxiety. Counselors call this gradual process of acceptance *working through.* The client comes to accept certain truths about how he deals with anxiety, truths that he has resisted accepting; after a time, he will also learn the reasons why he became so anxious in the first place. Sometimes unacknowledged wishes that one part of ourselves finds unacceptable cause anxiety, and other times anxiety results from repressed traumatic experiences. In addition, the client needs time to replace these maladaptive defenses with more appropriate ones. Should the tactless person become a counseling client, he might want to know why he was so anxious when he made a mistake or why he made so many tactless remarks to his friends.

I need to emphasize that defenses are adaptive responses to anxiety. We all need defenses to keep anxiety from overwhelming us and disrupting our functioning. At times it is helpful to deny anxiety. A mother's initial denial of her newborn's diagnosed disability helps her to maintain the maternal behavior necessary to ensure bonding to her child. But if she continues to deny her child's disability and pushes him to excel beyond his ability, then her denial is maladaptive. Similarly, the mother who, 6 months after her child's death, still hopes that her child will return to his unchanged room is now pathologically denying her child's death.

But what about a child who denies the reality of his rejecting parent's behavior? Is this denial pathological? I think not. This child has to deny reality, otherwise he will be overcome with fears for his own safety. He has to deny to survive. I will now turn to a detailed presentation of the various defenses with specific reference to children.

THE MOST PRIMITIVE DEFENSES

Introjection. When a child is made anxious by his mother's departure, he creates an inner image of her in his mind to soothe himself; he *intro-*

jects parts of her as a defense against anxiety. His sense of well-being and security depends on his utilizing this mechanism of defense. The sum total of a child's introjections contributes to his identification with adult caretakers. A child's identifications can be witnessed in his immature behavior and play; when he feeds his doll he is identifying with his mother's caring behaviors. When he spanks his doll he is identifying with her punishing behavior.

Denial. Denial is directed against acknowledgment of frightening or objectionable impulses, feelings, or preoccupations. It is a common defense of young children."I didn't do it." "I'm not afraid." "I'm not angry." Denial is not lying. The child firmly believes that what he is asserting is true. But after mulling things over and reaffirming his self-worth, as well as getting some distance from the situation, often he can begin to accept that the action he denied did, in fact, really happen. Constant denial is a sign of immaturity. The child can deny in words or in acts, or he can deny in fantasy. A child's defense structure sometimes is revealed in his fantasies and stories.

CHILD *(aged 3½):* The little rabbit went into the lady's garden to eat her lettuce. He didn't go into her garden to eat it. He goes into the woods to eat it. He chews the lettuce all up. He doesn't eat any more lettuce at all. He goes home to bed. He sleeps. He goes out to play.
CHILD *(aged 4):* Once the bear had a fire. And he got burned in the fire and had to go to the hospital. And he got better and had a new house. There was no flames in it. There was no burner burning. There were no stoves working. There was no heat coming out of the radiator. There were no rats in the basement. The end.

In the first story, the child attempts to deny the basic oral needs of the rabbit, while in the second, the child denies the initially frightened image of damage by fire. The second story is even more revealing when you discover that the child has just learned about an upcoming move to a new home.

More sophisticated denial in fantasy appears when the child's fantasies are the complete reversal of the real situation. The child who is frightened of the lion becomes the lion tamer. The child also transforms anxiety-provoking objects into friendly beings who either protect or obey him. Sometimes the child's fantasy becomes a play action invested with immense meaning. He wears a Daniel Boone hat or a Rambo shirt and becomes extremely upset if he cannot wear this protective garment. The garment has the same effect as a daydream of omnipotence, except that reliance on the garment is a more primitive mechanism because its effectiveness depends upon its concrete presence.

Negation. When a 2-year-old is embarrassed each time he soils his pants, he may deal with this unacceptable part of himself in denying his lack of toilet skill by making another child (or doll) the one who lacks this skill. "This is not like me." Many of us negate parts of ourselves. The child may not only negate unacceptable parts of himself, he may split off these parts so that they are never integrated into his sense of self. This is called *splitting.*

Splitting. When a child feels the pressure to express a forbidden impulse, he can suppress its expression and perhaps eventually repress its awareness. It goes underground. In the course of such repression, the anxiety-arousing aspects of what is repressed becomes "split off" from the child's conscious image of himself. Splitting serves the purpose of alienating from his self-image those parts of his feelings that are anxiety ridden. But when repression fails and anxiety is generated, the child's feeling is not "I feel this emotion," but "something alien to me operates within me" or "The bad me made me do it."

Splitting, then, is a form of negation: "This is not me." Negation also applies to the play actions the child displays. Children often display rather marked breakdowns in this defense. For example, if a child, in his magic omnipotence, accidentally hits another child too hard and sees that he has inflicted pain, his negation quickly disappears and he either displays wildly aggressive behavior or the opposite, instant lameness.

Splitting during play is a normal phenomenon. The play figure who kills or messes is not the child himself; as a result, the child is free from guilt or shame since he does not feel responsible for the action of the play figures. Over reliance on splitting to overcome anxiety, however, is pathological. A child can split off so many unacceptable parts of himself ("This is not me," "that is not me," etc.) that he has difficulty functioning without confusion. He appears fragmented.

Early in development a child splits his image of his caretakers. The same adults can be viewed one time as all good and another time as all bad. When they are givers, they are good, and when deniers, they are bad. Eventually the developing child learns to fuse the two images of the same person so that the person is no longer seen as all good or all bad— the person is seen independent of his function as a need satisfier. Yet we never truly outgrow the tendency to split. Romantic love also involves a similar process. Many lovers only see certain parts of each other. Others see each lover more objectively and often wonder what the lovers see in each other.

Externalization. When the child negates his split-off parts, he is externalizing them. Someone else becomes the bad parts the child denies and splits off from his sense of self. Many children externalize their unacceptable parts onto the counselor. He becomes the stupid one, the retard, and the counselor finds himself bombarded with insults.

Projections. A child is projecting when he attributes to another person the wishes or impulses he feels but that create anxiety in response to his internalized parental standards. The child therefore blames another for possessing these impulses. Often the child fears the counselor because he has projected his own unacceptable anger onto the counselor. He also fears his own parent for the same reason. The child often sees his parents as more rejecting than they are because he projects his retaliating anger onto them.

> A small group of children are watching television. A commercial for women's bras comes on and Jim hits Phil for no apparent reason. Jim is asked why he did that and he replies, "Philip said a nasty thing." The adult seated with the children heard no such comment from Phil. The staff hypothesized that Jim was sexually stimulated by the bra commercial and projected these feelings to Phil whom he then punished for having them.

Psychologists use projective techniques, such as the Rorschach Test (the child tells what ink blots look like) or the Thematic Apperception Test (the child tells stories to pictures) to measure need states. The child projects his needs and feeling states into these relatively ambiguous stimuli. If he sees violent, angry images or tells violent stories, he is felt to harbor violent and angry feelings. Projections also abound in children's fantasies. The king is the one with the angry bad impulses, not the good knight who slays him to free the people from tyrany.

Identification with the aggressor. In addition to incorporation of positive images of another, children also introject the threatening features of the parent. Being the threatener is less anxiety producing than being the person threatened. In the beginning, the child tends to split these two images, but later he fuses them into an identification with a prohibitive-protective figure as he learns that his parents' discipline is in his best interests. The child with a rejecting, critical parent will maintain this self-critical incorporation because it helps the child feel powerful. The incorporation is self-enhancing. At the same time, however, it is self-defeating because it makes the child feel worthless. Consequently, the child develops a method to handle this double-edged sword. He protects himself from external self-criticism by both *externalizing* his negative self-image and *projecting* his unacceptable impulses onto others. This process is called *identification with the aggressor.*

A three-year-old came for a preplacement visit to a therapeutic pre-school. In the playroom, the child immediately hit a baby doll with a drumstick, saying, "The baby is not going to bed, she needs a whipping," Then, dissatisfied with the drumstick, she asked the interviewer for his belt so she could beat the bad baby. Then she wanted to take the doll with her and bit the interviewer when he went to retrieve it from her.

Provocative behavior. When a child expresses his hostility against another by inducing the other to attack him first, his hostility appears as a self-defense. In this way he can express his hostility without internal conflict. The provocative behavior, however, may also occur as a defense against feeling guilty. By getting another to inflict punishment upon him the child can reduce or eliminate guilt feelings without becoming conscious of their nature.

Displacement. Expressing an emotion toward a substitute object is *displacement.* The child attacks Sally when he is really been angered by Bill (who is larger). The child who is angry at his mother becomes easily annoyed by his teacher's instructions. Displacement abounds in children's fantasies. The wicked witch stands for mother, the evil king for father, the wolf for himself. Fairy tales play on children's tendency to displace feelings. Fairy tales are full of masking symbols. When the child denies his fears in reality by making himself the lion tamer, the lion he tames is not always a lion; often it is the masked symbol for his father.

Regression. When a child reverts to earlier, less-mature patterns of behavior when overcome by anxiety, he is regressing in an effort to use previously successful coping strategies. Two of the most popular foods in hospitals are milktoast and oatmeal, foods many of us ate as children. Under the stress of hospitalization, earlier satisfactions help to ease our fears. Under stress, children will revert to more disruptive behavior, baby talk, thumb sucking, soiling, tantrums, and inability to understand schoolwork they knew earlier (*cognitive regression*). They revert to methods of need satisfaction they found successful in the past, and to the use of less mature defenses. Witness the following story;

CHILD (aged 9): He wanted to play the violin but he didn't know how. He asked his mother to teach him. She was too busy. He asked for her help, but she couldn't help, so he got out his Silly Putty and made snakes.

Regression occurs in counseling when the child wants to mess the finger paints or be pushed in a wagon, curls up on the counselor's chair, or sucks his thumb. With aggressive, macho children, such behavior may signal progress in developing trust. They have stopped inhibiting their needs for affection.

Oscillating behavior. Very often, both the defense and the direct expression of the unacceptable impulse occur simultaneously. A child may be excessively concerned about keeping his dresser drawers neat and orderly, and yet leave his clothes all over the floor. The child presents a picture of extreme disorder and extreme order, oscillating between defiant messiness and an anxious, self-righteous perfectionism. An article of clothing out of order in the drawer causes panic, while the same article is discarded on the floor after it is worn.

Many children referred to counseling utilize exclusively the defense mechanisms just reviewed. The children deny their shortcomings, fail to take responsibility for their feelings, split off and attribute their faults and wishes to others, and retreat to less mature behavior under stress. As a result, they have almost no energy to meet developmental challenges. They cannot move to the stage of initiative where a relatively calm, impulse-free state is needed to initiate and complete the tasks required to become the industrious children of the next stage.

THE MORE MATURE DEFENSES

When I speak of more mature defenses, I speak of those defenses whose use results in less resistance to socialization and educational practices. Their use is more adaptive. For example, the child who converts his anxious feelings into stomachaches may feel physically stressed and could develop an ulcerated condition. Nevertheless, he will elicit more caring feelings from adults than he would if he consistently used projection and displacement.

Somatization. When a child converts anxious feelings into bodily symptoms, it is called *somatization* or *inversion.* Somatization is a widely used defense against anxiety. Anywhere from 20% to 30% of adults who visit a medical doctor develop physical symptoms resulting from stress rather than from physical causes.

Avoidance. The child can avoid talking about painful feelings or facing painful situations. If afraid of the dark, he may act up at bedtime, trying to avoid sleeping alone. Avoidance can be subdivided into *inhibition, restriction,* and *distancing.* The child inhibits the expression of forbidden impulses and thereby constricts his functioning. In restriction, he limits his activities to ones he predicts will cause no anxiety. In inhibition, the child is avoiding painful feelings from within, while in restriction he is avoiding painful feelings stimulated by outside sources. Most aggressive children are avoiders, fearing failure, confusion, punishment, censure, and so on. They also inhibit their affectionate feelings because these wishes also cause anxiety. Children who distance from anxiety are those who make use of masking symbols to put what is feared in faraway places. Angry parents turn into angry monsters who dwell on distant planets.

Reversal. When the child attempts to mask anxious feelings by displaying behaviors seemingly incompatible with anxiety, he is using *reversal* as a defense. He may laugh or joke when hurt or punished. He may profess love when he feels hate.

Turning feelings against oneself. Instead of expressing anger or hatred against another, the hatred is turned against the self in the form of self-hate and self-accusation. Similarly, the feeling of love for another can be withdrawn and turned into self-love. Many aggressive children display marked self-love, often called self-centeredness or narcissism.

Undoing. When a child attempts to recant or undo the possible effects of an anxiety-producing thought or act, the defense is called *undoing.* This defense is most often employed when the child feels both anger and affection for the same person. It can also be used when the child both hates and fears the same person. The child who angers his mother and then offers to make amends by running errands could be employing undoing to handle his anxiety. The child has a hostile wish toward his baby sister and then continually checks the child to see if she is all right. He is "undoing" the possible effects of his hostile wishes. A child's removal of stones from a playground could be his effort o undo the hostility he feels in seeing them as dangerous objects. A child who destroys parental figures in his play and then rescues them in an ambulance is displaying undoing in his play. Childhood and superstition are full of undoing games. "Step on a crack, break your mother's back." The dreaded consequence of spilling salt is annulled by throwing a pinch over the left shoulder. Magical expiation has been used in religion since recorded history.

Overcompensation. The child makes use of an acceptable attitude to cover up an unacceptable one. Pity may cover up unconscious cruelty, shyness can serve as a defense against exhibitionism, or boastful conceit against feelings of inferiority. The conscious attitude is the polar opposite of the repressed unacceptable tendency.

Reaction formation. The child substitutes an acceptable feeling for an unacceptable one. He represses his angry jealous feelings towards his baby sister and substitutes solicitous behavior in its place. Children who were once fascinated with bodily functions and talked endlessly about "poopies, snot, and pee pee" now vehemently profess disgust with such talk. Reaction formation helps guarantee against expression of an unacceptable impulse by reinforcement of the opposite trend.

Rationalization. The child made anxious by failing to accomplish a task or to please another person now reinterprets the situation to excuse his behavior.

CHILD (aged 5): a cowboy rode a bucking horse and the horse ate the saddle. So the boy gave his horse to some Indians because Indians ride bareback.

Sublimation. In sublimation, the unacceptable impulse attains a certain amount of direct expression in a socially acceptable manner. The girl who desires to show off her body finds an outlet for these needs in dance or drama. The sexually curious child reads about sex instead of touching the opposite sex.

Anticipation. Very successful adults anticipate what will make them anxious and plan accordingly. It is the one defense that is consciously employed. Most disturbed children are excellent anticipators, but instead of planning an appropriate action to handle the anxiety, they avoid the feared situation. Public speaking, competition, or new social situations make us all anxious, so some of us take planful actions to handle the situations. Others of us simply avoid them and thereby restrict our opportunities for growth. Disturbed children do not know how to develop a plan or to carry the plan through to completion.

THE DEVELOPMENT OF MORE MATURE DEFENSES

I have organized defenses into the two chief categories of primitive and mature defenses. A summary list appears below:

Primitive	*Mature*
Incorporation	Somatization
Denial	Avoidance
Minimizing	Inhibition
Blaming	Restriction
Negation	Distancing
Splitting	Reversal
Externalization	Turning anger against

Projection	oneself
Identification with	Undoing
aggressor	Overcompensation
Provocative behavior	Reaction formation
Displacement	Sublimation
Regression	Anticipation

This organization of defenses suggests that the maladjusted child would progress if he made more use of the defenses in the "mature" category. Their use does not mean that the children are not free from problems. Quite the contrary, a school-phobic child or a child with ulcers can be quite disturbed. But he is typically more socialized.

The word *mature* is also used because some of these defenses help move the child from early stages of impulse expression into the period of development often characterized by a period of latency. These defenses help convert the child's behavior from the undifferentiated, massive drive discharge typical of regressed behavior (often referred to as *anal-sadistic*) into the controlled child who can profit from learning experiences. Sarnoff (1987) labels this group of defenses that modify aggressive behavior into states of calm assertiveness as the *mechanisms of restraint*. Among this group are the defenses of sublimation, undoing, reaction formation, and repression. Also utilized are obsessive-compulsive activities and symbol and fantasy formation. It is the activation of these mechanisms that produce the psychological state of calm, pliability, and educability that characterizes latency and allows the child to adapt to a world that requires social compliance and knowledge acquisition.

BUILDING DEFENSES

The disturbed child needs to make more effective use of the defenses he employs and to develop more mature defenses. A disruptive child immediately attempts to mess up the toys in the counselor's office ac.ompanying his efforts with the following chatter:

CHILD: I'm playing a game called "wreck everything." I'll wreck everything, then I'll be even stronger. It will make me even stronger; lifting weights makes me feel strong, too. I like doing things that are dangerous. If I fall, that wouldn't hurt me. I'm wrecking the "house." Bare naked, eee, eee, ha ha ha, make me angry [baby talk]; me wreck it, hee, hee.

The child proceeds to tell "playground jokes" about urination, defecation, and sexuality. The child's play (crashing cars together, dropping dolls off cliffs, burning down houses with people trapped inside) is chaotic and continually interrupted by his own thoughts and by flights into action or new play. Other than the most primitive defenses of "fight or flight," he appears to have no well-developed defenses against the expression of forbidden impulses.

In addition to exercising limit-setting communications, counseling needs to include efforts to help the child build a defensive structure. Efforts to build *displacement* would include encouraging expression of anger toward toy objects. The counselor can model hand puppets talking angrily to one another or miniature figures in sociodramatic situations. The counselor can draw soldiers fighting (stick figures for poor drawers). Forts can be built from blocks and toy soldiers employed to defend them. Toilet play can be modeled with miniature dolls bathing and toileting.

Efforts to teach *undoing* can include using a toy ambulance to rescue injured victims of the child's displaced aggression. Toy fire engines can rescue the people from the child's pretend fires. Army medical corps men or Red Cross dolls can rush injured soldiers to medical stations. Injured dolls can be fixed by the doctor kit, hugged, and given tender loving care.

Distancing is encouraged by labeling the male dolls as kings, witches, sorcerers, or robots and the destroying child as the barbarian warrior or knight who slays the sorcerer. By encouraging the child to displace and distance his anger from actions into play actions, we are also encouraging *splitting*. By verbalizing that the "lion has a right to be angry because the tiger attacked him," the child can split in his play and feel less overwhelmed by anxiety.

If the child begins to split adults into good or bad, or begins to split a preferred adult (sometimes the counselor), oscillating between clinging independence and angry defiance, this should be viewed as progress. Nevertheless, the extremely jealous, demanding child can be more difficult to manage than the indifferent, distrustful child and many children are "lost" during this stage of treatment.

With children who display some defenses (variable controls), the counseling effort is directed at reinforcing defenses used and introducing new ones for possible use.

CHILD: Once there was a witch who killed everyone in town and a burglar came and killed the witch. And a policeman came and killed the burglar. Then another burglar took the policeman to jail. Then one man, the chief of police, that was me, I killed them all. And I ate them all—meat and blood and guts. [*Child leaves play area to run around the room.*]

Here the child attempts to use both distancing and undoing, but they both break down. The policeman is not strong enough to overcome the burglars, and the child, identified with both the burglars and the police, becomes himself, and is made anxious by his own oral-aggressive fantasies.

COUNSELOR: It must be real scary to live in this town where all the good people are killed. Let's give the police chief some more deputies and together the chief and his deputies can round up all the burglars and witches and put them in jail.

A child is playing air raid. The child is the pilot and the counselor controls the airport. The child says:

CHILD: I am the pilot loaded with bombs and I am coming to bomb you.
COUNSELOR: Airport to pilot. You're about to bomb a friendly airport. Please divert mission and drop bombs into the sea.
CHILD: [Ignores airport controller and bombs town anyway.]
COUNSELOR: Attention, airport medical corps needed. Alert antiaircraft guns not to fire, repeat, do not fire. Pilot temporarily confused and mistakenly bombed airport as a result of angry confusion. Repeat, pilot is not an enemy.

Alongside modeling defenses, the counselor helps the child to feel good about his achievements and to reaffirm the child's present and past positive relationships. Often aggressive children hold sustaining fictions about themselves. These are beliefs about themselves or their past that are not true but maintain their sense of well-being. The counselor should acknowledge and reinforce these fictions.

It is especially important to save all the drawings and art works the child produces, as well as the counselor's process notes about each session. Periodically referring to these materials helps the child to develop a continuity of self and a past he can relate to his present. Progress can be concretely demonstrated. Each child's works should be kept in a locked file or file box used for just this purpose.

VERBALIZING ALTERNATIVE DEFENSES

The counselor can verbalize defenses he used as a child.

COUNSELOR: When I got upset because I didn't get an award, you know what I did?
CHILD: What?
COUNSELOR: I decided "who needs that stupid old ribbon anyway!"

. . .

COUNSELOR: When another child hit me and hurt me, instead of hitting him back, you know what I did?

CHILD: What?

COUNSELOR: I pretended that he hadn't hurt me a bit. By not hitting him back I was showing him that his blow didn't bother me at all, otherwise he might hit me again.

. . .

COUNSELOR: When my mom paid more attention to my sister and made me jealous of my sister and angry at my mom, instead of hitting my sister, I used to pretend that the doll in my room was her and I would make believe that all kinds of awful things happened to her. I also used to pretend that I really liked her and I would do nice things for her when my mom was around so Mom would notice me being good and praise me for it.

DISTINGUISH BETWEEN FEELING AND ACTION

When a child experiences angry feelings, a purely reflective response is one in which the counselor attempts to reflect the feeling beneath the anger. "It is upsetting to be treated unfairly." If the child experiences guilt over his angry feelings, a supportive response can be added. "It's all right to feel angry, everyone gets angry when someone is mean to them, but it's hard to be angry at someone you also love and need to take care of you." With the aggressive, undefended child, the painful feeling can be reflected and the angry reactive feelings legitimized, but the angry *retaliatory behavior must be met with disapproval.* Many adults fail to appreciate this difference and reprimand the child for his behavior without acknowledging his feelings. Below the counselor responds appropriately:

COUNSELOR: I can understand your feeling of being unfairly treated and your feeling angry in response, but hitting Billy is not acceptable. If you want to tell Billy or me how angry Billy made you feel, that's fine. But often when you do that you get even more angry in the telling and you want to leave me and hit Billy. I will deal with Billy after I hear your side of the story, but I won't be able to listen to you if you continue to try and leave me to seek revenge on Billy. Hitting Billy is not an acceptable way to handle your anger.

IN THE MILIEU

One role of the counselor is to help others to accept the child's defenses as the most adaptive defenses he can use at the time. Educational staff and parents should be advised not to confront the child's defenses since such tactics typically result in escalation of behavior into fight or flight, the most primitive responses to anxiety.

When a child angrily throws his schoolwork down and accuses the teacher of giving him work that is too hard (blaming denial), he should not be challenged.

ADULT: Maybe I did give you the wrong work. Come on up here and we will look through my lessons and pick the right one for you.

CHILD: I'm staying in my seat.

ADULT: Okay, I'll bring you several and you can choose one.

CHILD: I ain't doing no more work. You gave me the wrong lesson the first time so that's that. [*Child's refusal now less desperate, more calm*]

ADULT: Okay, so why don't I give you some Magic Markers and you can draw until you feel like working? But don't draw for too long because you get upset when you lose the opportunity to earn points for your schoolwork.

CHILD: I don't care about your lousy points.

ADULT: I can understand your feeling like that right now, but when I hand out points to the others, I feel bad when I can't give you any.

CHILD: That's your problem.

ADULT: Okay.

Some educators think that such tactics feed the child's sense of omnipotence and reinforces his use of his maladaptive defenses. Quite the contrary. When a child's defenses are continually confronted by adults, he typically increases their use. He becomes so busy defending himself and anticipating confrontation that he never develops more mature defenses. When adults sidestep or ignore a child's defenses, he has less need to bolster their use. Think about your own defense behavior. Think about what you do when confronted. You're so busy handling the confrontations that your anxiety and your defensiveness increases. Children are no different. Attack them and they will attack back. The counselor, either directly as the "ignorant interrogator," or indirectly as the "inquisitive wizard," can gently confront and interpret the child's defenses during counseling sessions. Others should be encouraged to avoid confrontations.

INCORPORATING POSITIVE IMAGES

The most difficult defense to modify is the child's identification with the aggressor. Only when the child has incorporated the more benign and supportive images of the counselor and other nonpunitive and protective adults can he begin to give up the threatening and hostile behavior he incorporated from his family members. Remember that the child also has incorporated a self-critical, self-punitive self-image, which he externalizes and projects onto others. He cannot give up directing his anger outwardly because he would become aware of his self-hate and marked depression would follow. Only when he has incorporated others' benign qualities and *self-forgiving traits* will he become less self-condemning.

The counselor staying calm in the face of the child's onslaughts contributes to the child's incorporation of calm in the face of his storms. Remember, too, that the child will resist efforts to incorporate the benign caring qualities of others because his self-criticism also serves to guard him against the overwhelming feeling that his parents reject him. The child will actively attempt to make the counselor, and other caring persons, act like the child's incorporated images of authority figures. He does so to reduce the tension resulting from changes in his incorporated images. The child projects his highly critical conscience onto neutral figures.

Change is easier for the child when his parents have been helped to be more supportive and have made progress with their own self-hate, which is aggravated by the child's noncompliant behavior. Elsewhere I have outlined basic principles to follow when working with parents of aggressive children (Mordock, 1988).

SUPPORT IS NOT SIDING WITH THE CHILD

Supporting the use of a defense is not siding with the child so that the defense is intensified. Siding with the child will diminish the child's awareness of the part he pays in provoking others. For example:

CHILD: My classmates all ganged up on me today and it wasn't my fault, I didn't start anything.
COUNSELOR: I would get angry, too—why can't they just leave you alone?
CHILD: That's right—they're all nothing but a bunch of bullies.

Here the counselor is not supporting the defense of denial, he is identifying with the child's plight and encouraging denial. His use of denial is a well-established defense, and now that the child is no longer actively engaged with his peers and not in danger of regression, the defense can be gently confronted by the ignorant interrogative approach.

COUNSELOR: I wonder why the whole class ganged up on you like that? That must have made you very upset.
CHILD: They had no right to pick on me.
COUNSELOR: So some of the kids who you thought were your friends turned on you?

CHILD: None of them are my friends.

COUNSELOR: That's sad, having no friends.

CHILD: I don't care.

COUNSELOR: There you go again—giving up on yourself and thinking you'll never make any friends. It gets pretty discouraging, huh?

CHILD: [*Silence*]

COUNSELOR: While sometimes you make trouble, you're not that awful a guy that kids should dislike you for no reason. I wonder if you didn't do something, maybe even accidentally, that upset the kids in your class, some of whom liked you last week.

REWARD MATURE COPING EFFORTS

When you notice a child using more mature defenses, actively comment on this improvement. Children with a long history of aggressive behavior get extremely pessimistic about their ability to change. They need reassurance when you see change. They need hope. Improvements come in steps so small that neither the child nor other adults notice them. Often a child's improvement is viewed as regression rather than progress. For example, when the pseudoautonomous child experiments with abandoning this behavior and giving in to his unfulfilled dependence needs, he often becomes a clinging child who talks baby talk and who, at times, seems confused and disoriented.

COUNSELOR: I wonder if you ever thought about what it would be like to be a baby again and to be taken care of. Lots of guys had to be tough to survive, but they never got the hugs and love they needed. I think you've made a lot of gains now that you can allow yourself to think about "soft" things rather than being your old, angry tough-guy self. But it's confusing and scary to feel such things. Real growth is hard—I'm proud of you.

A child who continually made demands on the counselor to give him things and who would respond to the counselor's refusal with angry, limit-testing behavior gradually replaces his angry behavior with requests to play a game. The child is displaying more mature behavior. Such behavior should be praised.

COUNSELOR: Did you know when I used to deny your requests to take things from the room you would get angry and play roughly with the dolls? Now when I deny your request, you ask to play a game. That really shows me how grown-up you can be.

Often a counselor confuses the development of a defense with resistance to counseling. A child who used to get very anxious, agitated, and disruptive every time the counselor would explore his relationship with his mother now states, "I don't want to talk about it." He has now initiated avoidance to handle his anxiety. That's actually progress rather than resistance.

COUNSELOR: You feel real nervous talking about your mother right now.
CHILD: I just don't want to!
COUNSELOR: So not talking, pulling back helps you not to feel so anxious. Is there anything else you are doing right now to prevent you from feeling anxious?

DEVELOPING DISPLACEMENT AND DISTANCING: TEACHING THE CHILD TO PLAY

Let's look more closely at the child's use of symbols to assist in maintaining the state of calmness that characterizes normal latency. A child's latency state can be overwhelmed or subjected to trauma if overstimulated. The child who has developed symbolization quells the humiliation of trauma and the excitement of over stimulation, and the latent fantasies they stir up, by actually reorganizing and resynthesizing these experiences into highly symbolized and displaced stories. By reliving the events couched in the symbols and stories of latency play, the child finds an outlet for his heightened drives.

The child without adequate symbolization skill acts out his conflicts. Fineman's (1962) observations of mother/infant interactions suggest that some children do not play because their mothers exert an inhibiting influence on their imaginative play. Children who constantly feel threatened by the loss of mother's approval and affection express this fear by being unable to relinquish what cannot be handled or touched. They simply play with the objects in ways dictated by the objects themselves; they do not make use of objects to represent or animate a fantasy.

Unlike some mothers, the counselor not only encourages fantasy play but actively models and rewards the child for playful behavior. Hopefully, the child will learn to play and his play will reveal some of the child's preverbal and presymbolization expressions that produce disturbing impulses and activities.

CHANGING MOOD

Some years ago, I administered the Thematic Apperception Test to a very anxious, disruptive child and found that almost all of the stories he told to the pictures were of violent, hostile interchanges between the figures depicted. In an effort to tap other feelings, I asked him to tell me new stories to each of the cards, but the "new rule" was that he could not tell me any violent or aggressive ones. To my surprise, he proceeded to do so. At the end of the day, his special class teacher asked me what I had done to him during testing because he came back calm and worked better than he had all week.

Pondering over what had taken place, I concluded that his telling of nonviolent stories must have changed his mood. He had to look into his memory and find images to project into the cards that were not violent ones. The process of searching for and finding these images calmed him. Perhaps the images were of positive times he had spent with care-takers, and thereby served to strengthen his positive feelings about him-self, or perhaps the images distracted him from the violent images that excited him. Whatever the reason, this serendipitous finding altered my approach to working with aggressive children. I began to teach them strategies to change their mood and to calm themselves.

I was encouraged in this effort by Singer's (1966) research. In contrast to the prevailing view that expression of aggression in fantasy helps re-duce aggressive behavior (*catharsis theory*), Singer found that individ-uals who are practiced daydreamers handle aggressive feelings by day-dreaming of pleasant and enjoyable states. They obtain relief from nega-tive affect following frustrating experiences by emoting fantasies that change their mood. Singer also discovered that individuals who rarely daydreamed tended to remain aggressive when frustrated. The calming strategy I taught children who became overly upset when frustrated was to remember those activities they enjoyed and to perform these activities when upset and angry. For some children, it is thinking about going to a ball game with a relative. For others, it is coloring with brightly colored crayons. Each child is helped to find and to utilize his own calming, mood-changing procedures. For some, it is images; for others, actions. For those for whom it is actions, an effort is made to find a symbolic equivalent. The child who is calmed only by eating is encouraged to draw foods and to color his drawings.

This effort to help the child to learn how to change his mood when angered is not incompatible with the effort to get the child who harbors specific, retaliating aggressive fantasies to relate them to you in detail. The first effort is used when the child is upset and the goal is to help the child develop calming skills. The second effort is employed when the child is calm and is designed to generate guilt or anxiety that will result in the inhibition of direct aggression. It is not hard to tell if the second effort is working. If the child delights in relating his specific hostile fantasies and regularly repeats them unchanged with vengeful relish, the effort has failed.

GETTING AT PREVERBAL CONCEPTS

There are two chief reasons to teach the child to play. First, the limited nature of the young child's experience leads him to group together events, feelings, and sensations that have occurred together in his real experience at different times and that have the same quality. They may or may not "belong" together in the way an adult would group them. These concepts are aggregations of sensations, emotions, and images grouped together in highly individual configurations long before the child developed speech. They resulted from the child's needs to make sense of, to introduce order into, his own experiences. Once these concepts are formed, the child acts as if they are true when in actual fact they may be false. For healthy later development, the child must have an opportunity to externalize these concepts in play. Lacking such an opportunity, the concepts become "stuck" and become the source of later pathology. For example, the child who has been force-fed as an infant may group together in his mind a spoon with other "painful" objects because of his strong nonverbal associations to a spoon. Similarly, the child does not realize why he is particularly anxious around adults who want him to eat all the food on his plate. The child never gets to test his highly personalized symbols against reality because his anxiety levels bring into play defenses that retard further cognitive growth.

STRUCTURING MEMORY

The second reason for teaching play is the fact that trauma disrupts even the verbal child's organizational abilities. A child exposed repeatedly to traumatic experiences fails to perceive and to register these experiences adequately. Even mild anxiety restricts and distorts perception. Such experiences, when repressed, are registered in the unconscious as poorly structured images, such as somatic memories or cognitive distortions, or, as has been repeatedly stated, the need to act or to be acted upon (*repetition compulsions*).

Traumatic experiences are imbued with painful feelings and are therefore different from normal memory traces. Cohen (1981) uses the term *deviant mental organization* to describe one's response to trauma. The disorganization trauma causes results not only in the formation of defensive wishes (wishes to avoid the trauma's repetition or wishes to control the experience by fantasies of active mastery), but also in the failure to develop normal wishes.

The child who plays out his traumas can be helped to understand his play as *forms of memory* and *defensive wishes* and to transform the feelings connected with them into forms that can be verbally expressed. The counseling task with many conflicted children is to uncover memories and wishes that were structured to begin with. With the repeatedly traumatized child, the task is to *construct memories*. The former task is an uncovering process, while the latter is a structuring one.

COUNSELOR: You want to hit me with the spoon because the spoon makes you anxious. You also get anxious around mealtimes, particularly with adults who want you to eat everything on your plate. [*Child has repeatedly force-fed dolls in the counseling room.*]

To the counselor's task of interpreting active defenses against the expression of unacceptable wishes is added the task of transforming pathological forms of memory into normal memories. A child's preoccupation with claws in his drawings and nightmares might be traceable to his mother's abuse of him as an infant.

The child resists efforts at transformation, partly because the feelings associated with the traumas are experienced as overwhelming and "crazy." The child actively avoids reexperiencing the frightening physical sensations that accompanied his trauma. He therefore resists understanding the fantasy elaborations that accompany his effort to master the traumatic experience. These elaborations become part of the deviant mental organization and makes it hard for the child to distinguish fantasy from reality. The counselor needs to help the child to make such distinctions.

COUNSELOR: The monster in your nightmares can't really hurt you anymore. You are too big for the daddy—people to smother you with a pillow like they did when you were little. You can run and call for help. Besides the daddy-people couldn't stand your screaming when you were little—you don't scream like that any more. Only babies scream like that. Now your dad hits you when you talk back and it hurts, but he has never hit you hard enough to kill you. Your big brother is still alive and I'll bet Dad hit him a lot.

Keep in mind that a child remembers by playing. When we introduce toys that stimulate his memory, and when we help him to elaborate on his play and thereby stimulate associations to the memory, we are helping the child to transform traumatic registrations into normal memories. Much of counseling involves modeling a different way to play with the materials selected. All normal latency-age children, because they cannot express drives directly act them out in fantasy. Consequently, we are helping the child to develop the symbolization he needs to construct need-fulfilling distant fantasies.

COUNSELOR: Let's make the little boy into Superman so he can capture his enemies and put them in jail. Here, put this little cape on the boy doll and fly him around.

. . .

COUNSELOR: The little boy can pretend to be a lion and he can growl ferociously at his enemy.

When a child can verbalize a feeling, he is encouraged to do so, but when he cannot, he is encouraged to draw the feeling on paper, mold it in clay, or re-create it in a miniature world.

Sarnoff (1987) presents an example of a child who felt compelled to look at smokestacks through binoculars. When asked to draw a picture of smokestacks, he indicated that there was something behind the smokestacks that he wished to see. Sarnoff then suggested that the child make clay figures of the smokestack. He made one with a hole in the base. The boy said that snakes went into the hole and he needed to watch them. He said that if his brother could see the stack he would say it looked like a penis. Two years earlier, the child had penile surgery for the correction of a congenital deformity. Whatever residual memory he had of his response to the injury was now part of his fear fantasy involving smokestacks. Working with clay, the child could be helped to deal more effectively with the feelings associated with this traumatic experience.

With younger children, the situation is more difficult. Typically, they cannot draw nor can they work in clay. Dollhouse equipment and miniature-world toys need to be utilized to help the very young child.

A 3-year old girl was referred for nighttime terrors of seeing "Monsters with different-colored hair." When encouraged to play with the dollhouse people, it became apparent that the "monsters" were all the different men her mother had been entertaining in her house, the majority of whom yelled at her or put her angrily in her room. The child was then asked what she would like to do with these "daddy people." who kept visiting her. She proceeded to bury them in the sandbox. She was also asked what she would like to do with the "mommy people." She treated the one mommy she had selected similarly, angrily burying her in the sand and telling her to "go to her room and stay there." Mother was also instructed to be more discreet with her boyfriends or to take the child to her grandmother when she entertained.

DEVELOPING MECHANISMS OF RESTRAINT

A large portion of counseling time is spent in helping the child to develop those defenses that Sarnoff (1987) groups under the heading of *mechanisms of restraint*. These defenses not only calm the child but help him to get some distance from himself so he can participate with the counselor in observing his behavior.

A lot of material in traditional play-therapy rooms stimulates regressive, immature behavior. Sandbox tables, finger paints, and clay are examples. With impulse-ridden children, the counselor should not keep a sandbox table in his room, and finger paint and clay should be stored in a locked cabinet where small amounts can be obtained when needed.

Miniature-world sand play can be introduced later when the child has gained some control over his impulses.

A portion of counseling can include encouragement of obsessive-compulsive activities that serve as calming behaviors. The child can be encouraged to collect rocks, baseball cards, coins, stamps, and so on, and to play repetitive meaningless games like organizing dominoes so that they fall down in sequence. Children can collect lollypop sticks to glue onto cardboard, pictures of athletic figures, and so on. Any elementary art teacher can give you ideas to employ. The child can draw and color geometric forms, with all the forms of one shape colored black, those of another shape colored red, and so on. If the child is in a special education or day-treatment center, the art teacher will usually help the child to develop these skills, freeing the counselor from this task. If the child is removed from class for disruptive behavior, he can calm himself by doing one of these tasks.

Children can be encouraged to sublimate their unacceptable impulses through study of special topics or participation in activities that are symbolic equivalents of their wishes. Aggressive children can study about wars and instruments of war, the purpose being to develop intellectualization as a defense. "The more I know about war and defense, the less anxious I will feel about my vulnerability." If the special education teacher cannot teach the child about such topics, the counselor can. Collecting war pictures and making war scrapbooks can be encouraged.

Games also can be used to develop mechanisms of restraint. The games should be simple repetitive ones like Candy Land, Chutes and Ladders, and occasionally, checkers. The value of games lies primarily in inculcating a sense of organization and adherence to regulations in a manner that can be pleasurable. They allow the child to engage in a calming activity while the counselor is helping the child to verbalize feelings aroused during problematic situations that have occurred during the week. The child plays while the adult talks.

Even better than games are the partially absorbing miniature "puzzles" that many children play, such as getting all the little balls in the holes on those plastic-enclosed frames. Pick-up Sticks and other "nonsense" games engage the child just enough to give him distance from the counselor's interpretative monologues about his feelings and behavior.

REFERENCES

1. Cohen, J. A. (1981). Theories of narcissism and trauma. *American Journal of Psychotherapy, 35,* 93–100.
2. Fineman, J. (1962). Observations on the development of imaginative play in early childhood. *Journal of the American Academy of Child Psychiatry,* 167–181.
3. Mordock, J. B. Working with parents of aggressive children. *The Pointer, 33,* 13–26.

4. Sarnoff, C. A. (1987.) *Psychotherapeutic strategies in the latency years.* Northvale, NJ: Aronson.
5. Singer, J. (1966). *Day dreaming: An introduction to the experimental study of inner experience.* New York: Random House.

FURTHER READINGS

Buckingham, R. W. (1990). *Care of the dying child* (2nd ed.) New York: Continuum.

Crenshaw, D. A. (1990). *Bereavement.* New York: Continuum.

Chetnick M. (1989). *Techniques of child therapy: Psychodymamic strategies.* New York: Guilford.

Coppolillo, H. (1987). *Psychodynamic psychotherapy of children.* Madison, CT: International Universities Press.

Group for the advancement of psychiatry. (1982). *The Process of child therapy.* New York: Brunner/Mazel.

Hammer, M. (Ed.). (1964). *The practice of psychotherapy with children.* Homewood, IL: Dorsey.

Haworth, M. R. (Ed.). (1964). *Child Psychotherapy.* New York: Basic Books.

James, B. (1989). *Treating traumatized children.* Lexington, MA: Lexington Books.

Jorgensen, E. C. (1990). *Breaking the deadly embrace of child abuse.* New York: Continuum.

Kernberg, P. F., & Chazan, S. E. (1991). *Children with conduct disorders: A psychotherapy manual.* New York: Basic Books.

Krall, V. (1989). *Play therapy primer: Therapeutic approaches to children with emotional problems.* New York: Human Science Press.

Mordock, J. B. (1991). *Counselling children.* New York: Continuum.

Sarnoff, C. A. (1987). *Psychotherapeutic strategies in the latency years.* Northvale, NJ: Jason Aronson.

Van Ornum, W., & Mordock, J. B. (1990). *Crisis counseling of children and adolescents.* New York: Continuum.

19

Counseling Victims of Child Abuse and their Families

WILLIAM VAN ORNUM, Ph.D.

JOHN B. MORDOCK, Ph.D.

> The plant cut down to the root
> Does not hate.
> It uses all its strength
> To grow once more.
> —Elizabeth Coatsworth
> *The Fair American*

The weekend is over. It is Monday morning, and Carl is at school before the doors have opened or the teachers have arrived. Throughout the morning he is anxious and preoccupied. Only later in the afternoon does he begin to settle down. One winter day it snowed so heavily that school was closed, but Carl came to school anyway. He was the only child present.

Every day Carl carries his gym shoes with his books so he can remain on the grounds after classes. Throughout the week, he lingers after school every afternoon until he is asked to leave. Friday afternoons are particularly difficult because he does not want to go home. He worries about getting hurt. Carl is an abused child.

By now most people are aware that child abuse is a significant part of our culture. Estimates of incidents are between 200,000 and 500,000 cases a year. This figure could approach 1.5 million if severe neglect and sexual abuse are included in the total.

This chapter is adapted from Van Ornum, W., and Mordock, J., *Crisis Counseling with Children and Adolescents.* (New York: Crossroad, 1991).

Suspected abuse and neglect evoke a crisis in the helper who is more entrenched in the school environment than in the mental health professions: Do I intervene or not? Can I document what I think is going on? If my intervention backfires, will it be taken out on the child? Besides these practical problems, issues of a more philosophical nature arise. For example, intervention attempts to alleviate harm, but it can violate the rights of privacy when harm is not substantial (Faller, Ziefert, & Jones, 1981).

Strains that Can Lead to Child Abuse
Single parents are overrepresented among abusive and neglectful parents. Many of them are adolescents, and more and more adolescents are becoming parents. For example, 30% of the births in New Orleans in 1982 were to teenage mothers. Most thoughts of adolescents center on themselves and they can be irrational and impulsive. Typically, they want the children to grow up so they can get on with their young lives. Consequently, they have grossly unrealistic expectations for their infants. Surveys of adolescents reveal that most expect children to be toilet trained before they are able (as early as 6 months of age), to walk earlier than possible, and to talk before they are ready. When children don't reach these milestones as expected, adolescent parents take it personally: "This child is deliberately defying me!" One teenage mother thought her infant was deliberately disobeying her because she repeatedly dropped objects from her high chair onto the floor. When adolescent parents' futile attempts to accelerate the development of their children are met with resistance, an interaction occurs that results in abuse. "I just couldn't stand his crying, and when he finally stopped I felt relief," a young mother admitted. The child stopped crying because he was beaten unconscious.

Adolescents have particular difficulty with an infant's demands. Teenage mothers have their own needs that are unmet and have little energy to meet the needs of a growing child. Usually a first unwanted child is followed by another, and the likelihood of abuse increases as the responsibilities rise. When the 25-year-old mother of three beats her youngest child, we often forget that it all began when her needs went unmet as a teenager and, in search of love, she became a young mother.

Different factors interact to produce abuse. Prematurity, mental retardation, physical handicaps, congenital malformities, and other disabilities cause increased stress in parents and therefore are ever-present in abused populations. Vulnerability in the infant, such as low birth weight or colicky behavior, can be heightened by a separation from the mother after birth. The mother herself may come from a poor environment and may be experiencing significant stress in her marriage.

Nevertheless, just because these factors are present does not mean that abuse will occur. "There is a complexity and subtlety of the many processes that interact to create the abuse" (Williams & Money, 1980).

HOW ABUSED CHILDREN FEEL

One of the things we sometimes fail to appreciate is that almost all children—no matter how abusive the parents—want to love their parents and remain at home. We may "objectively" judge the home life as unfit. Yet to the children their home offers as much love as they have ever known in the world, and they are afraid to leave this security. As the Wizard of Oz said to Dorothy when she wanted to go home, yet loved the Land of Oz: "I get it—you prefer the security of misery to the misery of insecurity!"

Abused children feel they are the cause of their abuse. They are yelled at and punished so frequently and told so many times that they are bad when they disobey or irritate that they come to believe it.

Typically, frequent screaming, tension, and upheaval characterize abusive families. Abused children are often demeaned by hostile name-calling: "devil," "bastard," or "whore." The affectionate nicknaming so common in healthy families is not present. The children are threatened with removal, eviction, or abandonment by their parents. When this happens, the children become painfully aware of their predicament. As one British 8-year-old said: "Nobody bloody wants me."

Abused children suffer from inconsistent and inappropriate punishment out of proportion to their behavior. Often normal behavior is regarded as a nuisance to the parents: "This child is out to get me!" claims a tired parent when her noisy child is simply playing like a normal 6-year-old. A child may be hit for a relatively minor action. Abused children learn to suffer silently. They often do not cry when punished, because if they did, parents would then beat them for crying.

Abused children are angry and full of rage. (One child said, "What makes me angry is when my father puts my head in the toilet.") However, they have learned to suppress these powerful feelings at home. They must deny the bitterness, resentment, fear, anger, and hatred that they feel toward their parents because expressing these emotions could cause more abuse. And they feel guilty because they fail to feel the full love they know they should have toward their parents.

Perhaps the greatest problem of abused children is the parents' expectation that they will nurture them. This role reversal is doomed to fail: what 4-year-old or 8-year-old or even 10-year-old can ever hope to meet the insatiable needs of the deprived adult?

No matter how well the abused children behave, they can never please their parents or meet their unrealistic expectations. They can dot every *i* and cross every *t* and still fall short. Their best is never good enough. They are always doing something wrong.

In families in which child abuse occurs, the children are blamed for all the woes. Frequently, they are viewed as the source of marital problems, economic problems, even medical problems: "I wouldn't have this cold if I didn't have to work so hard to be able to feed you." Abused children take the blame when their parents erupt. "Don't cry or I'll lose control and spank you, and it will be your fault."

Is it any wonder that some abused children withdraw? Any playtime activity may be perceived by the parent as a disruption, a direct attack. Consequently, abused children are afraid to try new things, afraid to explore, and afraid to volunteer unless asked. Since they are failures at home, every activity is a new threat to them.

Abused children need their parents and want to love them. But as they draw close to the parents, their violence pushes them away. They love and hate their parents at the same time and are forced to bear this painful ambivalence in solitude. Often these children provoke others in order to relieve the tension inside. Abused children often become defiant children, easily stimulated to tantrums and attack upon anybody who comes near.

HOW WE FEEL

News of child abuse shocks us. We feel indignant, outraged, and impatient. Talking with children who bear bruises from the previous evening can tear your heart out. Child abuse is cruel. It is unfair. But it is a crisis that many who work with children will encounter.

Sometimes we fail to be sympathetic with abused children because they are typically the children who attempt to abuse us. Violence begets violence. Children learn aggressive behavior from aggressive parents. Because interest in and empathy for others is learned from empathetic and caring parents, abused children are predominantly concerned with their own welfare and frequently seek it at the expense of others. Their frustration tolerance is low, their feelings are high, and their actions run rampant. As a result the teacher, child care worker, or other professional is too busy trying to manage these children to feel much sympathy for them.

Enormous amounts of time and effort are needed to make an impact on abusing families. Our common reaction is to want, indeed demand, that change come immediately. To witness suffering, especially in innocent and vulnerable children, is draining—but even more draining is harboring false expectations that our interventions will instantly rectify the situation.

Most child protective agencies remain overburdened and understaffed and are unable to attract highly trained personnel. They can place abused and neglected children only temporarily and lack the capacity to provide the intensive, long-term clinical support necessary to treat these children and their families.

Short-term treatment approaches are not satisfactory. Even intensive long-term treatment may not allay the powerful cultural and personal factors that contribute to abuse. A teacher usually has a child for an entire year; it generally takes that long for the abusive parent to develop a working relationship with a treatment agency.

One organization that makes an impact on abusing parents is Parents Anonymous, a self-help group similar in organization and philosophy to Alcoholics Anonymous. Yet even this very effective organization reaches only a few. Parents must decide to join and to commit themselves to the group. Change requires a period of support and encouragement and may end up being only minimal. As one abusing parent said, "Since I joined Parents Anonymous, I don't beat my kid anymore, but I still don't like playing with her. Every time I say we have to stop, she carries on and cries and I wish I hadn't started playing with her in the first place."

Once we enter the world of abused children, it is easy to become angry at the parents. A normal response is to want the children taken away. Unfortunately, acting on these angry impulses does little to help either the abused children or their family. A mature response needs to also take into consideration the world of the abusing parents.

HOW PARENTS FEEL

No matter how poor, how deprived, or how overwhelmed, most parents would rather not abuse their children. They become frustrated, they can't control their frustration, and they take it out on the youngster. They feel ashamed and guilty of their actions, but they can't seem to help themselves and may lack empathic skills.

Most abusing parents lead lives in which their own needs for safety and love are not met and never have been. "Wanting" characterizes their lives. Most have lost significant others early in life. An early death of a parent or a difficult divorce chokes emotional fulfillment during childhood and takes an even greater toll years later. Abusing parents grow up with unmet needs and look to their own children to satisfy their emotional deprivations. Instead of wanting to give, they expect to receive: "I have never really felt loved all my life. When the baby was born, I thought he would love me; but when he cried all the time, it meant he didn't love me, so I hit him" (Helfer & Kempe, 1968).

Frequently, abusing parents are poor; poverty breeds frustration. They suffer the violence, humiliation, and despair that accompany poverty in our society. They feel unable to meet life's daily demands.

Parents who abuse misunderstand the basic nature of children. When they were growing up, they lacked a positive role model of parenting. To be good at parenting, parents must express love, show tolerance, and serve as examples. Most parents who abuse were raised without seeing these in practice, and many were abused themselves.

One father whose severe disciplining included forcing his son to kneel on carpet tacks explained:

> It may seem cruel to you, but as children this is the type of punishment we received, my wife and I. We were just using the same type of punishment. If we did not care about him, we would not do this. (Paulson & Chaleff, 1973)

Parents who are abusers suffer.

> Child abusers are going through hell. We have a vision of how powerful our anger can be, the concept of where our anger will take us if we are pushed too far, and the constant dread . . . we will be pushed too far. [Abuse is not a singular incident but usually part of a consistent pattern.] We don't like being child abusers any more than society likes the problem of child abuse. (Reed, 1975)

Some child abusers would like to give their children up for foster care or even adoption. Unfortunately, their relatives pressure them to keep the children without supporting them. Giving up the children means loss of whatever little love they do get from their extended family. As one grandmother said to her daughter, "You give away my grandson and you're not welcome in my house anymore." Other statements are less direct but convey the same message: "Anyone who would put their child in a foster home is an unfit parent." Consequently, they keep the child in an effort to please their parents, but they find themselves continually criticized for mishandling the child.

WHEN YOU SUSPECT CHILD ABUSE: INTERVIEWING CHILDREN

Many adults feel uncomfortable when talking with children about suspected abuse. Some of these approaches might help.

First, mention that you see an injury on their body that may need attention. "Herb, I see you have a bruise on your arm. Should I have the nurse look at it?" Children who are reluctant to talk about their injury or to see the nurse are more likely to be those who have been abused.

Now the interview becomes more difficult. Most children are reluctant to take the blame for something that they didn't do. The adult can make statements that imply the child causes the accident, such as, "I guess you fell off your bicycle," or "I guess you lost a fight with some other boy," and note the response. Sometimes it works to simply say, "I guess your mom and dad must have gotten real mad at you for you to have a bruise like that—what did you do to make them that mad?" If the child responds with, "I didn't do nothin', and she hit me with the broom!" be empathic and reflect how angry she must feel at being hurt. Remember also that sometimes it is relatives or baby-sitters who abuse children, particularly in sexual abuse.

Children often reveal abuse through notes to teachers that are hastily written and unclear. When you go to talk with them about the note, they have second thoughts, sometimes saying they made it all up. They worry about the consequences of what they have done in a moment of desperation and clam up. They worry their parents will get into trouble, that they will be sent away, or that the abuse will get worse. No amount of reassurance can get them to change their mind.

In the vast majority of cases, children who mention, no matter how briefly, that they have been abused are telling the truth. Take them seriously. While your interview may get you no further, a thorough investigation needs to be made.

Never reassure children who report abuse to you that they won't get into trouble. Often they will. What you need to reflect is how difficult it must be for them to tell you this information, to risk getting hurt more, and how you hope you can assist them, but you can't make any promises. Remember, make no promises. Most likely the children will continue to be abused, and you want their trust throughout their ordeal so you can help them to deal with their painful environment. They won't turn to you if they think you lie.

ADULT: Maria, I'm glad you told me your dad hit you. You are angry at him and know I'm your friend. I'll have to talk to your dad about what you told me, and I can't promise he'll listen to me and not hit you again. He'll probably get angry at you for telling me. I hope I can convince him you're scared and need help. If he hits you again, someone else might have to come to your home and ask him if you need protection from him—sometimes we need protection even from the ones we love.

Many children from abusing families have been instructed *never* to mention abuse to outsiders. The parents hit the children, realize the mistake, and order the children to tell *no one:* "I'll hit you harder next time" or "You will be sent away for good." In addition to fearing harm, the children now worry about being sent away from home. They will be reluctant to provide you with a straightforward explanation about their bruises. Respect their position and terminate your interview.

There are other occasions when children will tell you about the abuse once but never again. One fourth-grade boy told his social worker that during a party at home his father's friend had burned him with a cigarette. The next day the boy had changed the story: "I backed into the cigarette accidentally." Later it was discovered that the father had threatened, "Say that it was an accident or I'll whip your butt good."

Once a protective service agency becomes involved, the children usually are blamed for the predicament: "If it weren't for you, I wouldn't be in this trouble," the parent wails. "And we wouldn't have people checking out our house for child abuse. So shut up. You misbehaved, you got your lickin', *now shut up!*"

Sometimes child abuse is a no-win situation for everyone involved. If the abuse goes undiscovered, it continues. But if discovered, sometimes parents can retaliate in greater force against the children. Keeping this in mind will help you understand children's reluctance to talk with you about their bruise marks.

Reporting Abuse

Most state laws require that suspected child abuse or neglect be reported, and the procedures vary from state to state. Some agencies funnel all reports through a specific individual: the principal, program director, school nurse, guidance counselor, designated social worker, and so on. Reporting suspected child abuse is a serious obligation, and persons mandated by law to report it leave themselves open to legal penalties if they fail to do so. This creates a dilemma for many workers when abuse is only suspected: "Will I do more harm than good by reporting this abuse?" Even if the abuse is substantiated, workers may question the effect of reporting on their relationship with the children and their families. If you face such a dilemma, seek out the support of your colleagues. Consultation with another mandated reporter in the area of child abuse can assist you in making the best possible decision, and support you throughout a difficult situation.

Reporting parents for child abuse when you have struggled so hard to establish a relationship with them is a frustrating requirement. Arrange for the principal, or another authority, to report the incident so that you might maintain your relationship during this period. Initially, the parents' anger will be directed at the entire school. Wait patiently, send positive notes home, inquire about the parents' welfare, tell them you miss them, and eventually your relationship with them may be renewed.

Interviewing Parents

Call a conference with the parents when you suspect neglect or abuse. While it is easier to simply call and officially report the abuse and hope the parents will think someone else is responsible, your own feelings about the parents will remain colored by impression rather than by fact. Suppose the parents actually aren't responsible. Talk with one of the parents first, even if you are required to report the suspected abuse. Explore the possibility that someone other than the parents is responsible. Sometimes it's siblings, baby-sitters, neighborhood children, or relatives.

ADULT: We've noticed lots of bruises on Glenn lately. Is he playing places he didn't used to, perhaps with older boys? He won't tell me how he got them.

PARENT: I don't know—I certainly don't abuse him. I smack him when he's bad, but I don't abuse him.

ADULT: Well, I hope you can find a way to prevent it. If it gets worse, we're obligated by law to report it to Child Protective Services, who will then come to your home and investigate the report. We certainly don't want to do that if you can handle it.

Such an interview alerts the parents, without accusation, to provide better supervision of the child, or if they are to blame, to curb their own impulses.

Sometimes children will tell you their parent hit them. If the bruise is serious, you must report the incident. Always call the parents first and ask for a conference. If they refuse, explain that by law you have to report the incident to Child Protective Services. If you can be of help, you will visit their home with the Child Protective Services worker. They will often hang up on you. Be prepared for their anger and respond empathically.

If the bruise is not serious, keep after them for a parent conference to explain some recent problems you've had with their child. Stress that it's really important that you see them, but don't mention exactly why. At the conference, express that you're troubled by their child's recent communications.

ADULT: Tim's been telling me that you hit him. This must have been hard for him to say 'cause I know he loves you. He's bragged about you before. What do you suppose is going on with him now? Is anything different going on in his life?

Sometimes children's play reveals concerns that require exploration with parents.

ADULT: We're somewhat concerned about Elliot. His play will dolls suggests he has some worries. He took a large man doll, pulled down its pants, and placed it on top of a baby doll he laid face down. When

I said the baby must have been scared, he quickly stopped playing. Do you think he's been playing with larger boys who have sexually molested him?

Sometimes the parents realize who the abuser is, don't say anything, but correct the situation on their own. They supervise the child more closely, severely admonish an older brother, kick the uncle out, or restrict visits to the grandfather—all done without your awareness.

Make sure all your interviews with parents start out in a nonaccusatory fashion. While this is rare, children sometimes try to elicit sympathy in ways that can get their parents in trouble. One child would change into filthy, ragged underwear, find some reason to see the school nurse, and then when she asked him to disrobe, he would "allow her" to discover his filthy underwear. He would then tell her his mother was too drunk to do the wash or too poor to buy him new underwear. Three children in a local children's home would hide their sweaters and socks during the winter so teachers would say, "What kind of a place is that children's home anyway, that they let children come to school dressed like this?" These children figured that if the home was forced to close, they could go home.

Parent-Teacher Conferences about other Issues

Most parents come to conferences anxious. They want to hear that their children have done well. If the teachers think the parents will challenge them, they are apprehensive. In a conference with a suspected abusing parent, anxiety will run high with both sides fearing each other. The parents expect to be scolded by the teachers for neglecting the child, and the teachers expect the parents to criticize their approach with the children. Both will be defensive and both could respond to this defensiveness by taking the offensive: "I'm going to be attacked anyway, so I'll attack first." The teachers want to convince the parents that their disinterest and neglect contribute to their problems with the children, and the parents want to avoid being reprimanded, so they blame the school for improper care or instructions: "What does he do here? Seems to me he hasn't learned anything." With this tack, an unproductive conference will result.

To avoid unproductive conferences, teachers can resist the temptation to defend themselves when attacked, and simply reflect the feeling the parent is conveying. "You're worried that Karin's not progressing fast enough, and her education is important to you. I can understand that!" or "Do you have any suggestions for me, things you feel are important for her to learn?" Teachers should let the parents be right to avoid an argument. The goal is to establish a relationship with them, not to defend skills. Insisting on being right will cost teachers the relationship and might make things harder for them in the classroom. When the parents learn that they are not going to be attacked, they will lighten up considerably and stop resisting. Then when the teachers show them the children's good work and don't emphasize the bad, they'll ease up more and eventually both will begin discussing the children's real problems as partners rather than as opponents ready to square off. Of course, if it's possible to start out talking about the children's strengths, so much the better.

Remember, don't let your anger get in the way! If you continually harbor anger toward abusive parents because the situation is not changing as fast as you would like, your effectiveness as a resource person will be diminished. The parents will feel your anger and avoid you. You will lose an opportunity to understand the family and be viewed by them as a source of support.

Another consideration is whether to call parents whom you suspect are abusive when the children have displayed inappropriate behaviors. With most parents, it is helpful to alert them to behavioral difficulties so that a consistent approach can be planned. When you know that children's parents have abused them, you should also remember that abuse occurs when the parents feel let down. Assess the situation thoroughly before you call parents in to discuss their children. Never discuss over the phone. As a general rule, avoid telling parents about the children's failures since the children's failures are parents' failures, and this feeling contributes to abuse. Send them regular notes about what they do well, no matter how insignificant. Many times you will want to write angry letters home, both about the children and the parents' seeming disinterest. You must restrain yourself—ventilation of anger on the parents can cause them to direct their anger toward the children.

Below is a letter written to a parent. At first, the writer wanted to chastise the parent for his uncooperative behavior, but instead tried to be more constructive:

> Dear Mr. Jones:
>
> I understand that one motive for your recent call to us was a visit from Child Protective Services regarding your difficulty with Tony. It would seem that you are under a great deal of pressure now from CPS, your ex-wife, family court, in addition to the problems with Tony, which can be overwhelming, such as his refusal to listen, his extreme restlessness, and so on.
>
> I would think you might need some rest from Tony just to keep your new family functioning. Astor Home in Rhinebeck runs a specialized foster home program for emotionally disturbed children that is supervised by a clinical staff. Foster parents are carefully selected and specially trained to handle disturbed kids, their problems following visits to parents, relating to schools, and so on. Perhaps you might

want to discuss such a service with us when our worker visits you. We know you want to be a good father and probably feel that Tony is best served at home with you. Sometimes, however, relationships get so strained that people need a break from them to work them out.

If you're not ready for such a step, then we will work with you to help Tony at home.

Becoming Too Involved

In working with parents of abused children, nonprofessional counselors often face this dilemma: "Where do I draw the line between working with these parents to providing therapy for them?" Professional counselors can help these workers by providing information.

Often these parents are more open and frank in talking with the empathic nonprofessional counselor than with the mental health worker. They realize that the former is less likely to confront them or try to make interventions in the home. Parents often view social workers as watchdogs. They are usually afraid that their children will be taken away if they discuss their true feelings about them or incidents that happen at home. They dread the thought of being labeled "bad parents."

A short-term ventilation of parents' feelings with you might be helpful, but if this continues over a period of time it may undercut the relationship they are building with their therapist.

An empathic attitude that shifts the parent back to the mental health professional is often the most therapeutic stance:

COUSELOR: Mrs. Harrison, you and your family have been under a great deal of stress lately. It sounds as though you feel overwhelmed, but you keep on trying. I appreciate your coming in to talk with me. But I want to encourage you to share your concerns with Mr. Samuels, your social worker. Since you will see him every week, I'm sure he can be a big help to you and your family.

It may be helpful to set up a meeting with yourself, the parent, and the social worker. In this way, you can gently define your role as one related to school matters, and the social worker's role as one concerning family problems and deep-seated personal issues.

HELPING ABUSED CHILDREN

Professional Treatment

Abused children convey a general feeling of depression, unhappiness, and sadness. They have problems forming attachments, as well as detaching from others. They can be aggressive, have poor self-concept, and have trouble relating to peers. But worst of all, their capacity to trust others is impaired.

Individual treatment of the abused child often takes two approaches: individual play therapy emphasizing a safe environment in which to express feelings, and therapy that educates the child to better cope with the reality of the abuse.

Many abused children have been deprived of the love and attention that all of us need. As a result they require a warm, nurturing relationship over a long period of time to help heal their wounds. In the safety of therapy, children will open up and reveal their feelings about being abused. In play the abuse situations can be re-created and discussed with the therapist.

Most abused youngsters believe at some level that they are the cause of the abuse. Abused children typically misbehave. This becomes a vicious circle: The children are abused, which leads to increased misbehavior. The parents, already with low stress tolerance, become even more abusive; children act out more, until their misbehavior becomes the "cause" of the abuse.

Many clinicians emphasize to children that perhaps their mom or dad is sometimes unreasonable and that the abuse would happen to them anyway. The goal of this tactic is to keep the children from internalizing the feeling that they are bad or worthless. They are not to blame. Unfortunately, the children typically feel at fault, and efforts to convince them otherwise fall on deaf ears. Another approach is to get the children to verbalize the things they feel cause their abuse. While the question, "What did you do that made Mom so mad?" may seem harsh, it needs to be asked so the children can begin to understand their role in the abuse.

One goal is to alert children to the cues that precede abuse by their parents and to the role their behavior plays in the parents' anger. If children are abused after parents fight, then they can remove themselves from the room rather than stay around to see how the fight develops. If their mother storms around the kitchen or living room when she is angry, then they can leave that area and to go their room. If their father comes home drunk and hates to see the television on, they can quietly read a book instead. These timely actions give children more control over the situation.

Abusive parents make unrealistic demands on their children. Even with professional intervention the demands may continue, and when the children fail to meet them they are abused. Some therapists teach children to meet these demands in order to dodge the abuse. If Ed's father beats him and keeps on beating him until he cries, then Ed can learn to cry right away. If Janice's mother gets mad at her for not cleaning the kitchen table, then she should clean the table. If Bobby's mom doesn't like him to tease the cat, then Bobby should not tease the cat. Educating children in this way gives them more power over a situation in which they were previously helpless. Since helplessness is a cornerstone of depression, this approach helps lift the children's unhappiness.

The Nonprofessional Counselor

Professional treatment requires a significant investment of time and energy. The approaches we have described must be repeated over and over again, with slight variations as in the theme of a symphony, for children to make them part of their thoughts, feelings, and behavior. Again, counselors can help the children by providing consultation to nonprofessional counselors.

Empathic statements communicate to abused children that they are understood and not alone. On Monday morning a teacher might pull fidgety Alice aside and say, "I know it must be hard for you to concentrate today." Or the recreation aide after school might say, "You'd probably like to stay here longer, but the basketball game is over. I know that you don't want to go home right now, but it's late, and it's time to leave."

Build in daily periods of intense physical activity in which these children can release their tension and aggression appropriately. You can also help these children by giving them I-messages. Let them know how their behavior affects you. For instance, help them see some of the things they do in your presence that infuriate you. If they do these same things at home, they are significantly contributing to their abuse. Teach children to see the relationship between their behavior and the feelings they evoke in adults:

ADULT: Leroy, I get very angry when I'm called names. I don't like being called a buffalo face. I get angry when you are disrespectful toward me.

or

ADULT: I wonder if your mommy gets mad when you call her names? Then she gets so angry that she hits you. You know your mommy has to learn not to hit you when she's angry. But you have to learn to change your behavior, too, and not call her names.

Developmental Considerations

Keep in mind children's developmental levels when you talk with them. Children in the magic years will attribute the parents' abuse to what they do. You can gently emphasize, over and over, that Mom or Dad has problems and that they are not to blame. Nevertheless, this message may not become incorporated into their thinking. Perhaps the best thing to do is to work with the protective service agency to guard them against abuse at home.

While children in the middle years believe they cause some of their parents' problems, it soon dawns on them that they do not cause most of them. They know they are not responsible for everything that's not working out. Discuss with the children the difference between problems they contribute to and problems beyond their control. Seek professional consultation. Since the children will probably tell the parents what you have discussed, be careful not to blame or disparage the parents.

Special issues arise in talking with abused adolescents. Their attitude is exactly the opposite of that held by magic years children: they know they are not the cause, blame their parents totally, and may refuse to acknowledge or discuss their role in the matter. "It's all their fault. I'm just gonna get the hell out of there."

Abused adolescents may confide in you that they plan to run away. In general, don't try to persuade them otherwise—there is no better way to inspire them to leave. Perhaps these youngsters should run away and thereby call attention to themselves and to their family. It is their way of saying, "Things are seriously wrong here, and we need to find solutions."

Be empathic with adolescents in this situation. Explore options with them. But try not to encourage or discourage them in either direction because you can never fully understand the condition in which they live. Your role is to help them make an intelligent decision. Appropriate self-disclosure may be helpful, not in the vein of "I can tell you what to do" but rather "I can appreciate the difficulty of your situation. I've had a slightly similar experience myself . . . "

If there is a theme for this chapter, it is that "things take time." Many who work with children are so busy planning activities and implementing them that they have little time for a heart-to-heart talk with a child. If you can listen to abused children and let them talk their feelings out, you help support them and lead them to a greater understanding of their lives. Likewise, if you have referred abused children to a mental health professional, beware of the illusion that therapy will work miracles with these children and their families over a brief period of time. It won't—but it is the most constructive approach to date in helping to break the vicious circle of child abuse.

FOR FURTHER READING (FOR CHILDREN)

Bradbury, B. (1972). *Those Traver kids.* Boston: Houghton Mifflin. (Ages 12 +)
Coolidge, O. E. (1970). *Come by here.* Boston: Houghton Mifflin. (Ages 11 +)
D'ambrosio, R. (1970). *No language but a cry.* New York: Doubleday. (Ages 13 +)
Greene, B. (1973). *The summer of my German soldier.* New York: Dial Press. (Ages 12 +)

Rabe, B. L. (1973). *Rass.* New York: Thomas Nelson. (Ages 12 +)
Smith, D. B. (1973). *Tough Chauncey.* New York: Dial Press. (Ages 12 +)

REFERENCES

Faller, K. C., Ziefert, M. & Jones, C. (1981). Treatment planning, process, and progress. In K. C. Faller (ed.), *Social work with abused and neglected children: A manual of interdisciplinary practice.* New York: The Free Press.

Geiser, R. (1973). *The illusion of caring. Children in foster care.* Boston: Beacon-Press.

Helfer, R. E. & Kempe, C. H. (1968). *The battered child.* Chicago: University of Chicago Press.

Paulson, M. J., & Chaleff, A. (1973). Parent surrogate roles: A dynamic concept in understanding and treating abusive parents. *Journal of Child Clinical Psychology, 2,* pp. 38–40.

Reed, J. (1975). Working with abusive parents: A parent's view. An interview with Jolly K. *Children Today, 4* 6–9.

Williams, G. J., & Money, J. (eds.) (1980). *Traumatic abuse and neglect of children at home.* Baltimore: Johns Hopkins University Press.

20

Counseling Adolescents

WILLIAM VAN ORNUM, Ph.D.
JOHN B. MORDOCK, Ph.D.

> I think what is happening to me is so wonderful and not only
> what can be seen on my body, but all that is taking place inside
> me. I never discuss myself or any of these things with anybody;
> that is why I have to talk to myself about them.
>
> —Anne Frank
> *The Diary of a Young Girl*

Adolescents are often absorbed in a world within themselves. They withdraw from contact with others and are limited by self-centeredness. "Are you deaf?" is a common plea from parents and teachers in response to their silence or sulking.

Adolescents react to an imaginary audience. When they feel self-critical, they assume others are equally critical of them. They feel particularly sensitive to shame. Because adolescents are more concerned with being observed than observing, with being interesting rather than interested, old friendships sustain them through this time as new friends are difficult to come by. Moves can be especially traumatic for this age group.

Adolescents regard themselves as unique and special—only they "can suffer such agonized intensity or exquisite rapture" (Elkind, 1965). They develop *personal fables,* stories they assume about themselves that aren't true. Learning to appreciate others' viewpoints helps adolescents see beyond their personal fables; they learn to integrate their own emotions with the feelings of others.

Because their social role is unclear, adolescents are inclined to shy-

---

This chapter is adapted from Van Ornum, W., and Mordock, J., *Crisis Counseling with Children and Adolescents* (New York: Crossroad, 1991). Chapter 3.

ness, sensitivity, and aggressiveness to mask their insecurity. Social fears are common, such as feeling rejected, being ignored, feeling disapproved of, looking foolish, losing control, speaking in public, being watched working. Because of their unstable sense of self, they fear unpleasant or peculiar people. They particularly fear those in authority. Some have described adolescence as a period of prolonged "sensitivity training."

Over two-thirds of adolescents express a desire to change their physical appearance. Girls think of themselves as too heavy or too tall, while boys feel they are too thin, particularly in their upper arms and chest (Frazier & Lisbondee, 1950). And God forbid if the girl should be small-breasted or the boy have any breast tissue! Acne brings humiliation. Because their bodies are changing, adolescents display fears of body injury, and fears of medical and dental treatment (Bamberg, 1973).

Adolescents' thinking is radically different from that of children. They are able to recognize possibilities as well as actualities. They can think conceptually in abstract and universal terms and tend to overidealize. Their new cognitive ability combined with a search for identity—the search for meaning in life is, after all, a search for identity—perhaps explains their preoccupation with issues of social justice, religion, morals, and values. Adolescents' powerful and almost nagging sense of idealism means that they *know* the way things should be; they expend a great deal of energy through anger and frustration when things are not working out the way they "should." By adulthood many of our views on sex, work, religion, and social values have crystallized into a lasting part of our personality. But for adolescents each day serves up new feelings and attitudes. One day they are attracted to traditional church worship and the next day to the scientific determinism of Bertrand Russell or the existential despair of Sartre.

Adolescents' impressions of themselves—their identity—comes from the feedback they get about themselves from others. They believe, and behave, differently in the company of different people. Sometimes adolescents even try to keep their different sets of friends apart and get nervous when they meet. The structure of adolescent identity is conceived as a group of characters. It includes all the people a youngster is with in different social situations. Adolescents copy people's speech unconsciously and surprise themselves by the way they behave. They play out roles expected of them, and much of what they play feels false, feels "not me." Some parts of the adolescent that feel true may be hidden or barely sensed. For example, should an American adolescent spend time in England, his or her speech will suddenly take on a British accent; should the adolescent strike up a close friendship in England, the English friend will want to be like the American and begin to speak "American."

Adolescents tend to place people in categories. Peers are "jocks," "druggies," "intellectuals," "nerds," "preps," or "vals." Adults are judged by the way they dress or by their professions, rather than by who they are. Such categorizations allow adolescents to ignore powerful issues or confrontations: "You people always ask questions like that."

Sexuality adds a new dimension to adolescents' thoughts and feelings. Happy, outgoing children become isolated and sad adolescents who doubt their sexuality. In early adolescence heterosexual relationships are conflictual, and in middle adolescence they are idealized. Adolescents judge their behavior in the context of sexual normalcy and abnormalcy.

Interviews with urban adolescents reveal that they show no resemblance to their popular stereotype. They are not mindless consumers, practitioners of violence and sensuality, or rebels against all authority. Most are seriously interested in being effective interpreters and performers in the social environments that are presently significant to them (Kitwood, 1980). So when they temporarily regress in the face of a crisis, have faith in them and they will resolve their difficulties.

Adolescents are idealists who tend to have unrealistic expectations for themselves and others. A crisis (divorce of parents, death of a loved one, broken romance, school failure) can lead to the subsequent loss of the ability to find value in things as they really are: " My parents split up; you can't count on anyone anymore."

Unlike depression, in which self-hate exists, disillusionment involves self-aggrandizement and degradation of others, interwoven with cynicism. The result is a powerful resistance to change, which can make a counselor feel hopeless.

CRISIS COUNSELING WITH ADOLESCENTS

Formal counselors are viewed by adolescents as people who will tell them they are not okay. They categorize counselors as shrinks who are weird themselves. They are definitely *not* glamorous adults. Weird people— and those who work with weird people—are to be avoided: "Psychologists are all nosy people" or "You shrinks are all the same. Same stupid couch . . . same stupid diplomas on the walls . . . same damn pictures of your family on the desk" (Gardner, 1975). Adolescents with problems are worried about being stigmatized, and referral to a counselor can intensify this feeling and add to their sense of alienation. The counselor is viewed not only as "one who deals with weirdos," but also as an authority figure—and so is doubly feared. An authority figure will discover their thoughts or private actions, intimate details about themselves that they feel are too horrid to mention. It is no wonder that adolescents reveal themselves to everyone but counselors!

Teachers, athletic coaches, supervisors of afterschool jobs, neighbors, church youth group coordinators are the people adolescents turn to as a first line of defense against the crises they face as part of growing up. Let's look at some of the approaches these adults (and formal counselors as well) can employ.

Confidentiality

It is best to discuss at the outset any limits to confidentiality so that you will not be setting the stage for a later accusation of betrayal. Richard Gardner (1975), a noted therapist, talks about how he handles the confidentiality issue. Early in treatment adolescents frequently ask him, "Are you going to inform my parents about what I tell you?" Gardner responds by saying that he won't divulge the things that are talked about in the sessions.

> However, I will also tell him that if he is involving himself in some kind of behavior that is extremely destructive *and* that he cannot stop after discussions with me and members of the treatment group, *then* I may very well have to resort to divulging what he tells me, even though he may not wish me to do so. (p. 62)

Gardner does not specify the kinds of things that will or will not cause him to break confidentiality, believing that this gives the adolescent food for thought.

Marshal Positive Forces

Remember that adolescents are attuned to negative reactions from others. If they are depressed, they will recall unpleasant memories more readily than pleasant ones. They will underestimate the positive feedback they receive and overestimate the negative. You need to focus on the positive, mirroring their hopeful feelings rather than their depressive ones. Use supportive approaches.

ADOLESCENT: I feel like I can't do anything right.
ADULT: Nothing seems to be working for you lately.
ADOLESCENT: Yeah, I'm really down in the dumps.
ADULT: I feel like that sometimes, a really lousy feeling.
ADOLESCENT: [*silence*]
ADULT: I usually go visit a friend when I feel depressed. What do you do?
ADOLESCENT: Nothing. Maybe go to sleep.
ADULT: Maybe you could try talking to a friend. You have some interesting ideas. I enjoy talking with you. So would others.

Remember, too, that you are an *enabler*, facilitating the development of strengths and making the person feel *more able*. Crisis states disrupt adolescents' problem-solving ability. They've solved difficult problems before. Help them to remember how they did it—get them in touch with their prior successes. Share with them your own personal thoughts and feelings in an effort to help them understand theirs. Reveal what has worked for you but be careful that your comments don't come across as advice or moralizing.

Adolescents often have what appear to others as silly ideas. Confronting them about these delusions only increases their intensity:

ADULT: That's why you got into trouble—because you have those ridiculous ideas.

or

ADULT: I can't follow your story. That idea is foolish.

Confrontations like these will alienate you from the youngster. Avoid disagreeing. Start with the least strongly held beliefs and offer other possible reasons why things are the way they are.

ADULT: You could be right, but I would like to discuss this with you in more detail. Why do you believe this?
ADOLESCENT: [*Gives explanation*]
ADULT: Do you think there might be other reasons? Might they not talk to you because . . .

Outline other possible explanations and encourage the young person to express alternative ideas.

Self-Disclosure

One of the most effective ways of facilitating discussion with adolescents may be to share some in-depth background about yourself, either presently or from a time when you were younger. This is not to be done in the preachy fashion of "when I was your age," but rather as a sincere attempt to bridge the gap between two people through honest sharing.

Self-disclosure may be used to help show that you understand a particular situation that may be painful to discuss. Tentatively phrased, it can be a starting point for further discussion on how the adolescent experiences the world:

ADULT: When I was in college, my parents split up—right before my graduation! You'd think they could have waited just a bit. I felt devastated, alone, and angry, even though I was an adult. You and your dad always seemed close to me. How has his leaving affected you?

or

ADULT: Next week I have been invited to a party where I know only the host. It really makes me nervous to talk to a group of complete strangers. Do situations like that ever make you nervous?

or

ADULT: When I was young, I never felt I could please my dad. Whatever I did never seemed good enough. Do you ever feel that way about yourself?

Some sources caution against becoming too "personally involved" with youth. Yet in my experience, it is often the staff who are willing to share personal material who are the most effective. Self-disclosure, when done appropriately, provides positive role modeling as well as an invitation to discuss things further.

Encourage Written Expression

Many adolescents experience difficulty in directly relating their feelings, especially positive ones, in a face-to-face manner. Encourage them to write. The private nature of writing helps them uncover feelings they have denied or avoided, which they can then openly express to others, or reread to themselves from time to time, unobserved and without interruption. Writing helps adolescents pay more attention to the situations they find themselves in and to differentiate among their various feelings. They can ponder their revelations in solitude, become actively involved without embarrassment, and review their positive qualities and problem-solve to meet challenges.

One activity that helps adolescents express themselves is keeping daily logs organized into two categories: *situations* and *myself*. Under *situations* adolescents write accounts of at least two things that happened to them that they had not initiated. They describe their reactions and how they feel about their reactions. Under *myself* they write actions or behaviors they had chosen to initiate, to involve themselves in, giving the reasons, reactions, and feelings. Following the successful completion of these logs and appreciation of their value, they can then make a "Feelings Workbook." The goal is to help youth learn how their feelings make them behave. They ask simple but reflective questions of themselves, such as "Why am I doing this?" and write their answers in the workbook (Tuzil, 1978).

Writing letters—which are never sent—helps adolescents become more aware of themselves. A young person could write a letter to someone he or she has difficulty with or strong feelings about. The process allows the writer to rehearse and prepare a script for a future conversation and reflect on what he or she is going to say. Writing letters that are never sent helps one to fully express feelings. Even writing to lost ones assists in the grieving process following a death, divorce, or romantic breakup.

Suggest Alternatives

When told what to do, most adolescents do the opposite. However, when their choices are respected and encouraged, they will often try to make a mature and intelligent decision. Providing alternatives for them helps clarify their thinking.

ADULT: You're very upset and don't know what to do. Some things you might want to consider are talking with your dad, going for a walk, or maybe going over to the gym to work out.

or

ADULT: You sure seem angry at Betty. You could tell her off, in front of everybody, let her know what you really think of her. Or you could go for a run and consider what to do later. Or you could write her a long letter about how you feel. You can think about these options and decide the best thing to do.

Explaining the consequences of a threatened action while withholding judgment can help an adolescent make a more informed decision.

ADOLESCENT: I'm going to run away to New York City. I don't have much money, but I can hitch a ride there.

ADULT: Be careful if you hitchhike. A lot of people take advantage of kids who hitchhike—they use them sexually.

When you talk with adolescents, concentrate on helping them see how they themselves may be the cause of their troubles. As long as they blame others, they can persist in inadequate problem-solving efforts. Steps toward constructive change come about once they see themselves as the "problem maker" and begin to accept responsibility for their actions. Even abused children can initiate their abuse. To break this pattern, they can learn to stop complaining when they know their father has been drinking. When individuals can admit that they bring about their own troubles (see their role in the matter), they realize they can bring about their own successes.

PRINCIPAL: Jan, you say that European history is so ancient, so boring and so useless—that's why you failed it. I think something else is going on. You don't even try to do the work. Remember how you didn't like computer programming but kept trying? You got a B and now you're in the advanced class. You know that you're the one in charge of doing well or doing poorly. Is something else troubling you?

Stay Empathic

Adolescents in crisis often behave in ways that elicit punishment from others. I strongly believe that firm and clear limits with consequences for going past them are crucial to any setting involving adolescents, be it a school dance, football game, or the home environment. However, when these sanctions are applied, it is equally important to be able to communicate to the youngster that you understand the feelings and experiences that his or her misbehavior is camouflaging.

Control by itself is of little influence in curbing nonconformist behavior. Nor is permissiveness effective. What matters is *support*—communicating to adolescents that you understand their feelings, are willing to listen to them time and time again to hear their point of view, that you care about them—and that your rules stand precisely because you care. Most nonconformist behavior results from strict, rigid, high-control parents who fail to convey support.

Adolescents need a firm but flexible set of standards and rules against which to define themselves. The controlling yet supportive family provides such standards. Control is most effective when it is accompanied by communication.

For example, adolescents undergoing stress often run away. To them, running away is a logical recourse in resolving problems. They are not only fleeing from a stressful situation, but also running toward something—usually toward less alienated feelings and more control of their lives. Alienated adolescents, disillusioned by a crisis, need to reestablish commitment bonds, to increase self-esteem, to find meaning and purpose in life. But before they can do this, they need to get over the shock state that blocks their motivation to find solutions. Further punishment by adults clearly does not contribute to this process. Exploration of feelings is a more effective approach.

ADULT: Last week you ran away. . . . Things were getting so difficult that you wanted out of the situation. How has being away made things different for you? Has anything improved?

A hiddent message often underlies the more extreme forms of adolescent behavior. Self-mutilating adolescents, through their deliberate behavior, express independence, autonomy, and personal freedom. It is their way of controlling their social environment. Self-mutilation can be an effort at control over fears of violence, aggressive impulses, sexual thoughts, as well as feelings of powerlessness and helplessness (Ross & McKay, 1979). One such girl, Melinda, put it succinctly: "It's my body, and I can do anything I want with it. It's mine—it's the only thing I can control completely. I'm the boss" (Ross & McKay, 1979). Adult-inspired programs that attempt to control behavior without dealing with the reality of these feelings inevitably fail.

Staying empathic means being able to apply sanctions and still be concerned about the feelings and experiences of the adolescent:

PRINCIPAL: Over the weekend you were caught by the police breaking windows and spray-painting the gym. You are going to have to make restitution for this, and there is a mandatory suspension, besides.

STUDENT: [long silence]

PRINCIPAL: Sometimes kids destroy things for fun. It's their way of having a good time. Other times they just go along with the group. Still other times they may be mad—really mad—about something, like maybe their parents aren't getting along, and it's tough to live at home with all the fighting and arguing.

STUDENT: [Starts to cry. Talks about divorce of his parents.]

Successful interviews with adolescents hinge on playing down differences in status. Both the interviewer and the adolescent should have similar chairs, perhaps pointed to each other at a 45° angle and without desk or table in between. This arrangement avoids making your meeting a face-to-face confrontation and conveys the impression of a *we* rather than a *me/you* relationship. The atmosphere should be that of two people working together, engaged in the discussion of a subject that concerns them both. Do not take notes. It may make the adolescent uncomfortable or suspicious.

You need to do most of the talking initially. Explain the reason for your meeting and talk about the counseling process as it relates to the young person's problem. You want the youth to develop a comfortable impression about you, about the person to whom he or she might reveal inner feelings. Remember that adolescents' initial fears, regardless of how they present themselves, are a major hurdle.

Some adolescents will be so reluctant to talk that indirect procedures will need to be employed. First, always reflect the youngster's silence, paying close attention to his or her movements.

ADULT: It's hard to know where to start—you're feeling particularly uneasy and feeling foolish just sitting there saying nothing, but you don't know who I am and what I'll think of you—lots of kids feel that way. We don't have to begin by discussing troubles. If you'd rather, you can tell me anything that interests you, or what you're good at.

Most quiet and reluctant adolescents are scared—scared of being overwhelmed by their own vulnerability, scared of being dominated in the interview, of revealing their unworthiness, of not being able to find words adequate to the task of self-description, of your being in collusion with their parents, or of others finding out what they have said.

Some adolescents respond angrily at being sent to counselors. Passive-aggressive ones refuse to take off their coats: "I'm here because I was told to see you, but I'm not going to say or do anything." Their anger is an attempt to distance themselves from the adult so that they will not become dependent. Counselors need to define the counseling process, to communicate their interest in helping youngsters but also their inability to do so for those who truly want no assistance.

ADULT: Some students refuse to talk to me, or to anyone else, for that matter. They feel they can solve their own problems—and they can. But most of us, when we're upset and angry, don't always think clearly. My job is to help you think about ways you can deal with your concerns. I can't tell you what to do. I know you don't want to be here—and being forced to do something I don't want to do would make me angry, too! But you're here, so let's work together to discover how we can make something positive out of this situation.

If the adolescent does talk initially, talk primarily when you are addressed. This gives the youngster the feeling that he or she can control the degree of your participation, which reduces anxiety. However, don't let silences between verbalizations become too long as silence creates pressure to talk, and you will need to reduce the pressure by talking yourself.

If the adolescent talks abstractly or intellectually, keep your comments in the same vein rather than looking for feelings or miscommunications. Again, this gives the adolescent the feeling that he or she can control the closeness of the relationship and that you respect his or her defenses. This helps the adolescent feel accepted.

ADULT: I guess you think I'm going to give you advice on how to handle your worries. Lots of people think we do that, or look for hidden motives and things. Actually, I try to help people look at things more clearly. I may tell you what I've learned from other adolescents who have helped me to learn about their problems, and if any of that fits your situation, then that's great. At other times you will be bouncing ideas off me that I will help you become clearer about. Sometimes counselors are like coaches. You study the videotapes of the games with your coach, and he helps you see your actions in such a way that you can improve next time. You may need to figure out how to present yourself better, or to make your ideas clearer to others, or to decide what strengths you have that will enable you to solve this thing.

Sometimes adolescents talk a lot but say nothing significant. They tell stories rather than describe genuine feelings. They try to fool you with the impression that they're okay. They comply in order to gain some other end; they respond with empty, practiced answers, or in a bored and unauthentic manner, slouched in their seat. Or they pursue every question with great interest. You need to address the adolescent's evasiveness in a direct and nonjudgmental manner:

ADULT: I get the feeling that what you say doesn't match up with how you really feel. It seems you're hiding the fact that you really don't want to be here. I can understand that, but how does it feel having to hide your real feelings?

If these efforts fail, you may need to be even more direct:

ADULT: Look, you can see me regularly and fool me if you want to. I'm no mind reader, but who are you really fooling? You've come to see me because people who care about you feel you're troubled. They could be wrong, but how would I know if you don't tell me? Not to deal with their concerns about you isn't helping—they'll just send you to someone else if I tell them you aren't working with me. Maybe you could tell me your side, at least, or just how you feel about having to hide that you don't want to be here.

Counselors as Advocates

Working with adolescents requires doing something practical for them. This can be a positive starting point in earning their trust, especially if they are being sent to you. Help them to negotiate the family, school, the courts, or other social systems. They need concrete assistance in managing disputes between themselves and adults in their environment. Consider also the need to make strategic changes for students, temporary efforts to reduce stress. Lessons can be changed, tests can be postponed, and even disciplinary measures can be altered to help the adolescent through the crisis.

Formal counselors need to become familiar with the student's family and its circumstances. Successful counselors of adolescents are those who clearly have the adolescents' permission to see their family and who explain the reasons for the contact.

GUIDANCE COUNSELOR: In order for me to continue seeing you, I need your parents' permission. Education law gives them the right to refuse counseling for you, even if you want it. How do you think I could approach them on this, or do you want to talk to them yourself?

Since counselors frequently need to communicate with parents about their son's or daughter's difficulties, or help teachers or principals better understand a student, discussing this possibility with the youngster beforehand lessens the chances of later accusations of betrayal.

In formal counseling, adolescents will frequently miss appointments. Because they are action oriented, they can become quickly disillusioned when the sessions do not immediately relieve their distress. A letter or phone call to the adolescent is helpful. Convey your concerns about any possible disillusionment. Explore the dissatisfactions and be prepared to modify your procedures to suit his or her needs.

FOR FURTHER READING

Egan, G. (1975). *The Skilled Helper.* Monterey, California: Brooks/Cole.

REFERENCES

Bamberg, J. H. (1973). Adolescent marginality—A further study, *Genetic Psychology Monographs, 88,* pp. 3–21.

Elkind, B. (1965). Egocentrism and adolescence. *Child Development, 38,* pp. 1025–34.

Frazier, A. & Lisbondee, L. (1950). Adolescent concerns with physique, *School Review, 58,* pp. 397–405.

Gardner, R. A. (1975). *Psychotherapeutic Approaches to the Resistant Child.* (New York: Jason Aronson).

Kitwood, J. (1980). *Disclosures to a stranger: Adolescent values in an advanced industrial society.* (London: Routledge and Kegan Paul).

Ross, R. R. & McKay, H. B. (1979). *Self-Mutilation.* (Lexington, Mass.: Lexington Books).

Tuzil, T. J. Writing: A Problem-Solving Process, (1978). *Social Work, 23,* pp. 63–70.

21

Counseling Persons
with Eating Disorders

KATHLEEN ZRALY, M.A.
DAVID SWIFT, M.D.

The analogy between eating disorders and an iceberg seems valid. It will be helpful for counselors, parents, and other readers to understand this metaphor in more detail. Those expert in such things tell us that over 90% of an iceberg lies hidden beneath the surface of the sea, leaving less than 10% available for easy observation. Furthermore, the submerged portion of an iceberg can vary greatly in its configuration, and the shape of the exposed portion is of little help in predicting the shape of what lies below. Eating disorders (and many other forms of emotional illness) are much the same. The symptoms and behaviors that are indicative of an eating disorder are relatively simple, straightforward, and observable. Yet the underlying personality structure may vary greatly from patient to patient despite surface similarities.

The *Diagnostic and Statistical Manual of Mental Disorders* (third edition, revised, DSM-III-R), published by the American Psychiatric Association (1987), identifies three categories of eating disorders that can occur during adult life: *anorexia nervosa, bulimia nervosa,* and *eating disorder not otherwise specified.*

Anorexia Nervosa
Anorexia nervosa is identified by the following criteria:

1. Refusal to maintain body weight over a minimal normal weight for age and height (e.g., weight loss leading to maintenance of body

---

This chapter is adapted from Zraly, K., and Swift, D., *Overcoming Eating Disorders* (New York: Crossroad, 1990).

weight 15% below that expected, or failure to make expected weight gain during period of growth, leading to body weight 15% below that expected.

2. Intense fear of gaining weight or becoming fat, even though underweight.

3. Disturbance in the way in which one's body weight, size, or shape is experienced (e.g., the person claims to "feel fat" even when emaciated, believes that one area of the body is "too fat" even when obviously underweight).

4. In females, the absence of at least three consecutive menstrual cycles when otherwise expected to occur *(primary or secondary amenorrhea)*. (A woman is considered to have amenorrhea if her periods occur only following hormone, e.g., estrogen, administration.)

Bulimia Nervosa

Bulimia nervosa is identified by the following criteria:

1. Recurrent episodes of binge eating (rapid consumption of a large amount of food in a discrete period of time).

2. A feeling of lack of control over eating behavior during eating binges.

3. The person regularly engages in either self-induced vomiting, use of laxatives or diuretics, strict dieting or fasting, or vigorous exercise in order to prevent weight gain.

4. A minimum average of two binge eating episodes a week for at least 3 months.

5. Persistent overconcern with body shape and weight.

Eating Disorder Not Otherwise Specified

These are disorders of eating that do not meet criteria for anorexia nervosa or bulimia nervosa. The DSM-III-R cites the following as examples of this category of eating disorder:

1. A person of average weight who does not have binge eating episodes, but frequently engages in self-induced vomiting for fear of gaining weight.

2. All of the features of anorexia nervosa in a female except absence of menses.

3. All of the features of bulimia nervosa except for frequency of binge eating episodes.

Compulsive overeating is not recognized as a separate clinical condition in the DSM-III-R and is, at present, generally classified under *eating disorder not otherwise specified.* Our experience working with compulsive overeaters has led us to see compulsive overeating as a distinct form of eating disorder. Typically, these people give a history of sustained, often daily, overeating for a prolonged period of time, resulting in gross obesity. They rarely attempt to lose weight by inducing vomiting or through the use of laxatives, diuretics, or exercise. Compulsive overeaters often attempt to lose weight by fasting or dieting, but generally fail and rapidly regain any weight they do succeed in losing. Eventually their obesity significantly impairs their physical health or ability to work and perform normal day-to-day tasks. Embarrassment and social withdrawal are common.

Anorexia nervosa occurs almost exclusively in females and most commonly begins during adolescence or early adulthood. In some studies the prevalence of anorexia nervosa has been reported to be as high as 1 in 90 adolescent girls. The severity and duration of this condition can vary widely. For a fortunate few, the condition may remit spontaneously after a few weeks or months. For most, anorexia nervosa is a chronic lifelong struggle that often results in severe physical debilitation or death unless adequate treatment is obtained.

Bulimia nervosa is much more common in females, although male bulimics are being identified with increased frequency. The female-to-male sex ratio appears to be approximately 50:1. In various studies of high school and college populations, the prevalence of bulimia nervosa has ranged from 8% to 20% of the female population and has been reported as high as 1.4% of the male population. Although some bulimics manage to control their symptoms and carry on fairly normal lives, for many others the illness greatly interferes with their ability to function.

Compulsive overeating occurs in both men and women. It often begins during childhood or adolescence but may develop later in life. Accurate statistics regarding the prevalence of compulsive overeating are not available but the condition is obviously quite common in our society.

Although each of these conditions has its own distinctive symptoms and signs, people suffering with eating disorders share much in common. Most obviously, they all suffer. Each, in her [1]own way, is a slave to food. Each is locked in a seemingly endless love/hate relationship with food that often becomes the most important, most time-consuming, and the most emotionally charged relationship in her life. People with eating disorders are always dissatisfied with their weight and the configuration of their bodies. They feel fat. The scales may read 80 pounds for the anorexic, 115 pounds for the bulimic, and 350 pounds for the compul-

---

[1] The use of the feminine pronoun in this chapter is for purposes of succinctness and is not intended to discriminate against persons of masculine gender, who also (though less commonly) have eating disorders.

sive overeater, but the numbers are irrelevant. Each is convinced that she is fat. Each feels out of control. Each judges herself to be a failure. Feelings of failure are often accompanied by pronounced embarrassment and shame and associated attempts to hide the problem from others. Social withdrawal is common. Bingeing and purging are done in secret. Loose-fitting clothes are worn to hide the fat—be it real or imaginary.

Depression is a frequent accompaniment of eating disorders. Patients often experience feelings of hopelessness and worthlessness. As they repeatedly fail in their efforts to control their weight or to stop bingeing and/or purging, they become increasingly self-critical and guilt-ridden. Suicidal impulses and suicide attempts are not uncommon. Many of the patients we have treated as inpatients were hospitalized following a suicide attempt, or because of severe depression accompanied by suicidal thoughts.

Finally, people with eating disorders are all risking their physical well-being. Ten to 15% of patients suffering from anorexia nervosa die as a direct result of their illness. They essentially starve themselves to death. Compulsive overeaters significantly damage themselves and shorten their life span as a result of the many well-known complications of obesity (bone and joint disease, cardiovascular disease, etc.). In bulimics, electrolyte imbalance brought about by laxative abuse, vomiting, and ingestion of substances to induce vomiting can result in death due to cardiac arrhythmias. Repeated vomiting sometimes results in rupture of the esophagus, and extreme bingeing can cause rupture of the stomach. Fortunately, these complications are rare.

All of these conditions have probably been present for centuries. Anorexia nervosa was recognized as a form of emotional illness more than 100 years ago. However, it is only during the past quarter-century that eating disorders have attracted widespread interest. Outpatient and inpatient programs designed specifically to treat eating disorders have mushroomed during the past 10–15 years in response to a dramatic increase in the incidence of eating disorders (especially bulimia nervosa), coupled with increased public awareness and openness regarding these conditions.

There is general agreement that the increased incidence of both bulimia and anorexia is largely the result of social pressure. Since World War II our society has placed increasing value on being thin and trim. Clothing styles have steadily evolved in a corresponding manner—tighter-fitting jeans, bikini swim wear, shorter skirts, and so on. Our changing ideas of health and beauty have encouraged people to lose weight by a multitude of means (diets, diet pills, health clubs, etc.). Unfortunately, an ever-increasing number of people have been encouraged to develop anorexia or bulimia as a way of conforming to social ideals and simultaneously handling (or at least trying to handle) their underlying psychological problems. At the same time, this change in society's definition of beauty and health has resulted in the compulsive overeater appearing (and feeling) more out of step with society and more isolated and uncomfortable.

It should be noted that we do not see all obesity as being the result of compulsive overeating. Many nonpsychological causes of obesity are known and others will probably be discovered in the future. Certain endocrine disorders and genetic illnesses can result in significant weight gain, and genetic inheritance is an important factor in determining each individual's "normal" body weight. Recent research indicates that people have a genetically determined "set-point" regarding weight, and that attempts to maintain weight greatly below the set-point will result in subjective discomfort, hunger, and the urge to eat. When we refer to compulsive overeaters we are talking about those individuals whose problems with food and excess weight are primarily the result of psychological factors and not due to physical illness or genetic inheritance.

CORE ISSUES

Dependence on Parents

Eating-disordered patients are often abnormally dependent on, or emotionally involved with, one or both parents. Their relationship with parents is characterized by immature patterns of thinking, feeling, and behavior that would be considered appropriate at a younger age but, given the patient's actual age, are inappropriate. In psychiatric terminology this is referred to as an unresolved symbiosis.

In the normal course of development, the child, initially totally helpless and dependent, gradually achieves a sense of separateness, autonomy, and self-confidence. Ideally, by late adolescence or early adulthood the child experiences herself as the emotional equal of her parents. Although they may not be equal in terms of material wealth, wisdom, or achievement, the child sees herself as being a separate adult entity, free to make independent choices, having equal rights, being responsible for her behavior and its consequences, and capable of succeeding in life without parental help. Patients with eating disorders have failed to achieve these goals. They remain dependent. They continue to see their parents through the eyes of a child.

This dependence is sometimes quite obvious. With other patients, the dependence may be less apparent. One patient, for example, had lived away from home for most of her adult life. She was highly critical of her parents, belittled them for their alleged shortcomings, and often insisted that she wanted nothing from them. But beneath that facade she felt hurt, alone, and afraid. Her dependence surfaced when her parents went away on a lengthy vacation trip while she was hospitalized. She then experienced intense anxiety and feelings of abandonment, which triggered an exacerbation of her eating disorder and other acting-out behaviors, including cutting herself.

Occasionally patients succeed in establishing what appears to be a high degree of separation and independence from parents. One of our patients, a married mother of two young children, had struggled with bulimia since the age of 20. Her relationship with her parents, while not especially close, had been cordial and outwardly conflict-free since adolescence. She entered treatment because of escalating symptoms after her father retired and her parents began devoting more time to their grandchildren. Initially, the patient insisted that she welcomed her parents' increased involvement and appreciated the attention they lavished on her children. She noted that it was "like having a free baby-sitter" and denied any emotional discomfort. As treatment progressed, however, this patient recognized that she deeply resented her parents for "giving my kids what they never gave me." Awareness of anger was soon followed by awareness of long-repressed loneliness and longing for parental love and acceptance. As this patient worked through these feelings in therapy, her bulimic symptoms subsided.

PROBLEMS WITH PROBLEM SOLVING

Healthy problem solving can be defined as activity that effectively ends or ameliorates an immediate difficulty; prevents or at least lessens the chance that the difficulty will recur; meets the real needs of all people concerned; and doesn't violate anyone's basic rights. A corollary to this definition is that when a problem concerns more than one person, all parties involved cooperate actively in the problem-solving process. Patients with eating disorders generally have not grown up in families where effective problem solving was modeled. As a result they lack good problem-solving skills and, more importantly, they lack faith that effective problem solving is possible. Although they may deal well with some problems, they believe, consciously or unconsciously, that other problems cannot be solved.

Many patients with eating disorders grow up in alcoholic families. Such families serve as models for passivity, the enabling of repetitive destructive behavior, and a lack of respect for individual rights. In short, alcoholic family systems model problem perpetuation rather than problem solving. Adult children of alcoholics (ACOAs) typically have poor self-esteem and problems with assertiveness. In their families of origin, aggression and/or passivity are the usual responses to stressful events. Their ability to trust that they or anyone else can effectively deal with difficult problems is seriously impaired.

Patients with eating disorders almost universally have failed to resolve their symbiotic attachment to one or both parents. Consciously or unconsciously, they want something from their parents that they didn't get as children. Their childhood needs were, in some degree, not met and they are vulnerable to regression (i.e., to slipping back into childlike ways of thinking, feeling, and behaving). This in itself is indicative of ineffective problem solving in the patient's family of origin. The universal problem of childhood, "How can I get my needs met in this family" went unsolved. In some significant way the needs of childhood were not met, the problem was not solved, faith and trust were damaged, and problem-solving skills were not learned.

Case example. Nancy's parents were quiet, emotionally distant, undemonstrative people. Nancy learned early in life that the only reliable way she could get their attention was to cause a crisis or be disruptive. She recalled in vivid detail how indulgent and attentive her parents were when, as a child, she severely lacerated her back falling out of a bunk bed. Her parents responded beautifully to the crisis and provided her with the best of care. Experiences of this type rapidly led Nancy to the belief that she could meet her needs for recognition and nurturing only by creating a crisis of self-injury. She continued to act out this belief over a period of many years. Nancy's "solution" to the problem was partially successful. She did get a degree of attention and recognition. But in doing so she violated her own rights and created unnecessary problems for others. Her method of problem solving could hardly be described as healthy or effective.

TRUST AND INTIMACY

Establishing and sustaining close, trusting relationships is often very difficult for patients with eating disorders. This appears to be the inevitable consequence when one's parents were unable to meet basic needs and successful problem-solving strategies were never learned; it logically follows that intimate relationships will be viewed with considerable anxiety. After all, intimate relationships present the greatest risks in terms of vulnerability and the possibility for being hurt if problems arising within the relationship are not solved.

In their work with many types of patients, therapists commonly encounter strong ambivalence toward close relationships. Many patients both want and fear intimacy, and employ a variety of defenses in their efforts to avoid intimacy and the anxiety that it evokes in them. Patients (and nonpatients as well) use deliberate withholding, intellectualization, and a host of other well-known consciously and unconsciously motivated tactics to avoid the risk of being hurt, rejected, or betrayed. In addition to these defenses, patients with eating disorders have a defense not generally used by others: talking about food and their bodies.

If allowed to, many people with eating disorders will talk endlessly about their illness. Even patients who try to hide their illnesses will do this once the ice has been broken in therapy. They often describe their symptoms in a highly self-critical and helpless manner that invites the other person—friend or therapist—to offer help in the form of suggestions, advice, or other kinds of support. It should be noted that storytelling of this sort generally reveals little of real importance about the patient and is a strategy often used by patients to avoid the risks of trust and intimacy.

PROBLEMS WITH ANGER AND ASSERTIVENESS

A number of factors may contribute to an eating-disordered person's difficulty with anger. Many come from families where their needs and feelings, especially angry feelings, were frequently discounted or ignored. Others grow up in families where angry feelings are judged as bad and as something to be ashamed of. Those from alcoholic or abusive families often report that they were verbally or physically punished for their normal childhood expressions of anger and frustration. Depending on their innate temperament, the influence of parents and siblings, and other factors beyond their control, people raised in such families may respond by retreating and keeping their feelings to themselves, or by attacking and exaggerating their feelings in an attempt to get their needs met. In the first instance, the result is passivity, withdrawal, and the expression of anger through indirect means. In the second instance, the result is aggressive demandingness that may escalate into high-level verbal or physical confrontation.

Most of the people we have worked with do some of both. That is, they often hide their anger (even from themselves) but will occasionally blow up and express anger in exaggerated and inappropriate ways. They often express anger in indirect, self-defeating ways. They have great difficulty finding a middle ground of healthy assertiveness. Eating-disordered patients need to learn assertive behaviors in order to give up their eating disorder. They need to learn how to express their needs and feelings in straightforward, appropriate ways.

THE OUTSIDE-IN ORIENTATION

People with eating disorders overvalue the outside world and devalue themselves. In general, they see power and goodness as residing in other people or things and they see themselves as weak and bad. Borrowing from the vocabulary of transactional analysis, they experience themselves as not-OK and other people as OK. It is important to note that this is a general orientation that may not apply across the board. Eating-disordered patients may identify some positive attributes in themselves and are capable of seeing other people in negative terms. On balance, however, this orientation is prominent in people with eating disorders.

One obvious result of this is that food is experienced as having immense power. A compulsive overeater experiences herself as powerless to resist it. Bulimics also see themselves as having no choices. They *have* to binge and they *have* to get rid of the food through some type of purging. Anorexics attribute so much power to food that they may avoid it to the point of starving to death. For all three groups, food dominates their lives. Food has power and they don't.

Another manifestation of the outside-in orientation is seen in the way eating-disordered patients use food to manipulate feelings. Food is experienced as needed in order to change or avoid unwanted feelings or to express feelings that the individual has difficulty expressing in more direct ways. For the eating-disordered patient, food serves much the same function as alcohol for the alcoholic. The most common example of this is the eating-disordered patient's use of food to relieve anxiety. Anorexics experience a lessening of anxiety when they abstain from food and achieve a loss of weight or a decrease in body size. Bulimics often report feeling peaceful and relaxed after bingeing and purging. Overeaters feel more relaxed after a binge.

Other uncomfortable feelings are handled in a similar manner. Borderline patients can numb their feelings of emptiness and abandonment by indulging in their eating-disordered behavior. Others use their symptomatic behavior to allay anger, grief, or any other emotion they see as threatening or undesirable. Food also serves as a medium for expressing feelings. Anger in particular can be expressed through the manipulation of food. Many bulimics leave enough "evidence" behind them to upset other people, and generally this is a deliberate (albeit sometimes unconscious) expression of anger.

Most eating-disordered patients blame themselves for being not-OK. They see themselves as failures and often judge both past and present behavior as "bad." Their bodies are bad (wrong size, shape, or weight); their eating disorder is bad (a sign of weakness and lack of self-control); past behavior is bad (too lazy, selfish, immoral, ungrateful, etc.). Self-perceptions of this sort are extremely common in eating-disordered patients and often give rise to strong guilt feelings. This guilt and the resulting need for punishment can be acted out through the eating disorder. Starving, bingeing, and purging can serve as a punishment for a multitude of "sins" and as a means of relieving, at least briefly, chronic feelings of guilt.

Food becomes a multipurpose medium for people with eating disorders—a kind of panacea much like drugs or alcohol for an addict. It provides reliable temporary relief for almost any form of distress. It also serves an additional purpose that deserves mention: that of self-validation.

It seems to be universally true that all of us, no matter what we believe, want the satisfaction of "proving" that our beliefs are correct. If we believe we are right about something, we want to get others to see things our way. Thus, a person who deeply believes that she is a bad person will seek validation of that belief. Despite "intellectual awareness" that the belief is probably incorrect, the person who truly believes that she is bad, or weak, or not competent in some respect is strongly driven to prove to herself and, if necessary, to others that her belief is right. Some part of us feels relieved and satisfied when we succeed in doing this. Eating-disordered patients validate their basic belief that they are not-OK every time they indulge in their symptomatic behavior. The very fact that they have an eating disorder and cannot control it "proves" that there is something wrong with them. The more entrenched the basic belief, the more difficult it will be for the patient to give up her eating disorder.

THE NEED FOR CONTROL

The need to be in control is strong in most people with eating disorders. Eating-disordered patients often report feeling "out of control" in many areas of their lives. They may see themselves as unable to control their weight, eating behaviors, feelings, impulses, social relationships, family relationships, and so on. During recovery they are reluctant to make significant life changes because in doing so, they experience fear and loss of control. The word "control" comes up repeatedly in therapy sessions, and maintaining a sense of control is a matter of great urgency for most eating-disordered patients. This is another result of the "outside-in" orientation.

A person with a healthy sense of self-confidence trusts that she will be able to deal with life's problems. She has received adequate nurturing, sound information, protection from excessive stress, and the needed support for dealing with age-appropriate stress. As a result, she has been able to internalize a sense of competency and experiences herself as a capable person. The healthy person believes, "I can deal with adversity; I can cope as well as other people." The person with an eating disorder, on the other hand, believes, "I'm defective; I can't cope as well as others." Since the person with an eating disorder feels weak and unable to respond effectively to problems, she strives to control her life. The key words here are *respond* and *control.* People who are confident of their ability to respond to life feel less need to control life.

PATHOLOGICAL SHAME

We will now turn our attention to what ultimately emerges as a major problem for many people with eating disorders—a problem that seems to underlie all the other problems that we have discussed. This is the problem of pathological shame.

It has been our experience that people who were subjected to a high degree of childhood trauma and who, early in life, came to believe in a global way that they were "bad" or "not-OK" have the greatest difficulty overcoming their eating disorder. Other people, whose self-esteem was less damaged, recover more rapidly. A few recover without treatment, given favorable circumstances. Whether recovery is rapid or gradual, an essential part of the recovery process is that the person modifies basic beliefs about herself and comes to see herself in more positive terms. To accomplish this, most patients must come to terms with a deeply embedded sense of personal shame.

The important role that shame plays in addictive illnesses has been highlighted by Bradshaw (1988), who defines addiction as "a pathological relationship to any mood-altering experience that has life damaging consequences" (p. 15). Since people with eating disorders use repetitive eating behaviors and obsessive thinking about food to alter their mood (i.e., to allay anxiety or to avoid unpleasant emotions), eating disorders clearly fall within his definition of addiction.

In doing long-term work with eating-disordered patients, what we have repeatedly seen is that beneath their other feelings and defensive behaviors these people feel ashamed. They see themselves as undeserving. They describe their underlying nature in such terms as "horrible," "worthless," and "a monster." Labels like "bad" and "not-OK" are far too bland to convey the inner experience of these patients.

Not all feelings of shame are inappropriate or pathological. People are, after all, limited beings incapable of perfection and prone to make mistakes. Some sense of shame is therefore understandable and appropriate. Pathological shame is inappropriate or irrational in the sense that it is based on a misunderstanding. More specifically, pathological shame results when the child incorrectly takes responsibility for something bad happening (i.e., when she says to herself something like, "The fact that this happened means I'm bad; this is my fault"). Many kinds of early experience can contribute to a child's sense of shame. Excessive punishment, overprotection, unrealistic parental expectations, parental unresponsiveness to the child's needs, neglect, physical abuse, sexual abuse—in short, negative strokes of any kind, if too frequent or extreme, can produce the same result.

THE BASIS OF EATING DISORDERS

It is generally agreed that anorexia nervosa and bulimia nervosa are reflective of intense ambivalence about something and that, although food is the immediate "something" in the here and now, the "real" or original object of ambivalence is something else. We see compulsive overeating as also being the outward manifestation of intense ambivalence. By ambivalence we mean that the person both likes and dislikes, wants and does not want, loves and fears someone or something. Strong contradictory attitudes therefore exist within the person, and a state of internal conflict is thereby established.

People suffering from bulimia, anorexia, and compulsive overeating express this ambivalence in somewhat different ways. The person with anorexia expresses primarily the negative or "I don't want" side of the ambivalence. Relatively speaking, her fear wins out over her hunger and the result is starvation, emaciation, and sometimes, death. The person suffering from bulimia represents a middle ground. At times the positive "I want" side wins out and a binge is the result. This is usually followed by a switch to the negative side, resulting in a period of purging and/or restricting. The compulsive overeater completes the spectrum. For her, the positive or "I want" side more often wins and the result is increasing obesity. Periodically the "I don't want" side will gain the upper hand and she will restrict or diet for a time. But in the long run, her needs win out over her fears.

The question then arises as to the source of the ambivalence demonstrated by these people. If we assume that food is the symbolic representation of something else, what is that something else? Is it just one thing or is it perhaps several; and is it the same thing or things for all eating-disordered people, or something more or less unique to each individual or diagnostic group? There are no universally agreed-upon answers to any of these questions.

Eating is one of the most primitive means by which people take in something from their environment and make it a part of themselves. Usually, within the first few hours after birth, the newborn is fed, and through the processes of digestion and metabolism, that which is "not self" becomes "self." The process of incorporating the outside world into the self also occurs through the physical senses of feeling, hearing, seeing, smelling, and tasting. These modes of taking in (especially feeling, seeing, and hearing) are of primary importance in the individual's psychological growth. But eating remains the most basic and essential mode of incorporation. With these observations in mind, it seems logical to conclude that eating disorders may be the end result of ambivalence about taking in something that the outside world is offering; something the individual needs and wants, but also dislikes and fears. Our view, which is shared by many others in the field, is that the feared "something" is best summed up by the words "parenting" and "intimacy," and that the original object of ambivalence is therefore the parents or other early care-givers.

The young patient-to-be, like all of us, needs nurturing and is dependent on parents or other care-givers for survival. A close, dependent attachment (or *infantile symbiosis*) is established with the parent or other care-giver. Initially this may be a healthy, comfortable, mutually gratifying relationship that fosters the development of intimacy and trust in the child. But then things begin to go wrong, and contact with the parent or other care-giver is increasingly experienced as painful. On both theoretical and clinical grounds we know that these painful experiences or traumas begin early, often during the first year of life, and almost certainly before age 4. The painful experiences may be the result of a number of factors: parental withdrawal or neglect, physical or sexual abuse, a high level of tension in the home secondary to parental conflict or alcoholism, overly critical, punitive, or demanding parental attitudes, and so on. The result is that the parent or other important care-giver is increasingly experienced as a source of physical and/or emotional pain. As a result the child begins to distrust the parent, and the seeds of chronic mistrust of all close relationships are planted. Increasingly, the child experiences the parent or other caregiver as someone to be feared and avoided. This sequence of events sets the stage for the development of ambivalence.

As the intensity of the child's discomfort increases, the child may initially react by becoming angry, having temper tantrums, crying, complaining, and so on. But when these normal and age-appropriate behaviors fail to solve the problem, the child begins to develop defenses against the pain that all too often accompanies contact with the parenting figure. We have labeled these defenses *avoidance*. This avoidance may take a variety of forms, depending on the age of the child and parental response. Physical withdrawal, verbal withholding, dissociation, repression, retreat into fantasy and magical thinking, and the development of obsessions and compulsive rituals are among the most commonly employed defenses. At the same time, because the child continues to be biologically dependent and in need of parental nurturing, she learns how to get her survival needs met despite the pain that contact with the parent or other care-giver frequently entails. She learns how to please the parent. She becomes "overadapted."

Overadapting means going along with or giving in to someone, even though one doesn't actually agree or feel comfortable doing so. Young children overadapt out of necessity. Since a young child is incapable of moving out of the home or calling the Department of Social Services when she becomes the target of abuse or neglect, she must give in and put up with the situation in order to survive. It is a case of "If you can't beat them, join them." So the young child may learn to smile in the face of adversity, or to be extremely hard-working and a high achiever at home and in school, or to keep her room neat and to help her mother prepare meals or care for younger siblings, or to be cute and seductive in relationships with men. But whatever form her overadapted behavior takes, it will be motivated by her need to survive and to avoid pain and will not be an expression of her true spontaneous self. Overadapted behavior therefore begins as an act. In time it becomes a habit, a part of the individual's personality structure. By the time the overadapted person reaches adulthood, she generally has little or no awareness of the fact that she is putting on an act. She has generally repressed or dissociated most of the traumas that originally motivated her overadapted behavior and experiences her behavior as comfortable and genuine. As adults, people with eating disorders are very often "people pleasers." They smile a lot. They are considerate of other people's needs and feelings. They generally take the role of caretaker in important relationships. This is especially true of people suffering from compulsive overeating and bulimia, but is a prominent personality trait in many anorexics as well.

The contradictory attitudes of attraction and avoidance experienced in relationship to the parent or other care-giver form the basis of the ambivalence that is so evident in people with eating disorders. If the child's avoidant and overadapted behaviors worked perfectly, all would be well and there would be no further problems. Unfortunately, this is never the case. Since overadapted behavior is an act and not an expression of the person's true self, it is never completely satisfying. Also, the various avoidant behaviors previously discussed serve to minimize pain, but never eliminate it. As a result, a continued state of conflict and anxiety persists.

Most eating-disordered people begin showing symptoms of their eating disorder during adolescence or early adulthood. Although some problems with eating and/or weight may be evident earlier, full-blown symptoms usually appear after the onset of puberty. It has long been postulated that the pressures to grow up, separate from parents, establish intimate relationships outside of the family, and eventually become self-supporting are what trigger the development of clinical illness. It is easy to see why this would be the case. Children destined to develop an eating disorder approach adolescence ill-prepared to negotiate the developmental steps that lie ahead. They have not yet mastered many of the tasks of earlier developmental stages. Their capacity for trust is impaired because their parents have not provided adequate parenting. Their capacity for intimacy is impaired because they associate intimacy with pain and anxiety. They have a poor sense of their own identity because they have had to repress and dissociate large portions of their experience, and because they have largely gotten along by pretending and overadapting. Their true self has not been allowed to develop. They truly do not know who they are, although they may pretend to know and may often believe that they do. They feel defective, bad, and ashamed. As adolescence and adulthood approach, their anxiety increases. On some level they recognize that they are not prepared to go on, that they cannot meet the demands of adult life.

REDUCING ANXIETY

One of the most important functions of behavioral symptoms is the reduction of anxiety. Phobias, compulsive rituals, obsessive thought patterns, addictions, and other repetitive abnormal or "symptomatic" behaviors serve to lessen the individual's level of anxiety. Although a symptom in and of itself may cause serious problems and significantly limit the individual's ability to function, one result of symptom formation is always to help the individual feel better. Were this not so—if behaving "normally" were more comfortable than being symptomatic— few people would ever become ill. Such problems as addictions, phobias, many forms of depression, and a host of other psychological illnesses would simply not exist. Organic illnesses and conditions primarily caused by genetic inheritance would still occur, but many illnesses, including eating disorders, would disappear.

People develop eating disorders therefore as a way of lessening anxiety. Although the person suffering from an eating disorder may be very uncomfortable and highly motivated to recover from her illness, it can be safely assumed that she feels less anxious with her illness than without it, and that any attempt to make her give up her illness will meet with significant resistance. The extreme life disruption that eating disorders often cause, and the high level of emotional discomfort that people with eating disorders experience as a result of their illness give us some sense of the level of anxiety that underlies their illness. As we see it, the roots of most eating disorders go back to earlier developmental stages where trust and autonomy were the crucial issues. Pressures to become sexually mature and active may serve to trigger the illness, but are not the basic cause of eating disorders.

Eating disorders serve to reduce anxiety in several ways. We have already noted that eating disorders provide a relatively safe, comfortable, and controllable object that substitutes for people, who are seen as unsafe and uncontrollable. Another mechanism by which anxiety is reduced is through regression. People with bulimia and compulsive overeating sometimes report that when they are bingeing they are "in another world" and have little awareness of what is going on around them. Their focus is entirely on food. All other concerns disappear and they seem to be, as one patient put it, "in a trance." Several patients refer to the subjective experience of bingeing as being "in la-la land." They feel much like what we presume a nursing infant feels: relaxed, oblivious to surroundings, focused on the act of eating and the comfort that it brings. Thus the act of bingeing fosters regression to an earlier infantile stage of developmental where the individual experienced comfort, safety, and trust.

Eating disorders also reduce anxiety by providing the person with an excuse for avoiding things. As one patient put it, "If I have binged or purged I can turn down social invitations without feeling guilty." She referred to her bulimic symptoms as her "cop-out," and recognized that her illness brought her relief from guilt. Finally, during their therapy, many eating-disordered persons become aware of how they use their illness in interpersonal situations. Like any illness, eating disorders can be used to control other people and to express anger or get revenge. Demands for attention and hostile impulses that the individual cannot express directly can be expressed through the illness itself, with resulting lessening of tension and anxiety. Thus a number of "secondary gains" are possible and, to the extent that such gains are present, the illness becomes more entrenched.

ISSUES IN THERAPY

Most eating-disordered people enter therapy with a strong sense of ambivalence. For most, problems with eating have been long-term, and the thought of living life without an eating disorder becomes not only a frightening thought, but also a seemingly unreal one. Giving up their eating disorder becomes the same as giving up their identity.

To date, we have not had an anorexic walk into our office and say, "I can't stand this anymore, I need help." Most often they are accompanied by a family member or friend who is at their wits' end as to how to help this person. The anorexic has found an identity within the eating disorder. The fear involved with acknowledging that a problem exists far outweighs the reality. (In speaking with the eating-disordered person who is well into the recovery process, it becomes more clear that an awareness of the unhealthy position they were in existed all along.) Denial becomes the single most difficult issue with the anorexic. Denial, for all intents and purposes, is the defense mechanism that enables the patient to avoid dealing with the fear involved in looking at herself from the inside out. The fear that they will not be accepted, approved of, or loved unless they are thin is paralyzing.

Bulimics most often seek treatment on their own. As they sit in the office recounting the years of bingeing and purging, there is a strong sense of guilt and remorse. Most bulimics have been able to carry on a seemingly "normal" life with little hint that something is wrong. By the time a bulimic seeks out treatment, she has had just about all she can take with this eating disorder.

Most bulimics will state that they are unclear as to whether they want to give up this disorder, but are clear in stating that they are mentally and physically exhausted from it. Like the anorexic, the bulimic has made this her identity. She finds it difficult to imagine life without it. Of the three disorders, bulimia is probably the most difficult to own for two reasons: First, the bulimic's weight does not signify that there is any difficulty inside or out, whereas the anorexic has a thin or emaciated body and the compulsive overeater has the heavier or obese body. Second, although starving or overeating are not condoned, both seem to be viewed in a more understanding manner than eating and throwing up.

Compulsive overeaters most often get caught in a whirlwind of "diets" and "miracle cures" to target their behavior of eating. They recognize they are overeating and often will only allow themselves to concentrate on getting their eating straighened out. This is not to say that the compulsive overeater does not seek treatment, but usually there is an underlying panic to "fix" the eating first. It is not unusual that as compulsive overeaters skip from diet to diet they also skip from therapist to therapist. Once they realize the therapist cannot fix them, and may ask them to look at underlying reasons for the overeating, compulsive overeaters seek out another way to lose weight.

Eating disorders work for the patient. It is the fear of giving up something that works, that keeps the eating disorder going. How do they work? With all three of the above-mentioned disorders the common thread is that the focus on food, weight, and meals is so consuming that it distracts and de-focuses from other thoughts and feelings that may be causing pain, discomfort, or confusion.

For the anorexic it is not the actual food the appears to relieve the tension, but the obsessive consuming thoughts about how to lose another pound, or the intense desire to compulsively exercise. For most humans, exercise can and does alleviate tension. They exercise until they feel somewhat more relaxed and in control, and can then look at whatever was creating the anxiety. It is important to point out that exercise, for the anorexic, serves as a way to defocus and distract herself from dealing with whatever is causing her this anxiety.

When the bulimic becomes anxious, the thoughts of bingeing usually increase quickly. When feelings start to surface, the bulimic becomes uncomfortable and frightened by those feelings. ("It's not-OK to feel.") The feelings are experienced as being pushed up from inside and threatening to spill out. Before the expression of these feelings actually comes out, she has begun a binge. As the food goes in, it pushes the feelings back down and out of the way. As the binge continues, the person's focus has now shifted from uncomfortable feelings to physical discomfort from the ingesting of a large quantity of food. Now, the only issues the person allows herself to experience are the guilt from eating all the food and the overpowering need to get rid of the food through purging. Once the purge is completed, the person returns to worrying, which will eventually lead her to become anxious once again. As with the anorexic, the process serves as a way to distract and de-focus from dealing with feelings.

Compulsive overeaters are similar to the bulimic, except they do not purge. The use of food as emotional comfort appears to stem from early life. If they weren't feeling well, the message became, "Have something to eat, you'll feel better." If they were sad the message was, "Don't be sad, go fix yourself something to eat." The compulsive overeater learned early on that no matter what uncomfortable feeling they were experiencing, food would fix it. Again, as with the anorexic and bulimic, it became a way to distract and de-focus from whatever was causing them this discomfort.

In the short run, the eating disorder works for the patient. The bingeing or starving temporarily makes the person feel better. The food or power she feels over it becomes her best friend—she can call on it any time. It doesn't argue or talk back and it's very reliable. In the long run, it is debilitating. Eating disorders are one of the most complex disorders to work with. Most patients are looking for a guarantee: "If I give this up you have to *promise* me everything will be OK and will work out." To date, we know of no guarantees.

If we take a look back at the outside-in theory, it becomes clear that eating-disordered persons are "re-acters," rather than "pro-acters." They will revolve their lives around others even if it means compromising their own belief system. They are people who fear their own feelings. Very often we encounter people in therapy who can express very clearly how they feel about an incident that may have created discomfort for them. When asked if they shared how they felt with the other person involved, they said, "Oh no, I could never let that person know how I feel; they might get mad." It becomes quickly evident, then, that what is being said to that other person most often does not match the patient's true feelings. Revealing their feelings is their primary fear, and seems to occur most often in intimate relationships.

When most eating-disordered people enter therapy, a prominent fear is that we will take the eating disorder from them. One of the first and clearest messages we give them is that we do not want to take their eating disorder away, but we would like to help them address their fears and develop healthy coping mechanisms. We also let them know that if they cannot, throughout the course of therapy, establish other ways of dealing with their fears, they can keep the eating disorder.

The reality is that no one can take away their eating disorder because they possess it, they control it. What they choose not to look at is that by seeking treatment, they have taken the first step in the process of letting go, not only of their eating disorders, but also of their fears.

The eating disorder serves as a cover-up. In most circumstances the patients we see come from a dysfunctional family system. Most often, as parents were fighting or discussions were being held, the message was "Everything is OK, go back to your room" or "Everything is not-OK; maybe when you're older we'll tell you more about it." Our experience has been that this is when fear becomes incorporated into the child's thinking process. In the first message, the child sees that there is something wrong, yet is being told that everything is OK. In the second message, the child learns something *is* wrong but that she is too young to understand. Both messages leave the child with feelings of not being able to handle issues. In turn, the child begins to question whether something is wrong with her—that she cannot handle a difficult situation. She grows up with the fear that something bad is going to happen, the fear that she's not-OK, and the fear that she may be abandoned if something is wrong.

On the opposite end of the spectrum is the message "You can handle everything and anything." We have found that many of our patients have learned to listen to one or the other parent's problems at an early age. The child becomes the therapist, the emotional support system. Here is where she learns to become the caretaker and protector.

The child who learns to swallow her feelings brings this trait into adolescence, when feelings become more confusing and difficult. She begins to experience anger and a sense of emptiness. Both feelings generate from her own needs not being met. She may feel unsupported by other siblings or family members in her quest to make everything OK. What begins to occur is that the feelings are turned inward, toward the self. "Maybe I can't handle it, maybe I am worthless. Why would anyone like me? And if they did like me, they wouldn't after they found out what I'm really like inside." All of the messages she perceived as a child are now being validated and reinforced. What makes it more difficult is that most people view her as "happy, peppy, and bursting with love." So she begins to live in her own world, tormented by this voice that is always doubting and questioning her worth as a person. Eventually, the tension created by the two worlds snaps. It is at this point that the eating disorder gets started. For most, it is not a conscious decision to abuse food, but one that takes on value gradually, like the alcoholic who starts out with one social drink and ends up drinking continuously.

Fear becomes her number one enemy. Since the message she has come to believe is that she is incapable of handling issues, she lives in fear of everything. We have heard many patients say, "I know what I need to do, I just can't get myself to do it." Facing and dealing with their fears takes time, patience and understanding on the part of therapists and patients alike. We can't help but mention that this is one of the most frustrating components in therapy. The therapist knows the patient will be OK, feel better, and maybe even believe in herself a little more, but she needs to experience it in her own space and time. When she beigins to let go of her fears, she also begins to let go of her eating disorder. Once she confronts her fears, the purpose served by the eating disorder loses its value. When a patient relapses and begins to hide behind the eating disorder once again, one of the first questions we address is "What are you afraid of?" When she owns that fear, the recovery process continues.

When the fear becomes too intense, the eating-disordered person begins to create a world of fantasy. This world cannot hurt her. It allows the eating-disordered person to create a warm, secure, fear-free environment. Unfortunately, she begins to believe it is reality. The patient's self-confidence and self-esteem both plummet.

RECOVERY

It's hard to say which is the most difficult part of recovery from the eating behavior: the beginning, the middle, or the letting go. The beginning seems almost impossible sometimes. For most, bingeing, purging, or restricting has been a major obsession that has consumed their thoughts for years. It also feels like a 24-hour-a-day job. The most common statement we hear at the beginning is that the patient has "screwed up" 6 out of the last 7 days. (This is probably a person who has binged, and/or purged, or eaten nothing on a daily basis for the last 2 or 3 years.) When we asked about the 1 good day, she almost looks surprised, as if that day doesn't really count in view of the 6 others that presented difficulty. Taking the eating-disordered person's black-and-white thinking into account, it makes sense that she disregards that 1 day. It either has to be 7 perfect days, or it doesn't count.

At the beginning of recovery, many people ask us to put them on a meal plan, feeling that if they could follow some regimen or know the right foods to eat, they would do better. We try not to get lost in this de-focusing technique. People with eating disorders could publish best-selling books on nutrition and healthy weight loss. Remember, this is their passion, so it's important not to get too caught up in what's being eaten or what's being done with it. The only time it does become an issue is when there are possible health risks involved. These need to be addressed immediately.

Unlike the alcoholic who, in treatment, learns "don't go to bars or hang out with your drinking and drugging friends," the eating-disordered person must learn throughout recovery to reincorporate food into her day with some sense of normalcy. The hard part is that the substance we need to survive has become the "enemy." Most people we have treated can recall a period of time before their eating disorder when they felt as though they had normal eating habits. It's important for the patient to remember that she wasn't born with an eating disorder. It entered into her life at a point where feelings were so painful that it seemed easier to self-destruct than to deal with these feelings.

The recovering patient will find herself experiencing a tremendous amount of frustration. Trial and error is not the easiest concept to deal with—mainly because trial and error takes patience and determination. Determination the eating-disordered person has. Patience—well, that's something else. During this middle phase, *everything* seems exaggerated. We had a patient in the hospital recently who reported that after leaving the grocery store she felt as though everything was louder, the noise, the people, even the colors on the food wrappers. It's important to remember that the eating-disordered person's awareness is increasing, while at the same time her head is clearing of many obsessive thoughts.

The eating-disordered person finds herself returning to old behaviors in situations where she's not feeling strong enough to reach out for better coping mechanisms. What we do know is that throughout the steps of recovery she will experience a return to old behaviors at least a few times, if not more. That's normal and part of the process. Remember, it's not the end of the world (although it can sure feel like that sometimes). Throughout this process food becomes more and more integrated into the patient's life. The key to this process is how she feels about herself. Food will always be there to hide behind. She has to be the one to decide to come out of hiding.

Fully letting go of the control eating has had over her life takes time, a lot of time. It's a normal and common part of the process to continue to have the thoughts of wanting to restrict, binge, and/or purge. The patient has to step back when these feelings overtake her and ask herself, "What am I really trying to communicate through my bingeing or restricting?" Also, it's important for her to understand that the bingeing may come upon her at a time when things seem as though they're going relatively well. She may not always be able to pinpoint or understand a reason for her bingeing. But people with eating disorders are wonderful during a crisis or times of undue stress. It's the delayed reaction (which can be a matter of a few hours or a few weeks) that creates uncomfortable feelings.

The second issue in the recovery process deals with the issue of relationships. Throughout recovery an integral part is the awareness of the relationships the eating-disordered person has experienced throughout her life. The most common and painful issue we hear regarding relationships is the feeling of not belonging. Most people we've encountered state that they always felt as though they were on the periphery of a group. This feeling is one of never fitting in as well as those who appear to be the center of the group. What makes looking at relationships a complex part of recovery is that the eating-disordered person almost always sees it only one way: "It must be something about *me* that people dislike." It's hard for her to recognize that a relationship always consists of more than one person. Recovery involves taking a very honest look at relationships. The patient will usually find that the relationships she has established involved either caretaking or control. When it was caretaking, it was easy to not allow the other to really know her, since the main focus was on taking care of that other. When it was trying to maintain control or have the upper hand, she allowed other people in only as far as she wanted them. Both represent lopsided relationships.

Isolation has also played a major role during the eating disorder, and therefore, most relationships have suffered in some way. Throughout recovery it is important to reevaluate past and present relationships. The most significant is the relationship with self. Until a sound relationship with self develops, it remains difficult to make amends with others. So much time has been spent by the eating-disordered person beating herself up that little room is left to put damaged relationships back together.

The third component deals with family. Of the dilemmas that deal with other people, family is the most difficult. Without mincing words, the family system has a major role in the eating disorder. Most people with eating disorders feel as though they don't fit into the family unit. Sometimes this is realistic and sometimes it's not. This is not to say the family is to blame. What we are suggesting is that the combination of the messages given to a young child and how this child perceives them is an important part of the foundation of an eating disorder. It's difficult for any of us to experience a family member in either emotional or physical pain—especially when this pain is self-imposed. Throughout recovery it becomes vital to take stock in relationships with family. Most often it is centered around parents and siblings. When working on this issue we often ask that the eating-disordered person begin to see her parents as people. They will always be Mom and Dad, but just as she is taking a step back to look at herself and the person she presents to the world, it's equally important to view her parents in the same way. What type of people are they and what traits do they bring into their own relationships? Unfortunately, she may not always like the people she sees. In the past, this was never questioned, but because recovery means questioning everything, it cannot go untouched.

The eating disorder itself has more than likely disrupted the family system. Even though it feels like the patient is the only person going through it, the family members in some way go through it with her. This in itself presents another dilemma. She can spend much of her time, energy, and effort feeling bad or guilty for having put them through this whole ordeal *or* she can accept that it has happened and continue on the yellow brick road. We're not saying it's as easy as it sounds, just offering a little "food for thought."

Our experience has been that dealing with family issues in and of itself creates a tremendous amount of upheaval. What the person with an eating disorder likes to disregard sometimes is that although family is family, they cannot read minds. The family only knows what she shares with them. Remember, in dysfunctional families a key component that is usually missing is the ability to communicate how one feels.

When the person in recovery looks at family issues, understands, and begins to confront them, frustration builds because the rest of the family may not have taken a look or changed their perspective on things. This is one of the most common omplaints we hear. And yet more dilemmas: stay in the family dwelling or leave, accepting that things aren't going to change; suggest family therapy or (what one experienced in the past) go back to the old behaviors because it's less painful—or seems so—than fighting the odds. Remember, recovery is a process. The patient may find herself doing all of the above at one time or another. The most important part is to take care of herself.

The eating-disordered person grieves for many things throughout the recovery process. Initially there is the loss of hiding behind a substance—food—to deal with life. There is a loss of some significant relationships. There is a loss felt from giving up whatever role she played in the family, and separating emotionally from those family members; and finally there is the loss of therapy and the therapist. All of these losses need to be addressed, for without fully grieving there remains a feeling of unfinished business.

With each loss there is a gain. Life without an eating disorder allows the person time to explore and to take from it what she may. New relationships are formed and the old ones are reintroduced. Separating and letting go is a healthy, normal part of life.

FOR FURTHER READING

Bradshaw, J. (1988). *Healing the shame that binds you.* Deerfield Beach, FL: Health Communications.

Erikson, E. (1968). *Childhood and society.* New York: Norton.
Kübler-Ross, E. (1969). *On death and dying.* New York: Macmillan.
Levenkron, S. (1979). *The best little girl in the world.* New York: Warner Books.
O'Gorman, P., & Oliver-Diaz, P. (1990). *Self-parenting 12 Step workbook.* Deefield Beach, FL: Health Communications.
Sandbek, T. (1986). *The deadly diet.* Oakland, CA: New Harbinger.
Siegel, M., Brisman, J., & Weinshel, M. (1988). *Surviving an eating disorder: Strategies for family and friends.* New York: Bantam Books.
Wholey, D. (1988). *Becoming your own parent: The solution for ACOA and other dysfunctional families.* New York: Bantam Books.
Woititz, J. (1985). *Struggle for intimacy.* Deerfield Beach, FL: Health Communications.

REFERENCES

American Psychiatric Association. (1987). *Diagnostic and statistical manual of mental disorders* (3rd ed., rev., DSM-III-R). Washington, DC: Author.
Bradshaw, J. (1988). *Healing the shame that binds you.* Deerfield Beach, FL: Health Communications.

22

Counseling College Students

JAMES ARCHER, Ph.D.

Psychologists, psychiatrists, and other mental health counselors spend years learning how to provide effective counseling and psychotherapy, yet much of the *basic* process of counseling is not all that complicated. As a faculty member, relative, friend, or advisor you can learn to be very helpful to college students by being a wise and understanding listener. Although the process of basic counseling and listening is not complicated, it is also not easy. You need to develop the skills and insight to do it well. The purpose of this chapter is to outline some of the basic skills and behaviors that make a good "counselor." I do this with some reservation because I know that many students need more than just "basic" counseling, and I know that there are many complex and useful theories of counseling and psychotherapy that go well beyond what I plan to discuss. Also, I should note that I am referring here to individual, one-on-one counseling, not group counseling.

Since my purpose is to help many different kinds of people learn to be better counselors to college students, I will outline some of the basic principles of good counseling and at the same time discuss limits and situations when more than just a basic approach is needed. For most college students, effective listening and support in sorting through alternatives and possible changes can be enormously helpful. Human beings, including college students, have great potential to improve and chart their own growth.

STEPS FOR EFFECTIVE COUNSELING

At the risk of greatly oversimplifying, I have outlined seven steps for effective counseling. These steps are basic, and have been described in

---

This chapter is adapted from Archer, J., *Counseling College Students* (New York: Crossroad, 1991).

various ways in many studies and books. These steps include the following:

1. Listen and establish a working relationship.
2. Develop a focus.
3. Contract to counsel the student or refer him or her to a professional.
4. Establish realistic alternatives and goals.
5. Devise an action plan.
6. End counseling and evaluate.

1. Listen and Establish a Working Relationship

Define the relationship. Before you can do any counseling, you have to provide the right setting and establish some agreement on what is going to occur. *Counseling* is defined as "one person helping another person." Therefore, you must agree on roles. Counseling is not a free-flowing conversation where each person tells about his or her problems. Not that this can't be helpful or enjoyable—it just isn't counseling. Counseling may evolve from a conversation, but there needs to be a clear signal that the interaction has moved from a conversation to counseling. For example, if a student is talking with a faculty member after class and begins to discuss a personal problem he or she has with another student, the faculty member should, at some point, decide whether or not he or she wants to counsel the student. If the faculty member does, then an appropriate statement might be, "It sounds like you would like to talk about your problems with anxiety. I have some time now. Would you like to talk?" An alternate response might be, "Look, I can tell that you need to talk with someone about your feelings. Can we set up a time tomorrow and I will be glad to discuss the situation with you?" Although it happens very frequently, I don't think that it is a good idea to slide into a counseling or helping role without some understanding and agreement by both parties. You don't have to be overly formal about it, but some acknowledgment is really useful. Even when two friends are talking and one is in need of counseling or just a sympathetic ear, one person needs to take the role of helper and one of helpee. One other important point: By agreeing to listen to what is troubling someone, you are not necessarily agreeing to spend the next three months being his or her counselor. In fact, you may very soon decide that you cannot deal with the problem and suggest a referral. You do, however, need to realize that once a person opens up to you, you have some obligation to help see him or her through, at least until he or she can find help elsewhere. If you don't really want to get involved, don't.

I said earlier that any friend, faculty member, college staff member, or family member can be helpful and serve in some capacity as a student's counselor. Let me include some reservations now that have to do with roles. In many close relationships it is difficult or impossible to serve as a counselor or helper to another person. Parents, for example, often cannot serve as counselors to their own children, or husbands to wives, or friends to each other. The emotional connections and closeness often make it difficult for the listener or counselor to perform effectively in that role. Keep in mind that emotional complications can make some helping relationships impossible. Also, remember that one of the great benefits of a professional counselor or therapist is that he or she is already in a kind of helping and objective role. Faculty members, student personnel workers, ministers, and student counselors provide a certain level of objectivity.

Once the parameters of a counseling relationship have been established, you need to worry about some mundane issues like where you are going to talk. Counseling sessions need to be held in a private place where there will be no interruptions. Again, some definition of what is going to occur will help you set the stage and find an appropriate setting. Privacy and attention help a person focus on his or her problems and they help you as the counselor attend to the person 100%. The issue of time is also important. If you are going to talk with a student about a particular issue, you need to think about how much time you have to give. Don't get started listening to a student who has an emotional issue to discuss if you only have 10 minutes to spare. Although it may be difficult not to be immediately responsive, you will be better off and more effective if you ask the student to come back when you can give him or her enough time.

Good listening is probably the most, or at least one of the most, crucial parts of counseling. In order to be a good listener you must be completely attuned to what the other person is saying. You must realize that your own needs to talk, share stories, and give advice will have to take second place, at least for the time being, in order to really hear the other person.

Attend to your nonverbal behavior. Your nonverbal behavior is very important. Some very good listeners don't say much at all. They express their caring and concern partly by the way they communicate without words. To do this you must face the person, have good eye contact, and express your interest and openness by your body. Head nods and other small gestures often communicate that you are listening and following. If you haven't had any formal training in counseling it may be difficult for you to assess just how well you communicate nonverbally. Consider two levels of this behavior. The first level involves your basic body orientation to the other person and is partly related to how you set up a counseling session. If you try to counsel students from behind a desk or in a setting that doesn't have comfortable chairs with a comfortable space between them, you are not providing a good, open counseling situation. Having a desk between you and someone you hope to counsel tends to decrease the effectiveness of nonverbal communication. If you are a professor, administrator, or someone who talks with students in your office where you also have a desk, you should arrange chairs somewhere else for counseling purposes.

Practice active listening. Nonverbal behavior, however, isn't enough by itself. The student must perceive that you understand what he or she is saying and feeling. Asking for help or telling someone about a personal problem can be quite scary, and the counselee often watches the counselor closely for signs that the counselor is really understanding him or her. Verbal responses that indicate the counselor's understanding are very important. The process of giving these verbal responses is called *active listening*. This means that you, as a listener, periodically let the other person know that you are following and understanding him or her. This is done most effectively by what is called a *reflection*. A reflection is basically paraphrasing what a person has just said. For counseling purposes, paraphrases usually focus on what feelings the other person has expressed. By letting the student know that you have some understanding of his or her feelings you are able to demonstrate your *empathic understanding* of him or her. Since every person and every student thinks and feels in some unique ways, it is essential for a counselor to try to understand this uniqueness and the student's special frame of reference. Following are two examples of paraphrasing and reflection of empathic understanding. (Note how the empathic responses encourage the student to explore the situation and his or her feelings further.)

Example 1

STUDENT: I just can't follow what the professor is saying. He goes so fast and never stops to see if anyone has any questions. Sometimes I think I will stand up in class and scream.

COUNSELOR: You are *really* frustrated with this situation and sometimes feel like you can't take it anymore.

Example 2

STUDENT: I don't know what is wrong. I just don't feel very happy anymore. I even start to cry for no reason.

COUNSELOR: You seem to be very sad and maybe depressed, and you can't seem to figure out why.

As you read these examples, remember that paraphrasing is something that you particularly need to do during step 1 of a counseling situation. It helps you establish rapport and build a working relationship. You wouldn't necessarily continue with this paraphrasing forever. By requiring you to come up with a succinct restatement of the students feelings, paraphrasing will challenge you to listen more closely. In other words, this method forces you to try harder to be empathic.

Don't give advice too soon. During the initial phase of counseling, there are a number of responses that tend to interfere with the development of a good working relationship. One very common mistake is to give advice too soon. Although a student may actually come to you for advice, unless you listen and really hear what is bothering him or her your advice will have limited value. Other students receive advice from too many others, when what they really want is to feel understood and to have someone help them figure out solutions for themselves. We all like to come up with our own solutions, and often a solution or course of action is only meaningful and useful after we have worked it out in our own minds. Premature advice giving in a counseling situation forecloses this possibility and it also prevents a listener from establishing an effective working relationship.

Don't be judgmental. Being judgmental can also abruptly stop the development of rapport that is the hallmark of a good counseling/helping relationship. If a student tells you about something that you believe is wrong, stupid, or dangerous, a judgmental response can stop communication. Following are two examples of *inappropriate* judgmental statements.

Example 1

STUDENT: After I took her home I went out and got really drunk, then I drove home and slept it off. Boy, did I have a hangover that next morning.

COUSELOR: Terry, I thought you were smarter than that. Don't you know that it is very dangerous to drink and drive?

Example 2

STUDENT: I am really scared about being pregnant. How can I have a baby when I'm not even finished with college? I don't know what to do or how I feel.

COUNSELOR: You do sound confused, but I am sure that you don't want to consider abortion. Let's talk about some other options.

In example 1, the counselor is certainly right; drinking and driving are very dangerous, but what needs to be explored at this point is Terry's feelings and his motivation for drinking. If Terry has an alcohol problem you, as the counselor, are much more likely to get him to confront his dangerous behavior *after* you have established a working relationship and have established yourself as someone who cares and understands some of the reasons for his drinking. In example 2, the counselor is more subtle about expressing her judgment. In this case, she steers the client away from considering all options and from freely expressing her feelings about these options. Although counseling is never really value-free, the counselor has an obligation not to impose his or her values on a student who is coming for help.

Don't talk about yourself. Focus on the person you are counseling. One other trap into which many novice counselors blunder is bringing in a similar situation or feeling from their own life. In general, this is not appropriate in the early stages of counseling. The focus must remain on the student who is being counseled. Bringing in your own experiences can be appropriate sometimes later on in counseling. However, in this early stage it will only distract you and the student from dealing with the problem at hand.

Don't ask too many questions. Generally it is better to paraphrase or nod your head to encourage a person to continue talking. Direct questions can distract the person and, at their worst, can block the development of empathy and rapport. If you must ask questions, make them short and open-ended. Questions can be useful and effective if used in moderation and if you don't get distracted into asking for irrelevant details. Following are some questions and phrases that can be helpful if they are used along with effective paraphrasing and reflecting:

Can you tell me more?
I don't think I understand. Can you go over that again?
Please go on.
Can you help me understand how you were feeling?
I don't think I am following you. Can you repeat that?
How were you feeling then?

2. Develop a Focus

After you have a good working relationship and a reasonable idea of what is bothering the student (and by the way, this won't always happen), it is time to help the student sort out and focus on the central issues. Often, students who seek counseling are overwhelmed by thoughts and emotions so that they can't really make any sense out of what is happening to them. A person serving as a counselor can help the student understand and identify the main issues at hand.

Consider the example of Janet: Janet comes to her English professor crying, and tells him that she feels depressed all of the time and can't get any work done. She reports that her friends are getting tired of her being down so much and are starting to avoid her. As her teacher talks with her, he begins to understand that much of Janet's sadness and depression is related to the loss of her mother. Her sadness centers around feeling alone and missing the closeness that she and her mother shared. She had a very close relationship with her mother (they talked on the phone several times a week), and she hasn't really had that kind of support since her mother died. Over the summer she was with the rest of her family and felt supported at home, but since coming back to school she hasn't had anybody with whom she can really talk.

The focus of counseling in this situation would probably be Janet's feelings about losing her mother, her loneliness for someone to support her, and her need to become more independent and function with the support of other friends.

Another illustration of developing a focus in counseling is that of Eric: Eric is a new college student. He is 28 and is just going back to college. He had been in the army for 6 years and finally decided that he wanted to go to school to become an engineer. By November of his first semester he is overwhelmed by the academic work of an engineering curriculum. He discusses the situation with his academic advisor, who notes that he seems very anxious. He reports that he hasn't been sleeping or eating well, and he says that he just can't get all of the work done. He is thinking about leaving school and feels like a failure. His decision to come back to school was a hard one, and now he feels like it was a mistake. As his advisor talks with Eric he realizes that Eric just doesn't know how to study or manage his time. He seems like a very bright student and does not have other problems that are interfering with his academic progress. (Note that the advisor learns about his lack of other problems by asking some questions and actively listening to Eric.)

This case illustrates a situation where the focus of counseling might be on developing study and time-management skills. By responding to this student's feelings, and listening to what he was feeling, the advisor was able to help Eric realize that his study-skill deficits and study behavior were the basic problems. The beginning step and patient listening were very important in order to determine an appropriate focus for counseling.

As another, extreme example, Mark was called in to talk with his residence hall advisor because the other students on the floor were worried about him. He was spending almost all of his time in his room and he often seemed very depressed. In the conversation with his residence advisor, he revealed the fact that he had been chronically depressed for a long time and that, as he put it, his family situation was really screwed up. He said that his father didn't love him and that both of his parents would just as soon not have to deal with him. He also expressed considerable self-hate and couldn't really believe that any of the students on his floor really liked him. Mark's situation illustrates a case where the issues are so complex that referral to a professional psychologist or psychiatrist is necessary.

3. Contract to Counsel the Student
or Refer Him or Her to a Professional

In all three of the previous examples, the faculty member or advisor reached a point early in the interaction where a decision had to be made about whether to continue or to make a referral. This decision should come as early as possible in the interaction. In other words, after the initial counseling is structured ("Yes, I have some time to talk to you about your feelings of sadness"), there is a decision point where the person taking on the counseling role must decide where to go next. This decision is not an easy one for a nonprofessional counselor, since it requires an assessment of the situation. In examples 1 and 2 in the previous section (Janet, the student who was depressed because she no longer had her mother to depend upon; and Eric, the 28-year-old new student who needed help with time-management and study skills), the counselor made an assessment that he or she could be helpful and was willing to spend some time counseling the student. In example 3 (the case of Mark who was chronically depressed), the advisor decided that he couldn't counsel the student after he learned more about the situation.

In all three cases discussed, and as a general principle, the need for referral or the agreement to continue with counseling should be explicit. A contract of some sort needs to be agreed upon before proceeding. This may seem too formal for a few help sessions between a teacher or advisor and student, but an understanding at the beginning about what will and will not happen can save considerable misunderstanding later.

The case of Mark, who needs to be referred, is more difficult. Don't let your need to help or your sympathy for a student override your own best judgment. It will be much fairer for the student in the long run if you get him or her to a professional when the need is there.

4. Establish Realistic Alternatives and Goals

Many novice counselors get impatient with step 1, where the major goal is to understand, express empathy, and get the story and feelings out. They want to do something, to get the student moving, to target some specific changes. Clearly there is a place for action in counseling, but only after you have sufficiently explored the problem and determined what kind of action really needs to happen. This can only come through discussion and mutual agreement by the student and counselor.

It is important to note here that there is not always a need in counseling for working on goals and alternatives. Sometimes all a student wants or needs is to be understood and heard. Many times when a student comes into my counseling office he or she already knows what needs to be done, but just doesn't have the courage or motivation to proceed. In reality, much of counseling is encouragement. As a counselor you encourage students to take risks and to develop themselves in positive ways. Usually the student needs help clarifying, articulating, and achieving goals, but sometimes just listening is enough.

When you are dealing with students with whom goals need to be defined and discussed, remember that these goals should be somewhat specific. Wanting to be happier and feel less depressed are certainly reasonable goals, but they are a bit too vague to focus on in counseling. In a case where a student articulated these goals for counseling, you would need to help the student get more specific. If you have spent time listening and building rapport with the student, you will probably have some ideas about what the student might do to improve his or her situation. Let's say that a student, John, is unhappy and depressed because he is not studying, is getting pressure from his parents to be more serious about school, feels that he is just floating, can't get motivated, and is not sure he even wants to be in school. He is very unhappy and depressed because of these problems. What can he do? The first step in goal setting is to have a student identify some goals (changed behaviors, activities, etc.) that he thinks would improve his situation. In this case John listed the following:

1. Get motivated and be more successful academically.
2. Get his parents to stop pressuring him.
3. Work out more (exercise).
4. Ask some girls out.

A student should be asked to spend some time thinking about the goals, so it was not at all unreasonable to ask John to bring in a list of goals to a counseling session. In this case, after reviewing these goals, the counselor raised a number of questions. First, does John really want to be in school? What is his academic/career goal? Since he is not certain about being in school, he probably doesn't really have a goal. This may be a factor that negatively affects his motivation and it may also precipitate some of the pressure from his parents. The goal to work out more may mean that he is generally apathetic and feels as if he needs to improve his general health, or it may mean that he wants to improve his appearance and be related to his desire to ask some girls out on dates. Wanting to ask some girls out probably means that he is not happy socially and that he may feel isolated and as if he is not where he should or wants to be with women.

So, John has a number of things to work on. After more discussion, the following goals were agreed on:

1. Make a clear decision about school—whether to stay and really try, or drop out and work.
2. Talk to his parents about his feeling of pressure and share his thinking about the decision as to whether to leave school.
3. In the meantime, no matter what the decision, work on health and physical fitness.
4. Get involved in career-choice and career-development activities.
5. Begin to ask some girls out on dates.

For each of these specific goals, then, the counselor and student need to generate alternatives. Take goal 1. Here are some possible alternatives:

1. Stay in school until the end of the semester and begin to look for a job that is in some way career-related.
2. Withdraw from school immediately and go home.
3. Drop out, work, and attend night school.
4. Drop out, travel, and find out what the world is really like.
5. Stay in school and work on achieving the other goals so that school will be a more positive and useful experience.

Setting goals and outlining alternatives, when appropriate, may take some time and effort. Some students are not used to the process of thinking and deciding for themselves. They may actually expect the person who is their counselor to make decisions for them or they may feel that, even if they do make a decision to do something, they can't actually do it.

In addition to understanding and empathy, persuasion and power are important aspects of a counseling relationship. The counselor must often persuade the student to try new behavior and to change faulty thinking and beliefs. A combination of understanding, encouragement, and persuasion is often necessary. Take the example of a student who has never been very sure of himself. His father is a very critical man and has always focused on his son's shortcomings and failings. The son grew up believing that he wasn't very competent and developed an overly cautious, conservative approach to most aspects of life. In college he is well liked and respected by his classmates, and several of his fraternity brothers have encouraged him to run for the presidency of his fraternity. He is afraid to become a candidate and is very confused about the situation. Counseling, in this case, will involve helping the student develop the courage to risk seeing himself differently. If the risk pays off, even if he doesn't win, he will probably learn a very valuable piece of information about himself that may have profound implications for his future. Understanding, persuasion, and encouragement will all be important factors.

Some attention to skills can also be helpful. In the above example, the student does not have some of the interpersonal skills that he thinks are important to run for his fraternity office. He may never have been in a similar situation because of his belief that he wasn't very competent, fostered by an overcritical father. The lack of skill could take the form of his being very nervous about making a required speech to the entire fraternity. Part of what the counselor does might be directed at helping him learn something about this kind of speech making and how to manage the attendant anxiety.

5. Devise an Action Plan

After the counselor and student have set up goals and considered different options for achieving the goals, it is time to devise an action plan. In this stage of counseling the counselor becomes a kind of coach, helping the student carry out a plan that will bring him or her closer to the established goals. There are several things to consider when working with a student on an action plan:

1. Create small steps so that the student has a good chance of success.
2. Reinforce and encourage success.
3. Plan for some failures.
4. Practice needed new verbal and other skills when necessary (i.e., rehearse conversations, practice taking notes, practice relaxation techniques).
5. Use available resources.
6. Set a timetable, but be flexible.

The key to much positive change and improvement is in being creative about setting steps toward a larger goal. What small action steps might be taken in pursuit of this goal? Often, making a start is the most important step in the counseling process. The use of reinforcement and encouragement can be a bit paradoxical in counseling, because the general goal of counseling is to help a student become self-sufficient and independent, not to rely upon another person for support. This kind of encouragement and reinforcement allows the student to develop confidence and skills, and to eventually learn how to become more self-sufficient.

Setting a timetable is one of the most difficult parts of an action plan. The counselor must respect the student's readiness, yet he or she needs to provide some impetus to get the student started. Many times there is considerable reticence and fear on the student's part. The best approach is to involve the student in setting a timetable and checking in with progress periodically. This provides some impetus to accomplish, and also allows the counselor to monitor progress and to deal with unexpected difficulties and circumstances as needed. Committing the timetable to writing in some form of contract can be helpful. Research has shown that when people commit themselves in writing they are more likely to carry through with their commitment. Be careful about trying to accomplish too many action steps at one time. For example, in this case the advisor was wise not to attempt to deal with the dating goal along with everything else. Often, the counselor and student must do some prioritizing to decide where to start.

6. End Counseling and Evaluate

I alluded to the problem of dependence when I discussed the paradox of providing considerable support and encouragement while at the same time working toward more self-sufficiency and independence. As a counselor, you must find the right time to end your counseling relationship when the student has made some progress and can go off and continue to use what he or she has learned in counseling. Sometimes counselors and students have a tendency to continue too long because they are both gratified by the relationship and the progress being made. Continuing too long is also impractical from a time standpoint for the counselor and can be harmful to the student if it gives the message that you, as the counselor, don't trust the student enough to go out on his or her own.

A gradual termination of counseling can be helpful. Some faculty members and others serving as counselors maintain a kind of as-needed relationship with students, seing them periodically to check on their progress. This system can work well if it is used judiciously. My own preference is for a kind of formal ending. In reality, the counseling relationship should be established with an ending in mind. Professionals often discuss "termination" issues when they finish counseling someone. These issues have to do with the difficulty both clients and counselors have in saying good-bye. A counseling relationship, by definition, is a close one that brings two people together to discuss very personal material. It is not unusual for both parties to develop affectionate feelings and to enjoy their contacts. Two things can help during the final few sessions: First, the counselor should remind the student that they will only be seeing each other once or twice more. This will allow both parties to begin to process their feelings and to prepare for the termination. Second, the counselor should encourage the student to talk about feelings and fears about going out on his or her own.

This entire discussion, with all of the steps and advice, may seem a bit too involved for much of the short-term counseling that faculty and other staff might do with students. In reality, you will often not be able to go through all of these desired procedures. I have presented them in the hope that they will help you understand a kind of basic model. Naturally, they may have to be modified according to individual student needs.

Some of the steps do seem especially crucial to me and I would recommend not bypassing them if at all possible. First, you must establish rapport and listen to what a student is saying. No matter how pressed you are for time, jumping in immediately with a solution, even if it seems most efficient, will not help in the long run. Second, make certain that you and the client have some agreement on process and goals. That is, you should both agree that you will provide some counseling toward some specified goals. Lastly, I urge you to gain familiarity with the mental health and other important resources on your campus. If you enter into even informal and apparently manageable counseling relationships, you will often find more complex and difficult problems under the surface. Be prepared to make referrals and to deal with this likelihood. It also helps to have a contact in the counseling center or some other comparable agency with someone whom you can use as a consultant when necessary. There is certainly no need to feel unsuccessful if a referral is necessary. If you help a student begin to deal with some more serious problem that is very likely to interfere with his or her life later on, you are doing that student a great service.

DEPRESSION AND SUICIDE

In over 20 years of counseling college students, my worst moments, by far, have been those few times when I have found myself talking with the parents of students who had committed suicide. Trying to help these parents understand why their children, in the prime of life, chose to end their lives is not something that I can recall without still feeling pain and sorrow. The circumstances in each of these cases were different, yet also similar. None of them had sought professional help (as is often the case), yet in retrospect they all gave out some signs of distress. The reasons for college student suicide are varied and complex. Sometimes students just tire and give up on dealing with a long-standing problem or feeling of failure. They may be unable to cope with an intense depression because of a lost love, or they just may not be able to cope with the pain of depression and hopelessness any longer.

Suicide is one of the leading causes of death for young people between 18 and 24, and there has been an increase in the number of completed suicides among people in this age group during the last several decades. Suicidal thoughts are not uncommon among college students. Thirty-two percent of the students questioned in one recent survey said that they had thought of committing suicide and 81% reported experiencing depression since attending college. In addition to clearly identifiable suicides, researchers have theorized that many automobile accidents and self-destructive behavior with drugs and alcohol represent suicidal behavior in college students.

Suicide and depression are difficult problems for professional psychologists and counselors to handle, and they are certainly problematic for nonprofessional counselors. Although nearly every student feels down and depressed at one time or another, assessment of student depression and its seriousness is difficult. The following information about depression and suicide should help you better understand student depression and its connection to suicidal thinking and behavior. As a general rule, a faculty member or other person acting as a counselor should consider referral for any student who is severely depressed or who has been depressed for more than a week or two, and for any student who exhibits any of the covert or overt signs of suicide.

Depression

Depression is considered a mood disorder by psychologists and psychiatrists. Because a person's mood tends to color his or her outlook on everything, being depressed has a significant impact on a student's entire life. It can be useful to view depression on a continuum with minor depression, often characterized as the blues or being in a bad mood on one end, and severe, life threatening hopelessness on the other. In severe depression a person tends to withdraw from the world and may even have trouble getting up out of bed in the morning. Traditional-age college students often feel depressed when they cannot adequately cope with all of the stressors they encounter. Sometimes the combination of trying to perform and satisfy all of the demands on their time, and slow or limited progress in major developmental task areas (development of a solid sense of identity and successful love relationships), create frequent depressions.

Usually it is not very difficult to tell when a student is depressed. Most of us show our depression in facial expressions and body language. However, some students do manage to hide depression and give no clues as to how bad they feel. In addition to physical appearance there are many signs of depression:

Frequent crying, uncontrolled sadness.
Feeling apathetic, not caring about anything.
Inability to have fun or experience positive feelings.
Feeling personally worthless, generally unsuccessful.
Loss of positive feeling about friends.
Withdrawal from friends.
Guilt and self-blame.
Failure to take care of self; disheveled appearance.
Lack of energy.
Loss of appetite or overeating.
Physical complaints (headaches and other aches and pains).
Reduced coping skills.
Poor concentration.

In assessing the seriousness of depression the clearest indicators are length of the depression, degree to which it interferes with a student's functioning, and the intensity as experienced by the student. If a student reports being depressed for more than a week or two, this is probably a signal that he or she has not been able to utilize normal coping mechanisms to overcome a depression. Current life circumstances, and the severity and complexity of stressors or problems, are important in assessing depression. Usually short-term and minor depressions are related to a particular situation, do not significantly interfere with a student's lfe, and will begin to lift as the student gains perspective and begins to cope with the situation.

The following is an example of one of these more typical situational depression periods: Mark, who was normally a very reliable graduate assistant and who took his responsibilities as a lab instructor very seriously, missed two lab sessions with his students in 2 weeks. His advisor noticed that he looked terrible, as if he hadn't slept well in several nights, and called him in for a talk. As the advisor began to inquire what was going on, Mark started to cry and reported that his best friend in high school, with whom he had kept in close touch, had been killed in an automobile accident 2 weeks ago. Mark said that he had been severely depressed since then, feeling that nothing really mattered. The advisor asked him about whether he had ever been this depressed before, and Mark could only remember one or two other times in his life when he felt so bad. The advisor helped Mark understand his grief reaction and suggested to him that he would probably feel sad for a long time about the loss of his friend. He asked Mark to talk about the friend and to tell him about some of the things that they did together in high school. The advisor also suggested that Mark go home for a few days to be with his parents and to spend time with his friend's family. Mark took this advice and upon his return he saw his advisor again and reported that he still felt sad, but that he felt able to go on with his life and his responsibilities.

This is an example of a fairly intense, but situational, depression. Although I suggested that depression might be viewed on a continuum, this example demonstrates that the intensity of the depression doesn't necessarily parallel the seriousness. In this case a situation created an intense depression that was an appropriate response to a real event. A less-intense depression that lasted for many weeks, in response to less well defined and more internal stressors, would be more serious. Mark was responding to his friend's death in an appropriate way, and he needed time to deal with his emotions about the death of his friend. His advisor wisely suggested that he seek some support from family and loved ones.

Harkum's situation is quite different: He had been coming into his honors seminar in American history looking depressed and somewhat disoriented for several weeks. He was apathetic and not involved in the class or with other students. He had also not completed the last three writing assignments. Upon being called in by his professor, he reported that he just couldn't get into the course. Further discussion revealed that he had few friends and that he didn't really have any particular goal or ambition for the future. He described his high school years as insignificant and said that few people liked him because he didn't talk about cars and athletics. He told the professor that he remembered being depressed on and off throughout much of his childhood.

This example of depression is quite different from the previous one. Harkum has been periodically depressed for many years, seems to be generally isolated, and may have a number of other psychological problems. In this case the professor would be wise to refer Harkum to a mental health or counseling center for evaluation and treatment.

Many other examples of student depression could be described here. Following are two very short descriptions with an indication of the potential seriousness: In the first case, Jan is a sophomore who has been depressed for several weeks because she has a general feeling that she is not living up to her potential. She has not found a major and isn't really certain what she should study in school. Although the causes of Jan's depression are not very well defined, this depression is probably not terribly serious and seems to be primarily a response to Jan's uncertainty about school. Some discussion about career and life goal choices, with career counseling and encouragement to take a more active approach to her situation, would probably help her depression. Of course, more information, particularly about her depression symptoms and previous history would be necessary before an accurate assessment of seriousness could be made.

Jeffrey, on the other hand, has bounced between his mother and father since he was 13, and he feels immature, and unwanted by his parents, and he has a low self-concept. He has few friends and feels that he will never really make it in college. He has been unhappy for several years and his feeling of depression has gotten worse since he came to college. Jeffrey is clearly a person who needs professional help. His depression is serious and is related to a number of personal psychological problems. It is not a reaction to a particular situation or set of events.

Isolation and the loss of a love relationship are probably the most frequent causes of depression. Students who lose a fiancé or lover often feel that they can never have another relationship as meaningful, and in extreme cases even contemplate suicide because of this loss. Also, students who have yearned for companionship, and someone to love and to love them, may finally stop being hopeful that they will ever find someone.

For common depressions, those related to a specific situation or loss or the feeling of blues and being down in the dumps that we all get, there are some simple, yet effective, ways to help students help themselves:

1. *Increase activity level.* One of the most effective ways to combat depression is to do something productive or enjoyable. Students often feel apathetic and have low energy when they are depressed. Forcing themselves to go out, start a project, call a friend, or anything requiring action and attention will help the depression.

2. *Work at regaining perspective.* Students who are depressed often start to see many different aspects of their lives in negative terms. Depression is often described as a kind of cloud hanging over the victim's head, affecting everything he or she does. Talking to a friend about depression and related feelings can help a student gain perspective. This doesn't mean that the friend can necessarily cheer him or her up, but a friend can help one to verbalize one's feelings and begin to gain a bit more control over them.

3. *Take a vacation—get away.* This isn't always possible, but even a day or two away from whatever is stressing a student can be very helpful. Perhaps a weekend away from campus or a short trip, even an inexpensive camping trip, will provide the necessary distance and perspective. Often, depressed students need a bit of a push to do this. Be careful not to suggest a trip alone for people who need companionship or who might be more depressed than they are admitting.

4. *Get back to regular exercise, decent meals, a reasonable schedule.* Usually students who are depressed have slipped out of a healthy and balanced lifestyle (if they had one originally). Just getting back into the routine of

a regular schedule that includes exercise, meals, and other scheduled activities can, in itself, be very therapeutic.

5. *Set a time limit.* Many students experience depression as a result of a difficult situation or personal setback. Depression and sadness is really an appropriate response to what has happened. The problem often is not being able to move out of the depression and get on with one's life. It can be helpful to set a time limit for depression. For example, if a student loses an opportunity for a really excellent internship that he or she had been counting on, it is certainly appropriate to feel depressed. It is not, however, appropriate to remain depressed for weeks. Sometimes it can be helpful to allow oneself a certain period to feel bad, and even to bask in self-pity a bit, if there is a clear limit to this activity. A student may be able to gain some control with this limit-setting strategy. Another variation of this technique is to have a student set aside specific times of the day to feel depressed and to experience sad feelings.

Depression can also be related to biochemical factors. Considerable advances have been made in the use of antidepressant medication in the treatment of depression, although much controversy still exists over the best way to treat various kinds of depression. Certain kinds of depression seem to be at least partly biochemical in nature, and a history of frequent depression can indicate that a student might profit from drug treatment. A history of depression in the immediate family can also be a strong indicator of possible biochemical depression.

Another biochemical factor to consider in assessing depression is the abuse of alcohol or other drugs. Depression and mood are, of course, clearly affected by all of the most common drugs on campus. Alcohol, marijuana, cocaine, amphetamines, and other drugs are most often used to induce pleasure. Students who are depressed and unhappy are particularly prone to look for chemical happiness. All of these drugs can provide temporary relief, in one way or another, for vexing problems and ongoing depression. Unfortunately, their continued use and abuse exacerbates depression and can lead to drug dependence. Students are particularly prone to use drugs and alcohol to cope with depression when they have no other coping skills.

Depression and the propensity toward being depressed is also related to a student's general personality and approach to life. Some students tend to see the negative side of life and to interpret events in a negative way. These students will experience depression frequently because they tend to see the dark side of most events. Often this approach to life is a rather ingrained personality characteristic and is not easily changed. These kinds of students can be very difficult to deal with in counseling because they often try to argue away any positive encouragement or interpretations offered by the counselor.

Suicide

Students who are depressed sometimes think about and attempt suicide. As a faculty member or person who is involved in counseling, you may uncover depression and suicidal thoughts when you are working with students. Frequently these thoughts and feelings are secret, and when students find someone they trust and who is able to listen and respond to their feelings, they may share painful and hidden thoughts and feelings. Students may also allude to these feelings without mentioning them very explicitly. For example, they may express feelings of hopelessness or make statements like "Well, it doesn't really matter," or "What's the use," or "I'm ready to give up." These feelings and statements don't necessarily mean that the student is suicidal, but they need to be explored. One good rule of thumb, whenever you have a feeling or intuition that a student has suicidal thoughts, is to ask directly. Generally you are better off to ask and risk being wrong. It is highly unlikely that your question will raise the issue for a student.

Suicide and suicidal behavior are much misunderstood. Like sexuality and other topics that we would rather not discuss, a number of myths have developed.

MYTH: *People who talk about suicide don't commit suicide.*

FACT: Most people who kill themselves do give some kind of verbal warning. Certainly many students and others talk about suicide and do not kill themselves, but it is inappropriate to assume that because a person talks about suicide he or she wouldn't carry out on a suicide.

MYTH: *Suicide happens without warning.*

FACT: People who commit suicide usually give clues and warning of their intentions. There are cases where a person gives no warnings, but these are the exception rather than the rule.

MYTH: *Suicidal people really want to die.*

FACT: Most suicidal people, particularly students, are terribly ambivalent about wanting to die. They usually vacillate back and forth, and only kill themselves in a period of extreme depression and hopelessness. Often people who unsuccessfully attempt suicide are very thankful soon after that they didn't succeed.

MYTH: *When a severe depression begins to lift, the risk of suicide is over.*

FACT: Sometimes a partial lifting of depression actually gives the person enough energy to decide on and carry out a suicide plan.

MYTH: *Anyone who is suicidal must be mentally ill.*

FACT: Most people who attempt suicide are not mentally ill. Suicide is usually the only way left that a particular individual can see to cope with his or her pain.

MYTH: *Suicide runs in families and the propensity is inherited.*

FACT: There is no direct evidence that the tendency toward suicide is inherited, although there is some evidence that biochemical depression is inherited, and statistically the probability of someone committing suicide is greater if a parent or other family member has committed suicide.

MYTH: *Most people are too strong to commit suicide.*

FACT: Given the right circumstances and feelings of hopelessness, almost anyone is capable of thinking seriously about suicide.

Clearly, as a faculty member, friend, or advisor of a student you are not in a position to make professional judgments about the severity of suicidal risk. Psychologists and mental health counselors have extensive training in risk assesment, and there are a number of psychological tests available to assess suicidal risk. Usually, if there is a substantial risk of suicide, a counselor or psychologist will intervene in some way and attempt to protect a student from harming himself or herself. The best strategy if you encounter students who are suicidal is to get them to see a professional.

Even though, as a friend, advisor, or faculty member, you are not professionally trained to assess suicidal risk, you will be forced to make decisions about how decisively to act when you become aware of a student who is, or might be, suicidal. First of all remember that you have no choice but to take suicidal talk, even in jest, seriously. Although you need to make every effort to get a professional evaluation, you may have to evaluate suicidal risk yourself. Following are some risk factors for which to be alert:

1. *Clear verbal statements of finality.* "I will be over this pain soon," "I won't have to worry about it much longer," and so on.
2. *Isolation.* Any student who is isolated, lives alone, and/or has no friends is at much greater risk.
3. *Suicide plan and means.* Any student who has a specific plan and who has the means at hand (i.e., has a gun and has thought about driving out into the country to shoot himself or herself, or has decided to do it late at night when his or her roommate is asleep and plans to get drunk and then take a large amount of sleeping pills) is at very great risk.
4. *Chronic depression and hopelessness.* Students who have been depressed a great deal in their lives tend to be less hopeful about

the future, and it may be more difficult for them to recover from serious depression.

5. *Previous attempts.* Students who have previously attempted suicide are more likely to make attempts than those who have not made previous attempts.

6. *Giving away possessions.* This can be a sign that a student has reached a decision to commit suicide and is preparing to die.

7. *Sudden lifting of depression and feeling at rest.* Another possible sign that a suicide decision has been reached.

8. *Terminal illness or very limiting accident/illness.* Students who are dealing with the news that they have a terminal illness or who have been maimed or learned that they will be seriously crippled or physically limited may be suicidal, particularly when they are initially dealing with this information.

9. *Alcohol or substance abuse.* Abusers are at greater risk, particularly for "accidental suicide."

In many of the situations where serious depression or suicide may be involved, it can be very helpful for someone who is not professionally trained to *consult* with a professional. Most psychologists, counselors, and psychiatrists working on college campuses are very cooperative and are willing to talk with faculty, staff, or friends on the phone or in person to help them decide upon a course of action regarding a particularly troublesome student.

Suicide and depression are among the most difficult kinds of student problems for anyone to handle. Although all of us who are part of campus communities do our best to get help for students who are depressed or suicidal, it is not always possible to prevent suicides. Although students usually signal their intent in some way, there are times when a suicide is virtually a complete surprise. It is important to realize that when a suicide occurs there are usually a number of people who are personally affected and who may need support and understanding. As a counselor of college students, you may be one of them. It is natural to feel fear and anxiety about students who are depressed and suicidal. Don't shoulder responsibility for dealing with a student in this situation; seek out consultation and support from professionals and attend to your own feelings.

23

Development in Adulthood

ESTHER LORING CRISPI, M.A.

CELIA B. FISHER, Ph.D.

Development is viewed today as an ongoing and modifiable process characterized by gradual transitions and overlapping tasks across childhood, adolescence, young adulthood, middle age, and old age. At each stage of life, new challenges help our growth and maturity. In addition, new problems and crises may arise.

There is no magical line that neatly separates adolescence from young adulthood. Teenagers do not automatically assume adult perspectives or responsibilities when they reach their 20th birthday. For some early maturing individuals, adulthood may be achieved during the teenage years, while for others circumstances such as a college education may delay young adulthood until the mid-20s.

LIFE-SPAN PERSPECTIVE

A life-span approach to adult development focuses on the growth and changes experienced by people from birth to death. Introduced to this country by Paul Baltes and colleagues, it is characterized by the idea that each of us exists on multiple levels of being, including biological, psychological, social, cultural, and historical levels, which dynamically influence each other over time. Some influences on development are a product of the accumulation of experiences common to an individual's social group and wider culture, and some are uncommon experiences unique to one individual. In addition, each of us brings into any social situation personal style, talents, and expectations. As a consequence of variation in characteristics and life history over the course of adulthood, individuals develop different perspectives and reactions to life events.

A life-span approach to adult development broadens the arena in which counselors can work with adult clients. For example, counselors can explore multiple levels of influence when they work with dual-earner families balancing the responsibilities of employment and child-rearing. In addition to examining the intrapsychic reactions to daily events, counselors can assist clients in considering (a) biological influences such as the relationship between changing energy levels and the physical demands of their jobs, (b) environmental influences such as economic resources and availability of substitute child care, (c) interpersonal issues such as spousal social support and reactions of the children to parental leave taking, and (d) cultural influences including the societal values related to maternal employment and the impact on the wife and husband's self-evaluations and attitudes.

Individual Differences and Variability

All individuals do not grow and develop at the same rate, nor do they experience the same cultural, historical, or age-related events. Individual developmental paths depend on the complex interplay between biological, psychological, and social influences. Physical capabilities, historic events, one's cultural/ethnic identification, and social class are just some of the factors that contribute to the unique development of each individual. Counselors need also keep in mind that the generalizability of current theories of adult development to ethnic minority individuals is still an unexplored area of research.

PSYCHOSOCIAL STAGES AND DEVELOPMENTAL TASKS OF ADULTHOOD

Psychologists often mark the passage from adolescence to young adulthood by achievement of various psychological tasks. Counselors may find it useful to refer to the work of Erik Erikson, who has developed a stage theory describing personality development across the life span. From this perspective personality develops through the resolution of crises marking eight psychosocial life stages. The stages sequentially progress from a focus on trust within early relationships, to development of an integrated self-image, to concern for future generations, and ultimately to a sense of one's place in humanity as a result of maturing social awareness. The stages that emerge after childhood are:

1. *Identity versus role diffusion* (adolescence). One who resolves the task positively has an integrated image of oneself as a complete individual; with negative resolution, the individual is ill at ease and has a shifting idea of self.
2. *Intimacy versus isolation* (early adulthood). With positive resolution, the individual has the ability to form close and intimate relation-

ships; with negative resolution, the individual avoids contact and intimacy.
3. *Generativity versus stagnation* (middle adulthood). The individual who resolves this task positively gains concern for family, society, and future generations; with negative resolution, the individual is self-indulgent and lacks a future orientation.
4. *Integrity versus despair* (aging years). With positive resolution, the individual becomes satisfied with life and has a sense of wholeness; with negative resolution, the individual is disappointed with life and feels futility.

The task characteristic of each stage must be at least partially resolved before the individual proceeds to the next stage, although the dynamics of problem resolution of each stage allow for reemergence of issues throughout the life span. The stages are interdependent, with a more satisfactory resolution of a prior level impacting the successful resolution of more current developmental stages. Since the individual has the capacity for growth and change throughout life, counselors working with adults need to view outcomes of childhood and adolescent psychosocial stages as changeable rather than static, and thus as potential areas of intervention in adulthood.

Psychosocial stages may also be conceptualized within the context of developmental tasks proposed by educator Robert Havighurst. According to Havighurst, successful completion of developmentally appropriate tasks leads to fulfillment and continued success with future tasks, whereas unsuccessful completion leads to personal unhappiness, societal disapproval, and difficulty with other related tasks. The tasks of early and middle adulthood are:

1. *Early adulthood*: selecting a mate, learning to live with a marriage partner, starting a family, rearing children, managing a home, getting started on an occupation, taking on civic responsibility, and finding a congenial social group.
2. *Middle adulthood*: achieving adult civic and social responsibility, establishing and maintaining an economic standard of living, assisting teenage children to become responsible and happy, developing leisure-time activities, relating to one's spouse as a person, accepting and adjusting to the physiological changes of middle age, and adjusting to aging parents.

Eriksonian psychosocial tasks and Havighurst's developmental tasks are interrelated. How an individual approaches Havighurst's tasks of adulthood depends on how one has resolved conflicts associated with psychosocial development. For example, the development of an integrated identity in late adolescence will influence the selection of both occupation and social group membership in early adulthood. Likewise, the ability to achieve intimacy with age peers will influence selection of a marriage partner. The remainder of this chapter will focus on the interplay between the resolution of Erikson's psychosocial stages and mastery of Havighurst's developmental tasks during young and mid-adulthood.

PERSONAL GROWTH IN YOUNG ADULTHOOD

As individuals leave late adolescence, developmental tasks of early adulthood coincide with the psychosocial challenges of identity formation and the ability to form close relationships. The establishment of one's own value system, beliefs, and preferences as well as the ability to form intimate relationships will influence major life choices of marriage and occupation. Individuals who can commit themselves to an intimate relationship have been found to enjoy better physical and mental health than those who cannot. Moreover, intimacy with another can lead to increased self-awareness, security, and attachment. Selection of a career path may reflect personal ideology and express individuality due to the diversity of occupations available to many young adults today. By contrast, individuals who select a career or a mate without having established a secure identity may be subject to confusion and distress.

Employment

Social psychology literature regarding occupational behavior has shown that job commitment is related to loyalty and identification with the place of employment. According to Erikson, these occupational or vocational choices are incorporated into individual ego identity.

Early employment choices may have long-range consequences. In delineating a future career trajectory and eliminating alternate paths, they may impact later personal growth, even in contributing to life satisfaction in old age. Thus, early career choices can influence resolution of Erikson's final psychosocial task, *integrity versus despair*, which entails life review and a determination as to whether one's life has been worthwhile.

Individuals beginning a career may be aware of the developmental aspects of career choices to a greater or lesser degree. Career guidance is often warranted when individuals find themselves in less than optimal job situations, such as underemployment or unemployment, or if they lack goal-directedness. Factors that need to be considered include the economic climate at the time as well as the individual's qualifications and the degree of realistic expectancy for career choice.

In early adulthood, career choices often entail an exploration of various roles. Individual temperament, capabilities, communicative ability, and values may be more or less well suited to a particular job. Both the demands of the job in particular and the expectations of other individuals within the job context can be explored in a counseling session.

Career choices may be viewed as expressions of individual identity; they may contribute to one's identity formation as well. Companies may instill loyalty by providing social activities and services such as day care, job training, and counseling. Loyalty and commitment to a place of employment can help shape an individual's vocational identity.

Newly employed young adults may find that occupational responsibility includes the performance of new roles that may conflict with existing ones. Individuals are known by the roles they play, and each role can reflect different aspects of a person's personality. A job may require one to be authoritative, assertive, and independent. Alternatively, the role of a parent may require one to be nurturing and understanding. Problems may occur when there is a conflict between roles and expectations.

The job may cause problems in other ways. Counseling issues that focus on family/occupational conflicts may include (a) management of the proportion of time spent at each location, (b) prioritization of social activities, (c) choice of friends, and (d) marital partner resentment resulting from noninclusion in work-related activities.

Friendship

A second developmental task of early adulthood is to find a congenial social group. Individuals are much more likely to become friends with those with whom they have close regular contact. Friendships are formed more often with people who live near each other, work together, and go to school together. It is more difficult to maintain long-distance friendships over time, and many friendships tend to diminish when individuals change locations or jobs. At long distances, interests diverge as do their experiences, and it is more of an effort to keep in touch.

The social group provides many things for the young adult. It is a reference group by which the individual can be identified, a source of support and validation for life choices, companionship for leisure-time activities, and comfort in time of need.

Friends are important to young adults, although there are individual differences with respect to the need for affiliation with others. Some individuals have a very high need to form friendships, and others tend to value their independence more. This need may be related to such things as temperament, upbringing, or self-esteem.

Sexuality

Patterns of sexual behavior in our culture are complex and multidimensional from a life span perspective. Individual sexual attitudes and behavior develop throughout life on numerous related levels. The counselor can explore sexual issues from the biological level, including sex drive and sexual orientation. One can also explore interpersonal psychological issues related to relevant past and present sexual relationships. Exploration of the social and cultural aspects of individual sexuality, including relevant value systems, may also be beneficial.

In general, Western cultural views regarding sexuality and premarital, homosexual, and extramarital sex have become more accepting in recent decades. Sexual standards for both males and females have changed toward more acceptance of a variety of sexual behaviors, but not toward acceptance of promiscuity. For an individual who has not yet achieved a stable identity, sexual behavior may reflect role exploration, pressure to conform to peer standards, or an attempt to test self-definition with another. For individuals who have achieved an integrated identity, sexual behavior may reflect an attempt to achieve intimacy with another in a relationship that offers love, friendship, mutuality and reciprocal understanding. Sexual behavior that is unsatisfactory to the young adult may be viewed in terms of individual struggles with Eriksonian intimacy issues and Havighurst's developmental task of selecting a mate.

Sex is generally an important part of early intimate relationships, including marriage. Pregnancy may change sexual behavior considerably. Studies have shown that women's sexual interests fluctuate throughout pregnancy and for a few months or more after giving birth, depending on health and the presence of other children in the household. Men may show decreased sexual interest during their partner's pregnancy and thereafter due to concern for the baby and possible decreased attraction toward their mate. One or both partners may find that sexual feelings seem incompatible with the new role as parent.

Sexual behavior varies according to individual living arrangements, sexual orientation, and commitment to another individual. Numerous young adults are not married, and live either alone, with another individual of the same or opposite sex, or in a group situation. Additionally, patterns of sexual behavior change throughout the life span depending on biological, psychological, and social factors, including gender, age, physical health, and marital status.

Starting and Maintaining an Intimate Relationship

Young adulthood is a time when individuals typically shift from living alone or with the family of origin to cohabitation. Interpersonal bonds may be loosened with parents and siblings and strengthened within the new relationship. According to 1989 U.S. Census figures, 95% of the population is married by age 46, totalling 2 million marriages. However, numerous types of intimate relationships, both sexual and platonic, are available to the young adult today including (a) unmarried cohabitation with a member of the same or opposite sex; (b) nontraditional marriages, including open marriages, where traditional assumptions regarding togetherness and/or fidelity are not adhered to; and (c) communal living.

Numerous studies in the social psychology literature have shown that successful couples have a lot in common. Similar values, leisure-time activities, desires for children, and similarities in sexual preferences and political opinions are all important.

Learning to live with a mate will involve adjustments no matter how well matched the individuals are on values and preferences. Each person brings into the relationship a lifetime of experiences and a unique set of expectations regarding intimate relationships. If intimacy is viewed in terms of sharing one's life and belongings as well as love, it can be seen that practical choices and compromises need to be made together regarding living arrangements, division of responsibilities, choice of friends, jobs, finances, recreation, extended family, and children.

One of the first major decisions in a relationship may be whether to cohabitate or marry. Counselors will find that conflicts on this matter will involve many dimensions including (a) individual experiences within the family of origin, (b) hopes and expectations for the future, (c) family values versus individual values, and (d) personal religious and moral values. Other issues that can be explored include the values of the culture or subculture with regard to cohabitation versus marriage. Counselors need to consider the age of the couple and sex differences in expectations. Marriage has traditionally involved more change in the woman's lifestyle than the man's, but that is changing now that more women remain in the work force after marriage.

The couple's relationship evolves over time whether or not they have children. Families with children tend to be more focused on their family needs, whereas those couples without children focus more on their careers than other aspects of their lives. In addition, childless couples tend to be urban, affluent, and well educated, and they often have better communication and more active sex lives than those with families. There is variation among couples, and adjustment may be related to the extent to which the couple has achieved the family configuration they had anticipated and sought.

Managing a Home
Another major developmental task of early adulthood, both for single adults and couples, involves managing a home. Some of the choices are obvious: decisions regarding buying or renting a home, where to live, and financial considerations. Other considerations include expected family expansion and future earning potential. Once a home has been established, issues arise regarding budgeting of finances, division of responsibilities, and furnishings.

Financial issues are often power issues. In some households, the individual who earns the highest salary, traditionally the male, may make the majority of decisions for the family, both financial and otherwise. Adjustments have been made in the traditional family now that the majority of women work outside the home. However, counselors should not assume that role equality automatically accompanies economic equality within a family.

Studies regarding dual-income families show that maternal satisfaction with the dual role of mother and breadwinner is related to the degree to which husbands share responsibilities of family and household, her comfort with child care arrangements, and both the husband's and wife's perception of the effect of maternal employment on child rearing. In dual-worker families, the fathers are often more involved in the housekeeping and child rearing than single-earner families. There are, however, indications that the division of labor within the home may still not be equal and that many women feel the strain of attempting to balance the traditional role with that of wage earner.

Parenting

A major task for those who have chosen to marry or cohabitate, and even for some single adults, is the determination of when to have children and how many to have. Conflict can arise when these issues are not well defined before the relationship is established, when one partner changes his or her mind, or when pregnancy is either unplanned or difficult to achieve.

The birth of a child, especially the first one, causes numerous changes within a household, and has differential effects on the parents. Roles must be redefined and daily routines altered.

According to family systems theory, the family system may break down to subsystem alliances in times of stress. In a family consisting of three individuals, a subsystem alliance is a dyad that can exclude the third member of the family triad. The alliances may shift depending on circumstances, at one time excluding a parent and at another time excluding the child. The establishment of boundaries around subsystems varies between families and may be appropriate in terms of providing privacy, such as when parents exclude children to maintain marital intimacy. Excessively shifting alliances or methodological exclusion of one family member may reflect a dysfunctional system. A counselor can explore these relationships within the family as well as the permeability of the boundaries surrounding each subsystem.

Raising children in our society today is complicated by the fact that both parents are usually employed. In the 1980s maternal employment reached 70%, with more than half of the women with infants under 1 year of age employed outside the home. This has caused profound changes in the dynamics of the contemporary family. No longer do the stereotypes of the patriarchal breadwinner and stay-at-home mother hold true. With the upsurge of dual-income families, the mother is no longer exclusive care giver to the children, nor is she a full-time home-maker. She has multiple roles that may be accompanied by stress, often because attitudes concerning maternal employment have not kept pace with the reality of the dual-income family. Spousal conflict over tradi-tional sex roles may negatively affect the employed mother's attitudes and satisfaction with her numerous roles.

A particular style of raising children may be appropriate for one fam-ily environment but not another, or for one child but not another. Simi-larly, a particular style of parenting may be appropriate at one stage in a child's development but not at another, depending on the child's temperament and needs at a particular stage. For example, a very active child may require more attention and control than a quieter child. This may affect not only the amount of time that a parent needs to spend with the child, but such other factors as day care choices, the quality of the parental relationship, and job choices.

Separation and Divorce
Child rearing and marital adjustment are critical life events that may lead to unsatisfactory conclusions. More than one-third of all first mar-riages today end in divorce. The figure rises to almost 40% when remar-riage is taken into account. Most divorces and separations occur within the first 3 years of marriage, although some studies show increased di-vorce rates among "empty-nest" couples. People who marry at older ages tend to stay married longer.

Many relationship difficulties such as separation and divorce, espe-cially those that occur in the early years of an intimate relationship, could reflect an inability to form the close bond necessary to achieve mature levels of intimacy. Additionally, identity issues may not have been resolved. Since the psychosocial tasks are interrelated, intervention may be effective working through conflicts on prior as well as current levels.

If the relationship or marriage ends, separation or divorce is a time of stress and readjustment. The family finds that there are changes in attachments, family roles, alliances, and social contexts. Counselors deal with a variety of issues related to self-concept, anger, resentment, and loss of love between partners. In addition, there are issues regarding children's reactions, financial problems, and domestic abuse.

PERSONAL GROWTH IN MIDLIFE

By the time adults reach their 40s, most are married with children who are approaching adulthood. Their parents are aging and dying, and they may become grandparents.

Development in midlife can be characterized by Erikson's psychosocial stage of *generativity versus stagnation*. Adults are generally at the peak of their careers and earning potential. Psychosocial concerns have shifted from intimacy toward considerations regarding their place in the world and accomplishments that can make the world better for themselves, their children, and future generations.

The process of generativity entails investing energy in skills and abilities, and applying that energy to ideas for future productivity. A sense of continuity with future generations is often expressed in civic responsibility. Those who are struggling unsuccessfully with this task are more lifeless and passive. Their activities are focused on a daily routine without concern or attention toward the future. Life becomes boring and dull, without vision, and the individual stagnates.

One of the tasks of middle age is assisting growing children or younger employees with their own developmental tasks, and assisting them to become independent, happy adults. A parental or mentoring style that is adaptable to the changing demands of growing children and young adults is optimal.

Inability to handle the challenges of midlife may precipitate what some call a *midlife crisis*, which manifests itself in depression, marital problems, excessive uncertainty, and feelings of futility. This is not an inevitable or universal phenomenon. Middle-aged adults face numerous turning points in life that can be called *midlife transitions*. These include but are not limited to the empty nest when all children have left the home, menopause, realization of mortality, and retirement. Individuals who are dealing with these turning points may feel uncertain or in conflict, but this is a normal and natural reaction to change.

Career Goals

As individuals reach middle adulthood, many reevaluate their career aspirations. They may assess the number of productive years remaining to them, current job conditions and satisfaction, more realistic employment goals, and shifting family responsibilities. Some find new jobs or make major career changes as they come to better know their career goals. Women who have not yet entered the job force tend to do so now.

Many middle-aged adults are satisfied with their jobs and career paths, and are at the peak of their careers, both financially and in terms of prestige. Others may wish to change careers, but remain in their jobs to maintain an economic standard of living, believing they have invested too much time in a career to change or that they are too old to alter career paths.

For some, individual abilities and goals may no longer match job requirements, and they may feel threatened by younger employees who possess more physical strength or technological skill. There may be internal or external pressure to retire early.

Counseling issues related to employment can include (a) vocational satisfaction as it relates to generativity; (b) stress, burnout, and overwork; (c) decreasing individual-job match due to technological advances in the workplace; (d) forced unemployment and layoffs; and (e) early retirement. This could include placing the older worker in a position of guidance of younger employees rather than the role of competitor. Identity and intimacy issues could also be explored.

Leisure time
Midlife adults may find that they have more time to develop leisure-time activities than when they were younger. With the children grown and greater economic security in hand, they are often able to nurture a new lifestyle that incorporates many things that have been postponed during the child-rearing years. Many of these leisure-time activities may be expanded more fully during retirement.

Havighurst stresses that some old leisure-time habits may not be appropriate for adults in mid-life. Early adulthood activities that are contingent upon physical strength and stamina may lose their attractiveness to older adults, and new hobbies and sports may need to take their place.

For some, leisure time is full of meaning, and choices may reflect hopes and unfulfilled dreams of childhood. For others, free time may produce boredom and frustration. Guidance in this area may include suggestions to include activities that address Eriksonian generativity issues. For example, volunteer work or assumption of civic responsibility may help an individual to feel productive and may compensate for an occupation that lacks these qualities.

Activities may be a major source of expressing oneself. If one's spouse shares the same interests, the time can be fulfilling. However, problems can arise when the two individuals develop conflicting interests. Counseling issues may include (a) exploration of individual interests and goals; (b) assessment of the degree to which each partner's individual goals, interests, and expectations match the other's; (c) effective use of leisure time; and (d) patterns of communication between partners.

Sexuality and Adjustment to Physical Changes
Adults in midlife find themselves in transition between youth and old age with respect to physical capabilities. Changes in the physical self become apparent, not only in sexual behavior but also in other areas of their lives. Acceptance of these physical changes and an understanding of the gradual nature of the changes over the life span can lead to a more satisfying aging process. Counselors can assist individuals to develop ways to compensate for decreases in certain capabilities or help them focus on less physically demanding activities.

Sexual activity tends to become less important in longer marriages.

However, there may be an upsurge in sexual activity after menopause due to cessation of pregnancy risks. Functional sexual capability needs to be viewed in relation to the couple's physical condition. Middle-age weight gain and sedentary lifestyle can contribute to both lower energy level and less physical attraction between partners. This change in physical condition can be advantageous, especially if it results in more compatible sexual needs.

Sexuality in middle adulthood can cause conflict within long-term relations in a number of ways. Long married couples may find that they are no longer compatible or are bored with each other. Individuals who seek to recapture the excitement of youthful sexuality or feel a sense of panic at impending aging may seek satisfaction outside the marital dyad. Individuals who do not have an intimate partner may feel that their chances are fading for finding someone with whom to share their aging years.

Parenting

Those individuals who have had children in their early 20s are faced with the task of redefining parenting as their children become adults themselves. As children grow away from their family of origin, the middle-aged adults find themselves with more time alone together. A major task of middle adulthood involves learning to live with and relate to one's spouse. The focus of the family gradually changes from raising children to living together as a couple again, or as a couple living with their now adult children.

Counseling issues may be focused on the "empty nest," the adjustment to children's leaving home, and parents may need to be educated to know that this is usually a desirable outcome. It has been found in studies of the empty nest that couples experience positive changes in their marriage as a result of children leaving home at the appropriate time.

One may find conversely that the children do not leave home on time but that they continue to be dependent on the parents. Clemens and Axelson refer to this as the "not-so-empty nest." This arrangement may be appropriate if it is due to economic necessity, to promote closer family ties, or to assist aging or ill relatives. Such arrangements may signal a dysfunctional, enmeshed family system, however, and counselors should explore the underlying reasons behind such family arrangements.

Conflict may occur when grown children remain living at home, and may include disagreements about rules, finances, privacy, and responsibilities. These can often be worked out through contracts or negotiations. Not so easy to resolve are the less overt problems regarding growth and development of both parents and children. Young adults who still live at home may or may not realize that the arrangement interferes with the developmental tasks of early adulthood. Middle-aged parents may be hindered in similar ways. Counselors who encounter such family arrangements may find it helpful to explore the appropriate developmental tasks for each age group and devise specific ways in which both generations can pursue appropriate developmental tasks.

Delayed childbearing. Childbearing patterns in adulthood show great variability. There is evidence of more delayed childbearing today than in previous generations. Some of the reasons include improved birth control and detection of genetic defects, women who want to establish careers prior to childbearing, the tendency toward smaller families, and couples who begin new families with second marriages.

Delayed childbearing can create new pressures and critical events within families. Primiparous parents in their late 30s and 40s tend to differ on many dimensions from first-time parents in their 20s. A counselor could explore both biological and social aspects of late childbearing. For example, the demands of parenting a young child may place more stress on middle-aged adults who are experiencing declines in general physical condition or other physiological changes, particularly those associated with menopause.

Late childbearing adults may need to make adjustments in choices of congenial companions. Many adults become friends due to the fact that their children are in close contact with one another. However, late childbearing adults may find that this social group consists of adults young enough to be their own children. Cohort differences may prevent friendships from forming under these conditions. The counselor needs to be able to help these new parents in their adjustment.

A helpful approach to take in counseling late childbearing adults would be to counter ageist myths regarding middle-aged declining health and skills. Adults in their middle years bring numerous advantages to childbearing and present compensations for what they lack in energy. They tend to have a clearer sense of who they are, who they want to spend their lives with, and what they want to accomplish and are therefore more able to provide a stable, consistent environment for raising a child.

Aging parents

As middle-aged adults continue to develop, they may find themselves adjusting to aging parents. They are often called the "sandwich generation" caring for teenagers or young adults who have not yet left home and aging parents. This can be a stressful transition time. Just as the middle-aged adult begins to feel that child-raising responsibilities are concluding and that time free from responsibility is imminent, aging parents become dependent emotionally, physically, and financially.

It may be especially stressful if the aging parent is ill. Financial burdens may be compounded and personal responsibility increased. If the parent returns to live with the children, numerous changes within the household can be expected as the family system expands to accommodate a new member.

Reactions to parent care vary widely. Each family differs with regard to history of individual experiences, patterns of interactions, and abilities to care for an aging parent. Family caregivers may find that the ability to cope with the situation is dependent upon social supports both within the family and in the community.

Middle-aged adults may find themselves distressed as their parents age. Some reasons for this may include anticipation of loss, regrets regarding an unsatisfactory relationship, burdens related to caregiving, and awareness of their own mortality. Counselors may help individuals to adjust to their own aging as well as that of their parents.

CONCLUSION

Individuals age at different rates and vary with regard to employment status, financial situation, cognitive ability, physical health, and family constellation. There is thus variability in the age at which adults begin to turn their attention away from the developmental tasks of midlife and begin instead to focus on the value of their own lives—what Erikson calls the psychosocial task of *integrity versus despair.*

As an individual approaches old age there is a time for reflecting. The individual who as a young adult married with dreams for the future and embarked afresh upon a career path, and who during mid-adulthood established family and career, now approaches the final years of life. The successful transition into old age depends largely on the extent to which an individual feels that he or she has lived a good life and accomplished personal goals.

A counselor's role can be enhanced through following a developmental perspective. This viewpoint leads counselors to specific things that can be done in counseling middle-aged adults. Five things for counselors to keep in mind include:

1. *Consider multiple levels of influence for intervention.* Problems may be solved more completely if levels other than individual psychological level are considered. Think of how biological, social, cultural, and historical factors may be targets of discussion and change.
2. *Think of various contexts in which the client is operating.* Behavior that is conflictual or inappropriate in one context, such as job, home, or organization, or in one relationship, such as with certain peers or family members, may be more appropriate in another context. A

counselor can strive to discover or restructure an environment for a client.

3. *Treat each client as a unique individual.* Be flexible in treatment strategies and be aware of the variability of clients.

4. *Use Havighurst's developmental tasks as a practical guide.* Counselors will find Havighurst's thoughts useful as they explore individual growth at various ages of adulthood. An individual's inability to handle any of these tasks may precipitate a need for counseling.

5. *Use Erikson's psychosocial stages in a broader, more general sense than Havighurst's.* Difficulties with these tasks are more basic and pervade a correspondingly larger portion of the individual's life. Seemingly different symptoms of dysfunction—such as, for example, self-indulgence, boredom, lack of future orientation, and depression—may all have roots in the ability to resolve the task of generativity versus stagnation.

FOR FURTHER READING

Rossi, A. (1980). Aging and parenthood in the middle years. In P. B. Baltes & O. G. Brim (Eds.), *Life-span development and behavior* (Vol. 3, pp. 137–205). New York: Academic Press.

Thomas, R. M. (1990). *Counseling and life-span development.* Newbury Park, CA: Sage.

Troll, L. E. (1982). *Continuations: Adult development and aging.* Monterey, CA: Brooks/Cole.

Trudell, T. M., & Fisher, C. B. (1992). Dual worker families. In M. E. Procidano & C. B. Fisher (Eds.), *Families: A handbook for school professionals.* (pp. 17–35). New York: Teachers College Press.

Turner, J. S., & Helms, D. B. (1991). *Lifespan development.* Orlando, FL: Holt, Rinehart, & Winston.

BIBLIOGRAPHY

Baltes, P. B., & Reese, H. W. (1984). The life-span perspective in developmental psychology. In M. H. Bornstein & M. E. Lamb (Eds.), *Developmental psychology: An advanced textbook.* (pp. 493–531). Hillsdale, NJ: Erlbaum.

Clemens, A. W., & Axelson, Z. J. (1985). The not-so-empty nest: The return of the fledgling adult. *Family Relations, 34,* 256–264.

Erikson, E. (1963). *Childhood and society* (2nd ed.). New York: Norton.

Havighurst, R. J. (1972). *Developmental tasks and education* (3rd ed.). New York: McKay.

Havighurst, R. J. (1980). More thoughts on developmental tasks. *Personal and Guidance Journal, 58,* 330–335.

24

Family Dynamics

JANE S. STURGES, M.S.W.

Family counseling had its roots in the growth and development of both the child guidance movement and professional marriage counseling in 1920–1930, and in the work of psychiatric researchers who studied the family and schizophrenia in the 1950s. In working with marital pairs, children's problems, and schizophrenia, researchers developed new ideas about the significance of family relations in the emergence and perpetuation of psychological and behavioral problems. Out of this grew the belief that effective help required the counselor to work simultaneously with both marital partners or with parents and child. By 1970 recognition of an integration of marriage and family counseling occurred when the American Association of Marriage Counselors (AAMC), founded in 1942, changed its name to the American Association of Marriage and Family Counselors (AAMFC). In 1978 the AAMFC became the American Association for Marriage and Family Therapy (AAMFT). Although *marriage counseling* is still a common term, professional family counseling is now most often referred to as *family therapy.*

In the past 20 years there has been a phenomenal growth of the family therapy movement, with development of theories and models of practice, establishment of centers for training and research, accreditation of schools to provide graduate training in marital and family therapy, recognition of marriage and family therapists through certification in a number of states, and a proliferation of journals and books in the field. Today family therapy and family counseling are practiced in child guidance clinics, mental health centers, family agencies, hospitals, employee assistance programs, and state agencies, and in the private offices of psychiatrists, psychologists, social workers, marital and family therapists, pastoral counselors, and nurses. (For a detailed history of the family movement see Goldenberg & Goldenberg, 1985, and Nichols, 1984.)

Out of the growth and development of marriage and family counseling and the professionalization of marriage and family therapy have come new ideas and practices, not only for the professional with a graduate degree, but for the counselor who works with families as well. This chapter includes a description of family therapy today, including theoretical concepts, models of practice, and current issues, followed by ideas for general practice for family counselors not specifically trained in family therapy.

DESCRIPTION OF FAMILY THERAPY

Family therapy is a form of psychotherapy that deals with interpersonal issues and involves in-person contact with members of a family. Problems and symptomatic behavior of individuals are viewed as the result of unhealthy interactions within the family, with each person playing a part, rather than of individual intrapsychic conflicts.

Seeking help is usually initiated by families at a time of heightened stress. Often there is particular concern about the problems of one family member identified as "the patient," rather than recognition of the need for help for the family as a whole. It is the role of the family therapist to suggest the idea that one family member's problem is a problem that involves everyone.

THEORETICAL CONCEPTS

Working with families requires a different perspective from working with individuals. Certain theoretical concepts that provide the foundation for all models of family therapy today are *the family as a system, circularity, triangles,* and *developmental stages of family life.*

The Family as a System
No family can be understood by analyzing the behavior of its members individually. That would be like trying to understand the workings of a complicated piece of machinery by disassembling it and studying each part separately, rather than learning how all the parts fit and work together as a whole. Just as with a piece of machinery, the members of a family in interaction with each other in interlocking patterns produce an entity greater than the sum of its parts. The family therapist's view is that an individual's problems can only be clearly understood within the context of his or her family system. Work with one family member may help, but the changes may be reversed, although not intentionally, within the context of repetitive psychological and social processes among mem-

bers of the family with which that member has the closest emotional and physical contact.

Circularity

Causality is thought of in circular rather than linear terms. For example, instead of thinking that A causes B, which subsequently affects C, interaction is thought of as a complex network of circular feedback loops in which everyone's behavior impacts on everyone else's with no clear sense of when and how the process began and with no one person considered blameworthy. More specifically, in the case of a mother-wife overly involved with her adult daughter distanced from the father-husband, which came first—the daughter's seeking extra attention from her mother, or the mother's excessive focusing on her daughter, sensing some special need of the child? Did this lead to the father-husband distancing himself, or did he distance himself first, leading to the overinvolvement of mother and daughter? The more distant father becomes, the more involved mother and daughter are. The closer mother and daughter become, the more father distances himself. This family problem is viewed then as occurring within the context of circular, interlocking loops in their collective relationships that become repetitive over time.

Triangles

This concept, developed by Bowen (1978), introduced the idea that when two people cannot handle the anxiety between them, they reduce the emotional intensity by forming a triangle with a third party. The classic example is when tension between husband and wife is defused, but not resolved, by focusing on one of their children. Instead of dealing with the problems between the two of them, they put much time and energy into the child. The more anxiety there is between the marital pair, the greater danger there is that one of them will become overly involved with a child, which may lead to symptoms in the child. Emotional triangles may include things, as well as people, such as drinking or overworking as one side of the triangle.

Developmental Stages of Family Life

Families change in both structure and function over the life cycle, and just as with individuals, they do so in an ordered sequence of developmental stages. In each stage of the life cycle of the traditional family (parents and children), from its formation to the deaths of the parents, there are specific tasks to be carried out for the healthy functioning of the family. Over the years the family will change in size, age composition, work status of family members, and financial condition. Expectable life changes, such as the oldest child starting to school, or the retirement of the chief breadwinner, can be as stressful and can require as much adjustment as sudden, unexpected events. If the family has difficulty dealing with a transitional phase, problems can develop.

Stages of the family life cycle of the traditional nuclear family (as described by Carter & McGoldrick, 1980) are:

1. the unattached young adult,
2. joining of families through marriage,
3. the family with young children,
4. the family with adolescents,
5. launching children and moving on, and
6. the family in later life.

MODELS OF FAMILY THERAPY

A number of models of family therapy have developed over time, with similarities as well as differences in concepts and practice. Their classifications include *object relations–intergenerational, Bowen, structural, experiential, communication,* and *psychoeducation.*

Object Relations–Intergenerational Model

The object relations–intergenerational model has its roots in psychoanalytic theory but has evolved specifically out of *object relations* theory, i.e., the belief that a person's basic motive in life is for satisfying relationships rather than instinctual drives. Therapists working from this perspective help family members recognize and deal with internalized representations from childhood relationships that get projected unconsciously onto other current relationships, with the family sometimes colluding in the process (*projective identification*). The work tends to focus more on family history and intergenerational issues than symptoms related to the initial problem for which the family sought help. Three followers of this general approach, with some variations, are Framo (1981), Boszormenyi-Nagy (1973) and Paul (1980).

Framo (1982) views intrapsychic and interactional processes as both essential to understanding the dynamic aspects of family life. He is interested in hidden transgenerational forces that influence current family relationships. Framo works with couples through a process of individual couples therapy, couples group therapy, and sessions that include the family of origin. He sometimes involves each individual (without the partner present) in sessions with his or her family of origin. The goal is to help individuals recognize the inappropriateness of projecting unresolved issues from old attachments onto current relationships.

Boszormenyi-Nagy (1982) and associates developed a family therapy approach that respects transgenerational legacies and influences and is written in the language of existentialism, emphasizing such issues as fairness, trustworthiness, and loyalty. In expanding his therapeutic approach, Boszormenyi-Nagy chose the name *contexual therapy*. This model takes into account individual dynamics as well as relationship dynamics over several generations. An important concept is the sense that every family keeps a "ledger," a kind of multigenerational accounting system of who, in psychological terms, owes what to whom. Whenever injustices occur there is the expectation of some later repayment or restitution. Problems in relationships develop when justice seems to move too slowly or in an amount too small to satisfy the other person. From this perspective dysfunctional patterns cannot be fully understood without looking at the history of the problem, the family "ledger," and "unsettled accounts."

Paul's (1980) theory is that unresolved issues in one generation inevitably distress subsequent generations. Unresolved grief for a death may affect not only the bereaved one and spouse but family members in future generations as well.

The Bowen Model

Bowen (1978) is considered by many the major theoretician in the field of family therapy. His theory encompasses the following interlocking concepts: *triangles, differentiation of self, the nuclear family emotional system, family projection process, emotional cut-off, multigenerational transmission,* and *sibling position.* One of his major contributions has been the concept of triangles described earlier in "Theoretical Concepts."

The functioning of a marital couple in the current nuclear family is viewed as highly affected by the extent to which they have resolved their individual relationships in the families in which they grew up. The central premise is that unresolved anxieties in the emotional attachment to one's family of origin will be projected onto one's relationships in the current nuclear family. Sibling position in one's family of origin influences both the marital relationship and relationships with children.

The goal of therapeutic work in the Bowen model is to help an individual resolve two sets of opposing forces, those that bind family members together and those that fight to break free enough from family to obtain differentiation of self. The therapist is a "coach" who helps an individual become more objective about family members by establishing one-to-one relationships with as many members as possible, rather than participating in triangles. The goal is to get the individual unstuck from powerful emotional forces and pull him toward fusion with the family without cutting off the family in doing so. The view is that the emotionally mature adult can move in and out of his family of origin's emotional sphere comfortably while holding onto his differentiation. Bowen therapists educate individuals with whom they work about the theory, that is, about triangles, multigenerational processes, the difference between reacting emotionally and thinking, and planning about oneself in the context of family. It is believed that work on oneself vis-à-vis one's family of origin is a lifelong task.

There are similarities between Bowen theory and object relations theory. Both are concerned with intergenerational processes and triangles. However, Bowenians work with individuals and couples rather than with the whole family. Another major difference is that individuals are "coached" to visit members of their families, ideally one-to-one, rather than to include them in family therapy sessions. (Bowen, 1978; Kerr & Bowen, 1988).

In recent years, until his death in October 1990, Bowen emphasized his belief that the human family is a naturally occurring emotional system governed by principles of nature rather than an entity created by the human brain. He worked toward having his theory accepted as a new science of human behavior.

The Structural Model
Minuchin (1974) and others (Minuchin & Fishman, 1981) developed the structural model, a short-term approach that focusses on rearranging the current organization and structure of the nuclear family to help solve the problem presented. This approach has become one of the most widely used concepts and practices in family treatment. Assessment is made of the organization and structure of the family through its transactional patterns, coalitions and alignments, subsystems, and boundaries between family members and with the external world. This assessment is made through observations by the therapist in action-oriented family therapy sessions. In the beginning the therapist joins with the family by going along with its style and organization and begins to reframe the problem from a one-person problem to a family problem. Then the therapist gradually encourages enactment of the dysfunctional ways of relating in the family sessions, making highly active, calculated moves to bring about change. The goal is to set up new, healthier alliances in which family members can experience each other differently and begin to cope better with the current problem.

The advantage of this approach, which grew out of Minuchin's early work with poor, disorganized families from inner city slums, is that it is cost effective. Families seeking help are viewed as being unable at the time to modify their structure to accommodate to a developmental or situational change. The belief is that if through reorganization of the family the current problem can be resolved, the healthier forces in the family will take over and no more therapy will be needed at the time. This model does not focus on family of origin issues or have as a goal insight about the root of the problem. A series of studies has shown this model to be effective in working with families of severely ill psychosomatic children and adult drug addicts.

The Experiential Model

Therapists working in the experiential model use the therapeutic relationship in family sessions to enhance the family's natural drive toward healthy growth. The goal is to help each family member and the family as a whole to fulfill its potential.

Whitaker (Napier & Whitaker, 1978), leading practioner of this model, stresses the value of a theoretical approach that emphasizes the value of an open, spontaneous, shared emotional experience between therapist and family that will loosen rigid patterns in the family and provide a growth-producing experience for therapist and family. His work, often with a co-therapist, uses both real and symbolic experiences to bring about changes in feelings and behavior. Symptoms are not dealt with directly. Goals are expansion of the experience of feelings; spontaneous, genuine interactions; decreased dependence; and more freedom of choice.

Kempler (1981) is also considered a practitioner of this model. A Gestalt family therapist, Kempler deals with moment-to-moment issues in the work between family members and himself. He confronts and challenges family members to explore how their blocked self-awareness prevents them from more satisfying and fulfilling relationships with each other.

The Communication Model

The communication model grew out of studies at the Mental Research Institute (MRI) in Palo Alto, California, in the 1950s. In this model human problems are viewed as interactional and as tied in with a set of circumstances within the family that keep them going. Bateson, Jackson, Haley, & Weakland (1956) laid the foundation for the interactional view of the therapeutic program at MRI. Strategic family therapy was developed by Haley (1976) and Madanes (1984) and systemic family therapy was developed by Selvini-Palazzoli (1978) and associates in Milan, Italy.

The emphasis of the communication model is on current interaction of family members, with no interest in causes or origins of the problem behavior. The goal is to change the rules of the current family system that maintain the ongoing problems. Techniques of these approaches include the use of paradoxical interventions for changing family relationship patterns. These interventions have their roots in the double-bind message described by Bateson, et al. (1956), in which one person issues to another a statement that simultaneously contains two logically inconsistent messages. In addition, there is a third message forbidding the receiver to comment on the inconsistency. The idea of the use of paradoxical interventions to help families solve their problems is that a family's paradoxical or double-bind messages can only be countered by a therapeutic double-bind or counterparadox. For example, clients are told not to change within a therapeutic setting where there is a built-in expectation for change. One paradoxical technique, *prescribing the symptom*, as used by Jackson (1959), is a way of undermining the resistance to change by making it unnecessary. (For the history of the communication model see Goldenberg & Goldenberg, 1985, and Nicohols, 1984.)

In the strategic family approach of Haley (1976) and Madanes (1984), carefully planned interventions and directives to the family are characteristic. Task assignments, "pretend" techniques, as well as paradoxical interventions bring about the willing abandonment of dysfunctional behavior by means of the family's refusal of the directive not to change (Selvini-Palazzoli, Boscolo, Cecchin, & Prata, 1978).

In the strategic family approach of Selvini-Palazzoli and colleagues (1978), carefully planned interventions, based on hypotheses as to what maintains the family's problem behavior, are given in the form of tasks based on paradoxical prescriptions. The family is seen by a team of therapists who together plan strategy. One or two of the therapists work directly with the family while the others observe behind a one-way mirror. Sessions with the family are usually spaced about a month apart. An attempt is made to label all behavior, no matter how problematic, as protective of the family (*positive connotation*). *Circular questioning* is used as an effective diagnostic and therapeutic tool to draw out differences in perceptions of family events and relationships among the family members. The Ackerman Institute in New York uses interventions similar to those of the Milan group, while also showing interest in the origins of symptoms within the history of the family.

The Psychoeducation Model
The psychoeducation model grew out of studies in the 1970s that provided evidence that schizophrenic patients from families who showed high expressed emotion (EE), a condition that is principally reflected in criticism and emotional overinvolvement, had larger relapse rates in the months immediately following discharge from a psychiatric hospital than patients who came from low EE families. Before the 1970s, the majority of schizophrenic patients were treated as outpatients with individual psychoanalytic psychotherapy, which did not include family members. While some traditional forms of family therapy did take place, particularly in the context of a psychiatric hospitalization, little information was provided for families about the nature of their ill family member's problems, and family members often felt they were at fault for the patient's schizophrenic illness.

The psychoeducation model developed largely by Falloon (Falloon,

Boyd, & McGill, 1984) and Anderson (Anderson, Reiss, & Hogarty, 1986), involves a collaborative relationship between therapist and family around understanding the illness and finding better ways to live with it (rather than focusing on etiological factors and family dynamics). Interventions include the provision of information about schizophrenia to families in a series of lectures and discussions. The model considers schizophrenia a biological disorder; families do not cause it but can influence the course of the illness. Ongoing meetings with the family are held to reinforce ways of coping. The approach is intended to decrease anxiety (and subsequently lower EE) and to increase self-confidence as family members find more constructive ways of relating to the patient and leading their own lives. Since the original studies of schizophrenia, the psychoeducation model has been found to be helpful with a variety of family problems, such as depression, substance abuse, and childhood autism.

PRACTICAL SUGGESTIONS

Many of the ideas from the various models of professional family therapy can be useful to the family counselor. How they might be used depends on the knowledge, experience, and skill of the counselor and the circumstances of the family needing help.

A family seeks help when its usual coping mechanisms are not working well enough to handle the current situation. Family problems may demonstrate themselves in the forms of behavior problems of a child, marital conflict, physical or emotional illness, substance abuse, family violence, or antisocial behavior. Although it may not be recognized immediately by family or counselor, the presenting problem may be related to a normal, expected event at a particular stage of family life (such as the birth of a child or the marriage of a family member), or to an unexpected situation (such as physical illness or loss of a job), or to intergenerational issues (such as expectations for the family from the previous generations).

Engagement of the Family and Evaluation of the Problem

The first step is to form a working relationship with the family and evaluate the presenting problem. Ways of doing this will vary according to the personalities and styles of family members and counselor, their relationship, and the nature of the problem and family members' reactions to it. Some initial approaches that are helpful under any circumstances are:

1. *Meet family members with respect, empathy, and acceptance.* Begin with what is most troublesome to the family at the time they seek help.

2. *Decide who should be included.* Reach out to those reluctant to be involved. Form an empathic bond with each family member.
3. *Carry out sensitive, nonjudgmental, thorough questioning about details of family members' lives related to the presenting problem.* Include each family member in the discussion, seeking out different perceptions of specific events and relationships.
4. *Reflect back what has been said for emphasis and clarification.*
5. *If the family is in a crisis and appears immobilized to take actions needed immediately, discourage excessive emotional expression.* Instead, give advice about the situation that will help them quickly get things under better control. Wait until the situation is calmer before trying to get a broader picture of the family and underlying issues.

Evaluation of the presenting problem precedes or accompanies counseling and may be accomplished in the process of listening to and observing family members as they talk about the problem in initial meetings or through more formal, structured assessment interviews. It is important to focus on interaction and behavior as well as thoughts and feelings. At the appropriate time a thorough assessment will also include a broader picture of other recent events that have affected family members, information about extended family, education, work, mobility, ethnicity, religion, financial resources, and health, as well as the effect of current societal events (e.g., economic recession, war, disease epidemics). One way of gathering history is to make a historical family diagram with the family, called a *genogram* (Kerr & Bowen, 1988; McGoldrick & Gerson, 1985). The genogram provides a useful map of family structure over several generations, including factual information (such as births, deaths, marriages, divorces, illnesses, and religious and other connections), as well as social changes that have affected the family system. The family members' participation with the counselor in creating the genogram can give members a sense of family history and structure, as well as a capacity to see themselves as a part of the process of family life.

Further evaluation will include both strengths and weaknesses in the following areas of family interaction that may influence efforts to solve the problem at hand: *communication, emotionality, leadership, boundaries,* and *task-goal performance.*

Communication. Each family has its unique style of communicating, both verbally and nonverbally. For a family to function effectively, clear communication channels are needed so that members can share a focus of attention and derive shared meaning from it. Unclear communication can contribute to problems in family functioning if the pattern is repetitive. Some of the ways the counselor can evaluate communication are to observe whether verbal and nonverbal messages are consistent, whether all family members are participants, and whether family members think abstractly or concretely, and to make note of what subjects are talked about and what subjects are considered taboo.

Emotionality. Emotionality takes into consideration the climate of the family, including the degree of emotionality; tolerance of feelings; modulation of aggression, criticism, and hostility; emotional over-involvement or underinvolvement; and interpersonal intimacy. Some families have trouble expressing warmth and caring. In such families members seem to connect with each other only through anger and criticism. Other families repress anger, acting as if everything is agreeable.

Leadership. Ideally parents share the main leadership functions, with flexibility and complementarity of roles. Leadership includes discipline, authority, and decision making. Problems will develop if a child is continually given too much power or responsibility.

Boundaries. Boundaries are defined by family rules as to who may participate in certain kinds of interaction and information sharing and who may not. There are appropriate boundaries between individuals and generations within the family and between the family and the outside world. For example, the parents are recognized in a healthy family to share a special degree of physical intimacy, privacy, and commitment that differs from each of the spouse's relationships with other family members. In some families boundaries are too loose; in others, too rigid. Examples of problems are overinvolvement of the previous generation in leadership in the nuclear family, one person always speaking for another, a child serving as a confidante for a parent, or too little contact between the family and the outside world.

Task-goal performance. General goals of the family are provision of basic physical needs, emotional support, assistance with mastery of separation, education, acculturation, leisure time use, and ability to negotiate and compromise differences. Certain tasks and goals are appropriate at each stage of individual and family development. In evaluating a family, the counselor should be aware of its stage of development and the tasks to be carried out at that time.

Interventions

A plan of intervention requires continued reflection and rethinking on the part of the counselor in the process of the evolving evaluation of the family. Interventions should be made with the family as a whole in mind and in collaboration with family members about what the problem is and what solution may work for them. Some general ideas for intervention are:

1. Encourage family members to look at the situation objectively, to view it from differing perspectives, and to consider various ways to handle it.
2. Make supportive comments, such as reassuring family members that it is common for people to react and feel the way they do under the circumstances. This helps families to feel more normal than pathological.
3. Partialize the problem by helping family members to determine which parts of their lives are going well and which part has the problem that is causing stress. Focusing on the strengths in the family enhances self-esteem and leads to better coping skills.
4. Find crucial points of intervention within the family. Seemingly small ones can have a big effect, bringing about changes throughout the family system.
5. Select with the family concrete tasks to carry out that will give a sense of mastery.
6. Help families identify and call on extra resources available for help (such as extended family members, friends, religious groups, and services in the community).
7. Educate families about family life, providing useful information in small bits rather than in a lecture.
8. Plan follow-up meetings to evaluate the progress of the family in solving the problem.
9. Assess whether the family is interested in and able to work on underlying issues.
10. Consider when it is appropriate to refer the family for more specialized help. Referrals need to be handled with sensitivity and a good, up-to-date knowledge of community resources.

CURRENT ISSUES AND CONCERNS

Current issues and concerns in the field of professional family therapy are the choice of model, or combination of models, of therapy that is the most effective, and social problems in society and their effect on families.

Among the leaders and practitioners of the various models of family therapy there are debates about the major dimensions in which the models differ vis-à-vis their overall effectiveness in helping families change. One of the chief questions raised is whether short-term focused approaches aimed at solving the presenting problem have long-term effects and, on the other hand, whether longer term approaches aimed at growth are cost effective. There are differing opinions about the value of the psychoeducation model over the communication model in working with families with a schizophrenic family member. Currently there is a trend toward integrating models, such as the structural model and the communication model, while others, such as the Bowen model, remain purist in approach.

Larger issues and concerns for both professional family therapist and family counselor are related to a number of major changes in society, which have occurred concomitant with the development of the family movement and which have significantly affected families. The women's liberation movement and changing economic conditions have led to the two-career family, raising the need for improved day care facilities for children. The increase in the breakdown of the traditional nuclear family through divorce has increased the number of one-parent families, often headed by women faced with increased responsibilities and economic hardship—and sometimes poverty. An increase in remarried families with stepchildren has also changed the structure of family life. Other types of new families have been formed by never married mothers and through cohabitation of heterosexual and homosexual couples, some of whom have children.

Abortion has been a controversial issue nationwide for several decades. An increase in substance abuse and the AIDS epidemic have brought new traumas to family life. Family violence has achieved epidemic proportions in this country as well. New policies for deinstitutionalization of the mentally ill have been largely supported by their families but have added extreme stress when development of community resources has not kept up with discharges of patients from state hospitals. Some of these mentally ill patients end up homeless along with thousands of others hard hit by economic conditions.

All of these major changes have brought with them new stresses for families and, in turn, new challenges for family therapists and counselors. Current foci in the literature and at professional conferences include dysfunctional families related to physical, sexual, and substance abuse; children at risk because of divorce, poverty, and abuse; families of the mentally ill; empowerment of women in families; and the effect of AIDS on the family. Questions are raised as to the limitations in scope of family counseling and therapy for some crisis-ridden families whose severe problems are rooted in the complexity of the social ills of society today.

RESOURCES FOR MORE INFORMATION

American Association for Marriage and Family Therapy
1100 Seventeenth Street N.W.
Washington, DC 20036-4601
(202) 452-0109
Publishes *Journal of Marital and Family Therapy*

Family Service America
11700 West Lake Park Drive
Milwaukee, WI 53224
(414) 359-1040
Publishes *Families in Society and Directory of Member Agencies*

National Alliance for the Mentally Ill (NAMI)
2101 Wilson Boulevard, Suite 302
Arlington, VA 22201
(703) 524-7600
With 1001 affiliates nationwide

National Coalition Against Domestic Violence
2401 Virginia Avenue N.W., Suite 302
Washington, DC 20037
(202) 293-8860

FOR FURTHER READING

Yale University Bush Center in Child Development and Social Policy & Family Resource Coalition (1983). *Programs to strengthen families: A resource guide.* New Haven, CT: Author.

REFERENCES

Anderson, C. M., Reiss, D. J. & Hogarty, G. E. (1986). *Schizophrenia and the family.* New York: Guilford Press.

Bateson, G., Jackson, D. D., Haley, J., & Weaklands, J. (1956). Towards a theory of schizophrenia. *Behavioral Science, 1*, 251–264.

Boszormenyi-Nagy, J. & Spark, S. M. (1973). *Invisible loyalties.* New York: Harper & Row.

Bowen, M. (1978). *Family therapy in clinical practice.* New York: Aronson.

Carter, E. A. & McGoldrick, M. (Eds.). (1980). *The family life cycle: A framework for family therapy.* New York: Gardner Press.

Falloon, I. R. H., Boyd, J. L., & McGill, C. W. (1984). *Family care of schizophrenia.* New York: Guilford Press.

Framo, J. L. (1982). *Explorations in marital and family therapy: selected papers of James L. Framo.* New York: Springer.

Goldenberg, I., & Goldenberg, H. (1985). *Family therapy: An overview.* Monterey, CA: Brooks/Cole.

Haley, J. (1976). *Problem-solving therapy.* San Francisco: Jossey-Bass.

Jackson, D. D. (1959). Family interaction, family homeostasis, and some implications for conjoint family therapy. In J. Masserman (Ed.), *Individual and Family Dynamics.* New York: Grune & Stratton.

Kempler, W. (1981). *Experiential psychotherapy within families.* New York: Brunner/Mazel.

Kerr, M. E., & Bowen, M. (1988). *Family evaluation.* New York: Norton.

Madanes, C. (1984). *Behind the one-way mirror.* San Francisco: Jossey-Bass.

McGoldrick, M. & Gerson, R. (1985). *Genograms in family assessment.* New York: Norton.

Minuchin, S. (1974). *Families and family therapy.* Cambridge: Harvard University Press.
Minuchin, S., & Fishman, H. C. (1981). *Family therapy techniques.* Cambridge: Harvard University Press.
Napier, A., & Whitaker, C. (1978). *The family crucible.* New York: Harper & Row.
Nichols, M. (1984). *Family therapy: Concepts and methods.* New York: Gardner Press.
Paul, N. L. (1980). Now and the past: Transgenerational analysis. *International Journal of Family Psychiatry, 1*, 235–248.
Selvini-Palazzoli, M. S., Boscolo, L., Cecchin, G. F., & Prata, G. (1978). *Paradox and counterparadox.* New York: Aronson.

25

Marriage and Marital Counseling

MICHAEL J. SALAMON, Ph.D.

MARRIAGE

As an institution marriage has existed for as long as there have been men and women. There are cultural, anthropological, psychodynamic, and object-relations explanations for the development of the institution of marriage. However, whether marriage developed for economic reasons, as an attempt to codify the division of labor between the sexes, as a method for male-dominated societies to traditionalize the subjugation of women, as a means of enhancing identity by defining oneself in relation to another, or simply as a technique to ensure procreation, most adult males and females will get married at least one time in their lives. The rates of marriage increased steadily from the 1950s through the early 1980s. Recent statistics indicate that presently over 2 million couples get married in the United States every year. Unfortunately, while the rate of marriage grew until it leveled off in the mid-1980s, rates of divorce doubled in that same period of time (Klagsbrun, 1985).

Couples bond together in marriage for many reasons. Often the reasons are sound and healthy, based upon reciprocal trust, respect, and love. Presently marriage is best defined as a relationship that encompasses an emotional impetus and that is solidified within a legal framework.

For marriages to endure both ontogenetically and over the centuries, a unified sense of satisfaction within the structure of marriage had to have developed. Simply put, marriage had to be satisfying to the marital partners in order for it to have endured. It is only recently that both research and clinical efforts have been directed to determine what makes up a satisfying marriage and how to remove the causes of dissatisfaction in troubled ones.

Marital Satisfaction

An early view of how happy marriages developed and were sustained was based upon the *strain toward consistency* theory. This theory suggested that the longer a couple remained together the more likely they were to develop similar views and values. This consistency in outlook was thought to lead to greater marital satisfaction (Kerchkoff, 1966).

While there is little doubt that shared values may lead to a greater sense of understanding between the partners in a marital relationship, other factors contribute to satisfaction. Anderson, Russell, and Schumm (1983) suggested that the course of marital satisfaction follows a U-shaped curve. Satisfaction is high both immediately after marriage and in late middle age. The stresses of child rearing, financial obligations, careers, and problems of raising teenagers and coping with elderly parents cause satisfaction to decline in the middle years of marriage.

Conflict is often cited as a primary cause for dissatisfaction in marriage. Intimacy without conflict is impossible; therefore, only specific types of conflict may indicate true marital discord. Conflict that is suggestive of defensiveness, stubbornness and withdrawal may be dysfunctional. According to Gottman and Krokoff (1989) the marital satisfaction of wives declines only if they exhibit sadness or fear during marital conflict. If, however, wives express anger and contempt during conflict with their husbands, who in turn are not stubborn or withdrawn but engage in the conflict in a similar vein, marital satisfaction of the wives improves. Conversely, if husbands refuse to approach conflict on an equal footing with their wives, using either passive or agressive communicative styles, satisfaction will decrease. To the degree that married people are able to express their needs clearly without negativity, benefits appear to accrue (Smith, Vivian, & O'Leary, 1990).

Long-term happy marriages have consistently been found to be characterized not only by shared values but by a strong sense of shared activities, companionship, and strong communication skills (Atchley & Miller, 1983; Mackinnon, Mackinnon, & Franken, 1984). In a series of interviews with older widows, Malatesta (1989) found that five factors tended to be reported by those who had successful marriages. First, a realistic view of the emotional intensity of marriage existed. Those with the most successful relationships reported that expecting "constant love" was not realistic. Rather, while love always existed, the intensity of the emotion tended to wax and wane. Interviewees also reported that spending time as a couple was important; however, private time or time alone was also necessary. Individuals whose self-esteem was strong also had good marriages. One interviewee indicated that "the marriage was only as good as how I felt about myself." The ability to compromise was a strong component of successful marriage. And finally, the ability to do new things together as a couple and avoid ruts aided the long-term success of marriage.

Thus, from the perspective of the counselor, teaching a couple ways to communicate in an assertive and direct fashion, along with specific techniques for enhancing time together should help as a first step toward increasing marital satisfaction.

Marital Discord

The causes of divorce are most often cited to be a lack of satisfaction in the relationship or marital discord. Poor communication is the most frequently reported problem of couples who seek marital therapy in an attempt to alleviate the discord (Smith et al., 1990). However, *communication* is a generic term that encompasses many subcomponents. Smith et al. (1990) reported that the emotional components of communication were more important indicators of the quality of the marital relationship than the actual communication. These researchers found that personality variables, as they interact with communication styles, combined with the stressors traditionally found in marriages (finances, sexual needs, etc.) are the best predictors of marital maladjustment.

Cognitive processes are contributing factors to the development and maintenance of marital maladjustment (Baucom, Epstein, Sayers, & Sher, 1989). These include selective attention, spouses' attributions as to why events occur, expectancies or predictions of what events will occur in the future, assumptions about the nature of events, personal characteristics, and personal standards about what "should be."

Communication is always lacking in couples who suffer from marital discord. The ability to recognize the contribution of personality factors and one's view of the world to marital satisfaction must, however, not be overlooked. Step two then for the counselor who seeks to alleviate marital discord is to address the personality variables and cognitive processes that have a negative impact on the communications in the marital dyad. Expectation and attributions must be realistic, and means of dealing with stress must be mutually agreed on by the spouses.

Marriage Counseling

When marital discord does develop, it may linger with tenacity. Many couples avoid dealing with the problems in their relationship, believing that this is the way marriage is meant to be or just hoping it will get better. Others, desirous of improving their marital lives, turn to therapists and counselors for marriage counseling. The history of the development of marital counseling is relatively recent, following theoretical changes in the field, and is evolving concurrently with the arbitrarily separate field of family therapy. Indeed there is an increasing tendency for marital therapy to become integrated with family therapy.

In the 1940s marital dysfunctions tended to be viewed from an intrapersonal perspective. The model evolved from psychoanalytic theory; thus, the psychodynamic view of marital discord emphasized unresolved individual conflicts as the cause and therefore the emphasis for intervention. In the 1950s and 1960s families began to be viewed as systems, composed of interrelated parts interacting within a social-ecological environment. A change in any one part of the system caused changes in another. An individual's problem was not within himself or herself, but rather within the context of a larger system. While this view of marital development went a long way toward recognizing factors beyond the marital dyad, the conceptualization was difficult to operationalize and therefore study. With the advent of behavioral and social learning theories in the 1960s and 1970s, scientific methods could be more readily applied to the field of marriage counseling. Unfortunately, rigid applications of these approaches tended to exclude intrapersonal factors as causative of distress. The 1980s began to see the development of rapprochement between social-learning, behavioral, and intrapersonal approaches to marital counseling.

Schools of Therapy
As recently as 1960 marriage counseling consisted primarily of seeing the marital partners individually. Presently, conjoint sessions are the predominant format for counseling regardless of the therapist's orientation. In fact, many therapists advocate involving spouses in therapy even when marital distress is not the presenting problem (Jacobson, Holtzworth-Munroe, & Schmaling, 1989).

While there are dozens of schools of family and marital therapy, there are overriding similarities between the schools; and almost all schools can be categorized as belonging to or having evolved from one of two theoretical orientations: *psychodynamic* models or *cognitive-behavioral* models.

Psychodynamic models. Insight-oriented (IOMT), intrapersonal, or the psychodynamic models of marriage counseling seek to assist the couple to overcome hidden or unconscious sources of conflict that developed earlier in life. These unresolved developmental crises adversely affect adult relationships in many ways. For example, when two partners unconsciously choose each other for marriage because of unresolved dependencies, collusion exists. This may occur when a male with unresolved dependence needs chooses an emotionally overpowering woman to marry, who in turn chose him because of her unresolved need for dominance. This couple may gain reinforcement for their underlying conflicts from the relationship, but they are locked in a struggle that causes additional distress.

Insight-oriented models of counseling seek to free the couple from their unresolved conflicts so that they can act in a more mature fashion. The techniques of change include interpretation and explanation by the therapist of the disordered interactions, communication training, instruction in clarifying communications, contracts between spouses to enhance communication and insight, quid pro quo negotiations, and task assignments such as daily speech.

Cognitive-behavioral models. The primary theoretical orientation for the cognitive-behavioral models (BMT, or behavioral marital therapy) of marital counseling is that all disordered behaviors are learned. The emphasis is on present rather than historical determinants of negative marital interactions. The general goals of BMT are to increase positive and decrease negative interactions and provide strategies for overcoming any future problems that may develop in the relationship.

BMT recognizes that couples in distress tend to reward each other less frequently, punish each other more often, and exhibit greater deficiencies in their ability to deal with conflict than couples not as disordered. The therapist acts as a model, encouraging rehearsal and feedback between the spouses. Specific techniques include a variety of methods to identify and eliminate aversive interactions. Problem-solving training helps the couple define the problem in a nonaccusational fashion. Solutions may then be generated and the best one selected. Communication training is especially important to enhance empathic listening and eliminate defensiveness and accusational posturing. Reframing, relabeling, or restructuring is a technique that helps the participants to carefully evaluate their own responses so that their reactions are not affected by distorted cognitions. For example, a wife may complain that her husband never expresses any love. Reframing may help her to see that the husband has simply not learned how to verbally express affection in the manner she would like.

Outcome Studies

The similarities between the two theoretical approaches IOMT and BMT are in the areas of therapist interventions. In almost all cases, therapists are active and directive, and the focus is on faulty communication as the primary problem in the marriage.

Over the last decade there have been several studies of the efficacy of the two approaches. One study (Hahlweg, Revenstorf, & Schindler, 1984) found that BMT was effective in changing the communication skills of couples in a positive fashion. This study reported that the positive outcome was not simply a statistical outcome based on the couples' reports but also of clinical relevance in that the verbal communication skills of those receiving BMT were improved to the point of equivalence with a control group of nondistressed couples.

Jacobson, Folleto, et al. (1984) reviewed four BMT outcome studies and reanalyzed the data from these studies for overall degree and rate of improvement. Statistically, there was a moderate rate of improvement in all four studies, with 55% of the couples reporting improvement. In about 40% of the couples, only one spouse reported positive change. In the 100 treatment control groups about 14% of the couples reported improvement, 17% deteriorated, and 70% reported no change.

Snyder and Wills (1989) studied 79 couples who were assigned to either BMT or IOMT. At the time of termination of therapy and at 6-month follow-up, the researchers found a general equivalence between the two types of therapy in producing positive changes both between and within the spouses. Interestingly, however, when the same couples were interviewed at a 4-year follow up, a significantly higher percentage of couples who had BMT had gone through divorce. Only 3% of the IOMT couples experienced divorce, while 38% of the BMT couples did (Snyder, Wills, & Grady-Fletcher, 1991a). The researchers concluded that apparently "sustained improvement in marital satisfaction may depend on spouses gaining insight and resolving preexisting emotional conflicts" (Snyder, Wills, & Grady-Fletcher, 1991b, p. 146).

Individuals enter marriage with unique backgrounds and history. The counselor must never lose sight of the fact that a complete assessment of the reasons for discord is necessary. In fact in some cases it may be appropriate to have a complete psychological evaluation of each of the spouses before initiating marital counseling. Understanding preexisting emotional conditions and gaining insight may not be sufficient when deeper psychopathology exists. Antisocial personality, significant depression, and alcohol and drug abuse, among other problems, can be exhibited as marital discord. While the discord is real, addressing the marital strife will not alleviate the deeper problem. Counselors should be aware of the need for more intensive forms of individual or medical therapy and make the appropriate referrals. Assessment can be performed by outside specialists. There are also many assessment tools to evaluate the degree of discord between spouses. Among these are the Marital Communications Inventory and Marriage Adjustment Form, available from Family Life Publications; the Marital Satisfaction Inventory and Marriage Adjustment Inventory, from Western Psychological Services; and the Marital Evaluation Checklist, from Psychological Assessment Resources (Lef-Sweetland & Keyser, 1986).

DIVORCE

As marriages form with an emotional impetus in a legal context, so do they end. When marriages can no longer endure and marital counseling is not attempted, not indicated, or no longer effective, divorce ensues. It should be noted that divorce is a legal action. Couples may decide to stay in a distressed marriage for any number of reasons rather than go through a legal divorce. Friedman (1981) has suggested that despite the fact that couples may not divorce well into midlife, their unhappiness was likely evident during the courtship years. Yet the results of remaining in an unsatisfying marriage may not be different from divorce (Salamon & Rosenthal, manuscript submitted for publication).

A relatively new approach to dissolving marriages through *divorce mediation* has evolved. The key to a successful divorce mediation is the mutual agreement between the spouses to end the marriage in a nonadversarial way. Divorce mediators, who may be attorneys, mental health professionals, or lay persons with specific training, attempt to resolve the primary issues in a legal framework that limits conflict and reduces emotional strain, and thus lessens the need for lengthy litigation.

While many speak of amicable divorces, clinically this appears not to be an accurate description. Rather, varying degrees of conflict within a divorce proceeding and ambivalence to the divorce process increase conflict.

The legal issues by which marriages are dissolved relate to family and finances. The family issues are almost exclusively child related and encompass the questions of with whom children reside, visitation, and degree of parental involvement. In those divorces where conflict is less intense, custody of the children is joint and visitation liberal. In the most difficult cases visitations may be supervised by a court-appointed third party for fear that the noncustodial spouse will abduct the child or children.

Financial components of divorce relate to the discussion of family-related assets. Decisions must be made regarding basic living costs, health needs, and financing the education of children. The costs of alimony and child support must be decided. Unfortunately, experience suggests that here too the degree of amicability between the partners has an impact on the outcome and degree to which the former spouses are able to agree and ultimately comply with any of the decisions. In some cases, because of divorce, financial situations change radically. Divorced women may become financially destitute if alimony and child support dry up. Even when divorced men do follow through with their financial obligations, the cost of supporting two homes can be overwhelming.

Perhaps the worst part of divorce is its impact on children (Ines, Fassler, & Lash, 1985). These children of divorce suffer from the emotional upheaval of the conflict for many years. The children often suffer guilt, fearful that they caused or contributed to the breakup. They may continue to fantasize that their parents will remarry, and they occasionally have difficulty forming and maintaining relationaships of their own. Divorce can mean that children may grow up without a proper role model or are forced to assume the role of the noncustodial parent. In most cases this means that a son living with his mother might feel obligated to tend to home repair, provide emotional care for the mother, or have unrealistic concerns about finances. Daughters express a great deal of emotion about their divorced fathers' social lives. These daughters may become too nurturant toward the father. Children are also emotionally threatened if they feel they failed the parents. These feelings arise if children believe that they can save the marriage or if they are put in a situation where parental frustration and anger is transferred onto them (Gardner, 1979). Children of divorce benefit from both individual and group therapy, where they learn how to overcome their negative emotions and form bonds with others.

The outcomes of divorce almost always result in a distressed life. Still, divorce may be the only alternative to living in a distressed marriage. When the counselor is involved in the process that can lead to divorce, it must be made clear that the final decision is the clients' and that it is made after all of the alternatives have been explored.

PRACTICAL POINTS FOR THE COUNSELOR

1. Marital discord does not occur in a vacuum, The counselor should try to discern any underlying psychopatholgy. If that pathology is significant, an appropriate referral should be made.
2. All counselling interventions, regardless of theoretical orientation, emphasize the importance of communication training and problem solving.
3. While problems with communication are the most frequent reported reason for couples to seek marriage counseling, communication means different things to different people.
4. When the communcation problem is due to the wife's inability to express her feelings without fear or sadness, it is necessary to teach her to be more assertive in her communications.
5. If the husband's communication style is either passive or aggressive, the counselor must teach him to be in more control of his reactions, addressing the issues more directly and evenly.
6. If both spouses' attributions, expectations, or assumptions get in the way of understanding between the couple, the counselor must make each spouse aware of these shortcomings.
7. Mutually agreed-on strategies for dealing with life's stressors should be developed. This will give the couple a plan to use in avoiding future conflicts.

8. The counselor must work to teach the couple how to develop insight into each other's moods and behaviors.
9. In some situations divorce is a reasonable option. When this is the case, the therapist must bear in mind that the decision is made by the couple.

REFERENCES

Anderson, S. A., Russel, C. S., & Schumm, W. R. (1983). Perceived marital quality and family life-cycle categories: A further analysis. *Journal of Marriage and the Family, 45*, 127–139.

Atchley, R. C., & Miller, S. J. (1983). Typles of elderly couples. In T.H. Brubaker (Ed.), *Family relationships in later life* (pp. 77–90), Beverly Hills, CA: Sage.

Baucom, D. H., Epstein, N., Sayers, S., & Sher, T. G. (1989). The role of cognitions in marital relationships: Definitional, methodological, and conceptual issues. *Journal of Consulting and Clinical Psychology, 57*, 31–38.

Friedman, H. J. (1981). The divorced in middle age. In J. G. Howells (Ed.), *Modern perspectives in the psychiatry of middle age* (pp. 103–115). New York: Brunner/Mazel.

Gardner, R. A. (1979). Divorce. In J.D. Noshpitz (Ed.), *Basic handbook of child paychiatry* (Vol. 4), (pp. 236–270). New York: Basic Books.

Gottman, J. M., & Krockoff, L. J. (1989). Marital interaction and satisfaction: A longitudinal view. *Journal of Counsulting and Clinical Psychology, 57*, 47–52.

Hahlweg, K., Revenstorf, D., & Schindler, L. (1984). Effects of behavioral marital therapy on couples' communication and problem-solving skills. *Journal of Consulting and Clinical Psycholgy, 52*, 553–556.

Ives, S. B., Fassler, D., & Lash, M. (1985). *The divorce workbook: A guide for kids and families.* Burlington, VT: Waterfront Books.

Jacobson, N. S., Folleto, W. C., Revenstorf, D., Hahlweg, K., Baucom, D. H., & Margolin, G. (1984). Variability in outcome and clinical significance of behavioral marital therapy: A reanalysis of outcome data. *Journal of Consulting and Clinical Psycholgy, 52*, 497–504.

Jacobson, N. S., Holtzworth-Munroe, A., & Schmaling, K.B. (1989). Marital therapy and spouse involvement in the treatment of depression, agoraphobia, and alcoholism, *Journal of Consulting and Clinical Psychology, 57*, 5–10.

Kerchoff, A. C. (1966). Norm-value clusters and the strain toward consistency among older married couples. In T. H. Simpson & J. C. McKinney (Eds.), *Social aspects of aging.* Durham, NC: Duke University Press.

Klagsbrun, F. (1985). *Married people: Staying together in the age of divorce.* New York: Bantam.

Lef-Sweetland, R. C., & Keyser, D. J. (Eds.). (1986). *Tests: A comprehensive reference for assessments in psychology education and business* (2nd ed.). Kansas City: Test Corporation of America.

Mackinnon, R. F., Mackinnon, C. E., & Franken, J. L. (1984). Family strengths in long-term marriages. *Alternative Lifestyles, Z*, 115–126.

Malatesta, V. J. (1989). On making love last in a marriage: Reflections of 60 widows. *Clinical Gerontologist, 9*, pp. 64–67.

Salamon, M. J., & Rosenthal, G. Cold marriage: Putting warmth back into a platonic relationship. Manuscript submitted for publication.

Smith, D. A., Vivian, D., & O'Leary, K. D. (1990). Longitudinal prediction of marital discord from premarital expressions of affect. *Journal of Consulting and Clinical Psychology, 58*, 790–798.

Snyder, D. K., & Wills, R. M. (1989). Behavioral versus insight-oriented marital therapy: Effects on individual and interpersonal functioning. *Journal of Consulting and Clinical Psychology, 57,* 39–46.

Snyder, D. K., Wills, R. M., & Grady-Fletcher, A. (1991a). Long-term effectiveness of behavioral versus insight-oriented marital therapy: A 4-year follow-up. *Journal of Consulting and Clinical Psychology, 59,* 138–141.

Snyder, D K., Wills, R. M., & Grady-Fletcher, A. (1991b). Risks and challenges of long-term psychotherapy outcome research: Reply to Jacobson. *Journal of Consulting and Clinical Psychology, 59,* 146–149.

FOR FURTHER READING

Bourn, M. (1978). *Family therapy in clinical practice,* New York: Aronson.

Herr, J. J., & Weakland, J. H. (1979). *Counseling elders and their families.* New York: Springer.

Ines, S. B., Fassler, D., & Lash, M. (1985). *The divorce workbook: A guide for kids and families.* Burlington, VT: Waterfront Books.

Jacobson, N. S., & Bussed, N. (1983). Marital and family therapy. In M. Hersen, A. E. Kazdin, & A. S. Bellack (Eds.), *The clinical psychology handbook* (pp. 611–630). New York: Pergamon Press.

Klagsbrun, F. (1985). *Married people: Staying together in the age of divorce.* New York: Bantam.

Minuchin, S. (1974). *Families and family therapy.* Cambridge, MA: Gardner Press.

Papp, P. (Ed.). (1977). *Family Therapy: Full-length case studies.* New York: Gardner Press.

Stuart, R. B. (1980). *Helping couples change.* New York: Guilford Press.

Wallerstein, J. S., & Kelly, J. B. (1980). *Surviving the breakup: How children and parents cope with divorce.* New York: Basic Books.

Wolman, B. B., & Stricker, G. (Eds.). (1983). *Handbook of family and marital therapy.* New York: Plenum Press.

26

Addictions Counseling

DAVID E. SMITH, M.D.
RICHARD B. SEYMOUR, M.A.

In the vast and bewildering pharmacopeia of drugs, none are more fascinating than the psychoactive drugs. While many of these substances are medications with recognized indications for medical treatment, others are used primarily for "recreational" purposes; that is, they are substances we have given ourselves permission to use in social and personal settings. Still others are illegal and their use or very possession is subject to criminal sanctions.

Psychoactive substances are so named because their principal action is on the psyche. Although many of them have far-reaching and profound effects on bodily functions, including heartbeat and respiration, these effects are a result of activities within the central nervous system (CNS). For that reason, psychoactive substances are also called *CNS drugs.* Many other substances, including both food and drugs, may have a peripheral effect on the psyche, but only psychoactive drugs have their primary effect on the psyche and in the central nervous system. These CNS effects can include alterations in mood, pain reaction, energy levels, physical and mental performance, and sense perceptions.

Current research on brain chemistry indicates that the molecular structure of psychoactive substances resembles that of endogenous "brain messengers," called *neurotransmitters,* that carry information and commands between the brain's nerve cells. The molecules of some psychoactive substances achieve their effects on brain cells by attaching to nerve cell receptor sites and tricking the cells into thinking that they have received messages from other parts of the brain. In this way, narcotics such as morphine and heroin take the place of endorphins (endogenous morphine). Others, like cocaine, attach to presynaptic sites and achieve their effects by stimulating the release of such endogenous neurotransmitters as the energy releasing epinephrine and norepinephrine. Some drugs, such as alcohol and the other sedative-hynotics, including benzodiazepines and barbiturates, and the so-called psychedelic drugs, produce a complex brain chemistry interaction that involves several different neurotransmitter systems.

ALCOHOL AND ALCOHOLISM

Alcohol is a psychoactive substance that can be produced naturally from fruits, grains, and other plant material through the process of fermentation. Fermentation is a process by which certain microorganisms called yeasts break down the sugar found in decaying plant material and excrete alcohol as a waste product. Ancient homonids probably discovered the psychoactive properties of alcohol by eating spoiled fruit and found that they enjoyed the effects produced by alcohol. The effect produced by small quantities of alcohol is *disinhibition euphoria,* a general feeling of well-being coupled with a lessening of personal inhibitions. Once these ancients grasped the principle of fermentation, they were able to produce a variety of wines, beers, and other alcohol-bearing concoctions. Some anthropologists maintain that the Neolithic Revolution, the shift from hunter-gatherer tribes to agricultural communities, took place as a means of facilitating the growing of grains for the production of beer.

Fermentation produced only a limited alcohol content, but during the middle ages, alchemists discovered that they could heat alcohol-bearing substances sufficiently to vaporize the alcohol, condense the alcohol vapor on a cool surface, such as the interior of a metal coil, and produce a much more concentrated and correspondingly potent substance. The process is distillation, and its discovery set Western civilization and those cultures affected by it on a path of intensified alcohol abuse that continues to this day. The abuse of alcohol did not start with the discovery of distilled spirits, however, nor is it limited to these. Even at the percentages found in wine and beer, alcohol can produce devastating physical and psychological effects.

Alcohol Abuse and Alcohol Dependence
Alcohol is one among a number of psychoactive substances that are called *sedative hypnotic drugs* and that have similar effects to one another. All of these drugs produce a greater or lesser degree of disinhibition euphoria, and prescription sedative-hynotics have a number of medical indications, including the treatment of anxiety, convulsions, and seizures. Until recently, alcohol had many medical indications as well, but now only has one: the treatment of acute methyl-alcohol poisoning. Alcohol is the only sedative-hynotic drug that a large part of humanity has given itself permission to use on a personal/social basis.

Most individuals use alcohol in moderation and in proscribed social settings as a "social lubricant." The practice of Christian and Jewish faiths involve the ceremonial use of small quantities of wine. Some sources maintain that for non-addiction-vulnerable individuals the moderate use of alcohol may even improve health.

For others, however, the use of alcohol can rapidly develop into abuse and even dependence. *Acute alcohol toxicity,* also known as being drunk, can produce slurred speech, slowed reactions, extreme emotional lability, motor impairment, and loss of good judgment. In extreme cases, heightened blood alcohol can result in coma and death. Much more frequently, the emotional lability can result in acts of violence, while the impaired motor facility, impaired reactions, bad judgment, and loss of consciousness can result in fatal accidents.

Incidents of alcohol intoxication may be just that—isolated incidents, such as getting inebriated at a New Year's Eve party. They may remain isolated incidents, if the individual is not vulnerable to addictive disease and has enough sense to learn from the experience or foresight to stay out of arguments and not to try to drive. When intoxication happens frequently or on a recurring basis, it becomes *alcohol abuse.* With abuse, there may or may not be a pattern or an escalation of use. The abuser is more apt to become involved in fights, or accidents, or alcohol-related interpersonal problems. The chronic abuse of alcohol can result in alcohol dependence.

As with all sedative-hypnotic drugs, the chronic abuse of alcohol produces tolerance, that is, the need for increasingly high dosages in order to produce the desired effects and susceptibility to withdrawal symptoms following abrupt cessation of use. A limited form of withdrawal often takes place following acute alcohol intoxication. This is the classic "hangover," characterized by headache, stomach disorder, feelings of anxiety, and general tremulousness. For the alcohol dependent, these symptoms can be greatly magnified and complicated, and may be life-threatening to the point of requiring hospitalization during the peak periods of withdrawal.

Detoxification
The most accepted medical treatment for alcohol dependence is *detoxification,* literally allowing the body to complete a process of withdrawal that results in fully eliminating alcohol from the system and then helping the body to return to normal function and a state of metabolic equilibrium. The process of alcohol detoxification is complicated by the fact that alcohol withdrawal like any withdrawal from a sedative-hynotic drug, can be life-threatening. There is a period during sedative-hypnotic withdrawal when the body is particularly vulnerable and prone to grand mal seizure, a major and life-threatening epileptic attack at-

tended by loss of consciousness. Such attacks may result from a reversal of the sedative-hypnotic role in suppressing seizure activity. Other withdrawal symptoms may include tremor, high temperature, and high blood pressure, and if the disease is progressed, convulsions, hallucinations, and delirium tremens (DTs). Because of the life-endangering nature of alcohol detoxification, especially in advanced stages of the disease, it is best to accomplish withdrawal in an inpatient program where the patient can be closely monitored and medical emergencies can be dealt with quickly.

Alcohol detoxification is usually accomplished through a process of substitution and withdrawal, or *taper*. In this process, a long-acting sedative-hynotic drug is substituted for the daily alcohol content and the dosage gradually reduced until full detoxification is accomplished and there are no further withdrawal symptoms. A variety of agents can be used for this process including librium (chlordiazepoxide), but the authors prefer the barbiturate phenobarbital. Essentially, phenobarbital is long-acting and dosages are easy to titrate. Once the patient is into withdrawal symptoms, the substitution agent is administered to a level where physiological signs of intoxication are just beginning to appear. The patient is then stabilized at that level and the step-down process is initiated. Reduction can be stopped and the patient restabilized at any point where overt withdrawal symptoms reemerge. Such medical treatment is effective; however, it only deals with the patient's physical dependence on alcohol. Most patients requiring alcohol detoxification are suffering from *alcoholism,* a disease that includes physical dependence but requries treatment and aftercare beyond that found in a purely medical protocol.

Alcoholism

Alcohol dependence is the physical component of the disease that has come to be known as alcoholism. Alcoholism has been described by Brissette (Brissette & Seymour, 1991; Seymour & Smith, 1987 a&b) as a "three-headed dragon," of which the first head is physical dependence and the other two heads represent psychological and spiritual components of the disease. The whole disease must be treated if there is to be any hope for success and long-term recovery. Treatment for alcoholism, as for any addiction, includes some form of detoxification, counseling that continues past detox, education on the nature of addiction and learning the "language of recovery," and institutional support, often leading to entry into a 12-step fellowship, such as Alcoholics Anonymous (AA).

In 1960, with publication of *The Disease Concept of Alcoholism,* Jellinek brought the medical nature of alcoholic disease to public consciousness. Many medical organizations endorsed Jellinek's basic concepts. Since that time, alcoholism has continued to be studied and treated as a medical, psychological, and spiritual malaise calling for detoxification, counseling, changes in lifestyle, often long-term aftercare, abstinence from all psychoactive substances, and supported recovery. Today, alcoholism is seen as one manifestation of *addictive disease*, a disease entity that involves both genetic and environmental factors and is characterized by compulsion, loss of control, and continued use in spite of adverse consequences.

It has become increasingly evident that there is a genetic factor in vulnerability to addiction, including alcoholism. Numerous studies have shown that individuals with a family history of alcoholism or other drug problems (i.e., parents or grandparents who are alcoholic) have a much higher incidence of addiction and alcoholism. The other primary contributor is environmental, including such factors as availability, cultural use and abuse, family use patterns, and so on: **Genetics + Environment = Addiction (Alcoholism)**.

The nature of alcoholism was anticipated in the development of a grass-roots fellowship of alcoholics known as Alcoholics Anonymous. The founders of AA, as it came to be called, were aware that the disease is progressive and incurable, and can only be brought into remission through abstinence and through the individual working a program of recovery that involves reliance upon a "higher power" and the development of spiritual maturity. Since its founding, AA has helped thousands of alcoholics into long-term sobriety with a minimum of relapse and today provides a verification of treatment efficacy. Much progress in the treatment of alcoholics, and of drug addicts, in the last two decades has been due to an increasing cross-understanding and cooperation between treatment personnel and facilities and the 12-step recovery fellowships represented by AA, Narcotics Anonymous (NA), and the growing number of fellowships involving recovery from a variety of specific psychoactive substances.

Alcoholics Anonymous

According to his own testimony, in early May 1933, Bill Wilson (AA, 1957), an unemployed New York stockbroker with a long history of alcohol abuse, stopped drinking with the help of an old friend, Ebby, a fellow alcoholic who had dried out through membership in an Oxford group, and was attempting to find a job. The Oxford movement was a spiritual fellowship that sought to recapture the values of early Christianity through a program of personal self-development. A proxy fight in Akron, Ohio, required a small group of aggressive hagglers to be on the scene. In that depression year, the newly sober Wilson jumped at the chance to demonstrate his field skills. The proxy failed and the others left Akron, but Wilson stayed on, having no job to which he could return.

On Saturday, May 11, the day before Mother's Day, Wilson thought about getting drunk and the thought threw him into a panic. Looking at the hotel's church directory, as far across the lobby as he could get from the bar, he saw a listing for an Episcopalian minister. Thinking of how his friend Ebby had been helped by the Oxford movement, Wilson promptly phoned the minister, who was busy writing a sermon but suggested that he call Henrietta Seiberling, an active member of the local Oxford group. Seiberling was not an alcoholic, but was deeply committed to the precepts of the Oxford movement. She was a Vassar graduate and the daughter-in-law of Harvey Firestone, the founder and one-time president of the Goodyear Rubber Company. The Akron group of the Oxford movement had come into being and developed largely through the efforts of Firestone.

Seiberling received Wilson's call with some excitement. In her private prayers, she had received "guidance" concerning an alcoholic surgeon and friend, Dr. Bob S. In a dilemma as to how to help her friend, she took Wilson's call as heavenly guidance. She invited Wilson to the Seiberling estate, where he told her his story and she in turn told him about Dr. Bob. The following Monday, Wilson and Dr. Bob met. Several weeks of interaction followed, culminating in the organization of Alcoholics Anonymous on July 11, 1935, two years after Bill Wilson—now called "Bill W."—stopped drinking.

Initially based on the Oxford precepts, AA developed as a fellowship of "anonymous drunks" meeting together to reinforce one another's sobriety. The fellowship established a blueprint for developing spiritual maturity, contained in the 12 Steps, and a group code of ethics, the 12 Traditions. The 12 steps provide a process that begins with the recognition that a problem exists. Alcoholism and other addiction is partly characterized by the alcoholic's inability to accept the fact that there is a problem. This is called "denial." There follows a further recognition that the problem can be dealt with through reliance on a higher power, and the exercise of working within that power to make the changes necessary to ensure long-term recovery from addiction/alcoholism. Most recovering individuals seek the help of a "sponsor," someone with established sobriety who will help them work the steps and generally strengthen the quality of their own recovery.

By 1939, Alcholics Anonymous had dissolved its close connections to the Oxford movement and was developing its own identity. Two additional AA groups had been established in Cleveland and New York. The *Big Book* (AA 1939), which has come to represent the ultimate AA authority, was completed and published.

Alcoholics Anonymous received a tremendous boost from the professional acceptance of the disease concept of alcoholism. In the years that have followed, AA has grown into a worldwide fellowship dedicated to helping alcoholics achieve and maintain sobriety. Along with AA, a variety of 12-step fellowships have come into being for other populations affected by addiction, and have spread in their own right. These include Narcotics Anonymous, Cocaine Anonymous, Marijuana Anonymous, Al-Anon, and Alateen. The last two are support fellowships for the relatives and other individuals close to alcholics who work on their own lives with the help of the 12 steps.

Fetal Alcohol Syndrome
Identified only 21 years ago, fetal alcohol syndrome (FAS) and fetal alcohol effect (FAE) are fully preventable diseases that result from a mother's use of alcohol during pregnancy. FAS is characterized by such symptoms as prematurity, low birth weight, and various physical and mental disabilities such as flatness of features and an inability to form cause-effect judgments on behavior. Some of these symptoms may be apparent at birth, but others do not appear until later in the growth process. While special education and other measures may help a little, the symptoms are often progressive and irreversible.

A very good book has been written about FAS. *The Broken Cord* (Dorris, 1989) is both a testament of the nearly 20-year relationship between Adam and Michael Dorris and the story of FAS in the Native American community. In this book, Dorris balances the objectivity of a trained anthropologist with the eye and ear of a novelist and the complex emotions of a concerned father to produce a clear and convincing narrative that is also very good reading. Chapters that could have been a dry recitation of facts and figures about FAS come to life as the author presents flesh-and-blood protagonists in the fight against the disease. Although the focus is on the Native American community, where FAS and FAE are rampant, the disease exists wherever women use alcohol during pregnancy. In all probability, we are only seeing the most visible cases. FAS may already be a multigenerational phenomenon, involving mothers and grandmothers who are incapable of understanding the consequences of their drinking.

Antabuse (Disulfiram)
Antabuse is a means of helping detoxified alcoholics avoid relapse by making them violently ill if they try to ingest alcohol. Its effects were discovered by accident when workers at a rubber factory found that they could not drink without experiencing such symptoms as flushing, throbbing head and neck ache, respiratory difficulty, nausea, vomiting, sweating, chest pain and breathing difficulty, vertigo, and other unpleasant reactions. Tetraethyliuram disulfide, a chemical used in processing rubber, was found to be the cause, and in 1940 disulfiram, now called Antabuse, was introduced into alcoholism treatment.

Alcoholics who are maintained on Antabuse are given a daily pill that has no effect so long as the alcoholic abstains from alcohol. Within a few minutes of ingesting even the small amount of alcohol found in a dose of cough syrup, however, a variety of unpleasant symptoms can occur with sufficient severity to discourage most attempts at alcohol use. Disulfiram works by interfering with the liver's metabolism of alcohol. A particularly virulent metabolite of alcohol, acetaldehyde, accumulates in the body to cause the distressing symptomatology.

Because it can produce a variety of side effects, antabuse treatment is still controversial. In their book *Under the Influence,* Milam and Ketcham (1981) point out that it does not represent a long-term deterrent to drinking and may detract from the recovering alcoholic's assumption of responsibility for staying sober. They recommend that Antabuse be used with extreme caution, including a detailed review of the client's medical history and weighing of the potential risks. Any client on Antabuse should be monitored regularly for adverse reactions, and clients with a history of congestive heart failure, liver and kidney disorders, diabetes, thyroid problems, brain damage, polyneuropathy, psychosis, or suicidal ideation should not be given this drug.

Adult Children of Alcoholics

Addiction/alcoholism is a family disease that has a profound negative effect on individuals who grow up within its aura. An increasing awareness of the long-term dysfunctionalities that can result has led to the adult children of alcoholics movement. Related to the 12-step fellowships, ACA or ACOA provided extensive support for adult children of alcoholics who are attempting to come to terms with their problems. Children of alcoholics have been characterized on the basis of their role within the alcoholic family. According to Black (1981), all children of alcoholics are affected by alcoholism within the family and need help. Problems can include personal dysfunctions resulting from violence and sexual abuse, seriously endangering the ACA's mental health, ability to gain emotional maturity, and spiritual development if not addressed. Numerous books have been written specifically for ACA readers, and a primary publisher of these is the Hazelden Foundation of Center City, Minnesota.

THE ROLE OF EDUCATION AND CERTIFICATION IN SUBSTANCE ABUSE TREATMENT

Until recently, drug and alcohol counseling was shunned by most health professionals. Alcoholism and addiction were not addressed in medical schools or in general counseling curricula. They were often considered untreatable afflictions of the terminally untouchables of our society (winos, bums, and junkies), and their symptoms were unseen and ignored when they appeared in "normal" patients. The increasing acceptance of a disease concept of alcoholism and the spread of drug addiction into the middle class began to soften these attitudes, but the helping professions were ill equipped to either diagnose or treat addictive disease. Until recently, most drug counselors were recruited directly from the ranks of the newly detoxified, and alcohol counselors were early-stage recovering alcoholics, practicing the 12th Step: "Having had a spiritual awakening as the result of these Steps, we tried to carry this message to alcoholics, and to practice these principles in all our affairs." In both cases, these "peer counselors" relied primarily on their personal experience with alcohol and other drugs and walked a tightrope between personal relapse and helping others. With the exception of these counselors' personal experience, however, little was known about the nature of alcoholism and other addictive diseases.

As more became known about the treatment and counseling of substance abuse and addiction clients, the need for professionally trained and certified practitioners increased. In the medical profession, physicians who referred to themselves as addictionologists won increasing recognition from the American Medical Association. These physicians and other health professionals had formed the American Medical Society for the Treatment of Alcoholism (AMSA). As drug addiction joined alcohol addiction within a general disease concept, AMSA changed its name to the American Medical Society for the Treatment of Alcoholism and Other Drug Dependencies (AMSAODD). As this title proved cumbersome, it was finally shortened to the present American society of Addiction Medicine (ASAM). Dedicated to seeking specialty status for addiction medicine, ASAM offers medical specialty certification and recertification through examinations given on an annual basis.

Certified Alcohol and Drug Abuse Counselor (CADC)

Certification of drug and alcohol counselors has long been a goal, but one that has encountered complications. Several attempts at setting national drug conselor guidelines and standards were initiated during the early 1970s by the National Institute on Drug Abuse, but it was alcohol counseling that first established itself at the state level through the development of a certified alcoholism counselor (CAC) designation in the early 1980s. Since then, the evolution has been toward combining drug and alcohol counseling into one, single certification process. In California, for example, the California Association of Alcohol Counselors (CAAC), started in the late 1970s, became the California Association of Drug and Alcohol Counselors (CADAC) in the mid-1980s. The National Association of Drug and Alcohol Counselors (NADAC) has championed the cause of providing a system of training and credentialing reciprocities for state programs on a national basis and has developed national accreditation standards. Their requirement is that state associations become 100% members of NADAC. All credentialed members in states that are aligned with NADAC are therefore members of both their state association and of NADAC. Many states have statewide credentialing examinations that include practicum requirements.

University-level drug and alcohol counseling certification programs have proliferated in the 1980s. In that many of the students who complete these programs and go on to state certification are themselves in long-term recovery, and often working in the field, these programs can provide the best of both worlds by providing academic information and exposure to treatment techniques to the already experientially adept and dedicated alcohol and other drug counselors.

ADDICTION

Primary addiction is a disease in and of itself and is characterized by compulsive use of a substance, loss of control over that use, and continued use in spite of adverse consequences, that is, disintegration of family and other relationships, loss of livelihood, medical problems that are a direct result of chronic use, and so on. The disease is chronic and progressive, and can be fatal if not treated. Addiction is incurable; that is, an addict, once he or she has crossed the line, cannot go back to controlled use (in AA parlance, "Once a cucumber, always a cucumber, but once you become a pickle, you can't go back to being a cucumber") but the addiction can be brought into remission through abstinence from all psychoactive substances and a program of supported recovery.

Physical Dependence
A major component of addiction is physical dependence, characterized by tolerance, or the need for increasing amounts of a drug in order to achieve desired effects, and the appearance of withdrawal symptomatology whenever the dependent individual attempts to stop using the drug. Until recently it was widely thought that *physical dependence* and *addiction* were synonymous, but the more that is learned about the nature of addiction, the more it becomes clear that although physical dependence is a major component, addiction includes genetic, environmental, psychological and spiritual components as well, all of which need to be addressed in order for the client to achieve long-lasting remission from the disease.

Physical dependence can exist without addiction. All it takes is enough exposure to certain psychoactive drugs to produce increased tolerance and susceptibility to withdrawal symptoms. Many individuals in a hospital postoperative setting develop a physical dependence on opioid analgesics and have to be detoxified before leaving. They experience the opioid drugs as an unpleasant necessity for curbing pain and are relieved when they no longer need to take them. In all likelihood, they will not turn to obsessive use of these drugs. For these individuals, the only problem is physical dependence, and it is dealt with through detoxification.

That is not the case, however, for addicts. Under the old physical Dependence = Addiction paradigm, detoxification was seen as the primary treatment. Today, detoxification is seen as the treatment for physical dependence, but only first step in a long process of treating addiction. While it can be said that addiction is addiction regardless of the primary drug of choice, consequently the bases of recovery and abstinence are not drug-specific, treatment approaches to detoxification and aftercare can be highly drug-specific. The following is a brief, general review of the four psychoactive categories, what the drugs in these groups have in common, and the addiction concerns for each.

The Four Psychoactive Categories
Psychoactive substances can be roughly grouped into four basic categories, each of which has similar effects and calls for similar acute detoxification and aftercare treatment. Two of these categories are "downers": *sedative-hypnotics,* which include alcohol, barbiturates, and benzodiazepines such as Valium, Librium, and Xanex; and *opioid painkillers,* which include such opium derivatives as codeine, morphine, and heroin, and such synthetics as darvon, methadone, and fentanyl. The third category, *stimulants,* or "uppers," includes caffeine and nicotine, amphetamines, and cocaine, while the fourth, *psychedelics,* is composed of all the "hallucinogenic" drugs, such as mescalline, psilocybin, lysergic acid diethylamide (LSD), methylenedioxyamphetamine (MDA), methylenedioxymethamphetamine (MDMA), and marijuana. Some psychoactive substances combine the attributes of two categories, such as the *psychedelic stimulants* MDA and MDMA. Phencyclidine (PCP) and its cogeners may produce symptoms of all except the opioids, depending on dosage and other factors (Inaba & Cohen, 1989).

Sedative-hypnotics. Alcohol, bromides, chloral hydrate, barbiturates, benzodiazepines, methaqualone, and so on. *Desired effects:* disinhibition euphoria (feeling good with lowered inhibitions, increased sociability, and decreased fear). *Acute toxic effects:* dysphoria, impaired judgment, motor impairment, unsteady gait, emotional lability, gastrointestinal distress; in extreme cases, unconsciousness, coma, death. *Chronic effects:* tolerance and the need to increase doses for desired effects, with eventual outweighing of positive effects by negative side effects as tolerance expands beyond the user's ability to assimilate the drug; onset of withdrawal symptoms, including insomnia, anxiety, tremors, high blood pressure, hallucinosis, and potentially life-threatening seizures. All sedative-hypnotics are cross-tolerant; that is, anyone developing tolerance to one will at the same time develop tolerance to all, even if they have never been used. Use of two or more sedative-hypnotic drugs at the same time can result in a multiplier effect that is responsible for most sedative-hynotic overdose fatalities. The addiction to sedative-hynoptics is typified by alcoholism.

2. *Opioid painkillers.* Opium, codeine, morphine, heroin, methadone, darvon, dilaudit, fentanyl, and so on. *Desired effects:* pain reduction, euphoria, sensation of "rush" sometimes described as being like an electric current or body orgasm. *Acute toxic effects:* analgesia or loss of pain, "nodding off" or semiconsciousness, respiratory and circulatory depression; in overdose, loss of consciousness, coma, death. *Chronic effects:* rapid development of tolerance, decreased sexuality, chronic constipation, onset of withdrawal symptoms that are not life-threatening but very uncomfortable.

3. *Stimulants.* Nicotine, caffeine, many antihistamines and decongestants, amphetamine, methamphetamine, ritalin, cocaine, and so on. *Desired effects:* performance enhancement, characterized by alertness, energy, ability to concentrate, and so on, and euphoria. (In high-dose intravenous use or smoking of amphetamines or cocaine, this rush is intense and probably the most important desired effect.) *Acute toxic effects:* rapid heartbeat and respiration, increased blood pressure, hyperthermia or increased temperature, anxiety, rage, paranoia, violent acting-out behavior. In advanced cases, vasoconstriction coupled with rapid respiration can lead to strokes. Non-dose-related idiosyncratic neurotransmitter reactions can cause potentially fatal heart attacks, respiratory arrest, and other complications. *Chronic effects:* Increasing lability marked by stimulant psychoses characterized by intense paranoia with ideas of reference, that is, "Someone (DEA, other users, yellow Volkswagens) is out to get me." This can be particularly problematic when the user is also a well-armed cocaine or amphetamine dealer. Unlike the sedative-hynotic or opioid narcotic addict, the stimulant addict doesn't develop steadily increasing tolerance. Instead, the potent stimulants use up quantities of neurotransmitters over relatively short periods of intense use and the drug becomes ineffective until these are restored. This gives more of an on-again, off-again binge pattern to the addiction. Although there is a withdrawal symptomatology, it doesn't fit the classical notions of physical dependence. Otherwise, however, cocaine and the amphetamine addiction is clearly within the paradigm of addictive dis-

ease, and is exacerbated by an intense drug craving that may appear during and after withdrawal.

4. *Hallucinogenics/psychedelics:* Marijuana, psilocybin mushrooms, peyote cactus, mescaline, LSD, MDA, and so. *Desired effects:* changes in consciousness characterized by altered sense perceptions and thinking patterns. *Acute toxic effects:* fear, anxiety, disturbing visions, loss of control over stimulus reactions, psychotomimetic episodes, release of underlying psychoses, accidents, bad judgment and confusion, distortions in space and time affecting motor control, and so on. Idiosyncratic potentially fatal reactions have been seen with some of these drugs, especially the stimulant psychedelics. *Chronic effects:* flashbacks (recurrence of drug effects up to a year after the drug has been eliminated from system); symptoms of emotional flatness and separation from reality that resemble delayed stress syndrome; psychosis. These drugs can definitely be addictive, but with the exception of marijuana, PCP, and the stimulant psychedelics, they rarely produce physical dependence.

Intoxication and Toxicity
All psychoactive substances are toxic, which means they are poisonous. Dosage levels that may cause human fatality have been established for these substances. The only exception is lysergic acid diethylamide (LSD), which is psychically potent at low microgram, or millionths of a gram, levels in humans and produces disabling psychological effects long before a fatal level can be reached. Consequently, psychoactive drugs fall within the realm of *toxicologists,* scientists who study poisonous materials. Some confusion can arise from the usage of the term *intoxicate.* In general parlance, it means to make drunk or inebriate. In medical terms, it means to poison or have a poisonous effect. A toxicologist would probably point out that there is really no difference between the two.

Polysubstance Abuse
Frequently, individual users will employ more than one substance in their abuse patterns. This is polydrug or *polysubstance abuse.* While there are some "garbage-heads" who will take anything that may change their consciousness or produce a rush, most polysubstance abusers follow a pattern. The most common pattern is the stimultaneous or series use of upper and downer drugs. Users find that each drug group mediates the less desirable effects and side effects of the other. In the early 1900s, this was the combined use of heroin and cocaine, known as a "speedball." Today there are many upper-downer users, for example, the barfly who

"powders his or her nose" with cocaine betwen drinks, or the individual who smokes both crack cocaine and high-purity heroin.

ADDICTION MEDICINE: AN INTERNATIONAL OVERVIEW

There is a general worldwide agreement that substance abuse is a global problem. This fact is brought home through ongoing communication with health professionals from around the world, all of whom report growing abuse of a variety of psychoactive substances. Specific substances used may vary from place to place, depending on route of supply, availability, and cultural attitudes. In general the more urban and industrialized areas have an increasing problem with pharmaceutical drugs, while rural, less industrialized cultures tend toward "green" drugs that are produced agriculturally and need little processing. With a few notable exceptions, alcohol abuse and alcoholism are pandemic. Throughout Europe, there is also a notable lack of concern and knowledge regarding the dangers of tobacco smoking.

While the medical etiology may be similar and the drug effects the same, and the abuse and addiction may follow basic clinical patterns, approaches to prevention, treatment, and recovery take place within a cultural context. In working with representatives from a variety of cultures, it has become clear that a treatment or prevention program that is successful in San Francisco may not be acceptable in Rome or Beijing, or that policies devised in Bangkok may be inappropriate in Zurich or Lima. There are, however, inferences that can be made, and cross-cultural syntheses make that much more achievable the ongoing prognosis for developing potentially successful approaches to prevention, intervention, treatment, and recovery.

Certain European cultural attitudes toward the role of wine as intrinsic to diet, for example, clash directly with American recovery beliefs in the need for abstinence from all psychoactive substances. On the other hand, the use of alcohol in certain Muslim cultures, especially in the Near East, is forbidden, while their view of opioid drug use is more permissive than that of Europeans or Americans.

Northern European cultures, viewing addiction primarily as a social and psychological problem, have often responded to drug problems with state-managed long-term and all-inclusive social programs. In parts of southern Europe, where individuals live and identify with extended family groups and often spend their lives in the same village, leaving only for school or military service, the emphasis may be on therapeutic community dynamics, often mediated by the church and carried on by the family. It has been theorized that 12-Step fellowships have not proliferated in these areas the way they have in North America because these peoples are less mobile and more inclined to have strong existing ties with which AA and other fellowships cannot compete. A competing observation is that AA, NA and others are strong and spreading in Western Europe but do not yet have the professional recognition and cooperation that they have gained in the United States and Canada. In France and other Western European coutries, the professional view is still that alcoholism and other addiction is a result of underlying psychopathology. Therefore, the emphasis is on psychotherapy. As of 1986, however, the *toxicomanes,* or addiction medicine professionals of Paris, were making strides in the study of brain chemistry and neurotransmitter-receptor site science, and may well be ahead of the United States in these areas.

Along with the other major changes now taking place in Eastern Europe, there is a distinct breakup of individual and cultural denial around substance abuse issues. Throughout Eastern Europe, but particularly within the former Soviet Union, AA and other 12-Step fellowships are being embraced by addicts and many health professionals as the means to recovery from alcoholism and other addictions. Public and private interactions are bringing a meaningful exchange of 12-Step approaches that includes visits to Eastern Europe by fellowship members and addiction medicine specialists to provide technical assistance.

The former Soviet Union presents a case where cultural presuppositions have been misleading. It was supposed by many in the West that a spiritually based program such as Alcoholics Anonymous would not stand a chance in a communist country. As it turns out, beneath an official antireligion facade, there runs a deep stream of individual spirituality that has responded positively to the AA recognition of a higher power and reliance on "God *as we understood Him.*"

It would be a mistake to discount the approaches taken by any nation or culture to its drug problems, or to view one approach as categorically superior or inferior to another. The field of addiction medicine is a young and rapidly growing field. We all have a lot to learn from one another.

REFERENCES

Alcoholics Anonymous World Services, Inc. (1957). *Alcoholics Anonymous comes of age: A brief history of AA.* New York: Author.

Alcoholics Anonymous World Services, Inc. (1939). *Alcoholics Anonymous.* New York: Author. (This is the "Big Book.")

Black, C. (1981). *"It will never happen to me."* New York: Ballantine.

Brissette, C. & Seymour, R. B. (1991). *Beyond the three-headed dragon.* Sausalito, CA: Westwind Associates.

Dorris, M. (1989). *The broken cord.* New York: Harper & Row.

Inaba, D. S., & Cohen, W. E. (1989). *Uppers, downers, and all arounders.* Ashland, OR: Cinemed, Inc.

Jellinek, E. M. (1960). *The disease concept of alcoholism.* New Haven, CT: Hillhouse Press.

Milam, J. R., & Ketcham, K. (1981). *Under the influence.* New York: Bantam.

Seymour, R. B., & Smith, D. E. (1987a). *Drugfree: A unique, positive approach to staying off alcohol and other drugs.* New York: Facts on File.

Seymour, R. B. & Smith, D. E. (1987b). *The physician's guide to psychoactive drugs.* New York: Haworth Press.

27

Health Counseling

MERLE A. KEITEL, Ph.D.

MARY KOPALA, Ph.D.

As of yet, health counseling has not been recognized as a speciality area within the field of counseling. No professional organization exists to provide a communication network for counselors interested in health issues, to promote the identity or interests of the health counselor, or to study issues particular to the area of health counseling. With the exception of certified alcoholism counselors (CACs), little professional literature exists regarding the employment, training, and types of services provided by master's-level health counselors. Nevertheless, it appears that it is a growing field and that more and more individuals trained at the master's level are choosing to attend to health-related issues. In fact, professional counseling journals are increasingly publishing articles relevant to health concerns.

More organized than health counseling as a discipline is the growing field of health psychology. *Health psychology* has been defined by Matarazzo (1980) as the contribution of the "discipline of psychology to the promotion and maintenance of health, the prevention and treatment of illness" (p. 815) and the identification of causes of health and illness. The preponderance of the research and interventions used for health-related issues comes from the writings of health psychologists or other psychologists who work in health-related facilities.

Why are more and more individuals concerned with health issues? Advances in medical technology have virtually eliminated some diseases. As a result, people live longer than ever before, but are more likely to contract diseases related to old age. This increased life span has led to a demand for an improved quality of life. Consequently, health care providers are becoming concerned with promoting good mental health in addition to physical health, and enhancing the quality of life one experiences when faced with disease. This has led to a collaborative approach among health care providers, patients, and their families. Although not all physicians and nurses practice this approach, there is increased interest in approaching health care from a collaborative rather than an expert perspective. Health counselors often provide the link between patient and physician in this model. In cases where medical personnel do not take a collaborative perspective, counselors may help patients to develop the appropriate assertiveness and communication skills so their needs are effectively met.

HOW COUNSELORS CAN HELP

The *holistic* approach to wellness defines good health as both the psychological and physical well-being of individuals. This movement views good health as more than simply an absence of disease. It recognizes that all of us have the potential to behave in ways that may result in poor health rather than good health. In order to promote a better quality of life and to help people maximize their state of health, health counselors might train health care providers in communication and relationship skills as well as provide direct services to patients and their families.

When providing direct services, health counselors intervene at four levels: *biological, affective, cognitive,* and *behavioral.* For example, at the biological level, health counselors might teach relaxation techniques in order to attempt to reduce the increased blood pressure that accompanies stress. At the affective level, they might provide emotional support to individuals undergoing treatment for a debilitating disease. Health counselors might intervene at the cognitive level by providing accurate information regarding an ailment experienced by the patient. Finally, at the behavioral level, the counselor can help the patient to institute lifestyle changes, for example, in nutrition, exercise, sexual behavior, time and stress management, and assertiveness.

These interventions can be both preventive and remedial in nature. Educational programs inform individuals of steps they can take to head off the development of health problems. Behaviors that sabotage good health and increase the likelihood of illness are identified. Individuals are helped to resolve emotional problems that may result from physical ailments, surgery, and/or disease.

Individual who provide health counseling may work in a variety of settings including drug and alcohol services, weight reduction programs, pregnancy counseling agencies, hospital wellness programs, and elementary, secondary, and postsecondary schools.

Problem areas such as stress disorders, appetitive disorders, infertility, premenstrual syndrome, menopause, pregnancy, and AIDS have been studied and addressed by health counselors and psychologists.

STRESS

Preliminary evidence suggests that stress is involved in the development of certain diseases and has been found to exacerbate symptoms in pre-existing conditions as well. Stress has been associated with a number of physical illnesses, including, but not limited to, migraine headaches, cardiovascular disease, cancer, skin problems, high blood pressure, and gastrointestinal distress. It has also been found to intensify symptoms in conditions that already exist, such as ulcers or asthma. To give you an idea of how prevalent stress is, two of the most frequently prescribed drugs in the United States are Inderal, a blood pressure medication, and Valium, a tranquilizer.

Stress is not a concept that has been well defined. Holmes and Rahe (1967) have developed a scale that measures the degree of stress associated with different life events. These researchers recognized that the amount of change required as a result of a life event is directly proportional to the amount of stress it produces. The death of a spouse has been rated as the most stressful life event one can experience because it necessitates change in so many facets of one's life. Since both positive and negative life events require change, both positive and negative events may be considered stressful. For example, although getting married, taking a vacation, and receiving a job promotion are happy events, they can also be considered stressful.

In addition to expected life events, traumatic events such as rape, natural disasters, war, and nuclear accidents have also been studied extensively. Posttraumatic stress disorder (PTSD) may develop in individuals who have experienced severe traumas. Following a trauma, nightmares, anxiety, and panic may occur. Individuals may also reexperience the event in a vivid fashion. It is not uncommon for these symptoms to appear long after the initial trauma.

On the other end of the continuum are the daily hassles of living, which are less powerful than the other stressors mentioned above, but which are stressful nonetheless due to their stable and repetitive nature. For example, your alarm clock fails to go off because you accidentally set it for P.M. rather than A.M. In the process of rushing to get ready for work, you spill a cup of coffee on yourself, then snap a shoelace as you are walking out the door. You rush madly to the train station in hopes of catching the train, but as you reach the platform you see your train pulling away. By the time you arrive at work, you are 45 minutes late and completely frazzled. None of these events by themselves are powerful stressors, but the pileup of these daily hassles may pose serious threats to your health and well-being.

Selye (1936) was the first person to introduce the stress concept to psychology. Selye described *stress* as a set of bodily responses that defend against any form of threat, whether it is psychological or physical. While Selye believed that all stressors automatically triggered bodily reactions, another researcher, Mason (1971), showed that different stressors may elicit somewhat different types of reactions or no reaction at all. Nevertheless, Selye labeled this reaction to "stressors" as "the general adaptation syndrome" (GAS). The GAS consists of three stages:

1. *The Alarm Reaction.* When an individual confronts a stressor, the body prepares to fight the enemy or run away—the fight or flight response. During the alarm reaction, secretions released by the adrenal system lead to quickened breathing, dilation of pupils, increased blood pressure, and increased blood flow to the arms and legs.
2. *Resistance.* Individuals employ various coping mechanisms to adapt. During this stage the body supplies a relatively constant resistance to the stressor at the same time that there is a decreased resistance to other stimuli.
3. *Exhaustion.* When the alarm reaction is experienced repeatedly and is followed by periods of resistance, or when a chronic stressor is experienced, the body's defenses or resistance to disease and so on become weakened and irreversible physiological damage may occur.

A very long time ago, when stressors primarily took the form of physical enemies or predators, such as when cavemen contronted wild animals, the fight or flight response was appropriate. When we confront the stressors of today (e.g., being stuck in a traffic jam, having a disagreement with a family member or friend), our body still undergoes the alarm reaction, but these phsyiological changes do not enable us to cope and are therefore maladaptive. Some researchers have suggested that prolonged periods of the fight or flight syndrome may result in a weakening of the immune system and consequently various illnesses may develop.

Stress reduction strategies include, but are not limited to, *coping skills training, progressive muscle relaxation (PMR) and imagery, biofeedback, exercise, time management, assertiveness training,* and *cognitive restructuring.*

Coping skills training. Counselors can help clients to accurately appraise situations so they can choose appropriate coping mechanisms. Coping skills training programs teach people effective skills for coping with situations that cause them stress. Many situations can be changed and problem-solving coping strategies, such as getting more information, talking to other people to resolve the difficulty, and so on, can be beneficial. If someone is anxious about an upcoming diagnostic procedure, for example, he or she can be taught to acquire information about the procedure, particularly sensory information, such as feelings the patient is likely to have. This reduces the ambiguity and, consequently, the anxiety.

Progressive muscle relaxation (PMR) and imagery. Progressive muscle relaxation (PMR) involves training clients to breathe deeply and then to alternately tense and relax each major muscle group in their bodies while focusing on the differences between how their bodies feel when their muscles are relaxed versus when they are tensed. Often clients are also trained to imagine peaceful settings complete with sounds and smells once they have achieved a relaxed state through PMR.

Biofeedback. Biofeedback machines assess physical levels of stress by providing information on muscle tension, respiration and heart rate, temperature, and release of perspiration. For example, some machines beep to indicate the degree of body tension. When a person is very tense, the beeping sound may be very rapid. As the individual utilizes relaxation techniques to lower tension, the beep may slow down or become less frequent. This feedback informs the individual when a relaxed state has been achieved. Ultimately, individuals are able to monitor their physical tension without the help of biofeedback machines. Biofeedback has been used for treating various conditions including migraine headaches, high or low blood pressure, anxiety, and Raynaud's disease.

Exercise. Physical exercise can be a very effective way to reduce stress. A regular program of aerobic exercise helps to reduce blood pressure and heart rate. Furthermore, endorphins are released after an extended period of exercise, and these natural chemicals released by the brain promote feelings of pleasure.

Time management. Feeling overwhelmed can be the result of procrastination, excessive environmental demands, and/or an inability to say no to the requests or demands of others. Learning how to prioritize responsibilities, plan schedules, make use of small bits of time, and maintain an appointment book can reduce stress and help clients find time for leisure activities. Individuals may also be taught to schedule in blocks of time each day for some relaxing activities such as meditation or exercise.

Assertiveness training. Interpersonal relationships are the source of stress for many people. Problems may develop when people are too passive or excessively aggressive. Developing assertiveness skills can help individuals to make their needs and wants known, and to say no when they mean no in a way that does not infringe on the rights of others. In this way, individuals can limit the amount of work and reduce the number of favors they agree to when asked by employers, friends, colleagues, and significant others.

Cognitive restructuring. Cognitive restructuring involves modifying one's self-talk, or internal dialogue. Many people experience the ill effects of stress when they do not accurately appraise whether or not they can have an impact on changing the situation. Individuals who are stuck in a traffic jam ultimately cause themselves physical damage when they silently seethe and get themselves more and more aggravated. Instead, since this is a situation that cannot be changed, it would be more beneficial to repeat words such as "There's nothing I can do to make this traffic jam disappear" or "I'll get there when I get there."

STRESS-RELATED DISORDERS

As discussed previously, stress can directly alter bodily processes. These physiological changes can be linked directly to certain types of illnesses that will be discussed below. The diseases covered are caused or facilitated, at least in part, by our responses and our behavior patterns. There is a great deal of evidence that the frequency of stressful life events is associated with the onset of illness. Stress that is ongoing or chronic eventually causes damage, perhaps by weakening the immune system.

Heart Disease

There are physical and psychosocial risk factors for the development of heart disease. Physical risk factors include age, sex, race, and family history. If you are an older male, black, and have a family history of heart disease, you are at higher risk. If you smoke and have high blood pressure and high cholesterol levels (both associated with obesity), you are at higher risk. Psychosocial risk factors include *occupational stress* and *Type A personality*.

Occupational stress, meaning high work demands combined with few opportunities for decision making and control (Karasek, Theorell, Schwartz, Pieper, & Alfredsson, 1982), has been associated with heart disease. The Framingham heart study (Haynes & Feinleib, 1980) showed that working women were more likely to develop heart problems as the number of children increased. Since this was not the case for unemployed mothers, the demand/control model was supported. Clerical workers who have little autonomy, working women with children, and women with unsupportive bosses were also more likely to develop heart disease (Haynes & Feinleib, 1980).

Type A personality, characterized by extreme competitiveness, impatience, hostility, and vigorous speech characteristics, has been related to increased coronary risk (Krantz & Manuck, 1984). Type B individuals are characterized by a more relaxed behavior pattern. In addition to the finding that Type A individuals are more likely to suffer a myocardial infarction (heart attack), Type A individuals with no coronary heart disease (CHD) seem to have many of the same biochemical abnormalities as individuals who are diagnosed with CHD. Type A persons are more reactive to stress than Type B's. For example, when confronted with the same stressful task, the Type A person will demonstrate larger increases in heart rate, blood pressure, and stress hormones than will Type B's. Some studies have shown that excessive reactivity to stress may in itself be a strong predictor of CHD. It should be noted that some recent studies did not support the relationship between Type A personality and CHD.

Interventions such as medication, exercise, and dietary changes have all been implicated in reducing the risk of CHD. The rate of heart attack recurrence has been found to be lower in individuals attending both Type A modification and cardiology counseling sessions as opposed to only a cardiology counseling group or a no-treatment control group (Friedman et al., 1984). Cognitive and behavioral methods to reduce Type A patterns, namely relaxing and smiling more often and doing things more slowly, rather than rushing around, were found to be effective supplements to the encouragement to stick with medication, diet, and exercise routines that were given to patients in the cardiology counseling group.

Hypertension
Hypertension, a condition in which blood pressure is chronically elevated, increases the risk of stroke, heart attack, and kidney and vascular disease. It is estimated that more than 35 million Americans have this condition. While excessive salt intake, obesity, and stress have been implicated in the development of hypertension, genetics and culture play a role. For example, in some populations, people with excessive salt intake will develop hypertension. Blacks and individuals of low *socioeconomic* status (SES), individuals living in stressful environments (e.g., high crime areas, crowded cities, neighborhoods with high divorce rates), and individuals in stressful occupations (e.g., where responsibility is high but authority is low) are more likely to be hypertensive.

The most common treatment for hypertension, medication, has some negative side effects, including impotency for men. Progressive muscle relaxation, meditation, yoga, and biofeedback have successfully lowered blood pressure without any side effects. These techniques can be used in combination with medication without adverse reaction. Of course, modifying one's diet and exercising may lower blood pressure enough so that medication is not needed.

The Immune System and Stress

Some diseases are believed to occur due to weakness in the immune system caused by exposure to acute stressors, although the research is inconclusive. Increased levels of cortisol (a stress hormone) have been found to destroy immune tissue and therefore impair immune system functioning. Some studies have shown poor immune functioning in men whose wives were dying, in people who are depressed, lonely, sleep deprived, or psychiatrically impaired, and in those taking stressful examinations. A study of elderly persons in a residential facility found that relaxation training heightened natural killer cell activity, and these individuals reported fewer stress-related symptoms compared to residents with no treatment or those provided only with increased social contact (Kiecolt-Glaser et al., 1985).

Cancer

Cancer is the second leading cause of death in the United States and is really an umbrella term for over 100 different diseases. Studies in cancer research have allowed substantial cure rates for some types of cancer, given early detection, while treatments for other cancers are not as effective. Smoking, diet, and environmental carcinogens, such as food additives, asbestos, radiation, and so on, have been implicated in the development of malignancies. There is some, but not conclusive, evidence that stress is implicated in the development of cancer. Natural immune cells actively look for signs of tumor growth and help to destroy them while they are small. Stress interferes with this process and tumors grow to the point that the immune system can no longer control them. The loss of a significant friend or family member has been associated with reduced immune competence and the development of cancer.

Just as personality traits have been suggested for coronary patients, such traits have been suggested for cancer patients as well. The inability to express anger and resentment, difficulty establishing and maintaining interpersonal relationships, self-pity, low self-esteem, and passivity have been observed by professionals who work with oncology patients. The cancer patient shows the world a polite and happy face, but inside he or she is lonely, depressed, helpless, insecure, and despairing. This personality pattern has not received strong empirical support as a key agent in the development of cancer; however, it has been implicated in disease progression. More aggressive people (fighters) have been shown to live longer than passive, apathetic, or depressed individuals. Compliance and cooperation in cancer patients have been associated with earlier deaths.

Medical treatments for cancer include chemotherapy, radiation, and surgery. Each is associated with side effects that may be more devastating than the disease itself. Health counselors can help by serving as information providers and by teaching relaxation training to reduce nausea, pain, and other side effects of chemotherapy. They can help patients and family members work through their feelings about the illness, and if the disease is terminal, to help them confront death in a more comfortable way. Some counselors encourage positive thinking by the use of imagery to actually combat the disease itself. In this technique, the patient is asked to visualize the cancer cells and then imagine them getting smaller and smaller until they disappear completely, or to imagine the chemotherapy drugs attacking the cells and killing them off in some way. There is no conclusive evidence for the efficacy of these treatments.

Headaches
Headaches can be divided into three major categories, namely, migraine headaches, muscle contraction or tension headaches, and a mixed category of headaches that don't fit neatly into either of the other types. Headaches appear to be instigated by stress. Migraine headaches, which are experienced by about 5% of Americans, generally occur *after* a stressful period, when constricted blood vessels expand resulting in a sharp and throbbing pain. Usually, the ache is on one side of the head and may be preceded by an aura (nausea, vomiting, or dizziness) that signals the headache's approach. Migraines can last from several hours to a few days.

Tension headaches are more common, in that they are experienced by 30% of all Americans. Sufferers report feeling as if they have "a tight band around their head." These headaches usually begin during a stressful period due to prolonged contraction of the head and neck muscles.

Health counselors can encourage headache sufferers to use the various stress reduction procedures discussed above, particularly relaxation training, imagery, and biofeedback.

APPETITIVE DISORDERS

Obesity and eating disorders, smoking, and substance abuse are major national public health problems. While a great deal of research has been conducted in these areas, there are many unanswered questions. Preliminary studies have found gender differences in the appetitive disorders, but more research is needed to achieve a more thorough understanding of the differences between women and men in regard to the etiology of these disorders and implications for treatment. Possible causes of and interventions for each of these health problems follows.

Obesity

Obesity has been defined as body weight that is at least 20% higher than levels deemed ideal given a person's height and body frame. Obesity also may be diagnosed when 20% of body mass is composed of fatty tissue. Physical correlates of obesity may be quite serious (e.g., hypertension, adult-onset diabetes, gout, obstetric complications, osteoarthritis, high cholesterol, dermatological problems, surgical complications, low back pain, respiratory illnesses, some cancers—colorectal and prostate cancers in men, and cancers of the breast, gall bladder, uterus, ovaries, and endometrium in women). While the physical consequences of severe obesity are very serious, being even slightly overweight may instigate negative psychological consequences. We live in a society that currently emphasizes that "thin" is in and discriminates against people who are overweight. Over time, such discrimination may lead to feelings of low self-esteem.

The absolute cause of obesity is still not known, however seven areas are frequently identified as contributing to being overweight: *genetics, fat cell theory, point theory, calorie intake and expenditure, metabolism, cultural factors, and stress.*

Genetics. Studies of twins reared together rather than apart show that individuals' adult weights are more highly correclated with the weights of their biological rather than their adoptive parents (Stunkard et al., 1986). A person whose biological parents are not obese has an 8% chance of being obese as an adult. Having one obese parent increases one's chance of being obese to 40%; and in persons with two obese parents, the chance of being obese rises even more, to 80%.

Fat cell theory. The number of fat cells is generally determined early in life. As an individual gains weight his or her fat cells continue to expand until the breaking point when the cells split in two. If the individual continues to ingest more calories than he or she expends, the cycle is repeated. Once fat cells are formed they do not disappear; they can only shrink. Fat cell theory is one explanation of why it is difficult for people who gain weight to permanently return to their previous weights.

Set point theory. This theory was constructed to help explain the apparent stability of a person's weight over time. The theory suggests that the body adjusts its basal metabolic rate to cause an individual to return to his or her previous weight (body-weight set points). Thus, when an individual loses weight, the body adjusts to the lowered energy (food) intake by lowering the rate of energy expenditure—a defensive response believed to guard people against the effects of starvation. Consequently, individuals are unable to lose weight past a certain point and when they do, the body will eventually return to the "set" weight.

Calorie intake and expenditure. When caloric intake exceeds the calories burned through physical activity (exercise), digestion (dietary thermogenesis), and other bodily functions (such as respiration, excretion, etc.), people gain weight. Surprisingly, more calories are burned through bodily funcitons than through physical exercise. Of course, one known way to lose weight is to decrease calorie intake and increase physical activity.

Metabolism. Few people with weight problems actually have thyroid irregularities; however, individuals with more sluggish metabolisms will not burn calories as quickly as those with higher metabolic rates. Aerobic exercise will temporarily increase metabolic rates during and for 24 hours after the activity, but will not have a lasting effect. Anaerobic exercise (e.g. body building), because it increases the ratio of muscle (lean body mass) to fat, does create a more permanent change in metabolism.

Cultural factors. The prevalence of high-fat food (e.g. pizza, hamburgers, ice cream, and potato chips) in the United States may help to explain the prevalence of obesity in this country. Other cultures (e.g. Asian) do not have the same degree of obesity because their diets are much lower in fat. When individuals from countries with low fat diets immigrate to the United States and adopt American food habits, their chances of becoming obese increase. In addition, different ethnic groups emphasize food to different extents. Some cultures, for example, push food as an answer to life's problems or to indicate nurturance and caring.

Stress. There have been contradictory results with respect to the connection between stress and eating. Animal studies have reported that different stressors may induce either overeating or restricted food intake. Studies of humans have shown that individuals who are "stressed" increase their consumption of food, particularly high-density sweet food, while other studies have failed to demonstrate these results. Both obese and nonobese individuals report decreases in anxiety after meals. When people eat carbohydrates, natural chemicals known as *opiates* are released by the brain. This process seems to reduce anxiety, pain, and stress.

Interventions with obese patients tend to be of four types, and are used singly or in combination: behavioral, cognitive-behavioral, social support systems, and nutrition education.

Behavioral interventions focus on teaching individuals to change their eating behaviors using various strategies. For example, individuals may be encouraged to remove junk foods from areas that are very visible such as counters or coffee tables. Eating from smaller plates, which automatically reduces the portion size while giving the impression of a full plate, can be substituted for regular dinner plates. Food shopping times can be changed to after mealtimes, when the shopper feels full.

Cognitive interventions focus on teaching individuals about the relationship between thoughts and behavior. Clients are initially taught to identify situations that may promote overeating. Then, clients are asked to brainstorm alternative self-statements (thoughts regarding food and their eating behavior) and to imagine other ways of dealing with the situation. Thoughts such as "I had a piece of candy; therefore, I may as well eat the whole box of candy" are common among individuals trying to lose weight or maintain weight loss. Individuals are taught to restructure this thought to one that refutes either/or thinking; that is, eating one piece of candy does not mean that the individual has binged and may as well give up on dieting. Rather, one learns that digressing from the proscribed foods does not make one bad, nor does it mean that the diet should be abandoned. In fact, individuals are encouraged not to view certain foods as forbidden, but rather to learn to eat such foods in moderation.

Counselors encourage clients to seek support from family and friends, and other individuals interested in losing weight or maintaining weight loss. Weight loss programs rely on support groups to varying degrees. Some programs such as Weight Watchers rely on their group members to provide support for one another, while other approaches include spouses and other family members as an integral component of the program. One reason to include family members is to prevent them from consciously or unconsciously sabotaging the dieter's efforts. In other cases, family members may model more appropriate eating behavior and/or praise the dieter when he or she makes wise food choices or eats smaller portions.

Nutritional education helps individuals to learn how to select foods so that meals are balanced and nutritious while being low in fat and calories. Those skills needed to make sound decisions regarding the selection of nutritious foods based on the information provided on the product label are also taught (Kolodner & DeLucia, 1990).

Eating Disorders

Counselors typically encounter two types of eating disorders: *bulimia nervosa* and *anorexia nervosa*. While these occur primarily among young women, eating disorders have been observed in men as well, although they are less common. Bulimia consists primarily of bingeing on a variety of foods (often junk food) and may or may not be followed by purging. Individuals who are anorexic tend to eat such tiny amounts of food that they become emaciated and may starve to death if not hospitalized and fed intravenously. These individuals may also engage in strenuous physical exercise to help lose weight. (See chapter 21, "Counseling Persons with Eating Disorders.")

Smoking

The U.S. Surgeon General reports that cigarette smoking is the single largest preventable cause of disease and premature death in the United States. Chronic smoking contributes to a variety of illnesses: lung cancer and several other cancers, bronchitis, emphysema, and coronary artery disease.

Many psychological, social, and behavioral theories have been suggested as to why people begin to smoke, especially given the dire health risks. Social learning theory suggests that adolescents begin to smoke because their friends, family members, and/or role models in the media, such as actors and athletes, smoke. Interpersonal or family theorists suggest that smoking is a form of rebellion against authority figures. Psychoanalytic approaches emphasize that smoking gratifies oral dependence needs. Psychosocial theorists believe that smoking is more likely to be initiated during adolescence when individuals are trying to establish a comfortable identity. Even infrequent experimentation in adolescence significantly raises the risk for adult smoking. Adolescents who begin smoking at a very young age and continue the habit uninterrupted are more likely to become regular smokers as adults.

We know that the maintenance of smoking behavior is based on a physical dependence on some components of tobacco, mainly nicotine. In addition, learning theorists believe that conditioning helps to maintain the habit. Many smokers report that smoking helps them to relax. Paradoxically, nicotine can be a stimulant. It is not the effect of the drug that is relaxing, but rather the action of inhaling deeply on a cigarette and then exhaling that people find calming. Some evidence, but not complete support, has been provided for the notion that smokers need to maintain a certain level of nicotine and that heavy smokers adjust their smoking rate to keep nicotine at an approximately constant level. Some researchers have found that cigarette urges increase when people experience stress.

Many different treatments, including medical treatments (e.g., nicotine gum, patches), hypnosis, and individual, group, and/or family therapy have been used, singly and in combination, to help people stop smoking. Behavioral techniques used in individual and group counseling will be the focus of the present discussion since research has provided some support for these commonly utilized techniques. Behavioral techniques such as tension reduction and aversion therapy, while commonly included in smoking cessation programs, are not without limitations and problems. Tension reduction techniques have not been particularly effective, and aversive techniques have had mixed success. Approaches that utilize several interventions in combination are the most promising, but in general, relapse rates for quitters are as high as 80%. Counselors have utilized the following interventions:

Cue identification and coping skills training. When a person smokes during many different activities, such as talking on the telephone, drinking coffee or liquor, or driving in a car, the activities by themselves become capable of triggering cigarette urges. Individuals who are attempting to quit smoking are encouraged to avoid as many of these kinds of activities as possible for as long as possible. In this way, the cues to smoke while engaging in these activities become less powerful. As a result, individuals become more comfortable both physically and psychologically in their identities as nonsmokers. When they do confront cigarettes, they are more confident that they can abstain. Naturally, people who quit smoking will have urges for cigarettes. Each time they experience an urge to smoke during a particular activity and they refrain from smoking, they are a step closer to breaking the association between that activity and having a cigarette. Consequently, these individuals are encouraged to find substitutes such as sucking on cinnamon sticks, chewing gum, eating carrot and celery sticks, drinking water, engaging in deep breathing exercises, and so on.

Reinforce nonsmoking. For example, individuals may be required to deposit a sum of money at the beginning of a smoking cessation program. This money is then returned only if the individual stops smoking. Another strategy is for individuals to save all the money that they would have spent on cigarettes and then buy something special with the money that they saved.

Introduce tension-reduction techniques. Imagery and relaxation training are techniques that may be used as substitutes when clients feel the urge to smoke. Clients are taught to imagine restful surroundings or concentrate on tensing followed by relaxing the body muscles instead of lighting up a cigarette.

Introduce aversive techniques. Examples of aversive techniques include rapid smoking, a technique where cigarettes are smoked at an extremely quick rate until no additional smoking can be tolerated. Another common aversive technique involves pairing actual or imagined smoking with electric shock, noise, and so on. Aversive techniques can pose serious risks and should only be used under the supervision of physicians.

Prevention programs are particularly important because smoking cessation programs have generally reported only short-term success. In other words, individuals may quit for a short time, but many people eventually do resume their smoking habits. Fortunately, decreases in smoking behavior are occurring. Decreased public tolerance for smoking and legislation against smoking have contributed to this phenomenon.

Substance Abuse
No one is really sure what prompts individuals to begin to abuse drugs and alcohol. Perhaps it is the relatively low cost of the substances and the ease with which one is able to obtain them that tend to promote their use. No one can dispute that some substances produce pleasurable effects. Clearly, this fact cannot be overlooked as contributing to use, abuse, and dependence. What about the influence of individuals we admire? Or the lifestyle we perceive users and abusers to lead? All of these factors may contribute to substance use, abuse, and dependence.

Mental health workers differentiate between individuals who abuse substances and those who are dependent on substances. When individuals use a substance such as alcohol in some regular manner and in excess so that they are no longer able to work or engage in normal social relationships or activities, they are diagnosed as being substance abusers. Those individuals, who are diagnosed as dependent on some substance, experience physiological withdrawal symptoms when they stop using the substance. Withdrawal symptoms might include nausea and vomiting, elevated blood pressure, anxiety, depression, and hallucinations. Individuals who develop a tolerance for a substance are also diagnosed as being dependent. In other words, these individuals find that they need to consume more and more of the substance in order to achieve the desired effect.

Individuals who are dependent on some substance find that they are unable to limit their intake of that substance. For example, someone who is dependent on alcohol may be unable to stop drinking even when the intent was to have no more than one drink. Further, dependent individuals spend a majority of their time planning how to get their next fix. These individuals often cut off relationships with family members or friends in order to spend more time with friends who are also users.

Causes of drug and alcohol use tend to fall into four main categories: *disease theories, progression theories, psychological theories,* and *psychosocial theories.*

Disease theories. These theories suggest that substance abuse is the result of an individual's physiology, metabolism, and genetic background. The tolerance-withdrawal model proposes that prolonged ingestion of the substance leads to tolerance and dependence such that withdrawal symptoms are experienced when the substance is no longer used. Because these withdrawal symptoms are so psychologically and physically painful, the individual ingests more of the substance. The situation seems to worsen; that is, substance use leads to increased tolerance and/ or withdrawal symptoms, which lead to even greater use of the substance. This theory has its shortcomings because not all drugs are physically addicting.

Another important disease theory suggests that some individuals have a genetic predisposition toward addiction. Some evidence exists to support his theory. Researchers cite examples of drinking behavior that crosses generations in families. This model suggests that an individual may crave alcohol if the brain is deficient in endorphins. This deficiency sets up a physiological need to ingest more alcohol. This condition does not exist to the same extent in nonusers. Although this theory has become widely accepted as a way to explain alcohol abuse, this type of reaction is really quite rare and occurs only in men.

Progression theories. These theories suggest that there is an orderly progression from using one drug to using another, and that all drug use is related to previous drug use. One may start off with caffeine in tea, coffee, or sodas (such as Jolt). Use of these drugs would lead to use of beer and cigarettes. Use of beer and cigarettes would lead to marijuana use, and so forth. Such theories do not explain why some individuals may use a particular substance but not graduate to harder drugs, nor do these theories explain why some individuals choose to use drugs while others choose not to use drugs or alcohol at all.

Psychological theories. Psychological theorists tend to believe that individuals use alcohol or drugs in order to escape from personal problems, to make up for personal shortcomings, to meet their personal needs, or to reduce anxiety and tension. Support for these theories is often contradictory. Although in some individuals the use of alcohol has resulted in decreased anxiety, it has also been shown to raise levels of anxiety and depression. Some personality theorists believe that substance abuse is related to personality type, although research has not demonstrated personality characteristics that differentiate substance abusers from nonabusers.

Psychosocial theories. Psychosocial theorists suggest that it is the interaction between one's personality and the environment in which he or she lives that may lead to drug or alcohol abuse. Personal problems, such as issues of low self-esteem, may interact with social situations, such as when peer pressure is great, to lead one to experiment with drug or alcohol use, and later to substance abuse. Attempts to become part of a group and fit in may necessitate use of a substance. As individuals become more and more involved with substance use, they may seek out other individuals who are part of a drug culture or who drink heavily.

Mixed support exists for all of these theories; no one theory seems to be better supported than any other. Yet each seems to offer some explanation for substance abuse for some individuals in some situations. Consequently, a combination of these theories may be necessary when trying to explain the causes of substance abuse.

Interventions

A number of interventions are based on the disease model. These approaches promote the belief that complete abstinence is the only effective treatment. Critics of the approach believe that this message is counterproductive at times because it implies that one is never able to fully overcome an abuse problem and that relapse is always a threat. For example, such a view may undermine a teenager's attempt to overcome an abuse problem, since adolescents are unlikely to remain completely abstinent and one slipup could signal that attempting to stop is futile.

Behavioral interventions include aversion therapy where clients are taught to associate unpleasant events with drinking and pleasant events with the absence of drinking. Contingency contracts are also used to decrease alcohol and drug use. In these contracts, clients agree to control their drinking and are reinforced to remain sober. Counselors may refer clients to inpatient units for treatments that may include drugs such as Antabuse that induce nausea and vomiting when alcohol is ingested.

Interventions rooted in a psychosocial approach to substance abuse depend on intervening not only in the environment in which the client lives and works, but also individually with the client. It is important for the counselor to understand conditions in which the client uses substances. With whom does he or she use drugs or alcohol? Where does the use occur? When does the use occur? Is drug or alcohol use an important way of gaining membership into some group? A systems approach can then be used. For example, the counselor may promote membership in groups where drugs are not used. Family counseling may be recommended to change communication patterns. If family members are "enabling" the drug user, those patterns are changed so that the abuser has a better shot at overcoming the problem. In addition, individual counseling would be provided to encourage self-exploration and resolution of psychological issues, for example, low self-esteem.

Prevention

Prevention may include community and school-based counseling programs that educate children and adolescents about the consequences of drug and alcohol use. Individual and group counseling programs can encourage children and adolescents to take personal responsibility, increase their self-esteem, and promote the development of problem-solving skills, self-reliance, and independence. In addition, teacher and parent effectiveness training programs may be implemented to teach adults how to interact with children and adolescents to promote healthy psychological development.

ISSUES RELATED TO HUMAN SEXUALITY

Infertility

Infertility has been defined as the inability to achieve a pregnancy after a year or more of regular unprotected intercourse, or the inability to carry a pregnancy to a live birth (Menning, 1980). Infertility problems may result in decreased sexual satisfaction, poorer marital adjustment and communication, and sometimes serious emotional and psychological distress. The infertile female has generally reported more distress than the infertile male; however, it is difficult to know whether men are not experiencing the distress or simply are uncomfortable expressing their feelings. Daniluk (1991) suggests that counselors can help infertile couples to express their feelings of grief and loss, and to accept that they do not have control over their fertility. They can remind their clients that they do have control over life choices and alternatives.

Premenstrual Syndrome (PMS)

Premenstrual syndrome, also known as PMS, is a phenomenon that is not well understood. Some women do not experience it at all, others have mild symptoms, and still others have severe symptoms that interfere with their functioning. Although PMS is generally thought of as a single clinical entity, there are actually several different clusters of symptoms that women may experience during the week or two before their periods, such as water-retention syndrome, hyperactivity syndrome, and depressive syndrome, in addition to less well-defined symptoms, such as extreme emotional responsiveness, irritability, sensitivity, anxiety, and sadness. Symptoms include breast tenderness and bloating, spasmodic and/or congestive cramping, backaches, moodiness, fatigue, and sometimes crying spells, nervousness, inability to concentrate, and feelings of being out of control. Some women report increased energy and productivity, the need for less sleep, and increased sexual desire in the week preceding their period.

Interestingly, correlations between menstrual mood fluctuations and religion have been found, with Catholic and Orthodox Jewish women reporting extreme changes in anxiety during their cycles and Protestant women describing little or no change. It's possible that negative cultural attitudes toward women in general, and menstruation more specifically, aggravate premenstrual symptoms. A recent study (Gallant, Hamilton, Popiel, Morokoff, & Chakraborty, 1990) was conducted on daily moods, well-being, physical symptoms, personal space, food cravings, and depression in healthy women who report no premenstrual or menstrual difficulties. During the week preceding menstruation, both women who were aware and those who were unaware that they were participating in a study on menstrual cycle effects reported a modest increase of physical symptoms, food cravings, and depression. Desires to be alone and stay at home were high during the premenstrual phase, a finding demonstrated in nonhuman primates as well. This study was significant in that it showed that even women who report no difficulties with PMS or menstruation actually do experience increased symptoms.

The diagnosis of *late luteal phase dysphoric disorder* (the clinical name for PMS) was not included in the American Psychiatric Association's (1987) *Diagnostic and Statistical Manual of Mental Disorders* (third edition, revised, DSM-III-R) because of insufficient data to support it as a clinical disorder. It was, however, added to the appendix of the manual. The acknowledgement of PMS as a disorder has sociopolitical implications. Some feminists believe that if this disorder is recognized, it could be used to keep women out of positions of power. Their argument suggests that once PMS is recognized as a psychiatric condition, some individuals might use it to keep women from holding responsible jobs. Other women are angry that the traditionally masculine medical establishment has not acknowledged the premenstrual symptoms that many women have reported. Historically, doctors have suggested to women that "it is all in their heads."

Counselors working with women who experience premenstrual symptoms tend to provide support, and behavioral and nutritional interventions. By providing information about the physical and psychological symptoms that may be experienced, women learn that they are not alone and they are not "crazy." Women can learn to understand their patterns by charting their moods and physical symptoms over several weeks. Women may be taught to plan their schedules so as to reduce stress as much as possible during the week preceding their periods. Understanding how changing hormone levels affect their feelings sometimes deters women from searching for other reasons to explain their feelings of agitation. For example, if a woman does not realize that she is premenstrual, but she is aware of a general feeling of negative emotional arousal, she may search for a psychosocial explanation, such as a problem in a relationship. Consequently, she may instigate an argument with her husband. If she had attributed her feelings to the hormonal changes, the argument may have been avoided.

Relaxation training and other stress management techniques may be helpful in promoting the extra rest that may be needed. Exercise and warm baths may also serve to reduce tension. Dietary changes, such as decreasing caffeine, sugars, salt, and processed artificial foods as well as taking vitamins, particularly, vitamins B, C, and E, may help PMS sufferers. If these interventions are not adequate, referrals may be made to physicians for hormone therapies, tranquilizers, or antidepressants.

Menopause

Menopause has been defined as one's last menstrual period, however, the ovaries actually start producing less estrogen when women are in their late 30s, with a gradual loss of estrogen until about age 50, when menstrual periods most commonly cease. This entire transitional period has been labeled the *climacteric*. Surprisingly, women may begin to experience premenopausal symptoms during their late 30s. Nearly one-third of women in the United States reach menopause through hysterectomies (the surgical removal of the ovaries). For these women, the physiological changes are sudden, may result in severe symptoms, and require hormone treatment.

There have been few studies of menopause and the climacteric, and those that have been done are not necessarily adequate. Results suggest that 10–15% of women have no problems with menopause, another 15% have more serious functional impairments, and the majority of women (70%) struggle with some difficulties or symptoms that occur periodically over a number of years.

Sheehy (1991) vividly describes the experience of menopause: ". . . at the dignified apex of one's adulthood, to have to worry about being hit with menstrual gushing, hot flushes, night sweats, insomnia, sudden bouts of waistline bloat, weight gain, heart palpitations, crying for no reason, temper outbursts, migraines, crawly skin, memory lapses—my God, what's going on?" (p. 254). To make matters worse, some women report that their sexual interest plummets, they experience vaginal dryness that makes sexual intercourse painful, they have difficulty concentrating, and they often experience a restlessness that makes it virtually impossible to sit still for any length of time. Although these symptoms are very real, physicians have historically misdiagnosed women who are in this transitional phase. As a result, inappropriate treatments such as sleeping medications, painkillers, and minor tranquilizers (e.g., Valium) have been over prescribed.

The most common treatment currently used for menopause is hormone therapy. Initially, women were treated with estrogen alone. Since the drug had not been tested adequately, it was later discovered that such treatment led to an increased risk of endometrial and breast cancers. Consequently, progestin, a synthetic progesterone, has been prescribed in addition to reduce that risk. Unfortunately, the addition of progestin may, in fact, block the positive effects of estrogen, resulting in a possible increased risk of heart disease and osteoporosis. At the same time, side effects of progestin may include migraines, bloating, breast tenderness, cramping, tension, sleeplessness, and sadness. We do not know how or whether progestin affects the increased risk of breast cancer that has been linked to estrogen. Clearly, the decision to undergo hormone treatment is a difficult one. Even in the medical community, the controversy rages over whether the risks of hormone treatment outweigh the benefits. Indicative of the ambivalence or confusion that women feel regarding hormone treatment is the fact that approximately one-third of women given prescriptions for hormones never have them filled. Additionally, of those women who are taking hormones, some women discontinue the progestin and resort to taking only the estrogen, while others simply discontinue the hormone treatment entirely.

As more baby boomers enter the climacteric and reach menopause, more women may seek the services of counselors who are knowledgeable about this transitional phase. Group and individual work where women can process their feelings about the physical changes they experience as well as the decisions they have made about hormone treatments may promote feelings of well-being. Counseling may help women develop mechanisms for coping with physical symptoms and emotional changes they are experiencing, as well as the external stressors that are commonly confronted by women in this age group. Research in this area is virtually nonexistent at this time, but political initiatives may result in the designation of funds to be targeted solely for research in this important area of women's health.

Pregnancy
Pregnancy is often a happy event; however, in some cases pregnancy is not planned and consequently may be unwanted. This may be especially true for adolescents. Teenage pregnancy has been called an epidemic in the United States, and counselors, particularly in schools, are in a unique position to prevent unplanned pregnancies. Teenage pregnancy has serious psychological and physical consequences for the mother and the infant. Because teenagers do not necessarily receive adequate prenatal care, low birth weight, cognitive and developmental lags or impairments, and decreased alertness and responsiveness to stimuli are common in infants of teenage mothers. Adolescent mothers often lack

the maturity to care properly for their offspring, and there is a higher incidence of abuse and neglect inflicted by teenage mothers than adult mothers. Personal and professional goals are less likely to be achieved by teenage mothers in that they often drop out of school in order to care for or support their children. Black teenage girls are more likely to carry their babies to term than are white teenagers.

Researchers have suggested many reasons for the high number of teenage pregnancies. Over the past 20 years, the structure of the family has broken down, leading to potentially inadequate parental supervision. There may also be unconscious determinants of teenage pregnancy. Some girls desire greater closeness with their mothers and may become pregnant to acieve that closeness. Alternatively, getting pregnant is for some girls an expression of rebellion against parental standards. Having a baby may fulfill their wishes to love and be loved by someone. Girls with low self-esteem may not have the assertiveness necessary to resist the pressure from boys or men for sexual activity. Teenage girls may erroneously believe that getting pregnant is the way to hold onto their boyfriends.

Other reasons for the high number of teenage pregnancies reflect the negative aspects some teens perceive regarding contraception. Boys may feel that using condoms is not "macho." Girls may not take responsibility for birth control because it destroys the fantasy of a spontaneous, romantic sexual liaison. After all, how can you hand a boy a condom? That would mean that you were planning to have sex and he might think that you are promiscuous. Purchasing birth control requires acknowledging that one is actively choosing to have sex.

Counselors often work with clients regarding issues of sexuality, reproductive health, and pregnancy. They may provide sex education and discuss options with women who are unsure whether they want to proceed with their pregnancies. Counselors working in family planning clinics, schools, colleges, and hospitals should be prepared to deal with sexuality and decisions regarding contraception, pregnancy, and sexual behavior. The role of a counselor is not to make decisions for clients, but to help clients to make decisions for themselves. Providing them with appropriate information and solid decision-making skills helps them to do so. It is critical, therefore, that counselors be knowledgeable about conception, pregnancy, and options, such as keeping the baby, giving it up for adoption, and having an abortion. Consequences of these options should be discussed.

Counselors can help clients to clarify their values (e.g., moral and religious issues, professional and personal goals, family dynamics, financial status, etc.). If a counselor strongly endorses only one or two options regarding reproduction, he or she should consider referring the client to a counselor with a more balanced perspective who could allow the client to make her own decision. If a client, particularly an adolescent client, decides to carry the baby to term, a counselor can be instrumental in reducing the negative consequences to the mother and infant by helping her to obtain adequate prenatal care and to plan her future.

Research is contradictory regarding the effectiveness of sex education programs for the prevention of pregnancy. In general, it appears that programs are most effective when they not only offer information about sex and contraception, but also allow individuals to share their views and feelings in a way that is personally meaningful and relevant. Counselors may teach skills for negotiating sexual encounters (e.g., saying no when you don't want to have sex, or insisting on using contraception). Allowing teenagers to rehearse these skills makes it much more likely that they will behave responsibly when confronting actual situations.

Helping teenagers to clarify their values regarding sex, intimacy, and relationships is helpful. Refusing to buckle to peer pressure, identifying psychological reasons that are perhaps unconscious for wanting to have a baby, and understanding the actual consequences of becoming a mother as opposed to the fantasy many teenagers have may be useful as preventive interventions. The realities of the demands infants make while giving little in return, the curtailment of the mother's freedom, and the financial costs of caring for a baby should be discussed. When unconscious motivations for wanting a baby are elicited, alternative ways of getting those needs met can then be pursued.

Human Immunodeficiency Virus (HIV), AIDS-Related Complex (ARC), and Acquired Immune Deficiency Syndrome (AIDS)

Human immunodeficiency virus (HIV) is a persistent disease of the immune system that progresses from initial infection (HIV positive) without symptoms (asymptomatic), to HIV with symptoms (symptomatic), also referred to as AIDS-related complex (ARC), to acquired immunodeficiency syndrome (AIDS) (Hoffman, 1991; Martin, 1989). Individuals who test positive for HIV have been infected with the virus and are able to transmit the disease to others even if no symptoms are present (Martin, 1989). AIDS is diagnosed only after the immune system can no longer defend the body against opportunistic infections such as Pneumocystic carinii pneumonia and cryptococcal meningitis (Hoffman, 1991).

Although drug treatments such as AZT have increased the life span of those infected, and other treatments are being developed, no cure has yet been developed. In most cases, individuals are aware of their HIV-positive status years before they become ill (Hoffman, 1991), and the disease ultimately results in early death. Because of the progressive nature of the disease, the physical, emotional, social, and professional functioning of the HIV-positive individual is seriously affected. In some cases, significant others are also affected. As a result, there has been an increased need for counseling services specifically directed toward the HIV-positive client and his or her significant others. (See chapter 30, "Counseling HIV + /AIDS patients.")

REFERENCES

American Psychiatric Association. (1987). *Diagnostic and statistical manual of mental disorders* (3rd ed., revised, DSM-III-R). Washington, DC: Author.

Daniluk, J. C. (1991). Strategies for counseling infertile couples. *Journal of Counseling and Development, 69*, 317–320.

Friedman, M., Thoresen, C., Gill, J., Powell, L., Ulmer, D., Thompson, L., Price, V., Rabin, D., Breall, W., Dixon, T., Levy, R., & Bourg, E. (1984). Alteration of Type A behavior and its effects on cardiac recurrences in post-myocardial infarction patients. *American Heart Journal, 108*, 237–248.

Gallant, S. J., Hamilton, J. A., Popiel, D. A., Morokoff, P. J., & Chakraborty, P. K. (1991). *Health Psychology, 10*, 180–189.

Haynes, S. G., & Feinlieb, M. (1980). Women, work, and coronary heart disease: Prospective findings from the Framingham heart study. *American Journal of Public Health, 70*, 133–141.

Hoffman M. A. (1991). Counseling the HIV-infected client: A psychosocial model for assessment and intervention. *The Counseling Psychologist, 19*, 467–542.

Holmes, T. H., & Rahe, R. H. (1967). The social readjustment rating scale. *Journal of Psychosomatic Research, II*, 213–218.

Kalodner, C., & Delucia, J. (1990). Components of effective weight loss progams: Theory, research, and practice. *Journal of Counseling and Development, 68*, 427–433.

Karasek, R. A., Theorell, T. G., Schwartz, J., Pieper, C., & Alfredsson, L. (1982). Job, psychological factors and heart disease: Swedish prospective findings and U.S. prevalence findings using a new ocupational inference method. *Advances in Cardiology, 29*, 62–67.

Kiecolt-Glaser, J. K., Glaser, R., Williger, D., Stout, J. C., Messick, G., Sheppard, S., Ricker, D., Romisher, S. C., Friner, W., Bonnell, G., & Donnerberg, R. (1985). Psychosocial enhancement of immunocompetence in a geriatric population. *Health Psychology, 4*, 24–41.

Krantz, D. S., & Manuck, S. B. (1984). Acute psychophysiologic reactivity and risk of cardiovascular disease: A review and methodologic critique. *Psychological Bulletin, 96*, 435–464.

Martin, D. J. (1989). Human immunodeficiency virus infection and the gay community: Counseling and clinical issues. *Journal of Counseling and Development, 68*, 67–72.

Mason, J. W. (1971). A reevaluation of the concept of *nonspecificity* in stress theory. *Journal of Psychiatric Research, 8*, 323–333.

Matarazzo, J. D. (1980). Behavioral health and behavioral medicine. *American Psychologist, 35*, 807–817.

Menning, B. (1980). The emotional needs of infertile couples. *Fertility and Infertility, 34*, 313–319.

Selye, H. (1936). A syndrome produced by diverse nocuous agents. *Nature, 138*, 32.

Sheehy, G. (1991, October). The silent passage: Menopause. *Vanity Fair*, pp. 222–227, 252–263.

Stunkard, A. J., Sorensen, T. I. A., Hanis, C., Teasdale, T. W., Chakraborty, R., Schull,

W. J., & Schulsinger, F. (1986). An Adoption study of human obesity. *New England Jouranl of Medicine, 314*, 193–197.

FOR FURTHER READING

Baum, A. & Grunberg, N. E. (Eds.), Gender and health [Special Issue], *Health Psychology, 10* (2), 79–153.

Gallant, S. J., Hamilton, J. A., Popiel, D. A., Morokoff, P. J., & Chakraborty, P. K. (1991). Daily moods and symptoms: Effects of awareness of study focus, gender, menstral-cycle phase, and day of the week. *Health Psychology, 10*, 180–189.

Gatchel, R. J., Baum, A., Krantz, D. S. (1989). *An introduction to health psychology.* New York: Random House.

Haynes, S. G., & Feinlieb, M. (1980). Women, work, and coronary heart disease: Prospective findings from the Framingham heart study. *American Journal of Public Health, 70*, 133–141.

Matarazzo, J. D. (1980). Behavioral health and behavioral medicine. *American Psychologist, 35*, 807–817.

28

Obsessive-Compulsive Disorder

FUGEN NEZIROGLU, Ph.D.
JOSÉ A. YARYURA-TOBIAS, M.D.

BEHAVIORAL TREATMENT

Acquisition and Maintenance Theory

The social learning theory of the acquisition of compulsive behavior is based on Mowrer's (1947) two-factor learning theory, which explains in general the acquisition of fear and avoidance. This theory has been applied by Dollard and Miller (1950) to the acquisition of obsessive-compulsive disorder (OCD). They suggested that the first type of learning is *classical conditioning;* the second, *operant conditioning.* Classical conditioning refers to the process whereby a neutral stimulus is paired with an unconditional stimulus that acquires the same properties as the unconditional stimulus and thus elicits anxiety. The second stage consists of a negative reinforcement paradigm, in which new responses are learned to decrease the anxiety in the presence of the conditioned (neutral) stimulus. These learned responses are termed *avoidance* or *escape* responses. They remove anxiety and therefore are negatively reinforcing.

How does this apply to obsessive-compulsive patients? For example, a conditioned stimulus may be a red mark on a doorknob that leads into a medical laboratory. The patient associates the red mark with death; therefore, the unconditioned stimulus is death. The unconditioned response is anxiety. Washing one's hands removes the anxiety that was elicited by the doorknob with the red mark; thus, hand washing becomes negatively reinforcing. It is this negative reinforcement that helps maintain the compulsive behavior.

The behaviorists do not have as eloquent an explanation for the acquisition or maintenance of obsessions. Rimm and Masters (1974) offer two explanations: First, obsessing is in some way rewarding for the individual, because most obsessive-compulsive individuals have above-average intelligence and therefore enjoy thinking, especially thinking that is of a problem-solving nature. Second, obsessions have an anxiety-reducing component. This does not, however, explain obsessions that are anxiety evoking. In fact, for most obsessive-compulsive patients obsessing is very aversive; rather than reduce anxiety, obsessiveness increases anxiety.

In our opinion these explanations do not seem plausible. Later on in this chapter we offer a biochemical hypothesis to explain the presence of obsessions and compulsions.

Development of Exposure and Response Prevention
In 1966, Meyer was the first to expose obsessive-compulsive patients to anxiety-evoking stimuli and to constant staff supervision to prevent ritualistic behavior. These procedures were derived from animal experimentation studies conducted by Maier (1949) and Baum (1966). This was the advent of the behavioral therapy approach now known as *exposure and response prevention* (ERP) or more commonly referred to as "flooding."

ERP is an effective treatment modality for approximately 60–75% of patients. We believe that when ERP is applied intensively with cognitive therapy, it yields the best treatment outcome. Treatment usually consists of 90-minute sessions for 5 days a week over 6 weeks, in which patients are exposed to their fears and then prevented from performing a compulsion. For example, to overcome an AIDS contamination fear, patients would be exposed to phobic stimuli and prevented from washing their hands, showering, or discarding shoes, clothes, and so on. In the case of double-checkers, they would be asked to practice walking out of the house without checking lights, stoves, and doors. Exposure in vivo combined with exposure in imagination is most efficacious since it allows patients to be exposed to all cues that elicit anxiety.

The mechanism by which ERP operates is known as *habituation*. Habituation occurs when the continual bombardment of sensory neurons results in fatigue and thereby in extinction of anxiety. In addition to ERP, cognitive therapy may be effective.

Cognitive Therapy Approach
Unfortunately, to date there are only a handful of investigations testing the efficacy of cognitive therapy in OCD (Emmelkamp, van der Helm, van Zanten, & Plochg, 1980; Emmelkamp, Visser, & Hoekstra, 1988; Neziroglu & Neuman, 1990; Salkovskis & Warwick, 1985;) Carr (1974) suggested that obsessive-compulsive individuals overestimate the probability of the occurrence of danger and that ritualistic behaviors are the most efficient strategy for reducing the probability of the unfavorable consequence. McFall and Wollersheim (1979) stated that the *primary appraisal* of threat is followed by a *secondary appraisal* of the individual's

perceived inability to cope with the threat. Thereby, anxiety and the avoidance of anxiety may be cognitively conceptualized as an outcome of appraisal.

A cognitive-behavioral formulation of obsessions was offered by Salkovskis and Warwick (1985). In the context of a cognitive approach, obsessions are cognitive intrusions, the content of which patients interpret or appraise as harm to themselves or others and which they are responsible to prevent from occurring.

In order to diminish the possibility of the occurrence of harm and their sense of responsibility, patients neutralize their thoughts, images, or impulses. Neutralizing is a voluntarily initiated activity that is overtly or covertly (through compulsive behavior or thought rituals) engaged in to reduce the perceived sense of responsibility (Salkovskis, 1989).

While Salkovskis (1989) gives illustrations of how obsessions are neutralized, not all obsessions can be appraised. Many obsessions do not have a content—for example repetition of a melody or number, which a patient cannot appraise—but they are nonetheless very anxiety provoking. Despite the lack of neutralizing, the obsession does not habituate. This may be partially explained by viewing the patient's beliefs about the uncomfortableness of the occurrence of the obsession, as a neutralizing strategy. The patient keeps thinking that he or she cannot tolerate the anxiety.

When direct ERP was compared to thought stopping and to a cognitive approach, specifically rational-emotive therapy (RET), RET was found to be significantly better than the other two approaches in treating obsessions (Neziroglu & Neuman, 1990).

Over the past decade we have identified several faulty beliefs in maintaining obsessions and compulsions (Neziroglu & Yaryura-Tobias, 1991.) They are the following:

1. I must have guarantees.
2. I can't stand the anxiety/discomfort.
3. I must not make mistakes.
4. I am responsible for causing harm.
5. I am responsible for not preventing harm.
6. Thinking is the same as acting.
7. It's awful, horrible, terrible to make wrong decisions.
8. There is a right and a wrong in every situation.
9. I must have complete control over everything at all times.
10. I am in continuous danger.
11. I am responsible for others.
12. I must be perfect.

Modification of these schemata may enhance therapeutic efficacy primarily in those who are treatment resistant.

Treatment Failure

Treatment failure is most prevalent in patients who are depressed and have overvalued ideas (Foa, Steketee, & Groves, 1979), and who have schizotypal personalities (Jenike et al., 1990).

The following factors were identified by Neziroglu and Yaryura-Tobias (1991) as modifying treatment outcome:

1. overvalued ideation
2. personality factors
3. other concomitant psychiatric disorders
4. prior level of functioning
5. lack of motivation
6. other immediate family members with OCD
7. secondary gains
8. procrastination

While knowledge about the behavioral treatment of OCD has increased tremendously in the past 25 years, many more studies are needed.

Proposed Mechanism of Behavior Therapy

It is our belief that the effectiveness of behavior therapy is probably due to its ability to modify the biochemistry of the patient, specifically serotonin activity. Preliminary findings suggested serotonergic activity change within 3 weeks of intensive ERP treatment (Neziroglu, Steele, Yaryura-Tobias, Hitri, & Diamond, 1990). However, more investigations are needed in the neurochemical processes involved with behavior therapy. In addition, new approaches are needed for those who do not respond to existing forms of treatment.

Behavioral versus Pharmacological Treatment

Since the early 1970s we have conducted a series of experiments to identify the etiology of OCD (Yaryura-Tobias & Neziroglu, 1983). It is our belief that the disorder may be caused by different biological or psychological etiologies. At this point, research should be channeled into identifying subgroups of obsessive-compulsive patients and isolating etiological factors. Few studies have investigated the behavioral treatment in combination with or against the drug therapies. L. Solyom, Sookman, C. Solyom, and Morton (1979) studied the effects of different antidepressant groups (clorimipramine, phenelzine, trimipramine, and doxepine) to four behavior therapy groups (flooding, thought stopping, aversion relief, systematic desensitization). Obsessional patients improved more on clorimipramine (CMI) than with behavior therapy (50% vs. 30%), respectively. However, compulsions improved between 30% and 40% with behavior therapy, CMI, phenelzine, and trimipramine. On doxepine a 40% increase in symptoms was noted. These results must be evaluated with caution. L. Solyom, Sookman, C. Solyom, and Morton (1979) did not fully explain how flooding was conducted. Since that time, research has indicated that ERP is the best behavioral approach to reduce compulsions. Thought stopping, aversion therapy, and systematic desensitization have been found to be ineffective behavioral methods. Therefore, it is not surprising that behavioral and drug therapy were equally effective in reducing compulsions and less so in obsessions, since the treatments used were not the most efficacious.

In another study, L. Solyom and Sookman (1978) indicated that there were negligible differences between CMI and behavior therapy. Contrary to other findings, they found that behavior therapy reduced depression scores more than the antidepressants, although the differences were not statistically significant. However, at a 3-year follow-up, those patients who had undergone behavior therapy continued to show increased improvement in their obsessive-compulsive symptomatology, while those on drugs such as CMI, phenelzine with trimipramine, and doxepine did not show further improvement. In several studies (Neziroglu, 1979; Neziroglu & Yaryura-Tobias, 1977; Neziroglu & Yaryura-Tobias, 1980), in which we looked at the combined effect of the CMI and behavior therapy (ERP), we found that the addition of behavior therapy to CMI administration increased the percentage of improvement. Patients were initially administered CMI for 4 weeks in order to enable them to start behavior therapy. At the end of 4 weeks, behavior therapy was instituted for ten 90-minute sessions on a weekly basis. We found a 60% reduction in obsessive-compulsive symptoms at the end of CMI administration and an 18.7% reduction of symptoms after 10 sessions of ERP. A 6-month follow-up showed that improvements were maintained with minimal patient supervision. At 1½-year follow-up, 9 out of the 10 patients were completely free from obsessions and compulsions. It appears that behavior therapy enables the patient to maintain improvement and reduce the possibility of relapse. Currently, one research group in addition to ours is studying the additive effects of ERP and CMI.

It is our experience that CMI enables many patients to undergo ERP by decreasing the urge to give in to a compulsion and thereby increasing their ability to resist avoidance.

Rachman, et al. (1979) studied the effects of exposure plus placebo, compared with CMI and placebo on 40 obsessive-compulsive patients. They concluded that behavior therapy and CMI were equally effective in reducing obsessive-compulsive symptomatology and that CMI improved the mood of the patients. Similar findings were reported by Marks, Stern, Mawson, Cobb, and McDonald (1980). They indicated that exposure produced significant improvement in rituals, but less change in mood. The therapeutic effects of CMI seemed to disappear once patients were discontinued, and improvement was observed again when they commenced taking the drug. Patients who were on a combined treatment, exposure and CMI, improved the most in their ritualistic behavior.

Christensen, Hadzi-Pavlovic, Andrews, and Mattick, (1987) conducted a meta-analysis, which is a form of assessment whereby many studies are pooled and the results of each of the studies are combined and an overall conclusion reached. In doing this meta-analysis, which used 38 trials, the researchers concluded that a variety of treatments have been shown to be of benefit to both obsessive-compulsive symptoms and to depression. Tricyclic medication, notably CMI and ERP treatments, did not seem to differ. Both were found to alleviate depression and obsessive-compulsive symptoms.

PHARMACOLOGICAL TREATMENT

Biological Theories
The neurochemical foundation for a theoretical posit has been limited to studies conducted on the indolaminergic pathway, notably, serotonin (5-HT). These studies were performed measuring neurotransmitters or their metabolites in blood, urine, and the cerebral spinal fluid (CSF) of OCD patients. Significantly lower whole 5-HT levels were found in OCD patients compared to normal controls (Yaryura-Tobias, Bebirian, Neziroglu, & Bhagavan, 1977) while total and free tryptophan (TRY), the 5-HT precursor, which was measured in plasma, and 5-hydroxyindolacetic acid (5-HIAA), a 5-HT metabolite, which was measured in a 24-hour urine sample, remained within normal limits (Yaryura-Tobias, Neziroglu, & Bhagavan, 1979). It has been shown that obsessive-compulsive patients who responded favorably to CMI treatment had significantly higher 5-HIAA baseline levels in CSF than those patients who did not respond well (Thoren, Asberg, Cronholm, Jornestedt, & Traskman, 1980). The efficacy of specific 5-HT reuptake blockers, mainly fluoxetine (Turner, Jacob, Beidel, & Himmelhoch, 1985) and fluvoxamine (Perse, Greist, Jefferson, Rosenfeld, & Dur, 1987), for the treatment of OCD gives further support to the serotonergic hypothesis (Yaryura-Tobias, 1977).

Historically, the encephalitis pandemia of 1915–1926 opened a biological window to the study of the psychopathophysiology of OCD. This was due to the presence of psychiatric symptoms in encephalitis. These symptoms appeared during the pseudoneurotic or second phase, where obsessions and compulsions were the clinical highlights. The OCD symptoms observed in postencephalitic patients included iterativeness, doubting, compulsions, and arithmomania. In encephalitis, the obsessions and compulsions seemed to be primitive and nonintellectual.

Cerebral lesions ranging from tumors to cerebrovascular accidents have been associated with OCD (Daumezon, Cor, & Moor, 1954). The anatomy of the brain has also been investigated by using computerized axial tomography. Computerized tomography has shown that the caudate nucleus volume in patients with OCD is less than that of controls (Luxemberg et al., 1988), while in adolescents with OCD mean ventricular-brain ratio was significantly higher than the controls (Behar et al., 1984).

Metabolic Studies
Glucose and oxygen are both the main nutrients of the brain. A faulty glucose metabolism in OCD has been reported in patients after a glucose load (5-hour oral glucose tolerance test, Yaryura-Tobias, 1988). Since glucose actively participates in the regulatory mechanisms of cerebral tryptophan (Fernstrom & Jacobi, 1975), a correlation between glucose and 5-HT may be considered.

Position emission tomography in an OCD population with childhood onset has shown an increase in glucose metabolism in left frontal, right sensorimotor, bilateral prefrontal, and anterior cingulate regions (Swedo et al., 1989), while in an adult population the areas affected were the left frontal gyrus and bilateral in the caudate nucleus (Baxter et al., 1987). These studies are instrumental in explaining some organic aspects of OCD.

Neurophysiological Aspects
Abnormal bifrontal electrical activity (Aslarov, 1970) and a left frontal dysfunction (Flor-Henry, Yeudall, Koles, & Howarth, 1979) have shown vegetative psychomotor and behavioral responses compatible with obsessive-compulsive symptomatology (Escobedo, Fernandez-Guardiola, & Solis, 1973). Neuropsychological testing has shown deficits consistent with frontal-parietal involvement (Neziroglu, Penzel, Vasquez, & Yaryura-Tobias, 1988).

Pharmacological Treatment and Management
Best treatment outcome is noted with an integrative approach consisting of drug, behavior, and cognitive therapy, with family participation. As a last resort if treatment fails, psychosurgical intervention may be considered. The need for comprehensive therapeutic management is indis-

pensable in long-term severe cases, with serious disruption of the patient's biopsychosocial environment.

Current access to anti-obsessive-compulsive agents with acceptable therapeutic track records will facilitate the task. These drugs are strong (clomipramine) or specific (fluoxetine, fluvoxamine, sertraline) serotonin (5-HT) reuptake blockers. The therapeutic efficacy of clomipramine (Yaryura-Tobias & Neziroglu, 1983; Clomipramine Collaborative Study Group, 1991), fluoxetine (Fontaine & Chouinard, 1989), fluvoxamine (Goodman et al., 1989), and sertraline (Jenike et al., 1990) has been published. Successful pharmacotherapeutic outcome averages are a rate between 30% and 50%.

L-tryptophan (L-TRY), the amino acid precursor of 5-HT, has been used in combination with pyridoxine and niacin (Yaryura-Tobias & Bhagavan, 1977), with lithium, and tranylcypromine (Yaryura-Tobias, 1981). It is, however, no longer available in the United States.

In refractory cases of OCD, moderately positive results have been reported following the use of clonazepam (Hewlett, Vinogradou, & Agras, 1990), fenfluramine (Hollander et al., 1990), and clonidine (Hollander et al., 1988).

Attempts, occasionally encouraging, were made prescribing multi-drug use (polypharmacy) for the following reasons: (a) to treat subset forms, (b) to act as therapeutic agents, after the failure of one single drug treatment, (c) to potentiate the action of the primary drug, and (d) to control secondary symptoms (e.g., severe anxiety).

Relapse following drug discontinuation ranges from 10% to 99% (Pato, Zohar-Kadouch, Zohar & Murphy, 1988). To lower the rate of relapse, we favor a combined drug and behavior therapy approach (Yaryura-Tobias, Neziroglu, Fuller, 1979). By doing so, two goals are obtained: (a) less medication is used, thus side effects are minimized, and (b) chances of relapse are diminished.

Psychosurgery

Surgical intervention of the brain for the treatment of OCD has been limited to those cases refractory to noninvasive treatment. It seems that patients with severe compulsions are better responders. The benefits appear to be symptomatic, and a period of at least 6 months is required before the full effect of treatment is observed. Treatment efficacy has been reported betwen 50% and 80%, with strong chances of relapse. Surgery of the orbital frontal and cingulum region has contributed to validate the organic hypothesis for OCD. Interestingly, stereotactic coagulation of intralaminar and medialthalmic nuclei was performed to treat compulsions, phobias, tics, and Tourette syndrome (Yaryura-Tobias & Neziroglu, 1983).

Family Intervention/Support Groups

Because OCD usually causes doubtfulness, patients often rely on relatives to make decisions and they usually need assistance to function and cope with life. As a result, a strong dependence bond may develop between the patient and the family, and subsequently, there may be secondary gains to maintaining the existing condition. Consequently, the patient's improvement may threaten the relationship. To preserve the bond, therapeutic sabotage may occur. Therefore, it is important to involve the family in the treatment. After recovery, a rehabilitation program should ensue to facilitate the patient's reinsertion into the social stream.

Support groups for both the family and patients are helpful. The group allows the patient and family to feel that they are not alone, to learn from the experiences of others, and to gain support from others with similar problems.

Course and Prognosis

The course of OCD follows an acute, subacute, or chronic evolution. Symptoms usually set insidiously with gradual increase in intensity and frequency. The illness usually occurs before the age of 25. This may be due to psychosocial changes in life, such as college, military draft, marriage, menopause, and mid-life crisis. OCD may be aggravated by stress, pregnancy, postpartum, divorce, economic losses, virosis, and major illnesses. Almost 40% of women with children have an onset during pregnancy (Neziroglu, Anemone, & Yaryura-Tobias, 1992). OCD does not follow seasonal cycles or a circadian rhythm.

Patients may report an increase of obsessions at nighttime or when they are alone, fatigued, and/or idling. OCD seems to be chronic, with spontaneous or long-term remissions a rarity. The duration of a relapse can be shortened in patients previously treated. Booster sessions are valuable.

Philosophical Outlook

OCD is associated with eating disorders, body dysmorphic disorder, hypochondriasis, self-mutilation, trichotillomania, and Tourette syndrome. The following disorders may demonstrate OCD symptoms but are not considered related disorders as those listed above: chorea, mental retardation, Parkinson's disease, schizophrenia, and epilepsy.

This multivariate disorder presenting so many clinical connections may be explained in terms of a pathological continuum. This continuum starts at a given point in the brain as a result of an impacting noxa. The impact produces a ripple effect that, in its trajectory, involves various histoelectrochemical subsystems, causing the observed mosaic of symptoms. As an example, we may use the concept of a Spanish fan where each fold represents one symptom. Thus, the stronger the impact, the larger the aperture, and the wider the presence of symptoms (Yaryura-Tobias, 1990). OCD might also be considered one model of the general system process.

FOR FURTHER READING

Neziroglu, F., & Yaryura-Tobias, J. A. (1991). Over and over again: understanding obsessive-compulsive disorder. New York: Lexington Books.
Yaryura-Tobias, J. A. (1990). A unified theory of obsessive-compulsive disorder. In C. N. Stefanis, C. R. Soldatos, A. D. Rabavilas (Eds.), *Psychiatry: A world perspective* (Vol. 1, pp. 568–571). Amsterdam: Elsevier.
Yaryura-Tobias, J. A. & Neziroglu, F. (1983). *Obsessive-compulsive disorder: Pathogenesis, diagnosis, and treatment.* New York: Marcel Dekker.

REFERENCES

Aslarov, A. S. (1970). In V. S. Rusinov (Ed.), *Electrophysiology of the central nervous system* (pp. 39–47). New York: Plenum Press.
Baum, M. (1966). Rapid extinction of an avoidance response following a period of response prevention in the avoidance apparatus. *Psychological Report, 18,* 55–64.
Baxter, L. R., Phelps, M. E., Mazziotta, J. C., Guze, B. H., Shwartz, J. M., & Selin, C. E. (1987). Local cerebral glucose metabolic rates in obsessive-compulsive disorder. *Archives of General Psychiatry, 44,* 211–218.
Behar, D. Rapoport, J. L., Denclka, M. B., Mann, L., Cox, C., Fedio, P., Zahn, T., & Wolfman, M. G. (1984). *American Journal of Psychiatry, 141,* 363–369.
Carr, A. T. A. (1974). Compulsive neurosis: A review of the literature. *Psychology Bulletin, 81,* 311–318.
Christensen, H., Hadzi-Pavlovic, D., Andrews, G., & Mattick, R. (1987). Behavior therapy and tricyclic medication in the treatment of obsessive-compulsive disorder: A quantitative review. *Journal of Consulting and Clinical Psychology, 55,* 701–711.
Clomipramine Collaborative Study Group (1991). Clomipramine in the treatment of patients with obsessive-compulsive disorder. *Archives of General Psychiatry, 48,* 730–738.
Daumezon, M. G., Cor, J., & Moor, L. (1954). Disparition de phénomènes obsessionnels grave après "autolobotomie" chez un grand déséquilibre [The disappearance of severe obsessional phenomena after "autolobotomy" producing a great disequilibrium]. *Annals of Medical Psychology, 112,* 93–97.
Dollard, J., & Miller, N. E. (1950). *Personality and psychotherapy: An analysis in terms of learning, thinking, and culture.* New York: McGraw-Hill.
Emmelkamp, P. M. G., van de Helm, M., van Zanten, B., & Plochg, J. (1980). Contributions of self-instructional training to the effectiveness of exposure in vivo: A comparison with obsessive-compulsive patients. *Behaviour Research and Therapy, 18,* pp. 61–66.
Emmelkamp, P. M. G., Visser, S., & Hoekstra, R. I. J. (1988). Cognitive therapy vs.

exposure in vivo in the treatment of obsessive-compulsives. *Cognitive Therapy and Research, 12,* 103–104.

Escobedo, F., Fernandez-Guardiola, A., & Solis, G. (1973). Chronic stimulation of the cingulum in humans with behavior disorders. In L. V. Lattinen & K. E. Livingston (Eds.), *Surgical approaches in psychiatry* (pp. 65–68). Baltimore: University Park Press.

Fernstrom, J. D., & Jacobi, J. H. (1975). Minireview: The interaction of diet and drugs in modifying brain serotonin metabolism. *Journal of General Pharmacy, 6,* 253–259.

Flor-Henry, P., Yeudall, L. T., Koles, Z. J., & Howarth, B. G. (1979). Neuropsychological and power spectral EEG investigations of the obsessive-compulsive syndrome. *Journal of Biological Psychiatry, 14,* 119–130.

Foa, E., Steketee, G., & Groves, G. A. (1979). The use of behavioral therapy and imipramine in a case of obsessive-compulsive neurosis with severe depression. *Behaviour Modification, 3,* 419–430.

Fontaine, R., & Chouinard, G. (1989). Fluoxetine in the long-term maintenance treatment of obsessive-compulsive disorder. *Psychiatric Annals, 19,* 88–91.

Goodman, W. K., Price, L. M., Rasmussen, S. A., Delgado, P. L., Henninger, G. R., & Charney, D. S. (1989). Efficacy of fluvoxamine in obsessive-compulsive disorder: A double-blind comparison with placebo. *Archives of General Psychiatry, 46,* 36–44.

Hewlett, W. A., Vinogradou, S., & Agras, W. S. (1990). Clonazepam treatment of obsessions and compulsions. *Journal of Clinical Psychiatry, 51,* 158–161.

Hollander, E., DeCaria, C. M., Schneier, F. R. (1990). Fenfluramine augmentation of serotonin reuptake blockade of antiobsessional treatment. *Journal of Clinical Psychiatry, 51,* 199–123.

Hollander, E., Fay, M., Cohen, B., Campeas, R., Gorman, J. M., & Liebowitz, M. R. (1988). Serotonergic and noradrenergic sensitivity in obsessive-compulsive disorder: Behavioral findings. *American Journal of Psychiatry, 145,* 1015–1017.

Jenike, M. A., Baer, L., Summergrad, P., Minichielli, W. E., Holland, A., & Seymour, R. (1990). *American Journal of Psychiatry, 47,* 923–928.

Luxemberg, J. S., Swedo, S. E., Flament, M. F., Friedland, R. P., Rapoport, J. & Rapoport, S. J. (1988). Neuroanatomical abnormalities in obsessive-compulsive disorder detected with quantitative X-ray computed tomography. *American Journal of Psychiatry, 145,* 1089–1193.

Maier, N. R. F. (1949). *Frustration: The study of behavior without a goal.* New York: McGraw-Hill.

Marks, I. M., Stern, R. S., Mawson, D., Cobb, J., & McDonald, R. (1980). Clomipramine and exposure for obsessive-compulsive rituals. *British Journal of Psychiatry, 136,* 1–25.

McFall, M. E., & Wollersheim, J. P. (1979). Obsessive-compulsive neurosis: A cognitive behavioral formulation and approach to treatment. *Cognitive Therapy and Research, 3,* 333–348.

Meyer, V. (1966). Modification of expectations in cases with obsessional rituals. *Behavior Research and Therapy, 4,* 273–280.

Mowrer, O. H. (1947). On the dual nature of learning: A reinterpretation of "conditioning" and "problem solving." *Harvard Educational Review, 17,* 102–148.

Neziroglu, F. (1979). A combined behavioral and pharmacotherapy approach to obsessive-compulsive disorders. In J. Obiols, C. Ballus, E. Gonzalez-Monclus, & J. Pujol (Eds.), *Biological psychiatry today* (pp. 591–596). Amsterdam: Elsevier.

Neziroglu, F., Anemone, M. A., & Yaryura-Tobias, J. A. (1992). Onset of obsessive compulsive disorder in pregnancy. *American Journal of Psychiatry, 149* (7), 947–950.

Neziroglu, F., & Neuman, J. (1990). Three treatment approaches to obsessions. *Journal of Cognitive Psychotherapy, 4,* 377–392.

Neziroglu, F., Penzel, F. I., Vasquez, J., & Yaryura-Tobias, J. A. (1988, November). Neuropsychological studies in obsessive-compulsive disorder. Presented at the *Association for Advancement of Behavior Therapy,* New York, N.Y.

Neziroglu, F., Steele, J., Yaryura-Tobias, J. A., Hitri, A., & Diamond, B. (1990). Effect of behavior therapy on serotonin level in obsessive-compulsive disorder. In C. N. Stefanis, C.R. Soldatos, A. D. Rabavilas (Eds.), *Psychiatry: A world perspective* (Vol. 3, pp. 707–710). Amsterdam: Elsevier.

Neziroglu, F., & Yaryura-Tobias, J. A. (1977). Usage of behavior therapy and chlorimipramine in the treatment of obsessive-compulsive and phobic behavior. Paper presented at the 11th annual meeting of the Association for the Advancement of Behavior Therapy, Atlanta, GA.

Neziroglu, F., & Yaryura-Tobias, J. A. (1980). Follow-up study on obsessive-compulsive patients on clomipramine and behavior therapy. *Pharmaceutical Medicine, 2,* 171–173.

Neziroglu, F., & Yaryura-Tobias, J. A. (1991). Over and over again: Understanding obsessive-compulsive disorder. New York: Lexington Books.

Pato, M. T., Zohar-Kadouch, R., Zohar, J., & Murphy, D. L. (1988). Return of symptoms after discontinuation of clomipramine in patients with obsessive-compulsive disorder. *American Journal of Psychiatry, 145,* 1521–1525.

Perse, T. L., Greist, J. H., Jefferson, J. W., Rosenfeld, R., & Dur, R. (1987). Fluvoxamine treatment of obsessive-compulsive disorder. *American Journal of Psychiatry, 144,* 1543–1549.

Rachman, S., Cobb, J., Grey, B., MacDonald, B., Mawson, D., Sartory, G., & Stern, R. (1979). The behavioral treatment of obsessional-compulsive disorders with and without clomipramine. *Behaviour Research and Therapy, 17,* 467–478.

Rimm, D. C., & Masters, J. C. (1974). *Behavior therapy: Techniques and empirical findings.* New York: Academic Press.

Salkovskis, P. M. (1989). Cognitive-behavioral factors and the persistence of intrusive thoughts in obsessional problems. *Behaviour Research and Therapy, 27,* 677–682.

Salkovskis, P. M. & Warwick, H. M. C. (1985). Cognitive therapy of obsessive-compulsive disorder: Treating treatment failures. *Behavioral Psychotherapy, 13,* 243–255.

Solyom, A., & Sookman D. (1978). A comparison of clomipramine HCL and behavior therapy in the treatment of obsessive neurosis. *Journal of International Medical Research, 5,* 49.

Solyom, L., Sookman, D., Solyom, C., & Morton, L. (1979). Obsessive-compulsive response to behavior therapy and to antidepressant drugs. J. Obiols, C. Ballus, E. Gonzales Monclus, & J. Pujol (Eds.), *Proceedings of the Second World Congress of Biological Psychiatry,* Amsterdam: Elsevier.

Swedo, S. E., Schapiro, M. B., Grady, C. L., Cheslow, D. L., Leonard, H. L., Kumar, A., Friedland, R., Rapoport, S. L, & Rapoport, J. L. (1989). Cerebral glucose metabolism in childhood: Onset of obsessive-compulsive disorder. *Archives of General Psychiatry, 46,* 518–532.

Thoren, P., Asberg, M., Cronholm, B., Jornestedt, L., & Traskman, L. (1980). Clomipramine treatment of obsessive-compulsive disorder. *Archives of General Psychiatry, 37,* 1281–1285.

Turner, S. M., Jacob, R. G., Beidel, D. C., & Himmelhoch, J. (1985). Fluoxetine treatment of obsessive-compulsive disorder. *Journal of Clinical Psychopharmacology, 5,* 207.

Yaryura-Tobias, J. A. (1977). Obsessive-compulsive disorders: A serotonergic hypothesis. *Journal of Orthomolecular Psychiatry, 46,* 36–42.

Yaryura-Tobias, J. A. (1981). Treatment of obsessive-compulsive disorder. In C. Perris, G. Struve, & R. Jansson (Eds.), *Biological psychiatry* (pp. 622–625). Amsterdam: Elsevier.

Yaryura-Tobias, J. A. (1988). Desorden obseso-compulsive primario: Aspectos bioquimicos. [Primary/Obsessive-compulsive disorder: Biochemical aspects]. In J. Ciprian-Ollivier (Ed.), *Psiquiatria biologica: Fundamentos y applicacion clinica* (pp. 120–127). Buenos Aires, Argentina: Cientifica Americana.

Yaryura-Tobias, J. A. (1990). A unified theory of obsessive-compulsive disorder. In C. N. Stefanis, C. R. Soldatos, A. D. Rabavilas (Eds.), *Psychiatry: A world perspective* (Vol. 1, pp. 568–571). Amsterdam: Elsevier.

Yaryura-Tobias J. A., Bebirian, R., Neziroglu, F., & Bhagavan, H. N. (1977). Obsessive-compulsive disorders as a serotonin defect. *Research Communications in Psychology, Psychiatry and Behavior, 2,* 279–286.

Yaryura-Tobias, J. A., & Bhagavan, H. N. (1977). L-tryptophan in obsessive-compulsive disorders. *American Journal of Psychiatry, 134,* 1298–1299.

Yaryura-Tobias, J. A., Neziroglu, F., & Bhagavan, H. N. (1979). Biochemical correlates in obsessive-compulsive disorders. In J. Obiols, C. Ballus, E. Gonzales Monclus, and J. Pujol (Eds.), *Biological Psychiatry Today, 1,* 574–580. Amsterdam: Elsevier.

Yaryura-Tobias, J. A., Neziroglu, F., & Fuller, B. (1979). An integral approach in the management of obsessive-compulsive patients. *Pharmaceutical Medicine, 1,* 170–173.

Yaryura-Tobias, J. A., & Neziroglu, F. (1983). *Obsessive-compulsive disorder: Pathogenesis, diagnosis, and treatment.* New York: Marcel Dekker.

29

Phobics and other Panic Victims

JANICE N. McLEAN, Ph.D.

SHEILA A. KNIGHTS, Psy.D.

Panic is a formidable enemy. For every direct panic victim, there are several secondary victims: the spouse or partner, the children, parents, close friends, sometimes even the employer and co-workers. In short, all of the people with whom the panic victim shares his life, all of the people whose own lives are affected by worrying about the victim and filling in for him or her, are secondary victims. They are the ones who are asked to be understanding when the victim can't do something he or she promised to try to do, things like taking a family vacation, or attending a son's awards ceremony or a husband's company dinner dance. These are the secondary, often forgotten, victims, of panic—and you may be one of them.

If you are a secondary victim of panic, you may be aware of the thoughts, feelings, and behaviors you experience in reaction to your husband's or wife's or parent's or friend's disorder. In fact, you may feel a little sheepish about the fact that some of those thoughts aren't so noble ("I don't deserve this blankity-blank hassle in my life!"). And some of your feelings may be a little more negative than you'd like ("I resent that I'm the one doing all the work when he's the one with the panic"!).

By now, the way you "fill in" for or help your victim with the panic may have become routine behavior (pick a vacation spot within 12 miles of home, stay by her side in the mall, ask him if he's okay when he gets quiet), and it has probably begun to test your patience. So besides getting

This chapter is adapted from McLean, J., and Knights, S., *Phobics and Other Panic Victims* (New York: Crossroad, 1989).

a firsthand look at how one person's panic can affect a whole series of people, you're also learning that there's a very human side to yourself.

THE PANIC PACKAGE

We use the term *panic package* to describe the far-reaching effects of a panic disorder and agoraphobia on not only the direct victim but the secondary victims as well—the family and other support people of the primary sufferer. These disorders don't victimize one person in isolation, but many people in a "ripple effect." In fact, in severe cases of these disorders, the ripple effect upon the support people may seem more like a tidal wave in the impact it has on the life of these secondary victims. Here's a typical example of how the panic package works:

For the direct victim of panic, it starts with a fluttery stomach, followed immediately by a rapid heartbeat, sweaty palms, warmth all over, rubbery knees, shakiness, a tightness in the chest, then dizziness, and a feeling of detachment, unreality, and doom. The victim is terrified at the thought of an impending heart attack, of losing control, of going crazy.

These are the frightening symptoms, thoughts, and feelings of the panic victim. Whether he or she is experiencing a panic attack for the first time or the thousandth time, the experience is just as frightening, just as frustrating. The worry of having a panic attack at any time, any place, without warning, results in a pattern of staying close to a "safe person," a person who can be counted on to help the victim in case of panic. It results in a pattern of avoiding places from which escape is difficult or delayed. It results in avoidance of social situations in which the victim might be scrutinized by others in the event of panic.

This avoidance is logical in a way, but in practice, the victims become prisoners of their own "what if's." For example, "What if I panic while driving?" (I'll drive off the bridge!) "What if I panic in the mall?" (I'll lose control and go screaming out of the store!) "What if I lose control at the party?" (I'll humiliate myself forever!)

What is the victim's solution to fighting these fears? The victim simply avoids any situation that might trigger such fears, avoids any situations involving separation from a safe person, avoids any situations involving delayed escape from public places, and avoids any social situations. In short, the victim develops his or her own set of commandments for minimizing the fear of losing control:

Don't drive alone.
Don't go into situations involving crowds.
Don't go into supermarkets.
Don't go to shopping malls.
Don't go to church.

Don't go to movies.
Don't go to parties.
Don't eat in restaurants.
Don't fly in airplanes.
Don't travel too far from home.

Of course, many panic victims are not at such a severe stage of avoidance. While they may enter into all of these situations, nevertheless they do so with a tremendous amount of anxiety. Panic victims within this group have the same commandments, but add a simple qualifier: "without feeling very anxious." Therefore, their commandments are as follows:

Don't drive alone without feeling very anxious.
Don't go into situations involving crowds without feeling very anxious.
Don't go into supermarkets without feeling very anxious.
. . . and so on.

If you are a secondary victim of panic, chances are that you have had to make some very significant changes in your own life to help your panic victim with his or her disorder. Think about it. For each of the commandments the panic victim has, there is someone, possibly you, who is called into play to enforce that commandment.

For example, let's take the first commandment of the panic victim: Don't drive, or in less severe cases, don't drive without feeling very anxious. Who is called upon to do the driving for the panic sufferer who does not drive? You! And who is called upon to be the safe person in supporting the nervous driver whose commandment is "Don't drive without feeling very anxious?" You! Refer back to those commandments lists for a moment or two. Take a look at the effect these commandments have on the lives of the support people, usually the spouse, children, and parents of the panic victim.

Who does the supermarket shopping for the wife who can't? Who attends the children's open school nights alone? You know the routine if you have lived with a panic victim for a while. And you know who usually "fills in" for the immobilized victim, or who adjusts his or her schedule to accompany the victim in each of the situations outlined. You do.

You may be the constant chauffeur of the panic victim. You may adjust your vacation plans to meet the safety zone of the victim. You may forgo the fun of attending country fairs, sporting events, movies, or any other situation involving crowds of people. You may give up eating at your favorite restaurant, or when you do, you yourself may feel so anxious about having to leave suddenly that you can't enjoy your meal. You may do the grocery shopping alone or starve! You may go to parties by your-self or miss them altogether, and it's difficult deciding which is harder. In fact, you may become an expert at making excuses why you must miss yet another party, wedding, or other event you wanted so much to attend.

Now who is the victim of panic? Everyone—the primary victim and his or her support system. Each and every victim succumbs to a predict-able combination of thoughts, feelings, and behaviors in response to the panic disorder.

THE THOUGHTS, FEELINGS, AND BEHAVIOR
OF THE DIRECT VICTIM

For the direct panic victim, their *thoughts* about their disorder usually fuel the strength of the disorder. Panic victims are known for their abil-ity to use their vivid imaginations to frighten themselves, rather than to calm themselves down. Dr. Arthur Hardy, an expert in the treatment of anxiety disorders, calls these thoughts "what if" statements. Here are some examples.:

> What if I have a heart attack?
> What if I panic in a store full of people and make a fool of myself?
> What if I go out by myself and feel faint—who will help me?
> What if I need to use the bathroom and can't find one in time?

The primary victims' feelings are their emotional responses to their thoughts about the disorder. The most common ones are fear and em-barrassment: the fear of having further attacks and the embarrassment of having others find out. Both of these feelings can keep people locked into the disorder. Here are other feeling statements:

> I feel angry with myself because I can't stop the phobia on my own.
> I'm worried that these attacks will happen again while I'm alone.
> I feel guilty because I can't do things or go places with my kids.
> I'm worried that people will reject me if I tell them about my disorder.

The *behavior* of the primary victim reflects an attempt to cope with these unsettling thoughts and feelings about the disorder. Here are ex-amples:

> I sit near the door in restaurants and near exits in movie theaters so I
>   can run out if I need to.
> I buy only four or five things at a time so I don't feel trapped in the
>   supermarket.

I tell people that I don't have my driver's license so I'm not expected to carpool the children.
I go shopping only with my husband and my mother.

THE THOUGHTS, FEELINGS, AND BEHAVIOR
OF THE SECONDARY VICTIMS

The *thoughts* the secondary victims have about the disorder and about the direct victim determine how they feel toward and behave with that victim. Such thoughts can be supportive, critical, or, more likely, a mixture of the two. Here are examples:

She needs me to do so many things. Who will take care of her if I get sick?
I have to be careful of what I say to him or I might trigger an attack.
This panic stuff is so childish!
I'm tired of always being the one to go grocery shopping.

The *feelings* of the secondary victims reflect both the supportive and critical thoughts they have about the disorder and its effect on the direct victim. Usually, this mixture of thoughts results in a combination of feelings about the disorder. Here are examples:

I feel helpless and scared when he has a panic attack.
I feel frustrated in having to do things alone that should be family activities.
I feel angry because she doesn't seem to be willing to do something about her problem.
I feel happy to be so needed.

The *behavior* of the secondary victim usually involves taking on duties the victim cannot perform. It also reflects making significant changes in their individual lifestyle to accommodate the limitations of the direct victim. Here are examples:

I have to do all the shopping—for food, clothes, and anything else we need.
I had to stop taking night courses for my college degree so that my wife wouldn't be home alone.
We spend all of our vacations in our backyard.
I've taken over the finances because he is so anxious he can't sit down long enough to fill out the paperwork.

At this point, you should appreciate the fact that panic is not a simple disorder that affects one individual, but rather a package of thoughts, feelings, and behaviors that involves both direct and secondary victims. For every thought the primary victim has about his or her disorder ("I can't stand being so disabled!"), the husband or child or parent has thoughts about the disorder ("If only she weren't so dependent on me!"). For every negative feeling the victim has ("I feel guilty that I can't attend my son's school play!"), the family member also has strong feelings ("If my mother *really* cared about me, she'd come to my play!") And for every behavioral change the victim makes in response to the disorder (avoiding grocery shopping to prevent panic), there is behavioral change in the victim's family (taking on the job of grocery shopping).

In clinical settings, recognizing this victimization of those beyond the direct victim is called taking a *systems approach*. Here, we might simply say that a panic disorder is a family affair. Given the fact that panic disorders significantly affect both the direct victim and the family and support people, two things become obvious: First, the direct victim owes it to these others as well as himself to seek comprehensive treatment. Second, recovery from these disorders is based on the family as well as the victim understanding the disorder, cooperating with comprehensive treatment, and making the necessary changes in behavior to hasten the recovery process. Therefore, while the primary victim of panic is the main focus of comprehensive treatment, these secondary victims must also be addressed to understand and change the system within which the panic thrives.

Let's begin with understanding these disorders; what we know about their development, comprehensive treatment, and how you personally can help the primary victim. As a secondary victim, you'll be helping yourself as well.

WHO IS MOST LIKELY TO EXPERIENCE A PANIC ATTACK?

Researchers in this field are unable to predict with certainty who will and who won't develop panic attacks leading to such disorders as panic disorder with or without agoraphobia. However, treatment experts such as Hardy, Zane, Weekes, Goldstein, and McCullough see a particular personality type as especially susceptible to the development of panic and the avoidance of panic-inducing situations. Based upon the work of such theorists, and our own experience with panic victims, we look at the development of such disorders within a recipe paradigm that states: An individual with a certain personality and a certain personal history is likely to develop such disorders under certain circumstances.

Confused? Let's fill in some information to make the recipe more understandable:

Take a certain personality type. Choose several or all of the following:

a people pleaser
a worrier
overly responsible
bottles up feelings
never really feels "grown-up"
superstitious
sees things as black and white
perfectionists
reacts strongly to mild stimuli
overly sensitive to criticism
tends to take on the problems of others
laughs or cries easily
overly affected by tragic headlines
sees self as just adequate as a person
very concerned about what others will think
overly conscientious at work and, in parenting, tries very hard to be
   "good"
has a strong sense of right, wrong, and fairness

Add a certain type of personal history. Choose two or more of the following:

loss of a parent or parental figure through death or perceived abandonment
sudden loss of support or a change in an important interpersonal relationship
difficulty separating from family: school phobias, sleepovers with
   friends, college homesickness
physical, sexual, and/or emotional abuse as a child
extreme attachment to a parent or parents
parental history of alcoholism
taught to bottle up feelings
childhood exposure to a yeller or screamer on a regular basis
childhood exposure to a worrier on a regular basis
childhood exposure to an overly demanding authority figure
other traumatic events in childhood and early adulthood

*Expose to one or more of the following events or adjustments in early adult-
hood.* These events usually occur in the victim's 20s or 30s:

death of a significant figure in the person's life
sudden loss or disruption of an important relationship

birth of a child
hospitalization resulting in dependence upon others
an argument with a significant figure in the victim's life
negative criticism from an authority figure
going away to college
entrapment in a physically or emotionally abusive relationship
a switching of gears from career to homemaking
divorce or separation
ongoing physical illness
perceived betrayal by a significant figure
a specific traumatic event: accident, physical assault, rape
loss of a significant relationship through argument, moving, breakup,
    and so on
social isolation due to geographical area, lack of friends, and so on

Yield: a person likely to experience a panic attack.

WHAT IS A PANIC ATTACK?

1. The victim of a panic attack experiences at least four of the follow-
    ing symptoms: the sudden onset of intense apprehension, fear, or
    terror; a feeling of impending doom; shortness of breath, or a
    smothering feeling; dizziness; heart palpitations or rapid heart
    rate; shaking or trembling; numbness or tingling sensation; chest
    pain or discomfort; feelings of depersonalization or unreality;
    sweating, nausea, or intestinal distress; a choking sensation; chills
    or hot flashes; and a fear of dying, going crazy, or losing control
    during the attack and doing something impulsive and embar-
    rassing.
2. As if this weren't enough, the victim experiences these symptoms
    unexpectedly, or out of the blue; and therefore with no warning to
    permit preparation. There is no clear reason for this transforma-
    tion. The victim might be picnicking with good friends, relaxing
    at home, or standing in line at the bank when the attack occurs.
3. Finally, these attacks are not the result of any organic disorders
    that could generate such symptoms, such as thyroid irregularities,
    caffeine intoxication, or amphetamine use.

For those readers who have suffered a panic attack, no further description of this frightening experience is necessary. For those who have
not, simply reading the previous description of the physical symptoms,
thoughts, and feelings comprising the panic attack should give you an

intellectual appreciation for the panic victim you know. But what about the feelings and sensations? How can you understand something you've never experienced? The answer, of course, is that you really can't understand it fully unless you have experienced such an episode. Just as those of us who have never been prisoners of war can never fully appreciate the torment and aftermath of such an experience, so are we unable to fully understand and sympathize with the torment of the panic victim. This is one of the most frustrating parts of having such attacks—the inability of others to understand what you are experiencing and the types of thoughts, feelings, and behaviors that you develop in reaction to such panic attacks.

This is why, in working with the spouse and family of panic victims, it is so important to explain the panic experience within a context that "hits home" for those support people. While you, the reader, may be lucky enough to have never experienced panic, consider the physical reactions, thoughts, and feelings you would expect to have in the following situations:

> You return home from work one evening to find several ambulances and police cars in your driveway, all with sirens wailing and lights flashing.
> While making a hairpin turn on a winding mountain road, you feel your car begin to skid, and realize there is no way to stop it from sliding over the cliff.
> You answer your doorbell late one night to find three men with masks and guns shoving you back into the house while shouting obscenities.

It's unpleasant to even *think* about such situations, isn't it? Now imagine experiencing your reaction to these situations over and over again, but without understanding why you are undergoing such a dramatic transformation; without the comfort of being able to say to yourself, "Well, of course I'm terrified—look what's going on!" This is the life of the panic victim.

WHAT IS PANIC DISORDER?

DSM-III-R, the *Diagnostic and Statistical Manual of Mental Disorders, American Psychiatric Association,* (1987), refers to this disorder as *panic disorder without agoraphobia.* Here, while the victim suffers recurrent panic attacks, this has little or no effect on that victim's social or occupational functioning. In other words, the victim suffers the attacks, but shows little or no avoidance of situations or settings from which escape might be difficult or delayed. The large majority of people with panic disorder do begin to avoid such situations, however, and in such cases the disorder usually progresses to *panic disorder with agoraphobia.*

What is Panic Disorder with Agoraphobia?

This disorder meets the criteria for panic disorder, but the victim has also developed a fear of being in situations or places from which escape might be difficult or embarrassing if the victim were to panic. Examples of such settings would be public transportation, driving, standing in line, grocery stores, situations involving crowds, shopping malls, or bridges. There is also usually a fear that help might not be available if a panic attack should occur in one of these settings. As a result of these fears, the person either needs a trusted companion when away from home, or the person restricts travel. There are three levels of agoraphobic avoidance:

1. *Mild:* In mild cases the victim shows only minimal avoidance in daily activities. Such individuals might travel unescorted to work or shopping, but otherwise avoid traveling alone. A mild level is also seen in people who enter all difficult situations, but do so with distress. Most victims of mild agoraphobia live a relatively normal lifestyle.
2. *Moderate:* In moderate cases the person's degree of avoidance results in a restrictive lifestyle. In such cases, the victim is able to leave home alone, but limits travel to within a few miles of home unless accompanied by a trusted companion.
3. *Severe:* In severe cases the person's pattern of avoidance results in an inability to leave home at all, or only in the company of a trusted companion. Sadly, while the lifestyle of the severe agoraphobic is the most restricted, the difficulty of leaving home is often an obstacle to this very needy person's reaching the comprehensive treatment that is required.

What is Agoraphobia without History of Panic Disorder?

As the name of this relatively rare disorder implies, the victim is agoraphobic, but has no history of panic disorder. While the person avoids situations from which to escape could be difficult or embarrassing, he or she does so out of fear of experiencing only selected symptoms of the panic attack. Since the person has never experienced a full panic disorder, his or her fear is largely that of "what if my limited attack develops into a full-blown panic attack?" This anticipatory anxiety maintains the pattern of avoidance.

What is Social Phobia?
Individuals with social phobia experience excessive and unreasonable anxiety in social situations where they are exposed to the scrutiny of others. The major fear here is not primarily of having a panic attack that could result in embarrassment, as with agoraphobia, but a fear of *acting* in a way that would be humiliating or embarrassing to them independently of a panic attack. Specific fears of the social phobic range from fear of speaking in public or choking on food while eating in front of others, to an inability to urinate in public rest rooms or trembling while writing in public. Therefore, social phobics avoid, or endure with significant distress, parties, speeches, or any other situation where they could be a focus of someone's attention.

Social phobia is diagnosed only if the avoidance of such situations of possible scrutiny interferes with job functioning, ordinary social activities, or relationships with others, or if there is significant distress about having this fear. This diagnosis does not apply to someone who fears public scrutiny due to another disorder, such as stuttering or the trembling that accompanies Parkinson's disease.

What is a Simple Phobia?
Simple phobias are also referred to as specific phobias. Rather than having a panic attack or suffering the scrutiny of others, the victim fears a specific object or situation. Simple phobias are rather common in the general population and include the fear of cats, dogs, snakes, mice, insects, closed spaces like elevators, exposure to blood or tissue injuries, heights, and airplane travel. Most people seek treatment for simple phobias only when they significantly interfere with their life. Accordingly, the elevator phobic transferred to a Manhattan skyscraper is more likely to seek treatment than the homemaker who only occasionally encounters an elevator, and even then can use the stairs.

QUESTIONS VICTIMS ASK ABOUT PANIC DISORDER

How does anxiety differ from panic? Anxiety symptoms are uncomfortable, but manageable; you can continue in your normal daily activities even while manifesting anxiety symptoms: dry mouth, stomach butterflies, shortness of breath. Indeed, there are times when a little anxiety is even good for us. Anxiety related to an upcoming exam spurs us to study a little harder. Anxiety about a job interview causes us to have a shoe shine or practice our handshake. Anxiety can sometimes give us that little edge that we need to improve our performance.

The feeling of panic seems to come out of the blue. It doesn't seem to be related to present activities. It lasts for discrete periods of time, departing as suddenly as it arrived; and there is a sharp rise, then an abrupt fall in the physical symptoms. While anxiety can last for days, it usually stays within manageable levels. Panic's intensity is self-limiting since the body cannot maintain that state of intensity for prolonged periods of time.

Could I have a heart attack or die from a panic attack? The answer is no. While the panic attack gives you physical symptoms, it is not connected to any medical condition, and medical tests run during the attack have shown that it does not cause any damage to the systems involved in a panic attack. Of course, we recommend that you see a physician at the start of psychological treatment to rule out any possible physical factors or medical conditions involved in your anxiety and panic. (Examples are thyroid irregularities and caffeine intoxication.) Your physician can also allay your worry by telling you under what circumstances your symptoms should be medically evaluated to rule out physical involvement.

Can I totally lose control during a panic attick? No! This is a common fear and one that keeps many panic victims from even attempting activities they fear might bring on a panic attack. Although most panic victims fear this total loss of control, most are unable to clearly define what they mean by "losing control." The general fear is of somehow "losing it" during an attack, and acting so dramatically that the victim is publicly humiliated forever. It is comforting to remember that, despite the panic victim's certainty that "everyone" can immediately detect their panic state, even panic disorder especialists have difficulty recognizing when a victim is experiencing a panic attack. The outward appearance of the victim appears normal even to the trained eye.

How long does a panic attack usually last? During a panic attack, your sense of time passing is lost and the attack seems to be never-ending. In reality, it usually lasts for only a few minutes. The body cannot sustain the intensity of the panic state for very long and will move to balance itself and relieve the panicky feeling. In rare cases, the panic continues for a longer period of time. However, comprehensive treatment teaches the victim to prevent anxiety from building to this·level.

How can I control my panic attack? Weekes (1972), in the book Peace From Nervous Suffering, tells the reader to "float through" the panic rather than fight it. Like a swimmer caught in a strong current, if you fight the current, you exhaust yourself and are overwhelmed. If you ride the current, you eventually drift to shore. This is one of many coping strategies that panic victims learn in comprehensive treatment.

Is there a relationship between panic attacks and inner ear disturbances, Mitral valve prolapse, and hypoglycemia? Although all of these disorders have been explored as possible generators of panic, statistics indicate that in fact none of these medical conditions occurs more frequently in phobia and panic victims than in the general public.

Are panic disorders and phobias hereditary? Can I pass them on to my children? Currently, research conducted on this question is inconclusive. While anxiety disorders may appear to "run" in families, it is unclear whether this is due to heredity or environment (learned behavior). Put more simply, the question is, Are you *born* with these disorders, or taught to react to life in such a way that you *develop* these disorders? For example, does an anxious and panicky mother unknowingly, by her example, "teach" her children to be anxious, or are her children born anxious? Another question of research interest is a cross between the previous two: Are some people born with a "predisposition," or the tendency to develop such a disorder under a certain set of circumstances? And what are those circumstances?

Confusing the picture are certain facts: Some people with these disorders have no known family history of such a disorder. And many anxious and panic-ridden parents have children who are easy-going and free from anxiety. Researchers continue to address this fascinating area, with current thinking leaning toward the predisposition theory.

What do I tell my children about my disorder? The truth! Often phobics and panic sufferers try to hide their disorder from their children. This is unfair to both parties. The panic victim feels guilty over missing family occasions as well as fear that the children will reject him or her for this "tragic flaw." The children are well aware that there is something wrong and may become resentful that no one is telling them the truth, or (perhaps worse) "play along" with the parents and pretend that everything is all right since this seems to be what makes the parent happy.

Children are very sensitive. In an alcoholic family, children as young as 4 or 5 are able to recognize that there is something wrong when the parent drinks, but may take the responsibility for that action upon themselves. "I must have been bad. That's why Daddy got drunk and hit me."

Remember that how you tell your children and people in general will determine how they react. Think of the build-up that television soap operas give before a dramatic scene. They can make the common cold seem like a terminal illness. When you talk about phobias and panic attacks, how you present it is how it will be perceived. Make the discussion of your disorder matter-of-fact, like a newspaper story rather than a tragic novel.

When children are made aware of a situation, they can deal with it much more capably than we generally assume. It is the *not* knowing what is being covered up or lied about that is so much more frightening to them. Children will love and accept us, even with our flaws or vulnerabilities, when they are allowed to share in the problem.

Talking about your disorder with your children will not only help them to understand you better, and alleviate their fears about "something" being wrong, but also help them to understand that you are missing family activities *because you are phobic, not because you don't love them.*

Children benefit from good role models, people who can communicate openly and share good coping strategies. By being honest about yor disorder and your pursuit of comprehensive treatment, you also teach your children that it is okay to have areas of difficulty, and that those areas can be improved with effort. A comprehensive treatment program will help you in explaining your disorder to your children.

GETTING HELP

What Is The First Step Toward Recovery?
Whether the panic victim has had the disorder for only months or for several years, recovery is possible. The first step to recovery is in the victim's acceptance of certain facts:

1. There is a name for what is happening to you.
2. You are not going crazy.
3. You are not alone. One out of 6 Americans is victimized by an anxiety disorder, and panic disorder is the most common disorder among those seeking treatment.
4. There is effective, comprehensive treatment for the disorder.
5. With determination and hard work, comprehensive treatment can help you reach recovery.

As the secondary victim, or the concerned professional or friend, you can help the primary victim take this first step. Your message is simple: Panic, the formidable enemy, can be conquered, and you are there to help.

Where Do I Get Help And How Will I Know It Is Effective?
Experts in the field of panic and phobia disorders agree that the most effective treatment for these disorders is a package or combination of behavior therapy, eduction about the disorder, peer group support, cognitive therapy, and medication, as appropriate. This is the standard

comprehensive treatment program offered at teaching hospitals, universities, and nationally known treatment centers. Such programs are usually staffed with psychologists, psychiatrists, social workers, and other mental health professionals. Many also utilize recovered panic patients to serve as role models for victims just entering a treatment program. To find a treatment program near you contact the Anxiety Disorders Association of America (133 Rollins Avenue, Suite 4B, Rockville, Maryland 20852-4004).

As the package of recovery methods may appear rather vague to the layperson, let's be more specific about what the panic victim could expect to be offered through comprehensive treatment.

The best comprehensive treatment programs include the following components:

1. *Time-limited treatment groups* (usually 8–16 weeks) that meet weekly
2. *Instruction in anxiety disorders and the reduction of anxiety* (instruction in the measurement and recording of symptoms, relaxation training, stress reduction training, cognitive coping strategies, and written materials)
3. *In vivo, systematic desensitization sessions* (in which a staff member accompanies the patient in entering difficult situations in a step-by-step way, e.g., grocery stores, driving, staying alone, separating in a mall, standing in lines, using elevators, and crossing bridges)
4. *Evaluation for medication* as appropriate by an affiliated psychiatrist
5. *Instruction in and discussion of related issues of importance* for panic patients (assertiveness, unresolved grief, anger, incomplete individuation, self-esteem, perfectionism, rigidity of thinking, pessimism, and feelings of powerlessness)
6. *An informational session conducted for the family and close support people of the panic viction* providing clarity about the disorder and their role in helping the victim
7. *Journal keeping* (documentation of thoughts, feelings, behavior, practive sessions, progress, and setbacks) that provides insight to the patient and monitoring for the therapist
8. *Homework assignments* (readings both directly and indirectly related to the disorder, e.g., self-help books, assertiveness readings, and practice assignments for extending limits with a practice partner)
9. *Individual psychotherapy and follow-up support groups* as needed to address individual issues and to enhance recovery

This list of treatment components is especially helpful in determining the comprehensiveness of a program a panic victim is considering. The candidates for such treatment should feel comfortable asking any potential therapist or treatment center which treatment components are offered in their program of recovery.

FOR FURTHER READING

McLean, J. N., & Knights, S. A. (1989). *Phobics and other panic victims: A practical guide for those who help them.* New York: Crossroad.

REFERENCES

American Psychiatric Association. (1987). *Diagnostic and stastical manual of mental disorders* (3rd DSM-III-R). Washington, DC: Author.
Weekes, C. *Peace from nervous suffering.* (1983). New York: Bantam.

30

Counseling
HIV + /AIDS Patients

FRANCIS D. PELTZ, C.S.W, C.R.C.
DAVID A. BRIZER, M.D.

AIDS, acquired immunodeficiency syndrome, is an infectious and therefore transmissible disease whose hallmark is a weakening of the body's immune system. The symptom profile may vary from one individual to another, but usually is a progressive, debilitating, and ultimately fatal disease.

AIDS, which is caused by the human immunodeficiency virus (HIV), is the last stage of what doctors now call *HIV disease*. HIV attacks certain populations of white blood cells—T cells—which ordinarily act to fight off infection and cancers. As a result of HIV infection, the T cells diminish in number and individuals with HIV disease are then far more susceptible to various types of infection and cancer. The time from infection with HIV to clinical AIDS is highly variable and can take 10 years or possibly longer. Most doctors currently consider HIV disease chronic and manageable.

Recent government estimates suggest that as many as 1 million Americans may be positive for human immunodeficiency virus (HIV). In the past 5 years there has been a dramatic increase in the absolute number of individuals infected with the virus, as well as increasing representation among the population of heterosexual nonaddicts.

AIDS is the ninth leading cause of death in the United States. The pandemic nature of HIV dictates that therapists and counselors familiarize themselves with the symptoms, course, treatment, and psychotherapeutic issues surrounding this illness.

What do we know about HIV? Over the past decade our knowledge has expanded enormously beyond the murky half-truths and rumors that surrounded what used to be called "GRID" (gay-related immune disease.) Now we know that all individuals—not just homosexual or intravenous drug users—can acquire the virus. We also know something about the course of the infection, its treatment, and perhaps most importantly, its prevention.

In 1981 physicians began diagnosing formerly rare diseases such as *Pneumocystis carinii* pneumonia (PCP) and Kaposi's sarcoma (KS) in previously healthy young homosexual men. Some of these patients were also found to have other infectious diseases—*opportunistic infections*, such as oral candidiasis (thrush)—which typically appears in individuals with compromised immune function. Two years later researchers identified the cause of this acquired immunodeficiency syndrome as a retrovirus, HIV. HIV, which is passed along in blood, semen, vaginal fluids, and possibly other body fluids, attacks specific populations of white blood cells (T cells) which play a crucial role in fighting off infections and cancer. Possible vectors of transmission include anal, vaginal, and oral sex; contaminated needles; contaminated blood products used in transfusions; and breast milk from an infected mother. Pregnant mothers with HIV can transmit the virus to the fetus.

Individuals with HIV infections may be symptom-free for 10 years or longer, may develop a less severe form of immunodeficiency, or go on to develop full-blown AIDS. Doctors are unable to predict when medical symptoms related to AIDS will appear in someone who is infected with HIV. Following initial infection the median time to symptom development is about 5 years. The clinical picture of HIV disease varies from one person to another, but usually includes any of the following symptoms:

- persistent fatigue or lowered energy, an inability to be as active as before, lasting several months
- weight loss (15 pounds or more, or 10% of the body weight) over a period of 3 months, in the absence of dieting or change in eating habits
- swollen lymph glands in the groin, the neck, and the armpits that last for several months and are without apparent cause
- persistent fever, without apparent cause
- chronic diarrhea
- night sweats (waking up at night to find that the bedclothes are soaked with perspiration)
- flulike symptoms that last for a month or longer
- a dry persistent cough that lasts for a month or longer and/or shortness of breath
- purple or reddish patches, lumps, or sores that appear on or beneath the skin (KS)
- a persistent thick, whitish coating on the tongue and/or inside the month (thrush)
- clusters of extremely painful small blisters surrounded by red-

dened itchy skin, typically found on the trunk or the back (shingles), or on the lips or mouth or genitals (herpes simplex)
* easy bruising and unexplained bleeding

AIDS patients may develop *Pneumocystis carinii* pneumonia (a fungal infection of the lungs); other infections of viral, fungal, or protozoal origin; Kaposi's sarcoma (a cancer that involves the skin and underlying connective tissue); and/or other types of cancers. Involvement of the central nervous system in HIV disease can result in memory loss, gait or balance difficulties, tremors, seizures, vision or hearing impairment, mood changes, and other neurological problems.

The course and duration of illness is also quite varied; however, AIDS is usually fatal. Although there is as yet no cure or vaccine for AIDS, treatments that may prolong life and limit suffering as well as strategies for disease prevention and health maintenance are definitely available.

Blood tests can detect the presence of HIV. The test detects the presence of antibodies to the virus. A positive enzyme-linked immunosorbent assay (ELISA) test can be confirmed with a second test, the Western blot. Although the test is extremely accurate, there can be false negative as well as false positive results. To obtain the most accurate results, individuals should be tested 6 months *after* possible exposure to HIV.

Many public health centers offer confidential testing services—increasingly important for individuals whose job security or health insurance coverage could be jeopardized by the finding of HIV positivity. Pre- and post–blood test counseling helps individuals understand the significance of test results and provides information on community resources such as clinics and support groups for those who test positive.

Treatment may include antibiotics (such as Bactrim for *Pneumocystis*, or Nystatin for oral candida, thrush) as well as agents such as AZT to halt further viral replication. Since AZT itself may cause side effects that are difficult to distinguish from the underlying illness, it is important that clients and their therapists remain fully informed on an ongoing basis by the treating physician. Stress management, adequate diet and exercise, and abstinence from alcohol and recreational drug use, which can further compromise immune function, are also vital measures in health maintenance.

Prevention of HIV infection involves two rather straightforward measures: use of condoms during sex (anal, vaginal, or oral) with a possibly infected partner, and abstention from needle sharing.

UNLIKE OTHER ILLNESSES

The diagnosis of AIDS has an entirely different valence from other potentially fatal diagnoses (such as cancer.) Individuals with HIV + /AIDS face a spectrum of responses from those around them that makes their experience unique. The following issues may confront the individual diagnosed with HIV infection or AIDS:

Stigma

Because AIDS is primarily transmitted by sexual contact and needle sharing—and because the groups identified at highest risk in this country are homosexuals and intravenous drug users—persons with HIV often face misunderstanding, stigmatization, hostility, and rejection. The incurable nature of the illness only compounds these reactions.

Fear of contagion is by no means limited to the uninformed. A lover, spouse, or friend may be justifiably concerned about infection, depending on the type of exposure (such as sexual contact) they may have had. Ostracization by friends and family members is not uncommon, despite assurances by health authorities that the virus is transmissible only by blood exchange or intimate sexual contact. Many individuals wonder whether it is safe to use common utensils or the toilet seat in the home of an HIV carrier. Similar (unfounded) concerns come up around everyday gestures such as handshakes and hugs.

Controversy surrounding the possible infectivity of HIV-positive health personnel such as doctors and dentists is rampant. Some physicians have chosen to minimize their contact with HIV-positive patients, especially during medical procedures that involve exposure to infected body fluids such as blood or feces. It is crucial that the care of persons with HIV disease be coordinated by a physician who is knowledgeable and affiliated with a network of health care resources specific to AIDS.

Revelations

Disclosure of HIV positivity or AIDS may also lead to other significant revelations. Infected persons may suddenly find themselves having to disclose and discuss long-standing secrets, such as homosexuality, episodes of promiscuity, and/or intravenous drug use.

Fear of mortality

Death is not an issue that is openly discussed in our society. When confronted with the possibility or imminence of death, we react with confusion, uncertainty, and varying degrees of denial. The death of an elderly (often chronically ill) relative is "normative," something we come to expect in the ordinary course of things, whereas the debility and death of young, recently vigorous friends and loved ones is disturbing, often unexpected, and extremely difficult to accept. Witnessing the untimely loss of those in the prime of life evokes the possibility of our own demise and can complicate the grieving process.

Abandonment
Individuals afflicted with terminal illnesses other than AIDS typically receive abundant support and care from family and friends. Persons with AIDS on the other hand may find themselves alone, ignored, and abandoned by significant others just when their need for support is greatest.

Avoiding the Real Issue
Frequently, the disclosure by a gay man to his family that he is infected with HIV may be met with shock, anger, and disbelief—that he is homosexual. This diverts attention from the real issue at hand, which is the life-threatening illness. The focus on homosexuality can lead to either short-term or permanent abandonment. Families can react much in the same way to the revelation of intravenous drug abuse. In the absence of involvement of family or friends, the therapist may be the only real source of support for the person with AIDS.

COPING WITH THE DIAGNOSIS

When a person learns that he or she has been diagnosed with HIV or AIDS it is almost always a devastating emotional experience. Even when aware that their behavior has placed them in a high-risk group, hearing the actual diagnosis can be overwhelming. Reactions can be complex and varied. One can react with anger, intense fear, denial and even numbness.

The therapist should be able to offer an empathic response rather than a merely sympathetic one. It's only when we experience what the patient is experiencing by vicarious introspection that we begin to truly understand the effect of the diagnosis on the person's life. It is vital that the therapist not view the diagnosis as a death sentence. Many persons with HIV +/AIDS remain medically compensated, leading useful productive lives for considerable periods of time lasting months and even years.

There's no simple formula for the optimal therapeutic response; one helpful approach is to explore the patient's understanding of the diagnosis, and his fears and concerns regarding the impact of the diagnosis on his or her life. For the therapist, this situation is not unlike the process of working through the initial stage of a patient's grief reaction.

Grieving, which is a normal response to imminent loss—of one's health, one's former way of life, or one's loved ones—is a *process* that unfolds over time. Bear in mind that clients may progress unevenly or remain stuck at any one of the following typical stages:

Denial

The individual first learning that he or she has HIV disease may react with disbelief or denial. Denial is a protective mechanism, it acts as a defense against potentially overwhelming realities. Denial provides the client time to adjust and develop coping strategies to deal with feelings.

Denial can take many forms. Clients may insist that their test results were erroneous, that the diagnosis is unfair ("This can't be happening to me, I've been clean and sober for 5 years") or that they have not been engaging in high-risk behaviors. Or they may minimize their reaction ("I'm HIV positive? That's okay. I expected it anyway"). When accepting the diagnosis becomes too painful, acting as if nothing is wrong also becomes a form of denial. Some individuals use the diagnosis as a launching point for additional drug use and/or promiscuity ("I'm going to have the party of my life. I don't care who I take with me."). Exclusive focus on other issues such as concurrent alcoholism or emotional problems can be a form of denial as well.

Therapist's Reactions. Denial is a normal and often appropriate reaction. Denial is a means that the client can use to protect himself from potentially overwhelming realities. It gives the client time to adjust, to work through feelings, and to develop adequate coping mechanisms. Denial can appear at any stage during or subsequent to the grieving process.

The therapist needs to be careful not to break down the patient's defenses prematurely. It's important for the therapist to respect the patient's denial. Clients require a certain level of emotional preparedness to cope with their anxiety and fears. It's equally important to remain attentive to signals from the patient regarding his or her willingness to confront reality.

It's equally important that the therapist be aware of the dangers associated with a client's persistent denial. Persistent denial may have multiple negative consequences on patients' behaviors and well-being. Patients in denial of their HIV illness may avoid seeking appropriate medical care. Denial of illness can also lead to behaviors that may prove detrimental to the client's health, such as unprotected sex, substance abuse, and poor self-care. (Repeat exposure to HIV in someone already infected with the virus can aggravate the course of illness.)

The therapist must ask questions in order to determine exactly how much the patient knows about his or her illness. The therapist's role here alternates from exploratory to supportive to educational. Therapists must be fully informed on all aspects of the diagnosis, including epidemiology, medical treatment, side effects of antivirals, and progno-sis, in order to provide adequate reality testing for their clients.

Distancing can be a subtle form of the therapist's denial. Upon learn-ing of his or her client's diagnosis, the therapist may feel a diminu-tion of attachment to or involvement with the patient. The therapist may minimize the full impact of the diagnosis on the patient and thereby avoid a thorough exploration and working through of the client's feelings.

"When my client first told me that he had HIV," said one therapist, "my initial reaction was to draw a blank. Somehow the meaning of what he was saying got lost on me. I found myself thinking about our previous session, about my other appointments later that day, and just about everything other than AIDS.

"Then it hit me. *My patient might die.* We might never get to complete working on the issues that we had struggled so long and hard to identify. As he went on talking about the diagnosis, I found myself wondering if there had been a mistake—a false positive or something. This couldn't be happening to *my* patient."

Fear

The diagnosis of HIV can provoke fear and terror. One of the first ex-pressed fears of newly diagnosed clients is that their lover or spouse or children may test positive for the virus. Shame and fear of exposure of a homosexual or drug-using lifestyle may be part of an individual's initial reaction to the diagnosis. The person with HIV faces the prospect of an intensely difficult, complicated, and uncertain future: What course will my illness take? How long before symptoms appear? Will I need to be taken care of by friends and family? Who will really be there for me? How will I pay my bills? Will I live to see a cure? This is often com-pounded by the client's having witnessed the difficult and sometimes agonizing struggles of friends and loved ones with AIDS.

Clients with HIV+/AIDS may decide to refrain from or may simply feel incapable of sexual activity. The abstention is often related to their fear of infecting their partner or their diminished sense of sexual at-tractiveness. Related issues—particularly in later stages of the illness—include diminished libido, sexual functioning, and self-perceived mas-culinity or feminity. Empathy and consistent acceptance on the part of the therapist is instrumental in helping the patient eventually come to terms with these changes and losses.

At first the person with HIV might feel overwhelmed by the illness and the attendant threat of loss of control. But once the patient starts working toward obtaining adequate medical care, some of the fear can be alleviated and the sense of control reestablished. Sometimes HIV pa-tients become inordinately preoccupied with concerns about minor health matters, such as a pimple or an insignificant amount of hair loss or weight change. All too frequently the accumulation of unanswered questions and uncertainty can prove more anxiety-provoking than the medical realities themselves.

Therapist's reactions. The client may question his or her ability to coexist with an infection for which there is no cure and that carries the implication of socially unacceptable behavior. The therapist's role here is to help the patient articulate his or her fears and uncertainties regarding the illness and its potential consequences. For some patients, the therapist may be the only source of noncritical, nonjudgmental comfort.

The disclosure of life-threatening illness in a patient may engender anxiety and other reactions in the therapist, such as the therapist's fear of his or her own mortality, fear of contagion, fear of abandonment, reminders of significant losses experienced by the therapist in the past, feelings of helplessness, and feelings of moralistic censure and disdain. For the therapist, repression and denial and avoidance all preclude empathy.

Therapists may find themselves struggling not only with the client's fears, but with their own irrational thoughts. Issues that can arise for the therapist include fear of contagion via mere physical proximity, or the use of bathroom facilities, crying, sneezing, coughing, or handshake. Therapists need to do some reality testing in regard to their own fears: what, for example, would the imagined mode of entry of the virus be? How would the virus make its way from the air or discarded tissue into the therapist's bloodstream? Access to information from informed professional sources can be extremely helpful in allaying these fears.

"At first my patient Sam talked about his HIV in the most placid, equable terms. He described his visits to the doctor and seemed well aware of the relevant medical issues. However, it soon became clear that all the rationality and medical expertise in the world couldn't shield him from awareness of the real possibility of imminent pain and death.

"Sam began sobbing and that made me want to cry. My immediate response, which was to move closer and somehow comfort him, was soon replaced by a growing sense of discomfort and then horror: there was live virus in those tears! For a moment I imagined myself growing ill and dying; I thought of all the people I had lost in my life and hated thinking that my patient could become one of them. By acknowledging that my fear of infection and dying were irrational, I was able to stay connected with the patient in the here and now."

Patients call upon therapists to validate or otherwise sanction unrecognized or fringe treatments. Again, the therapist should be prepared to refer his or her client to appropriate medical and community resources for further information.

Anger
Denial and fear may be superseded by anger, although anger may appear at or along with any of the other reaction stages.

Anger may be expressed toward the illness itself, the scientific/medical establishment, family, God, significant others (including the individual who they believe might have infected them), as well as at the lifestyle that put the individual at risk for HIV.

Acting out (promiscuity and alcohol or drug use) and depression can be psychological solutions to unprocessed anger. Not infrequently HIV positivity is experienced as a massive narcissistic injury. Clients become furious with themselves, at their sense of hopelessness, helplessness, and loss of control. Often the patient's anger is directed at the therapist.

Therapist's role. Narcissistic injury as described above, with its attendant anger, rage, and irrational thinking must be addressed. Upon learning of his or her diagnosis, a patient may attempt to somehow manipulate his fate: "I'll never drink or drug again" or "That's it; from now on I'll be faithful." The unspoken thought here, of course, is that a change of lifestyle can somehow undo the diagnosis.

Depression
Incomplete or complicated grieving—marked by failure of the grief work to progress from denial, anger, and bargaining to acceptance— can give way to depression. People are too often willing to accept the emergence of depression in the face of life-threatening illness such as AIDS ("If I had AIDS, I'd be depressed, too"). It's important to realize that depression is a maladaptive pathological response to loss; while sadness, preoccupation with anticipated changes, and life review are normative for the grieving process, depression is not.

Unlike the sadness associated with grieving, depression exacts a heavy psychological toll upon the self. Depression may include some or all of the following: insomnia, loss of appetite, hopelessness, helplessness, loss of self-esteem, chronic fatigue, impaired concentration, low energy, social withdrawal and isolation, anhedonia, diminished libido, and thoughts of suicide. There is a sense of the self's having been depleted.

Therapist's role. The distinction between grief and depression is critical, because the clinical approach to these differs. The therapist's role with the grieving client is facilitory, he or she will provide an empathic receptive setting for the evolution of the grief process. Clients may verbalize feelings of sadness and frustration related to anticipated losses and unrealized projects and ambitions. These issues of helplessness are experienced as a massive disruption of the self. Formerly stable coping mechanisms may break down and give way to earlier (more primitive) defenses, such as denial and projection.

The therapist needs to provide a setting in which the patient's anger can be safely ventilated. Ventilation should be safe for both patient *and* therapist: the therapist should not allow himself or herself to become diverted from the therapeutic task at hand. The therapist may feel compelled to rescue or otherwise alleviate the patient's suffering; however, the patient is entitled to his or her anger, and premature closure on this issue will prove countertherapeutic.

Anger expressed by borderline or narcissistic patients can be excessive, frightening, and potentially destructive to both patient and therapist. By providing a holding environment and setting appropriate limits, the therapist offers a safe arena for the ventilation of these affects. Negative outcomes of such anger in these patients can include "empty" depressions or aggression directed at the self (as in suicidal threats or gestures) and others. Not infrequently the therapist can find himself identifying with the patient and experiencing varying degrees of frustration, helplessness, and anger. The therapist should be able to relate these episodic angers to specific precipitating events and underlying concerns, and should also be prepared to offer increased contact and psychiatric referral for medication.

Bargaining
Bargaining can be understood as a variant of denial, or more typically as a form of magical thinking. Alternately, bargaining may be the first sign of an individual's acceptance of the diagnosis, albeit with associated denial and often provoke analogous feelings on the part of the therapist, which should be recognized and not allowed to hinder the therapeutic process.

Depressed clients on the other hand may require more specific support and/or education from the therapist. Interpretative interventions on the part of the therapist may be quite important in the psychotherapy of the depressed patient. Depressed patients—particularly those with severe persistent symptomatology including suicidal ideation—should be evaluated by a psychiatrist for medication or even possibly hospitalization.

Acceptance
Acceptance of the HIV+/AIDS diagnosis means that the patient has finally come to terms with a host of related issues. True acceptance is characterized by the absence of prominent denial, rage, acting out, bargaining, and depression. At this stage, the patient will be engaged in

adequate planning for the future, which can include realistic attempts to complete unfulfilled life goals, writing a will, and making funeral arrangements (when appropriate.) This is a time when patients may find themselves taking steps to consolidate relationships and/or make amends with friends and family members. It is not unusual for patients to find themselves consoling friends and family members around the anticipated loss.

True acceptance entails recognition that the illness is *not* a punishment for one's lifestyle; for gay men this ideally includes an analogous acceptance of their sexual orientation. Adequate grief work often results in an expanded awareness on the individual's part of his place in the larger scheme of people and things—a new or heightened sense of equanimity and spirituality and belonging. The patient who has truly accepted his illness is now in a position to make active conscious choices—choices related not only to career or lifestyle but to amount and type of medical care to be pursued in the future as well. Some individuals prefer to articulate their choices in a "living will," a legal document recorded by a person in a relatively good state of health that articulates choices that can be executed once illness and debility progress.

Therapist's role. The therapist's experience during this phase of the work in many ways parallels that of his or her patient. As the therapeutic relationship grows in importance for the patient, there is often a concomitant amplification of the therapist's attachment to and emotional investment in the patient. The therapist should now be able to find many opportunities to tie together significant life themes as they have emerged throughout the therapy.

Acceptance of illness and mortality sets the stage for the working through of the patient's other more long-standing issues related to separation and loss. This is a time during which the therapist may find herself grappling not only with survivor guilt ("How come my client is ill and not me? I'll be sitting here in this consulting room long after he's gone. It's not fair"), but with their own abandonment issues as well ("As our discussions of my client's HIV-related illness progressed, I found myself becoming increasingly anxious, more and more tense. I began to approach the sessions with dread. Eventually I realized that I was experiencing his illness as a very real imminent loss for me"). The therapist continues to provide support and education during this stage as well.

True acceptance of the illness makes for emotional growth for both patient and therapist. The therapist will find himself or herself coming to terms with his or her own mortality and limitations as a caretaker. Not uncommonly, therapists working with AIDS patients find themselves wondering about the quality of their *own* lives: are they living their lives to the fullest, living each day as if it might be the last? HIV+/AIDS patients embody the therapist's ultimate existential challenge: the prescriber of authentic living, of the philosophy of quality life lived one day at a time, must likewise accept and abide by those principles—or the therapeutic exchange will be less than real.

AS THE ILLNESS PROGRESSES

The therapeutic issues facing the patient with full-blown or end-state AIDS are quite different from those facing the individual who has just learned that he is HIV positive.

Aside from the grief work, which assumes increasing immediacy and relevance as the illness progresses, there are the numerous practical concerns surrounding medical care and communication with significant others. The therapist will need to decide how to approach kindred issues such as hospital visits, fees for visits, phone time, and appropriate level of involvement with medical personnel and friends and family of the patient. The therapist, who may well find himself or herself in a coordinating role, providing liaison and information to the extended network of care providers and significant others must decide at the outset what his or her level of involvement should be. There is no single formula or correct approach here; the therapist must evolve an approach that is human and empathic and that may depart from the analytic mode. This can include touching, hand holding, and even crying with the patient.

The fluctuating and sometimes erratic course of illness necessitates maximum flexibility on the part of the therapist. Regularly scheduled office sessions may be interrupted by hospitalization(s), and therapist and client must decide how to handle these to allow for continuity of the relationship: "When my client was hospitalized for what turned out to be PCP pneumonia, I found myself wondering what to do with our usual Tuesday afternoon hour. Should I save the time slot, in the hope that he would be able to resume his sessions soon? Or should I instead plan on visiting him during that hour? What if he became permanently bedridden? Would I be willing to make home visits? Or should I conduct our sessions by phone?"

With the client's increasing deterioration and attendant physical changes (thinness, pallor, skin lesions, hair loss), the therapist may feel alarmed, frightened, or repulsed. Recognition of these reactions can prevent distancing maneuvers and premature closure of the relationship by the therapist. AIDS patients often suffer cognitive decrements as well, with memory and speech deficits interrupting what had previously been a fluent dialogue. Some of the medications used at this stage of illness may also have adverse cognitive effects.

Some patients at this stage will express a desire to die. They may feel too exhausted to continue the struggle; because of pain or medical complications or general debility, they may feel that their quality of life has been overly compromised. If the patient's wish is neither impulsive nor arises out of a treatable depression, the therapist may be better able to support the patient's desire to die. Suicidal thinking should be thoroughly explored and further interventions such as involvement of significant others and a physician may be indicated.

Therapy with HIV disease patients is difficult yet gratifying work. The therapist will be confronted with a host of issues and clinical situations that are in some ways unique. Working with these patients has yielded enormous unexpected rewards for the authors: the resolution of unresolved personal grief, and the inspiration afforded by our patients' heroic struggles with their illness and their mortality. The presence of supportive, nurturing others empowers our patients to persist in their struggle; likewise, we as therapists must avail ourselves of a network of support.

BIBLIOGRAPHY

Brizer, D. (1993). *Psychiatry for beginners.* New York: Writers and Readers.

Markowitz, J. C., Kleman, G. L., & Perry, S. W. (1992). Interpersonal psychotherapy of depressed HIV-positive outpatients. *Hospital and Community Psychiatry, 43,* 885–890.

Martell, L., Peltz, F. & Messina, W. (1993). *When someone you know has AIDS* (2nd ed.). New York: Crown.

31

Personality Disorders

PAUL RETZLAFF, Ph.D.

SUSAN BROMLEY, Psy.D.

Personality disorders are different from clinical syndromes. While most psychological disorders are like medical ailments that have fairly fixed causes and relatively set courses, the personality disorders are far more enduring. In most individuals with personality disorders, problems have been evident since adolescence. Historically and in lay thought, the personality disorders are seen as characterological flaws. More accurately, personality disorders are maladaptive and severe variants of normal personality traits. While all people have personality traits, these may or may not rise to the level of a disorder that impairs one's social or occupational functioning.

THE ASSESSMENT OF PERSONALITY DISORDERS

The single biggest clinical error with regard to personality disorders is that they are not being identified. Counselors may go to great lengths to finely detail the subtleties of an anxiety or depression, yet fail to see an apparent personality disorder. Treating a patient for a clinical syndrome without understanding how a personality disorder is hindering treatment can lead to frustration and failure. Alternatively, far too many personality disorders are misdiagnosed as clinical syndromes.

All clients should be assessed for the presence of a personality disorder in order to efficaciously treat them. While the epidemiology of personality disorders is not yet precisely measured, it is safe to assume that a large number of patients have these disorders. The exact proportion is probably best viewed as a function of the particular patient population that a therapist serves. In prisons, probably 90–100% of patients have a personality disorder, and it is most likely an antisocial personality disorder. In a drug and alcohol setting, probably 50–70% have these disorders. In a general outpatient setting, a fair estimate would be 20–50%. A college counseling setting would be expected to have a lower percentage, such as 10–30%. While the overall prevalence will vary, so will the proportion of each specific type. A prison tends to have a high prevalence of personality disorders, most of which will be diagnosed as antisocial. A general outpatient clinic will have a more diverse sampling of personality disorders, with each particular type being in the low single digits of percentage.

THE PERSONALITY DISORDERS

There are eight basic personality disorders and three severe personality disorders currently delineated in the official diagnostic manual (DSM-III-R, American Psychiatric Association, 1987). While there are other personality disorders discussed in the literature to ensure common language, maintain diagnostic and treatment research integrity, and allow for third-party payment, only those in DSM-III-R should be used.

Schizoid personality disorder is primarily a disorder of social aloofness. These patients are indifferent to social interaction and relationships. They neither desire nor seek out the very basic human interactions that most people consider necessary. A second theme is one of restricted emotionality. Joy and sorrow are not felt. Little pleasure is apparent, and little emotional concern for others is expressed.

Often these patients are misdiagnosed as schizophrenics, or the social isolation may be seen as a depression.

Avoidant personality disorder is similar to schizoid due to a predominant symptom of social aloofness, but the driving force is one of social anxiety. These patients are so afraid of being hurt that they resist any social interaction. This often leads to a self-fulfilling prophecy when they are confronted with a social situation. Being more keenly aware of their anxiety, they often overinterpret what mild negative social response they get.

Those with avoidant personality diagnoses are also often misdiagnosed as suffering from schizophrenia, or they may be seen as having an anxiety disorder if the social anxiety is high enough and presented as the chief complaint.

Dependent personality disorder is marked by passive behavior. These individuals exhibit dependent and submissive behavior. They look to others to help them, make their decisions, and protect them. This often escalates, however, into a complete helplessness or a frank fear that whoever is providing for them may leave.

Dependence is not a disorder that is socially negative enough to become the focus of attention in and of itself. It is likely to be identified only after another complaint such as marital distress or medical complaint has brought the patient into treatment. Gender socialization is a complicating factor in this diagnosis.

Histrionic personality disorders are prevalent in Hollywood. These patients are the complete opposite of those with schizoid personality disorder. These people are too social and too outgoing. They seek attention excessively and are emotional. Further, for them everything is short-lived. They cry for 2 minutes and laugh for 2 minutes, all the time telling you that you are their best friend. They have too many "best" friends and as such lack insight and depth. They are also self-centered, sexually seductive and overly concerned with physical attractiveness.

Rarely do histrionics seek treatment because they are too outgoing. More often, the features of the disorder make treatment for other things more difficult, such as alcohol dependence.

Narcissistic personality disorder is a disorder of self-importance. These patients see themselves as unique and very important. They are interpersonally exploitive to acquire their own ends and lack interpersonal empathy.

Few patients refer themselves for "greatness," but narcissism makes the treatment of just about anything more difficult. Convicted felons will learn little from prison, and alcoholics will learn little from group therapy when they consider themselves above it all.

Antisocial personality disorder is an aggressive disorder. These patients are irresponsible in most areas of functioning. They may violate the law, lose jobs, be financially manipulative, lie, and be poor spouses and parents. They need immediate gratification and do what they want.

While many are treated via forensic placement, many others appear in marital, drug and alcohol, and compensation situations.

Obsessive-compulsive personality disorders are marked by perfectionism, and excessive preoccupation with rules and regulations. They are also often very socially correct and appear at first to be simply very proper people. This rigidity, however, masks a lack of affect, emotion, and especially, affection.

These people are usually referred for marital reasons or medical reasons such as heart attack.

Passive-aggressive personality disorder is traditionally seen in individuals who have a reluctance to work well and a tendency to impede others. In addition, they possess an interpersonal anger that is very aversive to most people. This anger is expressed through the patient's degrading of others and blaming of others for their situation.

This emotional presentation is often misdiagnosed as a depression, anxiety or situational reaction. Indeed, the passive-aggressive person is constantly distraught over something. They are quick to blame their situation or social relationships for their problems, whereas in actuality they are always this way as a characterological response to life's demands.

Schizotypal personality disorder includes a social aloofness as in the schizoid but goes farther. It is qualitatively a more severe disorder than the eight basic disorders. In addition to many of the symptoms of the schizoid, it includes a mild lack of reality. This almost psychotic process is seen as magical thinking, such as the belief in ESP or bizarre fantasies. The behavior is often "odd" and may be viewed as simply eccentric in non-threatening patients. Many odd street people are probably schizotypal.

These patients resemble schizophrenics, and classically it is believed that schizotypals may decompensate into schizophrenics. They may also be misdiagnosed as having paranoia or a delusional disorder.

Borderline personality disorder is a severe personality disorder. Much has been written about the borderline, primarily in psychodynamic circles (Waldinger, 1986). The cardinal feature of those with borderline personality disorder is instability. Their emotions are unstable, with wildly labile moods from glee to depression. Their social situation is unstable, and they lack clear occupational goals or desires for interpersonal intimacy. Finally, their thought processes are unstable, with illogical and contradictory cognitions and attitudes.

Borderline is the most misdiagnosed of all the personality disorders, and this misdiagnosis is the most dangerous. They, like the blind man assessing the elephant, often present only one symptomatic theme such as depression. It is only after a number of severe symptoms appear that the very deep and characterologically disturbed behavior pattern becomes evident.

Paranoid personality disorder is primarily a severe disorder of trust. Individuals with paranoid personality disorder are generally mistrustful of all people they encounter. They expect people to exploit them and harm them. As well, they read the "hidden, secret" message contained in the simple everyday behaviors of others. As such they do not become close to others and have poor social attachments.

The paranoid is most likely to come to the attention of a therapist for secondary reasons. The paranoid individual may arrive for marital therapy when his or her suspiciousness extends to spouse's fidelity. Or the paranoid may be referred for forensic purposes following harassing, following, or spying on a casual dating acquaintance.

PSYCHOLOGICAL TESTING FOR PERSONALITY DISORDERS

Personality disorders are usually difficult to diagnose, especially early in the assessment and treatment of an individual These symptoms may be overlooked or simply viewed as falling within the limits of normal personality. The best method of assessing a personality disorder to treat it is through psychological testing.

If a patient is suspected of having a personality disorder, he or she should be referred for or given an objective test of personality disorders. It has been only in the last few years that tests have focused on personality disorders. The MMPI (Butcher, Dahlstrom, Graham, Tellegen, & Kaemmer, 1989) is widely used to assess psychopathology, but it is primarily focused toward identification of clinical syndromes such as anxiety, depression, and schizophrenia. The best test for personality disorders is the Millon Clinical Multiaxial Inventory (MCMI, Millon, 1987). The MCMI is only 175 items long, and most patients can complete it in less than a half hour. It includes scales not only for the 11 personality disorders described above, but also for sadistic and self-defeating personalities. It further includes scales for the major clinical syndromes, such as anxiety, somatization, depression, and psychosis. The test has been shown to reliably assess these disorders and to validly predict the personality and clinical disorders as they are diagnosed on interview using DSM-III-R criteria.

THE TREATMENT OF PERSONALITY DISORDERS

Clients with personality disorders are difficult to treat because they usually think that their problems are caused by others, not by themselves, and because their problematic behaviors are so habitual that even minimal changes are accomplished slowly. Since all personality-disordered individuals have flawed interpersonal relationships, the treatment relationship is usually fraught with problems. Not only do patient and therapist usually disagree about what is wrong, but the patient is also adept at frustrating the therapist by resisting treatment and finding therapist weaknesses. Getting angry, feeling helpless or defensive, wanting to control or reject are common therapist reactions when treating those with personality disorders. Supervision or consultation is extremely important when treating these clients.

Determining specific treatments for each personality disorder is problematic due to lack of definitive research on treatment effectiveness, overlapping of the personality disorder diagnoses, confusion with Axis I disorders, and high treatment dropout rates (Gorton & Akhtar, 1990). Proponents of various modalities, such as psychoanalytic, cognitive, behavioral, and family systems, have all reported some treatment effectiveness. However, most professionals suggest that a combination of individual psychotherapy and other interventions is likely to be more effective.

Treatment combinations depend on the treatment targets defined by the therapist and the client, as well as by the decision whether to attempt personality restructuring or to treat problematic symptoms. Therapeutic attempts at personality reconstruction are long-term and expensive. They should be reserved for only the most experienced therapists and most motivated patients. Generally, treatment should be focused on symptom relief or containment of dangerous behavior. Medication is generally not helpful, and personality-disordered individuals are those most likely to have either compliance problems or spectacular side effects from psychopharmocological treatment.

Perry and Vaillant (1989) provide some general guidelines about what to do and what not to do as a therapist. The therapist should establish a collaborative rather than directive stance, set reasonable limits and structure that can be enforced in a calm and caring manner, be natural rather than neutral (a "blank screen" approach frightens these clients), avoid use of a contract unless addressing dangerous behavior, and be very careful about consistency in verbal and nonverbal messages to the client. The focus of treatment should be on client's present feelings and behaviors rather than on explanations and insights. The therapist's efforts are best directed to supporting the client's attempts to change instead of making explicit demands or contracts for change. The use of a reflective or problem-solving model is more effective than clarification or interpretation in working with clients with personality disorders. Counselors are advised to be careful not to reinforce repetitive complaints, as attending to complaints tends to increase their occurrence. Therapists should also avoid the tendency to rescue or to create dependence although these clients may make strong attempts to have therapists take charge.

Schizoid personality disorder is best treated through an active and self-disclosing therapeutic style. These clients often seek treatment due to some major change in life circumstances that upsets their fragile support systems. Initially it is advantageous to help build a support structure and then help clients decide if they can learn to develop relationships. If clients cannot manage close relationships, treatment efforts should focus on helping clients find satisfactory solitary pursuits. If some motivation and talent for developing relationships is evident, these clients often do well with carefully planned and executed behavioral training in assertiveness and social skills. They may do well in group settings if the group can tolerate the client's being silent for a long time before participating. The successful therapist is supportive and consistent and allows for some acting out.

Avoidant personality disorder is marked by the client's low self-esteem and anxiety regarding interpersonal relationships. These clients are quite vulnerable and are slow to trust but may become the most rewarding and successful clients if treated gently and with respect. Behavioral techniques for anxiety reduction and social skills as well as supportive group "growth" treatment may prove helpful. Higher func-

tioning clients in this group might have some success in psychodynamically oriented insight therapy.

Dependent personality disorder may best be treated by allowing the
patient to develop dependence on the therapist in order to build the
treatment relationship. Directive or authoritarian approaches are contraindicated. Behavioral treatment, such as assertiveness training, may
provide the quickest way to enhance interpersonal effectiveness, but
these patients also respond well to insight-based psychotherapy. Female
clients may respond to feminist therapy and consciousness-raising
groups because their behaviors are shaped, in part, by gender role
stereotypes (Widiger & Frances, 1985). Termination should be discussed
jointly, and the patient might need to return occasionally to develop a
strong sense of individuation. Premature termination or confrontive
challenge of dependence could lead to self-destructive acting out.

Histrionic personality disorder treatment should be marked by availability, consistency, firmness, and calmness. These clients are dramatic and
prone to have pseudoinsights. They seek total satisfaction from therapists as they do from others. Therapeutic skill derives from knowing
when to give and when to carefully frustrate the client. These clients
respond to psychodynamic treatment, which should be focused on helping them to differentiate real from false emotions and to learn what
they can realistically expect from others. Anxiety and depression are
common reactions to treatment. Suicidal behavior should be taken seriously. Gender bias in diagnosis and treatment is an important factor.
Chodoff (1982) and Kernberg (1980) provide good guidelines for assessment and treatment.

Narcissistic personality disorder is identified by the client's consistent de-
valuing of others, including the therapist. It is important to avoid defensiveness and to instead empathize with the pain or disappointment that
is the source of the patient's grandiosity. Personality restructuring involves long-term treatment to build self-esteem, diminish the defense of
projection, and deal with loss issues. Short-term treatment should focus
on strengthening, not restructuring, coping styles. Kohut (1971, 1977)
and Kernberg (1975, 1980) offer differing viewpoints about treatment
of these individuals, which are summarized by Russell (1985).

Antisocial personality disorder is not treated successfully through individual treatment. Therapists encounter these individuals most often in
prisons or treatment settings for addictions. The few helpful treatments
have been those in highly structured, closed settings conducted by
highly skilled therapists. A positive sign for limited treatment success is
evidence of depression in the client. Family therapy might prove helpful
for enmeshed adolescents. Further reading sources include Freeman
and Gunderson (1989) and Perry and Vaillant (1989).

Obsessive-compulsive personality disorder is different because these clients are often aware of their part in their problems and seek treatment for their distress. Therapists are warned to avoid battles of will, and instead to help clients develop and get in touch with their real feelings. These clients are skillful at intellectual discussions and might dupe inexperienced therapists. Group and behavioral treatment may help clients change maladaptive interactions, and the more motivated will succeed in insight-oriented therapy.

Passive-aggressive personality disorder is best treated through techniques that rechannel the client's anger away from resistance into more productive behavior. Assertiveness training, behavioral contracting, and explicit limit setting in dynamic therapy are such techniques. In general, the more resentful and vindictive the client, the more difficult the treatment. Pointing out consequences of behavior is more effective than interpretation of behavior. Suicide should be treated as a covert expression of anger and not as a depression. There may be high failure and dropout rates in this population.

Schizotypal personality disorder is harder to treat than schizoid personality disorder, but similar techniques may be used. Use of halfway houses and day treatment may be necessary if these clients are deteriorating. Supportive, educationally oriented groups might be of practical help in assisting these clients to function. These clients will not usually seek treatment, but they might learn some social skills in structured settings where their eccentricities are accepted.

Borderline personality disorder has been the most discussed in the treatment literature. Diagnosis and treatment is difficult because clients with this disorder display all the symptoms of Axis I disorders. In addition, their emotional liability is marked by self-destructive acting out and extensive interpersonal manipulations that are extremely frustrating for the therapist. These clients can create havoc in inpatient settings. Initial treatment efforts need to be focused on stabilizing external supports and creating realistic limits that the therapist can enforce. Family therapy with enmeshed families can be helpful. Inpatient treatment can help with stabilization of acting out behaviors, but must be monitored carefully to prevent regression of behavior. Long-term treatment conducted by skilled therapists might lead to some success in which the clients begin to resemble those with narcissistic personality disorders. For further information the reader is referred to Waldinger (1986) for a literature review of intensive treatment.

Paranoid personality disorder treatment has been universally unsuccessful. Clients with this disorder do not seek treatment unless they develop an Axis I disorder or unless they are forced by others. Due to their marked suspiciousness and/or hypersensitivity to attachments, these clients are likely to mistrust and find fault with the therapist. A professional, distant, formal, honest, and consultative stance by the therapist may allow for a sufficient relationship so that the client might return when more serious problems occur. Treatment requiring intimacy, group therapy, and behavioral treatment are all contraindicated and may be harmful because they may challenge the client's fragile autonomy and increase his or her mistrust.

SUMMARY

In summary, the personality disorders are very common. They are often misdiagnosed as clinical syndromes, and when a clinical syndrome does exist, the personality disorders often complicate the treatment of that chief complaint. Accurate diagnosis of personality disorders should include psychological testing. Finally, there is no single treatment of choice for these personality disorders. Treatment must be tailored to the specific disorder.

FOR FURTHER READING

Chodoff, P. (1982). The therapy of hysterical personality disorders. In J. H. Masserman (Ed.), *Current psychiatric therapies* (Vol. 21, pp. 59–65). New York: Grune & Stratton.

Freeman, P. S., & Gunderson, J. G. (1989). Treatment of personality disorders. *Psychiatric Annals, 19,* 147–153.

Millon, T. (1969) *Modern psychopathology.* Philadelphia: Saunders.

Perry, J. C., & Vaillant, G. E. (1989). Personality disorders. In H. O. Kaplan & B. J. Sadock (Eds.), *Comprehensive textbook of psychiatry/V* (Vol. 2, pp. 1352–1387). Baltimore: Williamson & Wilkins.

Reid, W. H. (1989). *The treatment of psychiatric disorders.* New York: Brunner/Mazel.

Widiger, T. A., Frances, A., Spitzer, R. L., & Williams, J. B. W. (1988). The DSM-III-R personality disorders: An overview. *American Journal of Psychiatry, 145,* 786–795.

REFERENCES

American Psychiatric Association. (1987). *Diagnostic and statistical manual of mental disorders,* (3rd Ed., DSM-III-R). Washington, D.C.: Author.

Butcher, J. N., Dahlstrom, W. G., Graham, J. R., Tellegen, A., & Kaemmer, B. (1989). *Manual for the restandardized Minnesota Multiphasic Personality Inventory: MMPI-2.* Minneapolis: University of Minnesota Press.

Chodoff, P. (1982). The therapy of hysterical personality disorders. In J. H. Masserman (Ed.), *Current psychiatric therapies* (Vol. 21, pp. 59–65). New York: Grune & Stratton.

Freeman, P. S., & Gunderson, J. G. (1989). Treatment of personality disorders. *Psychiatric Annals, 19,* 147–153.

Gorton, G. & Ahktar, S. (1990). The literature on personality disorders, 1985–88: Trends, issues and controversies. *Hospital and Community Psychiatry, 41* 39–51.

Kernberg, O. (1975). *Borderline conditions and pathological narcissism.* New York: Aronson.

Kernberg, O. (1980). *Internal world and external reality*. New York: Aronson.
Kohut, H. (1971). *The analysis of the self*. New York: International Universities Press.
Kohut, H. (1977). *The restoration of the self*. New York: International Universities Press.
Millon, T. (1987). *Manual for the MCMI-II*. Minneapolis: National Computer Systems.
Perry, J. C. & Vaillant, G. E. (1989). Personality disorders. In H. O. Kaplan & B. J. Sadock. *Comprehensive textbook of psychiatry/V* (Vol. 2, pp. 1352–1387). Baltimore: Williams & Wilkins.
Russell, G. A. (1985). Narcissism and the narcissistic personality disorder: A comparison of the theories of Kernberg and Kohut. *British Journal of Medical Psychology, 58*, 137–148.
Waldinger, R. (1986). Intensive psychodynamic psychotherapy with borderline patients: an overview. *American Journal of Psychiatry, 144*, 267–274.
Widiger, T. A. & Frances, A. (1985). Axis II personality disorders: Diagnostic and treatment issues. *Hospital and Community Psychiatry, 36*, 619–627.

32

The Paraphilias

EUGENE E. LEVITT, Ph.D.

Variety in human sexual behavior abounds. Many variations, once called *perversions* or at best, abnormalities, are currently classified as *paraphilias,* a term that retains the implication of deviation from a norm but without pejoration.

Each person develops a personal sexuality schema, what Money (1986) calls a *lovemap* and Gagnon (1990) refers to as a *script.* These schema, emerging primarily from early life experiences, determine sexual objects and behavior in adult life. Money's lovemap is "a developmental representation or template in the mind and in the brain depicting the idealized lover and the idealized program of sexuoerotic activity projected in imagery or actually engaged in with that lover" (Money, 1986, p. 290). For Gagnon, "The sequence of what ought to be done in a sexual act depends on the preexistence of a script that defines what is to be done with this or that person, in this or that circumstance, at this or that time and what feelings and motives are appropriate to the event . . . At the same time the script provides guidance as to what is or is not a sexual situation and contains those elements that link erotic life to social life in general" (Gagnon, 1990, p. 6).

The definition of a paraphilia is based on the assumption that the normative script/lovemap evokes what Money calls *normophilia*: sexual behavior with one peer member of the opposite sex, in a private place, the behavior including penetration of a female by a male in some fashion followed by ejaculation. From this base, paraphilia might be identified along two dimensions: 1) socially unacceptable choice of a sexual object, as a same-sexed or underaged or unconsenting person, a close relative, or an animal; 2) deviation in preferred sexual behavior, such as watching others (*voyeurism*), or exhibiting the penis publicly (*exhibitionism*).

The diagnostic manual used by most American mental health workers adds another criterion for identifying a paraphilia.

> The Paraphilias are characterized by arousal in response to sexual objects or situations that are not part of normative arousal-activity patterns and that in varying degrees may interfere with the capacity for reciprocal, affectionate sexual activity. (DSM-III-R, 1987, p. 279)

Since homosexuality often if not usually, does not "interfere with reciprocal, affectionate sexual activity," it is removed from classification as a paraphilia, despite fitting other criteria.

DSM-III-R adds further considerations in diagnosis: the paraphilia is characterized by "recurrent intense sexual urges and sexually arousing fantasies" which are either acted upon or are distressing.

The number of possible paraphilias varies considerably among expert sources. If prevalence and incidence are not considered as factors in identification, there may be as many as 40 (Money, 1986). DSM-III-R identifies 8 paraphilias, presumably on the basis of incidence. In view of the consensual adoption of this list, it will form the framework of this entry. Some content will also follow pages 279–290 of DSM-III-R.

According to DSM-III-R, paraphilias are "practically never diagnosed in females" except for an occasional case of sexual masochism (p. 281). Money (1986) suggests that this "greater paraphilic vulnerability of the male" is "somehow based on his greater dependency on the visual image for the arousal of erotic initiative" (p. 29). Money hints that constitutional inter-sex brain differences may also be involved.

A substantial minority of all paraphiliacs who could be classified as law violators have performed under the influence of alcohol but involvement of other drugs is rare (Gebhard, Gagnon, Pomeroy & Christenson, 1965). Alcohol involvement is more likely to occur with younger paraphiliacs.

As might easily be inferred, most paraphiliacs tend to be unhappy with their sexuality. If they are partnered, sexual adjustment in the relationship is likely to be poor. By most standards, the paraphiliac is considered sexually inadequate and, not infrequently, emotionally disturbed as well. In some cases it is clear that the emotional disturbance either causes the paraphilia or is a consequence of it. In many cases the relationship is unclear.

EXHIBITIONISM

Exhibitionism is the deliberate exposure of the body, almost always the penis, to a usually unwitting and unknown female, equally divided among adolescents and adults. Exhibitionists, always male, constitute a plurality among apprehended sex criminals, a reflection of the fact that most exposures occur in broad daylight in a public place; though exhibiting in front of an uncurtained window in the exhibitionist's dwelling is not unknown.

Patterns of exhibitionism vary. In some cases it occurs aperiodically, often associated with a time of great stress. There are also cases in which exposures occurred with a frequency as high as a 100 times per week. The penis may be flaccid or erect; spontaneous ejaculation may take place at the moment of exposure or the exhibitionist may masturbate immediately afterward. In some cases, there may be no immediate direct sexual reaction.

The typical exhibitionist is likely to be an anxious, passive individual with marked feelings of sexual inadequacy. If married, he will usually have a poor sexual adjustment. He is often socially uncomfortable and has always had difficulty carrying out the socially prescribed role with respect to the opposite sex.

The direct motivation of the exhibitionist is unclear. A common belief among mental health professionals is that exhibition is a hostile act and that the exhibitionist wishes to shock his victim or frighten his victim. A clinical study by Bray & Gigeroff (1977) suggests that *any* manifest reaction by the victim may be satisfying to the exhibitionist. It is also possible that the exhibitionist does not clearly perceive or accurately assess the victim's reaction; fantasy may guide his reaction. Exhibitionists rarely approach their victims and/or threaten sexual assault.

PEDOPHILIA

Pedophilia is the employment of a minor person by an adult for some form of sexual gratification. Every state has a law against pedophilia and the definitions of the key terms in the previous sentence vary among states. DSM-III-R, as a national, non-legal source, has been forced to adopt arbitrary definitions: *minor* is a prepubescent child; *adult* is a person who is at least 16 years of age and is at least five years older than the victim. This definition reflects the fact that most of the victims are younger than 13 years of age. However, an individual over the age of 21 who knowingly had sexual contact with a pubescent 14- or 15-year old would clearly be considered to have engaged in pedophilic behavior.

A majority of pedophiles are heterosexually oriented but most victims are male. This is a consequence of the finding that apprehended offenders against males report having had contact with over two hundred victims on the average while the same statistic for offenders against females is only two dozen. The ability of the pedophile to escape apprehension is a function of several circumstances.

In most instances, sexual behavior is limited to fondling and the victim is a relative or child of a friend, someone who is acquainted with the pedophile and therefore is less likely to perceive his behavior as wrong. The victim may not realize that the behavior is socially unacceptable. In some cases, the victim may be a willing participant. Thus, a large majority of pedophilic contacts are unreported.

When the victim is a relative (again, variably defined among state laws) the offense is called *incest.* Incest offenders are more often married and differ from the extrafamilial pedophiles in some minor ways associated with martial status. Otherwise, it makes little difference which classification is used.

There is a prevalent current belief that a prime cause of pedophilia is sexual molestation in childhood, i.e., victims of pedophilia become pedophiles. Pedophiles as a group have more often been victims than have normal persons, but the difference (25% against 10%) is small (Freund, Watson & Dickey, 1990). Childhood molestation obviously cannot be a *major* cause of pedophilia.

Another widespread view is that victims of pedophilia are invariably harmed. Again, the available research indicates that this perception is exaggerated. A review of thirty investigations by Constantine (1981) leads to the conclusion that there is no inevitable outcome of pedophilia. Every investigation found at least some unharmed victims; indeed, in almost half of the investigations, over half of the victims were unharmed. Outcome is more likely to be malignant when the victim is a reluctant or unwilling participant, and when he or she is sexually naive but is aware that sexual behavior is immoral. The least harm occurs when the victim is a willing participant, especially if he or she is sexually knowledgeable but has not yet "absorbed conventional moral negatives."

VOYEURISM

Voyeurism or "peeping" is "the act of observing unsuspecting people, usually strangers, who are either naked, in the process of disrobing or engaging in sexual activity" (DSM-III-R, p. 289). There are several important considerations that distinguish the paraphiliac voyeur from normal sexual arousal in observing. The peeper is usually alone in a place where he has no right to be and he is likely to find the illegality and privacy sexually stimulating. Despite the risk, he prefers this activity to any other form of sexual behavior. He has no interest in pursuing his observations and will gratify himself with masturbation. The man who becomes aroused while watching his partner undress before coitus, or is excited by commercial erotica, is a voyeur in the broadest sense of the word but is not a paraphiliac.

FETISHISM

Fetishism is the use of inanimate objects as a preferred or necessary tactic for obtaining sexual arousal. Some common fetish objects are women's lingerie and footwear or garments made entirely of rubber, leather or fur. The fetishist is likely to masturbate while rubbing or smelling the fetish object or he may require that his sexual partner wear the object in order for him to attain arousal.

Some sex experts extend the term to include any unusual circumstance of sexual arousal, such as become sexually excited by watching a woman smoke or by looking at her feet. The preoccupation with a part of the female body is called a partialism. Feet and breasts are the most common objects of partialism.

The critical consideration in diagnosis is the degree to which the fetish is required for sexual stimulation. The unquestionable fetishist is a man who is impotent in the absence of a particular fetish.

TRANSVESTISM

Transvestism is a special form of fetishism, sometimes called *transvestitic or cross-gender fetishism*. It involves dressing in women's clothing (female transvestites are rare), donning either one or more garments that are worn under ordinary male clothes ranging up to complete female attire, sometimes including a wig and cosmetics. Most transvestites never appear in public dressed as women. The woman's garment favored by transvestites is a nightgown.

Unlike other fetishists, transvestites have been subjected to careful objective investigation. Three classical studies (Prince & Bentler, 1972; Buhrich & McConaghy, 1977; Freund, Steiner & Chan, 1982) have revealed a number of characteristics of true transvestites. The primary facts are that most are heterosexual and have been, or are, married, and over half claim that their wives do not react negatively. Cross-dressing is sexually arousing; during this arousal, the transvestite is likely to fantasize being a woman or being treated like a woman by men. However, the transvestite has no interest in gender reassignment surgery, i.e., in becoming an actual anatomical female.

These conditions distinguish the transvestite from the *transsexual*, a man who usually believes that he is truly a woman trapped in the wrong body, and who may apply for gender reassignment surgery. Transsexuality is officially classified as a *gender identity disorder*, not a paraphilia. Transsexuals are more often single and homosexual. Cross-dressing is seldom reported as sexually arousing. The primary motivation for gender reassignment surgery in men is not sexual. The transsexual wishes to assume the conventional female social role, by contrast with the transvestite, whose interest is likely to be in playing the female role in sexual encounters.

The rarity of female transvestites is doubtlessly a function of women's greater latitude in socially accepted clothing. Certainly in recent decades, women have adopted almost all traditional male clothing including shirts, slacks and tailored suits. The prevalence of female-to-male transsexuals is somewhat higher, though far lower than male-to-female.

SEXUAL SADISM AND SEXUAL MASOCHISM

The essential characteristic of sexual sadism is sexual arousal evoked by causing suffering to another person. Sexual masochism is sexual arousal brought about by being the victim of sadistic behavior. These paraphilias are considered together because of this conjunction, plus the fact that both sadists and masochists tend to be "switchable," i.e., to enjoy the opposite role occasionally. The term *sadomasochism* (S/M) is a generic term for behaviors that stimulate sadists and masochists.

S/M behaviors cover a wide range. A classic report lists more than thirty (Moser & Levitt, 1987; see also Spengler, 1977; Breslow, Evans & Langley, 1986). Many are relatively benign such as bondage, spanking and humiliation. Ones that involving breaking the skin such as piercing with pins, burning, or severe whipping, approach the psychopathological.

An unusually deviant form of masochism is called *hypoxyphilia,* sexual arousal through oxygen deprivation, which is achieved by means of a ligature, head covering or a chemical. The unattended practice of hypoxyphilia is obviously dangerous. It has produced one or two reported deaths per million people in each recent year in the English-speaking countries.

Rape or sexual assault may be committed by the sadist. The identifying feature of *sadistic rape* is that the victim is damaged far more than is necessary to secure compliance. Extreme sadomasochistic behaviors are likely to be employed. This form of rape is distinguished from other rape motivations, especially *anger rape* in which the victim is also severely battered but the rapist is likely to be impotent or to neglect genital sexual behavior (see Crooks & Baur, 1987 for a sophisticated discussion of the various types of rape).

The continuum of dominance and submission plays an important part in sadomasochism. Degradation, whether physical or psychological is achieved through ultimate power or complete submission and helplessness. S/M "games" are usually scripted to bring about these extremes. The social roles acted out in the games are selected in an attempt to add a kernel of reality to the script: master-slave, teacher-pupil, guardian-child, etc.

Most sadists and masochists are male. True female sadists are rare. Those who do perform sadistic acts usually are servicing a masochistic male partner. There are true female masochists but still far fewer than among males.

OTHER PARAPHILIAS

DSM-III-R treats *frotteurism* or *toucherism* as a major paraphilia. Frotteurism is sexual arousal evoked by casual physical contact with a female stranger in a public place. The behavior rarely occurs in men past adolescence except in some Mediterranean countries of Europe where it is accepted behavior.

Some of the paraphilias listed by DSM-III-R under the "not otherwise specified" category and not discussed in detail actually belong in other paraphilias. *Coprophilia* (involvement of feces in sex), *urophilia* (or urolagnia-involvement of urine in sex), and *klismaphilia* (sexual arousal in response to an enema) are well-known aspects of the S/M scene. *Partialism* has already been noted as a fetish.

Zoophilia or *animal contact* (the preferred term) is largely restricted to young males living on farms but is not a major source of sexual arousal at any age. *Telephone scatophilia* is the attainment of sexual arousal by means of a telephone monologue with an unwitting respondent, using explicit vernacular sexual expressions. The behavior is not only rare but is seldom a preferred method of arousal.

Necrophilia is the desire to copulate with a corpse, probably the rarest of the identifiable paraphilias. Its significance lies in the fact that the necrophiliac must commit murder in order to gratify his sexual needs.

REFERRAL ISSUES

Paraphiliacs rarely seek professional remediation. Those few that are encountered by the mental health professional have fallen afoul of the law and therapy is an adjudicated alternative to imprisonment.

Consequently, few counselors or therapists have had experience in dealing with paraphiliacs. No proven treatment methods are available and formal investigation of remediation procedures is extremely difficult to implement. With or without endogenous motivation for change, clinical experience demonstrates that the paraphilias are treatment resistant.

Specific education and training in dealing with paraphiliacs is practically nonexistent, probably because of the shortage of available applicants for treatment and the absence of sound therapy procedures. There are several national organizations that certify professional practitioners as sex therapists or educators: the Society for Sex Therapy and Research, the American Board of Sexology and the American Association of Sex Educators, Counselors and Therapists. Such certification verifies substantial interest in sexual phenomena. It does not attest to either experience or competence in treating the paraphilias.

If a client referral is necessary, it must be on a personalized basis. The sophistication and practice of the therapist to whom one refers should be personally known to the referral source, insofar as it is possible to obtain such information. This admonition is admittedly somewhat dubious but there is no effective alternative recourse.

REFERENCES

Bray, R. M., & Gigeroff, A. (1977). *Exhibitionism: Facts, fictions, and solutions*. Toronto, Canada: Privately printed.

Breslow, N., Evans, L., & Langley, J. (1986). Comparisons among heterosexual, bisexual,and homosexual male sado-masochists. *Journal of Homosexuality, 13*, 83–107.

Buhrich, N., & McConaghy, N. (1977). The discrete syndromes of transvestism and transsexualism. *Archives of Sexual Behavior, 6*, 483–495.

Constantine, L. L. (1981). The effects of early sexual experience: A review and synthesis of research. In L. L. Constantine, & F. M. Martinson (Eds.), *Children and sex; New findings and new perspectives* (pp. 217–244). Boston: Little, Brown.

Crooks, R., & Baur, K. (1987), *Our sexuality (3rd ed.)*. Redwood City, CA: Benjamin-Cummings.

Diagnostic and statistical manual of mental disorders (3rd ed., revised). (1987). Washington, DC: American Psychiatric Association.

Freund, K., Steiner, B. W., & Chan, S. (1982). Two types of cross-gender identity. *Archives of Sexual Behavior, 11*, 49–63.

Freund, K., Watson, R., & Dickey, R. (1990). Does sexual abuse in childhood cause pedophilia: An exploratory study. *Archives of sexual behavior, 19*, 557–568.

Gagnon, J. H. (1990). The explicit and implicit use of the scripting perspective in sex research. In J. Bancroft (Ed.), *Annual review of sex research, Vol. 1* (pp. 1–43). Lake Mills, IA: Society for the Scientific Study of Sex.

Gebhard, P. H., Gagnon, J. H. Pomeroy, W. B., & Christenson, C. V. (1965) *Sex offenders*. New York: Harper & Row.

Money, J. (1986). *Lovemaps: Clinical concepts of sexual/erotic health and pathology, paraphilia, and gender transposition in childhood, adolescence, and maturity*. New York: Irvington Publishers.

Moser, C., & Levitt, E. E. (1987). An exploratory-descriptive study of a sadomasochistically oriented sample. *Journal of Sex Research, 23*, 322–337.

Prince, V. & Bentler, P. M. (1972). Survey of 504 cases of transvestism. *Psychological Reports, 31*, 903–917.

Spengler, A. (1977). Manifest sadomasochism of males: Results of an empirical study. *Archives of Sexual Behavior, 6*, 441–456.

33

Aging and Later Life

JANET K. BELSKY, Ph.D.

Nowhere are stereotypes more widespread, entrenched, and ruinous than in the area of older adults. The negative ideas linked to later life cut a wide swath, minimizing every aspect of humanity: in health ("Older people are disabled" or "Typically, they are in nursing homes"); in thinking ("Their mind goes"); and in personality ("Older people are depressed, childish, set in their ways"). These stereotypes apply to the main transitions of later life, too—retirement and widowhood. Each event oozes with connotations of unmitigated loss. As we will see in this chapter, this prism for viewing a whole phase of life is not only usually inaccurate, but poisonous, limiting human potential and fostering the very problems we expect.

Apart from theoretical perspective, counselors working with the elderly have a crucial role as purveyors of the truth. In approaching elderly clients it is important to understand the norm: what the research reveals about the life transitions and changes that occur in the later years. The counselor's job is to open up the possibilities for full and free living, armed with the studies demonstrating that optimal living is not an anomaly in later life. It is also crucial to know the facts about the losses that do occur so elderly clients can be taught to compensate and continue living as fully and freely as possible.

But first a comment about the value of working with this age group. The idea that counseling older people is boring, or useless, or depressing is just as much a myth as any other stereotype about old age. In fact, because the stereotypes older people themselves bring to therapy tend to be so erroneous, simple educational interventions can have a dramatic impact on an older client's life. This is not to say that counseling the elderly is simple and unexciting nor that it need be confined to educating clients and their families about the facts. From behavior therapy to psychodynamic interventions, the psychotherapy outcome evidence is clear. Older people do profit from every treatment. The diversity of strategies that have effectively been used with the elderly matches the diversity of this population in itself. (For an overview of this research evidence, see Smyer, Zarit, & Qualls, 1990.)

DIVERSITY AS THE HALLMARK OF AGING

The most basic fact about later life is the diversity that is its hallmark. Older people defy categorization. They may be beginning families or living in nursing homes. They may be at the brink of a new career or fit every preconceived notion of physical and mental frailty. In fact, the variety in life situation, in health, and in income among people lumped into the category of senior citizen is so great that many gerontologists feel that the elderly are the most diverse of *any* age group.

Furthermore, the vast majority of these people do not even fit our basic criteria for old: having physical or mental limitations and/or being close to death. The irony is that we have lowered the chronological marker for senior citizenhood (it is now age 60). At the same time we have pushed up the genuine entry point of old age.

A few generations ago, at 65 or 60 a person often did fit the stereotype of old. That person also had on average a mere handful of years left to live. Today the single digits have become decades. Women reaching age 65 can "on the average" expect to have close to 20 years more of life (U.S. Senate Special Committee on Aging, 1987–1988).

These are far from years spent in a nursing home. Contrary to common opinion, along with increasing longevity we have done just as good a job of pushing up the years of healthy life. We are arriving at age 65 physiologically resembling age 50. Physical frailty tends to strike in the 80s, not at 65.

The consequence is that people in their 60s and 70s live in a kind of limbo with regard to the concept of old. They say they feel middle-aged. Physiologically, socially, and psychologically they are middle-aged, too. Because of this gerontologists use a variety of terms for this vigorous, vital group: "third agers" or "the young-old." Even 80 is losing its once sure standing as an old age entry point. In one survey (Shanas, 1984) one-fourth of the men and one-fifth of the women over 80 said they did not feel old. They were not assaulted by serious health problems or doubled over by aches and pains. As one respondent in this large national survey mused: "The calendar tells me I'm old, but I still feel middle-aged."

This is not to deny the fact that some older people do have serious mental and physical impairments or that the incidence of illness and disability increases with age. But it is to underline a fundamental principle in approaching older clients. There is *no* age at which a person should be categorized on the basis of chronology. The key is how that person feels and most important how he or she acts.

The following focuses mainly on the minority of people who do need more unusual interventions—the frail elderly—and offers a brief overview of the surprising upbeat research to illustrate that full and free living should be an *expected* goal of therapy in later life.

WORKING WITH THE FRAIL ELDERLY; WHEN SPECIAL KNOWLEDGE IS NEEDED

"If you don't have your health, you don't have anything." It is a statement we have heard again and again. But the important thing to know about age-related physical conditions is that illness in itself is not what robs us of a satisfying life. That thief is disability: not being able to freely negotiate the world. The gerontological terms for disability is *functional impairment*: how able the person is to function in daily life.

A study in which researchers looked at predictors of morale among a group of frail older adults underlines just how crucial functional impairment is in determining the quality of life in old age (Osberg, McGinnis, DeJong, & Seward, 1987). Compared to other influences they examined, such as finances, social relations, and marital status, the extent of functional impairment was the factor most closely correlated with morale. In other words, the old saying should read: "We don't have anything if we don't have the ability to take care of ourselves."

Functional impairments are closely tied to illness, but the two are far from the same. For one thing, the incidence of these limitations in living is much lower than the incidence of disease. While one in two people over 65 suffers from some chronic illness, only one in four older people reports any problems negotiating life. Severe functional impairments, such as being bedridden by illness, are even more rare, affecting a mere 3% of men and 4% of women over 65 (U.S. Senate Special Committee on Aging, 1987). The incidence of functional impairments does rise with age, becoming more prevalent at 80 than at 65. But the important point is that the counselor must be very careful not to equate a chronic condition with a disability. Some people with heart conditions, arthritis, or diabetes are fully vital and active; some are genuinely limited by their disease.

The extent to which heart disease (or any other chronic problem) does limit life depends on the severity of the illness. But just as important it depends heavily on nonmedical factors, too, such as the person's own reaction to his problem (whether he responds by giving up and taking to his bed or going on) and the person's environment (whether it fosters dependence or promotes an independent life). In fact, the irony is that because functional impairments are *behavioral*, behavioral interventions made by nonphysicians (i.e., counselors) may have the most central role in treating the chronic ailments of aging.

TREATING EXCESS DISABILITIES

Many older people develop a condition psychologists label *excess disabilities*. Excess disabilities simply means the person is "excessively impaired," functioning more poorly in daily life than is warranted by his actual physical state. While most counselors probably are cognizant of the variety of intrapsychic reasons people might develop excess disabilities, it is important to understand that the outer context of life can foster this waste of human potential, too.

Excess disabilities tend to occur *any time* there is a mismatch between a person's life situation and his or her actual capacities. The environment is either overly supportive or not supportive enough. In working clinically with older people with chronic conditions, the key is to fit the environment to what the person can do.

Interpersonal causes. The main reason for an overly supportive environment is interpersonal relationships. Well-meaning relatives take over jobs the older person really could do on his or her own. In the typical scenario, Mrs. Smith's daughter is worried about her mother living alone so she asks her to move in with her. Within a few months the 80-year old woman can no longer cook or shop. While it seems her health has gone into a tailspin, her physical deterioration is artificial, not real. Her loving daughter has taken over the jobs that would strain Mother, and so has eased her entry into old age.

Taking over excessively is a predictible trap that well-meaning loved ones tend to fall into with elderly relatives who are beginning to show the frailties of age. Counselors working with this group and their caregivers need to be alert to this trap and educate families that the best intervention is one that preserves independence as long as possible. Taking over too much not only erodes self-esteem but exacerbates physical decline.

On a more concrete level, try to realistically assess what the person can do. Can he or she cook, dress, and so on. The validity of the assessment can be increased by collecting and correlating evaluations of several professional disciplines. For example, this assessment of the person's potential might be made by consulting with the older person's physician. Someone who genuinely knows the person's medical condition is in a fairly good position to give an opinion about the level of functioning that might be expected given chronic illness with severity X, Y, or Z. A geriatric nurse from a local long-term care facility can also evaluate the person's capacities using one of the standardized assessment scales developed to assess functional impairments.

Functional assessment scales can focus on activities of daily living (ADL) such as toileting, and bathing, or focus on instrumental activities of daily living (IADL) such as shopping and money management. Examples of such scales include the Katz ADL scale (Katz, Ford, Moskowitz, Jackson & Jaffe, 1963), the Instrumental Activities of Daily Living scale (Lawton & Brody, 1969), and the Older Americans Resources and Services (OARS) methodology (Pfeiffer, 1975). Other assessments can be included from psychologists, physical therapists, speech therapists, and so on. The more information that can be correlated regarding functional capacity, the better will be the judgment of what is excess disability for a specific older individual.

Another strategy might simply be to instruct families to reduce their level of caregiving for a few days. If a daughter is not there to prepare meals, will Mom actually do the cooking herself? If a child is not there to help, can Dad dress himself on his own? This strategy may have an important side benefit. It may directly demonstrate to loved ones that their parent may be more capable than they ever thought.

Work with families not to foster excess disabilities. Train them to be supportive without taking over everything. Educate the older person that "doing for myself" is essential, too. A host of studies show being as independent as possible for as long as possible promotes not only morale but also longevity (see Rodin, 1986a, 1986b, for reviews).

Environmental causes. One solution may lie in changing the actual physical environment. By modifying where the person lives, excessive interventions such as leaving home and moving in with children or to a nursing home may become unnecessary. This brings us to the second major cause for excess disabilities: too little, not too much, support. Typically, here the actual setting in which the person lives is fostering incapacity.

For instance, because climbing the hill to his apartment is too difficult, Mr. Jones does not go out as much. Yesterday, when he did leave the house, it was much harder to walk around the block. If he lived at the building at the bottom of the hill, he would be walking to the store every day. Similarly, because reaching the shelf for her pots is a strain, Mrs. Walker lets her husband take over the cooking. Soon she is even physically more depleted and unable to stand at all. In both cases minor disabilities are being transformed into life-threatening problems because the environment is too difficult and so works against an independent life.

Going into a person's home to make environmental suggestions is theoretically more alien to the role of the counselor, but this intervention can be surprisingly easy and effective. Common sense dictates that a home with poor lighting, high-pile rugs, or bare waxed floors may not be the right setting for a person who is having problems seeing or walking. Putting needed objects in easily reachable places or a low-pile carpet on a slippery bathroom floor may be all that is needed to make the difference between days fraught with peril and a comfortable life.

The counselor might do this home assessment or have the elderly client or family perform their own analysis with an eye to "what makes life easier." Counselors might also consult the physical or occupational therapy department of the local hospital or visit a medical supply store for information about the specific devices that exist to make homes more user friendly for people with problems reaching, walking, or getting around.

In dealing with elderly clients it also may be necessary to check into alternative living arrangements, which include a variety of residential options that exist for getting some care short of a nursing home. It is also important to explore the services that exist for keeping the person at home. Some of these different options are listed at the end of this chapter. Contact your local Office for the Aging to get information about the alternatives that exist. The object of all these services is to prevent that worst-case scenario, prematurely entering a nursing home.

Other causes. Be especially alert to excess disabilities after an acute illness. In this situation, the tendency is to assume that because someone is 70 or 90, improvement is impossible and the person should take to bed. Another frequent culprit is medications. The side effects of many drugs mimic the symptoms of old age. It is sometimes very tempting to attribute medication-induced drowsiness, or mental cloudiness, or unsteadiness to age. What compounds the problem is that drugs are metabolized more slowly by older people and the elderly are often taking several medications at a time. In fact, it has been estimated that 12–17% of all hospital admissions for the elderly are caused by adverse drug effects (Belsky 1985).

In summary, the basic principle in working with frail older people is to avoid what in cognitive behavioral terms might be labeled a depression engendering attributional style. Assume impairments are reversible and situational. Don't leap to the nihilistic assumption that they are fixed internal signs of old age.

SENSORY CHANGE

The need to rearrange the environment to enhance functioning is especially important in dealing with age-related sensory change. Vision and hearing changes that occur with age are far from intuitively obvious and have the potential to dramatically affect the quality of life. Furthermore, in this case, the counselor will not just be dealing with people with defined impairments. The principle of preventing excess disabilities also applies to the very minor changes in hearing and vision people normally experience by their 70s and beyond. (For a genuinely in-depth scholarly review of vision and hearing changes and their impact see Fozard, 1990.)

Hearing. Because conversation is the bridge that connects us as human beings, not being able to hear well has a potentially devastating impact in the interpersonal realm. Older people with hearing deficits may withdraw from relationships rather than risk always asking, "What did you say?" Another reaction is to turn suspicious, reading plots into whispers that are only half heard; or to feel rejected and convinced one is being shunned and avoided by loved ones. These impressions have more than a grain of truth. Friends and family members do begin to withdraw from people who are hearing impaired, simply because it is so exhausting to have to struggle to make themselves understood.

Older people often tend to put off acknowledging that they have hearing problems. Because the losses occur gradually over years, it is hard to define when a problem exists. Hearing troubles are easy to attribute to the environment: "People are speaking too softly. There is too much background noise." Poor hearing, emblematically a sign of old age, strikes at vanity. What compounds the problem is that the quality of the typical older person's hearing does tend to differ radically in different situations. Sometimes hearing is not a problem; sometimes it is practically impossible to hear.

The reason for this puzzling variability is that age-related hearing deficits do not involve a uniform loss for all sounds. People typically have a special problem hearing high-pitched tones. So if a tuba and piccolo are played with equal volume, the tuba will sound louder. It is the highness or lowness in pitch that is important, not loudness in itself.

Unfortunately, speech sounds tend to be in the higher pitched range. Background noise is lower pitched and so tends to differentially drown out the conversation that needs to be heard. This means noisy settings of any kind are anathema to people with hearing deficits. The drone of a car will make hearing very difficult; so will a noisy restaurant, a rattling air conditioner, or a fan. This selective loss also explains why hearing aids are often not all that effective in helping the millions of people who suffer from this third most common impairment of later life (see U.S. Senate Special Committee on Aging, 1987–1988). While technology is improving, it is hard to get a device that differentially dampens down the lower pitched frequencies and magnifies high-pitched tones. The classic hearing aids also were both a blessing and a bane because they magnified all sounds equally. Many people simply turned them off, to the consternation of family and friends.

This brings up the point that hearing deficits are especially prone to evoke a host of negative responses—not just withdrawal but irritation, too. Because their hearing does vary so much, older people may be accused of "faking," of deliberately turning hearing off. Another condition called *recruitment* reinforces this impression. A person suffering from recruitment first cannot hear and then hears perfectly after a sound reaches a certain level of loudness. While, mercifully, a minority of older people suffer from this age-related condition, it can exasperate friends and relatives who are told to "stop shouting" just after being instructed, "I can't hear that. Repeat what you said."

Once again, the key is using this knowledge constructively. The counselor needs to train a hearing-impaired client to actively select his environment. Avoid situations of high background noise—noisy restaurant, noisy air conditioner, or window fronting on a noisy street. Another strategy is to train the person to look at people when speaking in order to have the advantage of both visual and auditory cues. Installing carpeting or using double-paned windows can also cut down unwanted background noises in the person's home. Finally, the counselor might want to educate relatives that the person is not being malevolent when he or she cannot hear: "Selectivity is the nature of the problem itself."

Vision. The strategy is similar with vision problems. Know the nature of the deficit, then use this knowledge to help the client compensate. As with hearing, old-age vision impairments involve more than just the inability to see well. Environmental conditions affect vision greatly because the loss itself has a not-so-obvious form.

As people get older, a normally clear structure called the *lens* gets cloudy. (At its extreme this lens clouding results in the familiar condition called a *cataract*.) This loss of lens transparency plus other age-related changes means less light gets to the retina—the eye's back rim where the visual receptors are. The effect is to produce special trouble seeing in dim light. Twilight is gloomier and a dark night may be pitch black. The clouding also causes problems with glare. Older people are more prone to being blinded by a beam of light shining directly in their eyes.

Because brighter light is needed to see as well at 70 as at 20, increasing the wattage of light bulbs may aid vision. But incandescent lighting (regular household bulbs) should be used. Fluorescent lights (overhead tubular fixtures) may heighten seeing problems because they cause glare. (Unfortunately, the typical lighting in nursing homes, fluorescent lights shining on a bare floor, exacerbates age-related vision deficits.)

The older person should also be trained to take unusual care in glare-filled or dimly lit places. The client might be taught to get to the movies early or to go slower traversing fluorescent-lit passageways. He or she might be warned to take special care driving at night. Because other age-related problems are trouble shifting gaze and decreased peripheral vision, older people should be especially careful in situations when scanning a visual field is important, such as going down steps.

Impact on the Counseling Process
In addition to teaching the older person and families to understand and adapt to sensory loss, the counselor should be aware that these same age-related changes affect therapy, too. A dimly lit office so soothing to a younger person may have the opposite effect on an elderly client, evoking anxiety and discomfort, even the urge to flee. For an older person with hearing deficits, counseling in an office with background noise may become an exercise in communicating, an arduous trial for client and counselor alike.

Before seeing *any* older client, look carefully at the externals of the counseling milieu. Make it a policy to turn up office lighting, to turn down a noisy air conditioner, or to shut a window fronting on a street. Speak clearly; face the client; perhaps sit nearer to one another than customary. Understand the difficulties sensory loss can pose in simply getting to sessions, too. For instance, respect as reasonable, not irrational, a client's preference to come during daylight hours than to hazard evening appointments.

Unfortunately, as the above example implies, counselors are not immune from the same misinterpretations others make. In counseling an older person it may be easy to impute dynamic meaning to behavior that is just a consequence of sensory change. A client who refuses an evening session, or mishears a communication, may be judged "resistant." Worse, especially if the problem is a hearing deficit, the counselor may be tempted to falsely label, and then treat, the person as cognitively impaired.

In summary, in interpreting behavior of a client of 70 or 80, first consider the possibility of hearing and vision problems, not a deeper "cause." Also, keep firmly in mind that the same principles, pitfalls, considerations, and emotions that apply to the person's deficit outside the session apply within the session, too.

CAREGIVING

Up to this point, this chapter has focused on the disabled person. The discussion of caregivers has been limited to training them to make interventions that reduce excess disabilities. Yet clearly these other members of the dyad are important to involve in their own right. In fact, much counseling involving the frail elderly involves counseling caregivers and/

or reducing the stress of family members who struggle to cope with a functionally impaired loved one.

Luckily, over the past decade gerontologists have amassed a good deal of information on what makes a caregiver's job easy or difficult. They also know that caring for an impaired older relative, while not as normative as the media might have us believe, is indeed an occupational hazard of middle and later life. Finally, they know that families are emphatically not dumping their relatives in nursing homes. Study after study has documented that when a person has a living spouse or children, nursing home placement often occurs as a hated last resort when the older person's primary caregiver has gotten ill or simply been unable to manage caregiving (Brody, 1977). In fact, for every disabled person in a nursing home two equally impaired people are being cared for at home (U.S. Senate Special Committee on Aging, 1987–1988).

There is an unspoken line of command that governs family care. If a spouse is living, that person takes over the caregiving even if male and in frail health. If the person is widowed, the responsibility falls on the second line of defense against nursing home placement: children. It should come as no surprise that in this situation caregiving is gender linked. While sons may provide a bit of help, the responsibility for caring for an elderly parent falls almost exclusively on daughters or daughters-in-law (Brody, 1985; Gatz, Bengstson & Blum, 1990, Lang & Brody, 1983).

A host of studies have documented the emotional toll caregiving takes. Caregivers are more prone to physical and mental problems and low levels of morale (George & Gwyther, 1986). However, the interesting fact is that children, particularly daughters, as a group are especially at risk. Perhaps this is because the expectation in marriage is to take care of one another "in sickness and in health" while parent care seems to violate the natural order: "A mother cares for a child, not the reverse" (see Kuypers & Bengston, 1984). Perhaps because there are no competing responsibilities to one's own husband and children in spousal care, husbands and wives take on the burden with a freer heart, reporting less ambivalence, conflict, and stress than caregiving daughters and sons.

The importance of making distinctions between spouse and child caregivers is highlighted by a study in which researchers (Johnson & Catalano, 1983) compared the two types of relationships over time. When the caregiver was a spouse, the most common trajectory was one the researchers labeled *enmeshing*. As the husband or wife needed more care, the couple reduced outside involvements, withdrew from friends and relatives, and turned inward to the marriage to satisfy all of their needs. In contrast, when the caregiver was a child, *distancing* was the predominant pattern. The older person's needs and demands caused conflict. The relationship deteriorated as competing demands added to the friction and the child disengaged by either separating from the parents and going into therapy or deciding "I can't do anything" and turning exclusively to formal sources of help.

This is not to say that all children (or spouses) are equally stressed. Some are extremely unhappy and resentful; others find caregiving is on balance an enriching experience—one that actually enhances feelings of closeness and love (Fitting, Rabins, Lucas, & Eastham, 1986). Interestingly, rather than the severity of the person's objective problems, interpersonal aspects of the caregiving situation make the burden feel especially onerous. People who feel unsupported by family and friends, or who report having ambivalent or poor relationships with the person before the illness struck, tend to report being especially frustrated and unhappy in their role (Gatz, Bengston & Blum, 1990; George & Gwyther, 1986; Zarit, Orr & Zarit, 1985; Zarit, Todd, & Zarit, 1986).

There also are tantalizing gender differences in the amount of reported stress. A fairly consistent finding is that caregiving sons and husbands report less strain than caregiving daughters and wives (Fitting, Rabins, Lucas, & Eastham, 1986; Gatz, Bengston, & Blum, 1990). Perhaps this is because men are more likely than women to use formal sources of help rather than to feel compelled to do everything. Perhaps men get more accolades from others for undertaking an unaccustomed role. Or perhaps caregiving offers men a rare opportunity to be nurturant.

These findings have implications for counseling. The counselor should be aware that daughters, especially those with less supportive family and friends, are a group at special risk. In working with this group it seems especially important to intervene early to prevent the downward spiral described earlier. Attempt to encourage other family members to be more supportive, empathic, and appreciative of what is being done. Counselors who are working with the family as a whole might actively encourage them to take more of a role in care. Finally, counselors might encourage the primary caregiver to consider using the formal sources of help listed at the end of this chapter.

Interestingly, studies agree that help such as home care or day care or respite care tends to be underutilized, not just by daughters but by spouse caregivers, too (Arling & McAuley, 1984). One reason is the expense: If care is defined as chronic, Medicare will not pay the bill. Another is simple lack of knowledge about the options that actually exist. Finally, however, there is the misguided sense, particularly among women, that it is a badge of honor to do everything on one's own (see Brody, 1985).

Brody (1977, 1985), who has done considerable research on women in the middle, emphasizes that this emotion is endemic among caregiving daughters. No matter how much a woman feels she is doing for her mother or father, she feels she should be doing more. This guilt may partially arise from gender-linked injunctions such as that woman's job is to nurture at all costs. But partly it is due simply to mistakenly equating the past to now. A daughter remembers that her parents took Grandma in and berates herself for not insisting that her own mother move into her home. What she ignores is the reality that in the past people had to move in with children for economic reasons and that it was rare to live on requiring the kind of care many people do today.

The counselor might therefore need to be alert to attributions that may interfere with the tendency to get help: "I am not a good person if I don't do everything," "My parents would have behaved differently," or "Family care is always better than the care a stranger might give." Another guilt-inducing misperception is the idea that caregiving should be a pure labor of love. Parent care is tailormade to produce resentful feelings because it is inherently different from child care. We are indeed programmed to feel ambivalent and not quite comfortable about this reversal in roles (see Jarrett, 1985).

In conclusion, however, this does not imply that the job of the counselor is to convince people that seeking outside help is always the best course. As stated above, caregiving has multiple meanings. It is important to appreciate and respect the fact that the best choice for some people will be to do everything (or almost everything) for a loved one.

WORKING WITH THE NONFRAIL OLDER ADULT: THE CONTEXT FOR USING ANY INTERVENTION

Because the vast majority of older people do not fall into the category of disabled, any technique used with a 20- or 40-year-old is equally applicable to the problems in living that people in later life bring to counselors. Yet even when this is firmly grasped, stereotypes can still influence the expectations the counselor brings to the expectation of change. Here are some research findings to keep in mind in treating older adults:

Personality
There is a widespread assumption that as people age they become more rigid or set in their ways. Another common belief is that age equals emotional fragility and that depression is endemic in later life. These ideas, shared not only by older people but by many mental health workers, are false. The most methodologically sophisticated research on personality shows little evidence that people grow more childish or inflexible as they age. In fact, the dominant theme is consistency. If anything, people tend to stay the same as the years pass (see Costa & McCrae, 1980; Costa, McCrae, & Arenberg, 1983; McCrae & Costa, 1984). Furthermore, older people as a group are emphatically not more emotionally fragile.

While our strategies for coping with problems may change as we age, there is no evidence that they become any less mature. Several studies probing coping styles even suggest that people over age 40 tend to handle life's upsets in a more mature way (Irion and Blanchard-Fields, 1987). Finally, depression is far from endemic past age 65. In fact, contrary to common wisdom, some comprehensive epidemiological studies suggest this emotion problem is *no more prevalent* in later life than at any other life stage (see U.S. Senate Special Committee on Aging, 1984–1985.)

INTELLIGENCE AND MEMORY

The earliest studies using the Wechsler Adult Intelligence scale (WAIS) showed intelligence dramatically declined with age. But much of this loss turned out to be due to cohort factors: less well educated, less test-wise older people were being compared with young adults. The latest findings exploring age-IQ relationships suggest that IQ may increase through the middle years; after age 60 *on the average* there are indeed declines but much more modest ones than was thought (Hertzog & Schaie, 1988).

In truth, the relationship of intelligence and age has several trajectories. Any facet of thinking that involves speed does decline. Yet provided the older person remains intellectually interested, crystallized abilities (well-practiced skills and the fund of knowledge) can increase almost till the end of life. Currently psychologists are attempting to go beyond traditional IQ tests, which measure abstract school-oriented skills, to look at the aspects of intelligence likely to have an upward trajectory with age-wisdom, good sense, and knowledge of relationships. When we have good measures of these important facets of "life intelligence," we are likely to find that—as hoped—people do get more intelligent as they advance in years (Labouvie-Vief, 1985).

The findings are slightly less upbeat with regard to memory, yet here too we are revising our initially gloomy assessments of how performance shifts. The earliest laboratory research on memory abundantly confirmed the stereotype: older people were seriously deficient on any measure of memory compared to young or middle-aged adults. Yet more recent attempts to measure memory outside the laboratory in real-life contexts suggest that the traditional findings may in themselves have been off base. Older people in memory experiments are performing at their worst because they are likely to be excessively anxious. When the same people are observed in "real-life" situations, they show much less impairment than would have been predicted by their performance on traditional tests.

As we get older we seem to compensate naturally for the modest declines in memory that may occur. At 50 or 75 people take more time to memorize needed information, they tend to rely more on notes. So the *impact* of age-related changes in daily life need be really quite minimal, unless one has a genuinely pathological condition—Alzheimer's disease or a related disorder.

RETIREMENT AND WIDOWHOOD

The most important thing to know about retirement is that it is far from a life trauma for most middle-aged and elderly adults. In fact, researchers can find no statistical evidence that retiring has *any* net effect on health and morale (Palmore, Burchett, Fillenbaum, George, & Wallman, 1985). One reason is that the meaning of retirement has undergone a radical transformation in the past few decades. Instead of signifying "being put out to pasture," the end of life, today retirement often signals a new beginning, "The time of life to do just what I want to do." The fact is that the postwork phase of life has indeed changed from a few brief years before death to a genuine life era. People retire now in health and with adequate finances. In fact, on average, we now spend more years in retirement than in school.

Of course the meaning of that other age-linked transition, widowhood, has not changed. Yet perhaps because it is an expected passage during the later years, there is abundant evidence that older people *as a group* seem to handle this important life trauma better than the young (Breckenridge, Gallagher, Thompson, & Peterson, 1986). Elderly widows and widowers on average have less intense levels of distress during the first few months and do not show a high incidence of physical and emotional problems over the long term. Several studies show that this is particularly true of women. Of any group, elderly women are least likely to develop emotional or physical problems after their spouse dies.

Of course these are all averages. For some people retirement is a terrible trauma; for some older women, widowhood equals the end of life. But the findings relating to these life transitions underline an important fact: We should not view any transition of aging in tones of unmitigated gloom and doom. Healthy adaptation and optimal living should be the expected goal of treatment in later life, just as it is at any age.

SUMMARY

In conclusion, here are 10 summary principles to keep in mind in counseling older people:

1. Never use chronological age to judge a person's capacities. Never expect because a person is a certain age that he or she should be

impaired. Not only are the vast majority of older people healthy, they will profit from the same counseling strategies as the young. Do not assume differences that are not there.

2. At the same time, counselors working with the frail elderly need to be activists. They should become knowledgeable about services, get involved with families, make home visits, and do whatever is necessary to enhance independence.

3. Physical disabilities are intimately tied to emotional well-being in later life. Reducing "excess disabilities" should always be a basic goal in working with the infirm older adult.

4. Sensory changes can have widespread effects on the quality of life. It is important to be familiar with these changes and their impact on behavior. One thrust of counseling may be to help the person adjust to these normal age-related losses.

5. Keep in mind the impact of vision and hearing changes on the counseling process, too. Make changes in the physical milieu to enhance the client's comfort. Avoid the temptation to over interpret or to read things into certain actions. That seeming memory problem, personality deficit, or resistance may really be just poor hearing (or vision).

7. In working with caregivers, pay special attention to daughters, as they seem most at risk. Still, understand that caregiving for anyone is often a stress.

8. Explore the myths that may be underlying caregiving: "I have to do everything" and "I must be happy about what I am doing." These preconceived ideas may contribute greatly to the stress caregivers feel.

9. Encourage caregivers to utilize formal sources of support; work to get other family members involved. Yet, be sensitive to individual differences. Some primary caregivers genuinely want to do everything.

10. *Most importantly,* never assume that psychopathology or impaired thinking is normal in later life or succumb to the idea that the older person cannot change. *Change and growth should be the counselor's goal for a person of any age.*

SUPPORTS TO KEEP PEOPLE OUT OF NURSING HOMES

Alternative Living Arrangements

Congregate care housing. This includes a diverse array of residential settings offering supportive services to people who need some help living independently. Residents in congregate care take their meals in a common dining room and may have maid service, a nurse on call, and so on.

Continuing care retirement communities. As its name implies, this is housing that offers a continuum of living situations, from regular housing to congregate housing, to nursing home care. The person pays a substantial entry fee and monthly maintenance fees and then is assured for care that fits his functional capacities for life.

Supportive Services

Home care. This option is the most popular for older people who need some help living independently. A variety of home health agencies provide an array of services in one's home, from minimal housekeeping to 24-hour care.

Day care. With this less widely available option, the person goes out to a center where he or she gets medical and or social care during the day and returns home at night.

Respite care. The newest service, respite care is specifically designed to offer time off to family caregivers. The elderly person is admitted to an inpatient setting or gets intensive home care for a brief time so family caregivers can go on vacation or just get a break from 24-hour care.

RESOURCES FOR MORE INFORMATION

Area Agencies on Aging

These offices in every medium-sized city (addresses vary) serve as a clearinghouse for gerontological information, providing services and data on everything of interest to older adults in a particular community, from housing alternatives to information about Alzheimer's disease to work opportunities after age 65.

The American Association of Retired Persons

Headquartered at 601 E. St. NW, Washington, D.C. 20049, with branch offices in large cities, the AARP is *the* organization for older people in America. In addition to lobbying for older adults and advocating for the needs of the elderly nationwide, the AARP sponsors research, training, and services of a variety of types. It also offers a wealth of materials about opportunities. Among others, this important organization has special divisions devoted to widowed persons, lifetime learning, health care, and housing. It publishes numerous free pamphlets and practice-oriented directories and books, and serves as a clearinghouse for the latest information on aging.

National Institute on Aging
Bethesda, MD 20892.
A subdivision of the National Institute of Health devoted to aging, the NIA conducts research and training as well as funds research and training programs in aging across the country. It also publishes a variety of pamphlets informing the public about the latest, primarily biomedical, research in aging.

The Gerontological Society of America
1411 K St N.W.
Washington, DC 20005
The GSA is the multidisciplinary organization of professionals interested in aging. It publishes two major research-oriented journals, *The Journals of Gerontology* and *The Gerontologist*. It also sponsors an annual convention and publishes newsletters.

FOR FURTHER READING

Fozard, J. (1990). Vision and hearing in aging. In J. E. Birren & K. W. Schaie (Eds.), *Handbook of the psychology of aging* (3rd ed., pp. 150–170). New York: Academic Press.

Palmore, E. B., Burchett, B., Fillenbaum, G., George, L., & Wallman, L. M. (1985). *Retirement: Causes and consequences.* New York: Springer.

U.S. Senate Special Committee on Aging (1987–1988). *Aging America: Trends and projections.* Washington, DC: U.S. Department of Health and Human Services.

Zarit, S. H., Orr, N., & Zarit, J. (1985). *The hidden victims of Alzheimer's disease: Families under stress.* New York: New York University Press.

REFERENCES

Arling, G., & McAuley, W. J. (1984). The family, public policy, and long-term care. In W. H. Quinn & G. A. Hughston (Eds.), *Independent aging: Family and social systems perspectives* (pp. 133–148). Rockville, MD: Aspen.

Belsky, J. (1988). *Here Tomorrow.* Baltimore: Johns Hopkins Press.

Breckenridge, J. N., Gallagher, D., Thompson, L. W., & Peterson, J. (1986). Characteristic depressive symptoms of bereaved elders. *Journal of Gerontology, 41,* 163–168.

Brody, E. (1977). *Long-term care of older people.* New York: Human Sciences Press.

Brody, E. (1985). Parent care as a normative family stress. *Gerontologist, 25,* 19–29.

Costa, P. T., & McCrae, R. R. (1980). Influence of extaversion and neuroticism on subjective well-being: Happy and unhappy people. *Journal of Personality and Social Psychology, 38,* 668–678.

Costa, P. T., McCrae, R. R., & Arenberg, D. (1983). Recent longitudinal research on personality and aging. In K. W. Schaie (Ed.), *Longitudinal studies of adult psychological development* (pp. 222–265). New York: Guilford Press.

Fitting, M., Rabins, P., Lucas, M. J., & Eastham, J. (1986). Caregivers for dementia patients: A comparison of husbands and wives. *Gerontologist, 26,* 248–252.

Fozard, J. (1990). Vision and hearing in aging. In J. E. Birren & K. W. Schaie (Eds.),

Handbook of the psychology of aging (3rd ed., pp. 150–170). New York: Academic Press.

Gatz, M. Bengston, V. L., & Blum, M. J. (1990). Caregiving families. In J. E. Birren & K. W. Schaie (Eds.), *Handbook of the psychology of aging* (3rd ed. pp. 404–426). New York: Academic Press.

George, L., & Gwyther, L. (1986). Caregiver well-being: A multidimensional examination of family caregivers of demented adults. *Gerontologist, 26,* 253–259.

Hertzog, C., & Schaie, K. W. (1988). Stability and change in adult intelligence: 2. Simultaneous analyses of longitudinal means and covariance structures. *Psychology and Aging, 3,* 122–130.

Irion, J. C., & Blanchard-Fields, F. (1987). A cross-sectional comparison of adaptive coping in adulthood. *Journal of Gerontology, 42,* 502–504.

Jarrett, W. H. (1985), Caregiving within kinship systems: Is affection really necessary? *Gerontologist, 25,* 5–10.

Johnson, C. L., & Catalano, D. (1983). a longitudinal study of family supports to impaired elderly. *Gerontologist, 23,* 612–618.

Katz, S., Ford, A. B., Moskowitz, R. W., Jackson, B. A., & Jaffe, H. W. (1963). Studies of illness in the aged—the Index of ADL: A standardized measure of biological and social function. *Journal of the American Medical Association, 185,* pp. 914-919.

Kuypers, J., & Bengtson, V. L. (1984). Perspectives on the older family. In W. H. Quinn and E. V. Hughston (Ed.), *Independent aging: Family and Social Systems perspectives.* Rockville, MD: Aspen.

Labouvie-Vief, G. V. (1985). Intelligence and cognition. In J. E. Birren & W. K. Schaie (Eds.), *Handbook of the psychology of aging* (2nd ed. pp. 500–530). New York: Van Nostrand Reinhold.

Lang, A. & Brody, E. M. (1983). Characteristics of middle-aged daughters and help to their elderly mothers. *Journal of Marriage and the Family, 45,* 193–202.

Lawton, M. P., & Brody, E. M. (1969). Assessment of older people: Self-maintaining and instrumental activities of daily living. *The Gerontologist, 9,* 179–186.

McCrae, R. R. (1982). Age difference in the use of coping mechanisms. *Journal of Gerontology, 37,* 454–460.

McCrae, R. R., & Costa, P. T. (1984). *Emerging lives, enduring dispositions: Personality in adulthood.* Boston: Little, Brown.

Osberg, J. S., McGinnis, G. E., DeJong, G., & Seward, M. (1987). Life satisfaction and quality of life among disabled elderly adults. *Journal of Gerontology, 42,* 228–230.

Palmore, E. B., Burchett, B., Fillenbaum, G., George, L., & Wallman, L. M. (1985). *Retirement: Causes and consequences.* New York: Springer.

Pfeiffer, M. (1975). *Multidimensional functional assessment: The OARS methodology.* Durham, NC: Duke University Center for the Study of Aging and Human Development.

Rodin, J. (1986a). Aging and health: Effects of the sense of control. *Science, 233,* 1271–1276.

Rodin, J. (1986b). Health, control, and aging. In M. M. Baltes & P. B. Baltes (Eds), *Psychology of control and aging* (pp. 139–165), Hillsdale, NJ: Erlbaum.

Shanas, E. (1984). Old parents and middle-aged children: The 4- and 5-generation family. *Journal of Geriatric Psychiatry, 17,* 7–19.

Smyer, M., Zarit, S. H., & Qualls, S. (1990). Psychological intervention with the aging individual. In J. E. Birren & K. W. Schaie (Eds.), *Handbook of the psychology of aging* (3rd ed. pp. 375–403). New York: Academic Press.

U.S. Senate Special Committee on Aging (1984–1985). *Aging America: Trends and projections.* Washington, DC: U.S. Department of Health and Human Services.

U.S. Senate Special Committee on Aging (1987–1988). *Aging America: Trends and projections.* Washington, DC: U.S. Department of Health and Human Services.

Zarit, S. H., Orr, N., & Zarit, J. (1985). *The hidden victims of Alzheimer's disease: Families under stress.* New York: New York University Press.

Zarit, S. H., Todd, P. A., & Zarit, J. M. (1986). Subjective burden of husbands and wives as caregivers: A longitudinal study. *Gerontologist, 26,* 260–266.

34

Counseling about Behavior Problems in Alzheimer's and Other Organic Mental Disorders

RAYMOND VICKERS, M.D.

Most voluntary actions of human beings involving their skeletal muscles, including speech, can be regarded as behavior. Additionally, involuntary physiological responses, heart rate and breathing changes, sweating, and so on, which accompany purposive muscular actions, are also part of each behavior. Not included in discussions of behavior are reflex responses such as fright or those automatic bodily actions such as movement disorders and seizures, which are not responses to stimuli.

Whenever we look at the difficult behaviors we encounter in everyday life, where organic disorders are not usually our concern, we are particularly prone to try to analyze the thoughts and feelings we suspect as responsible for these actions. Indeed, what psychology knows about cognition and emotion is largely derived by inference from observing behavior as expressed by speech and action. Even when conscious volition does not seem to be responsible for a particular behavior, psychological theory may explain it by attributing unconscious "thoughts" as the cause. Thus we tend to assume that all behavior is "goal directed" to serve the dictates of mental processes even if neither the observer nor the subject can presently recognize what the goal may be. Our social, and indeed our legal system is founded on this assumption of "intent."

However, with certain illnesses, among them organic mental disorder, behavior may not reflect the current intent of the mind or of the affect at all. The subject may not be aware of his or her actions, and deny doing what has happened, or, perhaps more distressing, may be only too aware that what is occurring is outside the subject's control. Although in law, such an individual is not responsible for his or her actions, we often have difficulty in accepting this.

Among more unacceptable behaviors are many that can be recognized in simians and other mammals. Such behaviors include disrobing, urinating, or defecating in public. A noisy intolerance of frustration, unawareness of danger, fear of even momentary separation, and unpredictable patterns of sleep and activity may be related behaviors. Repetitive noises and actions, even if hurtful, such as head-banging, are also seen as primatelike as is incontinence when it is unassociated with bladder disease or neurological damage. Moaning, pacing, hollering, or fighting off restraints are also reminiscent of caged animals. Some of these behaviors are referred to as "primitive," although *primal* would be a better term. They also may be seen in infancy, only to be suppressed by the growth of intelligence; they would only be expected to reemerge later if a loss of the capacity to suppress them had occurred. Fearful attachment to the caregiver or constant requests to be allowed to "go home" are also common behaviors that have this infantile quality. Because of cultural prohibitions, the presence of any of these primal behaviors is unacceptable in public and forces a caregiver shamefully to exclude the sufferer from normal social settings.

Other unacceptable primal behaviors are attributed to an aggressive drive. Aggressive behaviors of this kind are often laid down on inherited templates that can be easily recognized as having provided our primitive ancestors with evolutionary advantages. These include intrusive, acquisitive, affrontive, threatening, combative, resistive, and retaliatory actions that largely threaten the equilibrium of the caring milieu. Although the aggressive drive is a major motivating force in man, acculturation has so "sublimed" its expression that it is difficult to detect the covert part it plays in everyday acceptable behavior. A subject who exhibits overtly violent episodes thus not only invokes the fear of injury, but may put a strain on our efforts to suppress our own aggression and retaliate. Such a breakdown of control may be related to the surprisingly high incidence of family abuse of organically ill relatives in their care.

One basic skill often heightened in dementia is the ability to read "body language." This can defeat the efforts of a caregiver to rely on verbal persuasion when their expression negates the message.

A particularly troublesome type of behavior is that of sexual aggression. Since the preponderance of caregivers are women, this usually takes the form of harassment by men in their care. The range extends from occasional unwelcome invitations to actual physical assault. Frequently there seems to be a preoccupation with the subject. One cannot often say that there is a contextual stimulus in the caregiver's behavior or in the circumstances of intimacy involved in bathing and dressing; more likely there is an absence of suppression of thoughts that would not previously have been expressed, even if experienced. A consideration of cultural styles might put a different interpretation on such behaviors. Of related importance is the subject of touch. This has both sexual and cultural aspects. The appropriate use of touching is of great value in reassuring an individual and obtaining his or her cooperation, but it has to be right for both people.

Other difficult behaviors seen in organic conditions are similar to those characteristic of other psychotic disorders. These include pathological suspiciousness, hallucinations, screaming, depression, and agitation. Paranoid delusions, silliness, and strange posturing, as seen in schizophrenia, may also occur.

Some researchers theorize that organically impaired individuals make errors in interpreting their environment, and that unwelcome behaviors are the innocent results of misperception, but this assumes a capacity for logical response that usually is not present. More often, aggressive behavior seems to be triggered by any number of random internal or external stimuli that are not in themselves threats, but that do place a strain on the individual. Some of these triggers are as follows:

Internal Triggers of Primal and Aggressive Behavior

- physical pain or discomfort (fever, fecal impaction, bladder distension, painful illness, or injury)
- sensory impairment (hearing, vision, or touch, especially if illusions occur)
- loss of sleep or fatigue
- dehydration (occasionally malnutrition)
- drugs and alcohol
- hallucinations, delusions, or paranoia

External Triggers of Aggressive Behavior

- catastrophic reaction (overstimulating, overdemanding environment)
- failure to recognize surroundings, people, or time (disorientation)
- transfer trauma (can occur without disorientation)
- separation anxiety
- sundowning (increasing agitation as the day wears on)

- being treated as impaired, scolded, argued with, doubted
- attempts at caregiving (feeding, dressing, bathing, or redirecting)

PRINCIPLES IN COUNSELING CAREGIVERS
OF THE ORGANICALLY DISTURBED

Abandon efforts to "understand" the behavior of organically impaired individuals. This is hard to do, both for the counselor, who is trained to analyze behavior by linear logic, and for the caregiver, who is reluctant to face the chaotic state the victim's mind is in. At times, intent does seem to be present, especially if old issues of conflict with significant others are relived, and families may slip into these quarrels from habit. This "raking over the coals" in which unresolved family issues are replayed should instead be interpreted as an effort by the victim to capture what memories he or she can. Emotionally charged memories are more easily recalled than mundane ones. Upsetting recollections are best handled by redirecting attention to more positive memories that serve the same reassuring purpose but are less contentious. It is totally nonproductive to try to argue.

Look for current "triggers" of behavior—welcome as well as unacceptable. A diary is often helpful in identifying patterns, and the counselor can learn a lot if this is brought into sessions. Especially difficult is the identification of internal triggers. A motivated medical professional may have to rely on a few unreliable symptoms in seeking out the presence of disturbing disorders. Infections, especially of the urinary tract, may be present in a demented person without fever or other telltale signs, yet cause marked behavioral disturbance. Other conditions, including fecal impaction and dehydration, may present with a high fever and behavioral disturbances but never develop the symptoms by which they usually can be diagnosed. The role of the counselor at such times may be to act as advocate to ensure that adequate medical attention is obtained and that the physician's findings are supplemented by the caregiver's perception of the symptoms. Especially elusive is pain. While dementia does not seem to alter the way an individual is aware of pain, memory is unreliable, and we must ask the sufferer for an account at frequent intervals to piece together the whole picture. Headache, dental and bone pain, angina, and abdominal pain are often minimized, yet all are potent causes of angry or withdrawn behavior.

In many cases the internal trigger is a medication. Many medications have toxic effects on the brain that are amplified by the fragile mental balance of organic brain loss. Such drugs include beta-blockers used for diseases of the heart and circulation, antispasmodics used in lung and bowel disorders, sedatives intended to produce sleep, and paradoxically, tranquilizers and antidepressants, which may produce agitation in the elderly and especially in those with dementia. Some common drugs, which do not usually cause mental symptoms except in overdose, can be toxic in quite low dosage to those with organic brain disease. An example of this is digoxin, a widely prescribed heart medication. Thus instead of rushing to find a drug to suppress unacceptable behavior, it may be wise to approach a drug-free state. In some cases, it takes weeks for the drug that is the cause of the behavior disturbance to be completely excreted. The counselor can help by confronting the tendency that many caregivers have of believing there is some drug that will suppress unwanted behavior without producing any adverse drug reactions. It is generally true that for every desirable drug action, there are two or more undesirable side effects potentially present in the same drug.

Remember that in addition to behaviors resulting from organic brain disease, various neuropsychiatric disorders may also be present. The commonest of these is depression, and this can take a number of behavioral varieties in the elderly. Hypoactive, withdrawn, forgetful, self-neglectful patients are readily diagnosed as depressed; indeed, the organic features may be difficult to elicit, although current research has suggested that the two conditions frequently coexist. Agitation, another common behavioral expression of late-life depression, is also difficult to distinguish from dementia. Antidepressant drugs increase the agitation of dementia, but may reduce that of depression, although several weeks of treatment may be needed to produce improvement. Another common condition that is often mistaken as agitation is *akathisia,* a syndrome of restlessness seen in Parkinson's disease and as a side effect of tranquilizers and antidepressants. Unfortunately, if akathisia is mistaken as agitation and these drugs are used, it becomes worse and a vicious cycle may be produced. Almost all the behavioral disorders seen in Parkinson's disease are due to l-DOPA and the other drugs used to treat it.

Look for evidence of misperceptions. Of course, we all can occasionally misname an acquaintance, but we are readily corrected. On the other hand, a mistake persistently cherished, such as in insisting that a caregiver is a daughter, is quite characteristic of dementia. Misperceiving objects, or by contrast, having visual hallucinations, is typical of delirium. In investigating misperceptions, the victim's vision and hearing should be checked—an often formidable challenge in a bewildered and suspicious subject!

Reduce the impact of environmental triggers on the demented individual. Simple surroundings with relatively few people and limited noise levels are best. Staff should not be rotated, and they should try to dress consistently. Shift changes should be planned to reduce surprises. Familiar objects brought from home are reassuring, and favorite hobbies should be considered, although old skills may be lost and produce frustration.

It is not necessary to "involve" subjects in conversation or activities, and demands should be kept to a minimum. A greeting and explanation should precede any encounter. Regularity and predictability of routines are helpful. However, the value of quite demanding exercise is well established; sleep from fatigue is better than that produced by drugs. If a time of day is "best" for some activity, such as bathing, or "worst" due to fatigue or sundowning, the plan should be modified accordingly. All care plans should include daily scheduling, and this should be reviewed regularly if unacceptable behavior is present.

Take a careful food history from the family and use it in the care plan. Mealtimes are fraught with difficulties. Mealtime for some men represented their family dominance, for others it was a battleground; these expectations may persist. For the individual with dementia, mealtimes emphasize many other losses. Institutional diets cannot emulate home cooking. Alzheimer's disease probably reduces the perception of flavor and aroma, the attention span is too short to finish the meal, and the disease and its drug treatment cause difficulties in swallowing.

Learn how to communicate with the subject. A pleasant, supportive approach with appropriate body language is imperative. This is very difficult when coming on the scene in which the patient has had a mishap, or when unacceptable behavior is occurring. Try to avoid a confrontation; rather, use avoidance or distraction. Scolding and finger-pointing are not productive, although it is appropriate to say "I don't like that; I am upset." It should not be necessary to emphasize your probity and decency by showing outrage at a display of unacceptable behavior.

Speak slowly, from in front of the individual. Use the first or the formal name according to the individual's preference. Do not ask questions that rely on memory for a reply. Wait for a reply; learn to listen. Try to sort out meaning from a garbled statement. Do not offer multiple choices. Use short sentences. Use language that is meaningful to the subject; even the vernacular term for body parts or functions may be preferable to the clinical one. Give instructions one step at a time, not in strings. Repeat often. Allow enough time. If catastrophic reaction threatens, back off.

Finally, recognize that some organic disorders are going to need organic therapies. Most of the bad reputation of drugs comes from their misuse, although some side effects are unpredictable. On the other hand, proper drug use can reduce the inner distress felt by the patient and enhance the effectiveness of caregiving. Before asking for medication, develop a goal for its use. No drug can do global good; in fact, a benefit usually has to be balanced against a disadvantage. For example, neuroleptics reliably reduce rage, but also invariably increase vulnerability to danger. Most psychotropic drugs achieve a therapeutic level slowly so should not be given in increasing doses simply because of impatience for their onset. When a satisfactory benefit is achieved, they should be reduced to avoid further buildup to toxic levels. Drug-free periods are important to maximize excretion and to review the need for resumption. Prophylactic use invites complications; tardive dyskinesia does not remit when the drug is stopped. Reliance on a "PRN" (as necessary) drug order has been rightly condemned, but initiating treatment in this way, with the caregiver administering each dose whenever the target symptoms are present, can be helpful in mapping a regular therapeutic regimen.

In summary, it is the role of the counselor to learn as much as possible about the characteristics of each phase of the manifestations of organic mental syndromes, to provide empathy for the anxiety and dread with which the caregivers respond to the progressive depersonalization of an individual to generate acceptance rather than explanation of disruptive activity, and to provide consultation, teaching, and support in modifying the emergence of unacceptable behaviors.

FOR FURTHER READING

Gwyther, L. (1985). Care of the Alzheimer's patient. In: *A manual for nursing home staff.* Chicago: American Health Care Association.

Mace, N., & Rabins, P., (1981). *The 36–hour day.* Baltimore: Johns Hopkins University Press.

Vickers, R. (1988). Medical aspects of aging. In L. W. Lazarus & L. Jarvik (Eds.), *Essentials of geriatric psychiatry.* New York: Springer.

35

Death and Dying

DAVID A. CRENSHAW, Ph.D.

Of all the challenges facing counselors, perhaps none is greater than helping the grieving or the terminally ill. It can be very taxing to counsel someone in the midst of excruciating pain as the result of the death of a loved one or someone facing imminent death because of serious illness. This task can be facilitated, however, by understanding the requirements of healthy grieving.

SEVEN TASKS OF MOURNING

There is general agreement in the field that healthy resolution of loss requires the person to grieve and to mourn. Drawing from the writing of leaders in the field of bereavement and from clinical experience, I propose seven important tasks of mourning (Crenshaw, 1990).

Task 1: Acknowledge the Reality of the Loss
A person cannot begin the grieving process until he or she has first accepted the reality of the loss. In the case of very painful or sudden unexpected losses, the need to deny the reality can be very strong.

Task 2: Identify and Express the Emotions of Grief
The bereaved must be helped to experience the pain of grief. This crucial aspect of the grief work consists of expressing in words the intense feelings that accompany the loss of someone important to us. The healing process is very much aided when the feelings are shared with a trusted person. When the bereaved share feelings of grief, they are not

This chapter is adapted from Crenshaw, D., *Bereavement* (New York: Crossroad, 1989).

just ventilating powerful painful emotions; more important in terms of the healing process, they are making an active declaration of trust.

Thus, the bereaved are taking a formidable risk. Grievers are confiding and unburdening their painful feelings and thereby are expressing the belief that their feelings can be accepted and understood by significant others. This declaration of trust removes barriers of isolation, cynicism, and mistrust that easily get erected after a tragic loss heightens our sense of vulnerability.

Task 3: Commemorate the Loss

All cultures have developed rituals and customs of mourning to assist the grieving process. Planning and participating in the funeral and burial services are helpful steps in honoring the memory of the deceased loved one. In addition the griever may need help in finding an acceptable way to remember and honor the life of the loved one that has died. This can be particularly helpful when there is an undue burden of guilt in relation to the death. When a family member commits suicide, for example, it can be very helpful for the surviving family to find a way to honor the memory of the deceased loved one by planning together projects through which they can carry on the unfinished work of the deceased. If, for instance, the suicide victim had been interested in conservation, the family could plan projects concerning the environment and in this way honor the memory of their deceased loved one as well as alleviate some of the unbearable guilt that is typically associated with suicide.

Task 4: Acknowledge Ambivalence

All relationships have their ups and downs. The bereaved need to recognize and acknowledge their conflicting feelings in relation to the deceased loved one. Denial of these conflicting feelings represents a considerable barrier to the resolution of grief. When a loved one dies, the death rarely leaves a clean wound. Almost always, there is a mixture of intense feelings. In addition to love of the deceased there may be anger related to the perception of desertion through death. Often the death of a loved one is emotionally experienced as abandonment by those left behind. This may be felt especially by children or adults who had a highly dependent relationship with the deceased. In addition there may be long-standing and unexpressed resentments related to disappointments in the relationship.

The acknowledgment of these feelings is a crucial step in the mourning process, but it is very difficult especially for children to recognize and accept such feelings in themselves, let alone share them with someone else—even a highly trusted person. This step then constitutes one of the greatest challenges to helping grieving children and adults alike.

Task 5: Resolve the Ambivalence

Once grievers are in touch with the negative feelings with respect to the deceased loved one, they frequently go overboard and lose perspective. They may ask themselves, "Did I really love my husband?" The griever must achieve a balance between the conflicting feelings so that both positive and negative feelings are fully recognized and then put into perspective. Some bereaved persons will express the positive feelings much more easily and will have a hard time recognizing and expressing the negative feelings. For such persons, the unacceptable and denied hostile feelings will block their attempts to resolve their grief. Counselors who have found it easy to get such individuals to talk about the things they missed about the deceased will then need to ask, "What don't you miss about the deceased?" (Worden, 1982).

Some grieving persons may experience the opposite. If their relationship was unfulfilling or perhaps depriving or abusive, they may find it far easier to express their hostile feelings than to express warm or loving ones. Yet in most cases, the warm, tender feelings exist unnoticed. It becomes a vital task for the grief counselor to bring these feelings into awareness and to help the mourner to achieve a realistic balance between them.

Task 6: Let Go

This task consists of saying good-bye on an emotional rather than an intellectual level. This can happen only after all the previous steps have been mastered. The bereaved must gradually withdraw their emotional investment in the deceased in order to go forward with their lives. It is very important, however, to emphasize that while the griever must let go of the physical person of the deceased, he or she can hold on to the loving memories and the positive influences that they have internalized. In this way the griever can continue to have a relationship with the deceased as long as the griever accepts that the relationship has changed significantly: that the griever can no longer have a relationship with the physical person.

Task 7: Move On

This step requires the adoption of a present and future orientation as hopes, dreams, plans and aspirations are restructured and reshaped in view of the new realities. This step can be exceedingly difficult because it involves relinquishing the hopes, dreams and aspirations that revolved around the deceased loved person. Sometimes this move forward can be blocked by what Bonime (1989) describes as *angry unwillingness,* the person's fight against the utilization of personal resources (Bonime, 1989).

In the context of bereavement, this resistance to moving on may result from anger that life has dealt the bereaved a cruel blow. The feeling of having been cheated may lead to stubborn refusal to go forward with life. Moving on can also be blocked by *faulty identifications*. For example, grievers may insist on viewing themselves as tragic figures. The bereaved must commit to full participation in life again, which may be difficult if they have received enormous gratifications from the solicitations of family and friends. These two dynamic elements can thwart the grief counselor's efforts to help grievers move ahead.

These seven tasks of mourning are impacted by developmental factors as well as other variables, including the circumstances and timing of the death and the preexisting personality of the griever. The younger the child, the more likely it is that he or she will have difficulty undertaking these tasks and that he or she will need adult modeling, guidance, and direction. When death is untimely and sudden, the first two tasks, recognition of the reality of the loss and identification and expression of feelings are likely to be especially difficult due to shock and denial. When the relationship between the deceased and the bereaved was highly conflicted, tasks 4, acknowledging ambivalence, and 5, resolution of ambivalence, are likely to pose significant challenges. When the bereaved experience undue guilt related to the loss, task 3, commemoration, becomes especially critical. When the bereaved was excessively dependent on the deceased loved one, he or she may find task 6, letting go, and task 7, moving on, to be particularly hard.

CHILDREN DIFFER FROM ADULTS IN GRIEVING

Some clinicians believe that the capacity to mourn is not fully developed until at least adolescence, if not adulthood (Wolfenstein, 1966). Other writers have noted the capacity of children as young as 3 and even 6 months of age to mourn (Furman, 1964). Children do mourn but in a manner quite different from adults that is determined by both the cognitive and emotional development of the child (Worden, 1982). Typically they are not capable of the prolonged and intense mourning that is typical of adult grieving. It takes them longer to accomplish the grief work because they can only do it in brief stages. They lack the ego resources to tolerate the painful affects that accompany the persistent grieving that we associate with adult mourning. Children can be assisted in the grieving process, and there are certain times when they are more open and receptive to focusing on these feelings and expressing them. Helpers should be alert to such windows of opportunity and also encourage parents to be sensitive to these occasions. These special opportunities may be associated with holidays, anniversaries, birthdays, or other meaningful family occasions. They may even be stimulated by watching on television something that reminds them of their deceased loved one.

THE CONSEQUENCES OF UNRESOLVED GRIEF

If the mourning process is skipped, avoided, or interrupted before closure, the person is at risk for manifesting *delayed* or *distorted* grief reactions. In delayed reactions the bereaved may show little or no outward signs of mourning at the time of the death, only to react with profound grief at a later time in response to a loss of seemingly less significance. In the case of distorted grief, the bereaved may show few signs of intense grief at the time of loss but later develop psychosomatic symptoms such as migraines or dizzy spells. They may become irritable and angry in their interpersonal relationships, sometimes leading to serious conflicts. A major goal of grief counseling is to prevent subsequent psychopathology by helping the bereaved to mourn their loss fully.

When we are unwilling or unable to mourn the loss of loved ones, we are at risk for distorted or delayed grief reactions. As we attempt to go forward with life, sooner or later an event occurs that brings the unresolved grief into focus, sometimes with startling intensity. These events can be thought of as "final straws" (Krueger, 1978). The final straw may be any subsequent loss, such as another death, divorce, abortion, or life transition. Life transitions may include pregnancy, relocation, a child leaving home, or perhaps a developmental step such as graduation from college. Whatever the precipitating event may be, the person's intense reaction is partly to the present stress but resonates with the earlier unresolved grief.

NORMAL AND PATHOLOGICAL BEREAVEMENT

Normal and pathological grief reactions can be distinguished on the basis of severity and duration (Worden, 1982). Thus, in acute grief, the bereaved experience all kinds of unsettling and sometimes frightening feelings such as the fear that they are losing their minds, as well as psychosomatic symptoms such as headaches and tightness in their chests. All of these reactions are common. If the symptoms of acute grief persist for more than 6 months, they may indicate pathological mourning. In general, if overt grief is completely absent, delayed or expressed in a distorted form such as acting out (e.g., abusing alcohol and drugs), or unusually intense or persistent, it indicates that the grieving process has taken an unhealthy form. While the acute symptoms of grief should resolve in the first 6 months, the total grief process can easily span 2 to

3 years. It typically takes longer in children, as previously mentioned, since they need to rework the grief at each developmental phase (Crenshaw, 1990). No one ever recovers from the loss of someone deeply loved. Recovery from grief means being able to face and bear the loss, but being permanently changed as the result of the experience. Some of these changes may be positive, as we may gain or discover strength within ourselves.

RISK FACTORS COMPLICATING BEREAVEMENT

Only a minority of the bereaved population develop intense and enduring pathological grief responses. The Harvard Bereavement Study has demonstrated a relationship between pathological grief and the following: *dependent attachment, conflicted attachment,* and *unexpected loss* (Parkes and Weiss, 1983). Thus, those who were quite dependent in their relationships with the deceased, those who had conflicted and highly ambivalent relationships with the deceased, and those suffering sudden and unexpected losses should be considered at risk for abnormal grief reactions. Sometimes the circumstances of the death can be so horrible as to be traumatizing. In the case of fatal accidents, murder, and suicide the grief is compounded by the sudden horror of these events and the rage "that something like this could happen in our family." The guilt can also be nearly unbearable, particularly in the case of childhood suicide, but also with accidents to the extent that they were perceived as preventable.

ISSUES IN COUNSELING THE GRIEVING

It is important to respond differentially, based on an assessment of the complicating factors in the grief. Failing to do so may make matters worse. Guidelines for responding differentially are spelled out in an earlier publication (Crenshaw, 1990). Whenever possible it is helpful to work with the bereaved in the context of their families. So much more can be accomplished by enlisting the natural healing forces that exist within families. Counselors must come to terms with their own anxiety about death. We cannot expect to be helpful when we ourselves have a need to deny our own mortality or avoid dealing with our own sense of loss or unresolved grief.

Caregivers need to avoid overcatastrophizing. If we expect trauma, especially with children and highly suggestible adolescents, we will get trauma. It is imperative to hold and convey the conviction that the bereaved person will survive the painful grieving experience. We should never assume that a particular death will be traumatic for a person lest it becomes a self-fulfilling prophecy. Research in resiliency indicates that certain individuals seem to thrive even in the case of extreme stressful situations.

Counselors need to empathize with the pain of the griever without overidentifying. In order to be helpful in counseling the breaved, we need to put ourselves in the place of grievers and feel their pain without losing our own sense of self. Helpers also need to be able to detach in order to maintain *objectivity*. If you can't express empathy, your responses to the bereaved are likely to be overly intellectualized and emotionally sterile. However, if you are unable to pull back and detach yourself you will lose objectivity. Thus, you must be able to strike a balance between empathy with the pain and sufficient detachment to achieve objectivity.

With young or nonverbal grievers, stimulate creative productions wherein the feelings of loss can be expressed. Young children—preschoolers and some of school age—may not be able to express their grief in words. In this case you can encourage the expression of feelings through creative productions such as symbolic play artwork, and drawings (Crenshaw, 1990).

Counselors should strive to be a guide and companion through the grieving process, rather than a representative of reality. This point is made by Bowlby in his writings on helping the breaved (Bowlby, 1979). The bereaved benefit much more from our attentive listening to and understanding of their feelings than from our rushing in to correct their distortions of reality. Confrontation may have a place in grief work but it is usually only helpful in later stages, such as when the excessively dependent griever gets stuck in accomplishing the task of moving on or letting go.

In the later stages of grief counseling it is important to enable mourners to relinquish old dreams in order to make room for new ones. The task of letting go and moving on requires giving up long cherished hopes and dreams and then daring to create new ones. This can be an exceedingly painful transition. Caregivers will need to review patiently the old dreams and plans until the emotional investment is gradually relinquished, at which point it becomes possible for the bereaved to entertain new possibilities.

Timing is critical with these interventions. Introduction of the idea of making new goals before mourning the lost aspirations and hopes will likely be experienced as insensitivity to the feelings of the griever. Failure to provide a "gentle push" when the bereaved are ready to move on may be experienced as desertion. It is vital to listen to the feelings behind the words so that we can really hear the messages of those we seek to help.

ISSUES IN COUNSELING THE TERMINALLY ILL

Kübler-Ross (1969) has beautifully and sensitively described the stages that the terminally ill typically go through in coping with their illness and impending death. She describes the stages of denial and isolation, anger, bargaining, depression, and acceptance. Not all terminally ill patients will reach the final stage of acceptance. Counselors, however, can play a vital role in assisting terminally ill patients to achieve a sense of peace and final acceptance of their fate. Kübler-Ross gives much emphasis to the role of hope and particularly warns against trying to predict the number of days, weeks, or months that the patient has to live. It is enough to validate for the patient, if they want to know, that their illness is very serious but that no one knows how much time they have left. This allows them to continue to hope for as long as needed to help them bear the painful medical procedures or the suffering of the illness itself until they reach that final state of acceptance and peace with the fact their life is coming to an end.

Kübler-Ross (1969) puts great emphasis on empathic listening and sharing with the terminally ill person and the family as well. Her approach seems to follow closely the recommendation of Bowlby (1979) that we are much more valuable in our role as companion and guide during the journey of terminal illness than as representatives of reality eager to confront whatever distortions the patient may have. These distortions may very well coincide with defenses the patient vitally needs. To challenge or confront these defenses may prevent the patient from calling on the hope needed to sustain the arduous journey. Terminally ill patients should not be pushed to confront feelings they are unwilling to face. The helper's role is to provide ample opportunities for those who are able and willing to talk about their experience and to share the accompanying feelings. At the very least this enables the patient not to feel so alone as he or she comes to the end of life. The counselor can also guide and instruct the family to follow the same approach, that is, being emotionally accessible to the patient when the terminally ill wish to talk, without pushing or forcing such exploration. In this way caregivers or family members can signal their readiness to talk about the impending death but always follow the lead of the terminally ill. In the process of counseling the terminally ill the counselor may be able to help them achieve what Erikson (1959) called *ego integrity*. They are then able to view their life as the only life they could have had and that they have done the best they could. The counselor will then have gone a long way toward helping them achieve Kübler-Ross's (1969) final stage of acceptance.

REFERENCES

Bonime, W. (1989). *Collaborative psychoanalysis.* Teaneck, NJ: Fairleigh Dickinson University Press.

Bowlby, J. (1979). *The making and breaking of affectional bonds.* London: Tavistock Publications.

Crenshaw, D. (1990). *Bereavement: counseling the grieving throughout the life cycle*. New York: Continuum Publishing Co.

Erikson, E. (1959). *Identity and the Life Cycle*. New York: Norton.

Furman, R. (1964). Death and the young child: some preliminary considerations. *Psychoanalytic study of the child. 15*, 9–52.

Krueger, D. (1978). Psychotherapy of adult patients with problems of parental loss in childhood. *Current concepts in psychiatry, 4*, 2–7.

Kubler-Ross, E. (1968). *On death and dying*. New York: MacMillan.

Parkes, C. & Weiss, R. (1983). *Recovery from bereavement*. New York: Basic Books.

Wolfenstein, M. (1966). How is mourning possible? *Psychoanalytic study of the child, 21*, 93–123.

Worden, L. (1982). *Grief counseling and grief therapy*. New York: Springer Publishing Co., p. 41.

Afterword:
The Counseling Profession

MARY KOPALA, Ph.D.

MERLE A. KEITEL, Ph.D.

The counseling profession has historically focused on the developmental issues that confront all people, such as choosing a career, parenting, academic problems, becoming more assertive and so on. Counseling has been referred to as the art of helping people of all ages, all physical capabilities, and all cultures to reach their maximum potential. Counselors provide remediation and prevention in various arenas, such as personal, social, occupational, and emotional.

A confusing array of mental health professionals provide counseling, such as (a) *professional counselors* (e.g., counselors in vocational rehabilitation, school, substance abuse/alcoholism, college student personnel, marriage and family, pastoral, career, employee assistance, and recreation), (b) *psychologists* (e.g., clinical, counseling, industrial/organizational, and school), (c) *psychiatrists,* and (d) *clinical social workers.* We will attempt to clarify the differences between these professionals.

Professional Counselors

Professional counselors typically have completed at least a master's degree program in counseling with course work that may emphasize a particular professional focus, such as school counseling or marriage and family counseling. The professional association that represents the numerous types of counselors is the American Counseling Association (ACA), a membership association that provides training, continuing education, and advocacy services for its members. It also publishes a bimonthly journal, *The Journal of Counseling and Development*; a monthly newspaper, *The Guidepost*; and ethical standards for counselors. It has many affiliates which are listed at the end of this chapter.

Psychologists

Psychologists who provide direct services to clients (e.g. counseling, clinical, school, industrial/organizational) generally have completed a doctoral level psychology program, including a one-year, full-time internship and dissertation. Other psychologists, such as experimental, cognitive, developmental, or social psychologists, are not trained to provide counseling. Clinical psychologists specialize in the diagnosis and treatment of mental illness, whereas counseling psychologists have a more developmental and preventive focus that is more aligned with the orientation of professional counselors. School psychologists assess, evaluate, and diagnose learning and social/emotional problems, intervene or refer, and consult with parents, teachers, and administrators. Industrial/organizational psychologists consult with business and industry regarding issues of employee motivation, interpersonal dynamics in the workplace, and environmental factors that affect productivity.

Psychiatrists

Psychiatrists are medical doctors who may prescribe medication such as antidepressants, antipsychotics, and mild tranquilizers for individuals diagnosed with biologically based mental illnesses. They attend medical school and then complete a residency in psychiatry. Psychiatrists often consult with counselors and psychologists when a client presents with serious pathology.

Clinical Social Workers

Individuals practicing in the profession of social work complete either an associate's, bachelor's, or master's degree in social work, depending on the states in which they practice. To be licensed, certified, or registered, social workers typically complete postdegree supervised experience and may be required to pass an examination. More than the other professions we have discussed, social workers emphasize environmental factors that influence mental health. Clinical social workers frequently intervene with individuals in the context of their social, cultural, and economic institutions.

LICENSURE, CERTIFICATION, AND REGISTRATION OF COUNSELORS

Counselors—either master's level or doctoral level—may or may not be licensed, certified, or registered, depending on the state in which they practice. These credentialing procedures define and legalize professions within states. Not every state in the United States licenses, certifies, or registers counselors. The purpose of these credentials is to protect the public's health, safety, and welfare from incompetent and/or unethical practices and to advance the profession.

As of December 1990, 34 states had established regulatory boards that govern the practice of professional counseling. The states that had not established such regulatory boards were Alaska, Connecticut,

Hawaii, Illinois, Indiana, Iowa, Kentucky, Minnesota, Nevada, New Hampshire, New Jersey, New Mexico, New York, Pennsylvania, Utah, and Wisconsin. Even within the 34 states that license counselors, the number of counselors applying for and receiving licensure is low, relative to the number eligible to apply. Those states with regulatory boards require at least a master's degree in counseling in addition to postmaster's supervised experience for certification, licensure, or registration. Master's degrees may require as few as 30 semester hours or as many as 60 semester hours. The amount of postmaster's experience ranges from as little as 6 months to as much as 4 years, with most states requiring 2 years' postmaster's experience.

Most states require an examination in order to be eligible for credentialing. A passing score on the National Board of Certified Counselors (NBCC) examination is accepted in most states. In other states, the examination of the Commission on Rehabilitation Counselor Certification (CRCC) or the Academy of Clinical Mental Health Counselors (ACMHC) are accepted in lieu of the NBCC examination. Texas and California require a passing score on a state-prepared examination only. Though Maine, Michigan, South Dakota, and Tennessee have an examination requirement, as of December 1990 the specific exam had not been defined. Most states require some form of continuing education postmaster's degree to renew the credential. It should be noted that critics of credentialing procedures believe that, in fact, credentials only ensure minimal competence and knowledge, and do not protect the public. The validity of licensure examinations has also been challenged.

Accreditation
Whereas licensing, certification, and registration refer to the credentialing of *individuals,* accreditation refers to the credentialing of an *academic program.* Various organizations are responsible for evaluating and accrediting programs in counseling, including state agencies (e.g., bureaus of professional and occupational affairs, and state education departments) and national accreditation organizations such as the Council for Accreditation of Counseling and Related Educational Programs (CACREP) and the Council of Rehabilitation Education (CORE). These accrediting bodies work to ensure the quality of the academic program. They establish standards for content and number of courses, the number of supervised practicum hours, the credentials of supervisors, and types of field settings.

ACADEMIC PROGRAMS IN COUNSELING

Master's degrees as well as doctorates in philosophy and education are offered in counseling and counselor education. Some programs are generic while others have a specific emphasis (e.g., elementary and secondary school counseling, college student personnel, rehabilitation, mental health, substance abuse, and marriage and family). As of 1990–1992, there were approximately 504 graduate programs (including counseling psychology) in the United States. Master's programs generally range from 30 to 72 credits. Most programs offer students a basic foundation in the following areas: (a) individual counseling, (b) group counseling, (c) career counseling, (d) assessment or measurement, (e) ethics and professional issues, (f) supervised practica or internships, and (g) research. Many programs are adding courses in multicultural counseling, substance abuse, marriage and family counseling, career and life planning, and consultation.

According to Hollis and Wantz (1990), programs in counseling are projecting the following trends:

1. Course work will emphasize substance abuse, marriage and family, rehabilitation, geriatric, and school counseling (particularly elementary school counseling), and consultation.
2. Multicultural/special population counseling will receive more attention, resulting in more courses offered.
3. Mental health/agency/community counseling programs will need to add course work and increase the requirements for clinical experience in order to meet CACREP standards.
4. Programs will need to modify their curricula in order to satisfy the specific states' requirements for certification/licensure.

COUNSELOR PREPARATION

Individual Counseling

Courses in individual counseling usually cover different theories of counseling, which may include, but are not limited to, psychodynamic, client-centered, cognitive, and behavioral. Some programs endorse a particular theoretical orientation, while others present several theories and allow students to select the theory that is most consistent with their views of human nature and development. Another focus of individual counseling courses is the process of counseling. Skills, such as how to open and close an interview, how to establish rapport with clients, how to recognize resistance, and how to promote client growth, are usually developed and practiced through laboratory training.

Group Counseling

Group counseling courses typically focus on types of groups, the stages of group development, the roles of the group leader and members, the development of group norms, process issues, and unique therapeutic factors that exist in groups. Groups may be particularly helpful because individuals are given an opportunity to play out their usual roles in life, and with the help of a counselor, to change aspects of their interpersonal behavior.

Career Counseling

Historically, an expertise in career counseling has been the distinguishing factor between the counseling profession and other mental health professions. Careers are an integral part of our lives and therefore strongly influence our personal well-being and family functioning. Courses in career counseling typically discuss how people choose their jobs. Some theories of career development focus on family influences, decision-making styles, chance factors, and/or intrapersonal dynamics as the factors that determine people's careers. Psychodynamic theorists, for example, might suggest that dentists are fulfilling oral aggressive needs.

Assessment/Measurement

Assessment courses typically discuss specific tests in personality, scholastic ability and achievement, and career inventories. Students might learn the answers to the following questions: Does a test measure what it is supposed to measure? Is the test reliable (i.e., if you administered the same test a second time to the same person, would the results be the same)? How can I help people to determine which career would be most satisfying? What kind of person am I and with whom would I be most compatible? Can I increase my standard test score if I take the examination over again? Skills in how to administer tests and interpret the results to clients are developed and practiced in assessment courses.

Ethics and Professional Issues

Counselors are responsible for the welfare of others, and it is therefore imperative that ethical issues be addressed. Different professional associations publish ethical codes and standards for practice that offer broad guidelines for counselor behavior. The examination of personal values and ethical decision-making models is encouraged so that students can make the best possible judgments when confronted by dilemmas. For example, a counselor may need to decide whether to break confidentiality in the case of a suicidal client. Other professional issues such as the status of certification and licensure, the roles and functions of counselors in different settings, the evaluation of counseling effectiveness, and other current issues are discussed. It is important to note that legal and ethical issues in counseling have only recently been added as a separate course in many counseling programs.

Supervised Practica and Internships

All counseling programs include some supervised field experience, but the number of required hours differs from program to program. Typically, students would choose field placements that are congruent with their career goals (e.g., schools, community mental health centers, hospitals, college counseling centers, and community agencies). Students practice under the supervision of professionals who are appropriately trained and/or credentialed. In addition to academic requirements, students should be aware that certifying bodies may have specific conditions that must be satisfied. It is the student's responsibility to investigate these requirements.

Research

Typically, master's level students complete introductory statistics and/or research courses. Such courses develop skills in conducting original research and evaluating existing studies. Basic courses focus primarily on descriptive statistics and elementary inferential statistics. Many potential counseling students initially feel frightened or intimidated by these courses; however, with a patient, understanding professor and some effort on the part of the student, not only do students survive some actually come to enjoy research.

Specialized Programs

Specialized programs in counseling generally require additional courses; for example, programs in rehabilitation counseling might require course work in the social and psychological impact of disabilities, medical information, and the classification of jobs. School counseling programs would offer courses in child and adolescent psychology, accountability, and administration of school counseling programs.

Doctoral Programs

Individuals who have completed a master's degree in counseling may decide to pursue further study. Typically, a student in counselor education would pursue a doctorate in either Philosophy or education. Such a program would allow the student to pursue the areas discussed earlier but in more detail. In addition, a strong emphasis on research skills, and the completion of an original piece of research distinguishes the doctoral level program from the master's level program. According to Hollis and Wantz (1991), the number of doctoral degree programs will continue to increase, with the degrees conferred being Ph.D.'s rather than Ed.D.'s. Completing a doctoral program would enable the counselor educator to teach at the university level, to direct counseling agencies, and to be credentialed in some states.

Applying to Counseling Programs

If you are interested in applying to master's or doctoral level graduate programs in counseling, please refer to Hollis and Wantz (1990) for additional information regarding detailed descriptions of counseling programs in the United States. Once you've selected those programs that appeal to you, request applications and information from those universities. Most programs will require you to send official undergraduate and graduate transcripts; some may require scores from the Graduate Record Examination or the Miller Analogies Test, letters of recommendation (academic or professional references are preferred), a goal statement, a personal interview, and a resume. Some schools may request the completion of undergraduate course work in psychology, sociology, and/or education. A personality test, completed prior to admission, may also be required. For doctoral level programs, it may be important to demonstrate a potential for conducting original research.

RESOURCES FOR MORE INFORMATION

American Counseling Association
5999 Stevenson Avenue
Alexandria, VA 22304–3300

American Counseling Association
(Direct correspondence to American Counseling Association at above address)
AACD Divisions and Organizational Affiliates:
Association for Counselor Education and Supervision (ACES)
National Career Development Association (NCDA)
Association for Humanistic Education and Development (AHEAD)
American School Counselor Association (ASCA)
American Rehabilitation Counseling Association (ARCA)
Association for Assessment Counseling (AAC)
National Employment Counselors Association (NECA)
Association for Multicultural Counseling and Development (AMCD)
Association for Religious and Values Issues in Counseling (ARVIC)
Association for Specialist in Group Work (ASGW)
International Association of Addictions and Offender Counselors (IAAOC)
American Mental Health Counselors Association (AMHCA)
Military Educators and Counselors Association (MECA)
Association for Adult Development and Aging (AADA)
International Association of Marriage and Family Counselors (IAMFC)

American College Personnel Association (ACPA)
1 DuPont Circle, Suite 360A
Washington, DC 20036-1110

FOR FURTHER READING

Baxter, N. (1990). *Opportunities in counseling and development*. Lincolnwood, IL: National Textbook Co.

Collison, B. B., & Garfield, N. J. (1990). *Careers in counseling and human development.* Alexandria, VA: American Association for Counseling and Development.

REFERENCES

Gerstain, L. H., & Brooks, D. K. (Feature Eds.) (1990). Helping professions' challenge: Credentialling and inter-disciplinary collaborations. *Journal of counseling and development 68,* no. 5, pp. 475–536. Available from American Counseling Association.

Hollis, J., & Wantz, R. (1990). *Counselor preparation 1990–1992: Programs, personnel, trends* (7th ed.). Muncie, IN: Accelerated Development.

Keim, M. C. R., & Graham, J. W. (1990). *Directory of graduate preparation programs in college student personnel.* Hanover, NH: Office of Residential Life, Dartmouth College.

Tryneski, J. (1990). *Requirements for certification: Teachers, counselors, librarians, and administrators for elementary schools, secondary schools, and junior colleges.* Chicago, IL: University of Chicago Press.

Notes on Contributors

James Archer, Jr. Ph.D., is director of the Counseling Center and professor in psychology and counselor education at the University of Florida. He is former president of the International Association of Counseling Services (IACS) and the Delaware Psychological Association, and former chairperson of the Association of University and College Counseling Center Directors (AUCCCD). Dr. Archer is the author of *Counseling College Students* and coauthor of *Multicultural Relations on Campus: A Personal Growth Approach.*

Michael Barnes, Ph.D., is associate professor of psychology at Hofstra University. He obtained his B.A. from Colgate University in 1973 and his M.A. and Ph.D. from Hofstra University in 1976 and 1980, respectively. A licensed clinical/school psychologist, he teaches courses in cross-cultural issues in professional psychology, measurement, and statistics. Dr. Barnes is the 1985 recipient of the Hofstra University Distinguished Teaching Award. He currently lives in Long Island.

Janet K. Belsky, Ph.D., assistant professor of psychology at Middle Tennessee State University, is the author of the college text *The Psychology of Aging: Theory, Research, and Interventions* and of *Here Tomorrow: An Omnibus Guide to Gerontological Research and Practice Written for the General Public and Practitioners.* She has lectured extensively in the psychology of aging to professional and nonprofessional groups and served on the faculties of Lehman College-CUNY and Yeshiva University School of Social Work. Currently Dr. Belsky is completing a college text in adulthood to be published by Harcourt Brace Jovanovic in late 1994.

Betty Bird, Ed.D., associate executive director for Direct Services at The Lighthouse, has worked in both the private and state agency sectors, spanning 15 years of management experience as well as direct service. She has been active in providing career counseling to adults and youth since she worked as the vocational counselor for visually impaired students at the University of Texas. Dr. Bird has been active in professional organizations at both the national and state levels, including the board of directors of the American Association of Workers for the Blind, The New York State Association for the Education and Rehabilitation of the Blind and Visually Impaired, and the United States Association for Blind Athletes.

Patrick J. Brice, Ph.D., is professor and co-director of the school counseling and guidance program in the department of counseling at Gallaudet University, Washington, D.C. He consults at various agencies and schools and maintains a private practice.

David Brizer, M.D., is medical director, inpatient psychiatry, Monmouth (New Jersey) Medical Center, with a private psychiatric practice in New York City. He has taught and written widely on the subjects of addiction, mood disorders, and mentally ill chemical abusers. He is editor of *Current Approaches to the Prediction of Violence* and author of *Psychiatry for Beginners*.

Susan Bromley, Psy.D., is an assistant professor of psychology at the University of Northern Colorado and a licensed clinical psychologist. Before this appointment, she was a therapist in medical settings and private practice for over 15 years. Dr. Bromley has published in the areas of hypnosis, pain management, and the personality of alcoholics.

Gerard B. Brooks, M.A., C.C.C., is a speech-language pathologist specializing in cognitive and speech therapies for the neurologically impaired adult. Senior associate and founder of speech and Language Associates, a private practice serving children and adults in Wappingers Falls, New York, Brooks is on staff at local hospitals and consults to an outpatient mental health clinic for developmentally disabled adults and to a Traumatic Brain Injury (TBI) project in New York's Mid-Hudson Valley.

David A. Crenshaw, Ph.D., is a clinical psychologist specializing in bereavement counseling. He is clinical director of The Astor Home for children in Rhinebeck, New York, and for the past 14 years has been in independent private practice in Rhinebeck. Dr. Crenshaw is the author of *Bereavement: Counseling the Grieving Throughout the Life Cycle* and has served as a consultant to schools, mental health agencies and community groups on issues related to death and dying.

Esther Loring Crispi, M.A., is a doctoral candidate in developmental psychology at Fordham University, Bronx, New York. She has a master's degree in counseling/community psychology from Marist College, Poughkeepsie, New York. Crispi is a psychological consultant to area nursing homes, where she assesses and counsels residents and conducts in-service education. She has been an educator for 15 years and is currently a part-time instructor at Marist College.

Frank M. Dattilio, Ph.D. is a clinical associate in psychiatry at the Center for Cognitive Therapy, the University of Pennsylvania School of Medicine. He is a licensed psychologist and listed in the National Register of Health Service Providers in Psychology. He is also an adjunct assistant professor in counseling psychology at Lehigh University and a clinical member and approved supervisor with the American Association for Marriage and Family Therapy. Dr. Dattilio maintains an active psychotherapy practice with Behavior Therapy Associates in Allentown, Pennsylvania.

Douglas M. Davidove, Ph.D., a Gestalt therapist in New York City, has been practicing Gestalt therapy for more than 20 years. For the past 11 years, Dr. Davidove has conducted continuing and short-term training workshops in the theory and practice of Gestalt therapy, in the United States and in Europe. He is the author of several articles on the subject and a fellow and past vice-president of the New York Institute for Gestalt Therapy.

Celia B. Fisher, Ph.D., associate professor and director of the Fordham University Graduate Program in Developmental Psychology, is current chair of the New York State Board for Psychology, a member of the American Psychological Association's Ethics Committee, and coeditor of *Ethics in Applied Developmental Psychology.*

Cyril M. Franks, Ph.D., is co-founder and first president of the Association for the Advancement of Behavior Therapy, and founder and first editor of *Behavior Therapy.* A distinguished professor emeritus of the Graduate School of Applied and Professional Psychology, Rutgers University, he is also a consulting licensed psychologist for the Carrier Foundation in Belle Meade, New Jersey. Dr. Franks is editor of *Child and Family Behavior Therapy,* and his publications include some 200 articles, chapters, and written or edited books.

Arthur Freeman, Ph.D., is associate professor of clinical psychiatry and director of The Cognitive Therapy Institute of the Department of Psychiatry in the School of Osteopathic Medicine, the University of Medicine and Dentistry of New Jersey. He is also clinical associate professor of psychology and psychiatry at the University of Pennsylvania, and senior consultant at the Center for Cognitive Therapy of the University of Pennsylvania. Dr. Freeman has published numerous books in cognitive therapy, which have been translated into Spanish, Swedish, German, Dutch, Norwegian, and Japanese. He is a diplomate in clinical psychology of the American Board of Professional Psychology and is a fellow of divisions 12 (Clinical Psychology), 29 (Psychotherapy), and 43 (Family Psychology) of the American Psychological Association. Dr. Freeman has lectured internationally and has presented workshops in 15 countries over the past 5 years.

Richard Friedman, Ph.D., is in private practice in New York City and a faculty member at New York University School of Social Work Post-Master's Certificate Program. He is a faculty member and training analyst at the New York Center of Psychoanalytic Training.

Thomas L. Hafemeister, J. D., Ph.D., is a staff attorney in the Research division of the National Center for State Courts and a member of its Institute on Mental Disability and the Law. He is also an adjunct professor with the Marshall-Wythe School of Law (where he has taught mental health law) and the department of psychology at the College of William and Mary. Previously he served as an assistant counsel in the Litigation Division of the Counsel's Office for the Office of Mental Health, State of New York. Dr. Hafemeister is currently completing work on a book chapter addressing legal aspects of the treatment of the mentally disordered offender and has published 27 articles or book chapters focusing primarily on mental health and health-related legal issues.

James J. Hennessy, Ph.D., professor and chair of the Division of Psychological and Educational Services in the Graduate School of Education, Fordham University, is a counseling psychologist with extensive experience in direct service provision with minors with serious behavior problems and young college-aged adults, and is the coauthor of *Criminal Behavior: A Process Psychology Analysis.*

Charles H. Huber, Ph.D., is an associate professor in counseling and educational psychology at New Mexico State University and a psychologist in private practice. He holds diplomates with the American Board of Behavioral Psychology in Cognitive-Behavior Therapy and the American Board of Professional Psychology in Family Psychology. Dr. Huber has authored numerous articles that have appeared in *Family Therapy* and the book *The 20-Minute Counselor: Transforming Brief Conversations into Effective Helping Experiences,* from which the topic of his chapter is taken.

Merle A. Keitel, Ph.D., received her doctorate in counseling psychology from the State University of New York at Buffalo. She is currently an assistant professor and acting director of training for the master's and doctoral programs in counseling and counseling psychology in the Graduate School of Education at Fordham University.

Sheila A. Knights, Psy.D., coauthor of *Phobics and Other Panic Victims,* is supervisor of the Psychology Department at United Cerebral Palsy of Ulster County in Kingston, New York, and has a private practice in Poughkeepsie, New York. She teaches counseling at Marist College.

Mary Kopala, Ph.D., received master of education in counseling in 1980 and a doctorate in counseling psychology in 1987 from Penn State. She has taught at Fordham University and currently is assistant professor at Hunter College of the City University of New York. Dr. Kopala has provided direct service to clients at the University of Delaware, Drexel University, and Georgia State University.

Mary Ann Lang, Ph.D., is director of The Lighthouse National Center for Vision and Child Development. She has served consecutively as director of children's services, professional training, and client programs before assuming her present position in January 1988. Dr. Lang has been a teacher of young children, the administrator of a preschool for children with multiple handicaps, and a university educator of professionals in the fields of blindness and visual impairment, as well as educational psychology and counseling. She has addressed national and international audiences on the impact of visual impairment and blindness on the development of children and adolescents; perspectives on working with families; and facilitating independence. Dr. Lang was also instrumental in developing the Lighthouse's program for persons with AIDS-related vision loss. Her publications include *AIDS, Blindness, and Low Vision: A Guide for Service Providers* with Carol Sussman-Skalka and Margaret Galligan and *AIDS, Blindness, and Low Vision: A Training Manual for Health Organizations,* coauthored with Kim Blakely.

Eugene E. Levitt, Ph.D. is professor emeritus of clinical psychology at Indiana University School of Medicine, having served as director of the section of psychology of the department of psychiatry for 30 years. Dr. Levitt is the author of 10 books, 21 book chapters, and 144 journal articles, including 31 publications in the area of human sexuality. He is a full clinical member of the Society for Sex Therapy & Research, founding clinical fellow of the American Academy of Clinical Sexologists, fellow and clinical supervisor of the American Board of Sexology, and member of the International Academy of Sex Research.

Barbara G. Love, Ph.D., is at the Kennedy Institute in Baltimore, Maryland, and in private practice.

Robert J. Lovinger, Ph.D. is a professor of psychology at Central Michigan University and director of the university's Psychological Training and Consultation Center, where he teaches in the clinical psychology doctoral program. He is author of several papers and publications on religious dimensions in therapy, and the book *Religion and Counseling.*

Helen B. McDonald, C.S.W., is coauthor of *Understanding Homosexuality: A Guide for Those Who Know, Love, or Counsel Gay and Lesbian Individuals.* She is a native of Minnesota, a resident of Saugerties, New York, and a practicing psychotherapist in New York City.

Janice N. McLean, Ph.D., is a clinical psychologist and the coauthor of *Phobics and Other Panic Victims.* She was formerly a four-county director of the Terrap Anxiety Program in New York. Dr. McLean currently teaches psychology at Dennison University in Ohio and works in outpatient counseling groups with persons with anxiety disorders.

John B. Mordock, Ph.D., A.B.P.P., directs The Astor Home and Child Guidance Clinics' community mental health programs in Dutchess County, New York. He has published widely in the area of child psychopathology. His books include *The Other Children: An Introduction to Exceptionality; Ego-Impaired Children Grow Up; Crisis Counseling with Children and Adolescents;* and *Counseling Children.*

Fugen Neziroglu, Ph.D., A.B.B.P., A.B.P.P., is a behavior and cognitive therapist who has been involved in the research and treatment of anxiety, depression, and aggression of over 18 years. She is a scientist and practitioner who has presented and published over 85 papers in scientific journals and books, and is coauthor of two books with Dr. Yaryura-Tobias. She has her diplomates in behavior therapy from the American Board of Behavioral Psychology (ABBP) and in clinical psychology from the American Board of Professional Psychology (ABPP). Dr. Neziroglu is an associate professor in the department of psychology at Hofstra University, and is on the scientific advisory board of the Obsessive-Compulsive Foundation.

Richard Panman, Ph.D., is chair of the Psychology Department, State University of New York, College at New Paltz. His special interest is in group dynamics, and he has conducted workshops for schools, businesses, and government agencies using the Tavistock model. Dr.

Panman is also a practicing psychologist who treats patients using transactional analysis, Gestalt, and rational-emotive therapies.

Sandra Panman, M.P.S., is an educational consultant, writer, and English instructor at the State University of New York, College at New Paltz. Panman, who does staff development training for schools, corporations, and professional organizations, uses the Tavistock model of group dynamics in her work with client groups. She is coauthor, along with Richard Panman, of educational textbooks that use a developmental approach to teach reading and writing.

Randy Ian Pardell, M.D., is clinical director at Craig House Hospital, and in private psychiatric practice in Poughkeepsie, New York. He divides his time between psychopharmacology, consultations, and psychotherapy practice. Dr. Pardell is a graduate of the New York University School of Medicine and trained at the St. Luke's–Roosevelt Hospital Center in New York City. Dr. Pardell also trained at the New York Psychiatric Institute in the department of clinical psychopharmacology and is an author of a number of papers on medication treatment for depression and abstinence syndromes.

Frances D. Peltz, C.S.W., C.R.C., is a practicing psychotherapist in New York City. She has worked with people with HIV+/AIDS and with care partners since 1982. Her publications include the book *When Someone You Know Has AIDS*. She is presently employed as a consultant in the psychiatry and chemical dependency units of Regent Hospital in New York City. She has also completed 4 years of analytical training at the Greenwich Institute.

Paul Retzlaff, Ph.D., is an associate professor of psychology at the University of Northern Colorado and a staff psychologist at the VA Medical Center in Cheyenne, Wyoming. He publishes extensively on personality disorders with a particular emphasis on differential diagnosis, comorbidities, and psychological testing.

Michael Salamon, Ph.D., is the executive director of the Adult Development Center, Inc. in New York City, and a consultant to a variety of professional groups in the United States and abroad. He is the author of two text books and the senior author of *Life Satisfaction in the Elderly Scale*. Dr. Salamon is on the editorial board of the *Journal of Clinical and Consulting Psychology* and the *Clinical Gerontologist*.

Richard B. Seymour, M.A., is president of Westwind Associates, a consultant at the Haight Ashbury Free Medical Clinics Drug Training and

Education Projects, and an instructor of psychopharmacology at Sonoma State University Rohnert Park and John F. Kennedy University in Orinda, California.

Milton F. Shore, Ph.D., A.B.P.P., is a diplomate in clinical psychology of the American Board of Professional Psychology and a fellow of the American Association for the Advancement of Science. He is former president of the American Orthopsychiatric Association and currently editor of its journal. He is the editor or author of 12 books and over 150 professional articles, including *When Your Child Needs Testing*. Formerly with the National Institute of Mental Health, he is currently in independent practice and is adjunct professor at Catholic University of America. Dr. Shore has worked with children and families for over 35 years and has been a visible advocate for including families actively in the care of children in pediatric hospitals.

Barbara Silverstone, D.S.W., is president of The Lighthouse, Inc., which includes among its diversified vision rehabilitation programs The Lighthouse National Center for Vision and Aging. Dr. Silverstone is a member of the National Association of Social Workers, a fellow and past president of the Gerontological Society of American, fellow of the American Orthopsychiatric Association, and formerly a member of the House of Delegates of the American Association of Homes for the Aging. Her professional experience has encompassed private practice and psychiatric and rehabilitation services, and has included individual and group psychotherapy with children, young adults, and the elderly and their families. Dr. Silverstone's publications include *You and Your Aging Parent*, coauthored with Helen Kandel Hyman, and the textbook *Social Work Practice with the Frail Elderly and Their Families*, coauthored with Ann Burack-Weiss.

David E. Smith, M.D., is president, medical director, and Founder of Haight Ashbury Free Clinics, Inc., and associate clinical professor of occupational medicine and clinical toxicology at the San Francisco Medical Center in the University of California.

Donna D. Stein, R.N., M.A., is a registered professional nurse who received her master of arts Degree in counseling psychology at the State University of New York, College at New Paltz. Her clinical experience has included providing psychological services to the college population at the psychological counseling center in New Paltz and coleading a group for the Survivors of Childhood Sexual Abuse. The recipient of numerous awards for her clinical accomplishments, Stein is interested in the integration of the disciplines of medicine and psychology.

Audrey I. Steinhorn, C.S.W., coauthor of *Understanding Homosexuality: A Guide for Those Who Know, Love, or Counsel Gay and Lesbian Individuals,* is a clinical social work psychotherapist with offices in Poughkeepsie, New York, and New York City.

Jane S. Sturges, M.S.W., is an assistant clinical professor of social work in psychiatry at the Yale School of Medicine, and is in private practice in New Haven, Connecticut. She received her master's degree from New York University and has had training in Bowen Family Systems Theory at Georgetown University. She is a past president of the Connecticut Society for Clinical Social Work and has published numerous articles in the field of family.

David Swift, M.D., is a staff psychiatrist and the director of an eating disorders program at Craig House Hospital in Beacon, New York. Dr. Swift is coauthor, with Kathleen Zraly, of *Counseling Persons with Eating Disorders.*

William Van Ornum, Ph.D., is assistant professor of psychology at Marist College in Poughkeepsie, New York, and coauthor of *Crisis Counseling with Children and Adolescents.* He is a fellow of the American Psychological Association.

Raymond Vickers, M.D., is clinical professor in the Geriatrics Division of the department of family medicine, East Caroline University School of Medicine. He is a former president of the Northeastern Gerontological Society and was a founding member of the American Association for Geriatric Psychiatry. Dr. Vickers has authored over two dozen articles in geriatrics and internal medicine. He has given over 200 presentations to professional audiences and the public in his distinguished career.

Ilene C. Wasserman, M.A.Ed., L.C.S.W., has been a psychotherapist for nearly 15 years, specializing in individual and couples therapy. She specializes in helping couples understand and celebrate differences such as gender, faith, and class. She also consults to corporations, universities, and religious institutions on valuing diversity, and has lectured on the subject of gender differences on numerous occasions.

Jose A. Yaryura-Tobias, M.D., is a biological psychiatrist and an internist with over 30 years' experience. He has pioneered research in the dopamine theory of schizophrenia and the biological theory of obsessive-compulsive disorder. He is coauthor of two books with Fugen A. Neziroglu, Ph.D., titled *Obsessive-Compulsive Disorder: Pathogenesis, Diagnosis, and Treatment* and *Over and Over Again: Understanding Obsessive-Compul-*

sive Disorder. He is also author of *The Integral Being* and has presented and/or published over 270 scientific papers and book chapters.

Kathleen Zraly, M.A., has her master's degree in developmental psychology. She is a clinical counselor and a certified eating disorder therapist, and is a doctoral candidate in an applied developmental program at Fordham University. Zraly has a private practice in New York and is co-author with David Swift of *Counseling Persons with Eating Disorders.*